WORD STUDIES

IN THE

NEW TESTAMENT

MARVIN R. VINCENT, D.D.

BALDWIN PROFESSOR OF SACRED LITERATURE IN UNION THEOLOGICAL SEMINARY
NEW YORK.

VOLUME IV.

THE THESSALONIAN EPISTLES
THE EPISTLE TO THE GALATIANS
THE PASTORAL EPISTLES
THE EPISTLE TO THE HEBREWS

HENDRICKSON PUBLISHERS

WORD STUDIES IN THE NEW TESTAMENT
4 Volume Set

Hendrickson Publishers
P.O. Box 3473
Peabody, MA 01961-3473

Printed in the United States of America

ISBN 0-917006-30-5

THE THESSALONIAN EPISTLES.

INTRODUCTION.

THE FIRST EPISTLE.

THESSALONICA was situated on the Thermaic Gulf, a fine harbour, affording anchorage for large ships directly in front of the city.* The situation commanded the trade of the Macedonian waters, and was connected inland with the plain of the Axius, one of the great levels of Macedonia, and with the plain of the Strymon, by a pass across the peninsula of Chalcidice. It was the chief station on the Via Egnatia, the great Roman road which ran from Dyrrhachium through Epirus, Macedonia, and Thrace to Byzantium.

In Paul's day it was a free city, the capital of the whole province and the most populous of its towns. Its extensive trade with all parts of the world accounts in part for the rapid spread of the news of the success of the gospel (1 Th. i. 8). The population consisted of the original Graeco-Macedonian inhabitants, mixed with many Romans and some Jews. The same heathen deities were worshipped as in other Graeco-Roman communities, and the worship of the Cabeiri had been introduced from Samothrace.†

Paul's first visit to Thessalonica is related in Acts xvii.; and the account must be filled out, as far as possible, by means

---

* "Medio flexu litoris." Pliny, *H. N.* iv. 10.

† The Cabeiri were Pelasgic deities worshipped in the islands between Euboea and the Hellespont, on the adjacent coasts of Asia Minor, and at Thebes and Andania in Greece. They were four in number, answering to Demeter, Persephone, Hades, and Hermes in the Greek mythology. Throughout the Roman period of Greek history the Cabeiric mysteries were held only second to the Eleusinian, and many Romans of high position were initiated.

of the references in the two letters. From the Acts it appears that he remained only three weeks ; but the first Epistle indicates that a large and flourishing church had been formed, chiefly of Gentiles (i. 8, 9); and from this, and from the facts that the Philippians, twice during his stay, sent him pecuniary aid (Philip. iv. 16), and that he labored for his own support, his visit would seem to have been longer.

According to the narrative in Acts, he secured some converts from among the Jews, but more from the pious Greeks or Proselytes, and many prominent women. Nothing is said of his labours among the heathen. The author of the Acts has, apparently, recorded the least important part of his work, which was evidently begun, according to his usual practice, in the synagogue. The principal part of it, however, was not done in the synagogue.

The cause of Paul's departure from Thessalonica was a persecution instigated by the Jews, who used the vulgar pagan rabble as their instruments. Most of the Christian converts were from the better classes, and the Politarchs were not disposed to interfere actively. But the riot was a serious matter. A powerful, dangerous, lasting sentiment was aroused in the class which fostered it (see ch. ii. 14). The charge against Paul was that of treason against the Emperor, and the Politarchs were forced to take active measures lest they should incur the charge of condoning treason. Their course was the mildest for which they could find precedent. The accused were bound over to keep the peace, and as security was exacted from Jason and the leading Christians of Thessalonica, it implied that they were under obligation to prevent Paul from coming to the city again.

Paul, after his departure, was distressed, lest his converts, who had been only partially instructed, might fall from their faith. He had twice made the attempt to revisit them, but in vain. He had sent Timothy to inquire into their condition and to establish and comfort them (iii. 2). Timothy had now rejoined him at Corinth, and the information which he brought called forth the first letter.

The letter, though official, is not stiff nor condescending.

It reveals a quick, intelligent sympathy with the burdens and sufferings of the church, and a full appreciation of their patience and fidelity. They are the subject of the Apostle's thoughts, wishes, and prayers; they are his joy and his crown. The tone of the Epistle, while peculiarly affectionate, is nevertheless decided, and exacting in moral demand. It has nothing of the legal or ecclesiastical character. It is pervaded, in parts, with the tension and anxiety of the interval between Paul's departure from Thessalonica and the reception of Timothy's report. Timothy's news had been substantially good. The church had remained true to the faith against all assaults. But a degree of mistrust had arisen concerning the sincerity of Paul's interest for the church, which must have come from the outside. Accordingly in the second chapter he takes on an apologetic tone. Some lack of religious steadfastness among the members has made itself evident, and some signs of not fully appreciating the relations of their faith to Christian morality. There has arisen a tendency to assume that the second coming of Christ is close at hand, and that all old relations and duties are therefore done away. On the other hand, an opposite tendency has shown itself, a reaction against the enthusiasm evoked by the expectation of the parousia, which calls for the admonitions, " Quench not the spirit : despise not prophesyings : prove all things : hold fast that which is good." Mistakes have become current respecting the lot of such Christians as may die before the Lord's coming. There is a possible hint of strained relations with the church-superintendents (v. 12–15) and of occasions given to the enemies of Christianity for malicious criticism (iv. 12). But the main objects of the letter are, to strengthen the bond between the writer and the church, to detach the church from the errors and abominations of heathen life, and to correct misunderstandings and give comfort as regards the dead in Christ.

The language of the letter is simple, taking on a rhetorical character only in certain isolated passages (ii. 19 f.; iii. 8 f.). It is not without picturesqueness (i. 8, 9; ii. 1, 6, 16, 17, 19, iii. 3, 8, 11; iv. 1, 6, 12; v. 2, 3, 5, 8, 19). There is an

occasional tendency to amplification (i. 2 f., 8; ii. 11, 13:
iii. 2, 7, 9, 10; v. 1, 3, 5, 23, etc.), and to round off the ends
of sentences with adverbial phrases (i. 5, 6; ii. 2, 16, 17;
iii. 3, 9, etc.). There is to be noted the frequent introduction
of expressions which recognise the knowledge and remembrance of the writer's correspondents, as καθὼς οἴδατε *even as
ye know:* also the forms of adjuration and comparison (ii. 5,
10; iii. 6). A certain ruggedness and lack of symmetry in
the structure of sentences appears at times (i. 2 ff., 8; ii. 10
ff., 17 f., 19 f.; iv. 1 f., 3 ff.). The vocabulary is relatively
small. Repetitions and similarities of expression occur.

There are no citations from the Old Testament, and no use
of apocryphal writings can be shown. The mode of expression
is thoroughly Pauline. The character of the Epistle does not
lead us to expect many of the technical terms of the Pauline
dogmatic; but such as we do find are Pauline, as ἐκλογή
election; καλεῖν *to call;* ἅγιοι *saints;* ἀγιασμός *sanctification;*
μὴ εἰδότες τὸν θεόν *not knowing God.* There are also to be
noted the characteristic play of words (ii. 4); paradox (i. 6);
mixed metaphor (v. 5), and antithesis of prepositions (i. 5;
iv. 7; ii. 3, etc.). There are relatively few hapaxlegomena,
some peculiar uses of words common in the New Testament;
possibly a dozen words and modes of expression which appear
only in the deutero-Pauline writings, and a few which are
almost exclusively confined to the writings of Luke and the
Epistle to the Hebrews.

The authenticity of the Epistle is generally conceded. It
has been assailed by Baur, Steck, Holsten, and Loman.

THE SECOND EPISTLE.

The authenticity and genuineness of this Epistle have
been challenged since the beginning of the present century.*
Its integrity has also been questioned on the assumed ground
of a combination of a genuine Pauline epistle with interpolated matter (P. W. Schmidt). It has been ascribed to

---

* J. E. C. Schmidt, DeWette, Kern, Baur, Hilgenfeld, Pfleiderer, Weizsäcker, Loman, Holtzmann, Schmiedel.

Timothy. Attempts have also been made to prove that it was earlier in date than the first Epistle (Ewald, Baur, Davidson); but there seems to be, on the whole, no sufficient reason for refusing it a place among the genuine Pauline Epistles. The external testimony in its favor is ancient and good, while the resemblances in manner and phraseology to the other Pauline writings cannot be evaded. The vocabulary is Pauline. The list of non-Pauline words is small and not important. As distinguished from all other Pauline letters, the two Thessalonian epistles exhibit a striking relationship, extending to sequences of thought, articulation of sentences, and peculiar expressions and usages. In not a few cases, the same subjects are treated with almost the same words.* Both letters have an eschatological drift; both exhibit, without specially emphasising it, the writer's apostolic consciousness; both treat moral questions from the religious point of view.†

The second Epistle appears to have been written some months after the first, because of some later information received by Paul, who was probably still in Corinth. The circumstances of the church were substantially the same, although there appears to have been a growth in faith and charity (i. 3, 4); but the idea of the imminent second coming of the Lord had assumed such proportions as to cause restlessness and impatience, and a measure of social disorganisation and fanaticism. A spurious epistle in Paul's name, announcing the immediate advent of the Lord, appears to have been circulated (ii. 2). The main design of this second letter is to correct false views concerning the second advent, and to rebuke the idleness and disorder into which some of the Thessalonian Christians had fallen.

---

* Comp., for instance, 2 Th. i. 1–7; ii. 13–17; iii. 1, 3, 12, and 1 Th. i. 3, 4 f., 6, 7; ii. 13, 15, 16; iii. 3, 4, 5, 8, 9, 10, 11, 12.

† The authenticity of the 2d Epistle is defended by Jowett, Godet, Weiss, Lünemann, Schenkel, Reuss, Bleek, Renan, Salmon, Klöpper, Jülicher, Bornemann, Zahn, McGiffert.

COMMENTARIES, ETC., ON THE THESSALONIAN LETTERS.*

GERMAN.

W. Bornemann. In the Meyer Series. 6th ed. *Die Thessalonicherbriefe*, 1894. P. W. Schmiedel, in the *Hand-Commentar zum Neuen Testament*, by Holtzmann, Lipsius, Schmiedel, and Von Soden, 1893. P. Schmid, *Der erste Thessalonicherbrief neu erklärt*, with Excursus on 2d Epistle, 1885. F. Zimmer, *Der Text der Thessalonicherbriefe, etc.* Textual Apparatus and Commentary, 1893.

ENGLISH.

J. B. Lightfoot, both Epistles, in *Notes on Epistles of St. Paul from Unpublished Commentaries*, 1895. C. J. Ellicott, *A Critical and Grammatical Commentary on St. Paul's Epistles to the Thessalonians*. B. Jowett, *The Epistles of St. Paul to the Thessalonians, Galatians and Romans. Translation and Commentary*, 3d ed. 1894. J. Eadie, *A Commentary on the Greek Text of the Epistles of Paul to the Thessalonians*, 1877. J. Hutchison, *Lectures, chiefly Expository, on Paul's 1st and 2d Epistles to the Thessalonians*, 1883. J. B. Lightfoot, *Biblical Essays*, chs. VI., VII. G. G. Findlay, in *Cambridge Bible for Schools*. J. Denney, in *Expositor's Bible*.

On Macedonia, L. Heuzey and H. Daumet, *Mission Archéologique de Macédoine*, 1876. Account of the expedition under the auspices of Napoleon III. for the exploration of Macedonia. M. R. Vincent, *Philippians and Philemon*, Introduction. *International Commentary*, 1897.

---

* No attempt is made to present an exhaustive catalogue of the Literature

8

THE FIRST EPISTLE TO THE THESSALONIANS.

CHAPTER I.

1. The address of the first Epistle is shorter than that of any of the Pauline letters. In the other Epistles Paul either indicates the contents of the letter, or adds details concerning the writer or his correspondents, or amplifies the apostolic greeting. The names of Silvanus and Timothy are added to that of Paul as the senders of the letter. They were with him at Corinth when it was written (Acts xviii. 5; 2 Cor. i. 19). They had assisted him in the foundation of the Thessalonian Church (Acts xvi. 1–3; xvii. 4, 10, 14). Paul's official title "Apostle" is omitted in the addresses of both Epistles, although in 1 Th. ii. 6 he uses ἀπόστολοι *apostles*, including Silvanus and Timothy under that title. The title appears in all the other Epistles except Philippians and Philemon. The reason for its omission in every case appears to have been the intimate and affectionate character of his relations with the parties addressed, which rendered an appeal to his apostolic authority unnecessary. Paul does not confine the name of apostle to the twelve.*

Silvanus. The Silas of the Acts, where alone the form Σίλας occurs. By Paul always Σιλουανός, of which Σίλας is a contraction, as Λουκᾶς from Λουκανός. Similar contractions occur in Class., as Ἀλεξᾶς for Ἀλέξανδρος; Ἀρτᾶς for

---

* See Rom. xvi. 7 ; 1 Cor. ix. 5, 6, and Bp. Lightfoot on "The Name and Office of an Apostle," *Com. on Galatians*, p. 92.

'Αρτεμᾶς, and that for 'Αρτεμίδωρος. Silas first appears in
Acts xv. 22, as one of the bearers of the letter to the Gentile Christians at Antioch. He accompanied Paul on his
second missionary tour, and was left behind with Timothy
when Paul departed from Macedonia after his first visit.
He was probably a Jewish Christian (see Acts xvi. 20), and
was, like Paul, a Roman citizen (Acts xvi. 37, 38). Hence
his Roman name. He cannot with any certainty be identified with the Silvanus of 1 Pet. v. 12.

Timothy. Appears in all the Pauline Epistles except Galatians and Ephesians. He was associated with Paul longer
than any one of whom we have notice. First mentioned Acts
xvi. 1, 2: comp. 2 Tim. iii. 10, 11. He accompanied Paul on
his second missionary tour (Acts xvi. 3), and was one of the
founders of the churches in Thessalonica and Philippi. He
is often styled by Paul "the brother" (2 Cor. i. 1; Col. i.
1; 1 Th. iii. 2; Philem. 1); with Paul himself "a bondservant of Jesus Christ" (Philip. i. 1); comp. 1 Tim. ii. 18;
2 Tim. i. 2. Paul's confidence in him appears in Philip. ii.
19-22, and is implied in his sending him from Athens to the
Thessalonian church to establish and comfort its members
(1 Th. iii. 2). Paul sent him again to Macedonia in company with Erastus (Acts xix. 22), and also to Corinth
(1 Cor. iv. 17). To the Corinthians he writes of Timothy
as "his beloved and faithful child in the Lord" who shall
remind them of his ways in Christ (1 Cor. iv. 17), and as
one who worketh the work of the Lord as he himself (1 Cor.
xvi. 10). He joined Paul at Rome, and his name is associated with Paul's in the addresses of the letters to the Colossians and Philemon. In every case where he is mentioned
by name with Silvanus, the name of Silvanus precedes.

To the church of the Thessalonians. This form of
address appears in 1st and 2d Corinthians, Galatians, 2d
Thessalonians. The other letters are addressed to "the
saints," "the brethren," "the saints and faithful brethren."
The use of the genitive of the national name is peculiar.

Comp. 1 Cor. i. 22; 2 Cor. i. 1; Gal. i. 2; Philip. i. 1; Col. i. 2.

The church (ἐκκλησία). From ἐκ *out*, and καλεῖν *to call* or *summon*. Originally with a secular meaning, *an assembly of citizens regularly summoned*. So Acts xix. 39. LXX uses it for the congregation of Israel, either as con vened for a definite purpose (1 Kings viii. 65; Deut. iv. 10; xviii. 16), or as a community (2 Chr. i. 3, 5; xxiii. 3; Neh. viii. 17). The verbs ἐκκλησιάζειν and ἐξεκκλησιάζειν *to summon formally*, which do not occur in N. T., are found in LXX with συναγωγὴν *gathering*, λαόν *people*, and πρεσβυτέρους *elders*. Συναγωγὴ is constantly used in LXX of the children of Israel as a body (Ex. xii. 6, 19, 47; Lev. iv. 13, etc.), and is the more common word in N. T. for a Jewish as distinguished from a Christian assembly; sometimes with the addition *of the Jews* (Acts xiii. 5; xiv. 1; xvii. 1). It is once used of a Christian assembly (Jas. ii. 2). Ἐπισυναγωγὴ *gathering together*, occurs 2 Th. ii. 1; Heb. x. 25. The Ebionites retained συναγωγὴ in preference to ἐκκλησία. The LXX translators found two Hebrew words for "assembly" or "congregation," עֵדָה and קָהָל, and rendered the former by συναγωγὴ in the great majority of instances. Ἐκκλησία does not appear as the rendering of עֵדָה. They were not as consistent in rendering קָהָל, since they used both συναγωγὴ and ἐκκλησία, though the latter was the more frequent: see Lev. iv. 13; Deut. v. 22, etc. The A. V. renders both words by "congregation" and "assembly" indiscriminately. Ἐκκλησία is only once used in N. T. of a Jewish congregation, Acts vii. 38; yet there are cases where there is an apparent attempt to guard its distinctively Christian sense against being confounded with the unconverted Jewish communities. Hence the addition ἐν Χριστῷ *in Christ*, Gal. i. 22; ἐν θεῷ πατρὶ καὶ κυρίῳ Ἰησοῦ Χριστῷ *in God the Father and the Lord Jesus Christ*, 1 Th. i. 1; comp. 2 Th. i. 1. In both Hebrew and N. T. usage, ἐκκλησία implies a community based on a special religious idea, and established in a special way. In N. T. it is also used in

a narrower sense, of a single church, or of a church confined
to a single place. So Rom. xvi. 5, etc.

In God the Father, etc. Const. with *the church*, and
comp. 2 Th. i. 1. The phrase "the church *in* God" is peculiar to the Thessalonian Epistles. Elsewhere "*of* God"
(1 Cor. x. 32; xi. 16, 22; xv. 9, etc.); "of the saints"
(1 Cor. xiv. 33). Lightfoot suggests that the word ἐκκλησία can scarcely have been stamped with so definite a
Christian meaning in the minds of these recent and early
converts as to render the addition "in God the Father," etc.,
superfluous.

Grace to you and peace (χάρις ὑμῖν καὶ εἰρήνη). In
Romans, 1st and 2d Corinthians, Galatians, Ephesians, Philippians, the salutation is, *Grace to you and peace from God
our Father and the Lord Jesus Christ:* Colossians omits the
last five words of this : 2 Thessalonians omits *our* before
Father. On the union of the Greek and Jewish forms of
salutation, see on 1 Cor. i. 3.

2. **We give thanks** (εὐχαριστοῦμεν). According to Paul's
habit, a thanksgiving follows the salutation, commonly with
the verb εὐχαριστεῖν, as here; but in 2d Corinthians and Ephesians, εὐλογητὸς ὁ θεός *blessed be God*. The thanksgiving is
omitted only in Galatians. The verb εὐχαριστεῖν occurs only
in later Greek, and there but rarely. In LXX only in
Apocr. See Judith viii. 25; 2 Macc. i. 11; x. 7; 3 Macc.
vii. 16. In the N. T. Epistles, P⁰. Originally *to do a good
turn ;* hence, *to return a favour*. The meaning *to give thanks*
is late. The kindred noun εὐχαριστία *giving of thanks*, is
found often in Paul. As a designation of the Lord's Supper
(*Eucharist*) it is not found in the N. T. Perhaps the
earliest instance of its use in that sense is in Ignatius. See
Philad. iv. ; Smyrn. vi., viii. ; Eph. xiii. Comp. Just.
Mart. *Apol.* i., 64, 65.

In *we give thanks*, it is not easy to decide whether Paul
uses *we* as plural, or in the sense of *I*. Rom. iii. 9 seems to

be a clear case of the latter usage.   In 1 Th. iii. 1, 2, ηὐδοκήσαμεν *we thought it good*, and ἐπέμψαμεν *we sent*, can, apparently, refer only to Paul; and similarly, in 1 Th. iii. 6, πρὸς ἡμᾶς *unto us*, can hardly include Silvanus who came with Timothy (comp. iii. 5). But it is significant that, in the Epistles which are written in Paul's name alone (Romans, Galatians, Ephesians), only *I* is used, unless we except Gal. i. 8, which is doubtful.   Paul and Timothy appear jointly as correspondents in Philippians, but the first person predominates throughout the letter.   The same is true of 1st Corinthians, where Paul and Sosthenes are associated in the address, but the singular pronoun is used almost throughout.   (See iv. 10–13; ix. 4, 5, 25, 26).   In Colossians Paul and Timothy appear in the address.   The plural prevails to i. 23, and alternates with the singular throughout the remainder.   The alternations in 2d Corinthians are very bewildering.

On the whole, I think that occasional instances of the epistolary plural must be granted.   It is not, however, Paul's habitual usage.   *We* is often employed as in ordinary correspondence or argument, where the writer or speaker associates himself with his readers or hearers.   Abundant illustrations of this may be seen in Rom. vi. and viii.; but in other cases, when Paul speaks in the plural, he usually associates his fellow-ministers, mentally, with himself.*

Making mention (μνείαν ποιούμενοι).   For the phrase see Rom. i. 9; Eph. i. 16; Philem. 4.   Always in connection with prayer.   In the sense of *remember* it appears in LXX, Job xiv. 13.   In Ps. cxi. 4, *to make a memorial*.   See further, on *without ceasing*, ver. 3.

In my prayers (ἐπί).   When engaged in offering my prayers. Ἐπί here blends the local with the temporal sense.

Prayers (προσευχῶν).   The more general term, and limited to prayer to God; while δέησις *petitionary* prayer, *supplica-*

---

* The discussion in detail may be found in Bornemann's *Thessalonicherbriefe*, p. 37 f. and p. 53.   See also Spitta, *Urchristenthum*, p. 120 f., and Lightfoot, *Notes on Epistles of St. Paul*, p. 22.

tion, may be addressed to man. Paul alone associates the two words. See Philip. iv. 6; Eph. vi. 18. In classical Greek the word does not occur in the sense of prayer. It is found in later Greek, meaning *a place for prayer*, in which sense it appears in Acts xvi. 13, 16. It signified either a *synagogue*, or an *open praying-place* outside of a city.*

3. Without ceasing (ἀδιαλείπτως). P⁰. In LXX see 1 Macc. xii. 11; 2 Macc. iii. 26; ix. 4; xiii. 12; xv. 7; 3 Macc. vi. 33. Should be construed with *making mention*, not with *remembering*, as A. V. and Rev. The salutations of Paul reproduce ordinary conventional forms of greeting. Thus the familiar Greek greeting χαίρειν *be joyful, hail, welcome*, appears in χάρις *grace*. This was perceived by Theodore of Mopsuestia (350–428 A.D.), who, in his commentary on Ephesians, says that in the preface to that letter Paul does very much as we do when we say " So and so to So and so, greeting " (ὁ δεῖνα τῷ δεῖνι χαίρειν). Deissmann gives some interesting parallels from ancient papyri. For instance, a letter dated 172 B.C., from an Egyptian lady to her brother or husband : " Isias to her brother Hephaestion, greeting (χαίρειν). If you are well, and other things happen as you would wish, it would be in accordance with my constant prayer to the gods. I myself am well, and the boy ; and all at home *make constant remembrance of you.*" Comp. Rom. i. 9; Eph. i. 16; Philem. 4. Again : " Ammonios to his sister Tachnumi, abundant greeting (τὰ πλεῖστα χαίρειν). Before all things, I pray that you may be in health ; and each day I make the act of worship for you." In these

---

* There has been some dispute as to whether it was applied to a synagogue, but the usage of Josephus and Philo seems decisive in favour of that meaning. See Jos. *Vita*, 54 ; Juvenal, *Sat.* III. 296 ; Schürer, *The Jewish People in the Time of Jesus Christ*, Div. II., Vol. II., p. 73 ; Wendt, *Apostelgeschichte*, on Acts xvi. 13. An inscription preserved in the Berlin Egyptian Museum testifies to the meaning *synagogue* as early as the third century B.C. Zenobia and Vaballath, about 270 A.D., decree the restoration of an inscription on a synagogue, as follows : Βασιλεὺς Πτολεμαῖος Εὐεργέτης τὴν προσευχὴν ἄσυλον *King Ptolemy Euergetes [decrees] that the place of prayer [be] an asylum.* See Deissmann, *Neue Bibelstudien*, p. 49.

specimens the conventional salutations in correspondence include the general greeting (χαίρειν) and the statement that prayer is made for the correspondent's welfare; and the words *constant* and *daily* are attached to the act of prayer. It is further to be noticed that many passages of Paul's Epistles give evidence of having been shaped by expressions in letters received by him from the parties he is addressing. In his answer he gives them back their own words, as is common in correspondence. Thus, *making mention of you* and *remembering your work*, etc., together with the statement that Timothy reports that *you have a good remembrance of us* (ch. iii. 6), all together suggest that Paul had before him, when writing to the Thessalonians, a letter which Timothy had brought from them. Other instances will be noted as they occur.*

Work — labour — patience (ἔργου — κόπου — ὑπομονῆς). Ἔργον *work*, may mean either the *act*, the simple transaction, or the *process* of dealing with anything, or the *result* of the dealing, — as a book or a picture is called *a work*. Κόπος *labour*, from κόπτειν *to strike* or *hew;* hence, *laborious*, *painful* exertion. Ὑπομονή *patience*, patient endurance and faithful persistence in toil and suffering. See on 2 Pet. i. 6; Jas. v. 7. The genitives, *of faith, love, hope*, mark the generating principles of the work and labour and patience, which set their stamp upon each; thus, *work* which springs from *faith*, and is characteristic of faith. The phrase *patience of hope* is found only here; but see Rom. v. 4; viii. 25; xv. 4; 1 Cor. xiii. 7; Heb. vii. 11, 12. For ὑπομονή in LXX, see 1 Chron. xxix. 15; Job xiv. 19; Ps. ix. 18; xxxviii. 7; Jer. xiv. 8. We have here the great triad of Christian graces, corresponding to 1 Cor. xiii. Hope is prominent throughout the two Epistles. The triad appears, 1 Th. v. 8; Gal. v. 5, 6; 1 Cor. xiii. 13; Eph. iv. 2–5;

---

* See an interesting article by J. Rendel Harris, *Expositor*, Vol. IV., No. III., 1898, "A Study in Letter-writing." Also an article by Walter Lock, *Expositor*, Vol. II., No. I., 1897, "1 Corinthians viii. 1–9. A Suggestion."

Col. i. 4, 5; Heb. x. 22–24; 1 Pet. i. 21–22.   Comp. 1 Th.
ii. 9; v. 8; 2 Th. iii. 5, 8; 1 Cor. xv. 10, 58; 2 Cor. xi. 27;
Apoc. ii. 2.

In our Lord, etc. (τοῦ κυρίου).   Lit. *of* our Lord.   For a
similar use of the genitive, see J. v. 42; 1 J. ii. 5, 15;
Acts ix. 31; Rom. i. 5; iii. 18, 22, 26, etc.   Connect with
hope only.

Before our God and Father.   Const. with *remembering*,
and comp. ch. ii. 19; iii. 9.

4. Election of God.   Incorrect.   Const. *of* or *by* (ὑπὸ)
God with *beloved*.   Ἐκλογὴ *election*, in N. T., mostly by Paul.
Elsewhere only Acts ix. 15, and 2 Pet. i. 10.   This, and
the kindred words, ἐκλέγειν *to choose*, and ἐκλεκτὸς *chosen* or
elect, are used of God's selection of men or agencies for
special missions or attainments ; but neither here nor elsewhere in the N. T. is there any warrant for the revolting
doctrine that God has predestined a definite number of mankind to eternal life, and the rest to eternal destruction.*
The sense in this passage appears to be defined by the succeeding context.   The Thessalonians had been chosen to be
members of the Christian church, and their conduct had
justified the choice.   See vv. 5–10.

5. For (ὅτι).   Incorrect.   Rend. *how that*.   It is explanatory of *your election*.   For similar usage see 1 Cor. i. 26.

Our gospel.   The gospel as preached by Paul and his
colleagues.   Comp. Rom. ii. 16; xvi. 25; Gal. i. 11; ii. 2;
1 Th. ii. 4.   *My gospel* is sometimes used in connection
with an emphasis upon some particular feature of the gospel,
as in Rom. ii. 16, where Paul is speaking of the judgment of
the world *by Christ;* or in Rom. xvi. 25, where he is referring to the extension of the messianic kingdom to the Gentiles.

---

* See the note in Vol. III., p. 133 ff.

In word (ἐν λόγῳ). The gospel did not appeal to them as mere eloquent and learned discourse.

In power (ἐν δύναμει). Power of spiritual persuasion and conviction : not power as displayed in miracles, at least not principally, although miraculous demonstrations may be included. Paul rarely alludes to his power of working miracles.

Assurance (πληροφορίᾳ). Assured persuasion *of the preacher* that the message was divine. The word not in pre-Christian Greek writers, nor in LXX. Only in one other passage in Paul, Col. ii. 2. See Heb. vi. 11 ; x. 22.

We were (ἐγενήθημεν). More correctly, *we shewed* or *proved ourselves.*

6. **Followers** (μιμηταί). More literally and better, *imitators.* Only once outside of Paul's writings, Heb. vi. 12. Comp. 1 Th. iii. 9 ; 2 Th. iii. 7 ; 1 Cor. iv. 16 ; xi. 1 ; Gal. iv. 12 ; Philip. iii. 17 ; iv. 9.

And of the Lord. Guarding against any possible imputation of self-assertion or conceit. Comp. 1 Cor. xi. 1.

Tribulation (θλίψει). See on Matt. xiii. 21. Referring especially to persecutions at the hands of the Jews (Acts xvii. 5 ff.), which probably continued after Paul's departure from Thessalonica.

7. **An ensample** (τύπον). See on 1 Pet. v. 3.

Macedonia and Achaia. Shortly after 146 B.C., all Greece south of Macedonia and Epirus was formed into a Roman province under the name of Achaia, and Macedonia with Epirus into another province called Macedonia.

8. **Hath sounded forth** (ἐξήχηται). N. T.°. LXX Joel iii. 14 ; Sir. xl. 13, of *thunder;* 3 Macc. iii. 2, of *a report.* It means a *loud, unmistakable* proclamation.

The word of the Lord (ὁ λόγος τοῦ κυρίου). The phrase in Paul only in these Epistles. Comp. 2 Th. iii. 1 ; iv. 15. Comparatively frequent in Acts. Paul has λόγος θεοῦ or τοῦ θεοῦ *word of God*, eight times, and λόγος τοῦ χριστοῦ *word of the Christ*, once, Col. iii. 16. The meaning here is *the gospel*, regarded either as the message *proceeding from* the Lord, or *concerning* him. It is the εὐαγγέλιον θεοῦ *the gospel of God:* see ch. ii. 2, 8, 9 ; Rom. i. 1 ; xv. 16 ; 2 Cor. xi. 7. As Professor Sanday remarks on Rom. i. 1, " it is probably a mistake in these cases to restrict the force of the genitive to one particular aspect : all aspects are included in which the gospel is in any way related to God and Christ."

In every place. A rhetorical exaggeration, signifying the whole known world. It is explained by the extensive commercial relations of Thessalonica. Comp. Rom. i. 8 ; Col. i. 6, 23 · 2 Cor. ii. 14.

Is spread abroad (ἐξελήλυθεν). Lit. and better, *has gone forth.**

9. **They themselves shew** (αὐτοὶ ἀπαγγέλλουσιν). *They themselves* in contrast with *we*, ver. 8. *We* need not speak of anything : *they themselves* volunteer testimony to your faith. *Shew*, more correctly *announce* or *report*.†

---

* Much discussion has arisen as to the proper connection of this passage. As punctuated and rendered in A.V. and Rev. the sequence is irregular. There is a clear antithesis between ἀλλ' *but* and οὐ μόνον *not only ;* and the sentence, if regular, would have closed with *in every place.* As it is, a new subject and predicate (*your faith—has gone forth*) is introduced with *in every place.* The simplest and best solution of the difficulty is to accept the irregular construction as characteristically Pauline. Others place a colon after *of the Lord*, and begin a new clause with *not only.*

† Dr. J. Rendel Harris offers as a conjectural reading ἀπαγγέλλετε *ye report*, taking the passage as an exact parallel to ch. ii. 1, *ye know that our entrance was not in vain.* He thinks that thus a reference would be shown to a letter from the Thessalonians to Paul, and that the difficulty would be relieved which grows out of the improbability of a newly founded church exerting so extensive an influence. *Expositor*, Vol. IV., No. III., 1898.

Entering in (εἴσοδον). Comp. ch. ii. 1. The thought of ver. 5 is resumed. The repetition of the word in ch. ii. 1, and of *in vain* in ch. iii. 5, may point to expressions in a letter of the Thessalonians.

Unto you (πρὸς). The preposition combines with the sense of *direction* that of *relation* and *intercourse*. Comp. Matt. xiii. 56; Mk. ix. 16; J. i. 1; Acts iii. 25; Col. iv. 5; Heb. ix. 20.

Ye turned unto God (ἐπεστρέψατε πρὸς τὸν θεὸν). Comp. Acts xiv. 15. The exact phrase only here. The verb is common in LXX, with both κύριον *Lord* and θεὸν *God*.

Idols. See on 1 Cor. viii. 3. The word would indicate that the majority of the converts were heathen and not Jews.

Living and true (ζῶντι καὶ ἀληθινῷ). The only instance in N. T. of this collocation. It does not occur in O. T. For ἀληθινὸς *genuine*, see on J. i. 9; iv. 37; vii. 28. Mostly in the Johannine writings.

10. To wait for (ἀναμένειν). N. T.º. Several times in LXX, as Job ii. 9; vii. 2; Isa. lix. 11. Paul's usual word is ἀπεκδέχομαι: see Rom. viii. 19, 23, 25; 1 Cor. i. 7; Philip. iii. 20.

From heaven (ἐκ τῶν οὐρανῶν). Lit. *from the heavens.* Comp. 1 Cor. xv. 47; 1 Th. iv. 16; 2 Th. i. 7. Paul uses the unclassical plural much oftener than the singular. Although the Hebrew equivalent has no singular, the singular is almost universal in LXX, the plural occurring mostly in the Psalms. Οὐρανός is from a Sanscrit word meaning *to cover* or *encompass.* The Hebrew *shamayim* signifies *height, high district, the upper regions.* Similarly we have in N. T. ἐν ὑψίστοις *in the highest* (places), Matt. xxi. 9; L. ii. 14: ἐν ὑψηλοῖς *in the high* (places), Heb. i. 3. Paul's usage is evidently coloured by the Rabbinical conception of a series of heavens : see 2 Cor. xii. 2 ; Eph. iv. 10. Some Jewish teachers held that there were seven heavens,* others three. The idea of a series of heavens appears in patristic writings, in Thomas Aquinas's doctrine of the celestial hierarchies, and in Dionysius the Areopagite. Through the scholastic theologians it passed into Dante's *Paradiso* with its nine heavens.† The words *to await his Son from heaven* strike the keynote of this Epistle.

Jesus which delivered (Ἰησοῦν τὸν ῥυόμενον). More correctly, *delivereth.* See on Matt. i. 21. Ῥύεσθαι to deliver, mostly in Paul. Lit. *to draw to one's self.* Almost invariably with the specification of some evil or danger or enemy. Σώζειν to save is often used in a similar sense, of deliverance from disease, from sin, or from divine wrath: see Matt. i. 21; Mk. vi. 56; L. viii. 36; Acts ii. 40; Rom. v. 9 : but σώζειν is a larger and more comprehensive term, including not only deliverance from sin and death, but investment with all the privileges and rewards of the new life in Christ.

The wrath to come (τῆς ὀργῆς τῆς ἐρχομένης). Lit. *the wrath which is coming.* The wrath, absolutely, of the wrath of God, as Rom. v. 9 ; xii. 19 ; 1 Th. ii. 16. Sometimes for the *punishment* which wrath inflicts, as Rom. xii. 4 ; Eph. v. 6 ; Col. iii. 6. See on J. iii. 36. The phrase *wrath to come* is found in Matt. iii. 7 ; L. iii. 7. *Coming* does not necessarily imply the thought of *speedy* or *imminent* approach, but the general tone of the Epistle points in that direction.

CHAPTER II.

1. **Was not in vain** (οὐ κενὴ γέγονεν). More accurately, *hath not proved vain.* Κενὴ is *empty.* Ματαία, also rendered *vain*, is *fruitless.*

---

* See Stanley's condensation of Wetstein, in *Com. on Corinthians*, on 2 Cor. xii. 2.

† See B. F. Westcott, *Religious Thought in the West.*

2. **Having suffered before** (προπαθόντες). N. T.º. Although we had suffered.

Having been shamefully entreated (ὑβρισθέντες). Comp. Matt. xxii. 6; L. xviii. 32; Acts xiv. 5. This may have been added because προπαθόντες alone might denote the experience of something good; but it is more probably intended as an expansion and illustration of that word. Paul's sensitiveness to personal indignity appears in the narrative in Acts xvi., which gives the historical explanation of the two words. It appears frequently in 2d Corinthians.

As ye know (καθὼς οἴδατε). One of the many characteristic expressions of these Epistles which indicate community of experience and sentiment on the part of Paul and his readers. See 1 Th. i. 5, 8; ii. 1, 5, 10, 11; iii. 3, 4, 12; iv. 1, 2, 6, 11; v. 1, 11; 2 Th. ii. 16; iii. 1, 2.*

Philippi. See Acts xvi. 19–40; Philip. 1, 30.

We waxed bold (ἐπαρρησιασάμεθα). Only once elsewhere in Paul, Eph. vi. 20. Frequent in Acts. Always in N. T. in connection with speaking. Derived from πᾶν *every*, and ῥῆσις *speaking*. Hence παρρησία *boldness*, bold *speaking out of every word*. The noun is very often used adverbially, as παρρησίᾳ *boldly* or *openly*, Mk. viii. 32; see also J. xviii. 20. In Acts always μετὰ παρρησίας *with boldness*, comp. Heb. iv. 16. Ἐν παρρησίᾳ *in boldness*, J. vii. 4; xvi. 29; Eph. vi. 19; Philip. i. 20. Both the verb and the noun are found in LXX. See Lev. xxvi. 13; Prov. x. 10; Wisd. v. 1; 1 Macc. iv. 18; Sir. vi. 11.

In our God (ἐν τῷ θεῷ ἡμῶν). Const. with *we waxed bold*. Their boldness was not mere natural courage, but was inspired by God. There is a slight emphasis on *our* God, as

---

* Dr. Harris says that the expression must be understood here in the sense "ye have admitted in your letter," or "ye have testified." I do not think that this can be shown. It looks a little like a piece of special pleading.

contrasted with the idols from which they had turned (ch.
i. 9). The phrase only here in N. T.

Gospel of God (εὐαγγέλιον τοῦ θεοῦ). For the phrase see
Mk. i. 14; Rom. i. 1; xv. 16; 2 Cor. xi. 7; 1 Th. ii. 8, 9;
1 Pet. iv. 17. It points to the monotheistic character of the
gospel.

In much contention (ἐν πολλῷ ἀγῶνι). Better *conflict.*
Comp. Col. ii. 1; Philip. i. 27; 1 Tim. vi. 12; Heb. xii. 1.
Ἀγών originally of a contest in the arena; but it is used of
any struggle, outward or inward.

3. **Exhortation** (παράκλησις). See on L. vi. 24 and 1 Cor.
xiv. 3. *Exhortation* or *counsel* is Paul's usual sense.

Of deceit (ἐκ πλάνης). Better, *of error.* It may imply
deceit as accompanying or causing error, but it does not
occur in the sense of *deceit.* Our exhortation did not proceed from any false teaching which we had ourselves received.
We were guided by "the spirit of truth"; see 1 J. iv. 6,
and comp. 2 Pet. i. 16.

Of uncleanness (ἐξ ἀκαθαρσίας). Ἀκαθαρσία in Matt.
xxiii. 27 of the corruption of the sepulchre. Elsewhere in
N. T. of sensual impurity. See Rom. i. 24; 2 Cor. xii. 21;
Eph. iv. 19. Here in the sense of impurity on the side of
*sordidness.** In Eph. iv. 19, Paul speaks of working *uncleanness* (ἀκαθαρσίαν) in a spirit of *selfish desire* (πλεονεξία), which
is the spirit of *covetousness.* In Eph. v. 3, uncleanness and
covetousness are closely associated. Paul means that his
exhortation did not proceed from greed for gain or lust for
power.

In guile (ἐν δόλῳ). While *uncleanness* expresses impure
purpose or *motive, guile* has reference to improper *means;*

---

* Lightfoot's view, that the word is used with a reference to the impuri-
ties of the worship of Aphrodite at Corinth and of the Cabeiri at Thessalonica, seems far-fetched.

plausible but insincere methods of winning converts; suppression of the truth; "huckstering the word of God" (see on 2 Cor. ii. 17); adulterating it for purposes of gain or popularity.

4. We were allowed (δεδοκιμάσμεθα). More correctly, *approved.* See on 1 Pet. i. 7. We came and spoke to you as *tested* men.

Pleasing (ἀρέσκοντες). As being those who seek to please. Comp. Gal. i. 10, and ἀνθρωπάρεσκοι *man-pleasers*, Eph. vi. 6; Col. iii. 22. Comp. LXX, Ps. lii. 5: "God hath scattered the bones of men-pleasers." The fourth Psalm of Solomon is entitled: *Against the men-pleasers* (ἀνθρωπαρέσκοις).

Who proveth (δοκιμάζοντι). Word-play with δεδοκιμάσμεθα *we were approved.*

5. Used we flattering words (ἐν λόγῳ κολακίας ἐγενήθημεν). Better, *were we found using flattering discourse.* Very literally and baldly it is, *we came to pass in discourse of flattery.* It means more than the mere fact that they were not flatterers: rather, they did not *prove to be* such in the course of their work. Similar periphrases with ἐν are found, L. xxii. 44; Acts xxii. 17; 2 Cor. iii. 7; Philip. ii. 7; with εἰς, Matt. xxi. 42; Mk. xii. 10; L. xx. 17; Acts iv. 11; 1 Th. iii. 5. Κολακία *flattery*, N. T.°. °LXX. Rare in Class. Λόγῳ is explained by some as *report* or *rumour.* Common report did not charge us with being flatterers. This meaning is admissible, but the other is simpler. Paul says that they had not descended to flattery in order to make the gospel acceptable. They had not flattered men's self-complacency so as to blind them to their need of the radical work which the gospel demands.

Cloke of covetousness (προφάσει πλεονεξίας). For πρόφασις see on J. xv. 22. Properly *pretext:* πρό before, φάσις a *word* or *saying.* Others, less probably, from προφαίνειν to

cause to shine forth or *before*.   Paul means that he had not
used his apostolic office to disguise or conceal avaricious
designs.

God is witness (θεὸς μάρτυς).   Comp. Rom. i. 9 ; 2 Cor.
i. 23 ; Philip. i. 8 ; 1 Th. ii. 10.   *God* or *the Lord is witness*
is a common O. T. formula: see Gen. xxxi. 44, 50 ; 1 Sam.
xii. 5, 6 ; xx. 23, 42 ; Wisd. i. 6.   For testimony to his *conduct*, he appeals to the Thessalonians (*as ye know*) : for testimony to his *motives*, he appeals to God.   Comp. ver. 10,
where there is the double appeal.

6. **Of men** (ἐξ ἀνθρώπων).   To extract glory *from* men.

When we might have been burdensome (δυνάμενοι ἐν
βάρει εἶναι).   Lit. *being able to be in weight*.   The phrase ἐν
βάρει *in weight* is unique in N. T., and does not occur in
LXX.   The better rendering here is *to be in authority*.   Paul
means that his position as an apostle would have warranted
him in asserting authority or standing on his dignity, which
he did not do.   Βάρος *weight*, in the sense of *influence*, is
found in late Greek.   Paul's Epistles were called *weighty*
(βαρεῖαι), 2 Cor. x. 10 : others explain as referring to the
apostolic right to exact pecuniary support.*

7. **Gentle** (ἤπιοι).   This reading is adopted by Tischendorf, Weiss, and the Rev. T.   Westcott and Hort read νήπιοι
babes.   This gives a stronger and bolder image, and one
which falls in better with the course of thought, in which
Paul is asserting his innocence of guile and flattery, and not
of *harshness*.

---

* This interpretation is urged on the ground that ἐπιβαρῆσαι, ver. 9, and
2 Th. iii. 8, κατεβάρησα, 2 Cor. xii. 16, and ἀβαρῆ, 2 Cor. xi. 9, all refer to
pecuniary support.   Accordingly these words are connected with *covetousness*, ver. 5.   But they are separated from πλεονεξία by a new idea, *seeking
glory*, with which their connection is *immediate*.   Moreover, it is unlikely
that Paul would have attached the idea of covetousness to a rightful claim
for support.   Our explanation is further favoured by the contrasted νήπιοι,
ver. 7.

Among you (ἐν μέσῳ ὑμῶν).   Better, and more literally, *in the midst of you*, which implies more intimate intercourse than *among* you.   Comp. L. xxii. 27.

Nurse (τροφός).   N. T.⁰.   In Class. sometimes of a mother, and so probably here.   See Gal. iv. 19.

Cherisheth (θάλπῃ).   P⁰.   Here and Eph. v. 29.   The verb originally means *to warm*.   See LXX, Deut. xxii. 6.

Her own children.   Note the inversion of metaphor.   Paul is first the babe, then the nurse or mother.   For similar instances see ch. v. 2, 4 ; 2 Cor. iii. 13–16 ; Rom. vii. 1 ff.   See Introduction to 2 Cor., Vol. III., p. xix.

8. **Being affectionately desirous** (ὁμειρόμενοι).   N. T.⁰.   Once in LXX, Job iii. 21.   The figure of the nursing mother is continued.   She is not satisfied with nursing the child, but interests herself affectionately in all that concerns it.

We were willing (ηὐδοκοῦμεν).   Better, *we were pleased.*   Imperfect tense : we *continued* to entertain and manifest our affectionate solicitude.   The verb occasionally in later Greek, and often in LXX.   In N. T. it is used of God's decrees, as L. xii. 32 ; 1 Cor. i. 21 ; Gal. i. 15 ; Col. i. 19 ; and of the free determination and plans of men, as Rom. xv. 26 ; 2 Cor. v. 8 ; 1 Th. iii. 1.

Souls (ψυχάς).   Better *lives.*   See on Rom. xi. 3 ; 1 Cor. xv. 45 ; Mk. xii. 30.

9. **Labour—travail** (κόπον— μόχθον).   The two words are associated in 2 Cor. xi. 27 ; 2 Th. iii. 8.   Μόχθος *travail*, P⁰.   Frequent in LXX.   Κόπος emphasises *fatigue*, μόχθος *hardship*.

Because we would not be chargeable (πρὸς τὸ μὴ ἐπιβαρῆσαι).   Incorrect.   Rend. *that we might not burden.*   Put you to expense for our support.   Comp. 2 Th. iii. 8.

10. **Holily — justly — unblameably** (ὁσίως — δικαίως — ἀμέμπτως). For ὁσίως *holily*, see on L. i. 75; for δικαίως *justly* or *righteously*, on Rom. i. 17; v. 7. Ἀμέμπτως *unblameably*, only in these Epistles. See ch. iii. 13; v. 23. For the distinction between ὅσιος and δίκαιος, see Plato, *Gorg.* 507.

11. **Comforted** (παραμυθούμενοι). The A. V. renders the three participles in this verse as finite verbs, *we exhorted*, etc. Rev. retains the participial construction. Better than *comforted, persuading*. Persuasion is the form which the exhortation assumed. Παράκλησις *exhortation*, and παραμύθιον *persuasion*, are associated in Philip. ii. 1. The verb παραμυθέομαι *to persuade* occurs only four times in N. T. See on Philip. ii. 1. Neither verb nor noun in LXX.

Charged (μαρτυρόμενοι). Rev. *testifying;* but the A.V. is more correct. Rend. *charging*. The verb means *to conjure*, or *appeal to* by something sacred. So Eph. iv. 17. Comp. Acts xx. 26; Gal. v. 3, and διαμαρτύρομαι *I charge*, 1 Tim. v. 21; 2 Tim. ii. 14; iv. 1. Comp. Thucyd. vi. 80.

12. **Walk** (περιπατεῖν). By Paul exclusively in the metaphorical sense of *behaving* or *conducting* one's self. Similarly in Hebrews. In the Synoptic Gospels, with one exception (Mk. vii. 5), of the physical act. Both senses in the Fourth Gospel, but only the metaphorical sense in John's Epistles. Once in the metaphorical sense in Acts, xxi. 21. In LXX almost exclusively literal; but see 2 K. xx. 23; Prov. viii. 20; Eccl. xi. 9. The phrase ἀξίως περιπατεῖν *to walk worthily*, in Eph. iv. 1; Col. i. 10.

Worthy of God (ἀξίως θεοῦ). Better *worthily*. For ἀξίως comp. LXX, Wisd. vii. 15; xvi. 1; Sir. xiv. 11. The formula ἀξίως θεοῦ is found among the Pergamum papyri. A priest of Dionysus is described as having performed his sacred duties ἀξίως θεοῦ. A priestess of Athene as having served ἀξίως τῆς θεοῦ καὶ τῆς πατρίδος *worthily of the goddess and of* *her fatherland.*   A chief herdsman as having conducted the divine mysteries ἀξίως τοῦ καθηγεμόνος Διονύσου *worthily of his chief, Dionysus.*   The dates of these papyri are from 141 B.C. to the beginning of the first century A.D.*

Kingdom and glory.   The only instance of this collocation. God's kingdom is here conceived as present — the economy of divine grace to which the readers are called as Christians. *Glory* is the future consummation of that kingdom.   For βασιλεία *kingdom,* see on L. vi. 20.   Δόξα *glory* is not used in N. T. in its primary, classical sense of *opinion* or *notion.* It signifies *reputation,* J. xii. 43; Rom. ii. 7, 10: *brightness* or *splendour,* Acts xxii. 11; Rom. ix. 4; 1 Cor. xv. 40. *Glory of God* expresses the sum total of the divine perfections.   The idea is prominent in redemptive revelation: see Isa. lx. 1; Rom. v. 2; vi. 4.   It expresses the form in which God reveals himself in the economy of salvation: see Rom. ix. 23; Eph. i. 12; 1 Tim. i. 11.   It is the means by which the redemptive work is carried on: see 2 Pet. i. 3; Rom. vi. 4; Eph. iii. 16; Col. i. 11.   It is the goal of Christian hope: see Rom. v. 2; viii. 18, 21; Tit. ii. 13.

13. **Also — we.**   *Also* may point to an expression of thanksgiving in a letter from the Thessalonians to Paul.   You say "we give thanks to God."   *We also* give thanks.   Comp. ch. i. 2.

When ye received the word of God which ye heard of us (παραλαβόντες λόγον ἀκοῆς παρ᾽ ἡμῶν τοῦ θεοῦ).   Rend. *when ye received the word of the message (which came) from us, even the word of God.*   The words *the word of the message from us* form one conception, governed by παραλαβόντες *having received* or *when ye received;* therefore *from us* is not to be taken as depending on *having received,* as Rev. *when ye received from us the word,* etc.   *Of God* (supply *the word*) is added in order to correct any possible false impression made

---

* Deissmann, *Neue Bibelstudien,* p. 75 f.

by *from us*. 'Ἀκοή in N. T. means *the sense of hearing*, as
Matt. xiii. 14; 1 Cor. xii. 17; 2 Pet. ii. 8: or *the organ of
hearing = ear*, as Mk. vii. 35; L. vii. 1: or *a thing heard, a
report, rumour*, as J. xii. 38; Rom. x. 16. The phrase λόγος
ἀκοῆς or τῆς ἀκοῆς *the word of hearing*, or *word of the message*,
signifies *the word which is heard*. Comp. Heb. iv. 2. See
on *the fame*, L. iv. 37.

Effectually worketh (ἐνεργεῖται). Referring to *the word*,
not to *God*. Comp. Philip. ii. 13. In the middle voice as
here, used only by Paul and James, and only of things. See
Eph. iii. 20; Col. i. 29; Jas. v. 16, and footnote on Col. i. 29.
The noun ἐνέργεια, Pᵒ. It means *power in exercise*, and is
used only of superhuman power.

14. **In Christ Jesus.** Seems to be added to distinguish
the Christian churches in Judaea from the synagogues of the
Jews, which would claim to be churches of God. Comp. Gal.
i. 22, and see on ch. i. 1. *In Christ Jesus, in Christ, in Jesus,
in the Lord, in him*, are common Pauline formulas to denote
the most intimate communion with the living Christ. These
phrases are not found in the Synoptic Gospels. 'Ἐν ἐμοί *in
me* (Christ) is frequent in the Fourth Gospel. The conception is that of a sphere or environment in which a Christian
or a church lives, as a bird in the air, or the roots of a tree in
the soil.*

Countrymen (συμφυλετῶν). N. T.ᵒ. ᵒLXX. Not in pre-
Christian Greek writers. Lit. *belonging to the same tribe* or
clan. The reference is to the Gentile persecutors who were
instigated by the Jews.

15. **Persecuted** (ἐκδιωξάντων). Rev. more literally and
correctly, *drave out*. The word only here, though it occurs
as an alternative reading, L. xi. 49. Probably with special
reference to his own expulsion from Thessalonica. Acts
xvii. 5–10.

---

* See G. A. Deissmann's excellent monograph, *Die neutestamentliche
Formel "in Christo Jesu."* Marburg. 1892.

Contrary to all men. Tacitus (*Hist.* v. 5) describes the Jews as stubborn in their faith, prompt in kindly offices to each other, but bitterly hostile toward everybody else. Juvenal (*Sat.* xiv. 102 f.) says that they observe and respect whatever Moses has taught in his mystical volume ; not to show the way except to one who practises the same rites, and to show the well only to the circumcised.

16. **To speak — that they might be saved** (λαλῆσαι ἵνα σωθῶσιν). Not, *to speak to the Gentiles in order that they might be saved*, but *to tell the Gentiles that they might be saved*. Comp. 1 Cor. x. 33.

To fill up (ἀναπληρῶσαι). The verb means the making up of what is lacking to perfect fulness ; the filling of a partial void. Comp. Philip. ii. 30. Once in LXX of filling up of sins, Gen. xv. 16. Always blind and stubborn, the Jews filled up the measure of their sins by their treatment of Christ and his apostles.

Alway (πάντοτε). Emphatically placed at the end of the sentence. At all times — before Christ, in Christ's time, now — the Jews by their resistance to the divine word fill up their sins.

Is come (ἔφθασεν). The verb not frequent in N. T. and used mostly by Paul. See on 2 Cor. x. 14, and comp. Rom. ix. 31 ; Philip. iii. 16.

To the uttermost (εἰς τέλος). This is not the meaning of the phrase in N. T. It is *to the end :* see Matt. x. 22 ; xxiv. 13 ; L. xviii. 5 ; J. xiii. 1. The wrath of God had *not* come upon them to the uttermost. The meaning is that the divine wrath had reached the point where it passed into judgment.*

---

* It has been urged that vv. 14–16 are unbecoming one who had been him-self a persecutor of the Jewish-Christian churches (so Baur, *Apostel Paulus*), and further that this diatribe is inconsistent with the patriotism which Paul displays in Rom. ix. xi. These considerations, it is claimed, go to show that

17. **Being taken from you** (ἀπορφανισθέντες). N. T.º.
ºLXX. Rev. better, *being bereaved of you*. From ὀρφανός
b reft. See Mk. xii. 40; J. xiv. 18; Jas. i. 27. The word
suggests the intimate personal fellowship of the writer with
his readers. The separation was like that between parents
and children. Comp. vv. 7, 8.

For a short time (πρὸς καιρὸν ὥρας). N. T.º. Lit. *for the
season of an hour*. Comp. Lat. *horae momentum*. Stronger
than the usual phrase πρὸς ὥραν *for an hour*: see 2 Cor. vii. 8;
Gal. ii. 5; Philem. 15. Comp. πρὸς καιρὸν *for a season*, L.
viii. 13; 1 Cor. vii. 5.

The more abundantly (περισσοτέρως). Rev. *the more exceedingly*. Paul uses this adverb very freely, and outside of
his letters it appears only Heb. ii. 1; xiii. 19. He is much
given to the use of comparatives, and sometimes heaps them
together: see Rom. viii. 37; 2 Cor. vii. 13; iv. 17; Eph.
iii. 20; Philip. i. 23.

18. **We would** (ἠθελήσαμεν). Implying more than a mere
inclination or desire. It was our *will* to come. See on Matt.
i. 19.

I Paul. Not implying any less desire on the part of his
associates, but emphasising his own. See on the use of the
epistolary plural, ch. i. 2.

Satan (Σατανᾶς). From the Aramaic *Sātanā, adversary*.
In the canonical LXX the name appears only three times,
1 K. xi. 14, 23, 25, and in each case is applied to a man.
In LXX διάβολος is used, almost without exception, as
the translation of the Heb. *Satan*. Of 22 instances of

---

the Epistle is a forgery, or at least that vv. 14–16 are interpolated. Such
criticism is hardly worthy of notice. Any allusion here to Paul's part in
Jewish persecutions would have been in singularly bad taste. As for Paul's
patriotism, genuine and deep though it was, it was secondary to his consuming
zeal for Christ and his gospel. What he here says about the Jews he had
long known, and his recent experience in Macedonia might have moved even
a patriot to fierce indignation against his own people.

διάβολος only 9 are outside of the book of Job. From the
more general conception of an adversary, there is, in the
O. T., a gradual development toward that of an evil per·
sonality. For instance, in 2 Sam. xxiv. 1, the numbering
of the people is ascribed to the anger of the Lord.   The
later historian, in 1 Chron. xxi. 1, ascribes the act to Satan.
See also Job, Wisd. ii. 24 ; Zech. iii. 1.   The specialising of
the conception was due, in part, to the contact of the Jews
with the religions of Babylon and Persia.   In N. T. Satan
appears as the personal spirit of evil — the same who is
called *the devil, the wicked one, the prince of the power of the
air, the prince of this world, the serpent, the god of this world,
the tempter.* He tempts to evil, opposes God's work, inspires
evil dispositions, torments God's people.   The word Satan
occurs only once in the Fourth Gospel, not in the Epistles,
but often in the Apocalypse.   Mark never uses διάβολος,
Matthew never Satan.   Paul seldom διάβολος, often Satan.
Satan alone in Pastorals.   Luke uses both.   It is clear
that Paul here as elsewhere employs the word in a personal
sense ; but any attempt to base the doctrine of a personal
devil on this and similar passages is unsafe.*

Hindered (ἐνέκοψεν).   See on 1 Pet. iii. 7.

19. **Hope**.   Used of the *object* of hope, as Col. i. 5 ;
1 Tim. i. 1 ; Heb. vi. 18.

Joy — crown (χαρὰ — στέφανος).   Comp. Philip. iv. 1.
The phrase *crown of rejoicing* or *boasting*, in Prov. xvi. 31 ;
Ezek. xvi. 12 ; xxiii. 42. Comp. Isa. lxxii. 3, στέφανος κάλλους
crown of beauty, and Soph. *Aj.* 465, στέφ. εὐκλείας *crown of
renown*.   The Thessalonians were " a chaplet of victory of
which Paul might justly make his boast in the day of the
Lord " (Ellicott).   For στέφανος see on Apoc. iv. 4.

Coming (παρουσία).   See on Matt. xxiv. 3, and on ἐπιφάνεια *appearing*, 1 Tim. vi. 14 and 2 Th. ii. 8.

---

* As Ellicott on this passage, who asserts that a denial of that doctrine
" can be only compatible with a practical denial of Scripture inspiration."

CHAPTER III.

1. Forbear (στέγοντες). Lit. no longer *forbearing*. See on 1 Cor. ix. 12: LXX, Sir. viii. 17. For Class. parall. Soph. *O. C.* 15; *Elec.* 1118; Eurip. *Hippol.* 844; *Ion* 1412. He means that his longing for some personal communication from the Thessalonians became intolerable.

To be left — alone (καταλειφθῆναι — μόνοι). Implying, as *we sent* (ver. 2) and *I sent* (ver. 5), the previous presence of Timothy with him at Athens.

2. Our brother. Comp. 2 Cor. i. 1; Col. i. 1; Philem. 1; Rom. xvi. 23; 1 Cor. i. 1; xvi. 12.

Minister (διάκονον). See on Matt. xx. 26; Mk. ix. 35. Not in the official sense of *deacon* which occurs only in the Pastorals. Διάκονος *minister* and διακονία *ministry* or *service* are common expressions of service to Christ or to men. Paul habitually uses them in this way. See Acts i. 25; vi. 4. Διάκονοι is used of ministers of Satan, 2 Cor. xi. 15, and διάκονος of the civil magistrate, Rom. xiii. 4. See Introduction to the Pastoral Epistles.*

Fellow labourer. Omit from text.†

To establish (στηρίξαι). See on L. xxii. 32; Introd. to Catholic Epistles, Vol. I., p. 625; 1 Pet. v. 10; 2 Pet. i. 12.

3. Moved (σαίνεσθαι). N. T.°. °LXX. In Class., as early as Homer, of dogs; *to wag the tail, fawn* (Hom. *Od.* x. 217; xvi. 6). Hence of persons, to *fawn* or *cringe*. The word is apparently used here in the original sense, *to be shaken.* ‡

---

* Also *International Commentary on Philippians and Philemon*, Excursus on "Bishops and Deacons."

† Weiss substitutes it for διάκονον.

‡ So Hesychius, who defines *moved, shaken, disturbed* (κινεῖται, σαλεύεται, ταράττεται).

We are appointed (κείμεθα). As L. ii. 34 (see note);
Philip. i. 17. Comp. Acts xiv. 22, in which occur four of
the words used here. For the thought, see Matt. v. 10;
x. 17; xvi. 24; 1 Pet. ii. 21 ff.; iv. 12; 2 Tim. iii. 12.

5. **The tempter** (ὁ πειράζων). Only here and Matt. iv. 3.
LXX. See on Matt. vi. 13.

In vain (εἰς κενόν). The phrase only in Paul. See 2 Cor.
vi. 1; Gal. ii. 2; Philip. ii. 16. The force of the preposition is fairly represented by *to* in the phrase *to no purpose.*
LXX has εἰς κενόν, εἰς τὸ κενόν, and εἰς κενά.

6. **Now** (ἄρτι). See on J. xiii. 33. Const. with *we were
comforted* (ver. 7), not with *came*.

Good remembrance (μνείαν ἀγαθὴν). Better *kindly* remembrance. Comp. Rom. v. 7 (see note); vii. 12; Tit. ii. 5;
1 Pet. ii. 18. See on ch. i. 3.

7. **Affliction** (ἀνάγκη). Rev. *distress*. The derivation
from ἄγχειν *to press tightly, to choke* (Lightfoot, Ellicott) is
doubtful. In the sense of *urgency, distress*, seldom in Class.
See 1 Cor. vii. 26; 2 Cor. vi. 4; xii. 10; L. xxi. 23.

8. **Stand fast** (στήκετε). The sense of *firm* standing is
derived from the context, and does not inhere in the word.
In Mk. iii. 31; xi. 25, it means simply *to stand*. Comp.
Philip. iv. 1. It does not occur earlier than N. T.

10. **Exceedingly** (ὑπερεκπερισσοῦ). Comp. Eph. iii. 20.
Paul is fond of compounds with ὑπέρ *above*. Of the 28 N. T.
words compounded with ὑπέρ, 22 are found in Paul, and 20
of them only there.

Perfect (καταρτίσαι). Primarily, *to adjust, fit together;* so
mend, Matt. iv. 21. Of the creation of the world, Heb. xi. 3.
See on Matt. xxi. 16; L. vi. 40; 1 Pet. v. 10; Rom. ix. 22.

11. **Direct** (κατευθῦναι). Lit. *make straight.* Only in Paul and Luke. See on L. i. 79, and comp. 2 Th. iii. 5. Frequent in LXX.

13. **With all his saints** (μετὰ πάντων τῶν ἁγίων αὐτοῦ). *Saints* is often explained as *angels;* but the meaning is *the holy and glorified people of God.* Οἱ ἅγιοι is uniformly used of these in N. T. and never of angels unless joined with ἄγγελοι. See L. ix. 26; Mk. viii. 38; Acts x. 22. It is doubtful if οἱ ἅγιοι is used of angels in LXX. Zech. xiv. 5, which is confidently cited as an instance, is quoted at the conclusion of the Didache (xvi. 7), clearly with the sense of glorified believers. Ἅγιοι ἄγγελοι appears Tob. xi. 14; xii. 15; Job v. 1. *Angels* has no connection with anything in this Epistle, but *glorified believers* is closely connected with the matter which was troubling the Thessalonians. See ch. iv. 13. This does not exclude the attendance of angels on the Lord's coming (see Mk. viii. 38; L. ix. 26), but when Paul speaks of such attendance, as 2 Th. i. 7, he says, *with the angels* (ἀγγέλων) *of his power.*

CHAPTER IV.

1. **Furthermore** (λοιπὸν). Rev. not so well, *finally,* although the word is sometimes rightly so rendered. The formula is often used by Paul where he attaches, in a somewhat loose way, even in the midst of an Epistle, a new subject to that which he has been discussing.

2. **Commandments** (παραγγελίας). Better, *charges.* Only four times in N. T. °LXX. The verb παραγγέλλειν *to command* or *charge* is frequent, and is often used in Class. of military orders. See Xen. *Cyr.* ii., 4, 2; Hdt. iii., 25.

3. **Fornication.** Paul wrote from Corinth, where sensuality in the guise of religion was rife. In Thessalonica, besides the ordinary licentious customs of the Gentiles,

immorality was fostered by the Cabeiric worship (see Introduction).   About the time of Paul, a political sanction was
given to this worship by deifying the Emperor as Cabeirus.

**4. That every one of you should know how to pos-
sess his vessel,** etc. (εἰδέναι ἕκαστον ὑμῶν τὸ ἑαυτοῦ σκεῦος
κτᾶσθαι).   The interpretation of vv. 3–6 usually varies
between two explanations: 1. making the whole passage
refer to fornication and adultery: 2. limiting this reference
to vv. 3–5, and making ver. 6 refer to honesty in business.
Both are wrong.   The entire passage exhibits two groups of
parallel clauses; the one concerning sexual, and the other
business relations.   Thus: 1. *Abstain from fornication:
deal honourably with your wives.*   2. *Pursue your business as
holy men*, not with covetous greed as the heathen: *do not
overreach or defraud.*   A comma should be placed after
σκεῦος *vessel*, and κτᾶσθαι *procure* or *acquire*, instead of being
made dependent on εἰδέναι *know*, should begin a new clause.
Render, *that every one of you treat his own wife honorably.*
Εἰδέναι is used Hebraistically in the sense of *have a care for*,
regard, as ch. v. 12, "*Know them that labour*," etc.: recognise their claim to respect, and hold them in due regard.
Comp. Gen. xxxix. 6 : Potiphar οὐκ ᾔδει τῶν καθ' αὑτὸν οὐδὲν
"*gave himself no concern* about anything that he had."
1 Sam. ii. 12 : the sons of Eli οὐκ εἰδότες τὸν κύριον "*paying
no respect* to the Lord."   Ex. i. 8 : Another King arose ὃς
οὐκ ᾔδει τὸν Ἰωσήφ "*who did not recognise* or *regard* Joseph":
did not remember his services and the respect in which he
had been held.   Σκεῦος is sometimes explained as *body*, for
which there is no evidence in N. T.   In 2 Cor. iv. 7 the
sense is metaphorical.   Neither in LXX nor Class. does it
mean *body*.   In LXX very often of *the sacred vessels of worship*: sometimes, as in Class., of *the accoutrements of war.*
In N. T. occasionally, both in singular and plural, in the
general sense of *appliances, furniture, tackling.*   See Matt.
xii. 29 ; L. xvii. 31 ; Acts xxvii. 17 ; Heb. ix. 21.   For the
meaning *vessel*, see L. viii. 16 ; J. xix. 20 ; 2 Cor. iv. 7 ;
Apoc. ii. 27.   Here, metaphorically, for *wife;* comp. 1 Pet.

iii. 7.   It was used for *wife* in the coarse and literal sense by
Rabbinical writers.   The admonition aptly follows the charge
to abstain from fornication.   On the contrary, let each one
treat honorably his own wife.   The common interpretation
is, "as a safeguard against fornication let every one know
how to procure his own wife."   It is quite safe to say that
such a sentence could never have proceeded from Paul.   He
never would have offset a charge to abstain from fornication
with a counsel to be well informed in the way of obtaining a
wife.   When he does touch this subject, as he does in 1 Cor.
vii. 2, he says, very simply, "to avoid fornication let every
man *have* (ἐχέτω) his own wife "; not, *know how to get one*.
Εἰδέναι *know*, as usually interpreted, is both superfluous and
absurd.   Besides, the question was not of *procuring* a wife,
but of living honorably and decently with her, paying her
the respect which was her right, and therefore avoiding
illicit connections.

**That he pursue his gain-getting in sanctification and
honour** (κτᾶσθαι ἐν ἁγιασμῷ καὶ τιμῇ).   As a holy and honorable man.   The exhortation now turns to business relations.   Κτᾶσθαι cannot mean *possess*, as A. V.   That would
require the perfect tense.   It means *procure, acquire*.   Often
buy, as Acts xvii. 28; LXX, Gen. xxxiii. 19; xxxix. 1;
xlvii. 19; xlix. 30; Josh. xxiv. 33; absolutely, Ezek. vii.
12, 13.

5. **Not in the lust of concupiscence** (μὴ ἐν πάθει ἐπιθυμίας).   Lit. *in passion of desire*.   Not with avaricious greed.
For ἐπιθυμία see on Mk. iv. 19.   Its meaning is by no means
limited to sensual lust; see, for instance, L. xxii. 15.   It is
used as including all kinds of worldly desires, as Gal. v. 16,
24; 1 J. ii. 17.   In Rom. vii. 7, especially of covetousness.

6. **That no man go beyond** (τὸ μὴ ὑπερβαίνειν).   Lit.
the not going beyond.   Dependent on *this is the will of God*,
ver. 3.   The verb N. T.°.   Often in LXX, mostly in the
literal sense of *overpassing limits*.   Also of *overtaking, passing*

by, *surpassing*, as in wickedness or cruelty.   It is an expansion of the preceding thought.   Pursue your business as holy men: do not overreach or defraud.

It is the *overstepping* of the line between mine and thine. It is used absolutely, being defined by the succeeding clause. The A. V. is literal, *go beyond*.   Rev. renders *transgress*. Weizsäcker and Bornemann "übergreife *overreach*."   So Rev. margin.   This last is the best.

Defraud (πλεονεκτεῖν).   P⁰.   See on 2 Cor. ii. 11, and *covetousness*, Rom. i. 29.   It emphasises gain as the motive of fraud.   Three times in LXX, Judg. iv. 11; Hab. ii. 9; Ezek. xxii. 27.   Often in Class.

In any matter (ἐν τῷ πράγματι).   Rev. correctly, in *the* matter.   Comp. 2 Cor. vii. 11.   The sense is *the* business in hand, whatever it be.   The τῷ does not stand for τινι *any*. For πράγματι *matter*, see on Matt. xviii. 19.   Those who connect this clause with the preceding, explain τῷ as *the* matter *just mentioned* — adultery.

Avenger (ἔκδικος).   P⁰.   Here and Rom. xiii. 4.   In LXX rarely, and in the same sense as here.   In this sense it occurs only in late Greek.   For the warning comp. Eph. v. 6; Col. iii. 6; Rom. xiii. 4; Gal. v. 21.

7. **Unto uncleanness** (ἐπὶ ἀκαθαρσίᾳ).   Better, *for* uncleanness; ἐπὶ denoting *aim* or *intention*.   The intention is viewed as the basis of the act (ἐπὶ *upon*).   Comp. Gal. v. 13; Eph. ii. 10.

In sanctification (ἐν).   Note the change of preposition. Sanctification is the characteristic life-element of the Christian, *in* which he is to live.   Comp. *in peace*, 1 Cor. vii. 15; *in hope*, Eph. iv. 4.

8. **Despiseth** (ἀθετῶν).   Better, *rejecteth*.   Setteth aside. Comp. Gal. ii. 21; iii. 15; 1 Cor. i. 19.   Used in N. T. both of persons and things.

His Holy Spirit (τὸ πνεῦμα αὐτοῦ τὸ ἅγιον). Solemn and emphatic : *His Spirit, the holy*.   Similarly, Acts xv. 8, 28; xix. 6; xx. 23 ; Eph. i. 13; iv. 30.

9. Taught of God (θεοδίδακτοι). **N.T.º. ºLXX.** Not in Class.

11. Study (φιλοτιμεῖσθαι). **Pº.** Make it your aim. Comp. Rom. xv. 20 (see note); 2 Cor. v. 9.   Often in Class.   Lit. *to be fond of honour :* hence *to strive for honour, to be ambitious.*

To be quiet (ἡσυχάζειν). Note the paradox, *strive* to be *quiet.* For similar instances see Rom. i. 20, *unseen* things *clearly seen :* Rom. i. 22, *wise*, be *fooled* (comp. Horace, *Od.* 1, 34, 2, *insaniens sapientia*) : 2 Cor. viii. 2, *poverty* abounded unto *riches :* 2 Cor. vii. 10, *repentance, not to be repented of.* The disturbances rebuked in the second Epistle may have begun to show themselves, so that there is a possible allusion to the idle busybodies of 2 Th. iii. 11.

12. Honestly (εὐσχημόνως). Pº. Better, *seemly.* From *εὐ well* and *σχῆμα figure* or *fashion.* The literal sense is suggested by the familiar phrase *in good form.* The contrast appears in ἀτάκτως *disorderly*, 2 Th. iii. 6. Paul has in view the impression to be made by his readers on those outside of the church. See on Rom. xiii. 13, and comp. 1 Cor. xiv. 40.

Of nothing (μηδενὸς). Either neuter, *of nothing*, or masculine, *of no man.* In the latter case it would refer to depending upon others for their support, which some, in view of the immediately expected parousia, were disposed to do, neglecting their own business.

13. I would not have you to be ignorant (οὐ θέλομεν ὑμᾶς ἀγνοεῖν). The Greek is, *we* would not, etc. A formula often used by Paul to call special attention to what he is about to say. See Rom. i. 13; xi. 25; 1 Cor. x. 1, etc. He

employs several similar expressions for the same purpose, as
θέλω ὑμᾶς εἰδέναι *I wish you to know* (1 Cor. xi. 3; Col.
ii. 1): γνωρίζω ὑμῖν *I declare unto you* (1 Cor. xv. 1; 2 Cor.
viii. 1; Gal. i. 11): γινώσκειν ὑμᾶς βούλομαι *I would have
you know* (Philip. i. 12).

Them which are asleep (τῶν κοιμωμένων).   Or, *who are
sleeping.*   See on Acts vii. 60; 2 Pet. iii. 4, and comp. 1 Cor.
vii. 39; xi. 30; xv. 6, 18, 20, 51; J. xi. 11, etc.   The dead
members of the Thessalonian church.

Ye sorrow (λυπῆσθε).   Opinions differ as to the possible
ground of this sorrow.   According to some, the Thessalonians supposed that eternal life belonged only to such as should
be found alive at the parousia, and therefore that those
already dead would not share the blessings of the second
advent.   Others, assuming an interval between the advent
and the general resurrection, think that the Thessalonians
were anxious lest their brethren who died before the advent
would be raised only at the general resurrection, and therefore would not share the blessings of communion with the
Lord during the millennial reign.   It is impossible to decide
the question from Paul's words, since he does not argue, but
only consoles.   The value of his consolation does not depend
upon the answer to the question whether the departed saints
shall first be raised up at the general resurrection, or at a
previous resurrection of believers only.   The Thessalonians
were plainly distressed at the thought of separation from
their departed brethren, and had partially lost sight of the
elements of the Christian hope — reunion with them and fellowship with the Lord.   These elements Paul emphasises in
his answer.   The resurrection of Jesus involves the resurrection of believers.   The living and the dead Christians shall
alike be with the Lord.

Others (οἱ λοιποί).   More correctly, *the rest.*   Paul makes
a sharp distinction between Christians and all others.

Who have no hope. Only believers have *hope* of life after death. The speculations and surmisings of pagan philosophy do not amount to a hope.

14. Them also which sleep in Jesus will God bring with him (καὶ ὁ θεὸς τοὺς κοιμηθέντας διὰ τοῦ Ἰησοῦ ἄξει σὺν αὐτῷ).

(1) *Which sleep* should be, *which have been laid asleep* or *have fallen asleep*, giving the force of the passive.

(2) Διὰ τοῦ Ἰησοῦ can by no possibility be rendered *in Jesus*, which would be ἐν Ἰησοῦ : see 1 Cor. xv. 18; 1 Th. iv. 16. It must mean *through* or *by means of* Jesus.

(3) The attempt to construe διὰ τοῦ Ἰησοῦ with τοὺς κοιμηθέντας *those who have fallen asleep by means of Jesus*, gives an awkward and forced interpretation. It has been explained by supposing a reference to martyrs who have died *by* Jesus ; because of their faith in him. In that case we should expect the accusative, διὰ τὸν Ἰησοῦν *on account of* or *for the sake of* Jesus. Moreover Paul is not accentuating that idea. Κοιμηθέντας would be universally understood by the church as referring to the death of Christians, so that *by Jesus* would be superfluous.

(4) Διὰ τοῦ Ἰησοῦ should be construed with ἄξει *will bring*. Rend. the whole : *them also that are fallen asleep will God through Jesus bring with him*. Jesus is thus represented as the agent of the resurrection. See 1 Cor. xv. 21; J. v. 28; vi. 39, 44, 54. *Bring* (ἄξει) is used instead of ἐγειρεῖ *shall raise up*, because the thought of separation was prominent in the minds of the Thessalonians.

15. By the word of the Lord (ἐν λόγῳ κυρίου). Or *in* the word. Λόγος of a concrete saying, Rom. ix. 9; xiii. 9. We do not say this on our own authority. Comp. 1 Cor. vii. 10, 12, 25. No recorded saying of the Lord answers to this reference. It may refer to a saying transmitted orally, or to a direct revelation to Paul. Comp. Gal. i. 12; ii. 2; Eph. iii. 3; 2 Cor. xii. 1, 9.

Remain (περιλειπόμενοι). Pº. and only in this Epistle. The plural *we* indicates that Paul himself expected to be alive at the parousia.*

Shall not prevent (οὐ μὴ φθάσωμεν). The A. V. misses the force of the double negative — shall *in no wise* prevent. *Prevent* in the older sense of *anticipate, be beforehand with*. See on Matt. xvii. 25, and 1 Th. ii. 16. The living shall not share the blessings of the advent sooner than the dead in Christ.

16. The word of the Lord, ver. 15, is apparently not intended to include the specific details which follow. In that word the revelation was to the effect that all believers simultaneously should share the blessings of the advent. The following description of the Lord's descent from heaven is intended to emphasise the fact that the reunion of dead and living believers will be accomplished by the Lord in person (αὐτὸς). Ὅτι does not indicate the contents of the word of the Lord (*that*, as A. V.), but means *for* or *because;* and the details are meant to strengthen the more general declaration of ver. 15. In the details themselves there are traces of certain O. T. theophanies, as Exod. xix. 11–18; Mic. i. 3.†

Shall descend from heaven. Used nowhere else of Christ's second coming. Frequently in the Fourth Gospel, of Christ's descent to earth as man. See iii. 13; vi. 33, 38, 41, etc. In Eph. iv. 9, of his descent by the Spirit in order to endow the church.

---

* The explanation that Paul uses the participle strictly in its present sense, and means *we who are now being left*, merely distinguishing himself and his readers from those who have died, is strained in the interest of a particular theory of inspiration. See Ellicott.

† Professor Ropes of Harvard, *Die Sprüche Jesu*, holds the opposite view. He thinks that ver. 15 is not cited as the word of the Lord, but that the beginning of the citation is indicated by ὅτι, ver. 16, and the end by air, ver. 17. He regards the citation as a free rendering of a *logion* of Jesus, akin to Matt. xxiv. 30 f.

With a shout (ἐν κελεύσματι). N. T.⁰. Once in LXX, Prov. xxiv. 62 (English Bib. xxx. 27). From κελεύειν *to summon*. Often in Class. Lit. *a shout of command*, as of a general to his army, an admiral to his oarsmen, or a charioteer to his horses.

Archangel (ἀρχαγγέλου). Only here and Jude 9. Not in O. T. The Pauline angelology shows traces of Rabbinical teachings in the idea of orders of angels. See Eph. i. 21; Col. i. 16; Rom. viii. 38. The archangels appear in the apocryphal literature. In the Book of Enoch (see on Jude 14) four are named, Michael, Uriel, Raphael, and Gabriel. Michael is set over the tree which, at the time of the great judgment, will be given over to the righteous and humble, and from the fruit of which life will be given to the elect. In Tob. xii. 15, Raphael appears as one of the seven holy angels. Comp. Apoc. viii. 2. See also on Jude 9, and comp. Dan. xii. 1.*

With the trump of God (ἐν σάλπιγγι θεοῦ). For the trumpet heralding great manifestations of God, see Ex. xix. 13, 16; Ps. xlvii. 5; Isa. xxvii. 13; Zech. ix. 14; Zeph. i. 16; Joel ii. 1; Matt. xxiv. 31; 1 Cor. xv. 52; Apoc. i. 10; iv. 1. *Of God* does not indicate the size or loudness of the trumpet, but merely that it is used in God's service. Comp. *harps of God*, Apoc. xv. 2; *musical instruments of God*, 1 Chron. xvi. 42. The later Jews believed that God would use a trumpet to raise the dead.

17. **Together with them** (ἅμα σὺν αὐτοῖς). Ἅμα *at the same time*, referring to the living. We that are alive shall *simultaneously* or *one and all* (comp. Rom. iii. 12) be caught up. Σὺν αὐτοῖς *along with them*, *i.e.*, the dead. Thus ἅμα is to be const. with *shall be caught up*. The A. V. and Rev. are inaccurate.† These are the important words as related to the disquietude of the Thessalonians.

---

* See O. Everling, *Die paulinische Angelologie und Dämonologie*, s. 80 ff.
† Lightfoot says that the combination ἅμα σὺν *together with*, is too common

Shall be caught up (ἁρπαγησόμεθα). By a swift, resistless, divine energy. Comp. 2 Cor. xii. 2, 4; Acts viii. 39.

In the air (εἰς ἀέρα). Rend. *into* the air, and const. with *shall be caught up.* Ἀὴρ *the atmosphere with the clouds*, as distinguished from αἰθὴρ *the pure ether*, which does not occur in N. T.

And so. After having met the Lord.

CHAPTER V.

1. Times — seasons (χρόνων — καιρῶν). See on Acts i. 7. With special reference to the Lord's coming. The plural is used because Paul is thinking of a number of incidents attending the preparation and accomplishment of the second advent, and occurring at different times. The collocation *times* and *seasons* only here and Acts i. 7. Καιρός is the *suitable* time, χρόνος the time *measured by duration.* Hence καιρός *a juncture, an occasion*, as Matt. xvi. 3. The distinction is so well marked that we have the phrases χρόνου καιρός *the right moment of the time*, and εὔκαιρος χρόνος *the opportune moment.* See Soph. *Elec.* 1292.

2. Perfectly (ἀκριβῶς). See on L. i. 3.

The day of the Lord (ἡμέρα κυρίου). The day of Christ's second coming. In Paul's Epistles this is expressed by ἡ ἡμέρα *the day*, absolutely, 1 Th. v. 4; 1 Cor. iii. 13; Rom. xiii. 12: ἡ ἡμέρα ἐκείνη *that day*, 2 Th. i. 10: ἡμέρα χριστοῦ *the day of Christ*, Philip. i. 10; ii. 16: ἡμέρα κυρίου or τοῦ κυρίου *day of the Lord*, 1 Cor. v. 5; 1 Th. v. 2; 2 Th. ii. 2:

---

to allow the separation of the two words. This is not the case. Liddell and Scott give only one instance, Eurip. *Ion*, 717. They give one other with μετὰ, Plato, *Critias*, 110 A, but here the words are separated. "Mythology and antiquarian research come *together* (ἅμα) into the cities, *along with* (μετὰ) leisure."

ἡμέρα τοῦ κυρίου ἡμῶν Ἰησοῦ (Χριστοῦ), 1 Cor. i. 8 ; 2 Cor. i. 14. These expressions refer to a definite time when the Lord is expected to appear, and Paul expects this appearance soon. Attempts to evade this by referring such expressions to the day of death, or to the advance toward perfection after death until the final judgment, are forced, and are shaped by dogmatic conceptions of the nature of Biblical inspiration.* In the O. T. the phrase *day of the Lord* denotes a time in which God will conspicuously manifest his power and goodness or his penal justice. See Isa. ii. 12 ; Ezek. xiii. 5 ; Joel i. 15 ; ii. 11 ; and comp. Rom. ii. 5. The whole class of phrases is rare in N. T. outside of Paul's Epistles.

As a thief (ὡς κλέπτης). Comp. Matt. xxiv. 43 ; L. xii. 39 ; 2 Pet. iii. 10 ; Apoc. xvi. 15, and see on Apoc. iii. 3.

In the night (ἐν νυκτί). The ancient church held that the advent was to be expected at night, on an Easter eve. This gave rise to the custom of vigils. Jerome, on Matt. xxv. 6, says: "It is a tradition of the Jews that Messiah will come at midnight, after the likeness of that season in Egypt when the Passover was celebrated, and the Destroyer came, and the Lord passed over the dwellings. I think that this idea was perpetuated in the apostolic custom, that, on the day of vigils, at the Pascha, it was not allowed to dismiss the people before midnight, since they expected the advent of Christ."

It is noteworthy how many of the gospel lessons on watchfulness are associated with the night and a visit by night. See Matt. xxiv. 43 ; xxv. 1–13 ; Mk. xiii. 35 ; L. xii. 35, 38 ; xvii. 34 ; xii. 20.

3. **When they shall say.** The prediction is thrown into dramatic form.

---

* See B. Jowett, "On the belief of the Coming of Christ in the Apostolical Age," in *Commentary on the Epistles of Paul.*

Cometh upon (ἐπίσταται). See L. xxi. 34, 36. Often in N. T. of a person coming suddenly upon another; as L. ii. 9; xxiv. 4; Acts iv. 1; xii. 7.

Travail (ὠδίν). Birth-throe. Only here in its literal sense. Elsewhere as a strong figure of sorrow or pain. See Matt. xxiv. 8; Mk. xiii. 8; Acts ii. 24. For the figure in O. T. see Isa. xiii. 6–8; xxxvii. 3; Mic. iv. 9; Hos. xiii. 3; Jer. xiii. 21.

Shall not escape (οὐ μὴ ἐκφύγωσιν). A. V. misses the force of the double negative. They shall *in no wise* escape.

4. **Overtake** (καταλάβῃ). See on *comprehended*, J. i. 5.

A thief (κλέπτης). Tischendorf, Weiss, and Rev. T. retain this reading. Westcott and Hort read κλέπτας *thieves*, but with κλέπτης in margin. The weight of textual evidence is in favour of the singular.

5. **Ye are all.** In the text γὰρ *for* should be inserted after πάντες *all*. Ye are not in darkness *for* ye are sons of light.

Children of light (υἱοὶ φωτός). More correctly, *sons* of light. See on Mk. iii. 17, and comp. L. xvi. 8; J. xii. 36; Eph. v. 8; Col. i. 12. The Christian condition is habitually associated in N. T. with light: see Matt. v. 14, 16; J. iii. 21; viii. 12; Acts xxvi. 18; 1 Pet. ii. 9; 1 J. i. 7. The contrary condition with darkness: see J. iii. 19, 20; Eph. v. 8; 1 Pet. ii. 9; Matt. iv. 16; vi. 23, etc.

Of the night — of darkness (νυκτὸς — σκότους). The genitive marks an advance of thought from ἐν σκότει *in* darkness, ver. 4. Ἐν indicates the element in which one is. The genitive, *of darkness*, points to nature and origin. To *belong to* darkness is more than *to be in* darkness.

6. **Others** (οἱ λοιποί). *The rest*, as ch. iv. 13.

Let us watch (γρηγορῶμεν). See on Mk. xiii. 35, and comp. Eph. v. 14.

Be sober (νήφωμεν). Primarily in a physical sense, as opposed to excess in drink, but passing into the ethical sense of *calm, collected, circumspect*. Alert wakefulness and calm assurance will prevent their being surprised and confused by the Lord's coming, as by a thief in the night.

7. **Be drunken** (μεθυσκόμενοι). Lit. who *are made drunk* or *get drunk*. See on J. ii. 10. In N. T. always of intoxication. In LXX, the Heb. *shekar strong drink* is several times rendered by μέθυσμα; Judg. xiii. 4, 7; 1 Sam. i. 11, 15.

8. **Putting on** (ἐνδυσάμενοι). The son of day clothes himself for the day's work or battle. The same association of ideas as in vv. 6, 8, is found in Rom. xiii. 12–14; Apoc. xvi. 15; 1 Pet. i. 13. Comp. LXX, Bar. v. 2.

Breastplate — helmet. Comp. Eph. vi. 14. The figures are not original with Paul. See Isa. lix. 17; Wisd. v. 18, 19. Notice that only defensive armour is mentioned, in accordance with the darkness and uncertainty of the last time; and that the fundamental elements of Christian character, faith, hope, and love, are brought forward again as in ch. i. 3; 1 Cor. xiii. 13. For the figure of the armed soldier, comp. also Rom. xiii. 12; 2 Cor. x. 4.

9. **For** (ὅτι). Special emphasis is laid on the hope of salvation. The exhortation to put it on is enforced by the fact that God's appointment is to salvation and not to wrath.

To obtain (εἰς περιποίησιν). More literally, *unto the obtaining*. See on Eph. i. 14. In three out of five instances in N. T. the word clearly means *acquiring* or *obtaining*. In Eph. i. 14 and 1 Pet. ii. 9, it is sometimes rendered *possession* (so Rev.). But in Ephesians the meaning is *redemption* or *acquisition*, or redemption which will give possession; and in

1st Peter a people *for acquisition.* The meaning here is *that we might obtain.* Comp. LXX, Mal. iii. 17.

10. Who died. Frequently the resurrection is coupled with the death of Christ by Paul, as ch. iv. 14 ; Philip. iii. 10 ; Col. ii. 12 ; iii. 1–4. Not so here ; but the thought of resurrection is supplied in *live together with him.*

Wake or **sleep.** Whether we are alive or dead at Christ's appearing. Comp. Rom. xiv. 9. Καθεύδειν in N. T. always literally of sleep, except here, and possibly Eph. v. 14. In Mk. v. 39 ; L. viii. 52, it is contrasted with death. In LXX in the sense of death, Ps. lxxxvii. 5 ; Dan. xii. 2 ; 2 Sam. vii. 12.

11. Comfort (παρακαλεῖτε). Rev. renders *exhort;* but comfort suits better the general drift of the passage, and corresponds with ch. iv. 18. There is some force in Bornemann's suggestion that the two meanings may be combined. Exhort each other to be of good heart.

Edify (οἰκοδομεῖτε). Lit. *build up.* See on Acts xx. 32. The metaphorical sense habitually in Paul. See 1 Cor. viii. 1, 10 ; x. 23 ; xiv. 4 ; Eph. ii. 20. In O. T. mostly in the literal sense. See however LXX, Ruth iv. 11 ; Ps. xxvii. 5 ; lxxxviii. 2 ; Jer. xxxi. 4.

12. Know (εἰδέναι). See on ch. iv. 4. Recognise them for what they are, and as entitled to respect because of their office. Comp. ἐπιγινώσκετε *acknowledge*, 1 Cor. xvi. 18 ; and ἐγνώσθης *takest knowledge*, LXX, Ps. cxliii. 3. Ignatius, Smyrn. ix., has ἐπίσκοπον εἰδέναι *to know the bishop*, to appreciate and honor him.

Are over (προϊσταμένους). Lit. *who are placed before you.* See on Rom. xii. 8. Used of superintendents of households, 1 Tim. iii. 4, 5, 12 : of the ruling of elders of the church, 1 Tim. v. 17. It does not indicate a particular ecclesiastical

office, but is used functionally. The ecclesiastical nomenclature of the Pauline Epistles is unsettled, corresponding with
the fact that the primitive church was not a homogeneous
body throughout christendom. The primitive Pauline church
consisted of a number of separate fraternities which were
self-governing. The recognition of those who ministered to
the congregations depended on the free choice of their members. See for instance 1 Cor. xvi. 15, 16. The congregation exercised discipline and gave judgment : 1 Cor. v. 3–5;
2 Cor. ii. 6, 7; vii. 11, 12; Gal. vi. 1.

Admonish (νουθετοῦντας). Only in Acts and Paul. See
on Acts xx. 31, and comp. ver. 14; Rom. xv. 14; 1 Cor.
iv. 14; Col. i. 28.

13. **Esteem** (ἡγεῖσθαι). Primarily *to lead*, which is the
only sense in the Gospels and Acts, except Acts xxvi. 2, in a
speech of Paul. To lead the mind through a reasoning process to a conclusion, and so *to think, to estimate*. Only in this
sense by Paul, Peter, and James. See 2 Cor. ix. 5; Philip.
ii. 3; Jas. i. 2; 2 Pet. iii. 9. In both senses in Hebrews.
See x. 29; xiii. 7.

Very highly in love. Const. *very highly* with *esteem*. *In
love* qualifies both words.*

For their work's sake (διὰ τὸ ἔργον αὐτῶν). Their esteem
for their superintendents is not to rest only on personal
attachment or respect for their position, but on intelligent
and sympathetic appreciation of their work. It is a good
and much-needed lesson for the modern congregation no less
than for the Thessalonian church.

14. **Them that are unruly** (τοὺς ἀτάκτους). N. T.º. The
A.V. is more vigorous and less stilted than Rev. *disorderly*.
From ἀ *not* and τάσσειν *draw up* or *arrange*. Those who are

---

* Others join *in love* with *esteem* as forming one conception ; but the
phrase ἡγεῖσθαι ἐν ἀγάπῃ is not warranted by usage.

out of line. Comp. the adverb ἀτάκτως *disorderly,* 2 Th.
iii. 6, 11. Probably referring to the idlers and busybodies
described there.

Feeble-minded (ὀλιγοψύχους). N. T.°. Better *faint-
hearted.* Ὀλίγος *little* and ψυχή *soul.* Those of little heart.
°Class. In LXX see Prov. xiv. 29; Isa. xxv. 5; liv. 6;
lvii. 15. Ὀλιγοψυχία *faint-heartedness,* °N. T. LXX, Ex.
vi. 9; Ps. liv. 8. Comp. Ps. of Sol., xvi. 11.

Support (ἀντέχεσθε). Comp. Matt. vi. 24; Tit. i. 9.
Ἀντί *against* and ἔχεσθαι *to hold one's self.* The primary
sense is, keeping one's self directly opposite to another so as
to sustain him.

15. That which is good (τὸ ἀγαθὸν). Not to be limited
to *profitable, beneficent* (as Lightfoot, Lünemann), although
ἀγαθός commonly includes a corresponding beneficent relation
of its subject to another subject, which is emphasised here by
to all men. See on Rom. v. 7. It may also include what is
absolutely, morally good, as Rom. ii. 10. So Heb. xiii. 21;
1 Pet. iii. 11 ; Rom. vii. 18.

17. Without ceasing (ἀδιαλείπτως). Comp. Rom. ∴. 9;
xii. 12; Eph. vi. 18; Col. iv. 2.

18. Will (θέλημα). In the sense of *requirement.* Comp.
ch. iv. 3.

19. Quench not the Spirit. Since he is the inspirer of
prayer, and the bestower of all gifts of grace on the Church.
Comp. Eph. iv. 30. The operation of the Spirit is set forth
under the image of fire in Matt. iii. 11; L. xii. 49; Acts ii.
3, 4. The reference here is to the work of the Spirit generally, and not specially to his inspiration of prayer or prophecy.

20. Prophesyings (προφητείας). The emphasis on prophesyings corresponds with that in 1 Cor. xiv. 1–5, 22 ff.
Prophecy in the apostolic church was directly inspired in-

struction, exhortation, or warning. The prophet received
the truth into his own spirit which was withdrawn from
earthly things and concentrated upon the spiritual world.
His higher, spiritual part (πνεῦμα), and his moral intelligence (νοῦς), and his speech (λόγος) worked in harmony.
His spirit received a spiritual truth in symbol: his understanding interpreted it in its application to actual events,
and his speech uttered the interpretation. He was not
ecstatically rapt out of the sphere of human intelligence,
although his understanding was intensified and clarified by
the phenomenal action of the Spirit upon it. This double
action imparted a peculiarly elevated character to his speech.
The prophetic influence was thus distinguished from the
mystical ecstasy, the ecstasy of Paul when rapt into the
third heaven, which affected the subject alone and was
incommunicable (2 Cor. xii. 1–4). The gift of tongues carried the subject out of the prophetic condition in which
spirit, understanding, and speech operated in concert, and
into a condition in which the understanding was overpowered
by the communication to the spirit, so that the spirit could
not find its natural expression in rational speech, or speech
begotten of the understanding, and found supernatural
expression in a tongue created by the Spirit. Paul attached
great value to prophecy. He places prophets next after
apostles in the list of those whom God has set in the Church
(1 Cor. xii. 28). He associates apostles and prophets as the
foundation of the Church (Eph. ii. 20). He assigns to
prophecy the precedence among spiritual gifts (1 Cor. xiv.
1–5), and urges his readers to desire the gift (1 Cor. xiv.
1, 39). Hence his exhortation here.

21. **Prove all things** (πάντα δοκιμάζετε). A general
exhortation, not confined to prophesyings; but Paul elsewhere insists that a test be applied to phenomena which
claim to be supernatural. See on *discerning of spirits*, 1 Cor.
xii. 10; xiv. 29, and comp. 2 Th. ii. 2, and 1 J. iv. 1–3.
For δοκιμάζετε *prove*, see on 1 Pet. i. 7. In LXX, Prov.
xxvii. 21 ; Ps. xi. 6, δοκίμιον is *a crucible* or *furnace*.

Hold fast that which is good (τὸ καλὸν κατέχετε).   These
words are associated in early Christian writers with an apocryphal saying ascribed to Jesus, and very frequently quoted,
γίνεσθε δὲ δόκιμοι τραπεζῖται *show yourselves approved money-
changers*.   By some ancient writers the two are cited together
as Paul's; by others they are distinguished, as by Origen,
who cites the saying as an injunction (ἐντολὴν) of Jesus, and
adds, "and also (observing) the teaching of Paul, who says,
'prove all things, hold fast the good, abstain from every form
of evil.'"   The saying about the money-changers is probably
a genuine *logion* of the Lord.   Some have thought that the
words added by Clement of Alexandria, "rejecting some
things but holding fast the good," formed part of the Lord's
saying, and that, accordingly, Paul's words here depend on
an original utterance of Jesus.   If this could be proved, εἶδος
form, ver. 22, might be explained as a figure of exchangers
distinguishing between genuine and false coins.*

22.   **Appearance** (εἴδους).   As commonly explained, abstain
from everything that even *looks like* evil.   But the word signifies *form* or *kind*.   Comp. L. iii. 22; J. v. 37, and see
nearly the same phrase in Joseph. *Ant*. x. 3, 1.   It never has
the sense of *semblance*.   Moreover, it is impossible to abstain
from everything that looks like evil.

Of evil (πονηροῦ).   To be taken as a noun; not as an
adjective agreeing with εἴδους *form* (from every evil form).
The meaning of πονηρός in N. T. cannot be limited to *active*
evil, *mischief*, though it often has that sense.   The same is
true in LXX, where it sometimes means *grudging* or *nig-
gardly*.   See Sir. xiv. 4, 5; xxxiv. 23.

23.   **The very God of peace** (αὐτὸς ὁ θεὸς τῆς εἰρήνης).
Better, *the God of peace himself*.   God's work is contrasted

---

* See J. H. Ropes, *Die Sprüche Jesu*, p. 141 f.; B. F. Westcott, *Introduction to the Study of the Gospels*, 5th ed., p. 454; J. B. Lightfoot, on
1 Th. v. 21, in *Notes on Epistles of St. Paul*.   Also the remarks of Bornemann on this passage.

with human efforts to carry out the preceding injunctions. The phrase *God of peace* only in Paul and Hebrews. See Rom. xv. 33; xvi. 20; Philip. iv. 9 ; Heb. xiii. 20. The meaning is, God who is the source and giver of peace. *Peace*, in the Pauline sense, is not mere calm or tranquillity. It is always conceived as based upon reconciliation with God. God is the God of peace only to those who have ceased to be at war with him, and are at one with him. God's peace is not sentimental but moral. Hence the God of peace is *the sanctifier*. "Peace" is habitually used, both in the Old and New Testaments, in connection with the messianic salvation. The Messiah himself will be Peace (Mic. v. 5). Peace is associated with righteousness as a messianic blessing (Ps. lxxii. 7; lxxxv. 10). Peace, founded in reconciliation with God, is the theme of the gospel (Acts x. 36). The gospel is *the gospel of peace* (Eph. ii. 17; vi. 15; Rom. x. 15). Christ is the giver of peace (J. xiv. 27 ; xvi. 33).

Sanctify (ἁγιάσαι). See on J. x. 36 ; xvii. 17. The primary idea of the word is *separation*. Hence ἅγιος, the standard word for *holy* in LXX is, primarily, *set apart*. Ἁγιάζειν is 1. *to separate from things profane and to consecrate to God;* 2. *to cleanse* or *purify* as one set apart to holy uses.

Wholly (ὁλοτελεῖς). N. T.°. So that nothing shall escape the sanctifying power. Ὅλος *complete*, and τέλος *end* or *consummation*.

Spirit, soul, body (πνεῦμα, ψυχὴ, σῶμα). It is useless to attempt to draw from these words a technical, psychological statement of a threefold division of the human personality. If Paul recognised any such technical division, it was more probably twofold ; the body or material part, and the immaterial part with its higher and lower sides — πνεῦμα and ψυχὴ. See on Rom. vi. 6; vii. 5, 23; viii. 4; xi. 3 and footnote.

Be preserved entire (ὁλόκληρον — τηρηθείη). This is the rendering of Rev. and is correct. A. V. joins ὁλόκληρον with

πνεῦμα, and renders *your whole spirit*. Ὁλόκληρον is predic
ative, not attributive.   It does not mean *whole*, but is derived
from ὅλος *whole* and κλῆρος *allotment*, and signifies *having the
entire allotment; complete in all parts*.   It occurs only here
and Jas. i. 4, where it is associated with τέλειοι *perfect*.   It
appears in LXX, as Lev. xxiii. 15 ; Deut. xvi. 9 ; xxvii. 6.
Joseph. *Ant*. iii. 12, 2, uses it of an unblemished victim for
sacrifice.   As distinguished from ὁλοτελεῖς *wholly*, ver. 23, it
is *qualitative*, while ὁλοτελεῖς is *quantitative*.   The kindred
ὁλοκληρία *perfect soundness*, only in Acts iii. 16.   For *preserved* see on 1 Pet. i. 4.

24. **Faithful** (πιστὸς).   Comp. 2 Tim. ii. 13, and see on
1 J. i. 9 ; Apoc. i. 5 ; iii. 14.

That calleth (ὁ καλῶν).   = *the caller*.   The emphasis is
on the person rather than on the act.   Comp. Rom. ix. 11 ;
Gal. i. 6, 15 ; v. 8 ; 1 Th. ii. 12 ; 1 Pet. v. 10 ; Jas. i. 5.

26. **Kiss.**   See on 2 Cor. xiii. 12.   Comp. Rom. xvi. 16 ;
1 Cor. xvi. 20 ; 1 Pet. v. 14.

27. **I charge** (ἐνορκίζω).   N. T.[o].   Rev. stronger and
more literal, *I adjure*.   [o]Class.   This strong appeal may perhaps be explained by a suspicion on Paul's part that a wrong
use might be made of his name and authority (see 2 Th.
ii. 2), so that it was important that his views should be
made known to all.   Lightfoot refers to 2 Th. iii. 17, as
showing a similar feeling in his anxiety to authenticate his
letter.

THE SECOND EPISTLE TO THE
THESSALONIANS.

CHAPTER I.

On vv. 1, 2, see on 1 Th. i. 1.

3. We are bound — as it is meet. The accumulation of cognate expressions indicates the apostle's earnestness.

Groweth exceedingly (ὑπεραυξάνει). N. T.º. See on 1 Th. iii. 10.

4. Glory (ἐνκαυχᾶσθαι). N. T.º. The simple verb καυχᾶσθαι *to boast*, and the kindred nouns καύχημα *ground of boasting*, and καύχησις *act of boasting*, are favorites with Paul.

5. A manifest token (ἔνδειγμα). N. T.º. Comp. ἔνδειξις, Philip. i. 28. The token is the patience and faith with which they endure persecution and tribulation. It is a token of the righteous judgment of God, in that it points to the future glory which God will confer at the final judgment, and the righteous award which will be dispensed to the persecutors. Similarly Philip. i. 28.

That ye may be counted worthy. The structure of the sentence is loose. These words should be directly connected with *righteous judgment*, and denote the purport of that judgment — their assignment to an inheritance in the kingdom of God.

Of the kingdom of God (τῆς βασιλείας τοῦ θεοῦ). The
phrase is not frequent in Paul. Βασιλεία θεοῦ four times ;
βασιλεία τοῦ χριστοῦ καὶ θεοῦ *kingdom of Christ and of God*,
once. Here in the eschatological sense — the future, consummated kingdom, the goal of their striving and the recompense of their suffering. See on L. vi. 20.

6. **Seeing it is** (εἴπερ). More literally, *if so be that.*
Confirming, in a hypothetical form, the assertion of God's
judgment upon persecutors, ver. 5. It implies no doubt,
but rhetorically puts a recognised fact as a supposition. So
Rom. iii. 30 ; viii. 9, 17 ; 1 Cor. viii. 5.

7. **Rest** (ἄνεσιν). See on *liberty*, Acts **xxiv. 23.** With
this exception only in Paul.

With us. According to Paul's habit of identifying his
experience with that of his Christian readers. See 1 Cor. iv.
8 ; Rom. viii. 23 ; Philip. i. 29, 30 ; ii. 18 ; iii. 20, 21 ; 2 Cor.
i. 7.

When the Lord Jesus shall be revealed (ἐν τῇ ἀποκαλύψει
τοῦ κυρίου 'Ιησοῦ). Lit. *in the revelation of the Lord Jesus.*
For ἀποκάλυψις *revelation,* see on Apoc. i. 1.

With his mighty angels (μετ' ἀγγέλων δυνάμεως αὐτοῦ).
Lit. *with the angels of his power.*

8. **In flaming fire** (ἐν πυρὶ φλογός). Lit. *in a fire of
flame.* Comp. 1 Cor. i. 13 ; 2 Pet. iii. 7.

Taking vengeance (διδόντος ἐκδίκησιν). Lit. *giving* or
rendering. *Vengeance* is an unfortunate rendering, as implying, in popular usage, personal vindictiveness. See on 2 Cor.
vii. 11. It is the full awarding of justice to all parties.

On them that know not God — obey not the gospel (τοῖς
μὴ εἰδόσι θεὸν — τοῖς μὴ ὑπακούουσιν τῷ εὐαγγελίῳ). To know
God is to know him as the one, true God as distinguished

from false gods ; to know his will, his holiness, his hatred of
sin, and his saving intent toward mankind.   Two words are
used of such knowledge, εἰδέναι and γινώσκειν.   Both are
applied to the heathen and to Christians, and both are used
of the Jews' knowledge of God. 'Εἰδέναι, of heathen, Gal.
iv. 8 ; 1 Th. iv. 5 ; 2 Th. i. 8.   Γινώσκειν, of heathen, Rom. i.
21 ; 1 Cor. i. 21.   'Εἰδέναι, of Christ and Christians, J. vii.
29 ; viii. 19, 55 ; xiv. 7.   Γινώσκειν, of Christ and Christians,
Gal. iv. 9 ; 1 J. ii. 13, 14 ; iv. 6, 7, 8 ; J. x. 15 ; xvii. 3.   In
John, γινώσκειν of Jews who do not know the Father, J. xvi.
3 ; viii. 55 : εἰδέναι, J. vii. 28 ; viii. 19 ; xv. 21.   The two
are combined, J. i. 26 ; vii. 27 ; viii. 55 ; 2 Cor. v. 16.   A distinction is asserted between γινώσκειν as knowledge grounded
in personal experience, apprehension of external impressions
— and εἰδέναι purely mental perception in contrast with con-
jecture or knowledge derived from others.   There are doubtless passages which bear out this distinction (see on J. ii. 24),
but it is impossible to carry it rigidly through the N. T.   In
the two classes, — those who know not God and those who
obey not the gospel, — it is not probable that Paul has in
mind a distinction between Jews and Gentiles.   The Jews
were not ignorant of God, yet they are described by John as
not knowing him.   The Gentiles are described by Paul as
knowing God, but as refusing to glorify him as God (Rom.
i. 21).   Paul rather describes here the subjects of God's
judgment as one class, but under different aspects.

9. **Shall be punished** (δίκην τίσουσιν).   The verb (N. T.°)
means *to pay* or *render*.   Lit. *shall pay penalty.*

Everlasting destruction (ὄλεθρον αἰώνιον).   The phrase
nowhere else in N. T.   In LXX, 4 Macc. x. 15.   Rev. properly, *eternal* destruction.   It is to be carefully noted that
eternal and *everlasting* are not synonymous.   See additional
note at the end of this chapter.

From the presence (ἀπὸ προσώπου).   Or *face.* 'Απὸ *from*
has simply the sense of separation.   Not *from the time of the*

Lord's appearing, nor *by reason of the glory of his presence.*
Πρόσωπον is variously translated in A. V. Mostly *face :* also
presence, Acts iii. 13, 19 ; v. 41 : *person*, Matt. xxii. 16 ;
L. xx. 21 ; Gal. ii. 6 : *appearance*, 2 Cor. v. 12 ; x. 1 : *fashion*, Jas. i. 11. The formula ἀπὸ προσώπου or τοῦ προσώπου
occurs Acts iii. 19 ; v. 41 ; vii. 45 ; Apoc. vi. 16 ; xii. 14 ;
xx. 11. In LXX, Gen. iii. 8 ; iv. 14, 16 ; Ex. xiv. 25, and
frequently.

Glory of his power (δόξης τῆς ἰσχύος αὐτοῦ). For *glory*
see on 1 Th. ii. 12. Ἰσχὺς *power*, not often in Paul. It is
indwelling power put forth or embodied, either aggressively
or as an obstacle to resistance : physical power organised or
working under individual direction. An army and a fortress
are both ἰσχυρὸς. The power inhering in the magistrate,
which is put forth in laws or judicial decisions, is ἰσχὺς, and
makes the edicts ἰσχυρὰ *valid* and *hard to resist*. Δύναμις is
the indwelling power which comes to manifestation in ἰσχὺς.
The precise phrase used here does not appear elsewhere in
N. T. In LXX, Isa. ii. 10, 19, 21. The power (δύναμις)
and glory of God are associated in Matt. xxiv. 30 ; Mk. xiii.
26 ; L. xxi. 27 ; Apoc. iv. 11 ; xix. 1. Comp. κράτος τῆς
δόξης αὐτοῦ *strength of his glory*, Col. i. 11.

10. To be glorified (ἐνδοξασθῆναι). Only here and ver.
12 in N. T. Repeatedly in LXX. See Ex. xiv. 4, 17 ; Isa.
xlv. 26. °Class.

11. Wherefore (εἰς ὃ). Better, *to which end*. Comp. Col.
i. 29. The end is, "that ye may be counted worthy of the
kingdom of God," ver. 5. The same thought is continued
in ver. 11.

Count — worthy (ἀξιώσῃ). Comp. 1 Tim. v. 17 ; Heb.
iii. 3 ; x. 29.

Your calling (τῆς κλήσεως). Including both the act and
the end of the Christian calling. Comp. Philip. iii. 14 ; 1
Th. ii. 12 ; Eph. iv. 1.

All the good pleasure of his goodness (πᾶσαν εὐδοκίαν
ἀγαθωσύνης). Wrong. Paul does not mean *all the goodness
which God is pleased to bestow*, but *the delight of the Thessalonians in goodness*. He prays that God may perfect their
pleasure in goodness. So Weizsäcker, *die Freude an allem
Guten*. The Rev. *desire* for εὐδοκίαν is infelicitous, and lacks
support. ᾿Αγαθωσύνη *goodness* (P⁰. see on Rom. iii. 12) is
never predicated of God in N. T. In LXX, see Neh. ix. 25,
35. ᾿Ευδοκία *good pleasure, delight*, is a purely Biblical word.
As related to one's self, it means *contentment, satisfaction :*
see Sir. xxix. 23 ; Ps. of Sol. iii. 4 ; xvi. 12. As related to
others, *good will, benevolence*. L. x. 21; Eph. i. 5, 9 ; Philip.
i. 15; ii. 13; Ps. of Sol. viii. 39.

12. **The name** (τὸ ὄνομα). In no case where it is joined
with Jesus, or Christ, or Lord Jesus, does it mean *the title* or
dignity.* Paul follows O. T. usage, according to which *the
name of the Lord* is often used for all that the name covers ;
so that *the name of the Lord* = the Lord himself.

ADDITIONAL NOTE ON ὄλεθρον αἰώνιον *eternal destruction*,
2 TH. I. 9.

᾿Αιών, transliterated *aeon*, is a period of time of longer or shorter duration, having a beginning and an end, and complete in itself. Aristotle
(περὶ οὐρανοῦ, i. 9, 15) says : "The period which includes the whole time
of each one's life is called the *aeon* of each one." Hence it often means
the life of a man, as in Homer, where one's life (αἰών) is said to leave him
or to consume away (*Il.* v. 685; *Od.* v. 160). It is not, however, limited
to human life; it signifies any period in the course of events, as the
period or age before Christ; the period of the millennium; the mythological period before the beginnings of history. The word has not "a
stationary and mechanical value" (De Quincey). It does not mean a
period of a fixed length for all cases. There are as many aeons as entities,
the respective durations of which are fixed by the normal conditions of
the several entities. There is one aeon of a human life, another of the
life of a nation, another of a crow's life, another of an oak's life. The
length of the aeon depends on the subject to which it is attached.

---

* As Lightfoot on Philip. ii. 9.

It is sometimes translated *world;* world representing a period or a series of periods of time. See Matt. xii. 32; xiii. 40, 49; L. i. 70; 1 Cor. i. 20; ii. 6; Eph. i. 21. Similarly οἱ αἰῶνες *the worlds,* the universe, the aggregate of the ages or periods, and their contents which are included in the duration of the world. 1 Cor. ii. 7; x. 11; Heb. i. 2; ix. 26; xi. 3. The word always carries the notion of *time,* and not of *eternity.* It always means a period of time. Otherwise it would be impossible to account for the plural, or for such qualifying expressions as *this* age, or the age *to come.* It does not mean something endless or everlasting. To deduce that meaning from its relation to ἀεί is absurd; for, apart from the fact that the meaning of a word is not definitely fixed by its derivation, ἀεί does not signify endless duration. When the writer of the Pastoral Epistles quotes the saying that the Cretans are *always* (ἀεὶ) liars (Tit. i. 12), he surely does not mean that the Cretans will go on lying to all eternity. See also Acts vii. 51; 2 Cor. iv. 11; vi. 10; Heb. iii. 10; 1. Pet. iii. 15. ʼΑεί means *habitually* or *continually* within the limit of the subject's life. In our colloquial dialect *everlastingly* is used in the same way. " The boy is everlastingly tormenting me to buy him a drum."

In the New Testament the history of the world is conceived as developed through a succession of aeons. A series of such aeons precedes the introduction of a new series inaugurated by the Christian dispensation, and the end of the world and the second coming of Christ are to mark the beginning of another series. See Eph. iii. 11. Paul contemplates aeons before and after the Christian era. Eph. i. 21; ii. 7; iii. 9, 21; 1 Cor. x. 11; comp. Heb. ix. 26. He includes the series of aeons in one great aeon, ὁ αἰὼν τῶν αἰώνων *the aeon of the aeons* (Eph. iii. 21); and the author of the Epistle to the Hebrews describes the throne of God as enduring unto the aeon of the aeons (Heb. i. 8). The plural is also used, *aeons of the aeons,* signifying all the successive periods which make up the sum total of the ages collectively. Rom. xvi. 27; Gal. i. 5; Philip. iv. 20, etc. This plural phrase is applied by Paul to God only.

The adjective αἰώνιος in like manner carries the idea of time. Neither the noun nor the adjective, in themselves, carry the sense of *endless* or *everlasting.* They may acquire that sense by their connotation, as, on the other hand, ἀίδιος, which means *everlasting,* has its meaning limited to a given point of time in Jude 6. ʼΑιώνιος means *enduring through* or *pertaining to a period of time.* Both the noun and the adjective are applied to limited periods. Thus the phrase εἰς τὸν αἰῶνα, habitually rendered *forever,* is often used of duration which is limited in the very nature of the case. See, for a few out of many instances, LXX, Ex. xxi. 6; xxix. 9; xxxii. 13; Josh. xiv. 9; 1 Sam. viii. 13; Lev. xxv. 46; Deut. xv. 17; 1 Chron. xxviii. 4. See also Matt. xxi. 19; J. xiii. 8; 1 Cor. viii. 13. The same is true of αἰώνιος. Out of 150 instances in LXX, four-fifths imply limited duration. For a few instances see Gen. xlviii. 4; Num. x. 8; xv. 15; Prov. xxii. 28; Jonah ii. 6; Hab. iii. 6; Isa. lxi. 17.

Words which are *habitually* applied to things temporal or material cannot carry in themselves the sense of endlessness. Even when applied to God, we are not forced to render αἰώνιος *everlasting*. Of course the life of God is endless; but the question is whether, in describing God as αἰώνιος, it was intended to describe the duration of his being, or whether some different and larger idea was not contemplated. That God lives longer than men, and lives on everlastingly, and has lived everlastingly, are, no doubt, great and significant facts; yet they are not the dominant or the most impressive facts in God's relations to time. God's eternity does not stand merely or chiefly for a scale of length. It is not primarily a mathematical but a moral fact. The relations of God to time include and imply far more than the bare fact of endless continuance. They carry with them the fact that God transcends time; works on different principles and on a vaster scale than the wisdom of time provides; oversteps the conditions and the motives of time; marshals the successive aeons from a point outside of time, on lines which run out into his own measureless cycles, and for sublime moral ends which the creature of threescore and ten years cannot grasp and does not even suspect.

There is a word for *everlasting* if that idea is demanded. That ἀΐδιος occurs rarely in the New Testament and in LXX does not prove that its place was taken by αἰώνιος. It rather goes to show that less importance was attached to the bare idea of everlastingness than later theological thought has given it. Paul uses the word once, in Rom. i. 20, where he speaks of "the *everlasting* power and divinity of God." In Rom. xvi. 26 he speaks of *the eternal God* (τοῦ αἰωνίου θεοῦ); but that he does not mean the *everlasting* God is perfectly clear from the context. He has said that "the mystery" has been kept in silence *in times eternal* (χρόνοις αἰωνίοις), by which he does not mean *everlasting* times, but the successive aeons which elapsed before Christ was proclaimed. God therefore is described as *the God of the aeons*, the God who pervaded and controlled those periods before the incarnation. To the same effect is the title ὁ βασιλεὺς τῶν αἰώνων *the King of the aeons*, applied to God in 1 Tim. i. 17; Apoc. xv. 3; comp. Tob. xiii. 6, 10. The phrase πρὸ χρόνων αἰωνίων *before eternal times* (2 Tim. i. 9; Tit. i. 2), cannot mean before *everlasting* times. To say that God bestowed grace on men, or promised them eternal life before endless times, would be absurd. The meaning is *of old*, as L. i. 70. The grace and the promise were given in time, but far back in the ages, before the times of reckoning the aeons.

Ζωὴ αἰώνιος *eternal life*, which occurs 42 times in N. T., but not in LXX, is not *endless* life, but life pertaining to a certain age or aeon, or continuing during that aeon. I repeat, life may be endless. The life in union with Christ *is* endless, but the fact is not expressed by αἰώνιος. Κόλασις αἰώνιος, rendered *everlasting punishment* (Matt. xxv. 46), is the punishment peculiar to an aeon other than that in which Christ is speaking. In some cases ζωὴ αἰώνιος does not refer specifically to the life beyond time, but rather to the aeon or dispensation of Messiah which succeeds the legal dispensation. See Matt. xix. 16; J. v. 39. John says that ζωὴ αἰώνιος is the *present* possession of those who believe on the Son of God, J. iii. 36; v. 24; vi. 47, 54. The Father's commandment *is* ζωὴ αἰώνιος, J. xii. 50; to know the only true God and Jesus Christ *is* ζωὴ αἰώνιος, J. xvii. 3.

Bishop Westcott very justly says, commenting upon the terms used by John to describe life under different aspects: "In considering these phrases it is necessary to premise that in spiritual things we must guard against all conclusions which rest upon the notions of succession and duration. 'Eternal life' is that which St. Paul speaks of as ἡ ὄντως ζωὴ *the life which is life indeed*, and ἡ ζωὴ τοῦ θεοῦ *the life of God*. It is not an end- less duration of being in time, but being of which time is not a measure. We have indeed no powers to grasp the idea except through forms and images of sense. These must be used, but we must not transfer them as realities to another order." *

Thus, while αἰώνιος carries the idea of time, though not of *endlessness*, there belongs to it also, more or less, a sense of *quality*. Its character is ethical rather than mathematical. The deepest significance of the life beyond time lies, not in endlessness, but in the moral quality of the aeon into which the life passes. It is comparatively unimportant whether or not the rich fool, when his soul was required of him (L. xii. 20), entered upon a state that was endless. The principal, the tremendous fact, as Christ unmistakably puts it, was that, in the new aeon, the motives, the aims, the conditions, the successes and awards of time counted for nothing. In time, his barns and their contents were everything; the soul was nothing. In the new life the soul was first and everything, and the barns and storehouses nothing. The bliss of the sanctified does not consist pri- marily in its endlessness, but in the nobler moral conditions of the new aeon, — the years of the holy and eternal God. Duration is a secondary idea. When it enters it enters as an accompaniment and outgrowth of moral conditions.

In the present passage it is urged that ὄλεθρον *destruction* points to an unchangeable, irremediable, and endless condition. If this be true, if ὄλεθρος is *extinction*, then the passage teaches the annihilation of the wicked, in which case the adjective αἰώνιος is superfluous, since extinction is final, and excludes the idea of duration. But ὄλεθρος does not always mean *destruction* or *extinction*. Take the kindred verb ἀπόλλυμι *to destroy, put an end to*, or in the middle voice, *to be lost, to perish*. Peter says, "the world being deluged with water, *perished*" (ἀπώλετο, 2 Pet. iii. 6); but the world did not become extinct, it was renewed. In Heb. i. 11, 12, quoted from Ps. cii., we read concerning the heavens and the earth as compared with the eternity of God, "they shall *perish*" (ἀπολοῦνται). But the perishing is only preparatory to change and renewal. "They shall be changed" (ἀλλαγήσονται). Comp. Isa. li. 6, 16; lxv. 17; lxvi. 22; 2 Pet. iii. 13; Apoc. xxi. 1. Similarly, "the Son of man came to save that which was *lost*" (ἀπολωλός), L. xix. 10. Jesus charged his apostles to go

---

* *The Epistles of St. John*, p. 205.

to the *lost* (ἀπολωλότα) sheep of the house of Israel, Matt. **x**. 6, comp. xv. 24. "He that shall *lose* (ἀπολέσῃ) his life for my sake shall find it," Matt. xvi. 25. Comp. L. xv. 6, 9, 32.

In this passage the word *destruction* is qualified. It is "destruction from the presence of the Lord and from the glory of his power," at his second coming, in the new aeon. In other words, it is the severance, at a given point of time, of those who obey not the gospel from the presence and the glory of Christ. Ἀιώνιος may therefore describe this severance as continuing during the millennial aeon between Christ's coming and the final judgment; as being for the wicked prolonged throughout that aeon and characteristic of it, — or it may describe the severance as characterising or enduring through a period or aeon succeeding the final judgment, the extent of which period is not defined. In neither case is αἰώνιος to be interpreted as *everlasting* or *endless*.

CHAPTER II.

1. By the coming (ὑπὲρ). More correctly *touching*. Comp. Rom. ix. 27; 2 Cor. i. 8. Ὑπὲρ never in N. T. in a formula of swearing.

Gathering together (ἐπισυναγωγῆς). Only here and Heb. x. 25. The verb ἐπισυνάγειν is used, as the noun here, of the Lord's gathering together his elect at his coming. See Matt. xxiv. 31; Mk. xiii. 27; comp. 2 Macc. ii. 7.

2. Shaken (σαλευθῆναι). From σάλος *the tossing* or *swell of the sea*. See L. xxi. 25. Comp. Matt. xi. 7; xxiv. 29; Acts iv. 31; Heb. xii. 26.

In mind (ἀπὸ τοῦ νοὸς). More correctly, *from your mind*. Νοῦς signifies *the judgment, sober sense*. Comp. 1 Cor. xiv. 15, and see on Rom. vii. 23. They are to "keep their heads" under the temptation to fanatical extravagances concerning the Lord's appearing.

Be troubled (θροεῖσθαι). From θροός *clamor, tumult*. The meaning is *be unsettled* or *thrown into confusion*.

By spirit (διὰ πνεύματος). By prophetic utterances of individuals in Christian assemblies, claiming the authority of divine revelations.

By word (διὰ λόγου). Oral expressions falsely imputed to Paul.

By letter as from us (δι᾽ ἐπιστολῆς ὡς δι᾽ ἡμῶν). Const. *as from us* with *word* and *letter*. The reference is to a letter or letters forged in Paul's name; not to the first Thessalonian Epistle, as misunderstood by the readers.

As that (ὡς ὅτι). Indicating the contents of such communications.

Is at hand (ἐνέστηκεν). Better than Rev. *is now present.* Lightfoot, happily, *is imminent.*

3. **Deceive** (ἐξαπατήσῃ). Better *beguile;* since the word means not only *making a false impression,* but *actually leading astray.*

Except there come a falling away. Before *except* insert in translation *the day shall not come.* Such ellipses are common in Paul.

Falling away (ἀποστασία). Only here and Acts xxi. 21. Comp. LXX, Josh. xxii. 22; 2 Chron. xxix. 19.

The man of sin — the son of perdition (ὁ ἄνθρωπος τῆς ἀνομίας, ὁ υἱὸς τῆς ἀπωλείας). See on *children of light,* 1 Th. v. 5. The phrase *man of sin (lawlessness)* does not occur elsewhere, either in N. T. or LXX. *Son of perdition* is found J. xvii. 12, °LXX: τέκνα ἀπωλείας *children of perdition* (A. V. *transgression*), Isa. lvii. 4. *The man of sin* has been thought to refer to Caligula, Titus, Simon Magus, Nero, the Pope of Rome, Luther, Mahomet, etc.

4. That is called God (λεγόμενον θεὸν). Above the true God and the false gods. The opposer claims divine honors for himself.

That is worshipped (σέβασμα). An object of adoration, including things as well as persons. Only here and Acts xvii. 23 on which see note under *devotions*.

Temple of God. According to some, a figure of the Christian Church. Others, the temple of Jerusalem.

Shewing (ἀποδεικνύντα). Publicly asserting divine dignity. Rev. *setting himself forth as God*.

6. What withholdeth (τὸ κατέχον). Better *restraineth*. The verb means *to hold fast*, as L. viii. 15: *to hold back*, as L. iv. 42. See on Rom. i. 18. He refers to some power which hinders the revelation of the man of sin or Antichrist.

In his time (ἐν τῷ αὐτοῦ καιρῷ). Better, *in his own season*. Not before his appointed season.

7. Mystery of iniquity (μυστήριον τῆς ἀνομίας). Better, *of lawlessness*. The phrase is unique in N. T. and °LXX. *Mystery* is found in various combinations, as *mystery of the kingdom of heaven*, Matt. xiii. 11: *of God*, 1 Cor. ii. 1: *of his will*, Eph. i. 9: *of Christ*, Eph. iii. 4: *of the gospel*, Eph. vi. 19: *of faith*, 1 Tim. iii. 9: *of godliness*, 1 Tim. iii. 16: *of the seven stars*, Apoc. i. 20: *of the woman*, Apoc. xvii. 7. A mystery does not lie in the obscurity of a thing, but in its secrecy. It is not in the thing, but envelops it. Applied to a truth, it signifies a truth once hidden but now revealed or to be revealed; a truth which without special revelation would be unknown. It is almost universally found in connection with words signifying publication or revelation. See on Matt. xiii. 11. The mystery of lawlessness is the mass of lawlessness yet hidden, but which is to reveal itself in the person and power of Antichrist. The position of the word is emphatic, emphasising the concealed character of the evil power.

Only (*μόνον*).   The sentence is elliptical: "only we must wait," or "only it must work in secret, until he that letteth," etc.   For a similar instance see Gal. ii. 10.   The collocation of A. V. is wrong.

Letteth (*κατέχων*).   The same word as *restraineth*, ver. 6. *Let* is old English for *hinder*, *prevent*.   Often in Chaucer.

> " May I him lette of that ? " (prevent him from it).
> > *Troil. and Cress.* ii. 732.

> "And bothe in love y-like sore they brente (burned)
> That noon of alle hir (their) frendes might hit lette."
> > *Legend of Good Women*, 731.

So Shakespeare :

> " What lets but one may enter ? "
> > *Two Gent. of Verona*, iii. 1.

> " I'll make a ghost of him that lets me."
> > *Ham.* i. 4.

" The flesh resisteth the work of the Holy Ghost in our hearts, and lets it." — Latimer, *Serm.*

8. **Consume** (*ἀνελεῖ*).   Better, *slay*, as Matt. ii. 16; L. xxii. 2; Acts v. 33.

Spirit (*πνεύματι*).   Better, *breath*.   Πνεῦμα, almost always translated *spirit*, is from *πνεῖν to breathe* or *blow*.   Frequent in class. in this sense.   Comp. J. iii. 8; Heb. i. 7.   LXX, Ps. cxlvii. 7; Ep. of Jer. 61.   Philo says: " *The spirit of God* signifies, in one sense, the air, the third element; and it is used in this sense in the beginning of Genesis . . . for air, being light, is borne up, and uses water as its basis.   In the other sense it is the pure wisdom in which every wise man participates " (*De Gigantibus*, 5).   See on Rom. viii. 4.

Shall destroy (*καταργήσει*).   See on *cumbereth*, L. xiii. 7, and *make without effect*, Rom. iii. 3.

With the brightness (τῇ ἐπιφανείᾳ). See on 1 Tim. vi.
14. Rev. correctly, *manifestation.* See LXX, Esth. v. 1;
Amos v. 22; 2 Macc. ii. 21; 3 Macc. ii. 9.   In class. (but
late) of deities appearing to a worshipper (Plut. *Themistocles*,
30): of the sudden appearance of an enemy (Polyb. i. 54,
2): of a manifestation of Providence (Diod. Sic. i. 15): of
the heathen gods assuming shape and appearing in order to
work mischief (Just. Mart. *Apol.* i. 5).   In N. T. of the
parousia.   See 1 Tim. vi. 14; 2 Tim. i. 10; iv. 1, 8; Tit.
ii. 13.   In 2 Tim. i. 10, of Christ's historical manifestation.
So ἐπιφαίνω, Tit. ii. 11; iii. 4.   Only here in Paul.

Coming (παρουσίας).   Or *presence*, which is the original
meaning.   In N. T. with a few exceptions, of the second
coming of Christ.   The combination *manifestation of his presence* (only here) appears to emphasise the resistless power of
the Son of man, not (as Lightfoot) his splendor and glory.
The mere *appearing* of his presence suffices to destroy his
adversary.

9. **After the working of Satan.**   The sense is that the
coming of Antichrist proclaims itself to be according to the
working of Satan by means of power, signs, etc.   'Ενέργεια
P°. *power in exercise*, used only of superhuman power.   See
Col. i. 29; ii. 12.

Signs and lying wonders (σημείοις καὶ τέρασιν ψεύδους).
Lit. *signs and wonders of a lie.*   *Of a lie* characterises the
three words, *power, signs, wonders.*   All bear the stamp of
fraud.   For *signs and wonders* see on Matt. xxiv. 24, and
mighty works, Matt. xi. 20.

10. **Deceivableness of unrighteousness** (ἀπάτῃ ἀδικίας).
Better *deceit* of unrighteousness; which is characteristic of
unrighteousness and is employed by it.

11. **Strong delusion** (ἐνέργειαν πλάνης).   Rev., literally
and correctly, *a working of error.*   See on *working* ver. 9.

The phrase is unique in N. T.   It means *an active power of misleading*.   For πλάνη *error which shows itself in action*, see on 1 Th. ii. 3.

A lie (τῷ ψεύδει).   Properly, *the* lie.   The article gives the generic sense, falsehood in all its forms.   Comp. J. viii. 44; Rom. i. 25; Eph. iv. 25.   Comp. the contrast of *truth* and *unrighteousness* in ver. 12.   All wrongdoing has an element of falsity.

12. **Might be damned** (κριθῶσιν).   More correctly, *judged*.   See on *damnation*, 1 Tim. v. 12.*

---

* I attempt no interpretation of this passage as a whole, which I do not understand.   The varieties of exposition are bewildering.   Convenient summaries may be found in Lünemann's *Meyer*, Dr. Gloag's *Introduction to the Pauline Epistles*, and Bornemann's *Commentary*.   Generally, it may be said that Paul seems to predict a great moral and religious defection which is to precede the coming of the Lord, and which is to reach its consummation in the appearance of an evil power described as *the Man of Sin*, the personal incorporation and concentration of wickedness.   His coming is denoted by the same word as the coming of Christ (παρουσία, ver. 9).   He is represented as sitting in the temple of God, exhibiting himself as God, and performing miracles of falsehood according to the working of Satan.   A restraining power is upon him, preventing his revelation before the proper time.   The two knots of the passage are the identification of *the man of sin*, and of *him that restraineth*.   The man of sin has been identified as Nero, the Pope of Rome, Luther, Mahomet, Caligula, Simon Magus, Titus.   By others, as representing not an individual, but the succession of popes, the Jewish nation, and especially the Sanhedrim.   The restraining power is explained as the Roman Empire; the German Empire; the Roman Emperor Vitellius; the Apostles; the chiefs of the Jewish nation against Simon the son of Giora; the Emperors Claudius and Vespasian; the pious Jews living at the time of the destruction of Jerusalem; James the Just.   Opinions differ as to whether the man of sin is an individual or an organisation.   Romanists discover him in some representative enemy of Romanism; Protestants in the Roman church and hierarchy.   Before any approach to a sound exegesis of the passage can be made, it will be necessary to define and settle the principles of apocalyptic interpretation, a matter which is still very much in the dark.   About the only valuable thing that can be fairly extracted from the passage is Paul's firm assurance that God's hand is ever on the work of evil, and that in whatever form or with whatever power it may reveal itself, it will inevitably be subdued and crushed by the power of Christ.

13. Hath chosen (εἵλατο). The only case in N. T. in which this word is used of God's election. LXX, Deut. xxvi. 18, of God's choosing Israel to be his peculiar people. Comp. Philip. i. 22; Heb. xi. 25.

From the beginning (ἀπ' ἀρχῆς). Not elsewhere in Paul. His usual expressions are πρὸ τῶν αἰώνων *before the ages* (1 Cor. ii. 7): πρὸ καταβολῆς κόσμου *before the foundation of the world* (Eph. i. 4) : ἀπὸ τῶν αἰώνων *from the ages* (Eph. iii. 9). *Before eternal times* (πρὸ χρόνων αἰωνίων) is found 2 Tim. i. 9; Tit. i. 2.

14. Our gospel. See on 1 Th. i. 5.

15. Traditions (παραδόσεις). See on 1 Cor. xi. 2. Not emphasising a distinction between written and oral tradition. Tradition, in the scriptural sense, may be either written or oral. It implies on the part of a teacher that he is not expressing his own ideas, but is *delivering* or *handing over* (παραδίδωμι) a message received from some one else. See 1 Cor. xi. 23. The prominent idea of παράδοσις is therefore that of an authority external to the teacher. Comp. *by word nor by letter*, ver. 2.

16. Through grace (ἐν χάριτι). Better, *in* grace, as the element of God's gift. Const. with *hath given*, not with *hath loved* and *hath given*.

CHAPTER III.

1. Finally (τὸ λοιπὸν). See on 1 Th. iv. 1.

May have free course (τρέχῃ). More literally, simply, and better, *may run.* Have swift progress through the world. An O. T. idea. See Ps. cxlvii. 15, and comp. Isa. lv. 11 and Acts xii. 24.

Be glorified (δοξάζηται). Acknowledged in its true power and glory. Comp. J. xii. 28. The phrase *the word of the Lord — be glorified*, only here.

2. **Unreasonable** (ἀτόπων). See on L. xxiii. 41, and comp. Acts xxv. 5; xxviii. 6. In LXX in a moral sense, *iniquitous*, Tob. iv. 8; xi. 11; xxxiv. 12. The word originally means *out of place*.

All men have not faith. See on Acts vi. 7; Gal. i. 23.

3. **From evil** (ἀπὸ τοῦ πονηροῦ). Possibly, *from the evil one*. Τὸ πονηρόν *evil* is found Rom. xii. 9; Matt. v. 39; but general N. T. usage favors the masculine, personal sense. See Matt. xiii. 19, 38; Eph. vi. 16; 1 J. ii. 13, 14; iii. 12; v. 18. In LXX, τὸ πονηρόν *evil* is very common: ὁ πονηρὸς a few times, but always of men. See Deut. xxiv. 7; Esth. vii. 6; Job xxi. 30. In Tob. iii. 8, 17, τὸ πονηρόν δαιμόνιον *the wicked demon*. The masculine is favored by the Jewish formularies, of which traces appear in the Lord's prayer; by the unanimous tradition of Greek interpreters; by the interpretations of Tertullian and Cyprian, and by the evidence of the Syriac and Sahidic Versions.*

5. **Hearts** (καρδίας). See on Rom. i. 21; x. 10; Eph. i. 18.

Patient waiting for Christ (ὑπομονὴν τοῦ χριστοῦ). Rather *patience of Christ*. The prayer is that their hearts may be directed to love God and to exhibit the patience of Christ.†

---

* For a full discussion, see Lightfoot, *On a Fresh Revision of the New Testament*. 3d ed. Appendix II.

† So Lünemann, Lightfoot, Weizsäcker, Ellicott, Bornemann. Schmiedel maintains the A. V. There is in N. T. no instance of ὑπομονή in the sense of *waiting for*, nor is the verb ὑπομένειν used in that sense. *Waiting for* or *awaiting* is expressed by ἀπεκδέχεσθαι (mostly Paul), ἀναμένειν (once in Paul), ἐκδέχεσθαι (twice in Paul), περιμένειν (not in Paul), προσδέχεσθαι (not in that sense in Paul), and προσδοκᾶν (not in Paul). In Rom. viii. 25 Paul has δι' ὑπομονῆς ἀπεκδεχόμεθα. In LXX both the noun and the verb are found in the sense of *awaiting* or *waiting for*. See Ezra x. 2; Ps. xxxviii. 7; Judg. iii. 25; 2 K. vi. 33; Tob. v. 7, etc. *Patient waiting for Christ* accords with the general drift of the Epistle. On the other hand see 1 Th. i. 3, and 1 Th. i. 10, where for *waiting for the Son* he uses ἀναμένειν.

6. **Withdraw yourselves from** (στέλλεσθαι ὑμᾶς ἀπὸ). Στέλλεσθαι, P⁰. In the active voice, *to place, arrange, equip*: in the middle voice, *to provide for, take care*. See 2 Cor. viii. 20. Here with ἀπὸ *from, to place one's self away from*.

Disorderly (ἀτάκτως). This adverb, the verb ἀτακτέω, and the adjective ἄτακτος are found only in Paul, and only in the Thessalonian Epistles. See on 1 Th. v. 14.

7. **Follow** (μιμεῖσθαι). Better, *imitate*. Comp. 1 Cor. iv. 16; xi. 1; Philip. iii. 17; 1 Th. i. 6.

8. **Any man's bread** (ἄρτον παρά τινος). Lit. *bread from any one*, or *at any man's hand*.

For nought (δωρεὰν). The word is a noun, meaning *a gift*. See J. iv. 10; Acts ii. 38; Rom. v. 15. The accusative often adverbially as here; *as a gift, gratis*. Comp. Matt. x. 8; Rom. iii. 24; Apoc. xxi. 6.

Labour and travail. See on 1 Th. i. 3.

Be chargeable (ἐπιβαρῆσαι). P⁰. Better, *burden*. By depending upon them for pecuniary support. Comp. 1 Cor. ix. 3–18, and see on 1 Th. ii. 6.

9. **Power** (ἐξουσίαν). Better, *right*. See on Mk. ii. 10; J. i. 12.

10. **If any would not work,** etc. A Jewish proverb.

11. **Working not at all — busybodies** (μηδὲν ἐργαζομένους — περιεργαζομένους). One of Paul's frequent word-plays. See on *reprobate mind*, Rom. i. 28. Not busy, but busybodies. Περιεργάζεσθαι (N. T.⁰.) is *to bustle about a thing*: here, *to be officious in others' affairs*. See on τὰ περίεργα *curious arts*, Acts xix. 19, and 1 Tim. v. 13.

12. **With quietness — work.** See on *study to be quiet*, 1 Th. iv. 11.

13. **Be not weary** (μὴ ἐνκακήσητε).   With one exception, L. xviii. 1, only in Paul.   To *faint* or *lose heart*.

Well doing (καλοποιοῦντες).   N. T.⁰.   According to the Greek idiom, *doing well, be not weary*.   Not limited to works of charity, but including Christian conduct generally, as, for instance, steadily attending to their own business, ver. 12.

14. **By this epistle.**   Connect with *our word*.   The message we send in this letter.   Not, as some, with the following words, *note that man in your epistle.*

Note (σημειοῦσθε).   N. T.⁰.   Lit. *set a mark on*.   The nature of the mark is indicated in the next clause.

Have no company with (μὴ συναναμίγνυσθαι).   P⁰.   See on 1 Cor. v. 9.

Be ashamed (ἐντραπῇ).   See on Matt. xxi. 37, and 1 Cor. iv. 14.

15. **Admonish** (νουθετεῖτε).   See on Acts xx. 31, and Eph. vi. 4.

16. **The Lord of peace** (ὁ κύριος τῆς εἰρήνης).   The only instance of the formula.

By all means (ἐν παντὶ τρόπῳ), or *in every way*.   The alternative reading τόπῳ *place* is rejected by the principal texts.

17. **The salutation of Paul with mine own hand** (ἀσπασμὸς τῇ ἐμῇ χειρὶ Παύλου).   Rev. properly, "the salutation *of me* Paul."   The genitive *of me* is contained, according to a familiar Greek idiom, in the possessive pronoun *my*.   Paul had apparently been employing an amanuensis.

In every epistle.   Comp. 1 Cor. xvi. 21; Col. iv. 18.

THE EPISTLE TO THE GALATIANS

THE EPISTLE TO THE GALATIANS.

INTRODUCTION.

By the churches of Galatia which Paul addresses (ch. i. 2) are most probably meant the churches in the Roman province of Galatia; those namely in Iconium, Pisidian Antioch, Lystra, and Derbe; and not the Christians living in the Galatian district lying to the north and east of Lycaonia and Phrygia, which formed only a part of the Roman province, and the chief cities of which were Ancyra, Tavium, and Pessinus. The Roman province was formed by Augustus, 25 B.C., and included Lycaonia, Isauria, southeastern Phrygia, and a portion of Pisidia. The churches in this province were founded by Paul in his first missionary tour, the account of which is given Acts xiii., xiv.*

The South Galatian hypothesis supplies a defect in the history of the Pauline churches, which, on the other, it is

---

* The view here given is known as the South Galatian hypothesis. The other view, which limits the application of the name Galatia to the Galatian district, the country of the Asiatic Gauls, is known as the North Galatian hypothesis, and is held by the majority of critics. The South Galatian hypothesis was propounded as early as 1825 by Mynster (*Introduction to the Galatian Epistle*); was maintained by the French archaeologist Perrot (*De Galatia Provincia Romana*, Paris, 1867), who was followed by Renan (*Paulus*, 1869); and has been defended by Hausrath, Weizsäcker, Zahn, Pfleiderer, Ramsay (*The Church in the Roman Empire*), and McGiffert (*Apostolic Age*). See also an article by Emilie Grace Briggs, "The Date of the Epistle to the Galatians," in the *New World*, March, 1900, and J. Vernon Bartlett, *The Apostolic Age.* Among the prominent advocates of the North Galatian hypothesis are Bishop Lightfoot (*Commentary on Galatians*), Lipsius (*Hand-Commentar*); Weiss and Jülicher (*Introductions to the N. T.*); Holsten (*Evangelium des Paulus*), Schürer (*Theologische Litteraturzeitung*, 1892, 1893, and *Jahrbücher für protestantische Theologie*, 1892), and Sieffert (*Der Brief an die Galater*, Meyer, 8 Aufl.).

difficult to account for. On the North Galatian hypothesis, although the Galatian churches were the scene of a violent conflict between Paul and the Judaising Christians, and the recipients of one of Paul's most important letters, and are therefore entitled to an important place in the history of the apostolic churches, — no mention of their origin or foundation occurs in the Book of Acts, while the founding of the churches of Pisidia and Lycaonia, which are nowhere named by Paul, is expressly narrated. On the other hypothesis, we have in Acts xiii., xiv., a detailed account of the foundation of the Galatian churches.

From the notices in the Acts and in the Epistle, it appears that Paul's preaching in Galatia met with a favorable reception. See Acts xiii. 42, 48, 49; xiv. 1; Gal. iv. 13. We do not know how long it was before the churches were invaded by Jewish emissaries, nor whence these came. They probably came from the Judaistic circles of the mother-church at Jerusalem, although it is held by some that they belonged to the Jewish Christian constituency of the churches in Galatia. They declared that Paul was not an apostle, but at most only a disciple of the apostles. He had had no personal knowledge of Christ: the contents of his gospel were derived from men, and therefore he was entitled to no authority. All questions should be referred to the mother-church in Jerusalem, especially to the great apostles of the circumcision, the pillars of the church, James, Peter, and John. Moreover, Paul's teaching that righteousness was based only upon faith in Christ and not upon circumcision and legal observance, contradicted the historical revelation of God, since God promised salvation to Abraham and to his seed on the ground of circumcision; and, in order to carry the promise into effect, made the covenant of the law forever with the people of Israel, who were to receive the divine blessing on condition of observing the divine commands. His teaching, moreover, encouraged moral license, and therefore contravened all moral principle (v. 13). They further accused him of being a man-pleaser, seeking a following and adapting his preaching to the tastes of his hearers; preaching circumcision to those who were inclined to accept it, and uncircumcision to such as wished to refuse it (v. 11).

These intruders were not proselytes, but born Jews, Jewish Christians, with a Pharisaic tendency like that of those who, in Antioch and Jerusalem, sought to impose circumcision and legal observance upon Gentile Christians (Acts xv. 1, 5; Gal. ii. 4). They demanded that the Gentile Christians should be incorporated by circumcision with the community of Israel, and should observe the leading requirements of the Mosaic law (v. 2, 11; vi. 12). They laid great stress on the observance of sacred seasons (iv. 10). "They prescribed a cultus with holy days and festivals, which contained a more seductive charm than the exposition of the word; for it offered compensation for the heathenism they had abandoned, and the old disposition once revived might easily have found in it a congenial home."* They did not emphasise the solemn duties which followed circumcision, and which Paul himself forcibly stated (v. 3; comp. iii. 10); but they recommended circumcision as an easy way of attaining salvation through mere formal incorporation with the true people of God, and also as a protection against persecution (vi. 12; comp. v. 11).

These efforts bore fruit among the Galatians. Having thrown off the corruptions of their heathen faith and worship, they again came into bondage to "the weak and beggarly elements" which they had outgrown (iv. 9). The slightest tendency to such a lapse was met and fostered by the daily appeal of the pagan cult amid which they lived, an elaborate and impressive system, fortified with a code of rules and administered by a powerful hierarchy, the whole presenting a striking external resemblance to the Jewish ceremonial system. As Professor Ramsay observes: "It is not until this is properly apprehended that Gal. iv. 3–11 becomes clear and natural. Paul in that passage implies that the Judaising movement of the Christian Galatians is a

---

* Weizsäcker.

recurrence to their old heathen type." Paul describes them
as arrested in a course of obedience to the truth which they
had been running well (v. 7) : as soon removed into a different gospel (i. 6) : as bewitched by an evil eye (iii. 1) : as
pervaded with an evil leaven (v. 9). They were beginning,
in part at least, to observe the Jewish ceremonial law : they
were depending upon the law for justification : they were
declining from a spiritual to a fleshly economy : they were
beginning to regard as an enemy the friend and teacher
whom, not so long ago, they had received as an angel of
God, and for whom they would have plucked out their own
eyes (iv. 14, 15).

To what extent the Galatian Christians had been prevailed
on to accept circumcision, we do not know. The writing of
this letter, however, implies that Paul did not regard this evil
as past arresting.

The letter itself is marked by unity of purpose, cohesion
of thought, and force and picturesqueness of diction. Like
2d Corinthians and Philippians it is intensely personal.
Like the former of those Epistles it reveals the apostle's keen
sensitiveness to the attitude of his readers toward himself.
It is indignant and severe, with dashes of bitterness, yet it
contains touches of affectionate reminiscence. It is pervaded
and controlled by the one purpose of meeting and correcting
the Galatian apostasy in its twofold form of repudiating his
apostolic right and the doctrine of salvation by faith. The
letter falls into three parts : chs. i., ii., maintaining the inde-
pendence and authority of his apostleship, and the divine
origin of his gospel. Chs. iii., iv., defending the intrinsic
truth of his gospel. Chs. v., vi., exhibiting the moral consequences which legitimately and logically result from his
gospel.

The relationship of the Epistle to the Roman letter is
marked, yet it has its special characteristics as distinct from
Romans. It bears the character of a letter more distinctly
than Romans, which is a treatise. It lays a more distinct emphasis upon the person and apostolic authority of Paul, and
its dominant conception is the freedom of the Christian, as

in Romans the dominant conception is justification by faith. Romans is more positively doctrinal; Galatians more apologetic and polemic as against Judaism. Romans treats circumcision as a question of practice; Galatians as a question of law. As in Romans, faith is emphasised over against the works of the law as the ground of justification before God; but equally with Romans the divinity and sanctity of the law are recognised. The law is holy, and just and good. It is the expression of God's sovereign and righteous will. It reflects his character, and if one could keep it he would live by it (iii. 12); all this, while it remains true that "by the works of the law shall no flesh be justified" (ii. 16).

Accordingly the ethics of the Epistle are stern and uncompromising. The picture of the works of the flesh is perhaps not as powerful and lurid as that in the first chapter of Romans. It is drawn in fewer lines, and is offset and enforced by a picture of the fruits of the Spirit. Yet the one is no less distinct and unmistakable than the other. In Romans the sins of the Gentile world are massed in a fearful catalogue; in Galatians single passages here and there afford glimpses of deeply-rooted evil tendencies in the life of the newly-converted Gentile, which show how hard it had been for him to divest himself of his pagan license, and which contain within themselves possibilities of future degeneracy. We see a conceit of higher knowledge and larger liberty which might readily seize upon "occasions to the flesh," and run into what some one has aptly styled "the bigotry of illumination," and the selfishness of fancied deeper insight (v. 15; vi. 2–5). The same conceit appears in the weakness and inconstancy which readily succumb to the flattering overtures of pretentious Jewish emissaries (iv. 12 ff.; v. 26). Yet with rigid severity against such tendencies there is blended a tender compassion for the erring, a reasonable and kindly appreciation of the weakness of the new convert.

Professor Sabatier (*l'Apôtre Paul*) says of the Epistle: "The style does not sustain the thought; it is the thought which sustains the style, giving to it its force, its life, its beauty. Thought presses on, overcharged, breathless and hurried, dragging the words after it. . . . Unfinished phrases, daring omissions, parentheses which leave us out of sight and out of breath, rabbinical subtleties, audacious paradoxes, vehement apostrophes,—pour in like surging billows. Mere words in their ordinary meaning are insufficient to sustain this overwhelming plenitude of thought and feeling. Every phrase is obliged, so to speak, to bear a double and triple burden."

The authenticity of the letter is generally conceded.*

---

* Galatians with Romans and the two Corinthian letters, were received as genuine and authentic by the Tübingen critics.   Some sixteen years ago they were attacked by a small coterie of critics, chiefly in Holland.   Allard Pierson and S. A. Naber ascribed the Pauline Epistles to one Paulus Episcopus, a Christian ecclesiastic, who appropriated large portions of certain reformed Jewish writings, and christianised them by means of changes and interpolations.   A. D. Loman asserted that Christianity was a messianic movement among the Jews; that Jesus had no existence, but was a purely mythical embodiment of a series of ideas and principles developed in the second century.   The four chief Epistles of Paul which contradict this hypothesis are spurious and legendary.   Out of the anti-Judaic and universalistic Gnosis of the early part of the second century, was developed a Paul-legend in the interest of a universalistic Christianity.   Romans, Galatians, and Corinthians were all written in Paul's name to recommend this Christianity.   These views obtained no currency, and were repudiated by even the radical critics of Germany.   Rudolph Steck of Bern (1888) held that none of the four letters were the work of Paul, but were the product of a Pauline party of the second century.   He revived the hypothesis of the dependence of the Pauline writings on Seneca.

COMMENTARIES ON GALATIANS.

ENGLISH.

J. B. Lightfoot, 10th ed., 1890: B. Jowett, *Epistles of St. Paul to the Thessalonians, Galatians, and Romans*, 3d ed., 1894. The essays are interesting and suggestive. C. J. Ellicott, *Critical and Grammatical Commentary on St. Paul's Epistle to the Galatians.* J. Eadie, *Commentary on the Greek Text of the Epistle of Paul to the Galatians,* 1869. Of a more popular character, J. A. Beet, *Commentary on Galatians,* 3d ed. Philip Schaff in *Schaff's Popular Commentary.*

GERMAN.

F. Sieffert, *Der Brief an die Galater*, Mey., 8 Aufl., 1894. R. A. Lipsius, "Der Brief an die Galater," in the *Hand-Commentar*, by Holtzmann, Lipsius, Schmiedel, and Von Soden.

For discussions of the Geographical question, see W. M. Ramsay, *The Church in the Roman Empire before A.D. 170:* Lightfoot in Commentary: Sieffert and Lipsius in Commentaries; E. Schürer, "Was ist unter Γαλατία in der Überschrift des Galaterbriefs zu verstehen?" *Jahrbücher für protestantische Theologie,* 1892, 460 ff.: C. Weizsäcker, *Das apostolische Zeitalter der christlichen Kirche.* Translation from 2d ed. by J. Millar, 1894: W. M. Ramsay's articles on "Galatia" and "Galatia, Regions of," in Hastings' *Dictionary of the Bible,* Vol. II., 1899: A. C. McGiffert, *The Apostolic Age,* 1897.

THE EPISTLE TO THE GALATIANS.

CHAPTER I.

1–5. The usual form of salutation is expanded by additions which answer to the occasion of the letter, and foreshadow its principal thoughts.

1. An apostle. This title is prefixed to Romans, 1st and 2d Corinthians, Ephesians, Colossians. Here with special emphasis, because Paul's apostleship had been challenged.

Of men — by man (*ἀπ' ἀνθρώπων — δι' ἀνθρώπου*). Better, *from* men — *through* man or a man. In contradiction of the assertion that he was not directly commissioned by Jesus Christ, like the twelve, but only by human authority. *From men*, as authorising the office; *through man*, as issuing the call to the person. He thus distinguishes himself from false apostles who did not derive their commissions from God, and ranks himself with the twelve. *Man* does not point to any individual, but is in antithesis to *Jesus Christ*, or may be taken as = *any man*.

By Jesus Christ. See Acts ix. 4–6; 1 Cor. ix. 1.

And God the Father. The genitive, governed by the preceding *διὰ by* or *through*. The idea is the same as *an apostle by the will of God :* 1 Cor. i. 1; 2 Cor. i. 1; Eph. i. 1. *Διὰ* is used of *secondary* agency, as Matt. i. 22; xi. 2; L. i. 70; Acts i. 16; Heb. i. 2. But we find *διὰ θελήματος θεοῦ by the will of God*, Rom. xv. 32; 1 Cor. i. 1; 2 Cor. i. 1, etc., and *διὰ θεοῦ by God*, Gal. iv. 7. Also *δι' οὗ* (God), 1 Cor. i. 9; Heb. ii. 10.

Who raised him from the dead (τοῦ ἐγείραντος αὐτὸν ἐκ νεκρῶν). It was the *risen* Christ who made Paul an apostle. For *resurrection* the N. T. uses ἐγείρειν *to raise up;* ἐξεγείρειν *to raise out of;* ἔγερσις *raising* or *rising;* ἀνιστάναι *to raise up;* ἀνάστασις and ἐξανάστασις *raising up* and *raising up out of.* With νεκρὸς *dead* are the following combinations: ἐγείρειν ἀπὸ τῶν νεκρῶν (never ἀπὸ νεκρῶν) *to raise from the dead;* ἐγ. ἐκ νεκ. or τῶν νεκ. *to raise out of the dead;* ἀναστῆσαι *to raise,* ἀναστῆναι *to be raised* or *to rise* ἐκ. νεκ. (never ἀπὸ); ἀνάστασις νεκ. or τῶν νεκ. *resurrection of the dead;* ἀνάστ. ἐκ. νεκ.; ἐξανάστασις ἐκ. νεκ. *rising* or *resurrection out of the dead* or *from among.* It is impossible to draw nice distinctions between these phrases.*

2. **Brethren — with me.** The circle of Paul's colleagues or more intimate friends. Comp. Philip. iv. 21, 22, where *the brethren with me* are distinguished from *all the saints* — the church members generally.

Unto the churches of Galatia. See Introduction. This is a circular letter to several congregations. Note the omission of the commendatory words added to the addresses in the two Thessalonian and first Corinthian letters.

3. **Grace to you, etc.** See on 1 Th. i. 1. He will not withhold the wish for the divine grace and peace even from those whom he is about to upbraid.

4. **Gave himself for our sins.** Comp. Matt. xx. 28; Eph. v. 25; 1 Tim. ii. 6; Tit. ii. 14. Purposely added with reference to the Galatians' falling back on the works of the law as the ground of acceptance with God. *For* or *with reference to* sins (περὶ) expresses the *general* relation of Christ's mission to sin. The *special* relation, *to atone for, to destroy, to save and sanctify its victims,* is expressed by ὑπὲρ *on behalf of.* The general preposition, however, may include the special.

---

* As, for example, Lightfoot on Philip. iii. 11.

Out of this present evil world (ἐκ τοῦ αἰῶνος τοῦ ἐνεστῶτος πονηροῦ). Lit. *out of the world, the present (world which is) evil.* For αἰών *age* or *period*, see on J. i. 9, and additional note on 2 Th. i. 9. Here it has an ethical sense, the course and current of this world's affairs as corrupted by sin. Comp. 2 Cor. iv. 4. Ἐνεστῶτος *present*, as contrasted with the world to come. Elsewhere we have ὁ νῦν αἰών *the now world* (1 Tim. vi. 17); ὁ αἰών τοῦ κοσμοῦ τούτου *the period of this world* (Eph. ii. 2); ὁ αἰών οὗτος *this world* or *age* (Rom. xii. 2). Ἐνεστῶτος, not *impending*, as some expositors, — the period of wickedness and suffering preceding the parousia (2 Th. ii. 3), which would imply a limitation of Christ's atoning work to that period. Comp. 2 Th. ii. 2; 2 Tim. iii. 1; 1 Cor. vii. 26. The sense of *present* as related to *future* is clear in Rom. viii. 38; 1 Cor. iii. 22; Heb. ix. 9. For the evil character of the present world as conceived by Paul, see Rom. xii. 2; 1 Cor. ii. 6; 2 Cor. iv. 4; Eph. ii. 2.

5. **To whom be glory, etc.** For similar doxologies see Rom. ix. 5; xi. 36; xvi. 27; Eph. iii. 21; 1 Tim. i. 17.

Forever and ever (εἰς τοὺς αἰῶνας τῶν αἰώνων). Lit. *unto the ages of the ages.* See additional note on 2 Th. i. 9, and comp. Rom. xvi. 27; Philip. iv. 20; 1 Tim. i. 17; 2 Tim. iv. 18. Often in the Apocalypse. In LXX habitually in the singular: see Ps. lxxxviii. 29; cx. 3, 30. In the doxology the whole period of duration is conceived as a succession of cycles.

6. **I marvel** (θαυμάζω). Often by Greek orators of surprise at something reprehensible. So in N. T., Mk. vi. 6; J. vii. 21; L. xi. 38; J. iv. 27.

So soon (οὕτως ταχέως). Better, *so quickly.* Paul does not mean so soon after a particular event, as their conversion, or his last visit, or the entry of the false teachers, — but refers to the rapidity of their apostasy; ταχέως being used absolutely as always.

Removed ($\mu\epsilon\tau\alpha\tau i\theta\epsilon\sigma\theta\epsilon$). A. V. misses the sense of the middle voice, *removing* or *transferring yourselves*, and also the force of the continuous present, *are removing* or *going over*, indicating an apostasy not consummated but in progress. The verb is used in Class. of altering a treaty, changing an opinion, desertion from an army. For other applications see Acts vii. 16; Heb. vii. 12; xi. 5. Comp. LXX, Deut. xxvii. 17; Prov. xxiii. 10; Isa. xxix. 17. Lightfoot renders *are turning renegades*.

Him that called ($\tau o\hat{v}$ $\kappa\alpha\lambda\acute{\epsilon}\sigma\alpha\nu\tau os$). God. Not neuter and referring to the gospel. Calling, in the writings of the apostles, is habitually represented as God's work. See Rom. viii. 30; ix. 11; 1 Cor. i. 9; Gal. i. 15; 1 Th. ii. 12; 1 Pet. i. 15; ii. 9; 2 Pet. i. 3.

Into the grace ($\acute{\epsilon}\nu$ $\chi\acute{\alpha}\rho\iota\tau\iota$). *Into* is wrong. It should be *by*.

Another gospel ($\acute{\epsilon}\tau\epsilon\rho o\nu$). Rather *a different, another sort of* gospel. See on Matt. vi. 24; L. xvi. 7; xviii. 10. In illustration of the difference between $\acute{\alpha}\lambda\lambda os$ *another* and $\acute{\epsilon}\tau\epsilon\rho os$ *different*, see 1 Cor. xii. 8–10; xv. 40; 2 Cor. xi. 4; Rom. viii. 23.

7. **Another** ($\acute{\alpha}\lambda\lambda o$). A *different* gospel is not another *gospel*. There is but one gospel.

But (ϵi $\mu\acute{\eta}$). Rev. *only*. As if he had said, "there is no other gospel, but there are some who trouble you with a different kind of teaching which they offer as a gospel."

Some that trouble ($o i$ $\tau\alpha\rho\acute{\alpha}\sigma\sigma o\nu\tau\epsilon s$). The article with the participle marks these persons as *characteristically* troublesome — *the troublers*. Comp. L. xviii. 9, of those who were characteristically self-righteous. For *trouble* in the sense of disturbing faith and unsettling principle, see Gal. v. 10; Acts xv. 24. Not necessarily, as Lightfoot, *raising seditions*.

8. **We.** See on 1 Th. i. 2.

Angel from heaven (ἄγγελος ἐξ οὐρανοῦ). The phrase only here. "Angels *in* heaven or the heavens," Matt. xxii. 30; Mk. xii. 25; xiii. 32. "Angels of the heavens," Matt. xxiv. 36.

Other than that (παρ' ὅ). Roman Catholic interpreters insist that παρ' should be rendered *contrary to*, though the Vulg. gives *praeterquam besides*. Some Protestant interpreters insist on *besides* as being against supplementing the gospel with traditions. The explanation is found in the previous words, *a different gospel*. Any gospel which is *different* from the one gospel, is both *beside* and *contrary to*.

Accursed (ἀνάθεμα). See on Rom. ix. 3, and *offerings*, L. xxi. 5. Comp. κατάρα *curse*, and ἐπικατάρατος *cursed*, Gal. iii. 13. In LXX always *curse*, except Lev. xxvii. 28, and the apocryphal books, where it is always *gift* or *offering*. By Paul always *curse*: see Rom. ix. 3; 1 Cor. xii. 3; xvi. 22. The sense of *excommunication*, introduced by patristic writers, does not appear in N. T.

9. As we said before (ὡς προειρήκαμεν). Comp. 2 Cor. xiii. 2; Philip. iii. 18. Not to be referred to the preceding verse, since the compound verb would be too strong, and *now* in the following clause points to an earlier *time*, a previous *visit*. Comp. Gal. v. 21; 2 Cor. viii. 3; xiii. 2; 1 Th. iv. 6.

10. For do I now persuade (ἄρτι γὰρ — πείθω). *For* introduces a justification of the severe language just used. The emphasis is on *now*, which answers to *now* in ver. 9. I have been charged with conciliating men. Does this anathema of mine look like it? Is it a time for conciliatory words *now*, when Judaising emissaries are troubling you (ver. 7) and persuading you to forsake the true gospel? *Persuade* signifies *conciliate, seek to win over*.

Or God. *Persuade or conciliate God* is an awkward phrase; but the expression is condensed, and *persuade* is carried for-

ward from the previous clause.   This is not uncommon in
Paul's style : See Philem. 5 ; Eph. i. 15 ; Philip. ii. 6, where
μορφὴ *form*, applied to God, is probably the result of μορφὴν
δούλου *form of a servant* (ver. 7) on which the main stress of
the thought lies.

11. **I certify** (γνωρίζω).   Or, *I make known.   Certify*,
even in older English, is *to assure* or *attest*, which is too
strong for γνωρίζειν *to make known* or *declare*.   This, which in
the N. T. is the universal meaning of γνωρίζειν, and the prevailing sense in LXX, is extremely rare in Class., where the
usual sense is *to become acquainted with*.   For the formula see
on 1 Th. iv. 13.

After man (κατὰ ἄνθρωπον).   According to any human
standard.   The phrase only in Paul.   See Rom. iii. 5 ; 1 Cor.
iii. 3 ; ix. 8 ; xv. 32.   Κατὰ ἀνθρώπους *according to men*,
1 Pet. iv. 6.

12. **Of man** (παρὰ ἀνθρώπου).   Better, *from* man.   Παρὰ
from emphasises the idea of transmission, and marks the connection between giver and receiver.   Comp. 1 Th. ii. 13 ;
iv. 1 ; 2 Tim. iii. 14 ; Acts x. 22.   In the Gospels and Acts
παραλαμβάνειν usually means *to take*, in the sense of causing
to accompany, as Matt. iv. 5 ; xvii. 1 ; Mk. iv. 36, etc.
Scarcely ever in the sense of *receive :* see Mk. vii. 4.   In
Paul *only* in the sense of *receive*, and only with παρὰ, with
the single exception of 1 Cor. xi. 23 (ἀπὸ).   The simple
λαμβάνω usually with παρὰ, but with ἀπὸ, 1 J. ii. 27 ; iii. 22.

By the revelation of Jesus Christ (δι' ἀποκαλύψεως
Ἰησοῦ Χριστοῦ).   Not, by Jesus Christ being revealed to
me, but, I received the gospel by Jesus Christ's revealing it to
me.   The subject of the revelation is the gospel, not Christ.
Christ was the revealer.   Rev. (*it came to me*) *through revelation of Jesus Christ*.

13. **Conversation** (ἀναστροφήν).   Better, *manner of life*.
See on 1 Pet. i. 15.

In the Jews' religion (ἐν τῷ Ἰουδαϊσμῷ). Only here and ver. 14. Lit. *in Judaism*. It signifies his national religious condition. In LXX, 2 Macc. ii. 21; viii. 2; xiv. 38; 4 Macc. iv. 26.

Beyond measure (καθ᾿ ὑπερβολὴν). Pᵒ. Lit. *according to excess*. The noun primarily means *a casting beyond*, thence *superiority*, *excellency*. See 2 Cor. iv. 7, 17. It is transliterated in *hyperbole*. For similar phrases comp. 1 Cor. ii. 1; Acts xix. 20; iii. 17; xxv. 23.

Wasted (ἐπόρθουν). Better, *laid waste*. In Class. applied not only to things — cities, walls, fields, etc. — but also to persons. So Acts ix. 21.

14. **Profited** (προέκοπτον). Better, *advanced*. See on *is far spent*, Rom. xiii. 12. Paul means that he outstripped his Jewish contemporaries in distinctively Jewish culture, zeal, and activity. Comp. Philip. iii. 4–6.

Equals (συνηλικιώτας). N. T.ᵒ. The A. V. is indefinite. The meaning is equals in *age*. So Rev., *of mine own age*.

Nation (γένει). Race. Not *sect* of the Pharisees. Comp. Philip. iii. 5; 2 Cor. xi. 26; Rom. ix. 3.

Zealous (ζηλωτὴς). Lit. *a zealot*. The extreme party of the Pharisees called themselves "zealots of the law"; "zealots of God." See on *Simon the Canaanite*, Mk. iii. 18. Paul describes himself under this name in his speech on the stairs, Acts xxii. 3. Comp. Philip. iii. 5, 6.

Traditions (παραδόσεων). The Pharisaic traditions which had been engrafted on the law. See Matt. xv. 2, 6; Mk. vii. 3, 13, and on 2 Th. ii. 15.

15. **It pleased** (εὐδόκησεν). See on *εὐδοκία good pleasure*, 1 Th. i. 11.

Separated (ἀφορίσας). Set apart: designated. See on Rom. i. 1, and *declared*, Rom. i. 4. The A. V. wrongly lends itself to the sense of the physical separation of the child from the mother.

From my mother's womb (ἐκ κοιλίας μητρός μου). Before I was born. Others, from the time of my birth. A few passages in LXX go to sustain the former view: Judg. xvi. 17; Isa. xliv. 2, 24; xlix. 1, 5. That view is also favored by those instances in which a child's destiny is clearly fixed by God before birth, as Samson, Judg. xvi. 17; comp. xiii. 5, 7; John the Baptist, L. i. 15. See also Matt. xix. 12. The usage of ἐκ as marking a temporal starting point is familiar. See J. vi. 66; ix. 1; Acts ix. 33; xxiv. 10.

Called (καλέσας). See on Rom. iv. 17. Referring to Paul's call into the kingdom and service of Christ. It need not be limited to his experience at Damascus, but may include the entire chain of divine influences which led to his conversion and apostleship. He calls himself κλητὸς ἀπόστολος an *apostle by call*, Rom. i. 1; 1 Cor. i. 1.

16. **To reveal his Son in me** (ἀποκαλύψαι τὸν υἱὸν αὐτοῦ ἐν ἐμοί). In N. T. ἀποκαλύπτειν *to reveal* is habitually used with the simple dative of the subject of the revelation, as L. x. 21. Once with εἰς *unto*, Rom. viii. 18: with ἐν *in* of the sphere in which the revelation takes place, only here, unless Rom. i. 17 be so explained; but there ἐν is probably instrumental. Render ἐν here by the simple *in:* in my spirit, according to the familiar N. T. idea of God revealing himself, living and working in man's inner personality. See, for instance, Rom. i. 19; v. 5; viii. 10, 11; 1 Cor. iii. 16; xiv. 25; 2 Cor. iv. 6; 1 J. ii. 5, 14, etc. Lightfoot explains, *to reveal his Son by or through me to others.* But apart from the doubtful use of ἐν, this introduces prematurely the thought of Paul's influence in his subsequent ministry. He is speaking of the initial stages of his experience.

Immediately (εὐθέως). Connect only with *I conferred not*, etc. Not with the whole sentence down to *Arabia*. Paul is emphasising the fact that he did not receive his commission from men. As soon as God revealed his Son in me, I threw aside all human counsel.

Conferred (προσανεθέμην). P°. and only in Galatians. Rare in Class. The verb ἀνατιθέναι means *to lay upon;* hence *intrust to*. Middle voice, *to intrust one's self to ; to impart* or *communicate* to another. The compounded preposition πρὸς implies more than *direction;* rather *communication* or *relation with*, according to a frequent use of πρὸς. The whole compound then, is *to put one's self into communication with*. Wetstein gives an example from Diodorus, *De Alexandro*, xvii. 116, where the word is used of consulting soothsayers.

Flesh and blood. Always in N. T. with a suggestion of human weakness or ignorance. See Matt. xvi. 17 ; 1 Cor. xv. 50; Eph. vi. 12.

17. **Went I up** (ἀνῆλθον). Comp. ver. 18. Only in this chapter, and J. vi. 3. More commonly ἀναβαίνειν, often of the journey to Jerusalem, probably in the conventional sense in which Englishmen speak of going *up* to London, no matter from what point. See Matt. xx. 17; Mk. x. 32; J. ii. 13; Acts xi. 2. In Acts xviii. 22 the verb is used absolutely of going to Jerusalem. The reading ἀπῆλθον *I went away* has strong support, and is adopted by Weiss. In that case the meaning would be *went away to Jerusalem* from where I then was.

Apostles before me. In point of seniority. Comp. Rom. xvi. 7.

Arabia. It is entirely impossible to decide what Paul means by this term, since the word was so loosely used and so variously applied. Many think the Sinaitic peninsula is meant (Stanley, Farrar, Matheson, Lightfoot). Others, the district of Auranitis near Damascus (Lipsius, Conybeare and Howson, Lewin, McGiffert).   Others again the district of Arabia Petraea.

18. To see (ἱστορῆσαι).   N. T.⁰.   1.   *To inquire into :* 2. *to find out by inquiring :* 3. *to gain knowledge by visiting ; to become personally acquainted with.*   In LXX, only 1 Esd. i. 33, 42, *to relate, to record.*   Often in Class.   The word here indicates that Paul went, not to obtain instruction, but to form acquaintance with Peter.

Cephas.   See on Matt. xvi. 18; J. i. 42; 1 Cor. i. 12.

19. Save James (εἰ μὴ).   With the usual exceptive sense. I saw none save James.   Not, I saw none other of the apostles, but I saw James.   James is counted as an apostle, though not reckoned among the twelve.   For Paul's use of "apostle," see on 1 Th. i. 1, and comp. 1 Cor. xv. 4–7.

The Lord's brother.   Added in order to distinguish him from James the son of Zebedee (Matt. iv. 21; x. 2; Mk. x. 35), who was still living, and from James the son of Alphaeus (Matt. x. 3).*   *The Lord's brother* means that James was a son of Joseph and Mary.   This view is known as *the Helvidian theory*, from Helvidius, a layman of Rome, who wrote, about 380, a book against mariolatry and ascetic celibacy. The explanations which differ from that of Helvidius have grown, largely, out of the desire to maintain the perpetual virginity of Mary.   Jerome has given his name to a theory known as the Hieronymian, put forth in reply to Helvidius, about 383, according to which the brethren of the Lord were the sons of his mother's sister, Mary the wife of Alphaeus or Clopas, and therefore Jesus' cousins.   A third view bears the name of Epiphanius, Bishop of Salamis in Cyprus (*ob.* 404),

---

* See *Introduction to the Catholic Epistles*, Vol. I., p. 615 f., and J. B. Mayor, *The Epistle of St. James*, XXXVI.-XLI.

and is that the Lord's brothers were sons of Joseph by a former wife.*

20. **I lie not.**   Comp. Rom. ix. 1; 2 Cor. xi. 31; 1 Tim. ii. 7.

21. **Regions** ($\kappa\lambda\iota\mu\alpha\tau\alpha$).   P°.   Comp. Rom. xv. 23 ; 2 Cor. xi. 10.   K$\lambda\hat{\iota}\mu\alpha$, originally *an inclination or slope of ground:* the supposed slope of the earth from the equator to the pole. The ancient geographers ran imaginary parallel lines from the equator toward the pole, and the spaces or zones or regions between these lines, viewed in their slope or inclination toward the pole, were $\kappa\lambda\iota\mu\alpha\tau\alpha$.   The word came to signify the temperature of these zones, hence our *climate*.   In Chaucer's treatise on the Astrolabe, chapter xxxix. is headed " Descripcion of the Meridional Lyne, of Longitudes and Latitudes of Citees and Townes from on to a-nother of Clymatz."   He says: " The longitude of a clymat is a lyne imagined fro est to west, y-lyke distant by-twene them alle. The latitude of a clymat is a lyne imagined fro north to south the space of the erthe, fro the bygynning of the firste clymat unto the verrey ende of the same clymat, even directe agayns the pole artik."   In poetical language, " climes " is used for regions of the earth, as Milton:

> " Whatever clime the sun's bright circle warms."

Syria and Cilicia.   Syria, in the narrower sense, of the district of which Antioch was the capital : not the whole Roman province of Syria, including Galilee and Judaea. Matt. iv. 24; L. ii. 2 ; Acts xx. 3.   This district was the scene of Paul's first apostolic work among the Gentiles. Cilicia was the southeasterly province of Asia Minor, directly adjoining Syria, from which it was separated by Mt. Pierius and the range of Amanus.   It was bordered by the Mediter-

---

* The reader who is curious about the matter may consult J. B. Mayor, *The Epistle of St. James*, ch. I.   He holds the Helvidian theory.   Also J. B. Lightfoot, *St. Paul's Epistle to the Galatians*, essay on " The Brethren of the Lord."   He holds the Epiphanian theory.

ranean on the south.   It was Paul's native province, and its
capital was Tarsus, Paul's birthplace.

22. **Was unknown** (ἤμην ἀγνοούμενος).   Better, *was still
unknown*, the imperfect denoting that he *remained* unknown
during his stay in Syria and Cilicia.

Of Judaea. The province, as distinguished from Jerusalem, where he must have been known as the persecutor of
the church. See Acts ix. 1, 2.

Which were in Christ. See on 1 Th. ii. 14.

23. **They had heard** (ἀκούοντες ἦσαν).   Correlative with
I was unknown, ver. 22.   Note the periphrasis of the participle with the substantive verb, expressing duration.   They
were hearing all the time that I was thus unknown to them
in person.

The faith. See on Acts vi. 7, and comp. 2 Th. iii. 2.   The
subjective conception of faith as trustful and assured acceptance of Jesus Christ as Saviour, tends to become objective,
so that the subjective principle is sometimes regarded objec-
tively.   This is very striking in the Pastoral Epistles.

24. **In me.** The sense is different from that in ver. 16,
see note.   Here the meaning is that they glorified God as
the author and source of what they saw in me.

CHAPTER II.

1. **Fourteen years after** (διὰ δεκατεσσάρων ἐτῶν).   Rev.
after the space of fourteen years.   Comp. δι' ἐτῶν πλειόνων
after several years, Acts xxiv. 17 ; δι' ἡμερῶν *after (some)
days*, Mk. ii. 1.   Διὰ means *after*, that is, a given number of
years being interposed between two points of time.   Not,
in the course of (Rev. marg.).

2. **By revelation** (κατὰ ἀποκάλυψιν). It was specially and divinely revealed to me that I should go. In what way, he does not state.

Communicated (ἀνεθέμην). Only here and Acts xxv. 14. 'Aνά up, τιθέναι to set. To set up a thing for the consideration of others: to *lay it before them*.

Unto them (αὐτοῖς). The Christians of Jerusalem generally.

Privately (κατ' ἰδίαν). The general communication to the Jerusalem Christians was accompanied by a private consultation with the leaders. Not that a different subject was discussed in private, but that the discussion was deeper and more detailed than would have befitted the whole body of Christians.

To them which were of reputation (τοῖς δοκοῦσιν). Lit. *to those who seem; are reputed.* Men of recognised position, James, Cephas, John. Not his adversaries who were adherents of these three. It is not to be supposed that he would submit his gospel to such. The expression is therefore not used ironically. Paul recognises the honorable position of the three and their rightful claim to respect. The repetition of the phrase (vv. 6, 9) may point to a favorite expression of his opponents in commending these leaders to Paul as models for his preaching; hardly (as Lightfoot) to the contrast between the estimation in which they were held and the actual services which they rendered to him. He chooses this expression because the matter at stake was his recognition by the earlier apostles, and any ironical designation would be out of place.*

Lest by any means I should run or had run in vain. Better, *should be running.* Comp. Philip. ii. 16. This is

---

* For the expression οἱ δοκοῦντες in Class., see Thucyd. i. 76; Eurip. *Hec.* 295; *Troad.* 609.

sometimes explained as implying a misgiving on Paul's part
as to the soundness of his own teaching, which he desired to
have set at rest by the decision of the principal apostles.
On this explanation μή πως will be rendered *lest in some
way or other*. But such a misgiving is contrary to Paul's
habitual attitude of settled conviction respecting that gospel
which he had received by revelation, and in the preaching
of which he had been confirmed by experience. In consulting the Christians at Jerusalem Paul had principally in
view the formal indorsement of his work by the church and
its leaders. Their formal declaration that he had not been
running in vain would materially aid him in his mission.
Μή πως is therefore to be taken as marking an indirect
question, *whether — not possibly;* and the sense of the whole
passage is as follows : "I laid before them that gospel which
I preach to the Gentiles, that they might examine and settle
for themselves the question *whether I am not possibly* running or had run in vain." The investigation was to be for
their satisfaction, not for Paul's.* *Run* (τρέχειν) is a favorite
metaphor with Paul. See Rom. ix. 16; 1 Cor. ix. 24, 26;
Gal. v. 7 ; Philip. ii. 16; iii. 13, 14.

3. **Neither** (οὐδὲ). More correctly, *not even*. So far were
they from pronouncing my labour in vain, that *not even* Titus
was compelled to be circumcised, although he was a Greek.
Though approving Paul's preaching, the apostles might, for
the sake of conciliation, have insisted on the circumcision of
his Gentile companion.

Being a Greek (Ἕλλην ὤν). Or, *although he was a Greek*.
Const. closely with σὺν ἐμοὶ *with me*. It was a bold proceed-

---

* This explanation is adopted by Sieffert, Meyer, and Weizsäcker. The
expositors generally admit that no doubt on Paul's part is implied (so Winer,
Alford, Lipsius, Ellicott, Lightfoot), but mostly insist on the first sense of
μή πως. The difficulty of reconciling these two positions, which is clearly
recognised by Ellicott, is evaded by referring τρέχω and ἔδραμον to the opinions of others. So Ellicott: "If others deemed Paul's past and present
course fruitless, it really must, in that respect, have amounted to a loss of
past and present labour."

ing for Paul to take an uncircumcised Gentile with him to
the conference at Jerusalem.

Was compelled to be circumcised (ἠναγκάσθη περιτμη-
θῆναι). That is, no constraint was applied by the Jerusalem
church and its authorities for the circumcision of Titus.
The statement is not that such an attempt was pressed but
successfully resisted, but that circumcision was not insisted
on by the church. The pressure in that direction came from
"the false brethren" described in the next verse.

4. **The false brethren** (τοὺς ψευδαδέλφους). Only here
and 2 Cor. xi. 26. Christians in name only; Judaisers;
anti-Paulinists. The article marks them as a well-known
class.

Unawares brought in (παρεισάκτους). N. T.º. Lit. *brought
in by the side*, and so *insidiously*, *illegally*. Vulg. *subintro-
ductos*. ºLXX. Strabo (xvii. 1) uses it as an epithet of
Ptolemy, "the sneak." Comp. παρεισάξουσιν *shall privily
bring in*, 2 Pet. ii. 1; and παρεισεδύησαν *crept in privily*, Jude
4. *Brought in*, not from Jerusalem into the church at
Antioch, nor into the Pauline churches generally, but into
the Christian brotherhood to which they did not rightfully
belong.

Who (οἵτινες). The double relative introduces the explanation of the two preceding epithets: false brethren, privily
brought in, *since they* came in privily to spy out our liberty.

Came in privily (παρεισῆλθον). Lit. *came in beside*. Only
here and Rom. v. 20, where it implies nothing evil or secret,
but merely something subsidiary. The aorist has a pluper-
fect sense, indicating the earlier intrusion of these persons
into the Christian community.

To spy out (κατασκοπῆσαι). N. T.º. In LXX, of spying
out a territory, 2 Sam. x. 3; 1 Chron. xix. 3.

Liberty (ἐλευθερίαν). Freedom from Mosaism through justification by faith.

Bring us into bondage (καταδουλώσουσιν). Only here and 2 Cor. xi. 20. Bring us into subjection to Jewish ordinances. The compound verb indicates *abject* subjection.

5. **We gave place by subjection** (εἴξαμεν τῇ ὑποταγῇ). *We*, Paul and Barnabas. *Gave place* or *yielded*, N. T.°. By *the* subjection which was demanded of us. The noun only in Paul and the Pastorals, and always in the sense of *self-subjection*. Comp. 2 Cor. ix. 13; 1 Tim. ii. 11; iii. 4.

6. Render the passage as follows : "But to be something from (at the hands of) those who were of repute, whatever they were, matters nothing to me (God accepteth not man's person), for those who were of repute imparted nothing to me."

To be something (εἶναί τι). Comp. ch. vi. 3; Acts v. 36; 2 Cor. xii. 11. To be in good standing as an evangelist or apostle, approved and commissioned by high authorities.

From those who were of repute (ἀπὸ τῶν δοκούντων). *From*, at the hands of; as receiving my indorsement or commission from them. Comp. ch. i. 1. *Of repute*, see on ver. 2.

Whatsoever they were (ὁποῖοί ποτὲ ἦσαν). Ποτέ in N. T. is invariably temporal, and points here to the preëminence which these apostles had *formerly*, up to the time of Paul's visit, enjoyed, because of their personal connection with Jesus.*

Maketh no matter to me (οὐδέν μοι διαφέρει). Paul does not say, as A. V. and Rev., that the standing and repute of

---

* Others, as Meyer, Ellicott, Sieffert, take ποτέ as strengthening the indefinite sense of ὁποῖοι like the Latin *cunque*. "Whatever *in the world* they were." This sense of ποτέ occurs in Class. but not in N. T.

the apostles were matters of indifference to him, but that he
was indifferent about receiving his commission from them as
recognised dignitaries of the church.   The construction is:
" To be something (εἶναί τι) at the hands of (ἀπὸ) those who
were of repute matters nothing to me."

God accepteth no man's person.   Or more strictly,
accepteth not the person of man.   Parenthetical.   Λαμβάνειν
πρόσωπον to receive or accept the face is a Hebraism.   See on
Jas. ii. 1.   In O. T. both in a good and a bad sense; *to be
gracious,* and *to show favour from personal or partisan motives.*
In N. T. only here and L. xx. 21, both in a bad sense.   Similar Hebraistic expressions are βλέπειν εἰς πρόσωπον to look at
the face, Matt. xxii. 16: θαυμάζειν πρόσωπα to admire the
countenances, Jude 16: καυχᾶσθαι ἐν προσώπῳ to glory in the
face, 2 Cor. v. 12.

For — to me.   Explaining the previous statement.   To be
of consequence because commissioned by those in repute matters nothing to me (God accepteth not man's person), *for*
although they might have asserted their high repute and
authority to others, *to me* they did not, as was shown by
their imposing on me no new requirements.

In conference added nothing (οὐδὲν προσανέθεντο).   *In
conference* is an attempt to conform the sense to ch. i. 16.
The verb without the accusative, as there, means *to confer
with.*   Here, with the accusative, the meaning is *laid upon*
or *imposed on.*   Rend. therefore, *imposed nothing on me.*
They imposed on me no new (πρὸς *additional*) requirements;
no conditions or limitations of my missionary work.*

7. **The gospel of the uncircumcision** (τὸ εὐαγγέλιον τῆς
ἀκροβυστίας).   The phrase only here in N. T.   The gospel

---

* It is objected that this meaning is precluded by the middle voice, which
requires us to render *undertook.*   But the word in the middle voice is used
in an active sense (see Xen. *Cyr.* viii. 5, 4).   It may mean *to lay upon
another for one's own use* or *advantage* (Xen. *Anab.* ii. 2, 4).   So here.   They
imposed no obligations in their own interest as Jewish Christians.

which was to be preached to the uncircumcised — the Gentiles. Lightfoot aptly says: "It denotes a distinction of sphere, and not a difference of type."

8. He that wrought effectually (ὁ ἐνεργήσας). See on 1 Th. ii. 13. Rev. omits *effectually*, but it is fairly implied in the verb.*   Comp. 1 Cor. xii. 6; Philip. ii. 13; Col. i. 29. The reference is to God, not to Christ.

In Peter (Πέτρῳ). Better, *for* Peter. *In* Peter would be ἐν Πέτρῳ.

Unto the apostleship (εἰς). Not merely *with reference to* the apostleship, but with the design of making him an apostle. Comp. 2 Cor. ii. 12; Col. i. 29. Observe how Paul puts himself on an equality with Peter.

Unto the Gentiles ʽεἰς τὰ ἔθνη). To make me an apostle to the Gentiles.

9. Who seemed to be pillars (οἱ δοκοῦντες στῦλοι εἶναι). Better, *who are in repute as pillars.* The metaphor of pillars, applied to the great representatives and supporters of an institution, is old, and common in all languages.†

The grace (τὴν χάριν). Including all the manifestations of divine grace in Paul — his mission, special endowment, success in preaching the gospel — all showing that he was

---

* So Weizsäcker, *wirksam war:* and Lipsius, *sich wirksam erwiesen hat.*
† See Pindar, *Ol.* ii. 146, of Hector; Eurip. *Iph. T.* 50, 55, of the sons of a house.   Hor. *Carm.* i. 35, 13, *stantem columnam,* of the public security and stability.   Chaucer, of the Frere, *Prol. to Canterbury Tales,* 214,

"Un-to his ordre he was a noble post."

Milton, *Par. L.* ii. 302, of Beelzebub:

"in his rising seemed
A pillar of state."

See also Clement, *ad Corinth.* V., and in N. T. 1 Tim. iii. 1⁵.; Apoc. iii. 12.

worthy of their fellowship.   He is careful to speak of it as
a gift of God, δοθεῖσαν.

They gave the right hands of fellowship (δεξιὰς ἔδωκαν
κοινωνίας).   The phrase only here in N. T.   A token of alli-
ance in the apostolic office of preaching and teaching.   The
giving of the right hand in pledge was not a distinctively
Jewish custom.   It appears as early as Homer.   Deissmann
cites an inscription from Pergamum, 98 B.C., in which the
Pergamenes offer to adjust the strife between Sardes and
Ephesus, and send a mediator δοῦναι τὰς χεῖρας εἰς σύλλυσιν
to give hands for a treaty.   See δεξιὰν or δεξιὰς διδόναι,
1 Macc. vi. 58; xi. 50, 62; xiii. 50; 2 Macc. xi. 26; xii. 11;
xiii. 22; and δεξ. λαμβάνειν *to receive right hand* or *hands*,
1 Macc. xi. 66; xiii. 50; 2 Macc. xii. 12; xiv. 19.*   The
custom prevailed among the Persians, from whom it may
have passed to the Jews.   See Joseph. *Antiq.* xviii. 9, 3.
Images of right hands clasped were sometimes exchanged in
token of friendship (see Xen. *Anab.* ii. 4, 1).   Tacitus
(*Hist.* i. 54) says : " The state of the Lingones had sent,
according to an ancient institution, right hands, as gifts to
the legions, a signal token of good will."   On Roman coins
often appear two hands joined, with various inscriptions, as
Exercituum Fides; Concordia; Consensus.   To give the hand
in confirmation of a promise occurs Ez. x. 19.   In Isa. lxii.
8, God swears by his right hand.

10. **Only.**   With only this stipulation.

We should remember (μνημονεύωμεν).   The only instance
in N. T. of this verb in the sense of beneficent care.   No
instance in LXX.   In Ps. ix. 12, there is the thought but
not the word.

---

* Lightfoot says that, in patriarchal times, the outward gesture which
confirmed an oath was different, and refers to Gen. xxiv. 2.   But this usage
is referred to in only one other place, Gen. xlvii. 29, and nothing is certainly
known as to the significance of the act.   See the interesting note on Gen.
xxiv. 2, in Lange's *Commentary.*

The poor (τῶν πτωχῶν). The poor Christians of Palestine. Comp. Acts xxiv. 17; Rom. xv. 26, 27; 1 Cor. xvi.
3; 2 Cor. ix. 1. For the word, see on Matt. v. 3. In LXX
ordinarily of those who are oppressed, in contrast with rich
and powerful oppressors, or of those who are quiet in contrast with the lawless.

The same which (ὃ — αὐτὸ τοῦτο). Lit. *which, this very
thing*. The expression is peculiarly emphatic, and brings
out the contrast between Judaising hostility and Paul's
spirit of loving zeal. Rev. *which very thing*.

11. **To the face** (κατὰ πρόσωπον). As Acts iii. 13. The
meaning is expressed in the familiar phrase *faced him down*.
It is, however, rarely as strong as this in N. T. Rather
before the face, or *in* the face of, meaning simply *in the sight*
or *presence of* (L. ii. 31), or *according to appearance* (2 Cor.
i. 7). The explanation that Paul withstood Peter only *in
appearance* or *semblance* (so Jerome, Chrysostom, Theodoret,
and other Fathers) is one of the curiosities of exegesis, and
was probably adopted out of misplaced consideration for the
prestige of Peter.

He was to be blamed (κατεγνωσμένος ἦν). A. V. is
wrong. Rev. correctly, *he stood condemned*. Not by the
body of Christians at Antioch; rather his act was its own
condemnation.

12. **Did eat with** (συνήσθιεν). A. V. misses the force of
the imperfect, marking Peter's custom. Not only at church
feasts, but at ordinary meals, in defiance of the Pharisaic
prohibition. Peter had been shown by special revelation
that this prohibition was not binding (Acts x. 28; xi. 8, 9),
and had defended that position in the apostolic conference
(Acts xv. 7 ff.).

Withdrew and separated himself (ὑπέστελλεν καὶ ἀφώριζεν
ἑαυτόν). Or, *began* to withdraw, etc. Ὑποστέλλειν only here

in Paul. It means, originally, *to draw in* or *contract.* Thus of furling sails, closing the fingers. Middle voice, *to draw* or *shrink back from through fear.* Hence, *to dissemble* or *prevaricate.* There seems to be no special reason for making it either a military metaphor, as Lightfoot, or a nautical metaphor, as Farrar. See on Acts xx. 20.

13. **Dissembled with him** (συνυπεκρίθησαν). N. T.°. Peter's course influenced the other Jewish Christians at Antioch, who had previously followed his example in eating with Gentiles.

Was carried away (συναπήχθη). Lit. was carried away *with them* (συν). In Paul only here and Rom. xii. 16, on which see note. In LXX once, Ex. xiv. 6.

With their dissimulation (αὐτῶν τῇ ὑποκρίσει). Not *to* or *over to* their dissimulation. Paul uses a strong word, which is employed only in 1 Tim. iv. 2. The kindred verb ὑποκρίνεσθαι *to play a part*, and the noun ὑποκριτής *hypocrite*, do not occur in his letters. Their act was *hypocrisy*, because it was a concealment of their own more liberal conviction, and an open profession of still adhering to the narrow Pharisaic view. It was "a practical denial of their better spiritual insight" (Wieseler).*

14. See additional note at the end of this chapter. **Walked not uprightly** (ὀρθοποδοῦσιν). Lit. *are not walking.* N. T.°. °LXX. °Class. Lit. *to be straight-footed.*

Being a Jew (ὑπάρχων). The verb means originally *to begin;* thence *to come forth, be at hand, be in existence.* It is sometimes claimed that ὑπάρχειν as distinguished from εἶναι implies an antecedent condition — being *originally.* That is true in some cases.† But, on the other hand, it sometimes

---

* See a striking passage in Arrian's *Epictetus*, ii. 9.
† See Thuc. iv. 18; vi. 86; Hdt. ii. 15. Comp. the meaning *to be taken for granted*, Plato, *Symp.* 198 D; *Tim.* 30 C.

denotes a present as related to a future condition.*   The
most that can be said is that it is very often used with a
relative meaning, but that it often is found simply in the
sense of *to be*.

Livest after the manner of Gentiles (ἐθνικῶς ζῇς).
'Εθνικῶς, N. T.º.   The force of the present *livest* must not
be pressed.   The reference is not strictly temporal, either as
referring to Peter's former intercourse with the Gentile
Christians, or as indicating that he was now associating with
them at table.   It is rather the statement of a general principle.   If you, at whatever time, act on the principle of living
according to Gentile usage.   At the time of Paul's address
to Peter, Peter was living after the manner of Jews ('Ιουδα-
ϊκῶς).

Compellest (ἀναγκάζεις).   Indirect compulsion exerted by
Peter's example.   Not that he directly imposed Jewish sepa-
ratism on the Gentile converts.

To live as do the Jews ('Ιουδαΐζειν).   N. T.º.   Once in
LXX, Esth. viii. 17.   Also in Joseph. *B. J.* ii. 18, 2, and
Plut. *Cic.* 7.   It is used by Ignatius, *Magn.* x.   Χριστιανίζειν
to practise Christianity occurs in Origen.

15. We, etc.   Continuation of Paul's address; not the
beginning of an address to the Galatians.   Under *we* Paul
includes himself, Peter, and the Jewish Christians of Antioch,
in contrast with the Gentile Christians.   The Galatians were
mostly Gentiles.

Who are Jews, etc.   The *who* is wrong.   Render *we are
Jews*.   The expression is concessive.   We are, I grant, Jews.
There is an implied emphasis on the special prerogatives and
privileges of the Jews as such.   See Rom. iii. 1 f.; ix. 1 ff.

---

* Hdt. vii. 144; Thuc. ii. 64.   Comp. Aesch. *Agam.* 961, *to be in store.*

Sinners of the Gentiles (ἐξ ἐθνῶν ἁμαρτωλοί). Lit. sinners *taken from* the Gentiles, or *sprung from*. *Sinners*, in the conventional Jewish sense; born heathen, and as such sinners; not implying that Jews are not sinners. The Jew regarded the Gentile as impure, and styled him *a dog* (Matt. xv. 27). See Rom. ii. 12; 1 Cor. vi. 1; ix. 21; Eph. ii. 12; L. xviii. 32; xxiv. 7. Possibly Paul here cites the very words by which Peter sought to justify his separation from the Gentile Christians, and takes up these words in order to draw from them an opposite conclusion. This is quite according to Paul's habit.

16. Justified (δικαιοῦται). See on Rom. iii. 20, 26. The meaning *to declare* or *pronounce righteous* cannot be consistently carried through Paul's writings in the interest of a theological fiction of imputed righteousness. See, for example, Rom. iv. 25; 1 Cor. vi. 11; and all passages where the word is used to describe justification by works of the law, as here, ch. iii. 11; v. 4. If one is justified by the works of the law, his righteousness is a *real* righteousness, founded upon his conformity to the law. Why is the righteousness of faith any less a real righteousness?

By the works of the law (ἐξ ἔργων νόμου). Lit. *out of* the works, etc. Comp. Rom. iii. 20. Works are characteristic of a legal dispensation. Paul often puts "works" alone as representing legal righteousness. See Rom. iv. 2, 6; ix. 11, 32; xi. 6; Eph. ii. 9.

But by faith (ἐὰν μὴ). As the Greek stands, it would read, "Is not justified by the works of the law *save through faith.*" So, unfortunately, Rev. This would mean, as the Romish interpreters, *not through works of the law except they be done through faith in Christ*, and would ascribe justification to works which grow out of faith. Paul means that justification is by faith *alone*. The use of ἐὰν μὴ is to be thus explained: A man is not justified by the works of the law: (he is not justified) *except* by faith in Jesus Christ. Ἐὰν μὴ

retains its exceptive force, but the exception refers only to
the verb. Comp. εἰ μὴ in Matt. xii. 4; L. iv. 26, 27; Gal.
i. 19; Apoc. xxi. 27.

By the faith of Jesus Christ (διὰ πίστεως Χριστοῦ Ἰησοῦ).
Properly, *Christ Jesus*. Faith *in* Jesus Christ, according to
a common usage. See J. v. 42; 1 J. ii. 5, 15; Acts ix. 31;
Mk. xi. 22; Rom. iii. 22; Gal. iii. 22. Paul uses different
prepositions in describing the relations of faith and works to
righteousness; probably not always with a distinct intention
of giving different shades of thought. Here, *through* (διὰ)
faith and *out of* (ἐξ) works. Here and Rom. iii. 30, *out of*
(ἐκ) faith. Philip. iii. 9, righteousness *through* (διὰ) faith,
and *from* (ἐκ) God, *resting upon* (ἐπὶ) faith. Διὰ marks faith
as the *medium* of justification; ἐκ as *the source;* ἐπὶ as *the
foundation*. Ἐξ is habitually used with *works*.

Flesh (σάρξ). See on Rom. vii. 5. For *no flesh* see on
Rom. iii. 20.

17. Are found (εὑρέθημεν). More correctly, *were* found:
were discovered and shown to be. See Rom. vii. 10; 1 Cor.
xv. 15; 2 Cor. v. 3; Philip. ii. 8; iii. 9.

Sinners (ἁμαρτωλοί). Like the Gentiles, ver. 15. Paul
assumes that this was actually the case: that, seeking to be
justified in Christ, they were found to be sinners. To seek
to be justified by Christ is an admission that there is no justification by works; that the seeker is unjustified, and therefore a sinner. The effort to attain justification by faith in
Christ develops the consciousness of sin. It compels the
seeker, whether Jew or Gentile, to put himself upon the
common plane of sinners. The Jew who calls the Gentile a
sinner, in seeking to be justified by faith, finds himself a sinner also. The law has failed him as a justifying agency.
But Paul is careful to repudiate the false inference from this
fact, stated in what immediately follows, namely, that Christ
is a minister of sin.

Minister of sin. A promoter of sin by causing us to abandon the law.

God forbid ($\mu\grave{\eta}$ $\gamma\acute{\epsilon}\nu o\iota\tau o$). See on Rom. iii. 4. Not a reply merely to the question "is Christ a minister of sin?" but to the whole supposition from "if while we seek." The question is not whether Christ is in general a minister of sin, but whether he is such in the case supposed. Paul does not assume that this false inference has been drawn by Peter or the other Jewish Christians.

20. I build again the things which I destroyed ($\hat{a}$ $\kappa\alpha\tau\acute{\epsilon}$-$\lambda\nu\sigma\alpha$ $\tau\alpha\hat{\nu}\tau\alpha$ $\pi\acute{a}\lambda\iota\nu$ $o\grave{\iota}\kappa o\delta o\mu\hat{\omega}$). Peter, by his Christian profession, had asserted that justification was by faith alone; and by his eating with Gentiles had declared that the Mosaic law was no longer binding upon him. He had thus, figuratively, *destroyed* or *pulled down* the Jewish law as a standard of Christian faith and conduct. By his subsequent refusal to eat with Gentiles he had retracted this declaration, had asserted that the Jewish law was still binding upon Christians, and had thus built again what he had pulled down. Building and pulling down are favorite figures with Paul. See Rom. xiv. 20; xv. 20; 1 Cor. viii. 1, 10; x. 23; xiv. 4, 17; Eph. ii. 20 f. For $\kappa\alpha\tau\alpha\lambda\acute{\nu}\epsilon\iota\nu$ *destroy*, see on Rom. xiv. 20; 2 Cor. v. 1.

I make myself ($\grave{\epsilon}\mu\alpha\nu\tau\grave{o}\nu$ $\sigma\nu\nu\iota\sigma\tau\acute{a}\nu\omega$). Better, *prove myself.* The verb originally means *to put together*: thence to put one person in contact with another by way of introducing him and bespeaking for him confidence and approval. *To commend*, as Rom. xvi. 1; comp. Rom. v. 8; 2 Cor. iii. 1; iv. 2; v. 12. As proof, or exhibition of the true state of a case is furnished by putting things together, the word comes to mean *demonstrate, exhibit the fact*, as here, Rom. iii. 5; 2 Cor. vi. 11.

A transgressor ($\pi\alpha\rho\alpha\beta\acute{a}\tau\eta\nu$). See on Jas. ii. 11, and on $\pi\alpha\rho\acute{a}\beta\alpha\sigma\iota s$ *transgression*, Rom. ii. 23. In reasserting the validity of the law for justification, which he had denied by seeking justification by faith in Christ, he proves himself a transgressor in that denial, that pulling down.

19. For (γὰρ). Justifying the previous thought that the reërection of the law as a standard of Christian life and a means of justification is a condemnation of the faith which relies on Christ alone for righteousness.

I, through the law, am dead to the law (ἐγὼ διὰ νόμου νόμῳ ἀπέθανον). For *am dead*, render *died*. Faith in Christ created a complete and irreparable break with the law which is described as *death* to the law. Comp. Rom. vii. 4, 6. The law itself was the instrument of this break, see next ver. 'Εγὼ is emphatic. Paul appeals to his personal experience, his decided break with the law in contrast with Peter's vacillation.

Might live unto God (θεῷ ζήσω). With death to the law a new principle of life entered. For the phrase, see Rom. vi. 10, 11.

20. I am crucified with Christ (Χριστῷ συνεσταύρωμαι). This compound verb is used by Paul only here and Rom. vi. 6. In the gospels, Matt. xxvii. 44; Mk. xv. 32; J. xix. 32. The statement explains how a believer dies to the law by means of the law itself. In the crucifixion of Christ as one accursed, the demand of the law was met (see Gal. iii. 13). Ethically, a believer is crucified with Christ (Rom. vi. 3–11; Philip. iii. 10; 1 Cor. xv. 31; 2 Cor. iv. 10), and thus the demand of the law is fulfilled in him likewise. Paul means that, "owing to his connection with the crucified, he was, like him, legally impure, and was thus an outcast from the Jewish church." * He became dead to the law by the law's own act. Of course a Jew would have answered that Christ was *justly* crucified. He would have said: "If you broke

---

* Professor C. C. Everett, *The Gospel of Paul*, p. 147. The reader will do well to study his interesting and suggestive discussion.

with the law because of your fellowship with Christ, it proved
that both he and you were transgressors." But Paul is
addressing Peter, who, in common with himself, believed on
Christ (ver. 16).

I live; yet not I (ζῶ δὲ οὐκέτι ἐγώ). The semicolon after
live in A. V. and Rev. should be removed. Rend. : *and it
is no longer I that live, but Christ*, etc. The new life of Christ
followed his crucifixion, Rom. vi. 9–11. He who is crucified
with Christ repeats this experience. He rises with Christ
and shares his resurrection-life. The old man is crucified
with Christ, and Christ is in him as the principle of his new
life, Rom. vi. 4–11.*

I now live. Emphasis on νῦν *now*, since the beginning of
my Christian life, with an implied contrast with the life in
the flesh *before* he was crucified with Christ. *Then*, the *I*
was the centre and impulse of life. *Now*, it is no longer *I*,
but Christ in me.

By the faith of the Son of God (ἐν πίστει τῇ τοῦ υἱοῦ
τοῦ θεοῦ). Better, as Rev., *in faith, the faith which is in the
Son of God.* Thus the defining and explicative force of the
article τῇ after πίστει is brought out. *In* faith is better than
by faith, although ἐν is sometimes used instrumentally. *In*
corresponds better with ἐν σαρκὶ *in the flesh*. It exhibits
faith as the *element* in which the new life is lived.

And gave himself (καὶ παραδόντος ἑαυτὸν). Καὶ *and* has
an explanatory force : loved me, *and, as a proof of his love*,
gave himself. For παραδόντος *gave*, see on *was delivered*,
Rom. iv. 25.

> "For God more bounteous was himself to give
>   To make man able to uplift himself,
>   Than if he only of himself had pardoned."
>   Dante, *Paradiso*, vii. **115–117.**

---

* See *International Commentary on Philippians and Philemon*, **Excursus**
on "Paul's Conception of Righteousness by Faith," p. **123** ff.

For me (ὑπὲρ ἐμοῦ). See on *for the ungodly*, Rom. v. 6.

21. **Frustrate** (ἀθετῶ). Annul or invalidate. Comp. Mk. vii. 9; 1 Cor. i. 19; Gal. iii. 15.

The grace of God (τὴν χάριν τοῦ θεοῦ). Χάρις is, primarily, that which gives *joy* (χαρά). Its higher, Christian meaning is based on the emphasis of *freeness* in a gift or favour. It is the free, spontaneous, absolute loving-kindness of God toward men. Hence often in contrast with the ideas of *debt, law, works, sin*. Sometimes for *the gift* of grace, *the benefaction*, as 1 Cor. xvi. 3; 2 Cor. viii. 6, 19; 1 Pet. i. 10, 13. So here: *the gracious gift* of God in the offering of Christ.

Is dead (ἀπέθανεν). More correctly, *died;* pointing to the historical incident.

In vain (δωρεὰν). Groundlessly, without cause. See on 2 Th. iii. 8. The sense here is not common. It is not found in Class., and in N. T. only J. xv. 25. In LXX, see Ps. xxxiv. 7, 19; cviii. 3; cxviii. 161; 1 Sam. xix. 5; Sir. xx. 23; xxix. 6. Comp. Ignatius, *Trall.* x. Paul says: "I do not invalidate the grace of God in the offering of Christ, as one does who seeks to reëstablish the law as a means of justification; for if righteousness comes through the law, there was no occasion for Christ to die."

ADDITIONAL NOTE ON VERSES 14–21.

The course of thought in Paul's address to Peter is difficult to follow. It will help to simplify it if the reader will keep it before him that the whole passage is to be interpreted in the light of Peter's false attitude — as a remonstrance against a particular state of things.

The line of remonstrance is as follows. If you, Peter, being a Jew, do not live as a Jew, but as a Gentile, as you did when you ate with Gentiles, why do you, by your example in withdrawing from Gentile tables, constrain Gentile Christians to live as Jews, observing the separative ordinances of the Jewish law? This course is plainly inconsistent.

Even you and I, born Jews, and not Gentiles — sinners — denied the obligation of these ordinances by the act of believing on Jesus Christ. In professing this faith we committed ourselves to the principle that no one can be justified by the works of the law.

But it may be said that we were in no better case by thus abandoning the law and legal righteousness, since, in the very effort to be justified through Christ, we were shown to be sinners, and therefore in the same category with the Gentiles. Does it not then follow that Christ is proved to be a minister of sin in requiring us to abandon the law as a means of justification?

No. God forbid. It is true that, in seeking to be justified in Christ, we stood revealed as sinners, for it was Christ who showed us that we could not be justified by the works of the law; that all our legal strictness only left us sinners. But the inference is false that Christ is thereby shown to be a minister of sin.

For to say that Christ is a minister of sin, is to say that I, at his bidding, became a transgressor by abandoning the law, and that the law is the only true standard and medium of righteousness. If I reassert the obligation of the law after denying that obligation, I thereby assert that I transgressed in abandoning it, and that Christ, who prompted and demanded this transgression, is a minister of sin.

But this I deny. The law is *not* the true standard and medium of righteousness. I did *not* transgress in abandoning it. Christ is *not* a minister of sin. For it was *the law itself* which compelled me to abandon the law. The law crucified Christ and thereby declared him accursed. In virtue of my moral fellowship with Christ, I was (ethically) crucified with him. The law declared me also accursed, and would have no more of me. The act of the law forced me to break with the law. Through the law I *died* to the law. Thus I came under a new principle of life. I no longer live, but Christ lives in me. If I should declare that righteousness is through the law, by reasserting the obligation of the law as you, Peter, have done, I should annul the grace of God as exhibited in the death of Christ; for in that case, Christ's death would be superfluous and useless. But I do not annul the grace of God.

CHAPTER III.

1. **Foolish** (ἀνόητοι). See on L. xxiv. 25. In N. T. and LXX always in an active sense. See L. xxiv. 25; Rom. i. 14; 1 Tim. vi. 9; Tit. iii. 3. Νοῦς is used by Paul mainly with an ethical reference, as *the faculty of moral judgment.* See on Rom. vii. 23. Ἀνόητος therefore indicates a folly which is the outgrowth of a moral defect. Paul is not alluding to a national characteristic of the Galatians.*

---

* As Lightfoot, *Introduction to Commentary on Galatians*, p. 15.

Hath bewitched (ἐβάσκανεν).   N. T.⁰.   In Class. with accusative, *to slander, malign;* with dative, *to envy, grudge, use ill words to another, bewitch by spells.** For the verb in LXX, see Deut. xxviii. 54, 56 ; Sir. xiv. 6, 8.   The noun βασκανία (not in N. T.) in LXX, Wisd. iv. 12 (*the bewitching*) ; 4 Macc. i. 26 (*the evil eye*) ; 4 Macc. ii. 15 (*slander*). See also Plato, *Phaedo,* 95 B (*evil eye*).   The adjective βάσκανος (not in N. T.) appears in LXX, Prov. xxiii. 6 ; xxviii. 22 (*having an evil eye*) ; Sir. xiv. 3 ; xviii. 18 ; xxxvii. 11 (*envious*).   See also Aristoph. *Knights,* 103 ; *Plut.* 571 (*slanderous, a calumniator*).   Ignatius (*Rom.* iii.) uses it of *grudging* the triumph of martyrdom.   The two ideas of *envy* or *malice* and the *evil eye* combine in the Lat. *invidere, to look maliciously.*   The ὀφθαλμὸς πονηρὸς *evil eye* is found Mk. vii. 22.   Paul's metaphor here is : *who hath cast an evil spell upon you?*   Chrysostom, followed by Lightfoot, thinks that the passage indicates, not only the baleful influence on the Galatians, but also the envious spirit of the false teachers who envy them their liberty in Christ.   This is doubtful.

Before whose eyes (οἷς κατ᾽ ὀφθαλμοὺς).   The Greek is stronger : *unto whom, over against your very eyes.*   The phrase κατ᾽ ὀφθαλμοὺς N. T.⁰, but quite frequent in LXX. Comp. κατὰ πρόσωπον *to the face,* Gal. ii. 11.

Hath been evidently set forth (προεγράφη).   The different explanations turn on the meaning assigned to προ : either *formerly,* or *openly, publicly.*   Thus *openly portrayed.*   The use of προγράφειν in this sense is more than doubtful.   *Previously written.*   In favour of this is the plain meaning in two of the three other N. T. passages where it occurs : Rom. xv. 4 ; Eph. iii. 3.   *Was posted up, placarded.*   It is the

---

* So Aristot. *Probl.* 20, 34.   The derivation from βάζω, βάσκω *to speak* or *talk* (Sieffert, Lightfoot, doubtfully, Thayer) is doubtful, as is also the connection with Lat. *fascinare to bewitch.*   Comp. Vulg. *fascinavit vos.*   See Curtius, *Greek Etymology,* Transl. 531, and Prellwitz, *Etymologisches Wörterbuch der griechischen Sprache,* sub βάσκανος.

usual word to describe public notices or proclamations.* The
more probable sense combines the first and third interpretations. Rend. *openly set forth.* This suits *before whose eyes,*
and illustrates the suggestion of the evil eye in *bewitched.*
Who could have succeeded in bringing you under the spell
of an evil eye, when directly before your own eyes stood
revealed the crucified Christ?

Crucified among you (ἐν ὑμῖν ἐσταυρωμένος). Ἐν ὑμῖν
among you is omitted in the best texts. *Crucified* emphatically closes the sentence. Christ was openly set forth *as
crucified.*

2. **This only.** I will convince you of your error by this
one point. Do you owe the gifts of the Spirit to the works
of the law, or to the message of faith?   *

Received ye, etc. The answer lies in the question. You
cannot deny that you received the gifts of the Spirit by the
message of faith.

The hearing of faith (ἀκοῆς πίστεως). See on ch. i. 23.
For *hearing,* render *message.* So, often in N. T. See Matt.
iv. 24; xiv. 1; xxiv. 6; J. xii. 38. LXX, 1 Sam. ii. 24;
2 Sam. xiii. 30; Tob. x. 13; Hab. iii. 2.†

3. **So foolish.** Explained by what follows. Has your
folly reached such a pitch as to reverse the true order of
things? Comp. 1 Cor. xv. 46.

Having begun (ἐναρξάμενοι). Pᵒ. Comp. Philip. i. 6;
2 Cor. viii. 6. Having commenced your Christian life. The

---

* See Aristoph. *Av.* 450; Just. Mart. *Apol.* 2, 52; Plut. *Camillus,* 11.
So, acc. to some, Jude 4, *registered* for condemnation. Comp. 1 Macc. x. 36,
enrolled.

† Many of the earlier interpreters, *the hearing of the faith,* *i.e.,* the reception of the gospel; but *the faith* is not used in the Pauline epistles as = *the
gospel.* Others, as Lightfoot and Lipsius, *hearing which comes of faith.* But
ἀκοή is habitually used in N. T. in a passive sense (see on 1 Th. ii. 13), and
the opposition is not between *doing* and *hearing,* but between the *law* and
faith.

verb is common in Class. in the sense of beginning a sacrifice or other religious ceremony ; but it is not likely that any such figurative suggestion is attached to it here, as Lightfoot.

In the Spirit (πνεύματι).   Or, *by means* of the Spirit. The Holy Spirit, as the inspirer and regulator of the life.

Are ye made perfect (ἐπιτελεῖσθε).   The word is found in connection with ἐνάρχεσθαι *to begin*, in 2 Cor. viii. 6; Philip. i. 6.   The A. V. and Rev. render here in the passive voice.   The active voice, always in N. T. with the object expressed, means *to bring to completion*.   See Rom. xv. 28; 2 Cor. vii. 1; Philip. i. 6; Heb. viii. 5.   The passive only 1 Pet. v. 9.   It is true that the verb in the middle voice is not found in either N. T. or LXX ; but it is not uncommon in Class. and answers better to the middle ἐναρξάμενοι *having begun*.   It implies more than bringing to an end ; rather to a *consummation*.   Rend.: *having begun in the spirit are ye coming to completion in the flesh?*   The last phrase has an ironical tinge, suggesting the absurdity of expecting perfection on the Jewish basis of legal righteousness.   The present tense indicates that they have already begun upon this attempt.

The flesh.   The worldly principle or element of life, represented by the legal righteousness of the Jew.

4. **Have ye suffered** (ἐπάθετε).   Or, *did ye suffer.*   The exact sense is doubtful.   By some it is held that the reference is to sufferings endured by the Galatian Christians either through heathen persecutions or Judaising emissaries. There is, however, no record in this Epistle or elsewhere of the Galatians having suffered special persecutions on account of their Christian profession.   Others take the verb in a neutral sense, *have ye experienced*, or with a definite reference to the experience of benefits.   In this neutral sense it is used in Class. from Homer down, and is accordingly joined with both κακῶς *evilly*, and εὖ *well.*   Paul habitually uses it in the

sense of suffering evil, and there is no decisive instance,
either in N. T. or LXX, of the neutral sense.   In Class.,
where it is used of the experience of benefits, it is always
accompanied by some qualifying word.   When it stands alone
it signifies *to suffer evil.*   The evidence on the whole makes
very strongly for the meaning *suffer;* in which case the reference is, probably, to the annoyances suffered from Judaising
Christians.   It must be said, on the other hand, that a reference to such annoyances seems far-fetched.   If we could
translate *did ye experience* (so Weizsäcker, Lipsius, Sieffert),
the reference would be to the impartation of the gifts of the
Spirit.

In vain (εἰκῇ).   So that ye have fallen from the faith and
missed the inheritance of suffering and the rich fruitage of
your spiritual gifts.   See Matt. v. 10–12; Rom. viii. 17;
2 Cor. iv. 17.

If it be yet in vain (εἰ γε καὶ εἰκῇ).   The A. V. misses
the force of the particles.   Καὶ should be closely joined with
εἰκῇ, with the sense of *really.*   *If, that is, it be really in vain.*

5. **Therefore** (οὖν).   Resumes the thought of ver. 2 (vv.
3, 4 being, practically, parenthetical), in order to adduce the
example of Abraham as a proof of justification by faith.
The thought of ver. 2 is further emphasised.   The gift of
the Spirit, and the bestowment of miraculous powers, is a
purely divine operation in believers, which is not merited
by legal works, but can be received and experienced only
through the message of faith.

He that ministereth (ὁ ἐπιχορηγῶν).   Or *supplieth.*   See
2 Cor. ix. 10; Col. ii. 19; 2 Pet. i. 5.   The idea of *abundant* supply (Lightfoot), if conveyed at all, resides, not in the
preposition ἐπὶ, which indicates *direction,* but in the simple
verb, which is used of abundant, liberal supply.   *He that
ministereth* is God.

Worketh (ἐνεργῶν).   See on **1 Th. ii. 18.**

Miracles (δυνάμεις). See on Matt. xi. 20. Either *miracles*, as Mk. vi. 2; 1 Cor. xii. 10, or *miraculous powers*, as 1 Cor. xii. 6; Philip. ii. 13; Eph. ii. 2. The analogy of these latter passages favours the second meaning.

Among you (ἐν ὑμῖν). So, if δυνάμεις is explained as *miracles*. If *miraculous powers*, render *in* you.

6. **Even as** (καθὼς). The answer to the question of ver. 5 is so obvious that it is not given. Paul proceeds at once to the illustration — the argument for the righteousness of faith furnished in the justification of Abraham. The spiritual gifts come through the message of faith, *even as* Abraham believed, etc.

Believed God (ἐπίστευσεν τῷ θεῷ). See on Rom. iv. 5. Believed God's promise that he should become the father of many nations. See Rom. iv. 18–21. The reference is not to faith in the promised Messiah.

It was accounted to him for righteousness (ἐλογίσθη αὐτῷ εἰς δικαιοσύνην). See on Rom. iv. 5. Ἐις does not mean *instead of*, but *as*. His faith was reckoned *as* righteousness — as something which it really was; since all possibilities of righteousness are included in faith.

7. **Know ye** (γινώσκετε). Imperative. It may also be rendered as indicative, *ye know*, but the imperative is livelier, and the statement in the verse is one of the points which the writer is trying to prove.

They which are of faith (οἱ ἐκ πίστεως). Ἐκ πίστεως *from* or *out of faith*, is found with the verb *to justify* (Rom. iii. 26, 30; v. 1): with other verbs, as *live* (Rom. i. 17); *eat* (Rom. xiv. 23): with the noun δικαιοσύνη *righteousness* (Rom. i. 17; ix. 30; x. 6): with other nouns, as *promise* (Gal. iii. 22), *law* (Gal. iii. 12). For parallels to the phrase οἱ ἐκ πίστεως, see Rom. iii. 26; iv. 16; xiv. 23; Gal. iii. 9.

It denotes believers as *sprung from*, or *receiving their spiritual condition from* that which specially characterises them. Comp. οἱ ἐξ ἐριθίας *they who are of faction*, Rom. ii. 8; οἱ ἐκ νόμου *they who are of the law*, Rom. iv. 14; ὁ ἐκ τῆς ἀληθείας *he who is of the truth*, J. xviii. 37.

8. The scripture (ἡ γραφὴ).   See on 1 Tim. v. 18.   The particular *passage* cited below.   See on Mk. xii. 10; J. ii. 22; v. 47 footnote.

Foreseeing (προϊδοῦσα).   The passage of Scripture is personified.   Comp. *hath concluded*, ver. 22.   The Jews had a formula of reference, "What did the Scripture see?"

Would justify (δικαιοῖ).   Better *justifieth*.   The present tense.   The time foreseen was the Christian present.   Comp. 1 Cor. iii. 13; Matt. xxvi. 2.

Preached before the gospel (προευηγγελίσατο).   N. T.°. An awkward translation.   Better, *preached the gospel beforehand*.

All nations (πάντα τὰ ἔθνη).   From Gen. xviii. 18; comp. Gen. xxii. 18, LXX.   Gen. xii. 3 reads πᾶσαι αἱ φυλαὶ all the *tribes*.   Τὰ ἔθνη was the collective term by which all non-Jews were denoted, and is more suitable to Paul's Gentile audience.

Shall be blessed (ἐνευλογηθήσονται).   In N. T. only here. LXX, Gen. xii. 3; xviii. 18; xxii. 18; xxvi. 4; Sir. xliv. 21.   The blessing is the messianic blessing of which the Gentiles are to partake — the imparting of the Spirit as the new life-principle and the pledge of future blessedness in Christ.   This blessing Abraham shared on the ground of his faith, and believers shall share it as the true spiritual children of Abraham.

In thee (ἐν σοὶ).   Not, *through thy posterity, Christ*, but in the fact that *thou* art blessed is involved the blessedness of

the Gentiles through faith, in so far as they shall be justified
by faith, and through justification receive the Holy Spirit.

9. **With** (σὺν). Not=*like* or *as*, but *in fellowship with*.
Believers are regarded as homogeneous with Abraham, and
as thus sharing the blessing which began in him.

Faithful (πιστῷ). Or *believing*, as Acts xvi. 1; 2 Cor. vi.
15; 1 Tim. v. 16. Those who are of the faith are one in
blessing with him whose characteristic was faith.

10. **Under the curse** (ὑπὸ κατάραν). Better, *under curse*.
There is no article. The phrase is general = *accursed*. Comp.
ὑφ᾽ ἁμαρτίαν *under sin*, Rom. iii. 9. The specific character
of the curse is not stated. It is not merely the wrath of
God as it issues in final destruction (Meyer); but it represents a condition of alienation from God, caused by violation
of his law, with all the penalty which accrues from it, either
in this life or the next.

Cursed (ἐπικατάρατος). Only here and ver. 13. °Class.
In LXX, see Gen. iii. 14, 17; Deut. xxvii. 16–20 ; Isa. lxv.
20 ; Wisd. iii. 12; xiv. 8, etc.

Continueth — in (ἐμμένει). The expression is figurative,
the book of the law being conceived as a prescribed district
or domain, in which one remains or out of which he goes.
Comp. *continue in the faith*, Acts xiv. 22 ; *in the covenant*,
Heb. viii. 9 ; *in the things which thou hast learned*, 2 Tim.
iii. 14.

11. **But** (δέ). Better, *now*. The δὲ continues the argument, adding the scripture testimony.

By the law (ἐν νόμῳ). Rather, *in the sphere of* the law;
thus corresponding with *continueth in*, ver. 10.

The just shall live by faith (ὁ δίκαιος ἐκ πίστεως ζήσεται).
Better, *the righteous*. Quoted from Hab. ii. 4, and appears

in Rom. i. 17, and Heb. x. 38. The LXX has μοῦ *my*, either
after δίκαιος, "*my* righteous one shall live, etc.," or after πίστεως, "by *my* faith or faithfulness." *

13. **Hath redeemed** (ἐξηγόρασεν). Pº. Better *redeemed*.
Comp. Gal. iv. 5; Eph. v. 16; Col. iv. 5. In LXX once,
Dan. ii. 8. See on Col. iv. 5.

Us. Referring specially to Jews.

Being made a curse (γενόμενος κατάρα). Better, *having
become*. See on ch. ii. 20.

It is written. From LXX of Deut. xxi. 23, with the
omission of ὑπὸ θεοῦ *by God* after *cursed*. Paul, as Lightfoot justly says, instinctively omits these words, since Christ
was in no sense accursed by God in his crucifixion. The
statement does not refer to Christ's enduring the curse in
our stead, but solely to the attitude in which the law placed
Christ by subjecting him to the death of a malefactor. The
law satisfied its demand upon him, and thus thrust him out
of the pale of the legal economy. We, by our fellowship
with him, are likewise cast out, and therefore are no longer
under curse.

Upon a tree (ἐπὶ ξύλου). Originally *wood, timber*. In
later Greek, *a tree*. In Class. used of *a gallows* (Aristoph.
Frogs, 736). Often of *the stocks* (Aristoph. *Clouds*, 592;
Lysistr. 680; *Knights*, 367). So Acts xvi. 24. Of *the cross*,
Acts v. 30; x. 39; 1 Pet. ii. 24. Ignatius (*Smyrn.* i.) says
that Christ was nailed up for our sakes — of which *fruit* are
we. That is, the cross is regarded as a tree, and Christians
as its fruit. Comp. *Trall.* ii. See the interesting remarks
of Lightfoot on the symbolism of the tree of life in Paradise
(*Apostolic Fathers*, Part II., Vol. II., p. 291).

---

* In Heb. x. 38, μοῦ after δίκαιος is retained by Tischendorf, Weiss, and
Rev. T., and is bracketed by WH. Vulg. has *justus autem meus.*

14. That (ἵνα). Marking the purpose of Christ in redeeming from the curse of the law.

That we might receive, etc. The second ἵνα is parallel with the first. The deliverance from the curse results not only in extending to the Gentiles the blessing promised to Abraham, but in the impartation of the Spirit to both Jews and Gentiles through faith. The εὐλογία *blessing* is not God's gift of justification as the opposite of the curse; for in vv. 10, 11, justification is not represented as the opposite of the curse, but as that by which the curse is removed and the blessing realised. The content of the curse is *death*, ver. 13. The opposite of the curse is *life*. The subject of the promise is the life which comes through the Spirit. See J. vii. 39; Acts ii. 17, 38, 39; x. 45, 47; xv. 7, 8; Rom. v. 5; viii. 2, 4, 6, 11; Eph. i. 13.

15. After the manner of men (κατὰ ἄνθρωπον). According to human analogy; reasoning as men would reason in ordinary affairs. The phrase is peculiar to Paul. See Rom. iii. 5; 1 Cor. iii. 3; ix. 8; xv. 32; Gal. i. 11. Comp. ἀνθρώπινος *as a man*, Rom. vi. 19.

Though it be — yet. The A. V. and Rev. give the correct sense, but the order of the Greek is peculiar. Ὅμως *yet* properly belongs to οὐδεὶς *no man:* " Though a man's covenant *yet* no man disannulleth it." But ὅμως is taken out of its natural place, and put at the beginning of the clause, before ἀνθρώπου, so that the Greek literally reads : " Yet a man's covenant confirmed no one disannulleth, etc." A similar displacement occurs 1 Cor. xiv. 7.

Covenant (διαθήκην). Not *testament*. See on Matt. **xxvi.** 28, and Heb. ix. 16.

Confirmed (κεκυρωμένην). Pᵒ. See 2 Cor. ii. 8. In LXX, Gen. xxiii. 20; Lev. xxv. 30; 4 Macc. vii. 9. From κῦρος *supreme power*. Hence the verb carries the sense of *authoritative* confirmation, in this case by the contracting parties.

Disannulleth (ἀθετεῖ).   See on *bring to nothing*, 1 Cor. i. 19.   Rev. *maketh void.*

Addeth thereto (ἐπιδιατάσσεται).   N. T.º.   Adds new specifications or conditions to the original covenant, which is contrary to law.   Comp. ἐπιδιαθήκη *a second will* or *codicil,* Joseph. *B. J.* ii. 2, 3 ; *Ant.* xvii. 9, 4.   The doctrine of the Judaisers, while virtually annulling the promise, was apparently only the imposing of new conditions.   In either case it was a violation of the covenant.

16.   The course of thought is as follows.   The main point is that the promises to Abraham continue to hold for Christian believers (ver. 17).   It might be objected that the law made these promises void.   After stating that a *human* covenant is not invalidated or added to by any one, he would argue from this analogy that a covenant of *God* is not annulled by the law which came afterwards.   But before reaching this point, he must call attention to the fact that the promises were given, not to Abraham only, but to his descendants.   Hence it follows that the covenant was not a mere temporary contract, made to last only up to the time of the law.   Even a man's covenant remains uncancelled and without additions.   Similarly, God's covenant-promises to Abraham remain valid ; and this is made certain by the fact that the promises were given not only to Abraham but to his seed ; and since the singular, *seed*, is used, and not *seeds*, it is evident that Christ is meant.

The promises (αἱ ἐπαγγελίαι).   Comp. Rom. ix. 4.   The promise was given on several occasions.*

Were made (ἐρρέθησαν).   Rend. *were spoken.*

---

* See Clement, *Ad Corinth.* x., who enumerates the different forms of the promise to Abraham, citing Gen. xii. 1–3 ; xiii. 14–16 ; and Gen. xv. 5, 6. See also Gen. xv. 18 ; xvii. 8 ; xxii. 16–18.

To his seed (τῷ σπέρματι αὐτοῦ). Emphatic, as making for his conclusion in ver. 17. There can be no disannulling by the law of a promise made not only to Abraham, but *to his seed*.

Not—to seeds (οὐ — τοῖς σπέρμασιν). He means that there is significance in the singular form of expression, as pointing to the fact that *one* descendant (*seed*) is intended — Christ. With regard to this line of argument it is to be said, 1. The original promise referred to the posterity of Abraham *generally*, and therefore applies to Christ individually only as representing these : as gathering up into one all who should be incorporated with him. 2. The original word for *seed* in the O. T., wherever it means *progeny*, is used in the singular, whether the progeny consists of one or many. In the plural it means *grains of seed*, as 1 Sam. viii. 15. It is evident that Paul's argument at this point betrays traces of his rabbinical education (see Schoettgen, *Horae Hebraicae*, Vol. I., p. 736), and can have no logical force for nineteenth-century readers. Even Luther says: "Zum stiche zu schwach." *

Of many (ἐπὶ πολλῶν). Apparently a unique instance of the use of ἐπὶ with the genitive after a verb of speaking. The sense appears in the familiar phrase "to speak *upon* a subject," *many* being conceived as the basis on which the speaking rests. Similarly ἐφ' ἑνός *of one*.

17. And this I say (τοῦτο δὲ λέγω). Now I mean this. Not strictly the conclusion from vv. 15, 16, since Paul does not use this phrase in drawing a conclusion (comp. 1 Cor. i. 12, and τοῦτο δέ φημι, 1 Cor. vii. 29; xv. 50). It is rather

---

* With this compare the words of Ellicott. "It may be true that similar arguments occur in rabbinical writers : it may be true that σπέρμα is a collective noun, and that when the plural is used 'grains of seed' are implied. All this may be so, — nevertheless, we have here an interpretation which the apostle, writing under the illumination of the Holy Ghost, has deliberately propounded, and which therefore, whatever difficulties may at first appear in it, is profoundly and indisputably true."

the application, for which the way was prepared in ver. 16, of the analogy of ver. 15 to the inviolable stability of God's covenant.

Four hundred and thirty years after. Bengel remarks: "The greatness of the interval increases the authority of the promise." *

To make of none effect (καταργῆσαι). See on Rom iii. 3.

18. In the analogy of ver. 15 there was contemplated the double possibility of *invalidation* or *addition*. With relation to God's promise, the Judaisers insisted on *addition;* since, while they preached faith in the promise and in its fulfilment in Christ, they made the inheritance of the promise dependent upon the fulfilling of the law. Paul, on the other hand, holds that the Judaistic *addition* involves *invalidation*. Salvation must rest *either* upon the promise *or* upon the law. The Judaiser said, upon the promise *and* the law. For God gave the inheritance to Abraham by promise. It has been shown that the law did not abrogate the promise. Hence, if the inheritance be of the law it is no more of the promise. Comp. Rom. iv. 14.

Gave (κεχάρισται). Freely bestowed as a gracious gift. See on L. vii. 21.

19. **Wherefore then serveth the law?** (τί οὖν ὁ νόμος;). Lit. *what then is the law*, or, *why then the law?* What is its meaning and object? A natural question of an objector, since, according to Paul's reasoning, salvation is of promise and not of law.

---

* The LXX of Ex. xii. 40 which Paul is assumed to follow, says that the sojourn of Israel in Egypt *and in the land of Canaan* was 430 years, according to one reading; but according to another, 435 years. Lightfoot says the 5 in the Vatican Ms. is erased, but Swete retains it in his edition of the LXX. The words *in the land of Canaan* are not in the Hebrew. In Gen. xv. 13 (comp. Acts vii. 6) 400 years are given.

It was added ($\pi\rho\sigma\epsilon\tau\epsilon\theta\eta$).   Comp. $\pi\alpha\rho\epsilon\iota\sigma\hat{\eta}\lambda\theta\epsilon\nu$ *came in beside*, Rom. v. 20.   Not as an addition to the promise, which is contrary to ver. 18, but as a temporary, intermediate insti-tution, in which only a subordinate purpose of God was expressed.

Because of transgressions ($\tau\hat{\omega}\nu\ \pi\alpha\rho\alpha\beta\acute{\alpha}\sigma\epsilon\omega\nu\ \chi\acute{\alpha}\rho\iota\nu$).   In order to set upon already existing sins the stamp of positive transgression of law.   Comp. Rom. iv. 5; v. 13.   Note the article, *the* transgressions, summing them up in one mass. Not, in order to give the knowledge of sins.   This, it is true, would follow the revelation of sins as transgressions of law (Rom. iii. 20; vii. 13); but, 1. the phrase *because of trans-gressions* does not express that thought with sufficient defin-iteness.   If that had been his meaning, Paul would probably have written $\tau\hat{\eta}\varsigma\ \epsilon\pi\iota\gamma\nu\acute{\omega}\sigma\epsilon\omega\varsigma\ \tau\hat{\omega}\nu\ \pi\alpha\rho\alpha\beta\acute{\alpha}\sigma\epsilon\omega\nu\ \chi\acute{\alpha}\rho\iota\nu$ *on account of the knowledge of transgressions*.   2. He meant to describe the office of the law as more than giving the knowledge of sins.   Its office was, in revealing sin as positive transgression, to emphasise the objective, actual, contrary fact of righteous-ness according to the divine ideal, and to throw sin into contrast with that grand ideal.

The seed.   Christ, whose advent was to introduce the fulfilment of the promise (ver. 16).

Ordained ($\delta\iota\alpha\tau\alpha\gamma\epsilon\grave{\iota}\varsigma$).   The verb means *to arrange, appoint, prescribe*.   Of *appointing* the twelve, Matt. xi. 1: of *enjoining* certain acts, L. viii. 55; xvii. 10; 1 Cor. vii. 17: of the *decree* of Claudius, Acts xviii. 2.   Here, describing the *form* or *mode* in which the law was added; the *arrangement* made for giving it.

By angels ($\delta\iota'\ \grave{\alpha}\gamma\gamma\acute{\epsilon}\lambda\omega\nu$).   Better, *through* angels as agents and intermediaries.   Comp. $\epsilon\grave{\iota}\varsigma\ \delta\iota\alpha\tau\alpha\gamma\grave{\alpha}\varsigma\ \grave{\alpha}\gamma\gamma\acute{\epsilon}\lambda\omega\nu$ *with refer-ence to arrangements of angels;* or *as it was ordained by angels*, Acts vii. 53.   The tradition of the giving of the law through angels appears first in Deut. xxxiii. 2 (but comp. LXX and the Hebrew). See Heb. ii. 2; Acts vii. 38, 53. In the later rabbinical schools great importance was attached to this tradition, and it was not without influence in shaping the doctrine of angelic mediation which formed one of the elements of the Colossian heresy. Josephus (*Ant.* xv. 5, 3) relates that Herod excited the Jews to battle by a speech, in which he said that they had learned the holiest of laws from God through angels. It is a general O. T. idea that in great theophanies God appears surrounded with a heavenly host. See Hab. iii. 8; Isa. lxvi. 15; Zech. xiv. 5; Joel iii. 11. The idea of an angelic administration is also familiar. See Ex. xxiii. 20; xxxii. 34; xxxiii. 14; Isa. lxiii. 9; Josh. v. 14. The agency of angels indicates the limitations of the older dispensation ; its character as a dispensation of the flesh.

In the hand of a mediator (ἐν χειρὶ μεσίτου). ’Εν χειρὶ *by the agency of*. A Hebraism. In this sense, not elsewhere in N. T. See LXX, Gen. xxxviii. 20; Lev. xvi. 21. *In the hand of Moses*, Lev. xxvi. 46; Num. iv. 37, 41, 45, 49. Comp. σὺν χειρὶ ἀγγέλου *with the hand of the angel*, Acts vii. 35. For μεσίτης *mediator*, see on 1 Tim. ii. 5, and comp. Heb. viii. 6; ix. 15; xii. 24. It is a later Greek word, signifying also *umpire, arbitrator*, and appears in LXX only in Job. ix. 33. The mediator here is Moses, who is often so designated by rabbinical writers. The object is not (as Meyer) to enable the reader to realise the *glory* of the law in the dignity and formal solemnity of its ordination, but to indicate the inferior, subordinate position held by the law in comparison with *the promise*, not *the gospel*. A glorification of the law cannot be intended, since if that were contemplated in the mention of angels and the mediator, the statement would tend to the disparagement of the promise which was given without a mediator. Paul, in the section iii. 6–iv. 7, aims to show that the law does not, as the Judaisers assume, stand in a relation to the divine plan of salvation as direct and positive as does the promise, and that it has not, like the promise and its fulfilment, an *eternal* significance. On the contrary, it has only a transitory value. This estimate of the law does not

contradict Paul's assertions in Rom. vii. 12–25. In representing the law as subordinate and temporary he does not
impugn it as a divine institution.

20. Now a mediator is not a mediator of one (ὁ δὲ μεσίτης
ἑνὸς οὐκ ἔστιν). Observe, 1. Δὲ is *explanatory*, not antithetic.
The verse illustrates the conception of mediator. 2. The article, *the* mediator, has a generic force : the mediator according
to the general and proper conception of his function. Comp.
the apostle (2 Cor. xii. 12); *the* shepherd, *the* good (J. x. 11).
3. 'Ἑνὸς *of one*, is to be explained by the following εἷς, so that
it is masculine and personal. We are not to supply *party* or
law. The meaning is : the conception of mediator does not
belong to an individual considered singly. One is not a
mediator of his single self, but he is a mediator between
two contracting parties; in this case between God and the
people of Israel, as Lev. xxvi. 46; thus differing from Christ,
who is called *the mediator of a new covenant* (Heb. viii. 6;
ix. 15; xii. 24). The new covenant, the gospel, was not a
contract. Accordingly ver. 20 serves to define the true conception of a mediator, and through this definition to make
clearer the difference between the law, which required a
mediator, and the promise, which is the simple expression
of God's will. The very idea of mediation supposes two
parties. The law is of the nature of a contract between God
and the Jewish people. The validity of the contract depends
on its fulfilment by both parties. Hence it is contingent,
not absolute.

But God is one (ὁ δὲ θεὸς εἷς ἐστίν). God does not need a
mediator to make his promise valid. His promise is not of
the nature of a contract between two parties. His promise
depends on his own individual decree. He dealt with Abraham singly and directly, without a mediator. The dignity of
the law is thus inferior to that of the promise.

21. Against the promises (κατὰ τῶν ἐπαγγελιῶν). Does
it follow from the difference between the law and the promises

that they are in antagonism?   Paul supposes this objection on
the part of a Jewish Christian.

God forbid (μὴ γένοιτο).   See on Rom. iii. 4.   This could
only be true in case the law gave *life*, for life must come
either through the promises or through the law.   If the law
is against the promises, and makes them invalid, it follows
that life must come through the law, and therefore righteousness, without which there is no life, would *verily* (ὄντως), just
as the Judaisers claim, be through the law.

By the law.   Tisch., Rev. T., Weiss, retain ἐκ νόμου *from*,
resulting from the law.   WH. read ἐν νόμῳ *in the law*.   The
meaning is substantially the same with either reading: in the
one case *proceeding from*, in the other *residing in* the law.

22.   But it is not true that the law gives life, for the law,
according to scripture, condemned all alike.

The scripture (ἡ γραφὴ).   Scripture is personified.   See
on ver. 8.

Hath concluded (συνέκλεισεν).   Better, *hath shut up*, as a
jailer.   Only in Paul, with the exception of L. v. 6.   Frequent
in LXX.   Not *included with others*, but confined as within an
enclosure, as L. v. 6, of the net *enclosing* the fish.   Comp.
Ex. xiv. 3; Josh. vi. 1; 1 Macc. iv. 31.   Scripture, in its
divine utterances on the universality and guilt of sin, is
conceived as a jailer who shuts all up in sin as in a prison.
Comp. Rom. iii. 10–19; xi. 32.

All (τὰ πάντα).   Neuter, *all things collectively* : = *all men*.
For the neuter in a similar comprehensive sense, see 1 Cor.
i. 27; Col. i. 20; Eph. i. 10.

That (ἵνα).   In order that.   That which is represented
through a personification as the act of Scripture, is the act of
God, according to a definite purpose that the promise should
be inherited by believers only, through faith in Jesus Christ.

The promise (ἡ ἐπαγγελία). That is, the thing promised; the *inheritance*, ver. 18.

By faith (ἐκ πίστεως). Const. with *the promise*, not with *might be given*. The promised gift which is the result of faith. The false teachers claimed that it was the result of works.

To them that believe (τοῖς πιστεύουσιν). Not tautological. Even the Judaisers held that salvation was intended for believers, but also that legal obedience was its procuring cause; against which Paul asserts that it is simply for those that *believe*.

23. But the office of the law as a jailer was designed to be only temporary, until the time when faith should come. It was to hold in custody those who were subjected to sin, so that they should not escape the consciousness of their sins and of their liability to punishment.

Faith (τὴν πίστιν). *The* subjective faith in Christ which appropriates the promise. See on ch. i. 23.

We were kept (ἐφρουρούμεθα). Better, *kept in ward*, continuing the figure in *shut up*, ver. 22. The imperfect tense indicates the continued activity of the law as a warder.

Under the law (ὑπὸ νόμον). Const. with *were kept in ward*, not with *shut up*. We were shut up with the law as a warder, not for protection, but to guard against escape. Comp. Wisd. xvii. 15. The figure of the law as pedagogue (ver. 24) is not anticipated. The law is conceived, not as the prison, but as the warder, the lord or despot, the power of sin (see 1 Cor. xv. 56; Rom. vii.), by whom those who belong to sin are kept under lock and key — under moral captivity, without possibility of liberation except through faith.

Shut up unto the faith (συνκλειόμενοι εἰς τὴν πίστιν). Εἰς *unto* or *for* expresses the object of keeping in ward. It is not temporal, *until*, which is a rare usage in **N. T.**, but *with a view to our passing into the state of faith.*

Which should afterwards be revealed (μέλλουσαν — ἀπο-καλυφθῆναι). The position of μέλλουσαν emphasises the future state of things to which the earlier conditions pointed. The faith was first revealed at the coming of Christ and the gospel.

24. **Wherefore** (ὥστε). Better, *so that.* Theological consequence of the previous statements.

Our schoolmaster (παιδαγωγὸς ἡμῶν). *Our.* Paul speaks as a Jew of Jews especially. *Schoolmaster* (παιδαγωγὸς P^o.) is an error. The word means an *overseer* or *guardian.* See on 1 Cor. iv. 15. *Tutor* (Rev.) is defensible on the ground of etymology, *tueri to look upon*, thence *to guard.* In civil law a tutor is a person legally appointed for the care of the person and property of a minor. So Bacon (*Adv. of Learning*, ii. 19): "the first six kings being in truth as *tutors* of the state of Rome in the infancy thereof." The later use of the word, however, in the sense of *instructor*, has so completely supplanted the earlier, that the propriety of the Revisers' rendering is questionable. The law is here represented, not as one who conducts to the school of Christ; for Christ is not represented here as a teacher, but as an atoner; but rather as an *overseer* or *guardian*, to keep watch of those committed to its care, to accompany them with its commands and prohibitions, and to keep them in a condition of dependence and restraint, thus continually bringing home to them the consciousness of being shut up in sins, and revealing sin as positive transgression.*

26. **For ye are all the children of God** (πάντες γὰρ υἱοὶ θεοῦ ἐστὲ). Better, *ye are all sons of God.* Note 1. The change of person, *ye* are. Comp. *we, our, us*, vv. 23, 24, 25.

---

* See an interesting passage in Plato, *Lysis*, 207, 208.

He now addresses the Galatians, who were mostly Gentiles, and includes all Christians, Jewish and Gentile.   2. The emphasis is on *sons of God* rather than on *all;* for his object is to show that, after the coming of faith, they are no more under the care of a guardian.   'Τιοὶ signifies sons of full age (comp. ch. iv. 1) who have outgrown the surveillance of the guardian; so that *sons* is emphasised as against *children.* Paul describes Christians both as τέκνα θεοῦ *children* of God (Rom. viii. 16, 21; ix. 8; Philip. ii. 15), and υἱοὶ θεοῦ *sons* of God (Rom. viii. 14, 19; ix. 26).   Both τέκνον and υἱός signify a relation based on parentage.   The common distinction between τέκνον as emphasising natural relationship, and υἱός as marking legal or ethical status, should not be pressed. In LXX both words are applied ethically to Israel as God's beloved people.   See Isa. xxx. 1; Wisd. xvi. 21; Joel ii. 23; Zech. ix. 13; and Isa. xliii. 6; Deut. xiv. 1; Wisd. ix. 7; xii. 19.   John never uses υἱός to describe the relation of Christians to God; but he attaches both the ethical relation and that of conferred privilege, as well as that of birth, to τέκνον. See J. i. 12; 1 J. iii. 1, 10; J. i. 13; iii. 3, 7; 1 J. iii. 9; iv. 7; v. 1, 4, 18.   Paul often regards the Christian relation from a legal point of view as υἱοθεσία *adoption,* a word used only by him.   See Rom. viii. 15, 23; Gal. iv. 5; Eph. i. 5; but in Rom. viii. 14, 17, we have both υἱοὶ and τέκνα, and both in the ethical sense.   In Rom. viii. 21 τέκνα has the legal sense.   In Rom. ix. 8; Eph. v. 1, the ethical sense. 3. *In Christ Jesus.*   Const. with *faith.*   The article before πίστεως *faith* may point back to the faith previously mentioned, or may have, as so often, a possessive force, *your* faith.

27. Were baptized into Christ (εἰς Χριστὸν ἐβαπτίσθητε). See on Matt. xxviii. 19.   Not *in relation* to Christ (Meyer), but into spiritual union and communion with him.   Comp. Rom. vi. 3 (see note); 1 Cor. xii. 12, 13, 27.   Paul here conceives baptism, not as a mere symbolical transaction, but as an act in which believers are put into mystical union with the crucified and risen Lord.   Comp. Rom. vi. 3–11.

(**You**) **put on Christ** (Χριστὸν ἐνεδύσασθε). The phrase only here and Rom. xiii. 14. The figurative use of the verb occurs only once in the Gospels, L. xxiv. 49, but often in Paul, 1 Cor. xv. 53; Eph. iv. 24; Col. iii. 10, 12, etc. Chrysostom (*Hom.* xiii. on Ephesians) remarks, "We say of friends, one *puts on* the other, meaning thereby much love and unceasing fellowship." In LXX quite often in the figurative sense, as Judg. vi. 34; 1 Chron. xii. 18; 2 Chron. vi. 41; Job viii. 22; xxix. 14; Ps. cviii. 18. Similarly in class., Plato, *Rep.* 620, of Thersites putting on the form of a monkey: Xen. *Cyr.* ii. 1, 13, of insinuating one's self into the minds of hearers. So the Lat. *induere:* Cicero, *De Off.* iii. 10, 43, to assume the part of a judge: Tac. *Ann.* xvi. 28, to take on the part of a traitor or enemy. To put on Christ implies making his character, feelings and works our own. Thus Chrysostom : "If Christ is Son of God, and thou hast put him on, having the Son in thyself and being made like unto him, thou hast been brought into one family and one nature." And again: "He who is clothed appears to be that with which he is clothed."

28. With this putting on of Christ, the distinctions of your ordinary social relations — of nation, condition, sex — vanish. Comp. Rom. x. 12; 1 Cor. xii. 13; Col. iii. 11.

There is (ἔνι). Only in Paul (1 Cor. vi. 5; Col. iii. 11) and Jas. i. 17. Ἔνι is the abbreviation of ἔνεστι *there is in* or *among.**

Male nor female (ἄρσεν καὶ θῆλυ). Comp. Matt. xix. 4. He has said "Jew *nor* Greek "; "bond *nor* free." Here he says "male *and* (καὶ) female "; perhaps because political and

---

* Ellicott and Lightfoot deny this, and say that ἔνι is the lengthened form of the adverbialised preposition ἐν, with which ἔστι must be supplied. But both retain in their texts the accentuation ἔνι, whereas the lengthened form of the preposition is ἐνί. In 1 Cor. vi. 5, and often in Class., ἔνι and ἐν are found together, showing that ἔνι stands independently as a compound word. See Xen. *Anab.* v. 3, 11; Hdt. vii. 112; Plato, *Phaedo*, 77 E.

social distinctions are alterable, while the distinction of sex is unalterable, though absorbed in the new relation to Christ. Yet see Col. iii. 11, where we find, "not Greek *and* Jew, circumcision *and* uncircumcision."

Ye are all one. One moral personality. The individual differences are merged in the higher unity into which all are raised by their common life in Christ. This is *the one new man*, Eph. ii. 15.

29. **Abraham's seed.** As being one with Christ. See vv. 7, 16. In Rom. iv. Paul shows that Abraham was justified by faith, and was thus constituted the spiritual father of all believers in Christ, whether circumcised or uncircumcised. The purpose of God in making the inheritance of the promise dependent on faith was that the promise might be sure to *all* the seed. Abraham, he says, is "the father of *us all*" (Rom. iv. 16). This spiritual paternity does away with the current Jewish notion of *physical* paternity. Physical relationship with Abraham is of no significance in the economy of salvation. The apostle "discovers the basis of Christian universalism in the very life of him in whose person theocratic particularism was founded. He has demonstrated the existence of a time when he represented Gentilism, or, to speak more properly, mankind in general; and it was during this period, when he was not yet a Jew, but simply a man, that he received salvation" (Godet).

CHAPTER IV.

The last words of ch. iii., "heirs according to the promise," are now further discussed. It is shown that the capability of heirship, which was first conferred through Christ, could not enter earlier into the history of mankind, because mankind was still in its minority; and its majority, its sonship, was first entered upon through Christ. The way of the law was not, as the Jews supposed, a *direct* way to the fulfilment

of the divine promise.   At the same time, it did not utterly
lead away from the true goal.   It was a roundabout way to
it.   Sabatier (*l'Apôtre Paul*) observes: "The law is neither
absolutely identical with the promise, nor absolutely opposed
to it.   It is not the negation of the promise, but is distinct
from it and subordinate to it.   Its final purpose lies in the
promise itself.   It is an essential but transitional element in
the historical development of humanity.   It must disappear
on attaining its goal.   'Christ is the end of the law.'"   But
why was this way necessary?   Why did not God open the
way of faith leading to the inheritance of the promise immediately after the promise was given?   The answer to this was
indicated in iii. 24–26.   It is now given more fully.

1. Now I say (λέγω δὲ).   Introducing a continued, explanatory discussion.   Comp. ch. iii. 17 ; v. 16 ; 1 Cor. i. 12.

The heir (ὁ κληρονόμος).   See on *inheritance*, 1 Pet. i. 4.
The article is generic as in *the mediator*, ch. iii. 20.

A child (ἤπιος).   A minor.   See on 1 Cor. iii. 1.   Used
by Paul in contrast with τέλειος *full grown*.   See Eph. iv. 13 ;
1 Cor. xiv. 20 ; Philip. iii. 15.   The Jews called proselytes
or novices *babes*.   See Rom. ii. 20.

Lord of all.   Legally, by right of birth, though not actually.

2. Tutors (ἐπιτρόπους).   Better, *guardians*.   See on L.
viii. 3.   Only here in Paul.   A general term, covering all
to whom supervision of the child is intrusted, and should not
be limited to παιδαγωγός (ch. iii. 24).   See 2 Macc. xi. 1 ;
xiii. 2 ; xiv. 2.

Governors (οἰκονόμους).   Better, *stewards*.   Lat. *dispens-
atores*.   More special than *guardians*, signifying those who
had charge of the heir's property.   See on L. xvi. 1.   In
later Greek it was used in two special senses : 1. The slave
whose duty it was to distribute the rations to the other slaves :

so L. xii. 42. 2. The *land-steward:* so L. xvi. 1. Comp. Rom. xvi. 23, ὁ οἰκονόμος τῆς πόλεως, commonly rendered *city-treasurer:* A. V. *chamberlain.** In Lucian, *Alex.* 39, the Roman procurators, or fiscal administrators, are called οἱ Καίσαρος οἰκονόμοι; comp. 1 Esdr. iv. 49; Esth. viii. 9. The *dispensator* in the Roman household had charge of the accounts and made the payments (see Cicero, *ad Att.* xi. 1; Juv. *Sat.* i. 91). He was commonly a slave. Christian teachers are called "*stewards* of the mysteries of God" and "of the grace of God" (1 Cor. iv. 1; 1 Pet. iv. 10), as those who have received the counsels of God and impart them to men. A bishop or overseer is also called "a *steward* of God" (Tit. i. 7).

The time appointed (προθεσμίας) N.T.°. °LXX. In Athenian law the term limited for bringing actions and prosecutions. Προθεσμίας νόμος *a statute of limitations.* It was also applied to the time allowed a defendant for paying damages, after the expiration of which, if he had not paid, he was called ὑπερήμερος, or ἐκπρόθεσμος, or ὑπερπρόθεσμος *one who had gone over his day of payment.* Whether Paul's figure assumes that the father is dead or living is a point which does not affect his argument. It is not easy to decide. As Alford justly remarks: "the antitype breaks through the type and disturbs it, as is the case wherever the idea of inheritance is spiritualised." Προθεσμία *an appointed time for the termination of the minority*, would seem to imply that the father is conceived as living; since, if he were dead, that matter would be regulated by statute.†

3. **We.** Not Jewish Christians only, but *all* Christians. For in ver. 5, Jewish Christians are distinctly characterised

---

* Hatch, *Essays in Biblical Greek*, p. 73, thinks that it means *the administrator of the city lands.* 'Οικονομία in papyri of the first and second centuries A.D. often signifies *record, document.*

† The *living* father, Meyer, Sieffert. Alford, Ellicott, Eadie, leave it undecided. The *dead* father, Lipsius, Lightfoot, with the majority of older interpreters.

as those under the law, while the following *we*, subjects of
Christian adoption, points back to the *we* in this verse. Again,
elements of the world is too wide a conception to suit the law,
which was given to Israel only.

Elements of the world (τὰ στοιχεῖα τοῦ κόσμου). For
the word στοιχεῖα in N. T. see Col. ii. 8, 20 ; Heb. v. 12 ;
2 Pet. iii. 10, 12. See on 2 Pet. iii. 10. Interpretations
differ. 1. *Elements of knowledge, rudimentary religious ideas.*
See Heb. v. 12. The meaning of *world* will then be, the
material as distinguished from the spiritual realm. Elements
of the world will be the crude beginnings of religion, suited
to the condition of children, and pertaining to those who are
not Christians : elementary religious truths belonging to
mankind in general. Thus the Jewish economy was *of the
world* as appealing to the senses, and affording only the first
elements of a spiritual system. The child-heir was taught
only faint outlines of spiritual truth, and was taught them
by worldly symbols. 2. *Elements of nature* — of the physical
world, especially the heavenly bodies. See 2 Pet. iii. 10, 12 ;
Wisd. vii. 17. According to this explanation, the point
would be that the ordering of the religious life was regulated
by the order of nature ; "the days, months, times," etc. (ver.
10), as well as the heathen festivals, being dependent on the
movements of the heavenly bodies. This was the patristic
view (Ambrose, Augustine, Chrysostom, Theodoret). 3. The
elements of the world are the *personal, elemental spirits.* This
seems to be the preferable explanation, both here and in Col.
ii. 8. According to Jewish ideas, all things had their special
angels. In the *Book of Jubilees*, ch. ii., appear, the angel of
the presence (comp. Isa. lxiii. 9); the angel of adoration ; the
spirits of the wind, the clouds, darkness, hail, frost, thunder
and lightning, winter and spring, cold and heat. In the *Book
of Enoch*, lxxxii. 10–14, appear the angels of the stars, who
keep watch that the stars may appear at the appointed time,
and who are punished if the stars do not appear (xviii. 15).
In the *Apocalypse of John* we find four angels of the winds
(xiv. 18); the angel of the waters (xvi. 5); the angel in the

sun (xix. 17). In Heb. i. 7 we read, "who maketh his angels *winds*." Paul also recognises elemental forces of the spiritual world. *The thorn* is "a messenger of Satan" (2 Cor. xii. 7) ; Satan prevents his journey to Thessalonica (1 Th. ii. 18) ; the Corinthian offender is to be "delivered to Satan" (1 Cor. v. 5) ; the Kingdom of God is opposed by "principalities and powers" (1 Cor. xv. 24) ; Christians wrestle against "the rulers of the darkness of this world ; against the spiritual hosts of wickedness in the upper regions" (Eph. vi. 12). In this passage *the elements of the world* are compared with *overseers and stewards*. This would seem to require a personal interpretation. In ver. 8, "did service to them which by nature are no gods," appears to be = "in bondage under the elements," suggesting a personal interpretation of the latter. The Galatians had turned again to the observance of times and seasons (ver. 10), which were controlled by the heavenly bodies and their spirits.*

4. **Fulness of the time** (τὸ πλήρωμα τοῦ χρόνου). The moment by which the whole pre-messianic period was completed. Comp. Eph. i. 10. It answers to *the time appointed of the Father* (ver. 2). For πλήρωμα see on J. i. 16. The meaning of the word is habitually passive — *that which is completed, full complement*. There are frequent instances of its use with the genitive, as "fulness of *the earth, blessing, time, the sea, Christ*," in all which it denotes the plenitude or completeness which characterises the nouns.†

Sent forth (ἐξαπέστειλεν). From himself : from his heavenly glory. This does not mean that God then, for the first

---

* See E. Y. Hincks, *Journal of Bibl. Lit.*, Vol. XV., 1896, p. 183. Otto Everling, *Die paulinische Angelologie und Dämonologie*, p. 65 ff. H. von Soden, on Col. ii. 8, in the *Hand-Commentar*. A. Ritschl, *Rechtfertigung und Versöhnung*, 3d ed., ii., p. 252. F. Spitta, *Der zweite Brief des Petrus*, etc., p. 263 ff. E. Kühl, Meyer series, *On Peter and Jude*. T. K. Abbott, *International Commentary*, on Col. ii. 8.

† See T. K. Abbott on Eph. i. 23, *International Commentary*, and comp. Lightfoot's detached note in *Commentary on Colossians*, p. 323.

time, embodied what had previously been a mere ideal, but
that he sent forth a preëxisting person. See Philip. ii. 6.*

Made of a woman (γενόμενον). Or *born*. Repeated, and
expressing the fact that Christ *became* a man, as distinguished
from his prehistoric form of being.

Under the law. The earthly being of Christ began under
the law. He was not only of *human* birth, but of *Jewish*
birth; subjected to all the ordinances of the law, as circumcision for instance, like any other Jewish boy.

5. **To redeem** (ἵνα ἐξαγοράσῃ). See on ch. iii. 13. To
redeem from the dominion and curse of the law. The means
of redemption is not mentioned. It cannot be merely the
birth of Christ of a woman and under the law. These are
mentioned only as the preliminary and necessary conditions
of his redeeming work. The means or method appears in
ch. iii. 13.

We might receive (ἀπολάβωμεν). Not receive *again* or
back, as L. xv. 27, for adoption was something which men
did not have before Christ; but receive *from* the giver.

The adoption (τὴν υἱοθεσίαν). Pᵒ. See on Rom. viii.
15, and comp. Rom. ix. 4; Eph. i. 5. Not sonship, but sonship *conferred*.

6. **Because** ye are sons (ὅτι). For ὅτι in this sense at
the beginning of a clause see Rom. ix. 7; 1 Cor. xii. 15; J.
xv. 19; xx. 29. The emphasis is on *sons*. The spirit would
not be given if ye were not *sons*. Others take ὅτι as demon-
strative, *as a proof that ye are sons;* but examples of such
usage are wanting. It is not a *proof* of the fact of sonship

---

* See *International Commentary on Philippians and Philemon*, p. 83, and
A. B. Bruce, *The Humiliation of Christ*, p. 431. Also W. Beyschlag, *Die
Christologie des Neuen Testaments*, and *Neutestamentliche Theologie*, 2 Aufl.,
Vol. II., p. 77 ff.

that the apostle is giving, but a *consequence* of it. Comp.
Rom. viii. 16, where the witness of the Spirit *attests* the
sonship.

The Spirit of his Son. The Holy Spirit which animated
Jesus in his human life, and which, in the risen Christ, is the
life-principle of believers. See 1 Cor. xv. 45, and comp. Rom.
viii. 9–11. The Holy Spirit is called *the Spirit of Christ*,
Rom. viii. 9, 10, where Paul uses *Spirit of God*, *Spirit of
Christ* and *Christ* as convertible terms. The phrase *Spirit of
Jesus Christ* only Philip. i. 19. In J. iii. 34 Christ is represented as dispensing the Spirit. He is fully endowed with
the Spirit (Mk. i. 10 ; J. i. 32) : he sends the Spirit from
the Father to the disciples, and he is the burden of the Spirit's
testimony (J. xv. 26 ; xvi. 7, 9, 10, 15). The Paraclete is
given in answer to Christ's prayer (J. xiv. 16). Christ
identifies his own coming and presence with those of the
Spirit (J. xiv. 17, 18). Paul identifies him personally with
the Spirit (2 Cor. iii. 17).

Our hearts. Note the interchange of persons : *we* might
receive, *ye* are sons, *our* hearts. Comp. Rom. vii. 4.

Crying ($\kappa\rho\hat{a}\zeta o\nu$). A strong word, expressing deep emo-
tion. The verb originally represents the sound of a croak or
harsh scream ; thence, generally, *an inarticulate cry ; an
exclamation of fear* or *pain*. The cry of an animal. So
Aristoph. *Knights*, 1017, of the barking of a dog : 285, 287,
of two men in a quarrel, trying to *bawl* each other down :
Frogs, 258, of the croaking of frogs. This original sense
appears in N. T. usage, as Matt. xiv. 26 ; xv. 23 ; xxvii.
50 ; Mk. v. 5, etc., and is recognised even where the word is
used in connection with articulate speech, by adding to it the
participles $\lambda\acute{e}\gamma\omega\nu$, $\lambda\acute{e}\gamma o\nu\tau\epsilon s$ *saying*, or $\delta\iota\delta\acute{a}\sigma\kappa\omega\nu$ *teaching*. See
Matt. viii. 29 ; xv. 22 ; Mk. iii. 11 ; J. vii. 28, etc. In Mk.
x. 47 the inarticulate cry and the articulate utterance are
distinguished. At the same time, the word is often used of
articulate speech without such additions, as Mk. x. 48 ; xi.
9 ; xv. 13, 14 ; L. xviii. 39 ; Acts vii. 60 ; xix. 34 ; Rom.

viii. 15. It falls into more dignified association in LXX, where it is often used of prayer or appeal to God, as Judg. iii. 9, 15 ; iv. 3 ; vi. 7 ; Ps. xxi. 2, 5 ; xxvii. 1 ; liv. 16 ; and in N. T., where it is applied to solemn, prophetic utterance, as Rom. ix. 27 ; J. i. 15, and is used of Jesus himself, as J. vii. 28, 37 ; xii. 44, and of the Holy Spirit, as here. The Spirit is represented as uttering the cry, because the Spirit gives the inspiration of which the believer is the organ. In Rom. viii. 15 the statement is inverted. The believer cries under the power of the Spirit.

Abba, Father. Comp. Mk. xiv. 36 ; Rom. viii. 15. Ὁ πατήρ *the Father*, is not added in order to explain the Aramaic *Abba* for Greek readers. Rather the whole phrase Ἀββά ὁ πατήρ had passed into the early Christian prayers, the Aramaic title by which Christ addressed his Father (Mk. xiv. 36) being very early united with the Greek synonym. Such combinations of Hebrew and Greek addresses having the same meaning were employed in rabbinical writings. Comp. also Apoc. ix. 11 ; xii. 9.

7. **Servant** (δοῦλος). Bondservant. See on Matt. **xx.** 26; Mk. ix. 35 ; Rom. i. 1.

Then an heir (καὶ κληρονόμος). Καὶ marks the logical sequence. Comp. Rom. viii. 17. The figure is based upon Roman, not upon Jewish, law. According to Roman law, all the children, sons and daughters, inherited alike. According to Jewish law, the inheritance of the sons was unequal, and the daughters were excluded, except where there were no male heirs. Thus the Roman law furnished a more truthful illustration of the privileges of Christians. Comp. ch. iii. 28.

Of God through Christ. The correct reading is διὰ θεοῦ *through God*, omitting *Christ*.

8. Over against their filial freedom in Christ, Paul sets their lapse into subjection to the elements of the world (ver. 3).

Knew not God.   See on 2 Th. i. 8.

Ye did service (ἐδουλεύσατε).   Better, *were in bondage* or *were slaves*.

By nature (φύσει).   Not denying their *existence* (comp. 1 Cor. viii. 5) but their *deity*.   Emphasis on *by nature*. Comp. 1 Cor. x. 20.

9. Rather are known of God.   *Rather* corrects the first statement, *have known God*, which might seem to attach too much to human agency in attaining the knowledge of God. The divine side of the process is thrown into the foreground by *are known*, etc.   *Known* does not mean *approved* or *acknowledged*, but simply *recognised*.   *Saving* knowledge is doubtless implied, but is not expressed in the word.   The relation of knowledge between God and his sons proceeds from God.   The Galatians had not arrived at the knowledge of God by intuition nor by any process of reasoning.   "God knew them ere they knew him, and his knowing them was the cause of their knowing him" (Eadie).   Comp. 1 Cor. xiii. 12 ; 2 Tim. ii. 19 ; Matt. vii. 23.   Dean Stanley remarks that "our knowledge of God is more his act than ours."   If God knows a man, that fact implies an activity of God which passes over to the man, so that he, as the subject of God's knowledge, comes into the knowledge of God.   In N. T. γινώσκειν often implies a personal relation between the knower and the known, so that knowledge implies influence.   See 1 Cor. ii. 8 ; J. i. 10 ; ii. 24 ; xvii. 3.   For a parallel to this interchange between the active and the passive, see Philip. iii. 12.

How (πῶς).   "A question full of wonder" (Bengel). Comp. *I marvel*, ch. i. 6.

Turn ye again (ἐπιστρέφετε πάλιν).   Better, the continuous present, *are ye turning*, as of a change still in progress. Comp. ch. i. 6.   Πάλιν *again*, according to N. T. usage, and

corresponding with πάλιν ἄνωθεν in the following clause.
Not *back*, which is the earlier sense and the usual classical
meaning.

Weak and beggarly elements (ἀσθενῆ καὶ πτωχὰ στοιχεῖα). For *elements* see on ver. 3. For πτωχὰ *beggarly*, see
on Matt. v. 3. The two adjectives express the utter impotence of these "elements" to do and to bestow what was done
and given by God in sending his Son into the world. Comp.
Rom. viii. 3 ; Heb. vii. 18.

Again (πάλιν ἄνωθεν). Ἄνωθεν (ἄνω *above*) adds to πάλιν
the idea of going *back to the beginning*. Its primary meaning
is *from above;* thence, *from the first*, reckoning in a descend-
ing series. So L. i. 3 ; Acts xxvi. 5.* Such combinations
as this are not uncommon in N. T. and Class. See, for
instance, Acts xviii. 21 ; Matt. xxvi. 42 ; Acts x. 15 ; J.
xxi. 16. But these additions to πάλιν are not pleonastic.
They often define and explain it. Thus, J. xxi. 16, πάλιν
marks the repetition of Jesus' question, δεύτερον the *number*
of the repetition. He asked *again*, and this was *the second*
time of asking.

Ye desire (θέλετε). It was more than a mere desire.
They were *bent* on putting themselves again into bondage.
See on Matt. i. 19.

10. **Ye observe** (παρατήρεισθε). See on Mk. iii. 2, and
J. xviii. 12, and comp. Joseph. *Ant.* iii. 5, 5, παρατηρεῖν τὰς
ἑβδομάδας *to watch the weeks*. The word denotes *careful*,
scrupulous observance, an *intent* watching lest any of the
prescribed seasons should be overlooked. A merely legal or
ritual religion always develops such scrupulousness.

Days. Sabbaths, fast-days, feast-days, new moons. Comp.
Rom. xiv. 5, 6 ; Col. ii. 16.

---

* Dr. Plummer on L. i. 3 is, I think, mistaken in explaining ἄνωθεν in
Acts xxvi. 5 as *radicitus* (thoroughly).

Months. Sacred months. Comp. Isa. lxvi. 23. In the preëxilic time the months were mostly not named but numbered *first, second, third,* etc., and this usage appears also in the post-exilic writings of the O. T. Only four months had special names : the first, Abib, the ear-month, which marked the beginning of harvest (Ex. xiii. 4 ; xxiii. 15 ; xxxiv. 18) : the second, Sif or Zîv, the flower-month (1 K. vi. 1, 37): the seventh, Ethanim, the month of streaming rivers fed by the autumnal rains (1 K. viii. 2) : the eighth, Bul, the month of rain (1 K. vi. 38). In the post-exilic time names for all the months came into use, the most of which appear in the Palmyrene inscriptions and among the Syrians. According to the Talmud, the returning Jews brought these names from Babylon. The names of all are found in a month-table discovered at Nineveh. Nîsan corresponds to Abib (Neh. ii. 1 ; Esth. iii. 7), answering to the latter part of March and April. Jjar answered to Zîv (Targ. 2 Chron. xxx. 2), our May. Tisri to Ethanim, the seventh month of the ecclesiastical, and the first of the civil year, corresponding to October. Marcheschwan (see Joseph. *Ant.* i. 3, 3) answered to Bul and November. Tisri, being the seventh or sabbatical month, was peculiarly sacred, and the fourth (Sîvan, June), fifth (Ab, August), and tenth (Tebeth, January) were distinguished by special fasts.*

Times (καιρούς). Better, *seasons.* See on Matt. xii. 1 ; Eph. i. 10, and comp. Lev. xxiii. 4. The holy, festal seasons, as Passover Pentecost, Feast of Tabernacles. See 2 Chron. viii. 13.

Years (ἐνιαυτούς). Sabbatical years, occurring every seventh year. Not years of Jubilee, which had ceased to be celebrated after the time of Solomon.

11. I am afraid of you (φοβοῦμαι ὑμᾶς). Not a felicitous translation, though retained by Rev. Rather, "I am

---

* See Ewald, *Antiquities of Israel* (trans.), p. 342 ff. Riehm, *Handw. des Bib. Alterth.*, Art. "Monate." Schrader, *Keilinschriften*, 2d ed. Wieseler, *Chronologie.*

afraid *for* you or *concerning* you." The second ὑμᾶς is not attracted into the principal clause so as to read, "I am afraid lest I have bestowed labour," etc. The two clauses are distinct. *I am afraid about you:* then the reason for the fear is added, *lest I have bestowed,* etc.

Upon you (εἰς ὑμᾶς). Lit. *into* you. The labour, though in vain, had borne directly upon its object. See the same phrase Rom. xvi. 6.

In vain (εἰκῇ). Comp. ch. iii. 4; 1 Cor. xv. 2, and εἰς κενὸν *to no purpose,* Philip. ii. 16; 2 Cor. vi. 1; Gal. ii. 2; 1 Th. iii. 5. After all my labour, you may return to Judaism. Luther says: "These words of Paul breathe tears."

12. **Be as I am** (γίνεσθε ὡς ἐγώ). Better, *become* as I am; free from the bondage of Jewish ordinances.

I am as ye are (κἀγὼ ὡς ὑμεῖς). Rather, *I became.* Supply ἐγενόμην or γέγονα. Become as I am, for I became a Gentile like you. Comp. Philip. iii. 7, 8. For the phrase γινέσθαι ὡς *to become as,* see Matt. vi. 16; Rom. ix. 29; 1 Cor. iv. 13; ix. 20–22.

Ye have not injured me at all (οὐδέν με ἠδικήσατε). This translation misses the force of the aorist, and conveys a wrong impression, that Paul, up to this time, had received no wrong at the hands of the Galatians. This was not true. The reference is to his earlier relations with the Galatians, and is explained by vv. 13, 14. Rend. *ye did not injure me at all.* Ye did not injure me then, do not do so now.

13. **Ye know** (οἴδατε δὲ). The A. V. omits δὲ which is wanting in some Mss. Δὲ not *oppositional* as commonly explained: "Ye did not injure me, *but on the contrary* ye know, etc."; but introducing an explanation of *ye did not injure me* by reference to the fact that they might easily have been moved to do him wrong by the unfavourable circumstances

under which he first preached the gospel to them (through infirmity of the flesh). The formulas οἶδα δὲ, οἴδαμεν δὲ, οἴδατε δὲ, are habitually used by Paul to introduce an explanation of what precedes, from a new point of view. See Rom. ii. 2; iii. 19; xv. 29; Philip. iv. 15. The general sense therefore is: " Ye did not wrong me at all as you might easily have been moved to do; *for* (δὲ) you know in what an unfavourable light my infirmities placed me when I first came among you."

Through infirmity (δι᾿ ἀσθένειαν).   On account of infirmity.   Referring to the fact that Paul, in his first journey, was compelled by sickness to remain in Galatia, and preached to the Galatians during this enforced sojourn.   This fact made their kindly reception the more commendable.*

At the first (τὸ πρότερον).   Either generally, *at an earlier time than the present* (as J. vi. 62; ix. 8; 1 Tim. i. 13), or *the first time* (as Heb. vii. 27).   Here in the latter sense. Paul had visited the Galatians twice before he wrote this letter.

14. My temptation which was in my flesh (τὸν πειρασ-μὸν ὑμῶν ἐν τῇ σαρκί μου).   The correct reading is πειρασμὸν ὑμῶν *your* temptation.   The trial to which they were subjected by his bodily infirmity (ver. 13), and which might have tempted them to treat him with indifference.

Ye despised not nor rejected (οὐκ ἐξουθενήσατε οὐδὲ ἐξεπτύσατε).   Commonly explained by making both verbs govern *your temptation*.   Thus the meaning would be: " You were tempted to treat my preaching contemptuously because of my bodily infirmity; but you did not despise nor reject that which was a temptation to you."   This is extremely far-fetched, awkward, and quite without parallel in Paul's writ-

---

* See Weizsäcker, *Apostolische Zeitalter* (trans.), i. 112. McGiffert, *The Apostolic Age*, p. 177 ff. Ramsay, *The Church in the Roman Empire*, p. 62 ff.

ings or elsewhere. It does not suit the following *but received
me*, etc. It lays the stress on the Galatians' resistance of a
temptation to despise Paul; whereas the idea of a temptation
is incidental. On this construction we should rather expect
Paul to say: " Ye *did* despise and repudiate this temptation."
Better, make *your temptation*, etc., dependent on *ye know*
(ver. 13); place a colon after *flesh*, and make both verbs
govern *me* in the following clause. Rend. "Ye know how
through infirmity of the flesh I preached the gospel to you
the first time, and (ye know) your temptation which was in
my flesh : ye did not despise nor reject me, but received me."
The last clause thus forms one of a series of short and detached clauses beginning with ver. 10.   'Ουκ ἐξουθενήσατε *ye
did not set at nought*, from οὐδέν *nothing*. The form οὐθέν occurs
L. xxii. 35 ; xxiii. 14 ; Acts xix. 27; xxvi. 26 ; 1 Cor. xiii. 2 ;
2 Cor. xi. 8.   For the compound here, comp. L. xviii. 9 ;
xxiii. 11; Acts iv. 11; 2 Cor. x. 10.   °Class. 'Εξεπτύσατε
spurned, N. T.°.   Lit. *spat out*.   A strong metaphor, adding
the idea of contempt to that of *setting at nought*.   Comp.
Hom. *Od*. v. 322; Aristoph. *Wasps*, 792.   The two verbs
express contemptuous indifference.   'Εμέσαι *to vomit*, as a
figure of contemptuous rejection, is found in Apoc. iii. 16.
The simple πτύειν *to spit* only in the literal sense in N. T.
Mk. vii. 33 ; viii. 23 ; J. ix. 6, and no other compound occurs.

As an angel. Bengel says : "The flesh, infirmity, temptation, are unknown to angels ; wherefore to receive as an
angel is to receive with great veneration."

As Jesus Christ. With even higher honour than an angel.
Comp. Matt. x. 40 ; J. xiii. 20.

15. **Where is then the blessedness ye spake of ?** (πού
οὖν ὁ μακαρισμὸς ὑμῶν).   Μακαρισμὸς, P°.   Comp. Rom. iv.
6, 9.   Not *blessedness*, but *pronouncing blessed, felicitation*.
" What has become of your self-gratulation on my presence
and teaching ? "   *Ye spake of* is an attempt to render ὑμῶν.
Better, " Where is then that gratulation *of yours ?* "

I bear you record (μαρτυρῶ). Better, *witness*. *Bear record* is common in A. V. for *bear witness*. *Record* is used both of a person, as *God is my record*, Philip. i. 8; *I call God for a record*, 1 Cor. i. 23, and in the sense of *evidence* or *testimony*. So Shaks. *Richard II.* I. i. 30:

> "First, Heaven be the *record* to my speech."

Plucked out (ἐξορύξαντες). Lit. *dug* out. Only here, and Mk. ii. 4, of digging up the roof in order to let down the paralytic before Jesus.

Your own eyes (τοὺς ὀφθαλμοὺς ὑμῶν). Better, *your* eyes. Eyes, as most treasured possessions. Comp. Ps. xvii. 8; Prov. vii. 2; Zech. ii. 8. Some have found here evidence that Paul was afflicted with disease of the eyes. See Dr. John Brown's *Horae Subsecivae*. Accordingly they explain these words, "You would have given me *your own* eyes to replace mine." But ὑμῶν is unemphatic, *your*. All attempts to connect the passage with Paul's "thorn in the flesh" (2 Cor. xii. 7) are to be dismissed as fanciful.

16. **Therefore** (ὥστε). Better, *so then:* seeing that your love for me has waned.

Your enemy (ἐχθρὸς ὑμῶν). Ἐχθρὸς *enemy*, in an active sense, as is shown by the next clause. Not passive, *an object of hatred*, which would have the pronoun in the dative.

Because I tell you the truth (ἀληθεύων ὑμῖν). Ἀληθεύειν, only here and Eph. iv. 15, means *to speak the truth* or *to deal truly*. The present participle refers to the same time as γέγονα *I am become*, the time of his second visit. The clause is usually construed as interrogative (A. V.). It is rather a direct statement with a slight interrogative suggestion. "So then, I am become your enemy, am I."

17. **They zealously affect you** (ζηλοῦσιν ὑμᾶς). They are zealously *paying you court* in order to win you over to

their side. *Affect*, in this sense, is obsolete. It is from
affectare, to strive after, earnestly desire. So Shaks. *Tam. of
Shr.* I. i. 40 :

> "In brief, sir, study what you most affect."

Ben Jonson, *Alchem.* iii. 2 :

> "Pray him aloud to name what dish he affects."

As a noun, *desire.* So Chaucer, *Troil. and Cress.* iii. **1391:**

> " As Crassus dide for his affectis wronge " (his wrong desires).

Comp. 1 Cor. xii. 31; xiv. 1.

Not well (οὐ καλῶς). Not in an honourable way.

Nay (ἀλλὰ). So far from dealing honourably.

They would exclude you (ἐκκλεῖσαι ὑμᾶς θέλουσιν).
From other teachers who do not belong to their party —
those of anti-Judaising views who formed the sounder part
of the church.

That ye might affect them (ἵνα αὐτοὺς ζηλοῦτε). So that
in your isolation from others, you might be led to seek affili-
ation with them.

18. **It is good — in a good thing.** Ζηλοῦσθαι *to be zealously sought*, in the same sense as before. It is passive. It
is good for you Galatians to be zealously sought. *In a good
thing* (ἐν καλῷ) answers to οὐ καλῶς *not honourably*, ver. 17.
In a good matter — the interest of the gospel. Thus Paul
would say : "These Judaisers zealously strive to win you over
to their views; but they do not do this in an honourable way.
There is no harm in seeking to interest and enlist you, provided it is in a good cause."

19. **My little children** (τεκνία μου). Only here in Paul,
but often in John. See J. xiii. 33; 1 J. ii. 1, 12, 28; iii. 7,
18, etc.* See on ch. iii. 26.

---

* The reading, however, is doubtful. Tischendorf, Weiss, Tregelles, read
τέκνα, which Westcott and Hort give in margin.

I travail in birth again (πάλιν ὠδίνω). Better as Rev. *of whom I am again in travail*. 'Ωδίνω only here and Apoc. xii. 2. Gal. iv. 27 is a quotation. The metaphorical use of the word is frequent in O. T. See Ps. vii. 14; Sir. xix. 11; xxxi. 5; xliii. 17; Mic. iv. 10; Isa. xxvi. 18; lxvi. 8. Paul means that he is for the second time labouring and distressed for the Galatian converts, with the same anguish which attended his first efforts for their conversion. The metaphor of *begetting* children in the gospel is found in 1 Cor. iv. 15; Philem. 10. It was a Jewish saying : "If one teaches the son of his neighbour the law, the Scripture reckons this the same as though he had begotten him."

Until Christ be formed in you (μέχρις οὗ μορφωθῇ Χριστὸς ἐν ὑμῖν). The forming of Christ in them, their attainment of the complete inner life of Christians, is the object of the new birth. By their relapse they have retarded this result and renewed Paul's spiritual travail. The verb μορφοῦν. N. T.⁰. The idea under different aspects is common. See Rom. viii. 9; 1 Cor. ii. 16; vi. 15; 2 Cor. iii. 18; Gal. ii. 20; Eph. iii. 17; Col. i. 27.

20. **I desire** (ἤθελον). Better, *I could wish*, the imperfect tense referring to a suppressed conditional clause, as *if it were possible*. Comp. Acts xxv. 22; Rom. ix. 3.

To change my voice (ἀλλάξαι τὴν φωνήν μου). To address you, not with my former severity, so as to make you think me your enemy, but affectionately, as a mother speaks to her children, yet still telling them the truth (ἀληθεύων).

I stand in doubt of you (ἀπορούμαι ἐν ὑμῖν). Lit. *I am perplexed in you*. For this use of ἐν, comp. 2 Cor. vii. 16 ; Gal. i. 24. Paul's perplexity is conceived as taking place *in* the readers. For the verb, see on Mk. vi. 20; 2 Cor. iv. 8. Paul means : "I am puzzled how to deal with you ; how to find entrance to your hearts."

21–31. Paul now defends the principle of Christian freedom from the law by means of an allegorical interpretation
of the history of Abraham's two sons. He meets the Judaisers on their own Old Testament ground, going back to the
statement of ch. iii. 7.

21. **Tell me.** He plunges into the subject without introduction, and with a direct appeal.

Desire (θέλοντες).   Are *bent on being* under the law. **See**
on ver. 9.

Under the law (ὑπὸ νόμον).   For νόμος with and without
the article, see on Rom. ii. 12.   Here, unquestionably, of the
Mosaic law.

Hear (ἀκούετε).   (Do ye not) hear what the law really
says: listen to it so as to catch its real meaning?   Comp.
1 Cor. xiv. 2; LXX, Gen. xi. 7; Deut. xxviii. 49.[*]

The law (τὸν νόμον).   In a different sense, referring to the
O. T.   For a similar double sense see Rom. iii. 19.   For
νόμος as a designation of the O. T. generally, see 1 Cor. xiv.
21; J. x. 24; xii. 34; xv. 25.

22. **For** (γάρ).   Your determination to be under the law
is opposed by Scripture, if you will understand it, *for* it is
written, etc.

A bondmaid (τῆς παιδίσκης).   *The* bondmaid, indicating
a well-known character, Hagar, Gen. xvi. 3.   The word in
Class. means also a free maiden; but in N. T. always a slave.
So almost always in LXX; but see Ruth iv. 12; Judith
xii. 13.

23. **Was born** (γεγέννηται).   *Has been* born, or *is* born:
perfect tense, treating the historical fact as if present.

---

[*] Others: " Do ye not hear it as it is read in your worshipping assemblies? "   The reading ἀναγινώσκετε *read aloud*, *read publicly*, is found in
DFG, and is followed by the Vulg., *non legistis*.

After the flesh (κατὰ σάρκα). According to the regular course of nature. Very common in Paul.

By promise (δι' ἐπαγγελίας). Most editors retain the article, *the* promise of Gen. xvii. 16, 19; xviii. 10. Comp. Rom. ix. 9. *In virtue* of the promise; for according to natural conditions he would not have been born.

24. **Are an allegory** (ἐστιν ἀλληγορούμενα). N. T.º. Lit. *are allegorised.* From ἄλλο *another,* ἀγορεύειν *to speak.* Hence, things which are so spoken as to give a different meaning from that which the words express. For *parable, allegory, fable,* and *proverb,* see on Matt. xiii. 3. An allegory is to be distinguished from a *type.* An O. T. type is a real prefiguration of a N. T. fact, as the Jewish tabernacle explained in Heb. ix., or the brazen serpent, J. iii. 14. Comp. Rom. v. 14; 1 Cor. x. 6, 11. An allegory exhibits figuratively the ideal character of a fact. The type allows no latitude of interpretation. The allegory lends itself to various interpretations. This passage bears traces of Paul's rabbinical training. At the time of Christ, Scripture was overlaid with that enormous mass of rabbinic interpretation which, beginning as a supplement to the written law, at last superseded and threw it into contempt. The plainest sayings of Scripture were resolved into another sense; and it was asserted by one of the Rabbis that he that renders a verse of Scripture as it appears, says what is not true. The celebrated Akiba assumed that the Pentateuch was a continuous enigma, and that a meaning was to be found in every monosyllable, and a mystical sense in every hook and flourish of the letters. The Talmud relates how Akiba was seen by Moses in a vision, drawing from every horn of every letter whole bushels of decisions. The oral laws, subsequently reduced to writing in the Talmud, completely overshadowed and superseded the Scriptures, so that Jesus was literally justified in saying : "Thus have ye made the commandment of God of none effect through your tradition."

Paul had been trained as a Rabbi in the school of Hillel, the founder of the rabbinical system, whose hermeneutic rules

were the basis of the Talmud. As Jowett justly says :
"Strange as it may at first appear that Paul's mode of
interpreting the Old Testament Scriptures should not conform to our laws of logic or language, it would be far
stranger if it had not conformed with the natural modes of
thought and association in his own day." His familiarity
with this style of exposition gave him a real advantage in
dealing with Jews.

It is a much-mooted question whether, in this passage, Paul
is employing an argument or an illustration. The former
would seem to be the case. On its face, it seems improbable
that, as Dr. Bruce puts it : "it is poetry rather than logic,
meant not so much to convince the reason as to captivate the
imagination." *   Comp. the argument in ch. iii. 16, and see
note. It appears plain that Paul believed that his interpretation actually lay hidden in the O. T. narrative, and that he
adduced it as having argumentative force. Whether he regarded the correspondence as designed to extend to all the
details of his exposition may be questioned ; but he appears
to have discerned in the O. T. narrative a genuine type, which
he expanded into his allegory. For other illustrations of this
mode of treatment, see Rom. ii. 24; ix. 33; 1 Cor. ii. 9|; ix.
9, 10; x. 1-4.†

For these are. Hagar and Sarah *are*, allegorically. Signify. Comp. Matt. xiii. 20, 38; xxvi. 26, 28; 1 Cor. x.
4, 16.

The one. Covenant.

From Mount Sinai (ἀπὸ ὄρους Σινᾶ). The covenant eman-
ating from Sinai : made on that mountain. The old covenant. See 2 Cor. iii. 14.

---

* *Paul's Conception of Christianity*, p. 68.

† On allegorical interpretation in general see F. W. Farrar, *History of
Interpretation*, Bampton, 1855. On the early training of Paul, Derenbourg,
Histoire de la Palestine d'après les Thalmuds, chs. xxi. xxii.

Which gendereth to bondage ($\epsilon i \varsigma$ $\delta o v \lambda \epsilon i a v$ $\gamma \epsilon v v \hat{\omega} \sigma a$). That is, the Sinaitic covenant places its children in a condition of bondage; note the personification and the allegorical blending of fact and figure.

Which is Hagar ($\accentset{\cdot}{\eta} \tau \iota \varsigma$ $\epsilon \sigma \tau \grave{\iota} v$ $\accentset{\cdot}{A} \gamma a \rho$). The Sinaitic covenant is that which, in Abraham's history, is Hagar: which is allegorically identified with Hagar the bondmaid.

25. **For this Hagar is Mount Sinai in Arabia** ($\tau \grave{o}$ $\delta \grave{\epsilon}$ $\accentset{\cdot}{A} \gamma a \rho$ $\Sigma \iota v \grave{a}$ $\accentset{\cdot}{o} \rho o \varsigma$ $\epsilon \sigma \tau \grave{\iota} v$ ϵv $\tau \hat{\eta}$ $\accentset{\cdot}{A} \rho a \beta i a$). The sentence is not parenthetical. This covenant is the Hagar of that allegorical history which is explained by the resemblance of her name to the Arabic name of Sinai. The Greek order is not $\accentset{\cdot}{o} \rho o \varsigma$ $\Sigma \iota v \grave{a}$, as ver. 24, but $\Sigma \iota v \grave{a}$ $\accentset{\cdot}{o} \rho o \varsigma$, in order to bring into juxtaposition the two names which are declared to coincide. The evidence, however, for the actual identity of the names is deficient. The proper name Hagar signifies *wanderer* or *fugitive* (Arab. *hadschar*, comp. *Hegira*, the term for the flight of Mahomet). It has probably been confounded with the Arabic *chadschar a stone* or *rock*, which cannot be shown to be an Arabic designation of Sinai. The similarity of the first two gutturals might easily lead to the mistake.[*]

Answereth to ($\sigma v v \sigma \tau o \iota \chi \epsilon \hat{\iota}$). N. T.[o]. The subject of the verb is Hagar, not Mount Sinai. Lit. *stands in the same row or file with*. Hence, belongs to the same category. See on *elements*, ch. iii. 3.[†]

Jerusalem which now is. As contrasted with "the Jerusalem above," ver. 26. The city is taken to represent the whole Jewish race.

---

[*] See Lightfoot's excursus in *Commentary on Galatians*, p. 190 ff.

[†] Lipsius explains the verb from the usage of grammarians, as *having letters of equal value*, and says that it is an example of the *Gematria* of the rabbinical schools, one of the methods of esoteric interpretation by which a numerical value was given to the letters of a word, and the word was connected with any other word the letters of which had the same numerical value, as *Mashiach Messiah*, and *nachash serpent*.

26. **Jerusalem which is above** (ἡ ἄνω Ἱερουσαλὴμ). Paul
uses the Hebrew form Ἱερουσαλὴμ in preference to the Greek
Ἱεροσόλυμα, which occurs Gal. i. 17, 18; ii. 1.   The phrase
Jerusalem which is above was familiar to the rabbinical teachers, who conceived the heavenly Jerusalem as the archetype
of the earthly.   On the establishment of Messiah's kingdom,
the heavenly archetype would be let down to earth, and would
be the capital of the messianic theocracy. Comp. Heb. xi. 10;
xii. 22; xiii. 14; Apoc. iii. 12; xxi. 2.   Paul here means the
messianic kingdom of Christ, partially realised in the Christian
church, but to be fully realised only at the second coming of
the Lord.   For ἄνω, comp. Philip. iii. 14; Col. iii. 1, 2.

Free (ἐλευθέρα).   Independent of the Mosaic law; in contrast with the earthly Jerusalem, which, like Hagar, is in
bondage.   The Jerusalem above therefore answers to Sarah.

Which is (ἥτις ἐστὶν).   The double relative refers to *the
Jerusalem which is above*, not to *free*.   That Jerusalem, as that
which is our mother, is free.

The mother of us all.   Render, *our mother*.   Πάντων *all*
does not belong in the text.

27. The last statement is proved from Scripture, LXX of
Isa. liv. 1, which predicts the great growth of the people of
God after the Babylonian exile.   It is applied to the unfruitful Sarah, who answers to the Jerusalem above, and who is a
type of God's dealings with her descendants.

Break forth (ῥῆξον).   In this sense not in N. T.   The
ellipsis is usually supplied by φωνήν *voice;* cause thy voice to
break forth.   Others prefer εὐφροσύνην *joy*, as suggested by
εὐφράνθητι *rejoice*.   Ῥήξει φωνὴν occurs Job vi. 5, of the lowing of the ox; and ῥηξάτωσαν, ῥηξάτω εὐφροσύνην in Isa. xlix.
13; lii. 9.   As these are the only instances in LXX in which
the verb is used in this sense, as the quotation is from Isaiah,
and as the verb occurs twice in that prophecy with εὐφροσύνην

joy, it seems better to supply that noun here.   *Cause joy to break forth.*

Many more children than (πολλὰ τὰ τέκνα — μᾶλλον ἤ).
Incorrect.   Not as Lightfoot and others for πλείονα ἤ *more than.*   Rather, "Many are the children of the solitary one in a higher degree than those of her which hath a husband." It is a comparison between two *manys.*   Both had many children, but the solitary had *a greater many.*

28. **As Isaac was** (κατὰ Ἰσαὰκ).   Lit. *after the manner of* Isaac.   See Rom. ix. 7–9, and, for this use of κατὰ, 1 Pet. i. 15 ; Eph. iv. 24 ; Col. iii. 10.

Children of promise (ἐπαγγελίας τέκνα).   Not *promised children,* nor *children that have God's promise,* but children who are not such by mere fleshly descent, as was Ishmael, but by promise, as was Isaac : children of the Jerusalem above, belonging to it in virtue of God's promise, even as Isaac was the child of Sarah in virtue of God's promise.

29. Notwithstanding this higher grade of sonship, the children of promise, the spiritual children of Abraham, are persecuted by the Jews, the mere *bodily* children of Abraham, as Isaac was persecuted by Ishmael.

Persecuted (ἐδίωκε).   Comp. Gen. xxi. 9, where Ishmael is said to have *mocked* Isaac (LXX, παίζοντα μετὰ) : but the Jewish tradition related that Ishmael said to Isaac : "Let us go and seek our portion in the field."   And Ishmael took his bow and arrows and shot Isaac, pretending that he was in sport.   Paul evidently meant something more than *jeering.*

After the Spirit (κατὰ πνεῦμα).   The divine Spirit, which was the living principle of the promise.   Comp. Rom. iv. 17. The Spirit is called "the Spirit of the promise," Eph. i. 13.

30. **What saith the Scripture?**   Giving emphasis to the following statement.   Comp. Rom. iv. 3 ; x. 8 ; xi. 2, 4.

Quotation from LXX of Gen. xxi. 10.   For the words *of this bondwoman — with my son Isaac*, Paul substitutes *of the bondwoman — with the son of the freewoman*, in order to adapt it to his context.   This is according to his habit of adapting quotations to his immediate use.   See 1 Cor. ii. **9 ;** xv. 55 ; Eph. v. 14, etc.

Shall not be heir (οὐ μὴ κληρονομήσει).   Or, *shall not inherit*.   One of the key-words of the Epistle.   See ch. iii. 18, 29 ; iv. 1, 7.   The Greek negation is strong : shall *by no means* inherit.   Comp. J. viii. 35.   Lightfoot says : "The law and the gospel cannot coexist.   The law must disappear before the gospel.   It is scarcely possible to estimate the strength of conviction and depth of prophetic insight which this declaration implies.   The apostle thus confidently sounds the death-knell of Judaism at a time when one half of Christendom clung to the Mosaic law with a jealous affection little short of frenzy, and while the Judaic party seemed to be growing in influence, and was strong enough, even in the Gentile churches of his own founding, to undermine his influence and endanger his life.   The truth which to us appears a truism must then have been regarded as a paradox."

CHAPTER V.

1. In the liberty wherewith.   This is according to the reading τῇ ἐλευθερίᾳ ᾗ.   Different connections are proposed, as with *stand fast*, as A. V.: or with the close of ch. iv., as, "we are not children of the bondwoman but of the free *with the freedom with which* Christ freed us " : or, "of her who is free *with the freedom with which*," etc.   But ᾗ *wherewith* must be omitted.   A new clause begins with τῇ ἐλευθερίᾳ.   Rend. *for freedom did Christ set us free.   For*, not *with* freedom. It is the dative of advantage ; that we might be really free and remain free.   Comp. ver. 13, and J. viii. 36.

Made (us) free (ἠλευθέρωσεν).   With the exception of **J.** viii. 32, 36, only in Paul.

Stand fast (στήκετε). Used absolutely, as 2 Th. ii. 15. Mostly in Paul. See on 1 Th. iii. 8.*

Be not entangled (μὴ ἐνέχεσθε). Or, *held ensnared.* By Paul only here and 2 Th. i. 4. Lit. *to be held within.* For an elliptical usage see on Mk. vi. 19.

Yoke (ζυγῷ). Metaphorical, of a burden or bondage. Comp. Matt. xi. 29, 30 ; Acts xv. 10 ; 1 Tim. vi. 1. Similarly LXX, Gen. xxvii. 40 ; Lev. xxvi. 13 ; 2 Chron. x. 4, 9, 10, 11, 14. So always in N. T. except Apoc. vi. 5, where it means *a pair of scales.* See note, and comp. Lev. xix. 35, 36 ; Prov. xi. 1 ; xvi. 11 ; Hos. xii. 7.

2. **Behold** (ἴδε). Imperative *singular*, appealing to each individual reader.

I Paul. Comp. 2 Cor. x. 1 ; Eph. iii. 1 ; Col. i. 23. Asserting his personal authority.

If ye be circumcised (ἐὰν περιτέμνησθε). Better, *receive circumcision.* The verb does not mean that they have already been circumcised. It states the case as supposable, implying that they were in danger of allowing themselves to be circumcised.

Christ will profit you nothing. Circumcision is the sign of subjection to the Jewish "yoke" — the economy of the law. The question with the Galatians was circumcision as a condition of *salvation.* See ch. ii. 3, 5 ; Acts xv. 1. It was a choice between salvation by law and salvation by Christ. The choice of the law involved the relinquishment of Christ.

---

* Lightfoot says that στήκω does not appear earlier than N. T. There are, however, three instances in LXX where it appears as a various reading: Ex. xiv. 13 ; Judg. xvi. 26 ; 1 K. viii. 11. In the two latter passages it is the reading of B, and is adopted by Swete. Lightfoot also says that it is found only in Paul, with one exception, Mk. xi. 25. It occurs Mk. iii. 31 ; J. i. 26. In J. viii. 44 and Apoc. xii. 4 there is a dispute between ἔστηκεν and ἑστηκεν. In both cases Westcott and Hort adopt the former, and Tischendorf the latter.

Comp. ch. ii. 21.   Chrysostom says : " He who is circumcised is circumcised as fearing the law : but he who fears the
law distrusts the power of grace; and he who distrusts gains
nothing from that which he distrusts."

3. **Again** (πάλιν).   Probably with reference to what he
had said at his last visit.

Every man. Emphasising and particularising the general
to you, you, in ver. 2.

A debtor (ὀφειλέτης).   In N. T. mostly of one under *moral*
obligation.   So in the sense of *sinner*, Matt. vi. 12 ; L. xiii.
4.   Comp. Rom. i. 14 ; viii. 12.   Similarly the verb ὀφείλειν
to owe, as L. xi. 4 ; xvii. 10 ; Rom. xv. 1, etc., though it is
frequent in the literal sense.

To do the law (ποιῆσαι).   Rare in N. T.   See J. vii. 19 ;
Rom. ii. 13, 25 (πράσσῃς).   Τηρεῖν *to observe* the law, the
tradition, the commandment, Matt. xix. 17 ; Mk. vii. 9 ;
J. xiv. 15 ; Acts xv. 5 ; Jas. ii. 10 : πληροῦν *to fulfil* the
law, Rom. xiii. 8 ; Gal. v. 14 ; comp. ἀναπληροῦν, Gal. vi. 2 :
φυλάσσειν *to keep* or *guard* the law, Acts vii. 53 ; xxi. 24 ;
Gal. vi. 13 : also with commandments, word of God or of
Christ, ordinances of the law, Matt. xix. 20 ; Mk. x. 20 ;
L. xi. 28 ; J. xii. 47 ; Rom. ii. 26.   Τελεῖν *to carry out* the
law, Rom. ii. 27 ; Jas. ii. 8.   Ποιῆσαι is *to perform* what
the law commands : τηρεῖν *to observe*, keep an eye on with the
result of performing : φυλάσσειν *to guard* against violation :
τελεῖν *to bring to fulfilment* in action.

The whole law (ὅλον).   Comp. Jas. ii. 10.   Submission
to circumcision commits one to the whole law.   It makes him
a party to the covenant of the law, and the law requires of
every one thus committed a perfect fulfilment, Gal. iii. 10.

4. **Christ is become of no effect unto you** (κατηργήθητε
ἀπὸ Χριστοῦ).   Incorrect.   Lit. *ye were brought to nought from*

Christ. Comp. Rom. vii. 2, 6.   Your union with Christ is dissolved.   The statement is compressed and requires to be filled out.   "Ye were brought to nought *and so separated* from Christ."   For similar instances see Rom. ix. 3 ; xi. 3. The ἀπὸ *from* properly belongs to the supplied verb of separation.   For the verb καταργεῖν see on Rom. iii. 3.

Ye are fallen from grace (τῆς χάριτος ἐξεπέσατε).   For a similar phrase see 2 Pet. iii. 17.   Having put yourselves under the economy of salvation by law, you have *fallen out* of the economy of salvation by *the* grace of Christ.   Paul's declarations are aimed at the Judaisers, who taught that the Christian economy was to be joined with the legal.   His point is that the two are mutually exclusive.   Comp. Rom. iv. 4, 5, 14, 16.   The verb ἐκπίπτειν *to fall out*, in the literal sense, Acts xii. 7 ; Jas. i. 11.   In Class. of seamen thrown ashore, banishment, deprivation of an office, degeneration, of actors being hissed off the stage.

5. **For we** (ἡμεῖς γάρ).   Γὰρ *for* introduces a proof of the preceding statement, by declaring the contrary attitude of those who continue under the economy of grace.   *Ye* who seek to be justified by the law are *fallen* from grace ; *for we*, not relying on the law, by faith wait for the hope of righteousness.

Through the Spirit (πνεύματι).   The Holy Spirit who inspires our faith.   Not as Lightfoot, *spiritually*.   The words πνεύματι ἐκ πίστεως are not to be taken as one conception, *the Spirit which is of faith*, but present two distinct and coördinate facts which characterise the waiting for the hope of righteousness ; namely, the agency of the Holy Spirit, in contrast with the flesh (comp. Rom. vii. 6 ; viii. 4, 15, 16 ; Eph. i. 13 ; ii. 22), and faith in contrast with the works of the law (comp. ch. iii. 3, and see ch. ii. 16 ; iii. 3 ; Rom. i. 17 ; iii. 22 ; ix. 30 ; x. 6).

By faith (ἐκ πίστεως).   Const. with *wait*, not with *righteousness*.

Wait for (ἀπεκδεχόμεθα).   Quite often in Paul, and only twice elsewhere, Heb. ix. 28 ; 1 Pet. iii. 20.   See on Philip. iii. 20.

The hope of righteousness (ἐλπίδα δικαιοσύνης).   *Hope* for *the object* of hope, as Rom. viii. 24 ; Col. i. 5 ; Heb. vi. 18 ; Tit. ii. 13.   The phrase means *that good which righteousness causes us to hope for.*   Comp. *hope of the calling* (Eph. i. 18 ; iv. 4) : *hope of the gospel* (Col. i. 23).*

6. **In Christ Jesus.**   In the economy of life which he inaugurates and inspires.

Availeth (ἰσχύει).   Has any significance or practical power. The verb in Paul only here and Philip. iv. 13.   See on 2 Th. i. 9.

Which worketh (ἐνεργουμένη).   See on 1 Th. ii. 13.   Middle voice, comp. Rom. vii. 5 ; 2 Cor. i. 6 ; iv. 12 ; 2 Th. ii. 7 ; Eph. iii. 20.   Not passive, as by many Roman Catholic expositors, *faith which is wrought by love.*

By love (δι᾽ ἀγάπης).   Not that justification is through love ; but the faith of the justified, which is their subjective principle of life, exhibits its living energy through love in which the whole law is fulfilled (ver. 14).   See 1 Tim. i. 5 ; 1 Th. i. 3 ; 1 Cor. xiii.

7. **Ye did run** (ἐτρέχετε).   Better, as giving the force of the imperfect, *ye were running.*   You were on the right road, and were making good progress when this interruption occurred.   Comp. ch. ii. 2 ; 1 Cor. ix. 24–27 ; Philip. iii. 14 ; 2 Tim. iv. 7.

Well (καλῶς).   Bravely, becomingly, honorably to yourselves and to the church.   Often in Paul.   See Rom. xi. 20 ; 1 Cor. vii. 37, 38 ; 2 Cor. xi. 4 ; Gal. iv. 17 ; Philip. iv. 14.

---

* Comp. ἐλπίδα προσδοκᾶσθαι, Demos. 1468, 13, and ἐλπίδα προσδέχωμαι, Eurip. *Alcest.* 130: προσδεχόμενοι τὴν ἔλπιδα, Tit. ii. 13.   Also LXX, Isa. xxviii. 10; 2 Macc. vii. 14.

Did hinder (ἐνέκοψεν).   See on 1 Pet. iii. 7.   Comp.
1 Th. ii. 18 ; Rom. xv. 22.

Obey the truth (ἀληθείᾳ πείθεσθαι).   The exact phrase
N. T.°.   *Disobey* (ἀπειθοῦσι) the truth, Rom. ii. 8 : *obedience*
(ὑπακοή) of the truth, 1 Pet. i. 22.

8. **This persuasion** (ἡ πεισμονὴ).   Or, *the* persuasion.
N. T.°.   °LXX, °Class.   It occurs in Ignatius, *Rom.* iii.
and Just. Mart. *Ap.* i. 53.   The sense is not passive, *your
being persuaded*, but active, the persuasion *which the Judaising teachers exert over you*.   Comp. 1 Cor. ii. 4, πιθοῖς λόγοις
persuasive words.   There may be a slight word-play on
πείθεσθαι and πεισμονὴ.   *Obedience* to the truth is the result
of the *persuasive power* of the truth.

Him that calleth (τοῦ καλοῦντος).   Very often applied to
God by Paul.   See Rom. viii. 30 ; ix. 11 ; 1 Cor. i. 9 ; vii.
15 ; Gal. i. 15 ; 1 Th. ii. 12 ; iv. 7 ; v. 24 ; 2 Th. ii. 14.
The persuasion to subject yourselves to the Jewish law does
not proceed from him who called you to freedom in Christ.

9. **A little leaven** (μικρὰ ζύμη).   A proverbial warning,
which appears also 1 Cor. v. 6.   It refers, not to the *doctrine*
of the false teachers, but to the false teachers themselves.
Comp. Mk. viii. 15.   With the single exception of the parable, Matt. xiii. 33, leaven, in Scripture, is always a symbol
of evil.   Comp. Ex. xii. 15, 19 ; xiii. 3, 7 ; xxiii. 18 ; Lev.
ii. 11 ; Deut. xvi. 3.   This, however, is no warrant for the
nonsense which has been deduced from it, as that Jesus' parable of the leaven contains a prophecy of the corruption of
Christianity.   Because leaven in Scripture is habitually the
type of corruption, we are " none the less free to use it in a
good sense as Christ did.   One figure need not always stand
for one and the same thing.   The devil is 'a roaring lion,'
but Christ is also ' the lion of the tribe of Judah ' " (Trench).
It is an apt figure of secret, pervading energy, whether bad
or good.   A new interest is given to the figure by Pasteur's

discovery that fermentation is a necessary consequence of the activity and growth of living organisms.*   A very few of these Judaising intruders are sufficient to corrupt the whole church.

Lump (φύραμα).   P⁰.   See on Rom. ix. 21.

10. **In the Lord.**   Const. with *I have confidence.*

Will be — minded (φρονήσετε).   The word denotes a general disposition of the mind rather than a specific act of thought directed at a given point.   Comp. Philip. iii. 15, 19 ; iv. 2 ; Rom. viii. 5 ; xi. 20 ; 1 Cor. xiii. 11 : and φρόνημα *mind*, Rom. viii. 6, 7, 27.   In Class. often with εὖ *well*, καλῶς *honourably*, ὀρθῶς *rightly*, κακῶς *mischievously*.   Τά τινος φρονεῖν is *to be of one's party.*

He that troubleth (ὁ ταράσσων).   Comp. ch. i. 7.   Not with reference to any particular individual, as Peter or James (Lipsius), but generally, of any possible person, "whoever he may be."   The verb is used by Paul only in this Epistle, and refers to disturbance of faith or unity.

11. **And I.**   In sharp contrast with the disturber.

If I yet preach circumcision (εἰ περιτομὴν ἔτι κηρύσσω).   Commonly explained as an allusion to a charge circulated by the Judaisers that Paul preached or sanctioned the circumcision of Gentile converts in churches outside of Galatia, as, for example, in the case of Timothy, Acts xvi. 3.†   But it is quite unlikely that any such charge was circulated.   The Judaisers would not have founded such a charge on an individual case or two, like Timothy's, especially in the face of the notorious fact that Paul, in Jerusalem and Antioch, had contested the demand for the circumcision of Gentile Christ-

---

* See Dr. William H. Thomson's admirable little volume, *The Parables by the Lake.*

† So Lightfoot, Meyer, Ellicott, Eadie.

ians ; and Paul's question, "Why do I suffer persecution?" would have been pertinent only on the assumption that he was charged with *habitually*, not *occasionally*, preaching circumcision.   Had the Judaisers actually circulated such a charge, Paul would have been compelled to meet it in a far more direct and thorough manner than he does here.   He would have been likely to formulate the charge, and to deal incisively with the inconsistency in his preaching which it involved.   The course of his thought is as follows : "He that troubleth you by preaching circumcision shall bear his judgment; but *I* am not a disturber — not your enemy (ch. iv. 16), for I do not preach circumcision ; and the proof of this is that I am persecuted.   If I preached circumcision, there would be no offence, and therefore no disturbance ; for the cross would cease to be an offence, if, in addition to the cross, I preached just what the Judaisers assert, the necessity of circumcision."

Yet (ἔτι).   As in the time before my conversion.   The second ἔτι is not temporal but logical, as Rom. iii. 7 ; ix. 19. What further ground is there for persecuting me ?

Then (ἄρα).   As a consequence of my preaching circumcision.

The offence of the cross (τὸ σκάνδαλον τοῦ σταυροῦ). Comp. 1 Cor. i. 23.   For *offence*, see on *offend*, Matt. v. 29.

Ceased (κατήργηται).   Lit. *been done away* or *brought to nought*.   See on ver. 4.   If Paul had preached circumcision as necessary to salvation, the preaching of the cross would have ceased to be an offence, because, along with the cross, Paul would have preached what the Judaisers demanded, that the Mosaic law should still be binding on Christians.   The Judaisers would have accepted the cross *with* circumcision, but not the cross *instead of* circumcision.   The Judaisers thus exposed themselves to no persecution in accepting Christ. They covered the offence of the cross, and conciliated unbe-

lieving Jews by maintaining that the law was binding upon
Christians. See ch. vi. 12.

12. **They were cut off** (ἀποκόψονται). More correctly,
would cut themselves off. Perhaps the severest expression in
Paul's Epistles. It turns on the practice of circumcision.
Paul says in effect : " These people are disturbing you by
insisting on circumcision. I would that they would make
thorough work of it in their own case, and, instead of merely
amputating the foreskin, would castrate themselves, as heathen
priests do. Perhaps that would be even a more powerful help
to salvation." With this passage should be compared Philip.
iii. 2, 3, also aimed at the Judaisers : " Beware of *the concision* " (τὴν κατατομήν), the word directing attention to the
fact that these persons had no right to claim circumcision in
the true sense. Unaccompanied by faith, love, and obedience,
circumcision was no more than physical mutilation. They
belonged in the category of those referred to in Lev. xxi. 5.
Comp. Paul's words on the true circumcision, Rom. ii. 28,
29 ; Philip. iii. 3 ; Col. ii. 11.

Which trouble (ἀναστατοῦντες). Only here in Paul, and
twice elsewhere, Acts xvii. 6 ; xxi. 38. °LXX. Stronger
than ταράσσειν *disturb.* Rather *to upset* or *overthrow.* The
usual phrase in Class. is ἀνάστατον ποιεῖν *to make an upset.*
Used of driving out from home, ruining a city or country.
See on *madest an uproar*, Acts xxi. 38. Rev. *unsettle* is too
weak.

13. **For** (γάρ). Well may I speak thus strongly of those
who thus overthrow your whole polity and enslave you, *for*
ye are called for freedom.

Unto liberty (ἐπ᾽ ἐλευθερίᾳ). Better, *for freedom.* See
on *unto uncleanness*, 1 Th. iv. 7. Ἐπὶ marks the intention.

Only (μόνον). For a similar use of the word, qualifying
or limiting a general statement, comp. 1 Cor. vii. 39 ; Gal.
ii. 10 ; Philip. i. 27 ; 2 Th. ii. 7.

Use not liberty (τὴν ἐλευθερίαν). *Use* is not in the Greek. We may supply *hold* or *make* or *turn*.

Occasion (ἀφορμὴν). See on Rom. vii. 8. Almost exclusively in Paul.

To the flesh (τῇ σαρκί). See on Rom. vii. 5. The flesh here represents lovelessness and selfishness. Christian freedom is not to be abused for selfish ends. Paul treats this subject at length in 1 Cor. viii. ; xii. 25, 26. Individual liberty is subject to the law of love and mutual service. Comp. 1 Pet. ii. 16.

By love (διὰ τῆς ἀγάπης). Or *through* love, through which faith works (ver. 6).

14. All the law (ὁ πᾶς νόμος). More correctly, *the whole law.* Comp. Matt. xxii. 40.

Is fulfilled (πεπλήρωται). Has been fulfilled. Comp. Rom. xiii. 8. The meaning is not *embraced in*, or *summed up in*, but *complied with*. In Rom. xiii. 9, ἀνακεφαλαιοῦται *is summed up*, is to be distinguished from πεπλήρωκεν *hath fulfilled* (ver. 8) and πλήρωμα *fulfilment* (ver. 10). The difference is between statement and accomplishment. See on *do the law*, ver. 3.

15. Bite and devour (δάκνετε καὶ κατεσθίετε). Strong expressions of partisan hatred exerting itself for mutual injury. Δάκνειν *to bite*, N. T.º. In LXX metaphorically, Mic. iii. 5; Hab. ii. 7. For κατεσθίειν *devour*, comp. Matt. xxiii. 13; 2 Cor. xi. 20; Apoc. xi. 5.

Be consumed (ἀναλωθῆτε). Rare in N. T. See L. ix. 54. Partisan strife will be fatal to the Christian community as a whole. The organic life of the body will be destroyed by its own members.

16. Walk (περιπατεῖτε). Frequent in a metaphorical sense for *habitual conduct*. See Mk. vii. 5; J. viii. 12; Acts xxi. 21; Rom. vi. 4; viii. 4; 1 Cor. iii. 3; Philip. iii. 18. Never by Paul in the literal sense.

In the Spirit (πνεύματι). Rather, *by* the Spirit, as the rule of action. Comp. Gal. vi. 16; Philip. iii. 16; Rom. iv. 12.

Fulfil (τελέσητε). Bring to fulfilment in action. See on *do the law*, ver. 3.

The lust (ἐπιθυμίαν). Frequent in Paul, and usually in a bad sense; but see Philip. i. 23; 1 Th. ii. 17, and comp. L. xxii. 15. The phrase *lust* or *lusts of the flesh* occurs also Eph. ii. 3; 2 Pet. ii. 18; 1 J. ii. 16. It means, not the mere sensual desire of the physical nature, but the desire which is peculiar to human nature without the divine Spirit.

17. Are contrary (ἀντίκειται). The verb means *to lie opposite to;* hence *to oppose, withstand*. The sentence *these — to the other* is not parenthetical.

So that (ἵνα). Connect with *these are contrary*, etc. Ἵνα does not express *result*, but *purpose, to the end that,* — the purpose of the two contending desires. The intent of each principle in opposing the other is to prevent man's doing what the other principle moves him to do.

Cannot do (μὴ ποιῆτε). A mistake, growing out of the misinterpretation of ἵνα noted above. Rather, each works *to the end that ye may not do*, etc.

The things that ye would (ἃ ἐὰν θέλητε). The things which you will to do under the influence of either of the two contending principles. There is a *mutual* conflict of *two* powers. If one wills to do good, he is opposed by the flesh: if to do evil, by the Spirit.

18. The question is, which of these two powers shall prevail. If the Spirit, then you are free men, no longer under the law. Comp. Rom. vi. 11, 14.

Under the law (ὑπὸ νόμον). The Mosaic law. We might have expected, from what precedes, *under the flesh.* But the law and the flesh are in the same category. Circumcision was a requirement of the law, and was a work of the flesh. The ordinances of the law were ordinances of the flesh (Heb. ix. 10, 13); the law was weak through the flesh (Rom. viii. 3). See especially, Gal. iii. 2–6. In Philip. iii. 3 ff. Paul explains his grounds for confidence in the flesh as his *legal* righteousness. The whole legal economy was an economy of the flesh as distinguished from the Spirit.

19. **Manifest.** You have a clearly defined standard by which to decide whether you are led by the Spirit or by the flesh. Each exhibits its peculiar works or fruits.

Adultery (μοιχεία). To be dropped from the text.

Uncleanness (ἀκαθαρσία). See on 1 Th. ii. 3.

Lasciviousness (ἀσέλγεια). See on Mk. vii. 22.

20. **Witchcraft** (φαρμακία). Or *sorcery.* Elsewhere only Apoc. xviii. 23. From φάρμακον *a drug.* In LXX, see Ex. vii. 11; Wisd. xii. 4; Isa. xlvii. 9. Comp. Acts xix. 19, περίεργα *curious arts,* note.

Wrath (θυμοί). Lit. *wraths.* See on J. iii. 36.

Strife (ἐριθίαι). More correctly, *factions.* From ἔριθος *a hired servant.* Ἐριθία is, primarily, *labor for hire* (see Tob. ii. 11), and is applied to those who serve in official positions for hire or for other selfish purposes, and, in order to gain their ends, promote party spirit or faction.

Seditions (διχοστασίαι). Better, *divisions*. Only here and Rom. xvi. 17. Once in LXX, 1 Macc. iii. 29.

Heresies (αἱρέσεις). In Paul only here and 1 Cor. xi. 19. See on 2 Pet. ii. 1. *Parties*, into which *divisions* crystallise.

21. Murders. Omit from the text.

Revellings (κῶμοι). Comp. Rom. xiii. 13; 1 Pet. iv. 3. In both passages coupled with *drunkenness* as here. See on 1 Pet. iv. 3.

I tell you before (προλέγω). Better *beforehand*, or as Rev. *I forewarn you.* P⁰. Comp. 2 Cor. xiii. 2; 1 Th. iii. 4.

The kingdom of God. See on L. vi. 20.

22. The fruit of the Spirit (ὁ καρπὸς τοῦ πνεύματος). The phrase N. T.⁰. *Fruit*, metaphorical, frequent in N. T., as Matt. iii. 8; vii. 16; J. iv. 36; xv. 8; Rom. i. 13; vi. 21, etc. We find fruit of *light* (Eph. v. 9); of *righteousness* (Philip. i. 11); of *labour* (Philip. i. 22); of *the lips* (Heb. xiii. 15). Almost always of a good result.

Love (ἀγάπη). Comp. *love of the Spirit*, Rom. xv. 30. In Class. φιλεῖν is the most general designation of *love*, denoting an inner inclination to persons or things, and standing opposed to μισεῖν or ἐχθαίρειν to hate. It occasionally acquires from the context a sensual flavour, as Hom. *Od*. xviii. 325; Hdt. iv. 176, thus running into the sense of ἐρᾶν which denotes sensual love. It is love to persons and things growing out of intercourse and amenities or attractive qualities. Στέργειν (not in N. T., LXX, Sir. xxvii. 17) expresses a deep, quiet, appropriating, natural love, as distinguished from that which is called out by circumstances. Unlike φιλεῖν, it has a distinct moral significance, and is not applied to base inclinations opposed to a genuine manly nature. It is the word for love to parents, wife, children, king or country, as one's own.   Aristotle (*Nic.* ix. 7, 3) speaks of poets as *loving* (στέργοντες) their own poems as their children. See also Eurip. *Med.* 87.   'Αγαπᾶν is to love out of an intelligent estimate of the object of love.   It answers to Lat. *diligere*, or Germ. *schätzen to prize*.   It is not passionate and sensual as ἐρᾶν.   It is not, like φιλεῖν, attachment to a person independently of his quality and created by close intercourse.   It is less *sentiment* than *consideration*.   While φιλεῖν contemplates *the person*, ἀγαπᾶν contemplates *the attributes* and *character*, and gives an account of its inclination. 'Αγαπᾶν is really the weaker expression for love, as that term is *conventionally* used.   It is judicial rather than affectionate.   Even in classical usage, however, the distinction between ἀγαπᾶν and φιλεῖν is often very subtle, and well-nigh impossible to express.

In N. T. ἐπιθυμεῖν *to desire* or *lust* is used instead of ἐρᾶν. In LXX ἀγαπᾶν is far more common than φιλεῖν.   Φιλεῖν occurs only 16 times in the sense of *love*, and 16 times in the sense of *kiss;* while ἀγαπᾶν is found nearly 300 times.   It is used with a wide range, of the love of parent for child, of man for God, of God for man, of love to one's neighbour and to the stranger, of husband for wife, of love for God's house, and for mercy and truth ; but also of the love of Samson for Delilah, of Hosea for his adulterous wife, of Amnon's love for Tamar, of Solomon's love for strange women, of loving a woman for her beauty.   Also of loving vanity, unrighteousness, devouring words, cursing, death, silver.

The noun ἀγάπη, °Class., was apparently created by the LXX, although it is found there only 19 times.*   It first comes into habitual use in Christian writings.   In N. T. it is, practically, the only noun for love, although compound nouns expressing peculiar phases of love, as *brotherly* love, love of *money*, love of *children*, etc., are formed with φίλος, as φιλαδελφία, φιλαργυρία, φιλανθρωπία.   Both verbs, φιλεῖν and ἀγαπᾶν occur, but ἀγαπᾶν more frequently.   The

---

* Deissmann, *Neue Bibelstudien*, p. 26 ff., holds that the word does not originate in Biblical Greek.   His remarks, however, are not conclusive.

attempt to carry out consistently the classical distinction between these two must be abandoned. Both are used of the love of parents and children, of the love of God for Christ, of Christ for men, of God for men, of men for Christ and of men for men. The love of man for God and of husband for wife, only ἀγαπᾶν. The distinction is rather between ἀγαπᾶν and ἐπιθυμεῖν than between ἀγαπᾶν and φιλεῖν.* Love, in this passage, is that fruit of the Spirit which dominates all the others. See vv. 13, 14. Comp. 1 Cor. xiii; 1 J. ii. 5, 9–11; iii. 11, 14–16; iv. 7–11, 16–21; v. 1–3.

Joy (χαρά). Comp. *joy of the Holy Ghost*, 1 Th. i. 6, and see Rom. v. 2; xiv. 17; xv. 13; 2 Cor. vi. 10; Philip. i. 25; iv. 4; 1 Pet. i. 8; 1 J. i. 4.

Peace (εἰρήνη). See on 1 Th. i. 1. Here of *mutual* peace rather than peace with God.

Long suffering (μακροθυμία). See on *be patient*, Jas. v. 7, and comp. Rom. ii. 4; 2 Cor. vi. 6; Eph. iv. 2; Col. i. 11.

Gentleness (χρηστότης). See on *good*, Rom. iii. 12; *easy*, Matt. xi. 30; *gracious*, 1 Pet. ii. 3. Better, *kindness;* a kindness which is *useful* or *serviceable*.

Goodness (ἀγαθωσύνη). P⁰. See on Rom. iii. 12.

Faith (πίστις). Trustfulness.

23. **Meekness** (πραΰτης). See on *meek*, Matt. v. 5.

Temperance (ἐγκράτεια). Only here by Paul. He alone uses ἐγκρατεύεσθαι *to have continency*, 1 Cor. vii. 9; ix. 25. See on *is temperate*, 1 Cor. ix. 25. The word means *self-control*, *holding in hand* the passions and desires. So Xen.

---

* See Professor Sanday's note on the history of ἀγάπη, *Commentary on Romans* (International), p. 374.

Mem. i. 2, 1, of Socrates, who was ἐγκρατέστατος *most temp-erate* as to sexual pleasures and pleasures of the appetite.

Such (τοιούτων). Such *things*, not *persons*.

There is no law (οὐκ ἔστιν νόμος). Against such virtues there is no law to condemn them. The law can bring no charge against them. Comp. 1 Tim. i. 9, 10.

24. **They that are Christ's** (οἱ δὲ τοῦ Χριστοῦ). The best texts add Ἰησοῦ *they that are of Christ Jesus.* Belong to him. The exact phrase only here. But see 1 Cor. i. 12; iii. 23; xv. 23; 2 Cor. x. 7; Gal. iii. 29.

Have crucified the flesh (τὴν σάρκα ἐσταύρωσαν). The phrase only here. Comp. ch. ii. 20; vi. 14; Rom. vi. 6. The line of thought as regards death to sin is the same as in Rom. vi. 2–7, 11; as regards death to the law, the same as in Rom. vii. 1–6.

Affections (παθήμασιν). Better, *passions.* Often *suffer-ings*, as Rom. viii. 18; 2 Cor. i. 5, 6, 7; Philip. iii. 10; Heb. ii. 9. Often of Christ's sufferings. Comp. *passions of sins*, Rom. vii. 5 (see on *motions*). °LXX, where we find πάθος in both senses, but mostly *sufferings.* Πάθος also in N. T., but rarely and Pᵒ. See Rom. i. 26; Col. iii. 5; 1 Th. iv. 5: always of evil desires.

25. Lipsius makes this verse the beginning of ch. vi. Weizsäcker begins that chapter with ver. 26. There seems to be no sufficient reason. Ver. 25 is connected naturally with the immediately preceding line of thought. "Such being your principle of life, adapt your conduct (walk) to it." The hortatory form of ver. 26, and its contents, fall in naturally with the exhortation to walk by the Spirit, and with the reference to *biting and devouring*, ver. 15, and *envy-ings*, ver. 21. The connection of the opening of ch. vi. with the close of ch. v. is not so manifest; and the address *brethren*

and the change to the second person (vi. 1) seem to indicate
a new section.

In the Spirit (πνεύματι). Better, *by* the Spirit, the dative
being instrumental as ver. 16.

Walk (στοιχῶμεν). A different word from that in ver. 16.
Only in Paul, except Acts xxi. 24. From στοίχος *a row.*
Hence, *to walk in line ;* to march in battle order (Xen. *Cyr.*
vi. 3, 34). Συνστοιχεῖ *answereth to,* Gal. iv. 25 (note). See
also on στοιχεῖα *elements,* Gal. iv. 3. Paul uses it very graphic-
ally, of *falling into line* with Abraham's faith, Rom. iv. 12.

26. **Desirous of vainglory** (κενόδοξοι). N. T.°. Better,
vainglorious. The noun κενοδοξία *vainglory* only Philip. ii. 3.
In LXX see Wisd. xiv. 14 ; 4 Macc. ii. 15 ; viii. 18. Originally, *vain opinion, error.* Ignatius, *Magn.* xi., speaks of falling into ἄγκιστρα τῆς κενοδοξίας *the hooks* or *clutches* of error.
Δόξα has not the sense of *opinion* in N. T., but that of
reputation, glory. This compound means *having a vain
conceit of possessing a rightful claim to honour.* Suidas defines *any vain thinking about one's self.* It implies a contrast
with the state of mind which seeks the glory of God. The
modes in which vainglory may show itself are pointed out in
the two following participles, *provoking* and *envying.*

Provoking (προκαλούμενοι). N. T.°. LXX, only 2 Macc.
viii. 11. Lit. *calling forth, challenging,* and so stirring up
strife. Very common in Class.

CHAPTER VI.

1. **Overtaken in a fault** (προλημφθῇ — ἔν τινι παραπτώ-
ματι). The verb means lit. *to take before ; to anticipate* or
forestall. Elsewhere only Mk. xiv. 8 ; 1 Cor. xi. 21. LXX,
Wisd. xviii. 17. Not, *be detected in the act* by some one else
before he can escape, but *surprised by the fault itself ;* hurried

into error. Thus πρό has the sense of *before he is aware*, and ἐν is instrumental, *by*.* For *fault* or *trespass*, see on Matt. vi. 14.

Spiritual (πνευματικοί). Comp. 1 Cor. iii. 1. Mostly in Paul. See 1 Pet. ii. 5. Those who have received the Spirit and are led by him. See ch. iii. 2, 3, 5, 14; iv. 6; v. 5, 16, 18, 25. He leaves it to the readers' own conscience whether or not they answer to this designation.

Restore (καταρτίζετε). See on Matt. iv. 21; xxi. 16; L. vi. 40; 1 Pet. v. 10. The word is used of reconciling factions, as Hdt. v. 28; of setting bones; of mending nets, Mk. i. 19; of equipping or preparing, Rom. ix. 22; Heb. x. 5; xi. 3; of manning a fleet, or supplying an army with provisions. Usually by Paul metaphorically as here. The idea of amendment is prominent: *set him to rights: bring him into line*. Comp. 2 Cor. xiii. 11; 1 Cor. i. 10.

Spirit of meekness. Comp. 1 Cor. iv. 21. Led by the Spirit of God, whose fruit is meekness (v. 23). For the combinations of πνεῦμα with genitives, see on Rom. viii. 4, p. 87.

Considering (σκοπῶν). Only in Paul, except L. xi. 35. The verb means *to look attentively;* to fix the attention upon a thing with an interest in it. See Rom. xvi. 17; 2 Cor. iv. 18; Philip. ii. 4; iii. 17. Hence, often, *to aim at* (comp. σκοπὸν *mark*, Philip. iii. 14). Schmidt (*Syn.*) defines: "To direct one's attention upon a thing, either in order to obtain it, or because one has a peculiar interest in it, or a duty to fulfil toward it. Also to have an eye to with a view of

---

* Interpreters differ in the explanation of πρό. Lightfoot, Ellicott, Eadie, Thayer, Alford, Weiss, say caught *in* the fault *before* he can escape. But this is an unusual meaning of the verb, which is certainly not settled by Wisd. xvii. 17. Ellicott objects to the meaning given in the note, that, in that case, πρό would seem to excuse, whereas καί appears to point to an aggravation of the offence. If that be true, then, on Ellicott's explanation, the aggravation of the offence would appear to be in being caught.

forming a right judgment." Notice the passing to the singular number — "considering *thyself.*" The exhortation is
addressed to the conscience of each. Before you deal severely
with the erring brother, consider your own weakness and sus-
ceptibility to temptation, and restore him in view of that fact.

2. **One another's burdens** (ἀλλήλων τὰ βάρη). The emphasis is on *one another's*, in contrast with the selfishness which
leaves others to take care of themselves. The primary reference in *burdens* is to *moral* infirmities and errors, and the
sorrow and shame and remorse which they awaken in the
offender.

So (οὕτως). By observing this injunction.

Fulfil (ἀναπληρώσατε). The verb denotes, not the filling
up of a perfect vacancy, as the simple πληροῦν, but the supplying of what is lacking to fulness ; the filling up of a partial
void. Comp. 1 Cor. xvi. 17 ; Philip. ii. 30 ; 1 Th. ii. 16.*

3. **Think** (δοκεῖ). Sometimes rendered *seems*, 1 Cor. xii.
22 ; 2 Cor. x. 9 ; Gal. ii. 9 ; but *think* is Paul's usual meaning. Comp. Matt. iii. 9 ; 1 Cor. xi. 16 ; Philip. iii. 4.

To be something (εἶναί τι). For the phrase see Acts v. 36 ;
viii. 9 ; 1 Cor. iii. 7 ; x. 19 ; Gal. ii. 6 ; vi. 15.

Deceiveth (φρεναπατᾷ). N. T.º. ºLXX, ºClass. See
the noun φρεναπάτης *deceiver*, Tit. i. 10. Denoting subjective
deception ; deception of the judgment. The simple ἀπατᾶν
to deceive, Eph. v. 6 ; 1 Tim. ii. 14 ; Jas. i. 26, and often in
LXX. Lightfoot thinks the compound verb may possibly
have been coined by Paul.†

---

* Quite a number of high authorities read ἀναπληρώσετε, future, *ye shall
fulfil.*

† Blass, however (*N. T. Gramm.*, p. 68, note), says that φρεναπάτης appears in a papyrus of the second century B.C. He refers to Grenfell, *An Alexandrian Erotic Fragment*, Oxford, 1896, p. 3. See also Sophocles, *Greek
Lexicon of the Roman and Byzantine Periods*, sub φρεναπάτης.

4. **Prove** (δοκιμαζέτω). In Class. of assaying metals Comp. LXX, Prov. viii. 10 ; xvii. 3 ; Sir. ii. 5 : also 1 Cor. iii. 13 ; 1 Pet. i. 7. It is the classical verb for testing money; see Plato, *Tim.* 65 C. Δοκιμάζειν and πυροῦσθαι *to burn* or *try by fire* occur together, Jer. ix. 7; Ps. xi. 6 ; lxv. 10. Generally, to *prove* or *examine*, as 1 Cor. xi. 28 ; 1 Th. v. 21. *To accept* that which is approved, 1 Cor. xvi. 3 ; 2 Cor. viii. 22; 1 Th. ii. 4.

Rejoicing (τὸ καύχημα). Better, as giving the force of the article, "*his* glorying." Καύχημα is *the matter* or *ground* of glorying, see Rom. iv. 2 ; 1 Cor. ix. 15 ; not the act (καύχησις), as Rom. iii. 27; 2 Cor. i. 12.*

In himself (εἰς ἑαυτὸν). Better, *with regard* to himself, or *as concerns.* For this use of εἰς see Rom. iv. 20 ; xv. 2 ; xvi. 6 ; Eph. iii. 16. Not, *he will keep his glorying to himself* or abstain from boasting. He means that if, on examination, one finds in himself anything to boast of, his cause of boasting will lie simply and absolutely in that, and not in his merit as compared, to his own advantage, with that of another.

Another (τὸν ἕτερον). Better, *the* other, or, as Rev., *his neighbour.* See on Matt. vi. 24.

5. **Bear ye one another's burdens: every man shall bear his own burden.** A kind of paradox of which Paul is fond. See Philip. ii. 12, 13 ; 2 Cor. vi. 8–10 ; vii. 10 ; xii. 10. Paul means, no one will have occasion to claim moral superiority to his neighbour, *for* (γὰρ) each man's self-examination will reveal infirmities enough of his own, even though they may not be the same as those of his neighbour. His own burdens will absorb his whole attention, and will leave him no time to compare himself with others.

---

* Still, this does not always hold. We find γέννημα, δίωγμα, θέλημα, ἴαμα, κήρυγμα, πλήρωμα for γέννησις, δίωξις, θέλησις, ἴασις, κήρυξις, πλήρωσις.

His own burden (τὸ ἴδιον φορτίον). For ἴδιον *own*, see on
1 Tim. vi. 1. With φορτίον *burden* comp. βάρη *burdens*,
ver. 2. It is doubtful whether any different shade of meaning is intended. Originally βάρη emphasises the *weight* of
the burden, φορτίον simply notes the fact that it is something to be *borne* (φέρειν), which may be either light or heavy.
See Matt. xi. 30 ; xxiii. 4 ; Ps. xxxvii. 4 ; L. xi. 46. Comp.
Acts xxvii. 10, *the lading* of a ship.

6. But, although each man is thus individualised as regards
his burdens, Christian fellowship in all morally good things
is to be maintained between the teacher and the taught. The
passage is often explained as an injunction to provide for the
temporal wants of Christian teachers.* But this is entirely
foreign to the course of thought, and isolates the verse from
the context on both sides of it. As vv. 1–5 refer to moral
errors, *in all good things* has naturally the same reference, as
do good in ver. 10 certainly has. The exhortation therefore
is, that the disciple should make common cause with the
teacher in everything that is morally good and that promotes
salvation. The introduction at this point of the relation of
disciple and teacher may be explained by the fact that this
relation in the Galatian community had been disturbed by
the efforts of the Judaising teachers, notably in the case of
Paul himself ; and this disturbance could not but interfere
with their common moral effort and life.

Him that is taught (ὁ κατηχούμενος). See on L. i. 4.

In the word (τὸν λόγον). The gospel. Usually in Paul
with some qualifying word, as *of God*. Comp. Acts iv. 4 ;
viii. 4 ; xi. 19 ; xiv. 25 ; xvi. 6 ; 1 Th. i. 6 ; Col. iv. 3.

Communicate (κοινωνείτω). Hold fellowship with ; partake with. Not *impart to*. The word is used of giving and
receiving material aid (Philip. iv. 15): of moral or spiritual

---

* So many ancient interpreters, and Lightfoot, Ellicott, De Wette, Eadie,
Alford.

participation (Rom. xv. 27; 1 Tim. v. 22 ; 2 J. 11): of participation in outward conditions (Heb. ii. 14): in sufferings (1 Pet. iv. 13).

7. Be not deceived (μὴ πλανᾶσθε). For the phrase see 1 Cor. vi. 9; xv. 33; Jas. i. 16. *Deceive* is a secondary sense; the primary meaning being *lead astray*. See on Mk. xii. 24. The connection of the exhortation may be with the entire section from ver. 1 (Eadie and Sieffert), but is more probably with ver. 6. The Galatians are not to think that it is a matter of no consequence whether their fellowship be with their Christian teachers who preach the word of truth, or with the Judaising innovators who would bring them under bondage to the law.

Is not mocked (οὐ μυκτηρίζεται). N. T.°. Quite often in LXX. See 1 K. xviii. 27 ; 2 K. xix. 21; Job xxii. 19; Prov. i. 30. Also the noun μυκτηρισμός *mockery*, Job xxxiv. 7; Ps. xxxiv. 16. See Ps. of Sol. iv. 8. The verb, literally, *to turn up the nose at.* Comp. Horace, *Sat.* i. 6, 5, *naso suspendis adunco*, ii. 8, 64 ; *Epist.* i. 19, 45.

That (τοῦτο). Most emphatic. *That* and nothing else. Comp. Matt. vii. 16; 2 Cor. ix. 6.

8. To his flesh (εἰς τὴν σάρκα ἑαυτοῦ). Rather, *his own* flesh. 'Εις *into:* the flesh being conceived as the soil into which the seed is cast. Comp. Matt. xiii. 22. *His own,* because the idea of personal, selfish desire is involved.

Corruption (φθοράν). Primarily, *destruction, ruin ;* but it also has the sense of *deterioration, decay,* as 1 Cor. xv. 42. Comp. Aristotle, *Rhet.* iii. 3, 4 : "And thou didst sow (ἔσπειρας) shamefully (αἰσχρῶς) and didst reap (ἐθερίσας) miserably (κακῶς)." See also Plato, *Phaedrus,* 260 D, and on *defile,* Rom. iii. 17.

The Spirit. The Holy Spirit : not the higher nature of man.

Eternal life (ζωὴν αἰώνιον). See on 2 Th. i. 9 (additional note).

9. **Be weary** (ἐνκακῶμεν). Lit. *faint* or *lose heart*. Comp. 2 Th. iii. 13.

In due season (καιρῷ ἰδίῳ). In the season which is peculiarly the harvest-time of each form of well-doing. See on ver. 5.

Faint (ἐκλυόμενοι). Only here in Paul. See Matt. xv. 32; Mk. viii. 3; Heb. xii. 3, 5. Lit. *to be loosened* or *relaxed*, like the limbs of the weary.

10. **As we have opportunity** (ὡς καιρὸν ἔχωμεν). As there is a proper season for reaping, there is likewise a proper season for sowing. As this season comes to us, let us sow to the Spirit by doing good. Comp. Eph. v. 16; Col. iv. 5.

Let us do good (ἐργαζώμεθα τὸ ἀγαθὸν). Let us *work* the good. For the distinctive force of ἐργάζεσθαι see on 3 J. 5; and for ποιεῖν to *do*, on J. iii. 21. Comp. Col. iii. 23 where both verbs occur. Τὸ ἀγαθὸν is, of course, the *morally* good as distinguished from what is merely *useful* or *profitable*, but includes what is *beneficent* or *kindly*. See Philem. 14; Eph. iv. 28; 1 Th. iii. 6; Rom. v. 7. Here, in a general sense, embracing all that is specified in vv. 1, 2, 3, 10.

Unto them who are of the household of faith (πρὸς τοὺς οἰκείους τῆς πίστεως). Πρὸς combines with the sense of *direction* that of *active relation with*. Comp. Matt. xiii. 56; Mk. ix. 16; J. i. 1; Acts iii. 25; xxviii. 25; 1 Th. iv. 12; Heb. ix. 20. Frequently in Class. of all kinds of personal intercourse. See Hom. *Od.* xiv. 331; xix. 288; Thucyd. ii. 59; iv. 15; vii. 82; Hdt. i. 61. 'Οικεῖοι *of the household*, rare in N. T. See Eph. ii. 19; 1 Tim. v. 8. Quite often in LXX of *kinsmen*. It is unnecessary to introduce the idea of a household here, as A. V., since the word acquired the general sense

of *pertaining* or *belonging to*.   Thus οἰκεῖοι φιλοσοφίας or
γεωγραφίας *belonging to philosophy* or *geography, philosophers,
geographers*.   So here, *belonging to the faith, believers.*

11. How large a letter (πηλίκοις γράμμασιν).   More correctly, *with how large letters*.   Γράμματα may mean *an epistle*,
as Lat. *literae*, or *epistles ;* but Paul habitually uses ἐπιστολή
for an epistle.   Γράμμασιν means *with characters*, and πηλίκοις refers to their size.   It is claimed by some that the large
characters are intended to call the attention of the readers to
the special importance of the close of the letter.   See below.

I have written (ἔγραψα).   The aorist may refer to the
whole of the preceding letter, or to the concluding verses
which follow.   In either case it is probably an instance of the
epistolary aorist, by which the writer puts himself at the time
when his correspondent is reading his letter.   To the correspondent, *I write* has changed itself into *I wrote*.   Similarly
the Lat. *scripsi*.   Ἔπεμψα *I sent* is used in the same way.
See Acts xxiii. 30 ; Philip. ii. 28 ; Col. iv. 8 ; Philem. 11.

With mine own hand (τῇ ἐμῇ χειρί).   The aorist ἔγραψα is
epistolary, and refers to what follows.   The concluding verses
emphasise the main issue of the letter, that the Judaising intruders are trying to win the Galatians over to the economy
of circumcision which is opposed to the economy of the cross.
It is therefore quite probable that Paul may have wished to
call special attention to these verses.   If so, this special call
lies in the words *with my own hand*, and not in *with how large
letters*, which would seem to have been added to call attention
to the apostle's handwriting as distinguished from that of the
amanuensis.   " Mark carefully these closing words of mine.
I write them with my own hand in the large characters which
you know."

12. To make a fair show (εὐπροσωπῆσαι).   N. T.°.
°Class.   °LXX.

In the flesh (ἐν σαρκί). Qualifying the verb *to make a fair
show.* The whole phrase is well explained by Ellicott : " To
wear a specious exterior in the earthly, unspiritual element in
which they move." 'Eν σαρκί is not = *among men*, nor *being
carnal*, nor *as regards fleshly things.* The desire to make a
good appearance irrespective of inward truth and righteousness, is prompted by the unrenewed, fleshly nature, and makes
its fair showing in that sphere.

They constrain (οὗτοι ἀναγκάζουσιν). Neither A. V. nor
Rev. gives the strong, definitive force of οὗτοι. It is *these* —
the Judaising emissaries, that constrain, etc. Comp. ch. iii. 7.

Only lest (μόνον ἵνα — μὴ). Or, *that they may not.* Having no other object, or only from the motive that, etc

For the cross (τῷ σταυρῷ). Better, *by reason of* the cross.
Because of preaching a crucified Messiah. See on ch. v. 11.
The Judaisers attempted to cover with the law — the require-
ment of circumcision — the "offence" of a crucified Messiah.

13. Neither they themselves who are circumcised (οὐδὲ
— οἱ περιτεμνόμενοι αὐτοὶ). For *neither*, translate *not even.*
Const. *themselves* with *keep the law.* The persons referred to
are the same as those in ver. 12. The participle tells nothing
as to the antecedents of these persons, whether Jewish or
heathen. It is general, those who are receiving circumcision.
It is = *the circumcision-party ;* and the present participle represents them as in present activity. They are circumcised
themselves, and are endeavouring to force circumcision upon
others.

Keep the law (νόμον φυλάσσουσιν). See on ch. v. 3.
They are in the same category with all who are circumcised,
who do not and cannot fully observe the law. Comp. ch.
iii. 10 ; v. 3. Hence, if circumcision develops no justifying
results, it is apparent that their insistence on circumcision
proceeds not from moral, but from fleshly motives.

That they may glory in your flesh (ἵνα ἐν τῇ ὑμετέρᾳ σαρκὶ καυχήσωνται).   May boast, not of your fulfilling the law, but in your ceremonial conformity ; your becoming legal zealots like themselves.   They desire only that you, like them, should make a fair show in the flesh.   For the formula καυχᾶσθαι ἐν *to glory in*, see Rom. ii. 17 ; v. 3 ; 1 Cor. i. 31 ; 2 Cor. x. 15.

14.   Contrast of Paul's own boasting and its ground with those of the false apostles.

By whom (δι' οὗ).   The relative may refer either to the cross, *by which*, or to Christ, *by whom*.   The cross was a stumbling-block to the Jews (ch. iii. 13), and it is the *crucified* Christ that Paul is emphasising.   Comp. ch. ii. 20 ; v. 24.

The world (κόσμος).   See on J. i. 9 ; Acts xvii. 24 ; 1 Cor. iv. 9.

15.   **A new creature** (καινὴ κτίσις).   Comp. 2 Cor. v. 17. For καινὴ *new* see on Matt. xxvi. 29.   For κτίσις on Rom. viii. 19 ; 2 Cor. v. 17.   Here of *the thing created*, not of *the act of creating*.   The phrase was common in Jewish writers for one brought to the knowledge of the true God.   Comp. Eph. ii. 10, 15.

16.   **Rule** (κανόνι).   Pᵒ.   See on 2 Cor. x. 13, 16.*   Emphasis on *rule* not *this*.

Peace be on them (εἰρήνη ἐπ' αὐτούς).   The only instance of this formula in N. T.   Commonly εἰρήνη with the simple dative, *peace unto you*, as J. xx. 19, 21 ; Rom. i. 7 ; 1 Cor. i. 3 ; Gal. i. 3, etc.   In the Catholic Epistles, with πληθυνθείη *be multiplied*.   See 1 Pet. i. 2 ; 2 Pet. i. 2 ; Jude 2.

Mercy (ἔλεος).   In the opening salutations of the Pastoral Epistles with *grace* and *peace;* also in 2 J. 3.   In Jude 2 with *peace* and *love*.

---

* For the history of the word see Westcott, *Canon of the N. T.*, Appendix A.

And upon the Israel of God. The καὶ *and* may be simply connective, in which case *the Israel of God* may be different from *as many as walk*, etc., and may mean truly converted Jews. Or the καὶ may be explicative, in which case *the Israel of God* will define and emphasise *as many as*, etc., and will mean the whole body of Christians, Jewish and Gentile. In other words, they who walk according to this rule form the true Israel of God. The explicative καὶ is at best doubtful here, and is rather forced, although clear instances of it may be found in 1 Cor. iii. 5; xv. 38. It seems better to regard it as simply connective. Then ὅσοι will refer to the *individual* Christians, Jewish and Gentile, and *Israel of God* to the same Christians, regarded collectively, and forming the true messianic community.

17. **Henceforth** (τοῦ λοιποῦ). Only here and Eph. vi. 10. Commonly τὸ λοιπόν. The genitive is temporal; *at any time* in the future as distinguished from *throughout* the future.

Trouble me (κόπους μοι — παρεχέτω). Lit. *give me troubles;* make it necessary for me to vindicate my apostolic authority and the divine truth of my gospel.

Bear in my body. Comp. 2 Cor. iv. 10.

Marks (στίγματα). N. T.º. The wounds, scars, and other outward signs of persecutions and sufferings in the service of Christ. Comp. 2 Cor. xi. 23 ff. The metaphor is *the brands* applied to slaves in order to mark their owners. Hence Rev., *I bear branded*. Brands were also set upon soldiers, captives, and servants of temples. See on Apoc. xiii. 16, and comp. Apoc. vii. 3; xiv. 1, 9, 11. The scars on the apostle's body marked him as the bondservant of Jesus Christ. The passage naturally recalls the legend of Francis of Assisi.

18. **The grace, etc.** The same form of benediction occurs Philem. 25.

Brethren. Rev. rightly puts the word at the end of the verse. The position is unusual. It would seem as if Paul intended to close this severe letter with an assurance that the "foolish Galatians" were still his brethren : They are addressed as "brethren," ch. iv. 12; v. 11; vi. 1. Comp. 1 Cor. xvi. 24.

THE PASTORAL EPISTLES.

THE PASTORAL EPISTLES.

INTRODUCTION.

THE two Epistles to Timothy and the Epistle to Titus are called the Pastoral Epistles because they consist chiefly of instructions and admonitions to pastors.

Their authenticity is disputed. The current of modern criticism is against their Pauline authorship, but it is supported by high authorities.

I. The three letters are closely allied, and stand or fall together. While each has its peculiarities, they contain considerable common matter; and their general situation and aim are substantially the same. They oppose heresies, seek to establish a definite church polity, and urge adherence to traditional doctrine. Their style is similar. Certain expressions which occur nowhere else in the N. T. are found in all three. Whole sentences are in almost verbal agreement.

II. They exhibit certain resemblances to the Pauline Epistles, notably to Romans. If the writer is not Paul, he is manifestly familiar with Paul's teachings.

III. As to the external evidence for these letters, there seems good reason to believe in the existence, at an early date, either of the letters in their present form, or of documents on which the letters were constructed later. Not much reliance can be placed on the traces which occur in

Clement's Epistle to the Corinthians : perhaps a little more on those in the Ignatian Epistles, although many of these are merely analogies of expression which may have been accidental, or echoes of current religious phraseology.   An unmistakable reminiscence appears in Polycarp's Epistle to the Philippians (*Philip.* iv; 1 Tim. vi. 7, 10).   There are no echoes in Hermas or in the Didache, and none of importance in Barnabas.   Justin Martyr has a few characteristic expressions of the Pastorals, which may be only accidental coincidences.   The Muratorian Canon enrols the three as canonical, and expressly justifies their reception because, being private letters, their canonicity might be called in question.   They are found in the Peshitto and Old Latin Versions, and are accepted and cited as Pauline by Clement of Alexandria, Irenaeus, and Tertullian.   At the end of the second century they have a recognised place among the Pauline Epistles.   It is, however, significant, that they were excluded from Marcion's Canon.   It cannot be positively affirmed that Marcion knew them, although his acquaintance with them would seem to be implied by Tertullian (*Adv. Marc.* v. 21), who says that it was strange how Marcion could have accepted a letter written to one man (Philemon), and have rejected the two to Timothy and the one to Titus.

On the assumption that they were known to Marcion, it is said that he cut and carved the New Testament Scriptures to suit his own views, and that there was therefore nothing strange in his rejecting the Pastorals.   But besides rejecting the whole of the New Testament with the exception of ten Epistles of Paul and the Gospel of Luke which he mutilated, Marcion applied the knife to the Pauline Epistles.   In view of his reverence for Paul as the only true apostle and representative of Jesus Christ, and for Paul's Epistles as containing the only true gospel, — it is strange that, knowing the Pastorals as Pauline, he should have rejected them *en masse*, instead of merely altering or abridging them to suit himself.   Tatian also rejected the two letters to Timothy, but accepted Titus, because it contained nothing adverse to ascetic practices.

IV. CHRONOLOGICAL CONSIDERATIONS. — Was Paul released from his first imprisonment and imprisoned a second time? Can a place be found for the three letters in his recorded history?

It is claimed that Paul was released from prison after his first confinement at Rome (Acts xxviii. 16–31) and that he then continued his missionary labours in Ephesus, Epirus, Macedonia, and Crete: that he was again arrested and imprisoned, and that the second imprisonment was terminated by his execution.

Of this there is no sound historical evidence whatever. The narrative of Acts leaves him in his first confinement. The ordinary course of argument forms a circle. The hypothesis of a second imprisonment can be sustained only by the Pastoral Epistles if they are authentic. Their authenticity can be shown only on that hypothesis. The only evidence adduced for the second imprisonment outside of these letters is, 1. A passage in Clement's Epistle to the Corinthians (V.), as follows: (Paul) "having preached the gospel both in the East and in the West, received the glorious renown due to his faith, having taught righteousness to the whole world, and having come to the boundary of the West, and having borne his testimony before the rulers. Thus he departed out of the world." The main point is *having come to the boundary of the West* (ἐπὶ τὸ τέρμα τῆς δύσεως ἐλθών). It is claimed that this expression refers to Spain, and that Clement thus records the fulfilment of the apostle's intention stated in Rom. xv. 24, 28. Others, however, hold that it refers to Rome.* Apart from this difference, which it is impossible to settle, the whole statement is general, vague, and rhetorical, and has no historical value.

2. The Muratorian Canon (about 170 A.D.) contains a passage apparently to the effect that Luke relates to Theophilus the things which fell under his own notice, and evidently declares as apart from his purpose the martyrdom of

---

* All that can be said in favour of the reference to Spain, is said by Bp. Lightfoot, *S. Clement of Rome,* ad loc.

Peter; but the departure of Paul setting out from the city to Spain — here the text is mutilated. How the writer intended to complete it can only be guessed. The passage is worthless as evidence. 3. After these two we have nothing until the fourth century, when Eusebius says that there was *a tradition* that the apostle again set forth to the ministry of his preaching, and having a second time entered the same city of Rome, was perfected by his martyrdom before Nero. That in this imprisonment he wrote the second Epistle to Timothy (*H. E.* ii. 22, 25). This is all. Jerome merely echoes Eusebius. Eusebius does not mention Spain. History does not show any apostolic foundation in Spain. Neither Irenaeus, Caius, Tertullian, nor Origen allude to such a mission; and although Irenaeus, Tertullian, and Origen mention the death of Paul at Rome, they say nothing of any journeys subsequent to his first arrival there. Dr. McGiffert remarks (note on Euseb. ii. 22, 2): "The strongest argument against the visit to Spain is the absence of any trace of it in Spain itself. If any church there could have claimed the great apostle to the Gentiles as its founder, it seems that it must have asserted its claim, and the tradition have been preserved at least in that church."

It is also said that 2 Tim. iv. 16, 17 implies that Paul had had a hearing and been discharged and permitted to preach. The assumption is entirely gratuitous. The words may have referred to a hearing during his first captivity, when he was delivered from imminent danger, but not set at liberty.

In short, historical evidence for a release from the first Roman imprisonment, a subsequent missionary activity, and a second imprisonment, is utterly wanting. It seems hardly conceivable that no traces of a renewed ministry should be left in history except these instructions to friends and pupils. If Paul was liberated from his first imprisonment, it is singular that Luke should not have recorded the fact as a triumph of the gospel.

Such being the case, it remains only to find a place for these letters in the recorded ministry of Paul. This cannot be

done.   There is no period of that ministry, from Damascus
to Rome, into which they will fit.*

V. STYLE AND DICTION. — The most formidable objection
to the Pauline authorship of these Epistles is furnished by
their style and diction, which present a marked contrast with
those of the Pauline letters.   That the three Pastorals contain 148 words which appear nowhere else in the N. T., and
304 which are not found in Paul's writings, are facts which,
by themselves, must not be allowed too much weight.   Hapaxlegomena are numerous in the several Pauline Epistles.
Second Corinthians has about 90 : Romans and 1st Corinthians each over a hundred : Ephesians about 40.   That
words like πολυτελής and οἰκουργός appear in the Pastorals
and not in Paul, counts for no more than that ὁλοτελής
occurs only in 1st Thessalonians, and ἀβαρής only in 2d
Corinthians.

But we are not dealing with individual letters, but with a
group of letters, nearly, if not absolutely, contemporaneous.
It *is* a striking fact that this entire group, closely allied in
all its three parts in vocabulary and style, presents, as a
whole, such marked variations in these particulars from the
accepted Pauline letters.   In their lexical peculiarities the
Pastorals form a class by themselves.

One who is thoroughly steeped in Paul's style and diction,
and who reads these letters out of hand, is at once impressed
with the difference from Paul.   He feels that he is in a strange
rhetorical atmosphere.   The sentences have not the familiar
ring.   The thought does not move with the accustomed rush.
The verve of Corinthians and Galatians, the dialectic vigour
of Romans, the majesty of Ephesians, are alike wanting.   The
association of ideas is loose, the construction is not compact,
the movement is slow and clumsy.   We miss the heavily-

* This is succinctly shown by Edwin Hatch, in his article "Pastoral Epistles," in the *Encyclopaedia Britannica;* and more in detail by von Soden, in
his introduction to the Pastorals in the *Hand-Commentar.*   The most recent
defence of the opposite view is by J. Vernon Bartlett, *The Apostolic Age,*
1899.

freighted utterance of Paul.   The thought is scanty in proportion to the volume of words ; as Holtzmann says : "We
miss those characteristic *dam-breakings* which the construction
suffers from the swelling fulness of thought." We miss the
frequent anacolutha, the unclosed parentheses, the sudden
digressions, the obscurities arising from the headlong impe-
tus of thought and feeling.   The construction of sentences
is simple, the thoughts are expressed without adornment,
everything is according to rule and easy, but without momentum or colour.   Strange compounds, great, swelling
words, start up in our path : a Pauline thought appears
in a strange dress : the voice is the voice of Jacob, but the
hands are the hands of Esau.

Some of these unusual compounds, for which the writer has
a great liking, occur neither in the N. T. nor in profane Greek.
High-sounding words are chosen where simpler terms would
have suited the thought better.   It seems, occasionally, as if
the diction were being employed to pad the meagreness of
the thought.   A class of words which occur principally in the
Pauline letters is wanting, as ἄδικος, ἀκαθαρσία, ἀκροβυστία,
γνωρίζειν, διαθήκη, περιπατεῖν, χρηστός, and σῶμα, which, in
the four principal Epistles alone, Paul uses 71 times.   We
miss entire families of Pauline words, as ἐλεύθερος, φρονεῖν,
πράσσειν, τέλειος, ἐνεργεῖν, περισσός, and the numerous deriv-
atives and compounds growing out of these.

Again, we look in vain for certain expressions most characteristic of the Pauline vocabulary, as ὑπακούειν, ἀποκαλύπτειν,
καυχᾶσθαι, and their kindred words.   Still more significant is
the fact that the article, which is freely used by Paul before
entire sentences, adverbs, interjections, numerals, and especially before the infinitive, is never so employed in the Pastorals.   Τοῦ with the infinitive disappears.   The prepositions,
the conjunctions, and especially the particles are quite differently handled.   The lively γάρ appears oftener in the Epistle
to the Galatians than in all the three Pastorals.   The movement of the Pauline thought indicated by ἄρα and ἄρα οὖν is
lacking.   Ἀντί, ἄχρι, διό, διότι, ἔμπροσθεν, ἕνεκεν, ἔπειτα, ἔτι,
ἴδε, ἰδού, μήπως, ὅπως, οὐκέτι, οὔπω, οὔτε, πάλιν, παρά with the

accusative, ἐν παντί, πότε, ποῦ, σύν, ὥσπερ — none of these
appear. There is no trace of Paul's habit of applying different prepositions to the same object in one sentence, for the
purpose of sharper definition. See Gal. i. 1; Rom. i. 17.

Similar ideas are differently expressed by Paul and in the
Pastorals. Comp. 1 Tim. i. 3 and 2 Cor. xi. 4; Gal. i. 6:
1 Tim. i. 9 and Gal. v. 18, 23; Rom. vi. 14: 1 Tim. i. 12 and
1 Cor. xii. 28. For Paul's ἐπιθυμεῖν or ἐπιποθεῖν the Pastorals give ὀρέγεσθαι. For Paul's ἄμωμος, ἄμεμπτος, ἀνέγκλη-
τος, the Pastorals give ἀνεπίλημπτος (not elsewhere in N. T.).
For ἐπιπλήσσω (not elsewhere in N. T.) Paul has ἐλέγχω,
though ἐλέγχω occurs several times in the Pastorals. For
ἀμοιβή (not elsewhere in N. T.) Paul has ἀντιμισθία or ἀνταπόδοσις. Paul uses ὄντως only adverbially (see 1 Cor. xiv.
25; Gal. iii. 21): in the Pastorals it is prefixed to a substantive, and converted into an adjective by means of an article,
and is used only in this way, a construction unknown to Paul
(see 1 Tim. v. 3, 5, 16; vi. 19).

To these should be added expressions in all the three Epistles which indicate a peculiar mode of thought and of literary expression on the part of the writer. Such are εὐσεβῶς
ζῆν to live godly; διώκειν δικαιοσύνην to pursue righteousness;
φυλάσσειν τὴν παραθήκην to guard the deposit; παρακολουθεῖν
τῇ διδασκαλίᾳ to follow the teaching; τὸν καλὸν ἀγῶνα ἀγωνίζεσθαι to fight the good fight. Also designations like ἄνθρωποι
κατεφθαρμένοι corrupt men; ἄνθρωπος θεοῦ man of God; con-
structions like διαβεβαιοῦσθαι περί τινος to affirm concerning
something; and the introduction of examples by ὧν ἐστίν of
whom are.

Many more might be added to these,* but these are amply
sufficient to show the wide gulf which separates the vocabulary and style of these letters from those of Paul.

By way of explaining away these facts we are reminded
that these are private letters; but even in his private letters
a man does not so entirely abjure his literary peculiarities,

---

* Full lists of peculiarities of style and diction will be found in Holtzmann,
Die Pastoralbriefe, ch. VII.

and the letter to Philemon exhibits no lack of distinctive Pauline characteristics.

It is further urged that Paul's style had developed, and that, in his advanced age, he had lost the vivacity once peculiar to him. One is tempted to smile at the suggestion of a development of style in the easy commonplaces of these Epistles over the nervous vigour of Romans, the racy incisiveness of Galatians and 2d Corinthians, and the majestic richness of Ephesians. As to a decline on account of age, Paul, on this showing, must have aged very rapidly. He styles himself "the aged" in Philem. 9. Colossians was written at the same time with Philemon, and Philippians and Ephesians shortly before or after. The Pastorals (assuming Paul's authorship) cannot have been written more than three or four years later than these; but the Epistles of the Captivity certainly betray no lack of vigour, and exhibit no signs of senility; and the differences between these and the Pastorals are far greater than between the former and Paul's earliest letters, written ten years before. The production of an old man may indeed exhibit a lack of energy or a carelessness of style, but an old writer does not abandon his favorite words or his characteristic turns of expression. After following Paul for a dozen years through ten Epistles, all marked by the essential features of his style, one finds it hard to believe that he should suddenly become a writer of an entirely different type, ignoring his own characteristic and favorite modes of expression. Surely the themes treated in the Pastorals would have furnished abundant occasion for υἱὸς θεοῦ, ἀπολύτρωσις, υἱοθεσία, δικαιοσύνη θεοῦ, and δικαιόω, which occurs only twice, and in one of these instances is applied to Christ.

VI. As to the character of the teaching, it is possible that the divergence of the teaching and of the Christian ideal of the Pastorals from those of the Pauline Epistles may have been somewhat exaggerated. On a fair construction, the Pastorals may be said to contain the essentials of the Pauline teaching, expressed or implied. More exaggerated, however, is the claim of Godet and Findlay, that the Pastorals repre-

sent an advanced and rounded expression of Pauline teaching, "bringing the doctrines of grace to a rounded fulness
and chastened ripeness of expression that warrants us in seeing in them the authentic conclusion of the Pauline gospel
of salvation in the mind which first conceived it" (Findlay).

No special pleading can get round the clear difference
between the types of Christianity and of Christian teaching
as set forth in the Pastorals and in the Pauline Epistles ;
between the modes of presenting the doctrine of salvation
and the relative emphasis on its great factors.

The death and resurrection of Christ are matters of allusion
rather than central truths.   As regards resurrection, the
Pastorals resemble the Epistle to the Hebrews.   The vital
union of the believer with Christ, which is the essence of
Paul's Christian ideal, may possibly be implied, but is not
emphasised, and certainly does not underlie the Pastoral
teaching.   The conception of Justification is not sharply
defined.   Δικαιοῦν occurs but twice, and in one of the cases is
predicated of Christ (1 Tim. iii. 16).   The teaching is pre-
dominantly ethical.   Its two key-notes are practical piety
and sound doctrine.   'Εὐσέβεια *piety* or *godliness* plays the
part which is borne by πίστις *faith* in the Paulines.   Πίστις
does not occupy the commanding and central position which
it does in Paul's teaching.   Only in 1 Tim. i. 16 ; 2 Tim.
iii. 15, does faith clearly appear as the means of the subjective appropriation of salvation.   In Tit. iii. 5, just where we
should expect it, we do not find faith set sharply over against
righteousness by works.   Faith is emphasised as confiding
acknowledgment of the truth, and sometimes as the virtue
of fidelity.   See 1 Tim. v. 12 ; Tit. ii. 10.   It appears either
as one of the cardinal virtues following in the train of *εὐσέβεια*, or as the acknowledgment of the *teaching* in which
εὐσέβεια finds expression.

These Epistles deal much with the character and attributes
of God, and exhibit them in terms which are mostly foreign
to Paul, such as *God our Saviour*.   This, however, may have
been partly due to the false representations of contemporary
heresies.   I cannot but feel that there is too much truth in

the remark of Schenkel, that "the image of Christ presented in the Pastorals is indeèd composed of Pauline formulas, but is lacking in the Pauline spirit and feeling, in the mystic inwardness, the religious depth and moral force, that live in the Christ of Paul." Still, the Pauline conception appears in the emphasis upon the manhood of Christ (1 Tim. ii. 5; 2 Tim. ii. 8), and the clear implication of his preëxistence (1 Tim. i. 15; iii. 16; 2 Tim. i. 10). In 1 Tim. iii. 16 the representation is nearer to that of John.

VII. THE WRITER'S ALLUSIONS TO HIMSELF AND HIS COMPANIONS. — Grave suspicions as to the Pauline authorship are awakened by the writer's mode of speaking of himself, and to intimate and trusted companions and disciples like Timothy and Titus. We know how near these two were to him, and how he confided in them (see Philip. ii. 19–22). It is strange that in writing to them he should find it necessary to announce himself formally as an apostle of Jesus Christ (comp. Philemon, δέσμιος *prisoner*), just as to the Galatians, who had impugned his apostolic authority, or to the Romans, to whom he was personally a stranger. Such an announcement is singularly out of place in a private letter, even though official. Equally strange is his assuring such friends that he is appointed of God to be a herald of the gospel; that he speaks the truth and does not lie; that he has served God from his fathers with a pure conscience. One might doubt his entire confidence in these trusted ministerial helpers and personal friends, when he feels it incumbent upon him to commend to them the most elementary and self-evident duties, as abstinence from youthful lusts. It is singular that he should exhort Timothy to let no man despise his youth, when Timothy had attended him for at least thirteen years, and must have been a mature man. And if Paul, before writing 1st Timothy and Titus, had recently been with them both (1 Tim. i. 3; Tit. i. 5), and had given them their commissions by word of mouth, why does he do the same thing so soon after, especially when he is looking forward to a speedy reunion (1 Tim. iii. 14; Tit. iii. 12)? Why does he picture the Cretans in such detail to Titus, who was in the midst of them, and who must have known their characteristics quite as well as himself?

VIII. The Heresies. — Before it can be decisively asserted that the heresies treated in these Epistles are later than Paul's time, it must be settled what these heresies were, and this, with our present knowledge, is impossible.   There are almost as many different views as there are critics.   In the Epistles themselves the statements regarding heresies are general and sweeping, and, taken together, do not point to any particular system.   It would seem that the writer was assailing, not a particular form of heresy, but a tendency, of which he does not discuss the details.   Indeed, the allusions to heresies appear intended principally to point the exhortations to hold fast sound teaching and the instructions concerning church polity, as safeguards against false teaching and immoral practice.   The moral developments of the heresies, rather than their doctrinal errors, are treated.   Their representatives are wicked men and impostors : they are deceiving and deceived : they are of corrupt mind, destitute of truth, with their consciences seared : they lead captive silly women, laden with sins, led away by divers lusts : they are greedy of gain.   At the root of the moral errors there seem to be indicated Gnostic tendencies and Jewish corruptions, and traits akin to those which appear in the Colossian heresy.   All of the writer's theology is anti-Gnostic.   Individual features of Gnosticism can be recognised, but a consistent reference throughout to Gnosticism cannot be shown.*   In any case, it is noticeable how the treatment of heresies and false teachers differs from that of Paul.   The treatment in the Pastorals is general, sweeping, vague, and mainly denunciatory.   No vital differences between the forms of error and between their teachers are defined, but all are indiscriminately denounced as concerned with foolish and ignorant question-

* See Pfleiderer, *Urchristenthum*, p. 801 ff., and Holtzmann, *Die Pastoralbriefe*, ch. IX.

ing, disputes about words, strifes about the law, fables, end-less genealogies, and profane babblings. This is quite unlike the controversial method of Paul, who defines what he assails, demonstrates its unsoundness, and shows the bearing of the gospel upon it.

IX. CHURCH POLITY. — The church polity of the Pastor-als is of a later date than Paul. Within the circle of the Pauline Epistles there is no trace of formally constituted church officers. The greeting to Bishops and Deacons in Philippians is unique, but it does not imply a polity differing substantially from that exhibited in 1st Corinthians and 1st Thessalonians. The greeting is to the church first, and the special mention of Bishops and Deacons by way of appendage is explained by the fact that the letter was called out by the pecuniary contribution of the Philippian church to Paul, of the collection and sending of which these functionaries would naturally have charge. The names Bishop and Deacon des-ignate functions and not official titles. In the formal list, in Eph. iv. 11, of those whom God has set in the church, neither Bishops, Elders, nor Deacons occur; and yet that Epistle was written within a short time of the writing of the Philip-pian letter. The offices in the Pauline church were charis-matic. The warrant of leadership was a divine, spiritual endowment. Paul recognises certain *functions* as of divine institution; and those functions are assumed in virtue of a special, divine gift in prophecy, speaking with tongues, teach-ing, healing, or helping, as the case may be (see 1 Cor. xii). There is no recognition of official distinctions, or of formal appointment to definite offices, in the Pauline Epistles. Apos-tles, prophets, teachers, powers, helps, healings, kinds of tongues, do not represent offices resting on the appointment of the church. The Pastorals recognise Bishops, Deacons, and Presbyters. The recognition of three distinct orders is not as sharp and clear as in the Ignatian Epistles (100–118 A.D.), but the polity is in advance of that of the Pauline churches as set forth in the Epistles of Paul. The Pastorals seem to mark a transition point between the earlier republican

simplicity and the later monarchical tendency.   If these letters are the work of Paul before his first imprisonment, their
notes of church polity do not consist with those of his other
letters written during that period.   If they were composed
by Paul a few years after his first imprisonment, the period
is too early for the change in polity which they indicate.

In view of all these facts, it seems unlikely that these Epistles are the work of Paul.   The writer was probably a Pauline Christian in the early part of the second century, who, in
view of the doctrinal errors and moral looseness of his age,
desired to emphasise the orthodox doctrine of the church, to
advocate a definite ecclesiastical polity as a permanent safeguard against error, and to enforce practical rules of conduct.
These counsels and warnings he issued in the name of Paul,
whose letters he evidently knew, whose character he revered,
and whose language he tried to imitate.   To this he was, perhaps, moved by the fact that contemporary heretics, in some
cases, laid claim to the authority of Paul, and in other cases
openly repudiated it.   It is probable that he based these letters upon genuine Pauline material — despatches, or fragments
of letters to Timothy and Titus, which had fallen into his
hands.   It may be conceded that the letters have a Pauline
nucleus.   The writer probably assumed that the addresses of
his letters to Timothy and Titus would attract attention and
carry weight, since these teachers were representatives of
churches.

To stigmatise such a proceeding as forgery is to treat the
conditions of that early time from the point of view of our
own age.   No literary fraud was contemplated by the writer
or ascribed to him.   The practice of issuing a work in the
name of some distinguished person was common, and was recognised as legitimate.   A whole class of writings, chiefly
apocalyptic, and known as pseudepigraphic or pseudonymous,
appeared in the times immediately preceding and succeeding
the beginning of the Christian era.   Such were the Book of
Enoch, the Sibylline Oracles, and the Psalter of Solomon.
Precedent was furnished by the Old Testament writings.
The Psalmists adopted the names of David, Asaph, and the

Sons of Korah. Neither Samuel nor Ruth nor Esther were supposed to be the authors of the books which bore their names. Koheleth, in the Book of Ecclesiastes, impersonates Solomon, and the Proverbs and the Canticles both bear his name.

The church of the second century thankfully accepted these three Epistles, and, inferior though they were in spiritual power and richness of idea to the genuine Pauline letters or the Epistle to the Hebrews, incorporated them with these among the New Testament writings. They are valuable in exhibiting to us certain features of post-Pauline Christianity. They testify to the energy and purity of the church's moral impulses as nourished by the religious principles of Christendom. They show us the causes out of which grew the increased emphasis upon authority and external regimen. By their strong attestation of the value of the inheritance from the apostolic age, by their high ethical character, based on religion and exhibiting the moral consequences of the Christian faith, by their emphasis upon the practical rather than the doctrinal edification of the church, upon the significance of the church, and upon the representation of Christianity by Christian personality — they justify their canonisation.

COMMENTARIES AND OTHER LITERATURE.

OPPOSERS OF THE AUTHENTICITY.

H. J. Holtzmann, *Die Pastoralbriefe kritisch und exegetisch behandelt*, 1880.

H. von Soden, "Introduction to Pastoral Epistles," *Hand-Commentar*, by Holtzmann, Lipsius, Schmiedel, and von Soden, 1893.

Samuel Davidson, *Introduction to the Study of the New Testament*.

C. von Weizsäcker, *Das apostolische Zeitalter der christlichen Kirche*, 1891. Transl. by Millar, 1894.

O. Pfleiderer, *Das Urchristenthum, seine Schriften und Lehren*, 1887. *Der Paulinismus*, 1890.

A. Sabatier, *L'Apôtre Paul.* Transl. by Hellier, 1890.

Ad. Jülicher, *Einleitung in das Neue Testament*, 1894.

Edwin Hatch, art. "Pastoral Epistles," *Encyclopaedia Britannica.*

A. McGiffert, *The Apostolic Age*, 1897.

Lemme, *Das echte Ermahnungschreiben des Apostels Paulus an Timotheus*, 1882.

F. H. Hesse, *Die Entstehung der neutestamentlichen Hirtenbriefe*, 1889.

DEFENDERS OF THE AUTHENTICITY.

B. Weiss, *Einleitung in das Neue Testament.* Transl. by Davidson, 1886.

G. Salmon, *A Historical Introduction to the Study of the New Testament.*

F. Godet, *Introduction au Nouveau Testament*, Pt. I. Transl. by Affleck, 1893.

W. M. Ramsay, *The Church in the Roman Empire before A.D. 170*, 1893.

J. E. Huther in Meyer's Commentary, 1875.

H. Wace, in Speaker's Commentary.

G. G. Findlay, Appendix to Transl. of Sabatier's *L'Apôtre Paul*, 1891.

F. W. Farrar, *Life and Work of St. Paul*, Vol. II., Excursus IX., 1879.

P. J. Gloag, *Introduction to the Pauline Epistles*, 1874.

Theo. Zahn, *Einleitung in das Neue Testament*, 1897.

Rud. Steinmetz, *Die zweite römische Gefangenschaft des Apostels Paulus*, 1897.

J. Vernon Bartlett, *The Apostolic Age*, 1899.

COMMENTARIES.

ENGLISH.

J. E. Huther, in Meyer's Commentary.   Transl.

C. J. Ellicott, *A Critical and Grammatical Commentary on the Pastoral Epistles.*

H. Wace, Speaker's Commentary.

P. Fairbairn, *The Pastoral Epistles*, Greek Text and Transl.

GERMAN.

B. Weiss, Meyer's Commentary, 1885.   Published separately.

H. J. Holtzmann, *Die Pastoralbriefe.*

H. von Soden, *Hand-Commentar*, Vol. III.

H. Koelling, *Der erste Brief Pauli an Timotheus.*

K. Knoke, *Praktisch-theologischer Kommentar zu den Pastoralbriefen des Apostels Paulus.*

THE FIRST EPISTLE TO TIMOTHY.

CHAPTER I.

1. An apostle of Jesus Christ. This title appears in the
salutations of Romans, 1st and 2d Corinthians, Galatians,
Ephesians, Colossians. In Philippians, Paul and Timothy
the servants of Jesus Christ. Philemon *a prisoner*. This
formal announcement of apostleship is strange in a private
letter.

By the commandment of God (*κατ' ἐπιταγὴν θεοῦ*). The
phrase in Rom. xvi. 26. *Κατ' ἐπιταγὴν* absolutely, *by commandment*, 1 Cor. vii. 6; 2 Cor. viii. 8. Paul uses *διὰ θελήματος θεοῦ by the will of God*. See 1 Cor. i. 1; 2 Cor. i. 1;
Eph. i. 1; Col. i. 1. Comp. 2 Tim. i. 1.

Our Saviour (*σωτῆρος ἡμῶν*). Comp. L. i. 47; Jude 25.
⁰P. Six times in the Pastorals. Used of both God and Christ
(see Tit. i. 3, 4; ii. 10, 13; iii. 4, 6). The saving of men
appears as God's direct will and act, 1 Tim. ii. 4; Tit. iii. 5;
2 Tim. i. 9: as Christ's work, 1 Tim. i. 15, comp. 2 Tim.
ii. 10. In LXX *σωτὴρ* occurs twenty times, and in all but
two instances, of God.

Jesus Christ which is our hope. The phrase is unique
in N. T. Comp. Col. i. 27, where, however, the construction is doubtful. 'Ελπὶς *hope* is predicated of Christ by
Ignatius, *Eph.* xxi; *Philad.* v. The salutation as a whole
has no parallel in Paul.

2. My own son in the faith (γνησίῳ τέκνῳ ἐν πίστει).
More correctly, "*my true child in faith.*" Comp. Tit. i. 4.
With these two exceptions, τέκνον or υἱός ἐν πίστει does not
occur in N. T. Ἐν πίστει or τῇ πίστει is not common in
Paul; see 1 Cor. xvi. 13; 2 Cor. viii. 7; xiii. 5; Gal. ii.
20; 2 Th. ii. 13. In the Pastorals, nine times. In Paul
joined with ζῆν to live, εἶναι to be, στήκειν to stand, βεβαιοῦσθαι to be established. For γνήσιος true, see 2 Cor. viii. 8;
Philip. ii. 20; iv. 3. It means *natural, by birth-relation,*
therefore *true* or *genuine.*

Mercy (ἔλεος). This addition to the usual form of salutation is peculiar to the Pastorals.

3. Even as (καθώς). An awkward construction, there
being nothing to answer to καθώς.

To abide (προσμεῖναι). To continue *on.* The compound
does not occur in Paul, but is found in Acts xi. 23; xiii. 43;
xviii. 18.

When I went (πορευόμενος). Better, *was going,* or *was on
my way.* The participle cannot refer to Timothy.

Might'st charge (παραγγείλῃς). See on Acts i. 4. Very
common in Luke and Acts, but not in Paul. In 1st Timothy alone five times.

Some (τισὶν). Note the indefinite designation of the
errorists, and comp. ver. 6; iv. 1; v. 15, 24; vi. 21. The
expression is contemptuous. It is assumed that Timothy
knows who they are. This is after the Pauline manner.
See Gal. i. 7; ii. 12; 1 Cor. iv. 18; xv. 12; 2 Cor. iii. 1;
Col. ii. 4, 8.

That they teach no other doctrine (μὴ ἑτεροδιδασκαλεῖν).
Better, *not to teach a different doctrine.* For ἕτερος *different,*
see on Gal. i. 6. The verb Past°. °LXX. °Class. The

charge is not to teach anything contrary to the *sound teaching* (ver. 10) or irreconcilable with it   Comp. Gal. i. 6; 2
Cor. xi. 4; Rom. xvi. 17.

4. **Give heed** (προσέχειν). °P. Frequent in LXX and
Class. Lit. *to hold to.* Often with τὸν νοῦν *the mind*, which
must be supplied here. It means here not merely *to give attention to*, but *to give assent to.* So Acts viii. 6; xvi. 14;
Heb. ii. 1; 2 Pet. i. 19.

Fables (μύθοις). Μῦθος, in its widest sense, means *word,
speech, conversation* or *its subject.* Hence the *talk of men,
rumour, report, a saying, a story*, true or false; later, *a fiction*
as distinguished from λόγος *a historic tale.* In Attic prose,
commonly *a legend of prehistoric Greek times.* Thus Plato,
Repub. 330 D, οἱ λεγόμενοι μῦθοι περὶ τῶν ἐν "Αἰδου *what are
called myths concerning those in Hades.* Only once in LXX,
Sir. xx. 19, in the sense of *a saying* or *story.* In N. T. only
in Pastorals, and 2 Pet. i. 16. As to its exact reference
here, it is impossible to speak with certainty. Expositors
are hopelessly disagreed, some referring it to Jewish, others
to Gnostic fancies. It is explained as meaning traditional
supplements to the law, allegorical interpretations, Jewish
stories of miracles, Rabbinical fabrications, whether in history or doctrine, false doctrines generally, etc. It is to be
observed that μῦθοι are called *Jewish* in Tit. i. 14. In
1 Tim. iv. 7, they are described as *profane* and *characteristic
of old wives.* In 2 Tim. iv. 4, the word is used absolutely,
as here.

Endless genealogies (γενεαλογίαις ἀπεράντοις). Both
words Past°. For γενεαλογία (°LXX) comp. Tit. iii. 9.
Γενεαλογεῖσθαι *to trace ancestry*, only Heb. vii. 6; comp. 1
Chron. v. 1, the only instance in LXX. Ἀπέραντος *endless*,
N. T.°. Twice in LXX. By some the genealogies are referred to the Gnostic *aeons* or series of emanations from the
divine unity; by others to the O. T. genealogies as interpreted allegorically by Philo, and made the basis of a psy-

chological system, or O. T. genealogies adorned with fables :
by others again to genealogical registers proper, used to
foster the religious and national pride of the Jews against
Gentiles, or to ascertain the descent of the Messiah. 'Aπέρ-
αντος from ἀ not, and πέρας limit or terminus. Πέρας may
be taken in the sense of object or aim, so that the adjective
here may mean without object, useless. (So Chrysostom, Holtzmann, and von Soden.)   Others take it in a popular sense,
as describing the tedious length of the genealogies (Alford);
and others that these matters furnish an inexhaustible subject of study (Weiss). " Fables and endless genealogies "
form a single conception, the καὶ and being explanatory, that
is to say, and the " endless genealogies " indicating in what
the peculiarity of the fables consists.

Which (αἵτινες).   Rather the which: inasmuch as they.

Minister (παρέχουσιν). Afford, furnish, give occasion for.
Only twice in Paul.   Elsewhere mainly in Luke and Acts.

Questions (ἐκζητήσεις).   Better, questionings.   N. T.º.
ºLXX. ºClass. The simple ζητήσεις in Pastorals, John and
Acts. The preposition ἐκ gives the sense of subtle, laborious
investigation: inquiring out.

Godly edifying.   According to the reading οἰκοδομίαν
edification.   So Vulg. aedificationem.   But the correct reading is οἰκονομίαν ordering or dispensation: the scheme or
order of salvation devised and administered by God : God's
household economy. 'Οικονομία is a Pauline word. With
the exception of this instance, only in Paul and Luke. See
Eph. i. 10; iii. 2, 9; Col. i. 25.

Which is in faith (τὴν ἐν πίστει).   See on ver. 2.   Faith
is the sphere or element of its operation.

5. **The end of the commandment** (τέλος τῆς παραγγελίας). The article with " commandment " points back to

might'st charge, ver. 3. Rend. therefore, *of the charge*. Τέλος
end, aim, that which the charge contemplates.

Love (ἀγάπη). See on Gal. v. 22. The *questionings*, on
the contrary, engendered *strifes* (2 Tim. ii. 23). Love *to
men* is meant, as commonly in N. T. when the word is used
absolutely. See Rom. xiii. 10.

Out of a pure heart (ἐκ καθαρᾶς καρδίας). Comp. L. x.
27, " Thou shalt love the Lord thy God *out of* thy whole
heart (ἐξ ὅλης καρδίας σου), and *in* or *with* (ἐν) thy whole
soul," etc. For *a pure heart*, comp. 2 Tim. ii. 22. Καθαρός
pure in Paul only Rom. xiv. 20. The phrase *a pure heart*
occurs, outside of the Pastorals only in 2 Pet. i. 22. For
καρδία *heart* see on Rom. i. 21.

A good conscience (συνειδήσεως ἀγαθῆς). Comp. 2 Tim.
i. 3. Συνείδησις *conscience* is common in Paul. See on 1 Pet.
iii. 16.

Faith unfeigned (πίστεως ἀνυποκρίτου). ’Ανυπόκριτος
unfeigned twice in Paul, Rom. xii. 9 ; 2 Cor. vi. 6, both
times as an attribute of love. In Jas. iii. 17, it is an attribute of wisdom, and in 1 Pet. i. 22, of brotherly love.
Notice the triad, *love, conscience, faith*. There is nothing
un-Pauline in the association of conscience and faith, although, as a fact, Paul does not formally associate them.
In 1 Cor. viii. 7, 10, 12, conscience is associated with knowledge.

6. Having swerved (ἀστοχήσαντες). Past⁰. In LXX,
Sir. vii. 19 ; viii. 9. It means *to miss the mark*.

Have turned aside (ἐξετράπησαν). ⁰P. Comp. 1 Tim.
v. 15 ; vi. 20 ; 2 Tim. iv. 4 ; Heb. xii. 13.

Vain jangling (ματαιολογίαν). N. T.⁰. ⁰LXX. ⁰Class.
The word illustrates the writer's fondness for unusual com-

pounds. *Jangling* is an early English word from the old
French *jangler*, comp. *jongleur a teller of tales.* Hence
jangling is *empty chatter.* So Chaucer,

> "Them that jangle of love."
>
> *Troil. and Cress.* ii. 800.

> "Thus jangle they and demen and devyse."
>
> *Squire's T.* 260.

And Piers Ploughman,

> " And al day to drynken
>   At diverse tavernes
>   And there to jangle and jape."
>
> *Vision, Pass.* ii. 1069.

Shakespeare,

> " This their jangling I esteem a sport."
>
> *Mids. Night's D.* iii. 2.

Wiclif, Ex. xvii. 7 (earlier version), uses jangling for
wrangling. " And he clepide the name of the place *Tempt-
ynge* for the jangling of the sons of Israel."

7. **Desiring** (θέλοντες). The participle is explanatory and
confirmatory of the preceding statement : *since they desire.*

Teachers of the law (νομοδιδάσκαλοι). °P. It occurs in
L. v. 17 and Acts v. 34. Νόμος is, apparently, the Mosaic
law. These teachers may have been arbitrary interpreters
of that law, but in what way, cannot be shown.

Understanding (νοοῦντες). Better, *though they understand.*

What they say — whereof they affirm (ἃ λέγουσιν — περὶ
τίνων διαβεβαιοῦνται). The latter expression is an advance on
the former, as appears not only from the verbs themselves,
but from the different pronominal expressions. They know
not *what* they say, nor what kind of things they are *of which*
they speak so confidently. The compound διαβεβαιοῦσθαι *to
affirm*, Past°. Comp. Tit. iii. 8. The false teachers announce their errors with assurance.

8. **Good** (καλός). Comp. Rom. vii. 16. Morally excellent
and salutary. See on J. x. 11. This is the only instance of
χρᾶσθαι *to use* with νόμος *law*.

Lawfully (νομίμως). Past°. °LXX. The nature of the
proper use of the law — use according to its design — is indicated by the next clause.

9. **Knowing** (εἰδὼς). The participle is connected with τὶς
one, a man, in the preceding clause.

Is not made (οὐ κεῖται). Lit. is not *laid down, set, appointed.* Comp. 1 Th. iii. 3. This is the only instance of
its use with νόμος *law.* That usage is frequent in Class. See,
for instance, Thucyd. ii. 37.

Righteous (δικαίῳ). Morally upright. Not in the Pauline
sense of justified by faith. Comp. 2 Tim. ii. 22; iii. 16.
This appears from the way in which the opposite of *righteous*
is described in the next clause.

Lawless (ἀνόμοις). Recognising no law; a sense which
accords better with the following context than *not having a
law,* as 1 Cor. ix. 21.

Disobedient (ἀνυποτάκτοις). Only in Pastorals and Hebrews. Better *unruly. Disobedient* is too specific. It means
those who will not come into subjection. It is closely allied
with *lawless.* In the one case no legal obligation is *recognised;*
in the other, subjection to law is *refused.*

Ungodly — sinners (ἀσεβέσι — ἁμαρτωλοῖς). The same
collocation in 1 Pet. iv. 18; Jude 15. See on *godliness,*
2 Pet. i. 3.

Unholy—profane (ἀνοσίοις—βεβήλοις). Ἀνόσιος *unholy,*
Past°. See on *holiness,* L. i. 75. Βέβηλος *profane,* comp.
ch. iv. 7; vi. 20; 2 Tim. ii. 16; Heb. xii. 16. The verb

βεβηλοῦν *to profane*, Matt. xii. 5; Acts xxiv. 6, and often in LXX. Derived from βηλός *threshold* (comp. βαίνειν *to go*). Hence the primary sense is *that may be trodden*. Comp. Lat. *profanus before the temple*, on the ground outside. What is permitted to be trodden by people at large is *unhallowed, profane.* Esau is called βέβηλος in Heb. xii. 16, as one who did not regard his birthright as sacred, but as something to be sold in order to supply a common need.

Murderers of fathers—murderers of mothers (πατρολῴαις —μητρολῴαις). Both words Past°. and °LXX. Both in Class. More literally, *smiters* of fathers and mothers, though used in Class. of parricides and matricides. Derived from ἀλοᾶν *to smite* or *thresh*. The simple verb, 1 Cor. ix. 9, 10.

Manslayers (ἀνδροφόνοις). N. T.°. Once in LXX, 2 Macc. ix. 28.

10. **Them that defile themselves with mankind** (ἀρσενο-κοίταις). Only here and 1 Cor. vi. 9. °LXX, °Class.

Menstealers (ἀνδραποδισταῖς). N. T.°. °LXX. Ellicott remarks that this is a repulsive and exaggerated violation of the eighth commandment, as ἀρσενοκοιτεῖν is of the seventh. The penalty of death is attached to it, Ex. xxi. 16.

Perjured persons (ἐπιόρκοις). N. T.°. Once in LXX, Zech. v. 3. See Lev. xix. 12.

Is contrary to (ἀντίκειται). Lit. *lies opposite to.* Used by Paul and Luke. See L. xiii. 17; Gal. v. 17.

The sound doctrine (τῇ ὑγιαινούσῃ διδασκαλίᾳ). A phrase peculiar to the Pastorals. Ὑγιαίνειν *to be in good health*, L. v. 31; vii. 10; 3 J. 2. °P. Quite frequent in LXX, and invariably in the literal sense. Often in salutations or dismissals. See 2 Macc. i. 10; ix. 19; 2 Sam. xiv. 8; Ex. iv. 18. In the Pastorals, the verb, which occurs eight times, is six

times associated with διδασκαλία *teaching*, or λόγοι *words*, and
twice with ἐν τῇ πίστει or τῇ πίστει *in the faith*. The sound
teaching (comp. διδαχή *teaching*, 2 Tim. iv. 2; Tit. i. 9)
which is thus commended is Paul's, who teaches in Christ's
name and by his authority (2 Tim. i. 13; ii. 2, 8). In all
the three letters it is called ἀλήθεια or ἡ ἀλήθεια *the truth*, the
knowledge (ἐπίγνωσις) of which is bound up with salvation.
See 1 Tim. ii. 4; 2 Tim. ii. 25; iii. 7; Tit. i. 1. As truth
it is *sound* or *healthful*. It is the object of *faith*. To be
sound in the faith is, practically, to *follow* (παρακολουθεῖν)
sound teaching or the truth. The subjective characteristic
of Christians is εὐσέβεια or θεοσέβεια *godliness* or *piety* (1 Tim.
ii. 2, 10; iii. 16; iv. 7, 8; vi. 6, 11); and the teaching and
knowledge of the truth are represented as κατ᾽ εὐσέβειαν *according to godliness* (1 Tim. vi. 3; Tit. i. 1). Comp. εὐσεβεῖν *to show piety*, 1 Tim. v. 4; εὐσεβῶς ζῆν *to live godly*, 2
Tim. iii. 12; Tit. ii. 12; and βίον διάγειν ἐν πάσῃ εὐσεβείᾳ *to
lead a life in all godliness*, 1 Tim. ii. 2. The contents of this
sound teaching which is according to godliness are not theo-
retical or dogmatic truth, but Christian ethics, with faith and
love. See 1 Tim. i. 14; ii. 15; iv. 12; vi. 11; 2 Tim. i. 13;
iii. 10; Tit. ii. 2. ᾽Αλήθεια *truth* is used of moral things,
rather than in the high religious sense of Paul. Comp., for
instance, Rom. iii. 7; ix. 1; 1 Cor. v. 8; 2 Cor. iv. 2; xi. 10;
Gal. ii. 5; Eph. iv. 21, 24; and 2 Tim. ii. 25, 26; iii. 7 (comp.
vv. 1–9); iv. 3, 4; Tit. i. 12 (comp. vv. 11, 15); Tit. ii. 4
(comp. vv. 1, 3); Tit. iii. 1. Whoever grasps the truth has
faith (2 Tim. i. 13; ii. 18; iii. 8; Tit. i. 3 f.). That the
ethical character of faith is emphasised, appears from the
numerous expressions regarding the false teachers, as 1 Tim.
i. 19; iv. 1; v. 8, 12; vi. 10, 21. There is a tendency to
objectify faith, regarding it as something believed rather than
as the act of believing. See 1 Tim. i. 19; iv. 1; vi. 10, 21;
Tit. i. 4. In comparing the ideal of righteousness (ver. 9)
with that of Paul, note that it is not denied that Christ is the
source of true righteousness; but according to Paul, the man
who is not under the law is the man who lives by faith in
Christ. Paul emphasises this. It is faith in Christ which

sets one free from the law.   Here, the man for whom the law
is not made (ver. 9) is the man who is ethically conformed to
the norm of sound teaching.   The two conceptions do not
exclude each other : the sound teaching is according to the
gospel (ver. 11), but the point of emphasis is shifted.

11. According to. The connection is with the whole foregoing statement about the law and its application, ver. 9 ff.
The writer substantiates what he has just said about the law,
by a reference to the gospel.   Comp. Rom. ii. 16.

The glorious gospel of the blessed God (τὸ εὐαγγέλιον
τῆς δόξης τοῦ μακαρίου θεοῦ).   More correctly, *the gospel of the
glory*, etc.   The phrase as a whole has no parallel in N. T.
The nearest approach to it is 2 Cor. iv. 4.   *Gospel of God* is
a Pauline phrase ; but μακάριος *blessed* is not used of God by
Paul, nor elsewhere outside of the Pastorals, where it occurs
twice, here and ch. vi. 15.   For *blessed* see on Matt. v. 3.
The appearing of the glory of God in Jesus Christ is the
contents of the gospel.   Comp. Tit. ii. 13.

Which was committed to my trust (ὃ ἐπιστεύθην ἐγώ).
Or, *with which I was intrusted*.   Comp. Tit. i. 3 ; Rom. iii.
2 ; 1 Cor. ix. 17 ; Gal. ii. 7 ; 1 Th. ii. 4.   The ἐγώ *I* emphatically asserts the authority of Paul against the " teachers
of the law " (ver. 7).

12. Hath enabled (ἐνδυναμώσαντι).   An unclassical word,
found in Paul and Acts.   See Acts ix. 22 ; Philip. iv. 13.
Three times in the Pastorals.

Counted (ἡγήσατο).   A common Pauline word.

Putting (θέμενος).   Better, *appointing*.   The participle
defines *counted me faithful*.   He counted me faithful *in that*
he appointed, etc.

Into the ministry (εἰς διακονίαν).   Better, appointing me *to
his service*.   The conventional phrase " the ministry " gives a

wrong impression. The term is general, covering every mode
of service, either to God or to men. Διάκονοι *ministers* is used
of the secular ruler, Rom. xiii. 4. See also 1 Cor. xii. 5 ; xvi.
15 ; 2 Cor. iii. 7, 8 ; Eph. iv. 12, and on *minister*, Matt. xx. 26.

13. **Blasphemer — persecutor — injurious** (βλάσφημον —
διώκτην—ὑβριστήν). Neither βλάσφημος nor διώκτης is used
by Paul. Βλάσφημος in Acts vii. 11 ; 2 Pet. ii. 11 ; διώκτης
N. T.°.; ὑβριστής in Rom. i. 30 only ; often in LXX. See
on *blasphemy*, Mk. vii. 22, and comp. 1 Cor. x. 30. Ὑβριστής
is one whose insolence and contempt of others break forth in
wanton and outrageous acts. Paul was ὑβριστής when he
persecuted the church. He was ὑβρισθείς *shamefully entreated*
at Philippi (1 Th. ii. 2). Christ prophesies that the Son of
man shall be *shamefully entreated* (ὑβρισθήσεται, L. xviii. 32).
Similar regretful references of Paul to his former career appear in Acts xxii. 4 ; Gal. i. 13, 23. Such a passage may
have occurred in some Pauline letters to which this writer
had access, or it may be an imitation.

I obtained mercy (ἠλεήθην). Comp. ver. 16. In speaking
of his conversion, Paul uses χάρις *grace*. See ver. 14, and
comp. 1 Cor. xv. 10 ; Gal. i. 15. In referring to his call to
the apostleship he speaks of himself as one who has obtained
mercy (ἠλεημένος) of the Lord to be *faithful*. 1 Cor. vii. 25 ;
comp. 2 Cor. iv. 1.

14. **Was exceeding abundant** (ὑπερεπλεόνασεν). Or
abounded exceedingly. N. T.°. °LXX. °Class. Paul is
fond of compounds with ὑπέρ, which, with a few exceptions, are found only in his writings. In the Pastorals
there are only three. See 1 Tim. ii. 2 ; 2 Tim. iii. 2.

With faith. For faith as treated in the Pastorals, see
Introduction, and *sound doctrine*, ver. 10.

15. **This is a faithful saying** (πιστὸς ὁ λόγος). Better,
faithful is the saying. A favourite phrase in these Epistles.
°P. See 1 Tim. iii. 1 ; iv. 9 ; 2 Tim. ii. 11 ; Tit. iii. 8.

Worthy of all acceptation (πάσης ἀποδοχῆς ἄξιος). The phrase only here and ch. iv. 9. Ἀποδοχή Past⁰. ⁰LXX. Comp. Acts ii. 41, ἀποδεξάμενοι τὸν λόγον *received* his word. Πάσης *all* or *every* describes the reception of which the saying is worthy as complete and excluding all doubt.

Came into the world (ἦλθεν εἰς τὸν κόσμον). The phrase is unique in the Pastorals, and does not appear in Paul. It is Johannine. See J. i. 9; iii. 19; xi. 27; xii. 46.

To save sinners (ἁμαρτωλοὺς σῶσαι). The thought is Pauline, but not the phrase. See L. ix. 56; xix. 10.

Chief (πρῶτος). Or *foremost*. Comp. 1 Cor. xv. 9, and Eph. iii. 8. This expression is an advance on those.

16. First (πρώτῳ). Not the chief sinner, but the representative instance of God's longsuffering applied to a high-handed transgressor. It is explained by *pattern*.

All longsuffering (τὴν ἅπασαν μακροθυμίαν). More correctly, "all *his* longsuffering." The A. V. misses the possessive force of the article. For *longsuffering* see on *be patient*, Jas. v. 7. The form ἅπας occurs as an undisputed reading only once in Paul, Eph. vi. 13, and not there as an adjective. Often in Acts and Luke. This use of the article with the adjective πᾶς or ἅπας is without parallel in Paul.

Pattern (ὑποτύπωσιν). Or, *ensample*. Only here and 2 Tim. i. 13. ⁰LXX. ⁰Class. An example of the writer's fondness for high-sounding compounds. Paul uses τύπος.

To them. The A. V. conveys the sense more clearly than Rev. "*of* them," which is ambiguous. The genitive has a possessive sense. He would be their ensample, or an ensample for their benefit.

Believe (πιστεύειν). This verb, so frequent in Paul, occurs six times in the Pastorals. In two instances, 1 Tim. i. 11;

Tit. i. 3, it is passive, in the sense of *to be intrusted with*. Here in the Pauline sense of *believing on Christ*. In 1 Tim. iii. 16, passive, of Christ *believed on in the world*. In 2 Tim. i. 12, of God the Father, in whom the writer confides to keep the trust committed to him. In Tit. iii. 8, of belief in God. With ἐπὶ *upon* and the dative, Rom. ix. 33 ; x. 11 ; 1 Pet. ii. 6 (all citations), and Rom. iv. 18 ; L. xxiv. 25.

Unto life everlasting (εἰς ζωὴν αἰώνιον). Better, *eternal life*. See additional note on 2 Th. i. 9. The conception of life eternal is not limited to the future life (as von Soden). Godliness has promise of the life which *now is*, as well as of that which is to come (1 Tim. iv. 8). The promise of eternal life (2 Tim. i. 1) and the words *who brought life and immortality to light through the gospel* (2 Tim. i. 10) may fairly be taken to cover the present life.

17. King eternal (βασιλεῖ τῶν αἰώνων). Lit. *the king of the ages*. Only here and Apoc. xv. 3. Comp. Heb. i. 2 ; xi. 3. In LXX, Tob. vi. 10. For kindred expressions in LXX, see Ex. xv. 18 ; 1 Sam. xiii. 13 ; Ps. ix. 7 ; xxviii. 10 ; lxxiii. 12 ; cxliv. 13 ; cxlv. 10. See also additional note on 2 Th. i. 9.

Immortal (ἀφθάρτῳ). Lit. *incorruptible*. In Paul, applied to God only, Rom. i. 23.

Invisible (ἀοράτῳ). Applied to God, Col. i. 15 ; Heb. xi. 27.

The only wise God (μόνῳ θεῷ). *Wise* should be omitted. Rend. *the only God*. Σοφῷ *wise* was interpolated from Rom. xvi. 27 — the only instance in which Paul applies the term to God. Comp. Jude 4, 25 ; L. v. 21 ; J. v. 44.

Honor and glory (τιμὴ καὶ δόξα). This combination in doxology only here and Apoc. v. 12, 13. Comp. Apoc. iv. 9. In doxologies Paul uses only δόξα *glory*, with the article, *the glory*, and with *to whom* or *to him* (be).

Forever and ever (εἰς τοὺς αἰῶνας τῶν αἰώνων). Lit. *unto the aeons of the aeons.* The formula in Paul, Rom. xvi. 27; Gal. i. 5; Philip. iv. 20. Also in Hebrews and 1st Peter, and often in Apoc. The doxology as a whole is unique in N. T.

18. **This charge** (ταύτην τὴν παραγγελίαν). See on ver. 5. It refers to what follows, *that thou might'st war*, etc.

I commit (παρατίθεμαι). The verb in the active voice means *to place beside.* In the middle, *to deposit* or *intrust.* Only once in Paul, 1 Cor. x. 27. Comp. 1 Pet. iv. 19.

According to the prophecies which went before on thee (κατὰ τὰς προαγούσας ἐπὶ σὲ προφητείας). Const. *according to* with *I commit: which went before* is to be taken absolutely, and not with *on thee:* const. *prophecies* with *on thee. On thee* means *concerning thee.* The sense of the whole passage is: "I commit this charge unto thee in accordance with prophetic intimations which I formerly received concerning thee." Prophecy is ranked among the foremost of the special spiritual endowments enumerated by Paul. See Rom. xii. 6; 1 Cor. xii. 10; xiii. 2, 8; xiv. 6, 22. In 1 Cor. xii. 28; Eph. iv. 11, prophets come next after apostles in the list of those whom God has appointed in the church. In Eph. ii. 20, believers, Jew and Gentile, are built upon the foundation of the apostles and prophets. According to 1 Tim. iv. 14, *prophecy* has previously designated Timothy as the recipient of a special spiritual gift; and *the prophecies* in our passage are the single expressions or detailed contents of the prophecy mentioned there. Προαγεῖν *to go before* is not used by Paul. In the Pastorals and Hebrews it appears only as an intransitive verb, and so in the only instance in Luke, xviii. 39. In Acts always transitive, *to bring forth.* See Acts xii. 6; xvi. 30; xvii. 5; xxv. 26.

That by them (ἵνα ἐν αὐταῖς). Ἵνα *that* denoting the purport of the charge. *By* them (ἐν), lit. *in* them; in their sphere, or, possibly, in the power of these.

Thou mightest war a good warfare (στρατεύῃ — τὴν καλὴν στρατείαν). More correctly, *the* good warfare. Στρατεία *war-fare* once by Paul, 2 Cor. x. 4. Not *fight* (μάχην), but covering all the particulars of a soldier's service.

19. **Holding** (ἔχων). Not merely *having*, but *holding fast*, as in 2 Tim. i. 13.

Faith and a good conscience (πίστιν καὶ ἀγαθὴν συνεί-δησιν). The phrase *good conscience* is not in Paul, although συνείδησις is a Pauline word. The phrase appears once in Acts (xxiii. 1), and twice in 1 Pet. (iii. 16, 21). In Hebrews *evil* (πονηρᾶς) conscience and *fair* (καλὴν) conscience; x. 22; xiii. 18. The combination *faith and good conscience* is peculiar to the Pastorals. Comp. 1 Tim. iii. 9.

Which (ἥν). Referring to good conscience.

Having put away (ἀπωσάμενοι). The A. V. is not strong enough. Better, *having thrust from them*. It implies wilful violence against conscience. Twice in Paul, Rom. xi. 1, 2, and three times in Acts.

Concerning faith have made shipwreck (περὶ τὴν πίστιν ἐναυάγησαν). Better, "concerning *the* faith *made* shipwreck." For a similar use of περὶ *concerning*, see Acts xix. 25 ; L. x. 40 ; 1 Tim. vi. 21 ; 2 Tim. ii. 18 ; iii. 8. It is noteworthy that περὶ with the accusative occurs only once in Paul (Philip. ii. 23). Ναυαγεῖν *to make shipwreck* only here and 2 Cor. xi. 25. Nautical metaphors are rare in Paul's writings.

20. **Hymenaeus and Alexander.** Comp. 2 Tim. ii. 17 ; iv. 14.

I have delivered unto Satan (παρέδωκα τῷ Σατανᾷ). See on 1 Cor. v. 5.

They may learn (παιδευθῶσι). Neither A. V. nor Rev. gives the true force of the word, which is, *may be taught by punishment* or *disciplined*. See on Eph. vi. 4.

CHAPTER II.

1. I exhort (παρακαλῶ). See on *consolation*, L. vi. 24.

First of all (πρῶτον πάντων). Connect with *I exhort*.
The only instance of this phrase in N. T.

Supplications be made (ποιεῖσθαι δεήσεις). The phrase
occurs L. v. 33; Philip. i. 4. °LXX. °Class. Δέησις is
petitionary prayer. Προσευχὴ *prayer* is limited to prayer
to God, while δέησις may be addressed to men. The two
are associated, 1 Tim. v. 5: the inverse order, Eph. vi. 18;
Philip. iv. 6.

Intercessions (ἐντεύξεις). Only here and ch. iv. 5. LXX,
2 Macc. iv. 8. The verb ἐντυγχάνειν, commonly rendered *to
make intercession*, Rom. viii. 27, 34; xi. 2; and ὑπερεντυγχάνειν
to intercede in behalf of, Rom. viii. 26. The verb signifies *to
fall in with a person; to draw near so as to converse familiarly.*
Hence, ἔντευξις is not properly *intercession* in the accepted
sense of that term, but rather approach to God in free and
familiar prayer. Ἐντυγχάνειν in the passages cited is not *to
make intercession*, but to *intervene, interfere*. Thus in Rom.
viii. 26, it is not that the Spirit pleads in our behalf, but that
he throws himself into our case; takes part in it. So Heb.
vii. 25: not that Jesus is ever interceding for us, but that he
is eternally meeting us at every point, and intervening in
all our affairs for our benefit. In ἐντεύξεις here the idea of
interposition is prominent: making prayers a factor in relations with secular rulers.

2. Kings (βασιλέων). In Paul only 2 Cor. xi. 32.

That are in authority (τῶν ἐν ὑπεροχῇ ὄντων). Ὑπεροχή
authority only here and 1 Cor. ii. 1. Several times in LXX.
Originally, *projection, prominence*: metaphorically, *preëminence, superiority*. In Byzantine Greek, a little like our *Excel-*

lency. This very phrase is found in an inscription of the early Roman period, after 133 B.C., at Pergamum. Paul has the phrase ἐξουσίαι ὑπερεχούσαι *higher powers*, Rom. xiii. 1 ; and οἱ ὑπερέχοντες *those in high places* is found Wisd. vi. 5.

We may lead (διάγωμεν). Past⁰. Comp. Tit. iii. 3.

Quiet and peaceable (ἤρεμον καὶ ἡσύχιον). Ἤρεμος, N. T.⁰. In Class. only the adverb ἠρέμα *quietly*. Ἡσύχιος *tranquil*, ⁰P. Only here and 1 Pet. iii. 4. In LXX once, Isa. lxvi. 2. Ἤρεμος denotes quiet arising from the absence of outward disturbance : ἡσύχιος tranquillity arising from within. Thus, ἀνήρ ἡσύχιος is the composed, discreet, self-contained man, who keeps himself from rash doing : ἤρεμος ἀνήρ is he who is withdrawn from outward disturbances. Hence, ἤρεμος here may imply keeping aloof from political agitations and freedom from persecutions.

Honesty (σεμνότητι). Better, *gravity*. *Honesty*, according to the modern acceptation, is an unfortunate rendering. In earlier English it signified *becoming deportment, decency, decorum*. So Shakespeare : " He is of a noble strain, of approved valour and confirmed honesty" (*Much Ado*, ii. 1). This noun and the kindred adjective σεμνὸς only in the Pastorals, except Philip. iv. 8. The adjective signifies *reverend* or *venerable ;* exhibiting a dignity which arises from moral elevation, and thus invites reverence. In LXX it is used to characterise the name of God (2 Macc. viii. 15) ; the Sabbath (2 Macc. vi. 11) ; the divine laws (2 Macc. vi. 28) ; the words of wisdom (Prov. viii. 6) ; the words of the pure (Prov. xv. 26).

Godliness (εὐσεβείᾳ). See on 1 Pet. i. 3, and *sound doctrine*, 1 Tim. i. 10. ⁰P. Mostly in the Pastorals.

3. **Acceptable** (ἀπόδεκτον). Past⁰. Compare ἀποδοχή *acceptation*, ch. i. 15, and Paul's εὐπρόσδεκτος *acceptable*, Rom. xv. 16, 31 ; 2 Cor. vi. 2 ; vii. 12.

4. **Who will have all men to be saved** (ὃς πάντας ἀνθρώπους θέλει σωθῆναι). Lit. *who willeth all men*, etc. Ὅς *who,
or seeing that he*, giving the ground of the previous statement.
Prayer to God *for all* is acceptable to him, because he wills
the salvation of all. Θέλει *willeth*, marking a determinate
purpose.

Come to the knowledge of the truth (εἰς ἐπίγνωσιν
ἀληθείας ἐλθεῖν). The phrase only here and 2 Tim. iii. 7.
Ἐπίγνωσις is a favorite Pauline word. See on Rom. iii. 20;
Col. i. 9; 1 Tim. ii. 4; iv. 3. It signifies *advanced* or *full*
knowledge. The difference between the simple γνῶσις and
the compound word is illustrated in Rom. i. 21, 28, and 1 Cor.
xiii. 12. In N. T. always of the knowledge of things ethical
or divine, and never ascribed to God. For ἀλήθεια *truth*,
see on *sound doctrine*, ch. i. 10. It appears 14 times in the
Pastorals, and always without a defining genitive. So, often
in Paul, but several times with a defining genitive, as truth
of God, of Christ, of the gospel. The logical relation in the
writer's mind between salvation and the knowledge of the
truth is not quite clear. Knowledge of the truth may be
regarded as the means of salvation, or it may be the ideal
goal of the whole saving work. See 1 Cor. xiii. 12; Philip.
iii. 8; J. xvii. 3. The latter is more in accord with the
general drift of teaching in these Epistles.

5. **For** (γὰρ). The universality of the grace is grounded
in the unity of God. Comp. Rom. iii. 30. One divine purpose for all implies one God who purposes.

One God. These Epistles deal much with the divine attributes. See 1 Tim: i. 17; vi. 13, 15, 16; iii. 15; iv. 10;
2 Tim. ii. 13; Tit. i. 2.

Mediator (μεσίτης). See on Gal. iii. 19. The word twice
in Paul, Gal. iii. 19, 20, once of Moses and once generally.
In Hebrews always of Christ; viii. 6; ix. 15; xii. 24. This
is the only instance in the Pastorals. As the one God, so

the one mediator implies the extension of the saving pur·
pose to all.

The man Christ Jesus. The phrase only here.

6. **Who gave himself** (ὁ δοὺς ἑαυτὸν). The phrase with
the simple verb only here, Gal. i. 4, and Tit. ii. 14. Paul
uses the compound verb παραδιδόναι, Gal. ii. 20 ; Eph. v. 2,
25. Comp. Rom. viii. 32.

Ransom (ἀντίλυτρον). N. T.°. °LXX. °Class. Λύτρον
ransom, Matt. xx. 28; Mk. x. 45, applied to Christ's life
given for many. But neither this nor any of its kindred
words is used by Paul. He uses ἀπολύτρωσις, but that
means the *act* not the *means* of redemption.

For all (ὑπὲρ). Ὑπὲρ does not mean *instead of* (ἀντὶ).
See on Rom. v. 6. Any idea of exchange or substitution
which may be implied, resides in ἀντίλυτρον; but it is press-
ing that unique word too far to find in it the announcement
of a substitutional atonement.*

To be testified in due time (τὸ μαρτύριον καιροῖς ἰδίοις).
Lit. (gave himself a ransom) *the testimony in its own times*.
That is, the gift of Christ as a ransom was to be the substance or import of the testimony which was to be set forth
in its proper seasons. Thus μαρτύριον *testimony* is in apposition with the whole preceding sentence, and not with *ransom* only. Μαρτύριον is used sometimes simply as *witness* or
testimony (Matt. viii. 4 ; Mk. vi. 11) : sometimes specially
of the proclamation of the gospel, as Matt. xxiv. 14 ; Acts
iv. 33 ; 1 Th. i. 10. The apostles are said μαρτυρεῖν *to bear
witness*, as eye or ear witnesses of the sayings, deeds, and
sufferings of Jesus (1 Cor. xv. 15). In 1 Cor. i. 6, μαρτύριον
τοῦ Χριστοῦ is practically = the gospel. In 2 Th. i. 10, τὸ
μαρτύριον ἡμῶν ἐφ᾽ ὑμᾶς *our testimony among you* is our public
attestation of the truth of the gospel. The idea of witness

---

* See Ellicott.

is a favorite one with John. See J. i. 7. The exact phrase
καιροῖς ἰδίοις *in its own times*, only in the Pastorals, here,
ch. vi. 15; Tit. i. 3. In Gal. vi. 9 καιρῷ ἰδίῳ *in due time*.
Comp. Gal. iv. 4.

7. I am ordained (ἐτέθην ἐγὼ). Better, *I was appointed*.
See on J. xv. 16.

A preacher (κῆρυξ). Lit. *a herald*. See on 2 Pet. ii. 5.
Paul does not use the noun, but the kindred verb κηρύσσειν
to proclaim or *preach* is very common in his writings. See
Rom. x. 8; 1 Cor. i. 23; 2 Cor. iv. 5; Philip. i. 15, etc.

I speak the truth in Christ and lie not. Omit *in Christ*.
A strange asseveration to an intimate and trusted friend.
Apparently an imitation of Rom. ix. 1.

A teacher of the Gentiles (διδάσκαλος ἐθνῶν). Paul does
not use this phrase. He expressly distinguishes between
teacher and *apostle*. See 1 Cor. xii. 28; Eph. iv. 11. He
calls himself ἐθνῶν ἀπόστολος *apostle of the Gentiles* (Rom.
xi. 13); λειτουργὸς Χριστοῦ Ἰησοῦ εἰς τὰ ἔθνη *minister of Christ
Jesus to the Gentiles* (Rom. xv. 16); and δέσμιος τοῦ Χριστοῦ
Ἰησοῦ ὑπὲρ ὑμῶν τῶν ἐθνῶν *prisoner of Jesus Christ for you
Gentiles* (Eph. iii. 1).

In faith and verity (ἐν πίστει καὶ ἀληθείᾳ). Or faith and
truth. The combination only here. Paul has *sincerity and
truth* (1 Cor. v. 8), and *sanctification of the Spirit and faith
of the truth* (2 Th. ii. 13). The phrase must not be explained *in true faith*, nor *faithfully and truly*. It means that
faith and truth are the element or sphere in which the apostolic function is discharged: that he preaches with a sincere
faith in the gospel, and with a truthful representation of the
gospel which he believes.

8. I will (βούλομαι). Better, *I desire*. See on Matt. i.
9, and comp. Philip. i. 12. Paul's word is θέλω *I will*. See
Rom. xvi. 19; 1 Cor. vii. 32; x. 20; xiv. 5, 19, etc.

Everywhere (ἐν παντὶ τόπῳ). Lit. *in every place*. Wherever Christian congregations assemble. Not every place indiscriminately.

Lifting up holy hands (ἐπαίροντας ὁσίους χεῖρας). The phrase is unique in N. T. °LXX. Among Orientals the lifting up of the hands accompanied taking an oath, blessing, and prayer. The custom passed over into the primitive church, as may be seen from the mural paintings in the catacombs. See Clement, *Ad Corinth.* xxix, which may possibly be a reminiscence of this passage. The verb ἐπαίρειν *to raise*, twice in Paul, 2 Cor. x. 5; xi. 20; but often in Luke. Ὁσίους *holy*, °P. See on L. i. 75.

Without wrath and doubting (χωρὶς ὀργῆς καὶ διαλογισμῶν). The combination only here. Ὀργὴ is used by Paul mostly of the righteous anger and the accompanying judgment of God against sin. As here, only in Eph. iv. 31; Col. iii. 8. Διαλογισμός in N. T. habitually in the plural, as here. The only exception is L. ix. 46, 47. By Paul usually in the sense of *disputatious reasoning*. It may also mean *sceptical questionings* or *criticisms*, as Philip. ii. 14. So probably here. Prayer, according to our writer, is to be without the element of sceptical criticism, whether of God's character and dealings, or of the character and behaviour of those for whom prayer is offered.

9. **In like manner** (ὡσαύτως). The writer's thought is still running upon the public assemblies for worship.

Adorn themselves (κοσμεῖν ἑαυτάς). Κοσμεῖν *adorn*, °P. Of female adornment, 1 Pet. iii. 5; Apoc. xxi. 2. In Matt. xxv. 7, of *trimming* the lamps. From κόσμος *order*, so that the primary meaning is *to arrange*. Often in LXX and Class. Prominent in the writer's mind is the attire of women in church assemblies. Paul treats this subject 1 Cor. xi. 5 ff.

In modest apparel (ἐν καταστολῇ κοσμίῳ). Καταστολή N. T.°. Once in LXX, Isa. lxi. 3. Opinions differ as to

the meaning. Some *apparel*, others *guise* or *deportment* =
κατάστημα *demeanour*, Tit. ii. 3. There seems, on the whole,
to be no sufficient reason for departing from the rendering
of A.V. and Rev.* Κοσμίῳ *modest, seemly*, Past⁰. Note the
word-play, κοσμεῖν κοσμίῳ.

With shamefacedness and sobriety (*μετὰ αἰδοῦς καὶ
σωφροσύνης*). 'Αιδώς, N. T.⁰. (*αἰδοῦς* in Heb. xii. 28 is an
incorrect reading). In earlier Greek, as in Homer, it sometimes blends with the sense of αἰσχύνη *shame*, though used
also of the feeling of respectful timidity in the presence of
superiors, or of penitent respect toward one who has been
wronged (see Homer, *Il.* i. 23). Hence it is connected in
Homer with military discipline (*Il.* v. 531). It is the feeling of a suppliant or an unfortunate in the presence of those

---

* It is difficult to determine the meaning decisively. The kindred verb
καταστέλλειν means (*a*) *to put in order* or *arrange*. Στέλλειν is *to put* or *place*,
and κατὰ probably has its distributive sense, denoting succession, relation, or
proportion of parts. (*b*) *To let down* or *lower*, κατὰ having its primary sense
of *down*. (*c*) Metaphorical, derived from the preceding, *to check* or *repress*.
Thus Acts xix. 25, 36. See also 2 Macc. iv. 31 ; 3 Macc. vi. 1. Hence ὁ κατεσ-
ταλμένος *the man of calm* or *sedate character* (Diod. i. 76 ; Arrian, *Epict.* iii.
23, 16). From these data two possible meanings are drawn : (1) *dress,
attire*. So Hesychius (περιβολή *garment*) and Suidas (στολή *raiment*). It is
used in Isa. lxi. 3 as the translation of מעטה *covering, wrapping*. The root
ath, in every case, points to *veiling*. Plutarch (*Pericles*, 5) has καταστολή
περιβολῆς *arrangement of dress ;* and Josephus, *B. J.* ii. 8, 4, καταστολή καὶ
σχῆμα σώματος *disposition and equipment of body*, which phrase is explained
by the following reference to details of dress. It must be admitted, however, that, with the exception of Isa. lxi. 3, there is no instance of the absolute use of καταστολή in the sense of *dress*. The meaning in Plutarch is
clearly *arrangement*, and in Josephus, σχῆμα may be rendered *dress*, while
καταστολή probably means the general arrangement of the person. It is
quite possible that from the use of καταστολή in these connections, it may
have come to mean *dress* by itself. A possible analogy is suggested by the
English *attire*, from the old French *atirier* or *atirer, to arrange, equip, deck,
dress*, cognate with Provençal *atierar* (*à tire*), *to bring into row* or *order*.
The sense of adjusting or regulating runs into that of adorning. The context
here, which refers to details of apparel, the fact that both Paul and Peter
specifically deal with the subject of female attire, the clear usage in Isaiah,
the association of καταστολή with dress, and the definitions of the old lexi-
cographers, all seem to point to the meaning *apparel*. So Holtzmann,
Huther, and Weiss.

from whom he seeks aid; of a younger man toward an older and wiser one. It is a feeling based upon the sense of deficiency, inferiority, or unworthiness. On the other hand, it is the feeling of a superior in position or fortune which goes out to an unfortunate. See Homer, *Il.* xxiv. 208; *Od.* xiv. 388; Soph. *Oed. Col.* 247. In the Attic period, a distinction was recognised between αἰσχύνη and αἰδώς : αἰδώς representing a respectful and reverent attitude toward another, while αἰσχύνη was the sense of shame on account of wrongdoing. Thus, "one αἰδεῖται *is respectful* to his father, but αἰσχύνεται *is ashamed* because he has been drunk." * Trench (*N. T. Synon.* § xix.) remarks that "αἰδώς is the nobler word and implies the nobler motive. In it is involved an innate moral repugnance to the doing of the dishonorable act, which moral repugnance scarcely or not at all exists in the αἰσχύνη. Let the man who is restrained by αἰσχύνη alone be insured against the outward disgrace which he fears his act will entail, and he will refrain from it no longer." † The A.V. *shamefacedness* is a corruption of the old English *shamefastness.* So Chaucer:

> "Schamefast chastite."
>
> *Knight's T.* 2057.

Shakespeare:

> "'Tis a blushing shamefast spirit that mutinies in a man's bosom."
>
> *Richard III.* i. 4.

It is one of a large class of words, as steadfast, soothfast, rootfast, masterfast, handfast, bedfast, etc. *Shamefaced* changes and destroys the original force of the word, which was *bound* or *made fast* by an honourable shame. Σωφροσύνη *sobriety*, ᴼP. Once in Acts, xxvi. 25. The kindred verb σωφρονεῖν *to be of sound mind*, Rom. xii. 3; 2 Cor. v. 13;

---

* Ammonius the Grammarian, fourth century. He wrote a work *On the Differences of Words of Like Signification*, which was appended to many of the older lexicons.

† The different uses of αἰδώς in Homer are discussed in a very interesting way in Gladstone's *Homer and the Homeric Age*, Vol. II., p. 431 ff. The best discussion of the word is by Schmidt, *Synonymik der griechischen Sprache*, Vol. III., § 140.

Tit. ii. 6.   Several representatives of this family of words
appear in the Pastorals, and with the exception of σωφροσύνη and σωφρονεῖν, nowhere else in N. T.   Such are σωφρον-
ίζειν *to be soberminded* (Tit. ii. 4); σωφρονισμός *discipline*
(2 Tim. i. 7); σωφρόνως *soberly* (Tit. ii. 12); σώφρων *sober-
minded* (1 Tim. iii. 2).   The word is compounded of σάος
or σῶς *safe, sound,* and φρήν *mind.*   It signifies entire command of the passions and desires; a self-control which holds
the rein over these.   So Aristotle (*Rhet.* i. 9): "The virtue
by which we hold ourselves toward the pleasures of the body
as the law enjoins."   Comp. 4 Macc. i. 31.   Euripides calls
it "the fairest gift of the gods" (*Med.* 632).   That it appears so rarely in N. T. is, as Trench remarks, "not because
more value was attached to it in heathen ethics than in
Christian morality, but because it is taken up and trans-
formed into a condition yet higher still, in which a man does
not command himself, which is well, but, which is better
still, is commanded by God."   The words *with shamefastness
and sobriety* may either be taken directly with *adorn themselves,* or better perhaps, as indicating moral qualities *accompanying* (μετὰ *with*) the modest apparel.   Let them adorn
themselves in modest apparel, having *along with this* shamefastness and sobermindedness.

With broidered hair (ἐν πλέγμασιν).   Lit. *with plaitings.*
N. T.°.   Rend. with *braided* hair.   *Broidered* is a blunder
owing to a confusion with *broided,* the older form of *braided.*
So Chaucer:

> " Hir yelow heer was broyded in a tresse,
> Bihinde hir bak, a yerde long, I gesse."
>
> *Knight's T.* 1049 f.

Costly array (ἱματισμῷ πολυτελεῖ).   Neither word in Paul.
Ἱματισμός signifies *clothing in general.*   Πολυτελής *costly*
occurs only three times in N. T.

10.   **Professing** (ἐπαγγελλομέναις).   In the sense of *professing* only in the Pastorals.   In Tit. i. 2, and everywhere
else in N. T. it means *promise.*   See Acts vii. 5; Rom. iv. 21:
Gal. iii. 19, etc.

Godliness (θεοσεβείαν). N. T.°. Several times in LXX. The adjective θεοσεβής *worshipping God*, J. ix. 31. It is = εὐσέβεια. See ver. 2. Const. *by good works* with *professing godliness*: omit the parenthesis *which — godliness;* take *which* (ὅ) as = *with that which* (ἐν τούτῳ ὅ) and construe it with *adorn.* The whole will then read: "That women adorn themselves in modest apparel, with shamefastness and sobriety; not with braided hair, or gold, or pearls, or costly array, but (adorn themselves) with that which becometh women professing godliness through good works." *

11. **Learn** (μανθανέτω). Comp. 1 Cor. xiv. 35.

In silence (ἐν ἡσυχίᾳ). See on *peaceable*, ver. 2. Rev. renders *quietness;* but the admonition concerns the behaviour of women in religious assemblies. Comp. 1 Cor. xiv. 34. The word is used in the sense of *silence*, Acts xxii. 2: with the broader meaning *quietness* in 2 Th. iii. 12.

12. **Suffer** (ἐπιτρέπω). Lit. *turn over to;* thence, *permit.* See 1 Cor. xiv. 34.

Usurp authority (αὐθεντεῖν). N. T.°. °LXX, °Class. It occurs in late ecclesiastical writers. The kindred noun αὐθέντης *one who does a thing with his own hand*, Wisd. xii. 6, and also in Herodotus, Euripides, and Thucydides. 'Αυθεντία *right*, 3 Macc. ii. 29. The verb means *to do a thing one's self;* hence, *to exercise authority.* The A. V. *usurp authority* is a mistake. Rend. *to have* or *exercise dominion over.*

13. **Was formed** (ἐπλάσθη). Comp. Rom. ix. 20. Strictly of one working in soft substances, as a potter in clay; *moulding* or *shaping.* Often in Class. and LXX.

---

* The other rendering proposed is to retain the parenthesis, and connect δι' ἔργων ἀγαθῶν *through good works* with κοσμεῖν *adorn.* Thus it will read: "*Adorn* themselves with good works." The objection to this is that κοσμεῖν is previously construed with ἐν (" *in* modest apparel, not *in* braided hair, gold, pearls, etc."), and we should therefore expect ἐν instead of δι' with *good works.* Further, it would be unsuitable to describe good works as an ornament when he is speaking of the demeanor of women in church assemblies.

14. **Was not deceived** (οὐκ ἠπατήθη). Once in Paul, Eph.
v. 6.   Comp. 2 Cor. xi. 3.   Rev. *beguiled*.   As it is evident
that Adam *was* beguiled, the interpreters have tried many
ways of explaining the expression, either by supplying πρῶτος
first, or by saying (as Bengel) that the woman did not *deceive*
the man, but *persuaded* him ; or by supplying *by the serpent*,
or *so long as he was alone;* or by saying that Eve was *directly*
and Adam *indirectly* deceived.

Being deceived (ἐξαπατηθεῖσα).   *Completely* or *thoroughly*
beguiled.

Was in the transgression (ἐν παραβάσει γέγονεν).   A. V.
misses the force of γέγονεν.   Γίνεσθαι ἐν often signifies the
coming or *falling into* a condition, as Acts xii. 11; xxii. 17;
Apoc. i. 10; 1 Cor. ii. 3; 2 Cor. iii. 7; 1 Th. ii. 5.   Rend.
hath fallen into transgression.

15. **She shall be saved in childbearing** (σωθήσεται διὰ τῆς
τεκνογονίας).   Better, "through *the* childbearing."   (1) *Saved*
is used in the ordinary N. T. sense.   (2) *She shall be saved* is
set over against *hath fallen into transgression*.   (3) It is difficult to see what is the peculiar saving virtue of childbearing.
(4) The subject of σωθήσεται *shall be saved* is the same as
that of ἐν παραβάσει γέγονεν *hath fallen into transgression*.   A
common explanation is that γυνή is to be taken in its generic
sense as referring to all Christian mothers, who will be saved
in fulfilling their proper destiny and acquiescing in all the
conditions of a Christian woman's life, instead of attempting
to take an active part as teachers or otherwise in public
religious assemblies.   On the other hand, *the woman*, Eve, may
be regarded as including all the Christian mothers.   Notice
the change to the plural, "if *they* continue."   She, though she
fell into transgression, shall be saved "by *the* childbearing"
(Gen. iii. 15); that is, by the relation in which the woman
stood to the Messiah.   This seems to be the better explanation.   Τεκνογονία *childbearing*, N. T.°.   °LXX, °Class.   Comp.
τεκνογονεῖν *to bear children*, 1 Tim. v. 14.   The expression is
utterly un-Pauline.

If they continue (ἐὰν μείνωσιν). *They*, the woman regarded collectively or as including her descendants. The promise does not exempt them from the cultivation of Christian virtues and the discharge of Christian duties.

Sanctification (ἁγιασμῷ). A Pauline word; but the triad, *faith, love, sanctification*, is unique in N. T.

CHAPTER III.

1. This is a true saying (πιστὸς ὁ λόγος). Better, *faithful is the saying.* See on ch. i. 15.

Desire (ὀρέγεται). Better, *seeketh.* Only here, ch. vi. 10, and Heb. xi. 16. Originally *to stretch forth, to reach after.* Here it implies not only desiring but seeking after. *Desire* is expressed by ἐπιθυμεῖ immediately following. The word implies eagerness, but not of an immoderate or unchristian character. Comp. the kindred word ὄρεξις with its terrible meaning in Rom. i. 27.

The office of a bishop (ἐπισκοπῆς). °P. Ἐπίσκοπος *superintendent, overseer*, by Paul only in Philip. i. 1. The fundamental idea of the word is *overseeing.* The term ἐπίσκοπος was not furnished by the gospel tradition : it did not come from the Jewish synagogue, and it does not appear in Paul's lists of those whom God has set in the church (1 Cor. xii. 28 ; Eph. iv. 11). Its adoption came about in a natural way. Just as *senatus*, γερουσία and πρεσβύτερος passed into official designations through the natural association of authority with age, so ἐπίσκοπος would be, almost inevitably, the designation of a superintendent. This process of natural selection was probably aided by the familiar use of the title in the clubs and guilds to designate functions analogous to those of the ecclesiastical administrator. The title can hardly be traced to the O. T. There are but two passages in LXX

where the word has any connection with religious worship,
Num. iv. 16; 2 K. xi. 18. It is applied to God (Job xx. 29),
and in N. T. to Christ (1 Pet. ii. 25). It is used of officers
in the army and of overseers of workmen. The prevailing
O. T. sense of ἐπισκοπή is *visitation* for punishment, inquisi-
tion, or numbering.*

He desireth (ἐπιθυμεῖ). See on 1 Pet. i. 12.

2. **Blameless** (ἀνεπίλημπτον). Or *without reproach:* one
who cannot be *laid hold of* (λαμβάνειν): who gives no ground
for accusation. °P. Only in 1st Timothy.

The husband of one wife (μιᾶς γυναικὸς ἄνδρα). Comp.
ver. 12; Tit. i. 6. Is the injunction aimed (*a*) at immor-
alities respecting marriage — concubinage, etc., or (*b*) at
polygamy, or (*c*) at remarriage after death or divorce? The
last is probably meant. Much of the difficulty arises from
the assumption that the Pastorals were written by Paul. In
that case his views seem to conflict. See Rom. vii. 2, 3;
1 Cor. vii. 39; viii. 8, 9, where Paul declares that widows are
free to marry again, and puts widows and virgins on the same
level; and comp. 1 Tim. v. 9, according to which a widow is
to be enrolled only on the condition of having been the wife
of but one man. The Pauline view is modified in detail by
the writer of the Pastorals. Paul, while asserting that
marriage is right and honourable, regards celibacy as the
higher state (1 Cor. vii. 1, 7, 26, 34, 37, 38). In this the
Pastoral writer does not follow him (see 1 Tim. ii. 15; iii. 4,
12; iv. 3; v. 10, 14). The motive for marriage, namely, protection against incontinency, which is adduced by Paul in
1 Cor. vii. 2, 9, is given in 1 Tim. v. 11-14. As in Paul,
the married state is honourable, for Bishops, Deacons, and
Presbyters are married (1 Tim. iii. 2, 12; Tit. i. 6), and
the honour of childbearing conferred upon the mother of

---

* See Introduction, and Excursus on "Bishops and Deacons" in *International Commentary on Philippians and Philemon.*

our Lord is reflected in the Christian woman of later times
(1 Tim. ii. 15). While Paul advises against second marriages
(1 Cor. vii. 8, 9, 27, 39, 40), in the Pastorals emphasis is laid
only on the remarriage of church-officers and church-widows.
In the Pastorals we see a reflection of the conditions of the
earlier post-apostolic age, when a non-Pauline asceticism was
showing itself (see 1 Tim. iv. 3, 4, 8 ; Tit. i. 15). The opposition to second marriage became very strong in the latter
part of the second century. It was elevated into an article
of faith by the Montanists, and was emphasised by Tertullian,
and by Athenagoras, who called second marriage "a specious
adultery " (εὐπρεπής μοιχεία).*

Vigilant (νηφάλιον). Only in the Pastorals. See ver. 11,
and Tit. ii. 2. °LXX. The kindred verb νήφειν means *to be
sober* with reference to drink, and, in a metaphorical sense, to
be *sober and wary ; cool and unimpassioned.* Thus Epichar-
mus, νᾶφε καὶ μέμνασ᾽ ἀπιστεῖν *be wary and remember not to be
credulous.* See on 1 Th. v. 6. In N. T. the meaning of the
verb is always metaphorical, *to be calm, dispassionate, and circumspect.* The A. V. *vigilant* is too limited. Wise caution
may be included ; but it is better to render *sober,* as A.V. in
ver. 11 and Tit. ii. 2, in the metaphorical sense as opposed
to youthful levity.

Of good behaviour (κόσμιον). °P. Only here and 1 Tim.
ii. 9, see note. Rend. *orderly.*

Given to hospitality (φιλόξενον). °P. Comp. Tit. i. 8 ; -
1 Pet. iv. 9. See note on *pursuing hospitality,* Rom. xii. 13.

Apt to teach (διδακτικόν). °P. Only here and 2 Tim.
ii. 24. °LXX, °Class. In the Pastorals the function of
teaching pertains to both Bishops and Elders (see 1 Tim.
v. 17; Tit. i. 9). It is at this point that the tendency to

---

* The reference to second marriages here is held by Holtzmann, Ellicott,
von Soden, Wace, and Pfleiderer. Huther and Farrar take it as simply
opposed to an immoral life, especially concubinage.

confound and identify the two reveals itself.   Bishops and
Presbyters are not identical.   Earlier, the teaching function
does not seem to have attached to the position of ἐπίσκοπος.
The office acquired a different character when it assumed that
function, which is not assigned to it in Clement's Epistle to
the Corinthians.   In the *Didache* or *Teaching of the Twelve
Apostles* (about 100 A.D.) the ministry of teaching is to be
assumed by the Bishops only in the absence of the Prophets
and Teachers (xiii. xv).

3. **Given to wine** (πάροινον).   Only here and Tit. i. 7.
The verb παροινεῖν *to behave ill at wine, to treat with drunken
violence*, is found in Xenophon, Aeschines, Aristophanes, and
Aristotle.   Once in LXX, Isa. xli. 12.   Rev. renders *brawler*,
which is not definite enough.   Better, *quarrelsome over wine*.
See Aristoph. *Acharn.* 981 : πάροινος ἀνὴρ ἔφυ, which Frere
renders "behaved in such a beastly way."   Cicero, *ad Att.*
x. 10, uses παροινικῶς = *insolently*.

Striker (πλήκτην).   Only here and Tit. i. 7.   Some soften
down the meaning into *a pugnacious* or *combative person*.   In
any case, it is a peculiar state of things which calls out such
admonitions to Bishops.

Not greedy of filthy lucre.   Omit.

Patient (ἐπιεικῆ).   Better, *forbearing*.   The word occurs
Philip. iv. 5, and ἐπιεικία *forbearance* in 2 Cor. x. 1, where it
is associated with πραΰτης *meekness*.   From εἰκός *reasonable*.
Hence, not unduly rigorous ; not making a determined stand
for one's just due.   In 1 Pet. ii. 18 ; Jas. iii. 17, it is associated with ἀγαθὸς *kindly*, and εὐπειθής *easy to be entreated*.
It occurs in LXX.

Not a brawler (ἄμαχον).   Better, *not contentious*.

Not covetous (ἀφιλάργυρον).   Only here and Heb. xiii. 5.
°LXX, °Class.   Φιλάργυρος *money-loving*, L. xvi. 14 ; 2 Tim.

iii. 2.   Rend. *not a money-lover.*   The word for *covetous* is
πλεονέκτης.   For the distinction see on Rom. i. 29.

This admonition is cited by some writers in support of the
view that the original ἐπίσκοπος was simply a financial officer.
It is assumed that it was prompted by the special temptations which attached to the financial function.   Admitting
that the episcopal function may have included the financial
interests of the church, it could not have been confined to
these.   It can hardly be supposed that, in associations distinctively moral and religious, one who bore the title of
overseer should have been concerned only with the material
side of church life.*

4. That ruleth (προϊστάμενον).   Mostly in the Pastorals,
but also in Rom. xii. 8; 1 Th. v. 12.   The participle means
placed in front.   Here in a general sense, but in 1 Th. i. 5
of church authorities, but only functionally, not as a title of
specially appointed officers.   It is characteristic of the loose
and unsettled ecclesiastical nomenclature of the apostolic age.

Having in subjection (ἔχοντα ἐν ὑποταγῇ).   The phrase
is unique in N. T.   Ὑποταγή *subjection* is a Pauline word:
see 2 Cor. ix. 13; Gal. ii. 5.   °LXX.

5. Shall he take care of (ἐπιμελήσεται)。   Only here and
L. x. 34.

6. Novice (νεόφυτον).   N. T.°.   From νέος *new* and φυτόν
a plant.   Comp. 1 Cor. iii. 6, 7; Matt. xv. 13.   Hence, *a
new convert, a neophyte.*   Comp. in LXX Job xiv. 9; Ps.
cxxvii. 3; cxliii. 12; Isa. v. 7.   Chrysostom explains it as
newly catechised (νεοκατήχητος); but a neophyte differed from
a catechumen in having received baptism.   Better the ancient
Greek interpreters, *newly baptized* (νεοβάπτιστος).   After the
ceremony of baptism the neophytes wore white garments for

---

* See Dr. Sanday, *Expositor,* 3d ser., V., 98, and Réville, *Les Origines de
l'Épiscopat,* p. 153 f.

eight days, from Easter eve until the Sunday after Easter,
which was called *Dominica in albis, the Sunday in white.*   The
Egyptian archives of Berlin give νεόφυτος in a Fayum papyrus
of the second century A.D., of *newly-planted palm trees.*   Comp.
LXX, Ps. cxxvii. 3: "Thy sons as νεόφυτα ἐλαιῶν *new plants
of olives.*"

Being lifted up with pride (τυφωθείς).   Only in the Pastorals.   See ch. vi. 4; 2 Tim. iii. 4.   The verb means primarily *to make a smoke:* hence, metaphorically, *to blind with
pride or conceit.*   Neither A. V. nor Rev. *puffed up*, preserves
the radical sense, which is the sense here intended — a
beclouded and stupid state of mind as the result of pride.

Fall into condemnation (εἰς κρίμα ἐμπέσῃ).   Κρίμα in
N. T. usually means *judgment.*   The word for *condemnation*
is κατάκριμα.   See especially Rom. v. 16, where the two are
sharply distinguished.   Comp. Matt. vii. 2; Acts xxiv. 25;
Rom. ii. 2; v. 18; 1 Cor. vi. 7.   However, κρίμα occasionally shades off into the meaning *condemnation*, as Rom. iii. 8;
Jas. iii. 1.   See on *go to law*, 1 Cor. vi. 7, and on 1 Cor. xi. 29.
Κρίμα is a Pauline word; but the phrase ἐμπιπτεῖν εἰς κρίμα
to fall into judgment is found only here.

Of the devil (τοῦ διαβόλου).   See on Matt. iv. 1, and on
Satan, 1 Th. ii. 18.   Paul uses διάβολος only twice, Eph. iv.
27; vi. 11.   Commonly *Satan.*   The use of διάβολος as an
adjective is peculiar to the Pastorals (see 1 Tim. iii. 11;
2 Tim. iii. 3; Tit. ii. 3), and occurs nowhere else in N. T.,
and not in LXX.   The phrase *judgment of the devil* probably
means the accusing judgment of the devil, and not the judgment passed upon the devil.   In Apoc. xii. 10 Satan is called
the accuser of the brethren.   In 1 Cor. v. 5; 1 Tim. i. 20, men
are given over to Satan for judgment.   In ver. 7 the genitive
διαβόλου is clearly subjective.   In this chapter it appears that
a Christian can fall into the *reproach* of the devil (comp. Jude
9; 2 Pet. ii. 11), the *snare* of the devil (comp. 2 Tim. ii. 26),
and the *judgment* of the devil.

7. **A good report** (μαρτυρίαν καλὴν). Comp. Acts vi. 3. Not only does καλός occur in the Pastorals nearly twice as many times as in Paul, but the usage is different. Out of 16 instances in Paul, there is but one in which καλός is not used substantively (Rom. vii. 16), while in the Pastorals it is, almost without exception, used adjectively. Μαρτυρίαν, better *testimony*. Comp. Tit. i. 13. Not in Paul, who uses μαρτύριον.

Of them which are without (ἀπὸ τῶν ἔξωθεν). Ἔξωθεν only once in Paul (2 Cor. vii. 5), and οἱ ἔξωθεν nowhere in Paul, and only here in Pastorals. Paul's phrase is ὁ ἔξω : see 1 Cor. v. 12, 13; 2 Cor. iv. 16; 1 Th. iv. 12.

Reproach (ὀνειδισμὸν). By Paul in Rom. xv. 3: only here in Pastorals : three times in Hebrews.

Snare (παγίδα). Comp. ch. vi. 9; 2 Tim. ii. 26. In Paul, Rom. xi. 9, see note. Both *reproach* and *snare* govern διαβόλου.

8. **Deacons.** The office of Deacon appears in the Pastorals, but not in Paul's letters, with the single exception of Philip. i. 1, where the Deacons do not represent an ecclesiastical office, though they mark an advance toward it. Clement of Rome (*ad Corinth.* xlii, xliv) asserts their apostolic appointment. But the evidence at our command does not bear out the view that the institution of the diaconate is described in Acts vi. 1–6. The terms διάκονος and διακονία are, in the Pauline writings, common expressions of servants and service either to Christ or to others. Paul applies these terms to his own ministry and to that of his associates. Διακονία is used of the service of the apostles, Acts i. 25; vi. 4. Διάκονος is used of Paul and Apollos (1 Cor. iii. 5); of Christ (Gal. ii. 17; Rom. xv. 8); of the civil ruler (Rom. xiii. 4); of ministers of Satan (2 Cor. xi. 15). The appointment of the seven grew out of a special emergency, and was made for a particular service; and the resemblance is

not close between the duties and qualifications of deacons in the Pastorals and those of the seven. The word διάκονος does not appear in Acts; and when Paul and Barnabas brought to Jerusalem the collection for the poor saints, they handed it over to the elders.

In like manner (ὡσαύτως). Rare in Paul (Rom. viii. 26; 1 Cor. xi. 25). Frequent in Pastorals.

Grave (σεμνούς). In Paul only Philip. iv. 8. See on σεμνότης *gravity*, 1 Tim. ii. 2.

Double-tongued (διλόγους). N. T.º. ºLXX, ºClass. Saying one thing and meaning another, and making different representations to different people about the same thing.

Given to much wine (οἴνῳ πολλῷ προσέχοντας). See on 1 Tim. i. 4. Total abstinence is not enjoined, even on a deacon. Comp. 1 Tim. v. 23.

Greedy of filthy lucre (αἰσχροκερδεῖς). N. T.º. ºLXX. The adverb αἰσχροκερδῶς *in a base, gain-greedy way*, 1 Pet. v. 2. From αἰσχρός *disgraceful* and κέρδος *gain*. Comp. Hdt. i. 187 : εἰ μὴ ἄπληστός τε ἔας χρημάτων καὶ αἰσχροκερδής *if thou hadst not been insatiable of wealth and ready to procure it by disgraceful means*. Aristoph. *Peace*, 622, alludes to two vices of the Spartans, ὄντες αἰσχροκερδεῖς καὶ διειρωνόξενοι *sordidly greedy of gain, and treacherous under the mask of hospitality*. Similarly Eurip. *Androm.* 451. Comp. *turpilucricupidus*, Plaut. *Trin.* 1, 2, 63.

9. **The mystery of the faith** (τὸ μυστήριον τῆς πίστεως). The phrase N. T.º. In the Gospels only, *mystery* or *mysteries* of the *kingdom of God* or *of heaven*. In Paul, *mystery* or *mysteries of God, of his will, of Christ, of the gospel, of iniquity, the mystery kept secret* or *hidden away*. Several times without qualification, *the mystery* or *mysteries*. See on 2 Th. ii. 7. *The mystery of the faith* is the subject-matter of the faith; the truth which is its basis, which was kept hidden from the

world until revealed at the appointed time, and which is a
secret to ordinary eyes, but is made known by divine revelation. Comp. Rom. xvi. 25; Eph. iii. 9; Col. i. 26; 1 Cor.
ii. 7. For *the faith* see on Gal. i. 23, and comp. Introduction
to these Epistles, VI.

In a pure conscience (ἐν καθαρᾷ συνειδήσει).   Comp.
2 Tim. i. 3, 5, 19.   Const. with *holding*.   The emphasis of
the passage is on these words.   They express conscientious
purity and sincerity in contrast with those who are described
as *branded in their own conscience*, and thus causing their followers *to fall away from the faith* (ch. iv. 1, 2).   The passage
illustrates the peculiar treatment of "faith" in these Epistles, in emphasising its ethical aspect and its ethical environment.   This is not contrary to Paul's teaching, nor does it
go to the extent of substituting morals for faith as the condition of salvation and eternal life.   See 2 Tim. i. 9; ii. 1;
Tit. iii. 5.   None the less, there is a strong and habitual
emphasis on good works (see 1 Tim. ii. 10; v. 10; vi. 18;
2 Tim. ii. 21; iii. 17; Tit. i. 16; ii. 7, 14; iii. 1, 8, 14),
and faith is placed in a series of practical duties (see 1 Tim.
i. 5, 14; ii. 15; iv. 12; 2 Tim. i. 13; 1 Tim. i. 19; ii. 7;
iii. 9; vi. 11; 2 Tim. ii. 22; iii. 10).   "Holding the mystery of the faith in a pure conscience" is a significant association of faith with ethics.   As Weiss puts it: "It is as if the
pure conscience were the vessel in which the mystery of the
faith is preserved."   The idea is sound and valuable.   A
merely intellectual attitude toward the mystery which, in
every age, attaches to the faith, will result in doubt, questioning, and wordy strife (see 1 Tim. vi. 4; 2 Tim. ii. 23;
Tit. iii. 9), sometimes in moral laxity, sometimes in despair.
Loyalty and duty to God are compatible with more or less
ignorance concerning the mystery.   An intellect, however
powerful and active, joined with an impure conscience, cannot
solve but only aggravates the mystery; whereas a pure and
loyal conscience, and a frank acceptance of imposed duty
along with mystery, puts one in the best attitude for attaining whatever solution is possible.   See J. vii. 17.

10. These also (καὶ οὗτοι δὲ). As well as the Bishops. No mention is made of a *proving* of the Bishops, but this may be fairly assumed. Comp. *not a novice*, ver. 6.

Be proved (δοκιμαζέσθωσαν). Common in Paul; only here in Pastorals. See on 1 Pet. i. 7. Not implying a formal examination, but a reference to the general judgment of the Christian community as to whether they fulfil the conditions detailed in ver. 8. Comp. 1 Tim. v. 22; 2 Tim. ii. 2.

Let them use the office of a deacon (διακονείτωσαν). Much better, *let them serve as deacons.* In this sense only in the Pastorals. Comp. ver. 13.* The verb is very common in N. T.

Being blameless (ἀνέγκλητοι ὄντες). Rather, *unaccused:* if no charge be preferred against them. In Paul, 1 Cor. i. 8; Col. i. 22. Comp. Tit. i. 6, 7. It is a judicial term. The participle ὄντες signifies *provided they are.*

11. Their wives (γυναῖκας). Probably correct, although some find a reference to an official class of women — deaconesses (so Ellicott, Holtzmann, Alford). But the injunction is thrown incidentally into the admonition concerning Deacons, which is resumed at ver. 12; and if an official class were intended we should expect something more specific than γυναῖκας *women* or *wives* without the article. A Deacon whose wife is wanting in the qualities required in him, is not to be chosen. She would sustain an active relation to his office, and by her ministries would increase his efficiency, and by frivolity, slander, or intemperance, would bring him and his office into disrepute.

13. Purchase (περιποιοῦνται). Only here, L. xvii. 33, and Acts xx. 28 on which see note. *Purchase* is unfortunate from the point of modern usage; but it is employed in

---

* Holtzmann and Huther add 1 Pet. iv. 11; but Huther says that it is not to be limited to the official ministry of the Deacon. It may fairly be taken in the general sense of *serve.* So von Soden.

its original sense of *to win, acquire,* without any idea of a bargain. So Bacon, *Ess.* iv. 14: "There is no man doth a wrong for the wrong's sake; but therby to *purchase* him-selfe profit, or pleasure, or honour, or the like." And Shake-speare:

> "Then, as my gift and thine own acquisition
> Worthily *purchased*, take my daughter."
>
> *Temp.* iv. 1, 14.

Rend. *acquire* or *obtain* for themselves.

A good degree (βαθμὸν καλὸν). Βαθμός, N.T.⁰. Prim-arily, *a step.* In LXX, 1 Sam. v. 5; Sir. vi. 36, *a thresh-old*: 2 K. xx. 9, *a degree on the dial.* In ecclesiastical writers, *order, grade, rank*: see, for instance, Eusebius, *H. E.* vii. 15. Also *degree of relationship* or affinity. Here the word apparently means a position of trust and influence in the church; possibly a promotion from the diaconate to the episcopate. Others (as De Wette, Ellicott, Pfleiderer) refer it to a high grade in the future life, which Holtzmann sar-castically describes as *a ladder-round in heaven* (*eine Staffel im Himmel*). John the Scholar, known as Climacus, a monk of the latter half of the sixth century, and Abbot of the Sinai Convent, wrote a mystical work entitled Κλίμαξ τοῦ Παρα-δείσου *the Ladder of Paradise.* The ladder, according to him, had thirty rounds.

Boldness (παρρησίαν). Primarily, free and bold *speaking;* speaking out *every word* (πᾶν, ῥῆμα). Its dominant idea is *boldness, confidence,* as opposed to *fear, ambiguity,* or *reserve.* The idea of *publicity* is sometimes attached to it, but as second-ary. Only here in the Pastorals: several times in Paul, as 2 Cor. iii. 12; vii. 4; Philip. i. 20. The phrase πολλή παρ-ρησία *much boldness* is also Pauline. An assured position and blameless reputation in the church, with a pure con-science, would assure boldness of speech and of attitude in the Christian community and elsewhere.

In faith. Connect with *boldness* only. It designates the boldness as distinctively Christian, founded on faith in Christ.

14. Shortly (ἐν τάχει). The adverbial phrase once in Paul, Rom. xvi. 20 : only here in Pastorals. Several times in Luke and Acts, and twice in Apocalypse.*

15. I tarry long (βραδύνω). Only here and 2 Pet. iii. 9.

Thou oughtest to behave thyself (δεῖ ἀναστρέφεσθαι). The verb ἀναστρέφεσθαι only here in Pastorals. In Paul, 2 Cor. i. 12 ; Eph. ii. 3. The reference is not to *Timothy's conduct* as the A.V. implies, but rather to the instructions which he is to give to church members. Rend. *how men ought to behave.* See on *conversation,* 1 Pet. i. 15.

House of God (οἴκῳ θεοῦ). An O. T. phrase, used of the temple. More frequently, house of *the Lord* (κυρίου); see 1 K. iii. 1; vi. 1 ; 1 Chron. xxii. 2, 11 ; xxix. 2, etc. Applied to the church only here. Paul has οἰκείους τῆς πίστεως *householders of the faith* (Gal. vi. 10), and οἰκεῖοι τοῦ θεοῦ *householders of God* (Eph. ii. 19), signifying members of the church. Christians are called ναὸς θεοῦ *sanctuary of God* (1 Cor. iii. 16, 17; 2 Cor. vi. 16); and the apostles are οἰκονόμοι *household stewards* (1 Cor. iv. 1). So of a Bishop (Tit. i. 7). See also Heb. iii. 6.

Church (ἐκκλησία). See on 1 Th. i. 1.

Pillar and ground of the truth (στύλος καὶ ἑδραίωμα τῆς ἀληθείας). Στύλος *pillar,* in Paul only Gal. ii. 9. In Apocalypse iii. 12; x. 1. Ἑδραίωμα *stay, prop,* better than *ground.* N. T.°. °LXX, °Class. The kindred adjective ἑδραῖος *firm, stable,* 1 Cor. vii. 37 ; xv. 58; Col. i. 23. These words are in apposition with *church.*† The idea is that the church is the *pillar,* and, *as such,* the *prop* or *support* of the truth. It

---

* The reading τάχιον or ταχεῖον *more quickly,* is preferred by Tischendorf and Weiss. The comparative would signify *sooner than these instructions presuppose.*

† Holtzmann makes an ingenious plea for apposition with θεοῦ *God,* though he does not decisively adopt it. Others explain as beginning the following clause, thus : " A pillar and stay of the truth, and confessedly great, is the mystery of godliness." This is quite inadmissible, as is the reference of the words to Timothy.

is quite beside the mark to press the architectural metaphor into detail. By giving to ἑδραίωμα the sense of *stay* or *prop*, the use of the two words for the same general idea is readily explained. The church is the *pillar* of the truth, and the function of the pillar is to *support.**

16. **Without controversy** (ὁμολογουμένως). Lit. *confessedly*. N. T.⁰.

The mystery of godliness (τὸ τῆς εὐσεβείας μυστήριον). (*a*) The connection of thought is with *the truth* (ver. 15), and the words *mystery of godliness* are a paraphrase of that word. The church is the pillar and stay of the truth, and the truth constitutes the mystery of godliness. (*b*) The contents of this truth or mystery is Christ, revealed in the gospel as the Saviour from ungodliness, the norm and inspiration of godliness, the divine life in man, causing him to live unto God as Christ did and does (Rom. vi. 10). See ch. i. 15; ii. 5; Col. i. 26, 27. According to the Fourth Gospel, Christ is himself *the truth* (J. xiv. 6). The mystery of godliness is the substance of piety = *mystery of the faith* (ver. 9). (*c*) The truth is called a mystery because it was, historically, hidden, until revealed in the person and work of Christ; also because it is concealed from human wisdom, and apprehended only by faith in the revelation of God through Christ. (*d*) The genitive, *of godliness*, is possessive. The mystery of godliness is the truth which pertains or belongs to godliness. It is not the property of worldly wisdom. *Great* (μέγα) means *important, weighty*, as Eph. v. 32.

God (θεὸς). But the correct reading is ὅς *who*.† The

---

* Dr. Briggs, *Messiah of the Apostles*, p. 229, thinks that the whole church is conceived as a pillar uplifting a *platform* or *basis* (ἑδραίωμα) on which the truth rests. Besides being contrary to the true sense of ἑδραίωμα, this explanation compels a very awkward metaphor.

† Those who are interested in the details of the controversy over this reading, may consult S. P. Tregelles, *An Account of the Printed Text of the Greek New Testament*, p. 165; and F. H. A. Scrivener, *Introduction to the Criticism of the New Testament*, 4th ed. Vol. II. 390–395.

antecedent of this relative is not *mystery*, as if Christ were
styled "the mystery," but the relative refers to *Christ* as an
antecedent ; and the abruptness of its introduction may be
explained by the fact that it and the words which follow
were probably taken from an ancient credal hymn.   In the
earlier Christian ages it was not unusual to employ verse or
rhythm for theological teaching or statement.   The heretics
propounded their peculiar doctrines in psalms.   Clement of
Alexandria wrote a hymn in honour of Christ for the use of
catechumens, and Arius embodied his heresy in his *Thalia*,
which was sung in the streets and taverns of Alexandria.
The Muratorian Canon was probably composed in verse.   In
the last quarter of the fourth century, there are two metrical
lists of Scripture by Amphilochius and Gregory Nazianzen.*

Was manifest (ἐφανερώθη).   More correctly, *was manifested*.   The verb is used J. i. 2; Heb. ix. 26; 1 Pet. i. 20;
1 J. iii. 5, 8, of the historical manifestation of Christ; and
of the future coming of Christ in Col. iii. 4; 1 Pet. v. 4;
1 J. iii. 2.

In the flesh (ἐν σαρκί).   Comp. J. i. 14; 1 J. iv. 2; 2 J. 7;
Rom. i. 3; viii. 3; ix. 5.   Σάρξ *flesh* only here in Pastorals.

Justified in the Spirit (ἐδικαιώθη ἐν πνεύματι).   The verb
δικαιοῦν, so familiar in Paul's writings, is found in the Pastorals only here and Tit. iii. 7.   Its application to Christ as
the subject of justification does not appear in Paul.   Its
meaning here is *vindicated, indorsed*, as Matt. xi. 19; L. x. 29.
Concerning the whole phrase it is to be said : (*a*) That the
two clauses, *manifested in the flesh, justified in the Spirit*,
exhibit a contrast between two aspects of the life of Christ.
(*b*) That ἐν *in* must have the same meaning in both clauses.
(*c*) That meaning is not instrumental, *by*, nor purely *modal*,
expressing the kind and manner of Christ's justification, but
rather *local* with a shade of modality.   It expresses in each

---

* See J. B. Lightfoot, *S. Clement of Rome*, Vol. II., p. 405 ff.

case a peculiar condition which accompanied the justification ;
a sphere of life in which it was exhibited and which gave
character to it.　In the one condition or sphere (the flesh)
he was hated, persecuted, and murdered.　In the other (the
Spirit) he was triumphantly vindicated.　See further the
additional note at the end of this chapter.

Seen of angels (ὤφθη ἀγγέλοις).　Better, *appeared unto*
or *showed himself to*, as Matt. xvii. 3 ; L. i. 11 ; Acts vii. 2 ;
Heb. ix. 28.　The same verb is used of the appearance of
the risen Christ to different persons or parties (1 Cor. xv.
5–8).　The reference of the words cannot be determined
with certainty.　They seem to imply some great, majestic
occasion, rather than the angelic manifestations during
Jesus' earthly life.　Besides, on these occasions, the angels
appeared to him, not he to them.　The reference is probably
to his appearance in the heavenly world after his ascension,
when the glorified Christ, having been triumphantly vindicated in his messianic work and trial, presented himself to
the heavenly hosts.　Comp. Philip. ii. 10 ; Eph. iii. 10, and,
in the latter passage, note the connection with "the mystery," ver. 9.

Was preached unto the Gentiles (ἐκηρύχθη ἐν ἔθνεσιν).
Better, *among the nations*.　There is no intention of emphasising the distinction between the Jews and other nations.

Was believed on in the world (ἐπιστεύθη ἐν κόσμῳ).　For
a similar construction see 2 Th. i. 10.　With Christ as subject this use of ἐπιστεύθη is unique.

Was received up into glory (ἀνελήμφθη ἐν δόξῃ).　Better,
received or taken up *in glory*.　'Αναλαμβάνειν is the formal
term to describe the ascension of Christ (see Acts i. 2, 22),
and the reference is most probably to that event.　Comp.
LXX, 2 K. ii. 11, of Elijah, and Sir. xlix. 14, of Enoch.
'Εν δόξῃ *in glory :* with attendant circumstances of pomp or
majesty, as we say of a victorious general, " he entered the

city *in* triumph." This usage is common in N. T. See
Matt. xvi. 27; xxv. 31; Mk. viii. 38; L. ix. 31; xii. 27;
1 Cor. xv. 43; 2 Cor. iii. 7, 8, 11.*

Additional Note on III. 16.

Christ's existence before his incarnation was purely spiritual (ἐν πνεύματι). He was in the form of God (Philip. ii. 6): He was the effulgence
of God's glory and the express image of his substance (Heb. i. 3), and
God is spirit (J. iv. 24).

From this condition he came into manifestation in the flesh (ἐν σαρκί).
He became man and entered into human conditions (Philip. ii. 7, 8).
Under these human conditions the attributes of his essential spiritual per-
sonality were veiled. He did not appear to men what he really was. He
was not recognised by them as he who " was in the beginning with God "
(J. i. 1, 2); as " the image of the invisible God " (Col. i. 15); as one with
God (J. x. 30; xiv. 9); as he who had all power in heaven and earth
(Matt. xxviii. 18); who was " before all things and by whom all things
consist " (Col. i. 17); who was " the king of the ages " (1 Tim. i. 17). On
the contrary, he was regarded as an impostor, a usurper, and a blasphemer.
He was hated, persecuted, and finally murdered. He was poor, tempted,
and tried, a man of sorrows.

The justification or vindication of what he really was did not therefore
come out of the fleshly sphere. He was not justified in the flesh. It came
out of the sphere of his spiritual being. Glimpses of this pneumatic life
(ἐν πνεύματι) flashed out during his life in the flesh. By his exalted and
spotless character, by his works of love and power, by his words of authority, in his baptism and transfiguration, he was vindicated as being
what he essentially was and what he openly claimed to be. These justifi-
cations were revelations, expressions, and witnesses of his original, essential
spiritual and divine quality; of the native glory which he had with the
Father before the world was. It was the Spirit that publicly indorsed him

---

* This explanation destroys the chronological order, since the appearing
to angels, the preaching among the nations, and the being believed on in the
world, followed the ascension. But I am not sure that the preservation of
the chronological order is absolutely essential, or that it might not have been
violated in the credal hymn. The fact of the formal use of ἀναλαμβάνειν by
Luke to describe the ascension seems to me to be significant, especially in
view of the numerous and striking affinities of vocabulary in Luke, Acts, and
the Pastorals. Besides, there is absolutely nothing else to which the word
can naturally be referred here. The explanation to which von Soden in-
clines, that Christ was taken up in glory by Christians, either in the ascrip-
tion of glory to him or in the glory thereby imparted to men, seems most
unnatural and forced.

(J. i. 32, 33) : the words which he spake were spirit and life (J. vi. 63) : he cast out demons in the Spirit of God (Matt. xii. 28) : his whole earthly manifestation was in demonstration of the Spirit.   These various demonstrations decisively justified his claims in the eyes of many.   His disciples confessed him as the Christ of God (L. ix. 20) : some of the people said "this is the Christ" (J. vii. 41) : others suspected that he was such (J. iv. 29).   Whether or not men acknowledged his claims, they felt the power of his unique personality.   They were astonished at his teaching, for he taught them as one having authority (Matt. vii. 28, 29).

Then followed the more decisive vindication in his resurrection from the dead.   Here the work of the Spirit is distinctly recognised by Paul, Rom. i. 4.   See also Rom. viii. 11.   In the period between his resurrection and ascension his pneumatic life came into clearer manifestation, and added to the vindication furnished in his life and resurrection.   He seemed to live on the border-line between the natural and the spiritual world, and the powers of the spiritual world were continually crossing the line and revealing themselves in him.

In the apostolic preaching, the appeal to the vindication of Christ by the Spirit is clear and unequivocal.   The spiritual nourishment of believers is "the supply of the Spirit of Jesus Christ" (Philip. i. 19) : the Holy Spirit is called "the Spirit of Christ" (Rom. viii. 9; Gal. iv. 6) : Paul identifies Christ personally with the Spirit (2 Cor. iii. 17); and in Rom. viii. 9, 10, "Spirit of God," "Spirit of Christ," and "Christ" are used as convertible terms.   The indwelling of the Spirit of Christ is the test and vindication of belonging to Christ (Rom. viii. 9).   Thus, though put to death in the flesh, in the Spirit Christ is vindicated as the Son of God, the Christ of God, the manifestation of God.

CHAPTER IV.

1. Now ($\delta\grave{\epsilon}$).   Better *but*, since there is a contrast with the preceding confession of the norm of faith.

Expressly ($\dot{\rho}\eta\tau\hat{\omega}\varsigma$).   N. T.°.   °LXX.   In express words.

In the latter times ($\dot{\epsilon}\nu$ $\dot{\upsilon}\sigma\tau\acute{\epsilon}\rho o\iota\varsigma$ $\kappa\alpha\iota\rho o\hat{\iota}\varsigma$).   The phrase only here.   For $\kappa\alpha\iota\rho\acute{o}\varsigma$ *particular season* or *juncture*, see on Matt. xii. 1 ; Acts i. 7.   Not the same as $\dot{\epsilon}\nu$ $\dot{\epsilon}\sigma\chi\acute{\alpha}\tau\alpha\iota\varsigma$ $\dot{\eta}\mu\acute{\epsilon}\rho\alpha\iota\varsigma$ *in the last days*, 2 Tim. iii. 1, which denotes the period closing the present aeon, and immediately preceding the parousia ; while this signifies merely a time that is future to the writer.   There is not the intense sense of the nearness of Christ's coming which characterises Paul. The writer does not think of *his* present as "the latter days."

Some (τινες). Not, as ch. i. 3, the heretical teachers, but those whom they mislead.

Shall depart from the faith (ἀποστήσονται τῆς πίστεως). The phrase only here. The verb in Paul only 2 Cor. xii. 8. Quite frequent in Luke and Acts. The kindred noun ἀποστασία (Acts xxi. 21; 2 Th. ii. 3) is almost literally transcribed in our *apostasy.*

Seducing (πλάνοις). Primarily, *wandering, roving.* Ὁ πλάνος a vagabond, hence *deceiver* or *seducer.* See 2 J. 7, and comp. ὁ πλανῶν *the deceiver,* used of Satan, Apoc. xii. 9; xx. 10; τὸ πνεῦμα τῆς πλάνης *the spirit of error,* 1 J. iv. 6. Once in Paul, 2 Cor. vi. 8, and in LXX, Job xix. 4; Jer. xxiii. 32. Evil spirits animating the false teachers are meant.

Doctrines of devils (διδασκαλίαις δαιμονίων). Better, *teachings of demons.* Comp. Jas. iii. 15. Διδασκαλία *teaching* often in Pastorals. A few times in Paul. See on 1 Tim. i. 10. Δαιμόνιον *demon* only here in Pastorals. Very frequent in Luke: in Paul only 1 Cor. x. 20, 21. Teachings proceeding from or inspired by demons. The working of these evil spirits is here specially concerned with striking at the true teaching which underlies godliness. It is impossible to say what particular form of false teaching is alluded to.

2. **Speaking lies in hypocrisy** (ἐν ὑποκρίσει ψευδολόγων). Wrong. Rend., *through the hypocrisy of men that speak lies.* Ὑπόκρισις *hypocrisy* once in Paul, Gal. ii. 13, see note. See also on Matt. xxiii. 13. The phrase ἐν ὑποκρίσει only here. Ψευδολόγος *speaking lies,* N. T.°. °LXX. Rare in Class.

Having their conscience seared with a hot iron (κεκαυστηριασμένων τὴν ἰδίαν συνείδησιν). Better, *branded in their*

own conscience. With a hot iron is superfluous. The verb
N. T.⁰. ⁰LXX, ⁰Class. The metaphor is from the practice
of branding slaves or criminals, the latter on the brow. These
deceivers are not acting under delusion, but deliberately, and
against their conscience. They wear the form of godliness,
and contradict their profession by their crooked conduct
(2 Tim. iii. 5). The brand is not on their brow, but on their
conscience. Comp. Tit. i. 15; iii. 11.

3. **Forbidding to marry and commanding to abstain
from meats** (κωλυόντων γαμεῖν, ἀπέχεσθαι βρωμάτων).
Κωλύειν, properly *to hinder* or *check*. Ἀπέχεσθαι *to hold one's
self off*. In Paul, 1 Th. iv. 3; v. 22; Philem. 15. *Commanding* is not expressed, but is implied in *forbidding.*
"Bidding not to marry and (bidding) to abstain from meats."
The ascetic tendencies indicated by these prohibitions developed earlier than these Epistles among the Essenes, an ascetic
Jewish brotherhood on the shores of the Dead Sea, who repudiated marriage except as a necessity for preserving the race,
and allowed it only under protest and under stringent regulations. They also abstained strictly from wine and animal
food. This sect was in existence in the lifetime of our Lord.
Strong traces of its influence appear in the heresy assailed in
Paul's Epistle to the Colossians. The Christian body received
large accessions from it after the destruction of Jerusalem
(70 A.D.). The prohibitions above named were imposed by
the later Gnosticism of the second century.

Hath created (ἔκτισεν). A common Pauline word. Only
here in the Pastorals.

To be received (εἰς μετάλημψιν). Lit. *for participation.*
N. T.⁰. ⁰LXX. It occurs in Plato and Aristotle.

Of them which believe and know the truth (τοῖς πισ
τοῖς καὶ ἐπεγνωκόσι τὴν ἀλήθειαν). The dative depends on
created for participation, and should be rendered "*for* them
which believe," etc., marking those for whom the food was

created.   The A. V. misses this by the rendering *to be received
of (by)*.   Πιστοῖς and ἐπεγκνωκόσι do not denote two classes,
but one.   Those who believe are described as those who have
full knowledge of the truth.

4. **Creature** (*κτίσμα*).   Not in Paul.   See Jas. i. 18;
Apoc. v. 13 ; viii. 9.   A created thing.   For *κτίσις creation* or
creature, frequent in Paul, see on Rom. viii. 19 ; 2 Cor. v. 17;
Col. i. 15.   Κτίσμα in LXX, Wisd. ix. 2 ; xiii. 5; xiv. 11;
Sir. xxxviii. 34 ; 3 Macc. v. 11.

Refused (*ἀπόβλητον*).   Lit. *thrown away*.   N. T.º.   In
ecclesiastical writings, *excommunicated*.   On the whole verse,
comp. Acts x. 15; Rom. xi. 15; 1 Cor. x. 25, 26, 30, 31.

5. **It is sanctified** (*ἁγιάζεται*).   Not *declared* holy, but
made holy.   The declaration confirms the last clause of ver. 4.
Thanksgiving to God has a sanctifying effect.   The food
in itself has no moral quality (Rom. xiv. 14), but acquires a
holy quality by its consecration to God ; by being acknowledged as God's gift, and partaken of as nourishing the life
for God's service.   Comp. Paul's treatment of the unbelieving husband and the believing wife, 1 Cor. vii. 14.

By the word of God (*διὰ λογοῦ θεοῦ*).   That is, by the
word of God as used in the prayer.   Scripture is not called
"the Word of God."   The Word of God includes much more
than Scripture : but Scripture *contains* the Word of God, and
the thanksgiving at table was in the words of Scripture.   See
Ps. cxlv. 15, 16.   The custom of grace at meat appears 1 Sam.
ix. 13.   Christ blessed the loaves and fishes (Matt. xiv. 19;
xv. 36) : Paul on the ship gave thanks for the meal which
the seamen ate (Acts xxvii. 35).   Ἐντεύξεως *prayer*, see on
ch. ii. 1.

6. **If thou put the brethren in remembrance of these
things** (*ταῦτα ὑποτιθέμενος τοῖς ἀδελφοῖς*).   The verb only
here and Rom. xvi. 4.   Lit. *to put under ;* so almost without

exception in LXX. See, for instance, Gen. xxviii. 18; xlvii. 29; Ex. xvii. 12. So Rom. xvi. 4. Hence, metaphorically, to *suggest*, which is, literally, *to carry* or *lay under*. Ταῦτα *these things* are those mentioned vv. 4, 5. In the Pastorals it is only here that ἀδελφοί *brethren* means the members of the church to whose superintendent the letter is addressed. In 2 Tim. iv. 21, they are the Christians of the church from which the letter comes; in 1 Tim. vi. 2, Christians in general; and in 1 Tim. v. 1, without any ecclesiastical sense.

Minister of Jesus Christ (διάκονος Χριστοῦ 'Ιησοῦ). Rendering Christ himself a service by setting himself against ascetic errors. For διάκονος *minister* see on ch. iii. 8. Here in the general sense of *servant*, without any official meaning. Paul's more usual phrase is *servant of God: servant* (διάκονος) *of Christ* twice, and διάκονος 'Ιησοῦ Χριστοῦ not at all. Paul uses δοῦλος *bond-servant* with *Jesus Christ*. See 2 Cor. xi. 23; Col. i. 7; and comp. Rom. i. 1; Gal. i. 10; Philip. i. 1.

Nourished up (ἐντρεφόμενος). Better, *nourishing thyself*. N. T.°. °LXX. The participle indicates the means by which Timothy may become a good minister. Comp. Heb. v. 12–14.

In the words of faith. The words in which the faith — the contents of belief — finds expression. Comp. ch. vi. 3; 2 Tim. i. 13. The phrase only here. Paul has τὸ ῥῆμα τῆς πίστεως *the word of the faith*, Rom. x. 8.

Whereunto thou hast attained (ᾗ παρηκολούθηκας). Wrong. Rend., *which thou hast closely followed*. Comp. 2 Tim. iii. 10. The verb means, primarily, *to follow beside*, *to attend closely*. In this literal sense not in N. T. *To attend to* or *follow up*, as a disease. So Plato, *Rep.* 406 B, παρακολουθῶν τῷ νοσήματι θανασίμῳ *perpetually tending a mortal disease*. To follow up a history or a succession of incidents, as L. i. 3. °P. The writer means that Timothy, as a disciple, has closely attended to his course of Christian instruction.

7. **Shun** (παραιτοῦ). Comp. 1 Tim. v. 11; 2 Tim. ii. 23; Tit. iii. 10. °P. The primary meaning is *to ask as a favour* (Mk. xv. 6; Heb. xii. 19). Mostly in this sense in LXX, as 1 Sam. xx. 6, 28. To *deprecate;* to prevent the consequences of an act by protesting against and disavowing it, as 3 Macc. vi. 27. To *beg off*, *get excused*, as L. xiv. 18, 19; 4 Macc. xi. 2. *To decline, refuse, avoid*, as here, Acts xxv. 11; Heb. xii. 25.

Profane. See on ch. i. 9, and comp. ch. vi. 20; 2 Tim. ii. 16; Heb. xii. 16.

Old wives' (γραωδεις). N. T.°. °LXX. From γραῦς *an old woman*, and εἶδος *form*.

Fables (μύθους). See on ch. i. 4, and comp. 2 Tim. iv. 4; Tit. i. 14; 2 Pet. 1. 16.

Exercise (γύμναζε). °P. Only here in Pastorals. Heb. v. 14; xii. 11; 2 Pet. ii. 14. From γυμνός *naked*. In Class. of training naked in gymnastic exercises; also, metaphorically, of training for or practising an art or profession.

8. **Bodily exercise** (ἡ σωματικὴ γυμνασία). With γυμνασία comp. γύμναζε, ver. 7. N. T.°. Σωματικός *bodily* only here and L. iii. 22. °LXX. The adverb σωματικῶς *bodily-wise*, Col. ii. 9. The words are to be taken in their literal sense as referring to physical training in the palaestra—boxing, racing, etc. Comp. 1 Cor. ix. 24–27. Some, however, find in them an allusion to current ascetic practices; against which is the statement that such exercise is *profitable*, though only for a little.

Profiteth little (πρὸς ὀλίγον ἐστὶν ὠφέλιμος). Lit. *is profitable for a little*. The phrase πρὸς ὀλίγον only here and Jas. v. 14. In the latter passage it means *for a little while*. Comp. Heb. xii. 10, πρὸς ὀλίγας ἡμέρας *for a few days*. According to some, this is the meaning here; but against

this is the antithesis πρὸς πάντα *unto all things*. The meaning is rather, the use of the athlete's training extends to only
a few things. 'Ωφέλιμος *useful* or *profitable*, only in Pastorals. Comp. 2 Tim. iii. 16; Tit. iii. 8. ᵒLXX.

Godliness (εὐσέβεια). See on ch. ii. 2, and Introduction,
VI.

Having promise (ἐπαγγελίαν ἔχουσα). The exact phrase
only here. Comp. 2 Cor. vii. 1; Heb. vii. 6. The participle is explanatory, *since it has* promise. For ἐπαγγελία *promise* see on Acts i. 4.

The life that now is (ζωῆς τῆς νῦν). According to the
strict Greek idiom, *life the now*. This idiom and the following, τῆς μελλούσης N. T.ᵒ. The phrase ὁ νῦν αἰών *the present
aeon*, 1 Tim. vi. 17; 2 Tim. iv. 10; Tit. ii. 12. 'Ο αἰών οὗτος
this aeon, a few times in the Gospels, often in Paul, nowhere
else. We have ὁ αἰών ὁ μέλλων *the aeon which is to be*, and
ὁ αἰών ὁ ἐρχόμενος or ἐπερχόμενος *the aeon which is coming on*,
in the Gospels, once in Paul (Eph. ii. 7), and in Hebrews
once, μέλλων αἰών without the article. 'Εν τῷ καιρῷ τούτῳ *in
this time*, of the present as contrasted with the future life,
Mk. x. 30; L. xviii. 30. 'Ο νῦν καιρός *the now time*, in the
same relation, Rom. viii. 18. For ζωή *life* see on J. i. 4.
The force of the genitive with ἐπαγγελία *promise* may be expressed by *for*. Godliness involves a promise for this life
and for the next; but for this life as it reflects the heavenly
life, is shaped and controlled by it, and bears its impress.
Godliness has promise for the present life *because* it has
promise for the life which is to come. Only the life which
is in Christ Jesus (2 Tim. i. 1) is *life indeed*, 1 Tim. vi. 19.
Comp. 1 Pet. iii. 10; 1 Cor. iii. 21–23.

10. Therefore (εἰς τοῦτο). More correctly, *to this end;* or
with a view to this.

We labour and strive (κοπιῶμεν καὶ ἀγωνιζόμεθα). Both
Pauline words. See on Col. i. 29, where the two are found

together as here. Also on κόπου *labour*, 1 Th. i. 3 ; and
κοπιῶντας *labouring*, 1 Th. v. 12.   Comp. ch. v. 17, and
2 Tim. ii. 6.   Both words denote strenuous and painful
effort.* The καὶ has an ascensive force : "we labour, *yea*
struggle."

We trust in (ἠλπίκαμεν ἐπί).   Better, *have set our hope on.*
The verb with ἐπὶ *upon* in Pastorals, in Paul, Rom. xv. 12,
a citation, and in 1 Pet. i. 13.

12. **Youth** (νεότητος). ⁰P. See L. xviii. 21. Acts xxvi. 4.
See Introduction, VII.   Timothy was probably from 38 to 40
years old at this time.

In word (ἐν λόγῳ).   Including teaching and verbal intercourse of every kind.

Conversation (ἀναστροφῇ).   Comp. Gal. i. 13 ; Eph. iv. 22 ;
Jas. iii. 13. A favourite word with Peter. See on 1 Pet. i. 15.

In spirit. Omit.

Purity (ἁγνίᾳ).   Only here and ch. v. 2. Ἁγνός *pure*,
1 Tim. v. 22 ; Tit. ii. 5. In Paul, 2 Cor. viii. 11 ; xi. 2 ; Philip.
iv. 8.   Also in James, Peter, and 1st John. Ἁγνότης *purity*,
2 Cor. vi. 6 ; xi. 3. ⁰LXX, ⁰Class. Ἁγνός always with a
moral sense ; not limited to sins of the flesh, but covering
purity in motives as well as in acts.   In 1 J. iii. 3, of Christ.
In 2 Cor. xi. 2, of virgin purity.   In Jas. iii. 17, as a characteristic of heavenly wisdom. Ἁγνῶς *purely* (Philip. i. 17),
of preaching the gospel with unmixed motives.   The verb
ἁγνίζειν *to purify*, which in LXX is used only of ceremonial
purification, has that meaning in four of the seven instances
in N. T. (J. xi. 55 ; Acts xxi. 24, 26 ; xxiv. 18).   In the
others (Jas. iv. 8 ; 1 Pet. i. 22 ; 1 J. iii. 3) it is used of
purifying the heart and soul.

---

* Holtzmann, von Soden, Weiss, and Ellicott, instead of ἀγωνιζόμεθα *we
strive*, read ὀνειδιζόμεθα *we suffer reproach.*

13. **To reading** (ἀναγνώσει). Three times in N. T. See Acts xiii. 15; 2 Cor. iii. 14. The verb ἀναγινώσκειν usually of public reading. See on L. iv. 16. So in LXX. In postclassical Greek, sometimes of reading aloud with comments. See Epictetus, *Diss.* 3, 23, 20. Dr. Hatch says : " It is probable that this practice of reading with comments . . . may account for the coördination of ' reading ' with ' exhortation ' and ' teaching ' in 1 Tim. iv. 13."

Exhortation (τῇ παρακλήσει). Often in Paul. See on *consolation*, L. vi. 24, *comfort*, Acts ix. 31, and *comforter*, J. xiv. 16.

14. **Neglect** (ἀμέλει). Rare in N. T. Only Matt. xxii. 5; Heb. ii. 3; viii. 9.

The gift that is in thee (τοῦ ἐν σοὶ χαρίσματος). Comp. 2 Tim. i. 6. Χάρισμα *gift* is a distinctively Pauline word, being found only three times outside of Paul's Epistles, and °LXX, °Class. See on Rom. i. 11. *That is in thee*, comp. τῆς ἐν σοὶ πίστεως *the faith that is in thee*, 2 Tim. i. 5. The meaning is the special *inward* endowment which qualified Timothy for exhortation and teaching, and which was directly imparted by the Holy Spirit.*

By prophecy (διὰ προφητείας). See on 1 Tim. i. 18. Προφητείας is genitive, not accusative. The meaning is *by the medium of prophecy*. The reference is to prophetic intimation given to Paul concerning the selection of Timothy for the ministerial office. These prophecies were given by the Holy Spirit who bestowed the "gift"; so that the gift itself

---

* After carefully studying Holtzmann's elaborate attempt to prove that χάρισμα means *office conferred by ordination*, I am unable to see in it anything but a most ingenious piece of special pleading. There is absolutely no instance of the use of the word in that sense. The meaning given above is confirmed by Paul's usage as well as by that of Justin Martyr, Clement of Alexandria, Tertullian, Origen, and Eusebius. Ἐν σοὶ *in thee* cannot be wrenched into *thy* by references to 2 Tim. i. 5 and Matt. vi. 23. "The office that is *in thee*" is quite inadmissible.

and the prophecy concurred in attesting the candidate for ordination.

With the laying on of the hands (μετὰ ἐπιθέσεως τῶν χειρῶν). Μετὰ *with* implies that the prophetic intimations were in some way repeated or emphasised in connection with the ceremony of ordination. We note the association of prophecy with ordination in the setting apart of Paul and Barnabas (Acts xiii. 2, 3); so that the case of Timothy has an analogue in that of Paul himself.* Ἐπίθεσις *laying on, imposition*, also Acts viii. 18; 2 Tim. i. 6; Heb. vi. 2, in each case with *of hands*. "The custom," says Lange, "is as old as the race." The Biblical custom rests on the conception of the hand as the organ of mediation and transference. The priest laid his hand on the head of the bullock or goat (Lev. i. 4) to show that the guilt of the people was transferred. The hand was laid on the head of a son, to indicate the transmission of the hereditary blessing (Gen. xlviii. 14); upon one appointed to a position of authority, as Joshua (Num. xxvii. 18–23); upon the sick or dead in token of miraculous power to heal or to restore to life (2 K. iv. 34). So Christ (Mk. vi. 5; L. iv. 40). In the primitive Christian church the laying on of hands signified the imparting of the Holy Spirit to the newly-baptized (Acts viii. 17; xix. 6; comp. Heb. vi. 2). Hands were laid upon the seven (Acts vi. 6). But the form of consecration in ordination varied. No one mode has been universal in the church, and no authoritative written formula exists. In the Alexandrian and Abyssinian churches it was by breathing: in the Eastern church generally, by lifting up the hands in benediction: in the Armenian church, by touching the dead hand of the predecessor: in the early Celtic church, by the transmission of relics or pastoral staff: in the Latin church, by touching the head.

Of the presbytery (τοῦ πρεσβυτερίου). The word is found in L. xxii. 66, where it denotes the body of representative

---

* Holtzmann says that this passage in Acts is the basis of the ordination-picture presented here.

elders of the people in the Sanhedrim, as distinguished from
the two other constituents of that body—the chief priests and
scribes.   Similarly Acts xxii. 5.   Here of the college or fra-
ternity of Christian elders in the place where Timothy was
ordained.   The word is frequent in the Epistles of Ignatius.*
According to this, Timothy was not ordained by a Bishop.
Bishop and Presbyter are not identical.   In 2 Tim. i. 6 we
read, "by the laying on of *my* hands."   The inconsistency is
usually explained by saying that Paul was associated with the
Presbyters in the laying on of hands.

15. **Meditate** ($\mu\epsilon\lambda\epsilon\tau\alpha$).   Only here and Acts iv. 25 (citation).   Often in Class. and LXX.   Most translators reject
the A. V. *meditate*, and substitute *be diligent in*, or *practise*, or
take care for.   *Meditate*, however, is legitimate, although in
Class. the word commonly appears in one of the other senses.
The connection between the different meanings is apparent.
Exercise or *practice* applied to the mind becomes *thinking* or
meditation.   In LXX it represents seven Hebrew equivalents,
and signifies *to meditate, talk of, murmur, delight one's self in,
attend to*.   Often *to meditate*, Josh. i. 8; Ps. i. 2; ii. 1;
xxxvii. 12; lxxii. 6; Sir. vi. 7.   Meditation is a talking
within the mind, and issues in speech; hence *to speak*, as
Ps. xxxiv. 28; xxxvi. 30; Isa. lxix. 3.   Similarly, $\lambda\acute{o}\gamma o\varsigma$
signifies both *reason* and *discourse*.   In Lat. *meditari*, "to
reflect," is also "to exercise in," "to practise," as Virgil, *Ecl.*
i. 2.   In the Vulg. *meditabor* is the translation of *murmur* or
mourn in Isa. xxxviii. 14.   The Heb. הָגָה means to *murmur,
whisper;* hence the inner whispering of the heart; hence *to
think, meditate, consider*, as Ps. lxiii. 7; lxxviii. 13.

Give thyself wholly to them ($\dot{\epsilon}\nu$ $\tau o\acute{u}\tau o\iota\varsigma$ $\ddot{\iota}\sigma\theta\iota$).   Lit. *be in
these things*.   The phrase N. T.°.   The only parallel in LXX
is Prov. xxiii. 17.   The meaning is that he is to throw himself wholly into his ministry.   Comp. "totus in illis," Horace,
Sat. i. 9, 2.

---

* *Eph.* ii; *Magnes.* ii, xiii; *Trall.* ii, vii; *Philad.* iv, v, vii; *Smyrn.* viii, xii.

Profiting (προκοπή). Better, *advance* or *progress*. Only here and Philip. i. 12. The verb προκόπτειν in 2 Tim. ii. 16; iii. 9, 13. In LXX, see Sir. li. 17; 2 Macc. viii. 8. The figure in the word is uncertain, but is supposed to be that of pioneers *cutting* (κόπτω) a way *before* (πρὸ) an army, and so *furthering* its advance. The opposite is ἐγκόπτειν *to cut into, throw obstacles in the way*, and so *hinder*. See Gal. v. 7; 1 Th. ii. 18; 1 Pet. iii. 7.

16. **Take heed** (ἔπεχε). Only here in Pastorals, and once in Paul, Philip. ii. 16. Quite frequent in LXX. Lit. *hold upon, fasten thy attention on*, as L. xiv. 7; Acts iii. 5; xix. 22. In LXX, in the sense of *apply*, as Job xviii. 2; xxx. 26; or *forbear, refrain*, as 1 K. xxii. 6, 15. In Philip. ii. 16, *to hold out* or *present*, a sense which is found only in Class.

Unto thyself and unto the doctrine (σεαυτῷ καὶ τῇ διδασκαλίᾳ). Better, *to thyself and to thy teaching*. The order is significant. Personality goes before teaching.

Continue in them (ἐπίμενε αὐτοῖς). See on Rom. vi. 1. In LXX only Ex. xii. 39. Ἀυτοῖς is neuter, referring to *these things*, ver. 15. A. V. *in them* is indefinite and ambiguous. Better, *continue in these things*.

CHAPTER V.

1. **Rebuke not an elder** (πρεσβυτέρῳ μὴ ἐπιπλήξῃς). The verb N. T.⁰. ⁰LXX. Originally *to lay on blows;* hence to *castigate* with words. Πρεσβύτερος *elder*, ⁰P., but frequent in Gospels, Acts, and Apocalypse. Modern critical opinion has largely abandoned the view that the original Christian polity was an imitation of that of the Synagogue. The secular and religious authorities of the Jewish communities, at least in purely Jewish localities, were the same; a fact which is against the probability that the polity was directly transferred to the Christian church. The preroga-

tives of the Jewish elders have nothing corresponding with them in extent in the Christian community. Functions which emerge later in the Jewish-Christian communities of Palestine do not exist in the first Palestinian-Christian society. At the most, as Weizsäcker observes, it could only be a question of borrowing a current name.*

Modern criticism compels us, I think, to abandon the view of the identity of Bishop and Presbyter which has obtained such wide acceptance, especially among English scholars, through the discussions of Lightfoot and Hatch.† The testimony of Clement of Rome (*Ep. ad Corinth.*) goes to show that the Bishops (ἡγούμενοι or προηγούμενοι) are distinguished from the Presbyters, and that if the Bishops are apparently designated as Presbyters, it is because they have been chosen from the body of Presbyters, and have retained the name even when they have ceased to hold office. For this reason deceased Bishops are called Presbyters. In Clement, Presbyters signify a class or estate — members of long standing and approved character, and not office-bearers regularly appointed. Among these the Bishops are to be sought. Bishops are reckoned as Presbyters, not because the Presbyter as such is a Bishop, but because the Bishop as such is a Presbyter. In the Pastorals, Bishops and Deacons are associated without mention of Presbyters (1 Tim. iii. 1–13). Presbyters are referred to in 1 Tim. v. 17–19, but in an entirely different connection. The qualifications of Bishops and Deacons are detailed in the former passage, and the list of qualifications concludes with the statement that this is the ordering of the church as the house of God (vv. 14, 15). The offices are exhausted in the description of Bishops

---

* The view that the original Christian polity was drawn from that of the Synagogue was maintained by Rothe, Baur, Lightfoot, Hatch, and others. The development of the view given above is largely due to Schürer, *Geschichte des jüdischen Volkes im Zeitalt r Jesu Christi*, 2 Aufl., Bd. II.   English trans. *A History of the Jewish People in the Time of Jesus Christ*, 2d divis., Vol. II., p. 56 ff.   Also, *Die Gemeindeverfassung der Juden in Rom in der Kaiserzeit*.

† For a more detailed examination of this subject I must refer the reader to my Excursus on "Bishops and Deacons" in the *International Commentary on Philippians and Philemon*.

and Deacons. Nothing is said of Presbyters until ch. v, where Timothy's relations to individual church-members are prescribed; and in Tit. ii. 2 ff. these members are classified as *old men* (πρεσβύτας), *old women, young men,* and *servants.* In 1 Tim. v. 17 are mentioned *elders who rule well* (οἱ καλῶς προεστῶτες πρεσβύτεροι). Assuming that Presbyters and Bishops were identical, a distinction would thus be implied between two classes of Bishops — those who rule well and those who do not: whereas the distinction is obviously between old and honored church-members, collectively considered, forming the presbyterial body, and certain of their number who show their qualifications for appointment as overseers. Presbyters as such are not invested with office. There is no formal act constituting a Presbyter. The Bishops are reckoned among the Elders, but the Elders as such are not officers.

Thus are to be explained the allusions to *appointed* Elders, Tit. i. 5; Acts xiv. 23. Elders are to be appointed as *overseers* or *Bishops*, for the overseers must have the qualifications of approved Presbyters. The ordination of Presbyters is the setting apart of Elders to the position of Superintendents. The Presbyterate denotes an honorable and influential estate in the church on the ground of age, duration of church membership, and approved character. Only Bishops are *appointed.* There is no appointment to the Presbyterate. At the close of Clement's letter to the Corinthians, the qualifications of a Presbyter are indicated in the description of the three commissioners from the Roman church who are the bearers of the letter, and to whom no official title is given. They are old, members of the Roman church from youth, blameless in life, believing, and sober.*

---

* The late Dr. Hort, in his *Ecclesia*, holds that "Bishop" was not the designation of an *office*, but of a *function*. It was a description of the Elder's function. He says: "It is now pretty generally recognised . . . that we have not here (in the word ἐπίσκοπος) a different office, held by one person in contrast to the plural *Elders*." And he adds: "It is hardly less erroneous to take ἐπίσκοπος as merely a second title, capable of being used convertibly with πρεσβύτερος" (p. 190).

2. **The elder women** (πρεσβυτέρας). N. T.º. Comp. πρεσβύτιδας *aged women*, Tit. ii. 3. The word indicates distinction in *age* merely, although some think that it points to an official position which is further referred to in the following directions concerning widows.*

3. **Honour** (τίμα). Not only by respectful treatment but by financial support. Comp. τιμήσει, Matt. xv. 5, and πολλαῖς τιμαῖς ἐτίμησαν, Acts xxviii. 10; and διπλῆς τιμῆς, 1 Tim. v. 17. Comp. Sir. xxxviii. 1. The verb only once in Paul (Eph. vi. 2, citation), and only here in Pastorals.

Widows (χήρας). Paul alludes to widows in 1 Cor. vii. 8 only, where he advises them against remarrying. They are mentioned as a class in Acts vi. 1, in connection with the appointment of the seven. Also Acts ix. 39, 41. In the Pastorals they receive special notice, indicating their advance from the position of mere beneficiaries to a quasi-official position in the church. From the very first, the church recognised its obligation to care for their support. A widow, in the East, was peculiarly desolate and helpless.† In return for their maintenance certain duties were required of them, such as the care of orphans, sick and prisoners, and they were enrolled in an order, which, however, did not include all of their number who received alms of the church. In Polycarp's *Epistle to the Philippians*, they are styled "the altar of God." To such an order the references in the Pastorals point. The Fathers, from the end of the second century to the fourth, recognised a class known as πρεσβύτιδες *aged women* (Tit. ii. 3), who had oversight of the female church-members and a separate seat in the congregation. The council of Laodicaea abolished this institution, or so modified it that widows no longer held an official relation to the church. ‡

---

* So Holtzmann, who finds in it a trace of " the Mothers of the Synagogue " in the synagogues of the Jewish dispersion. See *Pastoralbriefe*, p. 241.

† See Ignatius, *Ep. to Polycarp*, IV. Polycarp, *Ep. to Philippians*, VI.

‡ On the enrolment of virgins in this order see Lightfoot, *Ignatius*, Vol. II., p. 322 ff. (2d ed.).

Who are widows indeed (τὰς ὄντως χήρας). Comp. vv.
5, 16. Ὄντως *verily*, *truly*, twice in Paul, 1 Cor. xiv. 25;
Gal. iii. 21. See on 2 Pet. ii. 18. Wherever ὄντως is used
by Paul or by any other N. T. writer, it is used purely as an
adverb (see L. xxiii. 47; xxiv. 34): but in all the four
instances in the Pastorals, it is preceded by the article and
converted into an adjective. The meaning is, who are *absolutely* bereaved, without children or relations (comp. ver. 4),
and have been but once married. There is probably also an
implied contrast with those described in vv. 6, 11–13.

4. **Nephews** (ἔκγονα). N. T.°. Often in LXX. *Nephews*, in the now obsolete sense of *grandsons* or other lineal
descendants. Derived from Lat. *nepos*. Trench (*Select
Glossary*) remarks that *nephew* has undergone exactly the
same change of meaning that *nepos* underwent, which, in the
Augustan age, meaning *grandson*, in the post-Augustan age
acquired the signification of *nephew* in our present acceptation of that word. Chaucer:

> "How that my nevew shall my bane be."
> *Legend of Good Women*, 2659.

> 'His (Jove's) blind nevew Cupido."
> *House of Fame*, 67.

Jeremy Taylor: "Nephews are very often liker to their
grandfathers than to their fathers."

Let them learn. The subject is the children and grandchildren. Holtzmann thinks the subject is *any widow*, used
collectively. But the writer is treating of what should be
done to the widow, not of what she is to do. The admonition is connected with *widows indeed*. *They*, as being utterly
bereft, and without natural supporters, are to be cared for by
the church; but if they have children or grandchildren, these
should assume their maintenance.

First (πρῶτον). In the first place: as their first and nat
ural obligation.

To show piety at home (τὸν ἴδιον οἶκον εὐσεβεῖν). More correctly, *to show piety toward their own family*. *Piety* in the sense of filial respect, though not to the exclusion of the religious sense. The Lat. *pietas* includes alike love and duty to the gods and to parents. Thus Virgil's familiar designation of Aeneas, "*pius* Aeneas," as describing at once his reverence for the gods and his filial devotion. The verb εὐσεβεῖν (only here and Acts xvii. 23) represents filial respect as an element of godliness (εὐσέβεια). For τὸν ἴδιον *their own*, see on Acts i. 7. It emphasises their private, personal belonging, and contrasts the assistance given by them with that furnished by the church. It has been suggested that οἶκον *household* or *family* may mark the duty as an act of family feeling and honour.

To requite (ἀμοιβὰς ἀποδιδόναι). An entirely unique expression. Ἀμοιβή *requital, recompense* is a familiar classical word, used with διδόναι *to give*, ἀποτιθέναι *to lay down*, τίνειν *to pay*, ποιεῖσθαι *to make*. N. T.⁰. Paul uses instead ἀντιμισθία (Rom. i. 27; 2 Cor. vi. 13), or ἀνταπόδομα (Rom. xi. 9), or ἀνταπόδοσις (Col. iii. 24). The last two are LXX words.

Their parents (τοῖς προγόνοις). N. T.⁰. *Parents* is too limited. The word comprehends mothers and grandmothers and living ancestors generally. The word for *parents* is γονεῖς, see 2 Tim. iii. 2; Rom. i. 30; 2 Cor. xii. 14; Eph. vi. 1; Col. iii. 20. Πρόγονοι for *living* ancestors is contrary to usage. One instance is cited from Plato, *Laws*, xi. 932. The word is probably selected to correspond in form with ἔκγονα *children*.

Good and acceptable (καλὸν καὶ ἀποδεκτὸν). Omit καλὸν καὶ *good and*. Ἀπόδεκτος *acceptable* only here and 1 Tim. ii. 3. See note.

Before (ἐνώπιον). Frequent in N. T., especially Luke and Apocalypse. It occurs 31 times in the phrases ἐνώπιον τοῦ θεοῦ *in the sight of God*, and ἐνώπιον κυρίου *in the sight of the Lord*. ᵒLXX. Comp. ἔμπροσθεν τοῦ θεοῦ *before God*, Acts x. 4; 1 Th. i. 3; ii. 19; iii. 9, 13. Not in Pastorals, and by Paul only 1 Th. The difference is trifling. Comp. 1 J. iii. 19 and 22.

5. **And desolate** (καὶ μεμονωμένη). N. T.ᵒ. From μόνος *alone*. Explanatory of *a widow indeed*. One *entirely* bereaved.

Trusteth in God (ἤλπικεν ἐπὶ τὸν θεὸν). Strictly, *hath directed her hope at God*. Rev. *hath her hope set on God* implies ἐπὶ with the dative, as 1 J. iii. 3.

6. **Liveth in pleasure** (σπαταλῶσα). Only here and Jas. v. 5. See note. Twice in LXX, Sir. xxi. 15; Ezek. xvi. 49.

Is dead while she liveth (ζῶσα τέθνηκεν). Comp. Apoc. iii. 1; Eph. iv. 18. "Life in worldly pleasure is only life in appearance" (Holtzmann).

8. **Provide** (προνοεῖ). See on Rom. xii. 17.

His own — those of his own house (τῶν ἰδίων — οἰκείων). His own relations, see on J. i. 11. Those who form part of his family, see on Gal. vi. 10.

He hath denied the faith (τὴν πίστιν ἤρνηται). The verb not in Paul, but quite often in Pastorals. The phrase only here and Apoc. ii. 13. Faith demands works and fruits. By refusing the natural duties which Christian faith implies, one practically denies his possession of faith. "Faith does not abolish natural duties, but perfects and strengthens them" (Bengel). Comp. Jas. ii. 14–17.

Infidel (ἀπίστου). Better, *unbeliever*. One who is not a Christian, as 1 Cor. vi. 6; vii. 12, 13, etc. Even an unbeliever will perform these duties from natural promptings.

9. **Be taken into the number** (καταλεγέσθω).   Better, *enrolled* (as a widow).   N. T.°.   Very rare in LXX.   Common in Class.   Originally, *to pick out*, as soldiers.   Hence, to *enrol*, *enlist*.   Here, to be enrolled in the body of widows who are to receive church support.   See on ver. 3.

10. **Well reported of** (μαρτυρουμένη).   Lit. *borne witness to* or *attested*, as Acts vi. 3; x. 22; Heb. xi. 2.   Comp. μαρτυρίαν καλὴν ἔχειν *to have good testimony*, ch. iii. 7.

For good works (ἐν ἔργοις καλοῖς).   Lit. *in* good works; in the matter of.   Comp. 1 Tim. vi. 18; Tit. ii. 7; iii. 8, 14. In the Gospels, ἔργον *work* appears with καλὸς and never with ἀγαθὸς.   In Paul, always with ἀγαθὸς and never with καλὸς. In the Pastorals, with both.   The phrase includes good deeds of all kinds, and not merely special works of beneficence. Comp. Acts ix. 36.

If (εἰ).   Introducing the details of the general expression *good works*.

Have brought up children (ἐτεκνοτρόφησεν).   N. T.°. °LXX; very rare in Class.   The children may have been her own or others'.

Lodged strangers (ἐξενοδόχησεν).   N. T.°.   °LXX.   On the duty of hospitality comp. ch. iii. 2; Matt. xxv. 35; Rom. xii. 13; Heb. xiii. 2; 1 Pet. iv. 9; 3 J. 5.

Washed the feet.   A mark of Oriental hospitality bestowed on the stranger arriving from a journey, and therefore closely associated with *lodged strangers*.

Of the saints (ἁγίων).   Ἅγιος is rare in Class.   In LXX, the standard word for *holy*.   Its fundamental idea is *setting apart*, as in Class., *devoted to the gods*.   In O. T., *set apart to God*, as priests; as the Israelites consecrated to God.   In N. T., applied to Christians.   Ideally, it implies personal holiness.   It is used of God, Christ, John the Baptist, God's

law, the Spirit of God. Paul often uses οἱ ἅγιοι as a common
designation of Christians belonging to a certain region or
community, as Philip. i. 1 ; 2 Cor. i. 1 ; Col. i. 2. In such
cases it does not imply actual holiness, but holiness obligatory
upon those addressed, as consecrated persons, and appropriate
to them. What ought to be is assumed as being. In this
sense not in the Gospels (unless, possibly, Matt. xxvii. 52)
or in the Epistles of Peter and John. Rare in Acts.

Relieved (ἐπήρκεσεν). Only here and ver. 16. Comp.
1 Macc. viii. 26 ; xi. 35. Common in Class. Originally, to
suffice for, to be strong enough for, as in Homer, where it is
always used in connection with danger or injury. See *Il.* ii.
873 ; *Od.* xvii. 568. Hence, to *ward off, help, assist.*

The afflicted (θλιβομένοις). See on *tribulation,* Matt.
xiii. 21, and comp. 2 Cor. i. 6 ; iv. 8 ; 2 Th. i. 6, 7 ; Heb.
xi. 37.

Diligently followed (ἐπακο ουθησεν). Comp. ver. 24.
'Επὶ *after* or *close upon.* °P. Once in the disputed verses
at the end of Mk. (xvi. 20), and 1 Pet. ii. 21. Comp. the
use of διώκειν *pursue,* Rom. ix. 30 ; xii. 13 ; 1 Cor. xiv. 1 ;
1 Th. v. 15.

11. Younger (νεωτέρας). Almost in a positive sense,
young. Not, under sixty years of age.

Have begun to wax wanton (καταστρηνιάσωσιν). Not,
have begun, but rather, *whenever they shall come to wax wanton.* Comp. 2 Th. i. 10. The compound verb, signifying *to
feel the sexual impulse,* only here, and not in LXX or Class.
The simple verb, στρηνιᾶν *to run riot,* Apoc. xviii. 7, 9 ; and
the kindred στρῆνος *luxury,* Apoc. xviii. 3. See note.

Against Christ (τοῦ Χριστοῦ). Their unruly desire with-
draws them from serving Christ in his church, and is, therefore, *against* him.*

---

* Weizsäcker has it : *wenn sie trotz Christus in Begierde fallen.*

This is the only instance in the Pastorals in which *the Christ* is used without *Jesus* either before or after.   In Paul this is common, both with and without the article.

They will marry (γαμεῖν θέλουσιν).   Better, they *are bent on* marrying, or *determined* to marry.   The strong expression *wax wanton* makes it probable that θέλειν expresses more than a *desire*, as Rev.   See on Matt. i. 19.   Γαμεῖν *to marry*, in the active voice, of the wife, as everywhere in N. T. except 1 Cor. vii. 39.*

12. **Having damnation** (ἔχουσαι κρίμα).   The phrase only here.   See on 1 Tim. iii. 6.   *Damnation* is an unfortunate rendering in the light of the present common understanding of the word, as it is also in 1 Cor. xi. 29.   Better, *judgment* or *condemnation*, as Rom. iii. 8 ; xiii. 2.   The meaning is that they carry about with them in their new, married life a con·demnation, a continuous reproach.   Comp. ch. iv. 2 ; Gal. v. 10.   It should be said for the translators of 1611 that they used *damnation* in this sense of *judgment* or *condemnation*, as is shown by the present participle *having*.   In its earlier usage the word implied no allusion to a future punishment.   Thus Chaucer :

> " For wel thou woost (knowest) thyselven verraily
> That thou and I be *dampned* to prisoun."
> *Knight's T.* 1175.

Wiclif : " Nethir thou dredist God, that thou art in the same *dampnacioun?* "   L. xxiii. 40.   Laud. : " Pope Alexander III. condemned Peter Lombard of heresy, and he lay under that *damnation* for thirty and six years."   " A legacy by damnation " was one in which the testator imposed on his heir an obligation to give the legatee the thing bequeathed, and which afforded the legatee a personal claim against the heir.

---

* Holtzmann adds Mk. x. 12, after the reading of T. R. γαμηθῇ ἄλλῳ *be married to another*.   But the correct reading there is γαμήσῃ ἄλλον *have married another*.

They have cast off their first faith (τὴν πρώτην πίστιν ἠθέτησαν). Ἀθετεῖν is *to set aside, do away with, reject* or *slight*. See Mk. vi. 26; L. x. 16; Heb. x. 28. Often in LXX. Πίστιν is *pledge:* so frequently in Class. with *give* and *receive*. See, for instance, Plato, *Phaedr.* 256 D. In LXX, 3 Macc. iii. 10. The phrase πίστιν ἀθετεῖν N. T.º. ºLXX. There are, however, a number of expressions closely akin to it, as Gal. iii. 15, διαθήκην ἀθετεῖν to render a covenant *void*. In LXX with *oath*, 2 Chron. xxxvi. 13. Ps. xiv. 4: "He that sweareth to his neighbour καὶ οὐκ ἀθετῶν." Ps. lxxxviii. 34; cxxxi. 11; 1 Macc. vi. 62. The meaning here is, *having broken their first pledge;* and this may refer to a pledge to devote themselves, after they became widows, to the service of Christ and the church. The whole matter is obscure.

13. **They learn** (μανθάνουσιν). To be taken absolutely, as 1 Cor. xiv. 31; 2 Tim. iii. 7. They go about under the influence of an insatiable curiosity, and meet those who "creep into houses and take captive silly women" (2 Tim. iii. 7), and learn all manner of nonsense and error.

Going about (περιερχόμεναι). ºP. Comp. Acts xix. 13.

Tattlers (φλύαροι). N. T.º. Comp. 4 Macc. v. 10. The verb φλυαρεῖν *to prate*, 3 J. 10.

Busybodies (περίεργοι). In this sense only here. Comp. τὰ περίεργα *curious arts*, Acts xix. 19. The participle περιεργαζόμενοι *busybodies*, 2 Th. iii. 11. See note. Rend. the whole passage : "And withal, being also idle, they learn, gadding about from house to house; and not only (are they) idle, but tattlers also, and busybodies, speaking things which they ought not." *

---

* The construction is awkward at best. The most common explanation is to make ἀργαὶ *idle* depend upon μανθάνουσιν *they learn*, understanding εἶναι *to be: they learn to be idle*. Others take περιερχόμεναι with μανθάνουσιν; *they learn to go about*, which is not Greek. von Soden makes τὰ μὴ δέοντα *what they ought not* the object of both μανθάνουσιν and λαλοῦσαι *speaking*, which is clearly inadmissible.

14. **That the younger women marry** (νεωτέρας γαμεῖν). Better, *the younger widows*. This seems to be required by οὖν *therefore*, connecting the subject of the verb with the class just described. They are enjoined to marry, rather than to assume a position in the church which they might disgrace by the conduct described in vv. 11–13. Comp. 1 Cor. vii. 8, 9.

Bear children (τεκνογονεῖν). N. T.⁰. ⁰LXX, ⁰Class. Comp. τεκνογονία *childbearing*, 1 Tim. ii. 15.

Guide the house (οἰκοδεσποτεῖν). Better, *rule* the house. N. T.⁰. ⁰LXX, ⁰Class. Ὀικοδεσπότης *master of the house* is quite common in the Synoptic Gospels.

Occasion (ἀφορμὴν). See on Rom. vii. 8.

To the adversary (τῷ ἀντικειμένῳ). The one who is *set over against*. Not Satan, but the human enemy of Christianity. Comp. Philip. i. 28, and ὁ ἐξ ἐναντίας *he that is of the contrary part*, Tit. ii. 8.

To speak reproachfully (λοιδορίας χάριν). Lit. *in the interest of reviling*. Const. with *give no occasion*. Λοιδορία *reviling* only here and 1 Pet. iii. 9. For the verb λοιδορεῖν *to revile* see J. ix. 28; Acts xxiii. 4; 1 Cor. iv. 12; and note on J. ix. 28.

16. **Man or woman that believeth** (πιστὸς ἢ πιστὴ). Lit. *believing man or woman*. But πιστὸς ἢ should be omitted. Read, *if any woman that believeth*.

Have widows (ἔχει χήρας). If any Christian woman have relatives or persons attached to her household who are widows

The church be charged. Holtzmann quotes an inscription in the chapel of the Villa Albani at Rome : "To the good Regina her daughter has erected this memorial : to the good Regina her widowed mother, who was a widow for sixty years

and never burdened the church after she was the wife of one
husband.   She lived 80 years, 5 months, and 26 days."

17. **The elders that rule well** (οἱ καλῶς προεστῶτες πρεσβύτεροι).   For *that rule well*, see on καλῶς προϊστάμενον *ruling
well*, 1 Tim. iii. 4.   The phrase is peculiar to the Pastorals.
See on ver. 1.

Double honour (διπλῆς τιμῆς).   This at least includes pecuniary remuneration for services, if it is not limited to that.
The use of τιμή as *pay* or *price* appears Matt. xxvii. 6, 9;
Acts iv. 34; vii. 16; 1 Cor. vi. 20.   *Double*, not in a strictly
literal sense, but as πλείονα τιμὴν *more honour*, Heb. iii. 3.
The comparison is with those Elders who do not exhibit equal
capacity or efficiency in ruling.   The passage lends no support
to the Reformed theory of two classes of Elders — ruling and
teaching.   The special honour or emolument is assigned to
those who combine qualifications for both.

Those who labour (οἱ κοπιῶντες).   See on ch. iv. 10.   No
special emphasis attaches to the word — *hard* toiling in comparison with those who do not toil.   The meaning is, those
who faithfully discharge the arduous duty of teaching.   Comp.
Heb. xiii. 7.

In word and doctrine (ἐν λόγῳ καὶ διδασκαλίᾳ).   Better,
word and *teaching*.   *Word* is general, *teaching* special.   *In
word* signifies, in that class of functions where speech is concerned.   The special emphasis (μάλιστα *especially*) shows the
importance which was attached to teaching as an antidote of
heresy.

18. **The Scripture** (ἡ γραφή).   Comp. 2 Tim. iii. 16.   To
the Jews ἡ γραφή signified the O. T. canon of Scripture; but
in most cases ἡ γραφή is used of a particular passage of Scripture which is indicated in the context.   See J. vii. 38, 42;
Acts i. 16; viii. 32, 35; Rom. iv. 3; ix. 17; x. 11; Gal.
iii. 8.   Where the reference is to the sacred writings as a

whole, the plural γραφαὶ or αἱ γραφαὶ is used, as Matt. xxi.
42; L. xxiv. 32; J. v. 39; Rom. xv. 4.   Once γραφαὶ ἅγιαι
holy Scriptures, Rom. i. 2.   Ἑτέρα γραφὴ *another* or *a different
Scripture*, J. xix. 37; ἡ γραφὴ αὕτη *this Scripture*, L. iv. 21;
πᾶσα γραφὴ *every Scripture*, 2 Tim. iii. 16.   See on *writings*,
J. ii. 22.   The passage cited here is Deut. xxv. 4, also by
Paul, 1 Cor. ix. 9.

Thou shalt not muzzle (οὐ φιμώσεις).   In N. T. mostly in
the metaphorical sense of *putting to silence.*   See on *speechless*,
Matt. xxii. 12, and *put to silence*, Matt. xxii. 34.   Also on
Mk. iv. 39.   On the whole passage see note on 1 Cor. ix. 9.

That treadeth out (ἀλοῶντα).   More correctly, *while he is
treading out.*   The verb only here and 1 Cor. ix. 9, 10.   Comp.
ἄλων *a threshing-floor*, Matt. iii. 12; L. iii. 17.   An analogy
to the O. T. injunction may be found in the laws given to the
Athenians by the mythical Triptolemus, one of which was,
" Hurt not the labouring beast."   Some one having violated
this command by slaying a steer which was eating the sacred
cake that lay upon the altar, — an expiation-feast, *Bouphonia*
or *Diipolīa* was instituted for the purpose of atoning for this
offence, and continued to be celebrated in Athens.   Aristophanes refers to it (*Clouds*, 985).   A labouring ox was led
to the altar of Zeus on the Acropolis, which was strewn with
wheat and barley.   As soon as the ox touched the grain, he
was killed by a blow from an axe.   The priest who struck the
blow threw away the axe and fled.   The flesh of the ox was
then eaten, and the hide was stuffed and set before the plough.
Then began the steer-trial before a judicial assembly in the
Prytaneum, by which the axe was formally condemned to be
thrown into the sea.

The labourer is worthy, etc.   A second scriptural quotation would seem to be indicated, but there is no corresponding
passage in the O. T.   The words are found L. x. 7, and, with
a slight variation, Matt. x. 10.   Some hold that the writer
adds to the O. T. citation a popular proverb, and that Christ

himself used the words in this way. But while different
passages of Scripture are often connected in citation by καὶ,
it is not according to N. T. usage thus to connect Scripture
and proverb. Moreover, in such series of citations it is
customary to use καὶ πάλιν and again, or πάλιν simply. See
Matt. iv. 7; v. 33; J. xii. 39; Rom. xv. 9–12; 1 Cor. iii.
20; Heb. i. 5; ii. 13. According to others, the writer here
cites an utterance of Christ from oral tradition, coördinately
with the O. T. citation, as Scripture. Paul, in 1 Th. iv. 15;
1 Cor. vii. 10, appeals to *a word of the Lord;* and in Acts
xx. 35 he is represented as quoting "it is more blessed to
give than to receive" as the words of Jesus. In 1 Cor. ix,
in the discussion of this passage from Deuteronomy, Paul
adds (ver. 14) "even so hath the Lord ordained that they
which preach the gospel should live of the gospel," which
resembles the combination here. This last is the more probable explanation.

19. Receive not an accusation (κατηγορίαν μὴ παραδέχου).
Neither word in Paul. For *accusation* see on J. v. 45. It
means a formal accusation before a tribunal. The compound
verb with παρὰ emphasises the *giver* or *transmitter* of the
thing received : to receive *from* another.

But (ἐκτὸς εἰ μή). Except. A pleonastic formula, *except
in case.* The formula in 1 Cor. xiv. 5; xv. 2.

Before (ἐπί). Or *on the authority of.* On condition that
two witnesses testify. The O. T. law on this point in Deut.
xix. 15. Comp. Matt. xviii. 16; J. viii. 17; 2 Cor. xiii. 1.

20. Them that sin (τοὺς ἁμαρτάνοντας). Referring to
Elders, who, by reason of their public position (προεστῶτες),
should receive public rebuke.

Rebuke (ἔλεγχε). Comp. 2 Tim. iv. 2; Tit. i. 9, 13; ii.
15. See on *reproved*, J. iii. 20.

Others (οἱ λοιποί). More correctly, *the rest.* His fellow-
Elders.

May fear (φόβον ἔχωσιν). May *have* fear, which is stronger than A. V.

21. I charge (διαμαρτύρομαι). In Paul 1 Th. iv. 6 only. See on *testifying*, 1 Th. ii. 12. For this sense, *adjure*, see L. xvi. 28; Acts ii. 40; 2 Tim. ii. 14.

Elect angels (ἐκλεκτῶν ἀγγέλων). The phrase N. T.º. The triad, God, Christ, the angels, only L. ix. 26. It is not necessary to suppose that a class of angels distinguished from the rest is meant. It may refer to all angels, as special objects of divine complacency. Comp. Tob. viii. 15; Acts x. 22; Apoc. xiv. 10.

Observe (φυλάξῃς). Lit. *guard*. In the Pauline sense of *keeping* the law, Rom. ii. 26; Gal. vi. 13.

Without preferring one before another (χωρὶς προκρίματος). A unique expression. Πρόκριμα *prejudgment*. N. T.º. ºLXX, ºClass. Rend. *without prejudice*.

By partiality (κατὰ πρόσκλισιν). N. T.º. ºLXX. According to its etymology, *inclining toward*. In later Greek of joining one party in preference to another. In Clement (*ad Corinth*. xli, xlvii, 1) in the sense of factious preferences.

22. Lay hands on. Probably with reference to that rite in the formal restoration of those who had been expelled from the church for gross sins.*

Suddenly (ταχέως). Better, *hastily*.

Neither be partaker of other men's sins (μηδὲ κοινώνει ἁμαρτίαις ἀλλοτρίαις). Better, *make common cause with*. See on *communicating*, Rom. xii. 13. Comp. Rom. xv. 27; 1 Pet.

---

* Variously explained, of ordination; of reception into the communion of the church; of the reception of heretics who, having been excluded from one congregation, should present themselves to another as candidates for membership.

iv. 13 ; Eph. v. 11.   By a too hasty and inconsiderate restoration, he would condone the sins of the offenders, and
would thus make common cause with them.

Keep thyself pure (σεαυτὸν ἁγνὸν τήρει).   Comp. ch. vi.
14.   Enjoining positively what was enjoined negatively in
the preceding clause.   For *pure* see on 1 J. iii. 3.   For
keep see on *reserved*, 1 Pet. i. 4.   The phrase ἑαυτὸν τηρεῖν *to
keep one's self*, in Jas. i. 27 ; 2 Cor. xi. 9.

23.   **Drink no longer water** (μηκέτι ὑδροπότει).   The
verb N. T.⁰.   ⁰LXX.   Rend. *be no longer a drinker of water*.
Timothy is not enjoined to abstain from water, but is bidden
not to be a *water-drinker*, entirely abstaining from wine.   The
kindred noun ὑδροπότης is used by Greek comic writers to
denote a mean-spirited person.   See Aristoph. *Knights*, 349.

But use a little wine (ἀλλὰ οἴνῳ ὀλίγῳ χρῶ).   The reverse
antithesis appears in Hdt. i. 171, of the Persians : οὐκ οἴνῳ
διαχρέονται ἀλλ᾽ ὑδροποτέουσι *they do not indulge in wine but
are water-drinkers*.   Comp. Plato, *Repub.* 561 C, τοτὲ μεν
μεθύων — αὖθις δὲ ὑδροποτῶν *sometimes he is drunk — then he
is for total-abstinence*.   With *a little wine* comp. *much wine*,
ch. iii. 8 ; Tit. ii. 3.

For thy stomach's sake (διὰ στόμαχον).   Στόμαχος N. T.⁰.
⁰LXX.   The appearance at this point of this dietetic pre-
scription, if it is nothing more, is sufficiently startling ; which
has led to some question whether the verse may not have been
misplaced.   If it belongs here, it can be explained only as a
continuation of the thought in ver. 22, to the effect that Timothy is to keep himself pure by not giving aid and comfort
to the ascetics, and imperilling his own health by adopting
their rules of abstinence.   Observe that οἶνος here, as everywhere else, means *wine, fermented* and *capable of intoxicating*,
and not a sweet syrup made by boiling down grape-juice,
and styled by certain modern reformers " unfermented
wine."   Such a concoction would have tended rather to

aggravate than to relieve Timothy's stomachic or other infirmities.

Thine often infirmities (τὰς πυκνάς σου ἀσθενείας).   This use of *often* as an adjective appears in earlier English.   So Chaucer: "Ofte sythes" or "tymes ofte," *many times.* Shakespeare: "In which my *often* rumination wraps me in a most humourous sadness" (*As you like it*, IV. i. 19).   And Ben Jonson:

> "The jolly wassal walks the *often* round."
>
> *The Forest*, iii.

Even Tennyson:

> "Wrench'd or broken limb — an *often* chance
> In those brain-stunning shocks and tourney-falls."
>
> *Gareth and Lynette.*

Πυκνός *often*, very common in Class.   Originally, *close, compact*, comp. Lat. *frequens.*   In this sense 3 Macc. iv. 10, τῷ πυκνῷ σανιδώματι the *close planking* of a ship's deck.   In N. T., except here, always adverbial, πυκνά or πυκνότερον *often* or *oftener*, L. v. 33; Acts xxiv. 26.   'Ασθένεια *weakness, infirmity*, only here in Pastorals.   In the physical sense, as here, L. v. 15; viii. 2; J. v. 5; Gal. iv. 13.   In the ethical sense, Rom. vi. 19; viii. 26.

24.   **Open beforehand** (προδηλοί).   A. V. wrong in giving πρό a temporal force, whereas it merely strengthens δηλοί *evident, manifest.*   The meaning is *openly manifested to all eyes.*   In N. T. only here, ver. 25, and Heb. vii. 14.   In LXX, see Judith viii. 29; 2 Macc. iii. 17; xiv. 39.

Going before to judgment (προάγουσαι εἰς κρίσιν).   Προάγειν, [O]P.   In N. T. habitually with a local meaning, either intransitive, as Matt. ii. 9; xiv. 22; Mk. xi. 9; or transitive, as Acts xii. 6; xvii. 5.*   The meaning here is that these open sins go before their perpetrator to the judgment-seat like her-

---

* A temporal meaning is sometimes claimed for Heb. vii. 18 (so Holtzmann), but without sufficient reason.   *The commandment* there is represented as an introduction to a greater and final ordinance.

alds, proclaiming their sentence in advance. Κρίσιν, not specifically of the judgment of men or of the final judgment of
God, or of the sentence of an ecclesiastical court — but indefin-
itely. The writer would say : no judicial utterance is necessary to condemn them of these sins. The word in Paul, only
2 Th. i. 5.

They follow after (ἐπακολουθοῦσιν). The verb only here,
ver. 24, 1 Pet. ii. 21, and (the disputed) Mk. xvi. 20. The
sins follow up the offender to the bar of judgment, and are
first made openly manifest there.

25. **Otherwise** (ἄλλως). N. T.º. Not, otherwise than
good, but otherwise than *manifest*.

Be hid (κρυβῆναι). In Paul only Col. iii. 3. The good
works, although not conspicuous (πρόδηλα), cannot be entirely
concealed. Comp. Matt. v. 14–16. It has been suggested
that these words may have been intended to comfort Timothy
in his possible discouragement from his "often infirmities."
von Soden thinks they were meant to encourage him against
the suspicion awakened by his use of wine. By persevering
in his temperate habits (οἴνῳ ὀλίγῳ) it will become manifest
that he is no wine-bibber.

CHAPTER VI.

1. **As many servants as are under the yoke** (ὅσοι εἰσὶν
ὑπὸ ζυγὸν δοῦλοι). Incorrect. Rather, *as many as are under
the yoke as bondservants*. *As bondservants* is added in explanation of *under the yoke*, which implies a hard and disagree-
able condition. *Yoke* is used only here of the state of slavery.
In Gal. v. **1**: Acts xv. 10, of the Mosaic law. See on Matt.
xi. 29.

Their own (τοὺς ἰδίους). Lit. *private, personal, peculiar*,
as 1 Cor. iii. 8; vii. 7. Sometimes *strange, eccentric*. Con-

trasted with δημόσιος *public* or κοινός *common*. See Acts iv.
32. Sometimes without emphasis, substantially = possessive
pronoun, just as Lat. *proprius* passes into *suus* or *ejus*, or
οἰκεῖος *belonging to one's house* into the simple *one's own*. See
on Gal. vi. 10, and comp. Matt. xxii. 5; xxv. 14. In LXX
commonly with the emphatic sense. Very often in the
phrase κατ' ἰδίαν *privately*, as Mk. iv. 34; L. ix. 10; Gal.
ii. 2, but nowhere in Pastorals.

Masters (δεσπότας). Comp. Tit. ii. 9, and see on 2 Pet.
ii. 1. Not in Paul, who styles the master of slaves κύριος
lord. See Eph. vi. 9; Col. iv. 1.

Count (ἡγείσθωσαν). Implying a more conscious, a surer
judgment, resting on more careful weighing of the facts.
See Philip. ii. 3, 6.

Be not blasphemed (μὴ — βλασφημῆται). Or *be evil
spoken of*. See on *blasphemy*, Mk. vii. 22, and *be evil spoken
of*, Rom. xiv. 16; 1 Cor. x. 30. Paul uses the word, but
not in the active voice as in the Pastorals.

2. **Partakers of the benefit** (οἱ τῆς εὐεργεσίας ἀντιλαμβαν-
όμενοι). The verb means *to take hold of;* hence, to take
hold *for the purpose of helping; to take up for*, as L. i. 54;
Acts xx. 35. °P. Ἐνεργεσία *benefit* only here and Acts iv. 9.
Better, *kindly service*. Rend. *they that busy themselves in
the kindly service.** The reference is to the kindly acts which
the masters do to their slaves; not to the benefits received
by the slaves. Comp. Gal. v. 13.

3. **Teach otherwise** (ἑτεροδιδασκαλεῖ). See on ch. i. 3.

Consent (προσέρχεται). Lit. *draw nigh*. To approach
as one who confidingly accepts another's proffer. Hence, *to*

---

* So Weizsäcker : *sich des Wohlthuns befleissigen*. Similarly, Holtzmann,
von Soden, and Huther.

assent to.   Comp. Acts x. 28; 1 Pet. ii. 4; Heb. iv. 16; x. 22.   Often in LXX, and habitually in the literal sense. The figurative sense, Sir. i. 27, 30; iv. 15; vi. 26.   °P. The phrase only here.

Of our Lord, etc.   Either *concerning* our Lord, or *spoken by* him.   Probably the latter, according to N. T. usage, in which *word of the Lord* or *word of God* commonly means the word that proceeds from God.   The phrase *words of our Lord Jesus Christ* only here.

Doctrine which is according to godliness (τῇ κατ᾽ εὐσέβειαν διδασκαλίᾳ).   The phrase only here.   See on 1 Tim. i. 10.   For εὐσέβεια, on 1 Tim. ii. 2.

4. **He is proud** (τετύφωται).   See on ch. iii. 6.

Knowing nothing (μηδὲν ἐπιστάμενος).   Although he knows nothing.   °P.   Very frequent in Acts.   Comp. ch. i. 7.

Doting (νοσῶν).   N. T.°.   Lit. *sick.*   Comp. ὑγιαίνουσι *healthful,* ver. 3.

Questions (ζητήσεις).   °P.   °LXX.   Quite often in Class. Lit. *processes of inquiry;* hence, *debates.*   Comp. ch. i. 4.

Strifes of words (λογομαχίας).   N. T.°.   °LXX, °Class. One of the unique compounds peculiar to these Epistles. The verb λογομαχεῖν 2 Tim. ii. 14.

Surmisings (ὑπόνοιαι).   N. T.°.   See Sir. iii. 24.   Ὑπὸ *under* and νοῦς *mind, thought.*   A hidden thought.   The verb ὑπονοεῖν *to suppose,* only in Acts.   See xiii. 25; xxv. 18; xxvii. 27.

5. **Perverse disputings** (διαπαρατριβαί).   N. T.°.   °LXX, °Class.   Παρατριβή is *a rubbing against.*   Διὰ signifies *con-*

tinuance. The meaning therefore is *continued friction.* Hence *wearing discussion; protracted wrangling.**

Of corrupt minds (διεφθαρμένων τὸν νοῦν). More correctly, *corrupted in mind.* The verb not common in N. T. In Paul only 2 Cor. iv. 16. Only here in Pastorals. Διαφθορά *corruption* only in Acts. Comp. κατεφθαρμένοι τὸν νοῦν *corrupted in mind,* 2 Tim. iii. 8.

Destitute of the truth (ἀπεστερημένων τῆς ἀληθείας). Rev. *bereft* of the truth. In N. T. commonly of *defrauding,* Mk. x. 19; 1 Cor. vi. 7, 8; vii. 5. The implication is that they once possessed the truth. They put it away from themselves (ch. i. 19; Tit. i. 14). Here it is represented as *taken* away from them. Comp. Rom. i. 28.

Gain is godliness (πορισμὸν εἶναι τὴν εὐσέβειαν). Wrong. Rend. *that godliness is a way* (or *source*) *of gain.* Πορισμὸς, only here and ver. 6, is *a gain-making business.* See Wisd. xiii. 19; xiv. 2. They make religion a means of livelihood. Comp. Tit. i. 11.

6. Contentment (αὐταρκείας). Only here and 2 Cor. ix. 8. The adjective αὐτάρκης *self-sufficient,* Philip. iv. 11. Comp. Sir. xl. 18. Αὐτάρκεια is an inward self-sufficiency, as opposed to the lack or the desire of outward things. It was a favourite Stoic word, expressing the doctrine of that sect that a man should be sufficient unto himself for all things, and able, by the power of his own will, to resist the force of circumstances. In Ps. of Sol. v. 18, we read: " Blessed is the man whom God remembereth with a suffic-

---

* The A.V. *perverse disputings* grew out of the reading of T. R. παραδιατριβαί, in which παρά was taken in the sense of *neglect* or *violation.* Some of the Greek Fathers supposed that the word involved the idea of moral or mental *contagion,* and illustrated it by mangy sheep, which communicate disease by rubbing against each other. It is suggestive that διατριβή *a wearing away* or *waste of time* gradually passed into the meaning of *argument.* *Diatribe,* from the sense of *disputation,* passed into that of *invective* or *philippic.*

iency convenient for him" (ἐν συμμετρίᾳ αὐταρκεσίας); that
is, with a sufficiency proportioned to his needs.

7. And it is certain we can carry, etc. Omit *and* and
certain. Rend. ὅτι *because.* The statement is : We brought
nothing into the world *because* we can carry nothing out.
The fact that we brought nothing into the world is shown
by the impossibility of our taking with us anything out of it;
since if anything belonging to us in our premundane state
had been brought by us into the world, it would not be separated from us at our departure from the world. Comp. Job
i. 21; Eccl. v. 15 ; Ps. xlix. 17.

8. Food (διατροφὰς). N. T.º.

Raiment (σκεπάσματα). N. T.º. ºLXX. It means *cov-*
ering generally, though the reference is probably to clothing.
von Soden aptly remarks that a dwelling is not a question of
life with an Oriental.

Let us be content (ἀρκεσθησόμεθα). More correctly, *we*
shall be content. Once in Paul, 2 Cor. xii. 9. A few times
in LXX. Comp. Ps. of Sol. xvi. 12 : " But with good will
and cheerfulness uphold thou my soul ; when thou strength-
enest my soul I shall be satisfied (ἀρκέσει μοι) with what thou
givest me."

9. They that will be rich (οἱ βουλόμενοι πλουτεῖν). Better,
they that desire to be rich. It is not the *possession* of riches,
but the *love* of them that leads men into temptation.

Fall (ἐμπίπτουσιν). ºP. Lit. fall *into ;* but invariably in
N. T. with εἰς *into.*

Temptation (πειρασμὸν). See on Matt. vi. 13.

Foolish (ἀνοήτους). *Foolish* answers to several words in
N. T., ἀνόητος, ἀσύνετος, ἄφρων, μωρός. Ἀνόητος *not under-*

standing; a want of proper application of the moral judgment or perception, as L. xxiv. 25 ; Gal. iii. 1.   See notes on both. Ἄφρων is *senseless, stupid,* of images, beasts.   Comp. L. xii. 20, note.   Ἀσύνετος approaches the meaning of ἀνόητος *unintelligent.*   See Sir. xxii. 13, 15; xxvii. 12.   It also implies a moral sense, *wicked,* Wisd. i. 5; xi. 15; Sir. xv. 7.   On the etymological sense, see on Matt. xi. 25; Mk. xii. 33; L. ii. 47.   Μωρός is *without forethought,* as Matt. vii. 26 ; xxv. 3 ; *without learning,* as 1 Cor. i. 27; iii. 18; with a moral sense, *empty, useless,* 2 Tim. ii. 23 ; Tit. iii. 9; and *impious, godless,* Matt. v. 22 ; Ps. xciii. 8 ; Jer. v. 21.

Hurtful (βλαβεράς).   N. T.⁰.   LXX once, Prov. x. 26.

Drown (βυθίζουσι).   Only here and L. v. 7, note.   A strong expression of the results of avarice.

Destruction (ὄλεθρον).   See on 1 Th. i. 9, and additional note.

Perdition (ἀπώλειαν).   It is unsafe to distinguish between ὄλεθρος *destruction in general,* and ἀπώλεια as pointing mainly to destruction *of the soul.*   Ἀπώλεια sometimes of spiritual destruction, as Philip. i. 28; but also of destruction and waste in general, as Mk. xiv. 4; Acts viii. 20.   One is reminded of Virgil, *Aen.* iii. 56 :

> "Quid non mortalia pectora cogis,
> Auri sacra fames ? "

10. **Love of money** (φιλαργυρία).   N. T.⁰.   See 4 Macc. i. 26.   Rare in Class.

The root (ῥίζα).   Better, *a root.*   It is not the only root. In Paul only metaphorically.   See Rom. xi. 16, 17, 18.

Coveted after (ὀρεγόμενοι).   See on ch. iii. 1.   The figure is faulty, since φιλαργυρία is itself a *desire.*

Have erred (ἀπεπλανήθησαν). More correctly, *have been led astray.* ᵒP.

Pierced through (περιέπειραν). N. T.ᵒ ᵒLXX.

Sorrows (ὀδύναις). See on Rom. ix. 2.

11. **Man of God** (ἄνθρωπε θεοῦ). The phrase only in Pastorals. Comp. 2 Tim. iii. 17. Not an official designation.

Righteousness (δικαιοσύνην). See on Rom. i. 17. Not in the Pauline dogmatic sense, but as Eph. v. 9, *moral rectitude* according to God's law.

Meekness (πραϋπαθίαν). N. T.ᵒ. ᵒLXX. Meekness of *feeling* (πάθος). The usual word is πραΰτης, often in Paul. See on *meek*, Matt. v. 5. With the whole verse comp. Tit. iii. 12.

12. **Fight the good fight** (ἀγωνίζου τὸν καλὸν ἀγῶνα). A phrase peculiar to the Pastorals. Comp. 2 Tim. iv. 7. Not necessarily a metaphor from the gymnasium or arena, although ἀγών *contest* was applied originally to athletic struggles. But it is also used of any struggle, outward or inward. See Col. ii. 1; iv. 12.

Lay hold (ἐπιλαβοῦ). ᵒP. Frequent in Luke and Acts. Occasionally in this strong sense, as L. xx. 20; xxiii. 26; Acts xviii. 17, but not usually. See Mk. viii. 23; L. ix. 47; Acts ix. 27.

Professed a good profession (ὡμολόγησας τὴν καλὴν ὁμολογίαν). Both the verb and the noun in Paul, but this combination only here. For the use of καλός *good* see ch. i. 18, and ver. 12. Rend. *confessed the good confession,* and see on *your professed subjection,* 2 Cor. ix. 13. It is important to preserve the force of the article, a point in which the A. V. is often at fault.

13. **Quickeneth** (ζωογονοῦντος). °P. Rend. *who pre-serveth alive*. *Quickeneth* is according to the reading ζω-οποιοῦντος *maketh alive*. Comp. LXX, Ex. i. 17; Judg. viii. 19. This association of God as the preserver with confession is noteworthy in Matt. x. 28–33.

Witnessed a good confession (μαρτυρήσαντος τὴν καλὴν ὁμολογίαν). Better, *the* or *his* good confession. The phrase is unique. The good confession is the historical confession of Jesus before Pilate, which is the warrant for the truthful-ness of Timothy's confession. Christ is called "the faithful and true *witness*" (μάρτυς), Apoc. i. 5; iii. 14. It is true that μάρτυς was used very early of those who laid down their lives for the truth (see Acts xxii. 20; Apoc. ii. 13), and Polycarp speaks of τὸ μαρτύριον τοῦ σταυροῦ *the witness of the cross* (Philip. vii.); but this did not become general until after the end of the second century.*

Before Pontius Pilate. The mention of Pontius Pilate in connection with the crucifixion is of constant occurrence in early Christian writings. See Ignatius, *Magn.* xi; *Tral.* ix; *Smyrn.* i. It has been supposed that these words were taken from a liturgical confession in which the Christian faith was professed.

14. **Commandment** (ἐντολὴν). Usually of a single com-mandment or injunction, but sometimes for the whole body of the moral precepts of Christianity, as 2 Pet. ii. 21; iii. 2. The reference may be explained by ἡ παραγγελία *the com-mandment*, ch. i. 5, meaning the gospel as the divine standard of conduct and faith. Comp. 2 Tim. i. 14. The phrase τηρεῖν τὴν ἐντολὴν *to keep the commandment* is Johannine. See J. xiv. 15, 21; xv. 10; 1 J. ii. 3, 4; iii. 22, 24; v. 3.

Without spot (ἄσπιλον). Unsullied. Comp. Jas. i. 27; 1 Pet. i. 19; 2 Pet. iii. 14.

---

* See Hegesippus in Eusebius, *H. E.* iii. 20, 32, and the Epistle of the churches of Vienne and Lyons to the churches of Asia and Phrygia, Eusebius, *H. E.* v. 1.

Appearing (ἐπιφανείας). See on 2 Th. ii. 8. In the Books of Maccabees it is used to describe appearances and interventions of God for the aid of his people. See 2 Macc. ii. 21; iii. 24; xiv. 15; xv. 27; 3 Macc. v. 8, 51. In 2 Tim. iv. 18, and Tit. ii. 13, it denotes, as here, the second coming of Christ. In 2 Tim. i. 10, his historical manifestation, for which also the verb ἐπιφαίνειν is used, Tit. ii. 11; iii. 4. For the Lord's second advent Paul commonly uses παρουσία *presence;* once the verb φανεροῦν *to make manifest* (Col. iii. 4), and once ἀποκάλυψις *revelation* (2 Th. i. 7). It is quite possible that the word ἐπιφάνεια, so characteristic of these Epistles, grew out of the Gnostic vocabulary, in which it was used of the sudden appearing of the hitherto concealed heavenly aeon, Christ. This they compared to a sudden light from heaven; and Christ, who thus appeared, though only docetically, without an actual fleshly body, was styled σωτήρ *saviour*, although his oneness with the God of creation was denied. The Creator and the Redeemer were not the same, but were rather opposed. Christ was only a factor of a great cosmological process of development. As Neander observes: "The distinctive aim of the Gnostics was to apprehend the appearance of Christ and the new creation proceeding from him in their connection with the evolution of the whole universe."

15. **In his times** (καιροῖς ἰδίοις). Better, *his own seasons*, or *its* own seasons. Either the seasons proper to the appearing, or the seasons which God shall see fit to select. See on ch. ii. 6.

Potentate (δυνάστης). Only here of God. Very often in LXX. See Sir. xlvi. 5; 2 Macc. xii. 15, etc. In Class. applied to Zeus (Soph. *Antig.* 608). In Aesch. *Agam.* 6, the stars are called λαμπροὶ δυνάσται *bright rulers*, as the regulators of the seasons.

Of kings (τῶν βασιλευόντων). Lit. *of those who rule as kings*. Only here for the noun βασιλέων. Βασιλεὺς βασιλέων *king of kings*, Apoc. xvii. 14; xix. 16.

Of lords (κυριευόντων). Lit. *of those who lord it.* Only here for the noun κυρίων. See κύριος κυρίων *lord of lords,* Apoc. xix. 16; comp. LXX, Deut. x. 17; Ps. cxxxv. 3. Probably liturgical.

16. Who only hath immortality (ὁ μόνος ἔχων ἀθανασίαν). Comp. ἀφθάρτῳ *incorruptible,* ch. i. 17. It has been suggested that there is here a possible allusion to the practice of deifying the Roman emperors, with an implied protest against paying them divine honours. In the Asian provinces generally, this imperial cultus was organised as the highest and most authoritative religion. Domitian (81–96 A.D.) assumed the titles of "Lord" and "God," and insisted on being addressed as *Dominus et Deus noster* in all communications to himself. Trajan (98–117 A.D.) forbade his subjects to address him as "Lord" and "God," but Pliny (112 A.D.) required the citizens of Bithynia to pay divine honours to Trajan's statue. Hadrian (117–138 A.D.) allowed the worship of his statues.*

In light. Comp. Ps. ciii. 2; 1 J. i. 5, 7; Jas. i. 17.

Which no man can approach unto (ἀπρόσιτον). More simply, *unapproachable.* N. T.º. ºLXX.

17. Them that are rich in this world (τοῖς πλουσίοις ἐν τῷ νῦν αἰῶνι). Forming one conception. Chrysostom says: "Rich in this world, for others are rich in the world to come." Comp. L. xvi. 25. Πλούσιος *rich,* by Paul only metaphorically. See 2 Cor. viii. 9; Eph. ii. 4. The phrase ὁ νῦν αἰών *the now age,* only here and Tit. ii. 12, the usual expression being ὁ αἰὼν οὗτος *this age* or *world,* which is not found in Pastorals.

Be not highminded (μὴ ὑψηλοφρονεῖν). The verb N. T.º. ºLXX, ºClass. Comp. Rom. xi. 20; xii. 16.

---

* See W. M. Ramsay, *The Church in the Roman Empire before A.D. 170,* and the monograph of E. G. Hardy, *Christianity and the Roman Government,* the best treatise on the subject in English.

Uncertain riches (πλούτου ἀδηλότητι). A rendering which
weakens the sense by withdrawing the emphasis from the
thought of *uncertainty*. Rend. *the uncertainty of riches*. For
a similar construction see Rom. vi. 4. Ἀδηλότης *uncertainty*,
N. T.⁰. ⁰LXX. Originally *obscurity*. Πλοῦτος *wealth*, frequent in Paul, but never in the material sense. The play
upon the word *rich* in this and the next verse will be noticed.

To enjoy (εἰς ἀπόλαυσιν). Lit. *for enjoyment*. Only here
and Heb. xi. 25. See 3 Macc. vii. 16. In Class. occasionally, but the verb ἀπολαύειν *to have enjoyment* or *benefit* is
common. A contrast is implied between being highminded
on account of wealth — cherishing and worshipping it — and
rightly enjoying it. The true character of such enjoyment
is shown in the next verse.

18. **Do good** (ἀγαθοεργεῖν). In this uncontracted form,
N. T.⁰. ⁰LXX, ⁰Class. Comp. Acts xiv. 17. The usual
word is ἀγαθοποιεῖν, see Mk. iii. 4; L. vi. 9, 33, 35; 1 Pet.
ii. 15. ⁰P. who has ἐργάζεσθαι τὸ ἀγαθὸν *to work that which
is good*, Rom. ii. 10; Gal. vi. 10; Eph. iv. 28.

Good works (ἔργοις καλοῖς). For καλός see on ch. iii. 7,
and J. x. 11: for ἀγαθός on Rom. v. 7.

Ready to distribute (εὐμεταδότους). N. T.⁰. ⁰LXX,
⁰Class. For the verb μεταδιδόναι *to impart* to the poor, see
L. iii. 11; Eph. iv. 28.

Willing to communicate (κοινωνικούς). N. T.⁰. ⁰LXX.
See on *fellowship*, Acts ii. 42, and comp. κοινωνεῖν *to partake*,
1 Tim. v. 22, and κοινός *common*, Tit. i. 14. Stronger than
the preceding word, as implying a personal share in the
pleasure imparted by the gift.

19. **Laying up in store** (ἀποθησαυρίζοντας). N. T.⁰.
Laying *away* (ἀπό).

Eternal life (τῆς ὄντως ζωῆς). More correctly, *the life which is life indeed*, or *that which is truly life*. See on ch. v. 3.

20. **That which is committed to thy trust** (τὴν παρα-θήκην). Only in Pastorals. Comp. 2 Tim. i. 12, 14. From παρὰ *beside* or *with*, and τιθέναι *to place*. It may mean either something put *beside* another as an addition or appendix (so Mk. vi. 41; Acts xvi. 34), or something put *with* or *in the keeping of* another as a trust or deposit. In the latter sense always in LXX. See Lev. vi. 2, 4; Tob. x. 13; 2 Macc. iii. 10, 15. Hdt. vi. 73, of giving hostages; ix. 45, of confidential words intrusted to the hearer's honour. The verb is a favorite with Luke. The meaning here is that teaching which Timothy had received from Paul; the "sound words" which he was to guard as a sacred trust, and communicate to others.

Vain babblings (κενοφωνίας). Only in Pastorals. °LXX, °Class. From κενός *empty* and φωνή *voice*.

Oppositions of science falsely so called (ἀντιθέσεις τῆς ψευδωνύμου γνώσεως). Better, *oppositions of the falsely-named knowledge*. Ἀντίθεσις, N. T.°. °LXX. Used here, in its simple sense, of the arguments and teachings of those who opposed the true Christian doctrine as intrusted to Timothy. Γνῶσις *knowledge* was the characteristic word of the Gnostic school, the most formidable enemy of the church of the second century. The Gnostics claimed a superior knowledge peculiar to an intellectual caste. According to them, it was by this philosophic insight, as opposed to faith, that humanity was to be regenerated. Faith was suited only to the rude masses, the animal-men. The intellectual questions which occupied these teachers were two : to explain the work of creation, and to account for the existence of evil. Their ethical problem was how to develop the higher nature in the environment of matter which was essentially evil. In morals they ran to two opposite extremes — asceticism and licentiousness. The principal representatives of the school were Basilides, Valentinus, and Marcion. Although Gnosticism as a distinct system did not reach its full development until about the middle of the second century, foreshadowings of it appear in the heresy at which Paul's Colossian letter was aimed.   It is not strange if we find in the Pastoral Epistles allusions pointing to Gnostic errors; but, as already remarked, it is impossible to refer these allusions to any one definite system of error.   The word γνῶσις cannot therefore be interpreted to mean the Gnostic system; while it may properly be understood as referring to that conceit of knowledge which opposed itself to the Christian faith. Ψευδώνυμος *falsely-named*, N. T.⁰.   ⁰LXX.   It characterises the γνῶσις as claiming that name without warrant, and as being mere *vain babbling*.   Comp. Col. ii. 8.

21. Professing.   See on ch. ii. 10.

Erred (ἠστόχησαν).   See on ch. i. 6, and comp. 2 Tim. ii. 18.

Grace be with thee.   The correct reading is μεθ' ὑμῶν *with you*.   Although addressed to an individual, he is included in the church.   This brief benediction occurs in Paul only in Colossians.

THE SECOND EPISTLE TO TIMOTHY.

CHAPTER I.

1. An apostle by the will of God. So 2d Corinthians, Ephesians, Colossians. 1st Corinthians adds *called* or *by call* (κλητὸς).

According to the promise, etc. (κατ᾽ ἐπαγγελίαν). Ἀπόστολος κατὰ does not appear in any of the Pauline salutations. In 1 Tim. κατ᾽ ἐπιταγὴν *according to the commandment*, and in Titus κατὰ πίστιν, etc., *according to the faith*, etc. Κατ᾽ ἐπαγγελίαν, though in other connections, Acts xiii. 23; Gal. iii. 29. Ἐπαγγελία, primarily *announcement*, but habitually *promise* in N. T. In Pastorals only here and 1 T. iv. 8. With the promise of the life in Christ goes the provision for its proclamation. Hence the apostle, in proclaiming "ye shall live through Christ," is an apostle according to the promise.

Of life which is in Christ Jesus. The phrase *promise of life* only here and 1 Tim. iv. 8. ^OP. Life in Christ is a Pauline thought. See Rom. viii. 2; 2 Cor. iv. 10; Rom. vi. 2–14; Gal. ii. 19, 20; Col. iii. 4; Philip. i. 21. It is also a Johannine thought; see J. i. 4; iii. 15; xi. 25; xiv. 6; 1 J. v. 11.

2. Dearly beloved (ἀγαπητῷ). Better, *beloved*. Comp. 1 Cor. iv. 17. In 1 Tim. i. 2, Timothy is addressed as γνήσιος *true*, and Titus in Tit. i. 4.

3. I thank God (χάριν ἔχω τῷ θεῷ). Lit. *I have thanks to God.* The phrase in L. xvii. 9; Acts ii. 47; ^OP. unless

2 Cor. i. 15;* 1 Tim. i. 12; Heb. xii. 28; 3 J. 4. Paul
uses εὐχαριστῶ *I give thanks* (not in Pastorals) or εὐλογητὸς ὁ θεός *blessed be God* (not in Pastorals). The phrase
χάριν ἔχω is a Latinism, *habere gratiam*, of which several are
found in Pastorals.†

I serve (λατρεύω). In Pastorals only here. Comp. Rom.
i. 9, 25; Philip. iii. 3. Frequent in Hebrews. Originally,
to serve for hire. In N. T. both of ritual service, as Heb.
viii. 5; ix. 9; x. 2; xiii. 10; and of worship or service generally, as L. i. 74; Rom. i. 9. Especially of the service
rendered to God by the Israelites as his peculiar people, as
Acts xxvi. 7. Comp. λατρεία *service*, Rom. ix. 4; Heb.
ix. 1, 6. In LXX always of the service of God or of heathen
deities.

From my forefathers (ἀπὸ προγόνων). Πρόγονος, Past[o].
See on 1 Tim. v. 4. The phrase N. T.[o]. For the thought,
comp. Acts xxiv. 14; Philip. iii. 5. He means, in the spirit
and with the principles inherited from his fathers. Comp.
the sharp distinction between the two periods of Paul's life,
Gal. i. 13, 14.

With pure conscience (ἐν καθαρᾷ συνειδήσει). As 1 Tim.
iii. 9. The phrase, Past[o]. Heb. ix. 14 has καθαριεῖ τὴν
συνείδησιν ἡμῶν *shall purge our conscience.*

That without ceasing (ὡς ἀδιάλειπτον). The passage is
much involved. Note (1) that χάριν ἔχω τῷ θεῷ *I thank God*
must have an object. (2) That object cannot be that he
unceasingly remembers Timothy in his prayers. (3) That
object, though remote, is ὑπόμνησιν λαβών *when I received
reminder* (ver. 5). He thanks God as he is reminded of the

---

* Where Westcott and Hort read χαρὰν *joy;* Tischendorf and Weiss χάριν
thanks.
† As δι' ἣν αἰτίαν *quam ob rem* (2 Tim. i. 6, 12; Tit. i. 13): ὃν τρόπον
quemadmodum (2 Tim. iii. 8): οἵους *quales* (2 Tim. iii. 11). Little or nothing can be inferred from these instances as to the composition of these Epistles at Rome.

faith of Timothy's ancestors and of Timothy himself. Rend.
freely, " I thank God whom I serve from my forefathers
with pure conscience, as there go along with my prayers an
unceasing remembrance of thee, and a daily and nightly longing, as I recall thy tears, to see thee, that I may be filled with
joy — I thank God, I say, for that I have been reminded of
the unfeigned faith that is in thee," etc. Ἀδιάλειπτον *unceasing*, only here and Rom. ix. 2. Ἀδιαλείπτως *unceasingly*,
Rom. i. 9; 1 Th. i. 3; ii. 13; v. 17.

   I have remembrance (ἔχω τὴν μνείαν). The phrase once
in Paul, 1 Th. iii. 6. Commonly, μνείαν ποιοῦμαι *I make
mention*, Rom. i. 9; Eph. i. 16; 1 Th. i. 2; Philem. 4.

   Night and day (νυκτὸς καὶ ἡμέρας). See 1 Tim. v. 5.
The phrase in Paul, 1 Th. ii. 9; iii. 10; 2 Th. iii. 8. Const.
with *greatly desiring.**

   4. Greatly desiring (ἐπιποθῶν). Better, *longing*. Pastorals only here. Quite frequent in Paul. See Rom. i. 11;
2 Cor. v. 2; ix. 14; Philip. i. 8, etc. The compounded preposition ἐπὶ does not denote intensity, as A. V. *greatly*, but
direction. Comp. ch. iv. 9, 21.

   Being mindful of thy tears (μεμνημένος σου τῶν δακρύων).
The verb μιμνήσκεσθαι in Paul, only 1 Cor. xi. 2. In Pastorals only here. The words give the reason for the longing to
see Timothy. The allusion is probably to the tears shed by
Timothy at his parting from Paul.† One is naturally
reminded of the parting of Paul with the Ephesian elders at
Miletus (Acts xx. 17 ff., see especially ver. 37). Holtzmann
remarks that Paul's discourse on that occasion is related to
this passage as programme to performance. Bonds await the

   * Others with *I have remembrance ;* but *without ceasing* would make it
superfluous. Comp. 1 Th. iii. 10.
   † According to Hofmann, they are *epistolary tears* (!) — a letter of Timothy to Paul, expressing his distress at the apostle's imprisonment, and, therefore, an occasion of thanksgiving to Paul.

apostle (Acts xx. 23), and Paul appears as a prisoner
(2 Tim. i. 8).   He must fulfil his course (Acts xx. 24);
here he has fulfilled it (2 Tim. iv. 7).   He bids the overseers
take heed to the flock, for false teachers will arise in the
bosom of the church (Acts xx. 29, 30); these letters contain directions for the guidance of the flock, and denuncia-
tions of heretical teachers.

That I may be filled with joy.   Const. with *longing to
see you.*

5. **When I call to remembrance** (ὑπόμνησιν λαβὼν).
The object of χάριν ἔχω, ver. 3.   Lit. *having received a
reminding.*   The phrase, N. T.⁰. Ὑπόμνησις *reminding* (but
sometimes intransitive, *remembrance*), only here, 2 Pet. i. 13;
iii. 1.   In LXX three times.   As distinguished from ἀνάμνησις *remembrance* (1 Cor. xi. 24, 25) it signifies a reminding
or being reminded by another; while ἀνάμνησις is a recalling
by one's self.

Unfeigned faith that is in thee (τῆς ἐν σοὶ ἀνυποκρίτου
πίστεως).   See on 1 Tim. i. 5.   For the peculiar collocation
of the Greek words, comp. Acts xvii. 28; Rom. i. 12; Eph.
i. 15.   The writer's thought is probably not confined to
Christian faith, but has in view the continuity of Judaism
and Christianity.   In ver. 3 he speaks of serving God from
his forefathers.   In Acts xxiv. 14 Paul is represented as
saying that even as a Christian he serves the God of his
fathers, *believing* all things contained in the law and the
prophets.

Dwelt (ἐνῴκησεν).   Paul uses the verb with *sin, the divine
Spirit, God, the word of Christ,* but nowhere with *faith.*   The
phrase *faith dwells in,* N. T.⁰.   According to Paul, Christians
are or *stand in* faith; but faith is not represented as dwelling
in them.   *Christ* dwells in the heart *through* faith (Eph.
iii. 17).

First (πρῶτον). With reference to Timothy, and with a comparative sense, as Matt. v. 24; vii. 5; Mk. iii. 27; 1 Th. iv. 16, etc. This is shown by the last clause of the verse. The writer merely means that faith had already dwelt in Timothy's grandmother and mother before it did in him. How much farther back his believing ancestry went he does not say. Comp. Acts xvi. 1.

Grandmother (μάμμῃ). N. T.⁰. Once in LXX, 4 Macc. xvi. 9. Later Greek. The correct classical word is τήθη. See Aristoph. *Ach.* 49; Plato, *Repub.* 461 D. From the emphasis upon Timothy's receiving his training from his Jewish mother, it has been inferred that his father died early. That he was the child of a mixed marriage appears from Acts xvi. 1.

I am persuaded (πέπεισμαι). The verb in Pastorals only here and ver. 12. Often in Paul.

6. **Wherefore** (δι᾿ ἣν αἰτίαν). Lit. *for which cause.* Ἀιτία not in Paul. The phrase in ver. 12; Tit. i. 13; also in Luke, Acts, and Hebrews. Paul's expression is διό or διὰ τοῦτο.

Stir up (ἀναζωπυρεῖν). N. T.⁰. LXX, Gen. xlv. 27; 1 Macc. xiii. 7. In Class., as Eurip. *Electra,* 1121, ἀν᾿ αὖ σὺ ζωπυρεῖς νείκη νέα *you are rekindling old strifes.* From ἀνά *again,* ζωός *alive,* πῦρ *fire.* Τὸ ζώπυρον is *a piece of hot coal, an ember, a spark.* Plato calls the survivors of the flood σμικρὰ ζώπυρα τοῦ τῶν ἀνθρώπων γένους διασεσωσμένα *small sparks of the human race preserved.* The word is, therefore, figurative, *to stir* or *kindle the embers.* Ἀνά combines the meanings *again* and *up,* *rekindle* or *kindle up.* Vulg. only the former, *resuscitare.* Comp. ἀνάπτειν *kindle up,* L. xii. 49; Jas. iii. 5. It is not necessary to assume that Timothy's zeal had become cold.

The gift of God (τὸ χάρισμα τοῦ θεοῦ). See on 1 Tim. iv. 14.

The laying on of my hands. See on 1 Tim. iv. 14.

7. Spirit of fear (πνεῦμα δειλίας). Better, *of cowardice.*
N. T.º. Comp. Rom. viii. 15, and see on *the Spirit*, Rom.
viii. 4, § 5.

Of power (δυνάμεως). Found in all the Pauline Epistles
except Philemon. In Pastorals only here, ver. 8, and ch.
iii. 5. Not used by our writer in the sense of *working miracles*, which it sometimes has in Paul. Here, the power to
overcome all obstacles and to face all dangers. It is closely
linked with the sense of παρρησία *boldness.*

Of love (ἀγάπης). See on Gal. v. 22.

Of a sound mind (σωφρονισμοῦ). N. T.º. ºLXX, ºClass.
Not *self-control*, but *the faculty of generating it in others* or *in
one's self*, making them σώφρονες *of sound mind*. Comp. Tit.
ii. 4. Rend. *discipline*. See on σωφροσύνη, 1 Tim. ii. 9.

8. Be not ashamed (μὴ ἐπαισχυνθῇς). See on L. ix. 26.

Testimony (μαρτύριον). See on 1 Tim. ii. 6.

His prisoner (δέσμιον αὐτοῦ). Paul styles himself *the
prisoner of the Lord*, Eph. iii. 1 ; iv. i ; Philem. i. 9. Only
here in Pastorals. Not in a figurative sense, *one who belongs
to Christ*, but *one who is imprisoned because of his labours as an
apostle of Christ*. On Paul's supposed second imprisonment,
see Introd. IV.

Be partaker of the afflictions (συνκακοπάθησον). Only
here and ch. ii. 3. ºLXX, ºClass. The compounded σύν
with, not *with the gospel*, as Rev., but *with me*. Share afflictions with me *for* the gospel.

According to the power of God. Which enables him to
endure hardness. Connect with *be partaker*, etc.

9. Who hath saved us. Salvation is ascribed to God. See on *our Saviour*, 1 Tim. i. 1.

Called (καλέσαντος). Comp. 1 Tim. vi. 12, and see Rom. viii. 30; ix. 11; 1 Cor. i. 9; Gal. i. 6; 1 Th. ii. 12. It is Paul's technical term for God's summoning men to salvation. In Paul the order is reversed: *called, saved.*

With a holy calling (κλήσει ἁγίᾳ). Κλῆσις *calling*, often in Paul; but the phrase *holy calling* only here. In Paul, κλῆσις sometimes as here, with the verb καλεῖν *to call*, as 1 Cor. vii. 20; Eph. iv. 1, 4.

Purpose (πρόθεσιν). See on Acts xi. 23; Rom. ix. 11.

Grace which was given (χάριν τὴν δοθεῖσαν). Comp. Rom. xii. 3, 6; xv. 15; 1 Cor. iii. 10; Eph. iii. 8; iv. 7. The phrase only here in Pastorals.

Before the world began (πρὸ χρόνων αἰωνίων). See additional note on 2 Th. i. 9. In Pastorals the phrase only here and Tit. i. 2. Not in Paul. Lit. *before eternal times.* If it is insisted that αἰώνιος means *everlasting*, this statement is absurd. It is impossible that anything should take place *before* everlasting times. That would be to say that there was a *beginning* of times which are *from everlasting.* Paul puts the beginnings of salvation in God's purpose before the time of the world (1 Cor. ii. 7; 1 Pet. i. 20); and Christ's participation in the saving counsels of God prior to time, goes with the Pauline doctrine of Christ's preëxistence. The meaning, therefore, of this phrase is rightly given in A.V.: *before the world began*, that is, before time was reckoned by aeons or cycles. Then, in that timeless present, grace was given to us *in God's decree*, not *actually*, since we did not exist. The gift planned and ordered in the eternal counsels is here treated as an actual bestowment.

10. Made manifest (φανερωθεῖσαν). See on 1 Tim. iii. 16. In contrast with the preceding clause, this marks the histor-

ical fulfilment in time of the eternal, divine counsel. Comp.
Tit. i. 3.   There is an implication that the divine counsel
was hidden until the fitting time: comp. Eph. iii. 5, and see
Col. i. 26.

By the appearing (διὰ τῆς ἐπιφανείας). See on 2 Th. ii. 8;
1 Tim. vi. 14.

Who hath abolished (καταργήσαντος).   Better, *since he
made of none effect*. In Pastorals only here. Frequent in
Paul. See on *make without effect*, Rom. iii. 3, and comp. *is
swallowed up*, 1 Cor. xv. 54. Notice the association of the
verb with ἐπιφάνεια *appearing* in 2 Th. ii. 8.

Brought to light (φωτίσαντος).   Only here in Pastorals.
In Paul, 1 Cor. iv. 5 ; Eph. i. 18 ; iii. 9.

Immortality (ἀφθαρσίαν).   Better, *incorruption*. With this
exception, only in Paul. See Wisd. ii. 23 ; vi. 9 ; 4 Macc.
ix. 22 ; xvii. 12.

11. **A teacher of the Gentiles** (διδάσκαλος ἐθνῶν).   Omit
of the Gentiles. Comp. 1 Tim. ii. 7, from which the words
were probably transferred when the three Epistles were
jointly edited. Paul calls himself *an apostle*, and describes
himself as *preaching* (κηρύσσων); but he nowhere calls himself διδάσκαλος *a teacher*, although he uses διδάσκειν *to teach*,
of himself, 1 Cor. iv. 17 ; Col. i. 28.   He also uses διδαχή
teaching, of matter given by him to the converts, Rom. vi. 17;
xvi. 17 ; 1 Cor. xiv. 6.   He distinguishes between the apostle and the teacher, 1 Cor. xii. 28 ; Eph. iv. 11.

12. **I am not ashamed.** Comp. ver. 8, and Rom. i. 16.

Whom I have believed (ᾧ πεπίστευκα).   Or, *in whom I
have put my trust*. See on J. i. 12 ; ii. 22 ; Rom. iv. 5.

Able (δυνατός).   Often used with a stronger meaning, as
1 Cor. i. 26, *mighty ;* Acts xxv. 5, οἱ δυνατοὶ *the chief men:*

as a designation of God, ὁ δυνατός *the mighty one*, Luke i. 49 : of preëminent ability or power in something, as of Jesus, δυνατός ἐν ἔργῳ καὶ λόγῳ *mighty in deed and word*, L. **xxiv. 19** : of spiritual agencies, "The weapons of our **warfare are** δυνατὰ *mighty*," etc., 2 Cor. x. 4.   Very often in LXX.

That which I have committed (τὴν παραθήκην μου). More correctly, *that which has been committed unto me :* my sacred trust.   The meaning of the passage is that Paul is convinced that God is strong to enable him to be faithful to his apostolic calling, in spite of the sufferings which attend it, until the day when he shall be summoned to render his final account.   The παραθήκη or thing committed to him was the same as that which he had committed to Timothy that he might teach others (1 Tim. vi. 20).   It was the form of sound words (ver. 13); that which Timothy had heard from Paul (ch. ii. 2); that *fair deposit* (ver. 14).   It was the gospel to which Paul had been appointed (ver. 11); which had been intrusted to him (1 Tim. i. 11 ; Tit. i. 3 ; comp. 1 Cor. ix. 17 ; Gal. ii. 7 ; 1 Th. ii. 4).   The verb παρατιθέναι *to commit to one's charge* is a favourite with Luke. See L. xii. 48 ; Acts xx. 32.   Sums deposited with a Bishop for the use of the church were called παραθῆκαι τῆς ἐκκλησίας *trust-funds of the church*.   In the Epistle of the pseudo-Ignatius to Hero (VII) we read : "Keep my *deposit* (παραθήκην) which I and Christ have *committed* (παρθέμεθα) to you.   I *commit* (παρατίθημι) to you the church of the Antiochenes."

That day (ἐκείνην τὴν ἡμέραν).   The day of Christ's second appearing.   See on 1 Th. v. 2.   In this sense the phrase occurs in the N. T. Epistles only ch. i. 18; iv. 8; 2 Th. i. 10; but often in the Gospels, as Matt. vii. 22; xxvi. 29; Mk. xiii. 32, etc.   The day of the Lord's appearing is designated by Paul as ἡ ἡμέρα, absolutely, *the day*, Rom. xiii. 12 ; 1 Cor. iii. 13 ; 1 Th. v. 4 : ἡμέρα τοῦ κυρίου *the day of the Lord*, 1 Cor. i. 8 ; 2 Cor. i. 14 ; 1 Th. v. 2 ; 2 Th. ii. 2 : *the day of Jesus Christ* or *Christ*, Philip. i. 6, 10 ; ii. 16 : *the day when God shall judge*, Rom. ii. 16 : *the day of wrath and revelation* *of the righteous judgment of God*, Rom. ii. 5 : *the day of redemption*, Eph. iv. 30.

13. **The form** (ὑποτύπωσιν). Pasts⁰. ⁰LXX, ⁰Class. See on 1 Tim. i. 16.

Of sound words (ὑγιαινόντων λόγων). See on 1 Tim. i. 16.

In faith and love. The teaching is to be held, preached, and practised, not as a mere schedule of conduct, however excellent, but with the strong conviction of faith and the fervour of love.

14. **That good thing which was committed** (τὴν καλὴν παραθήκην). That fair, honourable trust, good and beautiful in itself, and honourable to him who receives it. The phrase N. T.⁰. See on ver. 12. Comp. *the good warfare*, 1 Tim. i. 18 ; *teaching*, 1 Tim. iv. 6 ; *fight*, 1 Tim. vi. 12 ; *confession*, 1 Tim. vi. 12.

15. **In Asia.** Proconsular Asia, known as *Asia Propria* or simply *Asia*. It was the Roman province formed out of the kingdom of Pergamus, which was bequeathed to the Romans by Attalus III (B.C. 130), including the Greek cities on the western coast of Asia, and the adjacent islands with Rhodes. It included Mysia, Lydia, Caria, and Phrygia. The division Asia Major and Asia Minor was not adopted until the fourth century A.D. Asia Minor (Anatolia) was bounded by the Euxine, Aegean, and Mediterranean on the north, west, and south ; and on the east by the mountains on the west of the upper course of the Euphrates.

Have turned away (ἀπεστράφησαν). Not from the faith, but from Paul.

16. **Onesiphorus.** Mentioned again, ch. iv. 19.

Refreshed (ἀνέψυξεν). N. T.⁰. Several times in LXX ; often in Class. 'Ανάψυξις *refreshing*, Acts iii. 19 ; and καταψύχειν *to cool*, L. xvi. 24.   Originally *to cool ; to revive by fresh air.*

Chain (ἅλυσιν). Once in Paul, Eph. vi. 20. Several times in Mark, Luke, and Acts. It may mean *handcuffs* or *manacles* (see Lightfoot, *Philippians*, ed. of 1896, p. 8), but is not limited to that sense either in classical or later Greek. See Hdt. ix. 74 ; Eurip. *Orest.* 984. Mk. v. 4 is not decisive.

18. **Very well** (βέλτιον). N. T.[o]. The sense is comparative ; *better* than I can tell you.

CHAPTER II.

1. **Therefore** (οὖν). In view of what has been said in the previous chapter.

Be strong (ἐνδυναμοῦ). In Paul, Rom. iv. 20 ; Eph. vi. 10 ; Philip. iv. 13. Lit. *be strengthened inwardly.*

In the grace (ἐν τῇ χάριτι). Grace is the inward source of strength. Comp. the association of grace and strength in 2 Cor. xii. 9.

2. **Among many witnesses** (διὰ πολλῶν μαρτύρων). Διὰ *through the medium of*, and therefore *in the presence of.*

Commit (παράθου). As a trust or deposit (παραθήκη). See on ch. i. 12, 14. In Paul only 1 Cor. x. 27.

Faithful (πιστοῖς). Not *believing*, but *trusty*, as appears from the context. See on 1 J. i. 9 ; Apoc. i. 5 ; iii. 14.

Able (ἱκανοί). In Pastorals only here. Very common in Luke and Acts : a few times in Paul. See on *many*, Rom. xv. 23.

3. Endure hardness (συνκακοπάθησον). Comp. ch. i. 8. A. V. fails to give the force of συν *with*. Rend. *suffer hardship with me*.

Soldier (στρατιώτης). Only here in Pastorals. °P. Frequent in Acts.

4. That warreth (στρατευόμενος). Better, *when engaged in warfare*. Rev. *no soldier on service*. In Paul, 1 Cor. ix. 7; 2 Cor. x. 3. In Pastorals only here and 1 Tim. i. 18.

Entangleth himself (ἐμπλέκεται). Only here and 2 Pet. ii. 20 (see note). This has been made an argument for clerical celibacy.

In the affairs of this life (ταῖς τοῦ βίου πραγματίαις). Better, *affairs of life*. Not as A. V. implies, in contrast with the affairs of the next life, but simply the ordinary occupations of life. In N. T. βίος means either *means of subsistence*, as Mk. xii. 44; L. viii. 43; 1 J. iii. 17; or *course of life*, as L. viii. 14. Βίος °P.

Him who hath chosen him to be a soldier (τῷ στρατολογήσαντι). N. T.°. °LXX. Better, *enrolled him as a soldier*.

5. Strive for masteries (ἀθλῇ). N. T.°. °LXX. Paul uses ἀγωνίζεσθαι (see 1 Cor. ix. 25), which appears also in 1 Tim. iv. 10; vi. 12; 2 Tim. iv. 7. *For masteries* is superfluous. Rev. *contend in the games;* but the meaning of the verb is not limited to that. It may mean to contend *in battle;* and the preceding reference to the soldier would seem to suggest that meaning here. The allusion to *crowning* is not decisive in favour of the Rev. rendering. Among the Romans crowns were the highest distinction for service in war. The *corona triumphalis* of laurel was presented to a triumphant general; and the *corona obsidionalis* was awarded to a general by the army which he had saved from a siege or

from a shameful capitulation.   It was woven of grass which
grew on the spot, and was also called *corona graminea.*   The
corona myrtea or *ovalis*, the crown of bay, was worn by the
general who celebrated the lesser triumph or *ovatio.*   The
golden *corona muralis*, with embattled ornaments, was given
for the storming of a wall ; and the *corona castrensis* or *val-
laris*, also of gold, and ornamented in imitation of palisades,
was awarded to the soldier who first climbed the rampart of
the enemy's camp.

Is he not crowned (οὐ στεφανοῦται).   The verb only here
and Heb. ii. 7, 9.   For στέφανος *crown*, see on Apoc. ii. 9 ;
iv. 4 ; 1 Pet. v. 4.   Paul has στέφανον λαβεῖν, 1 Cor. ix. 25.

Lawfully (νομίμως).   Past⁰.   See 1 Tim. i. 8.   According
to the law of military service which requires him to abandon
all other pursuits.   So the law of the ministerial office requires
that the minister shall not entangle himself with secular pursuits.   If he fulfils this requirement, he is not to trouble himself about his worldly maintenance, for it is right that he
should draw his support from his ministerial labour : nay,
he has the *first* right to its material fruits.

6. **The husbandman that laboureth** (τὸν κοπιῶντα γεωρ-
γὸν).   The verb implies *hard, wearisome* toil.   See on 1 Th.
i. 3 ; v. 12.   Γεωργός *husbandman*, only here in Pastorals.
⁰P.   See on J. xv. 1.

Must be first partaker (δεῖ πρῶτον — μεταλαμβάνειν).
Better, *must be the first to partake.*   His is the first right
to the fruits of his labour in the gospel.   The writer seems
to have in his eye 1 Cor. ix. 7, where there is a similar
association of military service and farming to illustrate the
principle that they who proclaim the gospel should live of
the gospel.   Μεταλαμβάνειν to *partake*, ⁰P, and only here in
Pastorals.   Paul uses μετέχειν.   See 1 Cor. ix. 10, 12 ; x. 17,
21, 30.

7. **Consider** (νόει).   Better, *understand.*

And the Lord give thee understanding (δώσει γάρ ὁ κύριος σύνεσιν). More correctly, *for the Lord shall give.** For σύνεσιν *understanding*, see on Mk. xii. 33; L. ii. 47; Col. i. 9.

8. Remember that Jesus Christ — was raised, etc. Incorrect. Rend. *remember Jesus Christ raised from the dead.* Μνημόνευε *remember*, only here in Pastorals : often in Paul. Ἐγείρειν *to raise*, very often in N. T., but only here in Pastorals. The perfect passive participle (ἐγηγερμένον) only here. The perfect marks the permanent condition — raised and still living.

Of the seed of David. Not referring to Christ's human descent as a humiliation in contrast with his victory over death (ἐγηγερμένον), but only marking his human, visible nature along with his glorified nature, and indicating that in both aspects he is exalted and glorified. See the parallel in Rom. i. 3, 4, which the writer probably had in mind, and was perhaps trying to imitate. It is supposed by some that the words *Jesus Christ — seed of David* were a part of a confessional formula.

According to my gospel. Comp. Rom. ii. 16 ; xvi. 25, and see 1 Cor. xv. 1 ; 2 Cor. xi. 7; Gal. i. 11; ii. 2; 1 Tim. i. 11.

9. Wherein I suffer trouble (ἐν ᾧ κακοπαθῶ). *Wherein* refers to the gospel. Κακοπαθεῖν only here, ch. iv. 5, and Jas. v. 13. LXX, Jon. iv. 10.

As an evildoer (ὡς κακοῦργος). Only here and in Luke. Better, *malefactor.* The meaning is technical. Comp. L. xxiii. 32, 33, 39.

Unto bonds (μέχρι δεσμῶν). Comp. Philip. ii. 8, μέχρι θανάτου *unto death :* Heb. xii. 4, μέχρις αἵματος *unto blood.* Const. with *I suffer trouble.*

---

* The A. V. follows T. R. δῴη *may* (*the Lord*) *give.*

But the word of God is not bound (ἀλλὰ ὁ λόγος τοῦ θεοῦ οὐ δέδεται). Nevertheless, although I am in bonds, the gospel which I preach will prevail in spite of all human efforts to hinder it. *Word of God* often in Paul. In Pastorals, 1 Tim. iv. 5; Tit. ii. 5. *Bound*, in Paul metaphorically, as here, Rom. vii. 2; 1 Cor. vii. 27, 39.

10. Therefore (διὰ τοῦτο). Because I know that God is carrying on his work.*

That they may also (ἵνα καὶ αὐτοὶ). More correctly, *they also may*, etc. *Also*, as well as myself.

Obtain the salvation (σωτηρίας τύχωσιν). The phrase N. T.⁰. Paul has περιποίησις σωτηρίας *obtaining of salvation*, 1 Th. v. 9.

Which is in Christ Jesus. The phrase *salvation which is in Christ Jesus*, N. T.⁰. For other collocations with *in Christ Jesus* in Pastorals, see 1 Tim. i. 14; iii. 13; 2 Tim. i. 1, 9, 13; ii. 1, 3, 15.

With eternal glory (μετὰ δόξης αἰωνίου). The phrase *eternal glory* only here and 1 Pet. v. 10. Paul has αἰώνιον βάρος δόξης *eternal weight of glory*, 2 Cor. iv. 17. *Glory* here is the eternal reward of Christians in heaven.

11. It is a faithful saying. Better, *faithful is the saying*. See on 1 Tim. i. 15. It refers to what precedes — the eternal glory of those who are raised with Christ (ver. 8) which stimulates to endurance of sufferings for the gospel.

For (γὰρ). Faithful is the saying that the elect shall obtain salvation with eternal glory, *for* if we be dead, etc.†

---

* Others connect with what follows : I endure — on this account, namely, that the elect may obtain salvation. *For the elects' sake* is not against this connection, since God's election does not do away with the faithful efforts of his servants.

† Others refer *faithful is the saying* to what follows, and render γὰρ *namely*.

The following words to the end of ver. 12 may be a fragment
of a hymn or confession, founded on Rom. vi. 8; viii. 17.

If we be dead with him (εἰ συναπεθάνομεν). A.V. misses
the force of the aorist. Better, *if we died*, etc. Comp. Rom.
vi. 8; Col. ii. 20. For the verb, comp. Mk. xiv. 31; 2 Cor.
vii. 3.

12. **If we suffer we shall also reign with him** (εἰ ὑπομένο-
μεν, καὶ συνβασιλεύσομεν). For *suffer*, rend. *endure*. Συν-
βασιλεύειν *to reign with*, only here and 1 Cor. iv. 8. Comp.
L. xix. 17, 19; xxii. 29, 30; Rom. v. 17; Apoc. iv. 4; v. 10;
xxii. 5.

If we deny him he also will deny us (εἰ ἀρνησόμεθα, κἀκεῖ-
νος ἀρνήσεται ἡμᾶς). The verb °P. *Him* must be supplied.
The meaning of the last clause is, *will not acknowledge us as
his own*. Comp. L. ix. 26; Matt. x. 33.

13. **If we believe not** (εἰ ἀπιστοῦμεν). Better, *are faith-
less* or *untrue* to him. Comp. Rom. iii. 3. In Pastorals
only here.

Faithful (πιστὸς). True to his own nature, righteous character, and requirements, according to which he cannot accept
as faithful one who has proved untrue to him. To do this
would be to deny himself.

14. **Put them in remembrance** (ὑπομίμνησκε). °P. See
on ὑπόμνησιν *reminding*, ch. i. 5.

Charging (διαμαρτυρόμενος). In Paul only 1 Th. iv. 6.
Very frequent in Acts. See on Acts ii. 40; xx. 23. The
sense is rather *conjuring* them by their loyalty to God. Paul
uses the simple μαρτύρεσθαι in a similar sense. **See Gal.
v. 3**; 1 Th. ii. 12 (note); Eph. iv. 17.

Before God (ἐνώπιον τοῦ θεοῦ). See on **1 Tim. v. 4.**

Strive about words (λογομαχεῖν). N. T.⁰. ⁰LXX, ⁰Class. Comp. λογομαχίας *disputes of words*, 1 Tim. vi. 4, and see 1 Cor. iv. 20.

To no profit (ἐπ᾽ οὐδὲν χρήσιμον). Lit. *to nothing useful*. Ἐπ᾽ οὐδὲν, ⁰P. He uses εἰς κενόν to no purpose. See 2 Cor. vi. 1; Gal. ii. 2; Philip. ii. 16; 1 Th. iii. 5. Χρήσιμος *useful*, N. T.⁰.

To the subverting (ἐπὶ καταστροφῇ). Ἐπὶ does not mean here *to* or *for* (purpose or object), but indicates the ground on which the unprofitableness of the wordy strife rests. Unprofitable *because* it works subversion of the hearers. Καταστροφή *subversion*, transliterated into *catastrophe*, only here and 2 Pet. ii. 6. In LXX of the *destruction* or *overthrow* of men or cities. Καταστρέφειν *to overturn*, Matt. xxi. 12; Mk. xi. 15; Acts xv. 16, cit. Paul uses καθαίρεσις *pulling down*, 2 Cor. x. 4, 8; xiii. 10.

15. **Study** (σπούδασον). Originally, *make haste*. In Paul, Gal. ii. 10; Eph. iv. 3 (note); 1 Th. ii. 17.

To shew thyself approved (σεαυτὸν δόκιμον παραστῆσαι). Παραστῆσαι, better, *present*. In Pastorals only here and ch. iv. 17. Often in Acts and Paul. See on Acts i. 3; Rom. xvi. 2; Eph. v. 27. Δόκιμον *approved*, only here in Pastorals, five times by Paul. See on Jas. i. 12. On δοκιμή *approvedness*, Rom. v. 4; and on δοκιμάζειν *to approve on test*, 1 Pet. i. 7.

A workman (ἐργάτην). In Paul, 2 Cor. xi. 13; Philip. iii. 2. In Pastorals, 1 Tim. v. 18.

That needeth not to be ashamed (ἀνεπαίσχυντον). N. T.⁰. ⁰LXX, ⁰Class. Lit. *not made ashamed*, as Philip. i. 20. A workman whose work does not disgrace him.

Rightly dividing (ὀρθοτομοῦντα). N. T.⁰. ⁰Class. In LXX, Prov. iii. 6; xi. 5; both times in the sense of direct-

ing the way.   From ὀρθός *straight* and τέμνειν *to cut*.   Hence,
to cut straight, as paths; *to hold a straight course*; generally,
to make straight; to handle rightly.   Vulg. *recte tractare*.
The thought is that the minister of the gospel is to present
the truth rightly, not abridging it, not handling it as a char-
latan (see on 2 Cor. ii. 17), not making it a matter of wordy
strife (ver. 14), but treating it honestly and fully, in a
straightforward manner.   Various homiletic fancies have
been founded on the word, as, to *divide* the word of truth,
giving to each hearer what he needs : or, to separate it into
its proper parts : or, to separate it from error : or, to cut
straight through it, so that its inmost contents may be laid
bare.   Others, again, have found in it the figure of dividing
the bread, which is the office of the household steward ; or of
dividing the sacrificial victims ; or of cutting a straight fur-
row with the plough.

16. **Shun** (περιΐστασο). ⁰P.   In Pastorals, here and Tit.
iii. 9.   Originally, *to place round ; to stand round*.   In the
middle voice, *to turn one's self about*, as for the purpose of
avoiding something : hence, *avoid, shun*.   Often in Class.,
but in this sense only in later Greek.

Profane and vain babblings (βεβήλους κενοφωνίας).   For
profane, see on 1 Tim. i. 9.   *Vain* is superfluous, being
implied in *babblings*.   For *babblings*, see on 1 Tim. vi. 20.
Babble is a word of early origin, an imitative word, formed
on the efforts of a young child to speak, and having its coun-
terparts in many languages.   It appears very early in English, as in Piers Plowman :

> "And so I bablede on my bedes."
> *Vis.* 2487.

Bacon :
> "Who will open himselfe to a blab or a babler ? "
> *Ess.* vi.

Shakespeare :
> "Leave thy vain bibble babble."
> *Twelfth N.* iv. 2.

They will increase (προκόψουσιν).   See on Rom. xiii. 12,
and Gal. i. 14.

Ungodliness (ἀσεβείας). The opposite of εὐσέβεια *godliness*, for which see on 1 Tim. ii. 2. In Pastorals, Tit. ii. 12. In Paul, Rom. i. 18 ; xi. 26, cit.

17. **Will eat** (νομὴν ἕξει). Lit. *will have pasturage*, and so *grow*. Νομὴ πυρός is *a spreading of fire :* a sore is said νομὴν ποιεῖσθαι to spread. Comp. Acts iv. 17, διανεμηθῇ *spread*, of the influence of the miracle of Peter, from the same root, νέμειν *to distribute* or *divide ;* often of herdsmen, *to pasture*. Νομὴ only here and J. x. 9.

Canker (γάγγραινα). Transliterated into *gangrene*. *An eating sore ; a cancer.* N. T.⁰. ⁰LXX. Comp. Ovid :

> " Solet immedicabile cancer
> Serpere, et illaesas vitiatis addere partes."
>
> *Metam.* ii. 825

18. **Have erred** (ἠστόχησαν). See on 1 Tim. i. 6.

The resurrection (ἀνάστασιν). Only here in Pastorals.

19. **Nevertheless** (μέντοι). Mostly in John. ⁰P. Only here in Pastorals.

The foundation of God standeth sure (ὁ στερεὸς θεμέλιος τοῦ θεοῦ ἕστηκεν). Wrong. Στερεὸς *sure* is attributive, not predicative. Rend. *the firm foundation of God standeth*. The phrase *foundation of God*, N. T.⁰. Θεμέλιος *foundation* is an adjective, and λίθος *stone* is to be supplied. It is not to be taken by metonymy for οἰκία *house* (ver. 20), but must be interpreted consistently with it,* and, in a loose way, represents or foreshadows it. So we speak of an endowed institution as *a foundation*. By " the sure foundation of God" is meant *the church*, which is " the pillar and stay of the truth " (1 Tim. iii. 15), by means of which the truth of God is to withstand the assaults of error. The church has its being in

---

* In LXX, אַרְמוֹן *palace, fortress, citadel, hall,* is rendered by θεμελία. See Hos. viii. 14 ; Amos i. 4, 7, 10, 12, 14 ; Jer. vi. 5 ; Isa. xxv. 2.

the contents of "the sound teaching" (1 Tim. i. 10), which is
"according to godliness" (1 Tim. vi. 3), and which is deposited in it.   "The mystery of godliness" is intrusted to it
(1 Tim. iii. 16).   Its servants possess "the mystery of the
faith" (1 Tim. iii. 9).   In 1 Cor. iii. 11, Christ is represented as "the chief corner-stone."   In Eph. ii. 20, the
church is built "upon the foundation of the apostles and
prophets," with Christ as the corner-stone, and grows into a
"holy temple (ναὸν) in the Lord."   Here, the church itself
is the foundation, and the building is conceived as a great
dwelling-house.   While the conception of the church here
does not contradict that of Paul, the difference is apparent
between it and the conception in Ephesians, where the church
is the seat of the indwelling and energy of the Holy Spirit.
Comp. 1 Cor. iii. 16, 17. Στερεός *firm* only here, Heb. v. 12,
14, and 1 Pet. v. 9 (note).   Ἕστηκεν *standeth*, in contrast
with *overthrow* (ver. 18).

Seal (σφραγῖδα).   Mostly in the Apocalypse.   Only here
in Pastorals.   In Paul, Rom. iv. 11; 1 Cor. ix. 2.   Used here
rather in the sense of *inscription* or *motto*.   Comp. Deut. vi.
9; xi. 20; Apoc. xxi. 14.   There are two inscriptions on the
foundation stone, the one guaranteeing the *security*, the other
the *purity*, of the church.   The two go together.   The purity
of the church is indispensable to its security.

The Lord knoweth them that are his (ἔγνω κύριος τοὺς
ὄντας αὐτοῦ).   The first inscription : *God knows his own.*
Comp. Num. xvi. 5; 1 Cor. xiii. 12.   For ἔγνω *knoweth*, see
on Gal. iv. 9.   *Them that are his*, his ἐκλεκτοὶ *chosen;* see
ver. 10; Tit. i. 1; Rom. viii. 33; Col. iii. 12; 1 Pet. ii. 9;
Apoc. xvii. 14.   Not, however, in any hard, predestinarian
sense.*   Comp. J. x. 14; Matt. vii. 23; L. xiii. 25, 27.

* As in the Westminster Confession, where this passage is cited as a proof-
text of the dogma that those "angels and men" who are "predestinated and
foreordained" to everlasting life or death, "are particularly and unchange-
ably designed: and their number is so certain and definite that it cannot be
either increased or diminished." Ch. III., Sect. iv.

Let every one that nameth the name of Christ depart from iniquity. The second inscription, concerning the purity of the church. For *of Christ* rend. *of the Lord* (κυρίου). Ὀνομάζων *nameth*, only here in Pastorals. It means *to give a name to, to style*, as Mk. iii. 14 ; L. vi. 14 ; 1 Cor. v. 11 : *to pronounce a name as having a special virtue*, as in incantation, as Acts xix. 13 : *to utter a name as acknowledging and appropriating what the name involves, as a confession of faith and allegiance.* So here. Comp. Rom. xv. 20 ; 1 Cor. v. 11 ; Isa. xxvi. 13. For ὄνομα *name*, see on 1 Th. i. 12. Ἀποστήτω ἀπὸ ἀδικίας *depart from iniquity.* For the verb, see on 1 Tim. iv. 1. Mostly in Luke and Acts. Comp. Num. xvi. 26 ; Isa. lii. 11. Whatever may be implied in God's election, it does not relieve Christians of the duty of strict attention to their moral character and conduct. Comp. Philip. ii. 12. The gift of grace (Eph. ii. 8) is exhibited in making one a coworker with God (1 Cor. iii. 9). The salvation bestowed by grace is to be "carried out" (Philip. ii. 12) by man with the aid of grace (Rom. vi. 8–19 ; 2 Cor. vi. 1). What this includes and requires appears in Philip. iii. 10 ; iv. 1–7 ; Eph. iv. 13–16, 22 ff. ; Col. ii. 6, 7.

20. But the church embraces a variety of characters. Unrighteous men steal into it. So, in a great household establishment there are vessels fit only for base uses.

House (οἰκίᾳ). As θεμέλιος *foundation* indicates the inward, essential character of the church, οἰκία exhibits its visible, outward aspect. The mixed character of the church points to its *greatness* (μεγάλῃ).

Vessels (σκεύη). See on Matt. xii. 29 ; Mk. iii. 27 ; Acts ix. 15 ; xxvii. 17 ; 1 Pet. iii. 7.

Of wood and of earth (ξύλινα καὶ ὀστράκινα). Ξύλινος *wooden*, only here and Apoc. ix. 20. Ὀστράκινος *of baked clay*, only here and 2 Cor. iv. 7 (note). Comp. the different metaphor, 1 Cor. iii. 12.

Some to honour and some to dishonour. After Rom. ix. 21.

21. Purge (ἐκκαθάρῃ). Only here and 1 Cor. v. 7. The meaning is, *separate himself from communion with.*

From these (ἀπὸ τούτων). From such persons as are described as " vessels unto dishonour." Some attempt to relieve the awkwardness of this figure by referring *these* to persons mentioned in vv. 16, 17.

Unto honour (εἰς τιμήν). Const. with *vessel*, not with *sanctified*.

Sanctified (ἡγιασμένον). Comp. 1 Tim. iv. 5. Set apart to noble and holy uses, as belonging to God. See on ἁγιασμός *sanctification*, Rom. vi. 19. For ἅγιος *holy*, see on 1 Tim. v. 10.

Meet (εὔχρηστον). From εὖ *well* and χρᾶσθαι *to use*. Hence, *easy to make use of, useful.* The A.V. *meet*, is *fit, suitable.* Rend. *serviceable.* In contrast with *to no profit*, ver. 14. See Philem. 11, where the contrast with ἄχρηστος *useless* is brought out. Only here, ch. iv. 11, Philem. 11.

For the master's use (τῷ δεσπότῃ). *Use* is superfluous. Rend. *for the master.* The master of the household. See on 1 Tim. vi. 1.

Prepared (ἡτοιμασμένον). In Paul, 1 Cor. ii. 9; Philem. 22. Only here in Pastorals. Comp. Tit. iii. 1.

Every good work. The phrase in Paul, 2 Cor. ix. 8; Col. i. 10 ; 2 Th. ii. 17. In Pastorals, 1 Tim. v. 10; 2 Tim. iii. 17; Tit. i. 16; iii. 1.

22. Youthful lusts (νεωτερικὰς ἐπιθυμίας). Νεωτερικὸς *youthful*, N.T.°. For ἐπιθυμία *desire, lust*, see on Mk. iv. 19;

1 Th. iv. 5. Such counsel from Paul to Timothy seems strange.

Follow (δίωκε). *Pursue.* Stronger than *follow.* A favourite word with Paul to denote the pursuit of moral and spir·· itual ends. See Rom. ix. 30, 31; xii. 13; 1 Cor. xiv. 1; Philip. iii. 12.

Peace (εἰρήνην). Not a distinct virtue in the list, but a consequence of the pursuit of the virtues enumerated. Const. with *with them that call,* etc. For *peace* with διώκειν *pursue,* see Rom. xiv. 19; Heb. xii. 14, and Ps. xxxiv. 14, cit. 1 Pet. iii. 11.

Call on the Lord (ἐπικαλουμένων τὸν κύριον). A Pauline phrase, only here in Pastorals. See Rom. x. 12, 13, 14; 1 Cor. i. 2. See also Acts ii. 21; ix. 14; xxii. 16.

Out of a pure heart (ἐκ καθαρᾶς καρδίας). Const. with *call on the Lord.* The phrase, 1 Tim. i. 5; 1 Pet. i. 22. Comp. Matt. v. 8.

23. **Foolish** (μωρὰς). In Pastorals only here and Tit. iii. 9. Μωρός means *dull, sluggish, stupid :* applied to the taste, *flat, insipid :* comp. μωρανθῇ *have lost his savour,* Matt. v. 13. In Pastorals never substantively, *a fool,* but so in 1 Cor. iii. 18; iv. 10. Comp. ἄφρων, 1 Cor. xv. 36.

Unlearned (ἀπαιδεύτους). Rev. *ignorant* is better; but the meaning at bottom is *undisciplined :* questions of an *untrained* mind, carried away with novelties : questions which do not proceed from any trained habit of thinking.

Questions (ζητήσεις). Better, *questionings.* See on 1 Tim. vi. 4.

Avoid (παραιτοῦ). See on 1 Tim. iv. 7. Better, *refuse* or *decline.*

Gender (γεννῶσι). Only here in Pastorals. In Paul, metaphorically, 1 Cor. iv. 15; Philem. 10; Gal. iv. 24.

24. The servant of the Lord (δοῦλον κυρίου). The teacher or other special worker in the church. Comp. Tit. i. 1; Rom. i. 1; Gal. i. 10; Philip. i. 1; Col. iv. 12. Of any Christian, 1 Cor. vii. 22; Eph. vi. 6. The phrase is often applied to the O. T. prophets as a body: see Amos iii. 7; Jer. vii. 25; Ezra ix. 11; Dan. ix. 6. To Joshua, Judg. ii. 8; to David, Ps. lxxvii. 70.

Must not (οὐ δεῖ). Moral obligation.

Gentle (ἤπιον). Only here and 1 Th. ii. 7 (note).

Apt to teach, patient (διδακτικόν, ἀνεξίκακον). Διδακτικός *apt to teach*, only here and 1 Tim. iii. 2 (note). 'Ανεξίκακος *forbearing*, N. T.º. 'Ανεξικακία *forbearance*, Wisd. ii. 19. Rend. *forbearing*.

25. In meekness (ἐν πραΰτητι). A Pauline word, only here in Pastorals, but comp. πραϋπαθία *meekness*, 1 Tim. vi. 11 (note). Const. with *instructing*.

Instructing (παιδεύοντα). See on 1 Tim. i. 20. Better, *correcting*.

Those that oppose themselves (τοὺς ἀντιδιατιθεμένους). N. T.º. ºLXX. Class. only late Greek. *Themselves* is wrong. The meaning is, those who oppose the servant of the Lord; who carry on the ἀντιθέσεις *oppositions* (1 Tim. vi. 20);=*gainsayers* (ἀντιλέγοντες, Tit. i. 9). Paul's word is ἀντίκεισθαι *to oppose*: see 1 Cor. xvi. 9; Gal. v. 17; Philip. i. 28; 2 Th. ii. 4.

Repentance (μετάνοιαν). Only here in Pastorals. See on *repent*, Matt. iii. 2.

To the acknowledging of the truth (εἰς ἐπίγνωσιν ἀληθείας). More correctly, *the knowledge*. The formula Pastº.

See 1 Tim. ii. 4 (note) ; 2 Tim. iii. 7.   For εἰς *unto* after μετάνοια *repentance*, see Mk. i. 4; L. iii. 3; xxiv. 47; Acts xi. 18; xx. 21; 2 Cor. vii. 10.

26. **May recover themselves** (ἀνανήψωσιν).   Lit. *may return to soberness.*   N. T.⁰.   See on *be sober*, 1 Th. v. 6.   A similar connection of thought between coming to the knowledge of God and awaking out of a drunken stupor, occurs 1 Cor. xv. 34.

Out of the snare of the devil (ἐκ τῆς τοῦ διαβόλου παγίδος). Comp. Ps. cxxiv. 7.   The phrase *snare of the devil*, only here and 1 Tim. iii. 7 (note).   The metaphor is mixed ; return to soberness out of the snare of the devil.

Who are taken captive (ἐζωγρημένοι).   Or, *having been held captive.*   Only here and L. v. 10 (note on *thou shalt catch*).

By him (ὑπ' αὐτοῦ).   The devil.

At his will (εἰς τὸ ἐκείνου θέλημα).   Better, *unto* his will : that is, to do his (God's) will.

The whole will then read : " And that they may return to soberness out of the snare of the devil (having been held captive by him) to do God's will." *

CHAPTER III.

1. Comp. the beginning of 1 Tim. iv.

This know (τοῦτο γίνωσκε).   The phrase N. T.⁰.   Comp. Paul's γινώσκειν ὑμᾶς βούλομαι *I would have you to know,* Philip. i. 12; and θέλω δὲ ὑμᾶς εἰδέναι *I would you should know,* 1 Cor. xi. 3.

---

* Some, as A.V., make both αὐτοῦ and ἐκείνου refer to the devil.   Others explain : "having been taken captive by him (the servant of God) to do his (God's) will."   Others again, " having been taken captive by him (God) to do his (God's) will."

In the last days (ἐπ' ἐσχάταις ἡμέραις). The phrase only here in Pastorals, Acts ii. 17, Jas. v. 3. Similar expressions are ἐν καιρῷ ἐσχάτῳ *in the last season*, 1 Pet. i. 5: ἐπ' ἐσχάτου τῶν χρόνων *at the last of the times*, 1 Pet. i. 20: ἐπ' ἐσχάτου χρόνου *at the last time*, Jude 18: ἐπ' ἐσχάτων τῶν ἡμερῶν *at the last of the days*, 2 Pet. iii. 3: ἐν ὑστέροις καιροῖς *in the latter seasons*, 1 Tim. iv. 1. The times immediately preceding Christ's second appearing are meant. Comp. Heb. i. 2; Jas. v. 3.

Perilous times (καιροὶ χαλεποί). Only here and Matt. viii. 28. Lit. *hard times: schwere Zeiten*. Καιρός denotes a definite, specific season. See on Matt. xii. 1; Acts i. 17.

Shall come (ἐνστήσονται). Or *will set in*. Mostly in Paul. Only here in Pastorals. See on Gal. i. 4.

2. **Lovers of their own selves** (φίλαυτοι). Better, *lovers of self*. N. T.°. °LXX. Aristotle, *De Repub.* ii. 5, says: "It is not loving one's self, but loving it unduly, just as the love of possessions."

Covetous (φιλάργυροι). Better, *lovers of money*. Only here and L. xvi. 14. For the noun φιλαργυρία *love of money*, see on 1 Tim. vi. 10. Love of money and covetousness are not synonymous. *Covetous* is πλεονέκτης; see 1 Cor. v. 10, 11; Eph. v. 5. See on Rom. i. 29.

Boasters (ἀλαζόνες). Or *swaggerers*. Only here and Rom. i. 30. See on ἀλαζονείαις *boastings*, Jas. iv. 16.

Proud (ὑπερήφανοι). Or *haughty*. See on ὑπερηφανία *pride*, Mk. vii. 22.

Blasphemers (βλάσφημοι). See on 1 Tim. i. 13. Better, *railers*. See also on βλασφημία *blasphemy*, Mk. vii. 22.

Unthankful (ἀχάριστοι). Only here and L. vi. 35.

Unholy (ἀνόσιοι). Only here and 1 Tim. i. 9 (note).

3. **Without natural affection** (ἄστοργοι). Only here and Rom. i. 31. ⁰LXX. See on ἀγάπη love, Gal. v. 22, under στέργειν to love with a natural affection.

Truce-breakers (ἄσπονδοι). N. T.⁰. ⁰LXX. Rend. *implacable*. From ἀ not, and σπονδαί a treaty or truce. The meaning is, *refusing to enter into treaty, irreconcilable.**

Incontinent (ἀκρατεῖς). Or *intemperate, without self-control*. N. T.⁰. Once in LXX, Prov. xxvii. 20. Ἀκρασία *incontinence*, Matt. xxiii. 25; 1 Cor. vii. 5; 1 Macc. vi. 26; Ps. of Sol. iv. 3.

Fierce (ἀνήμεροι). Or *savage*. N. T.⁰. ⁰LXX. Comp. ἀνελεήμονες *merciless*, Rom. i. 31.

Despisers of those that are good (ἀφιλάγαθοι). Better, *haters of good*. N. T.⁰. ⁰LXX, ⁰Class. Comp. the opposite, φιλάγαθον *lover of good*, Tit. i. 8.

4. **Traitors** (προδόται). Or *betrayers*. Only here, L. vi. 16; Acts vii. 52.

Heady (προπετεῖς). Precipitate, reckless, headstrong in the pursuit of a bad end under the influence of passion. Only here and Acts xix. 36. In LXX, *slack, loose*, hence *foolish*, Prov. x. 14, and *dividing* or *parting asunder*, as the lips; of one who opens his lips and speaks hastily or thoughtlessly, Prov. xiii. 3. Comp. Sir. ix. 18.

Highminded (τετυφωμένοι). Better, *besotted* or *clouded* with pride. See on 1 Tim. iii. 6, and comp. 1 Tim. vi. 4.

Lovers of pleasure more than lovers of God (φιλήδονοι μᾶλλον ἢ φιλόθεοι). Pleasure-lovers rather than God-lovers. Both words N. T.⁰. ⁰LXX.

---

* So Aeschylus, *Agam.* 1235, of Clytaemnestra, ἄσπονδόν τ' ἀρὰν φίλοις πνέουσαν "breathing an *implacable* curse against her friends."

5. **A form** (μόρφωσιν). Only here and Rom. ii. 20. Μορφὴ *form* (for the want of any other rendering) is the expression or embodiment of the essential and permanent being of that which is expressed. Μόρφωσις, lit. *forming* or *shaping.* Yet the meaning differs in different passages. In Rom. ii. 20, μόρφωσις is the truthful embodiment of knowledge and truth as contained in the law of God. Here, the mere outward semblance, as distinguished from the essential reality.

The power (τὴν δύναμιν). The practical virtue. Comp. 1 Cor. iv. 20. It is impossible to overlook the influence of Rom. i. 29–31 in shaping this catalogue.

Turn away (ἀποτρέπου). N. T.⁰. Comp. παραιτοῦ *avoid,* ch. ii. 23 ; ἐκτρεπόμενος *turning away,* 1 Tim. vi. 20 ; and ἐκκλίνετε *turn away,* Rom. xvi. 17.

6. **Of this sort** (ἐκ τούτων). Lit. *of these.* The formula often in Paul.

Which creep (οἱ ἐνδύνοντες). N. T.⁰. Thrust themselves into. Comp. Jude 4, παρεισεδύησαν *crept in privily* (see note); 2 Pet. ii. 1 (note), παρεισάξουσιν *shall privily bring in ;* and Gal. ii. 4, παρεισάκτους *brought in by stealth.*

Lead captive (αἰχμαλωτίζοντες). Only here in Pastorals. See on *captives,* L. iv. 18 ; and 2 Cor. x. 5.

Silly women (γυναικάρια). N. T.⁰. ⁰LXX. *Silly* is expressed by the contemptuous diminutive. Comp. Vulg. *mulierculas.*

Laden (σεσωρευμένα). Only here and Rom. xii. 20, citation. In LXX, see Judith xv. 11, of *loading* a wagon with the property of Holofernes. It implies *heaped up; heavily laden.*

Led away (ἀγόμενα). *Away* is superfluous.   It is only an inference.   The meaning is *under the direction of.*   Comp. Rom. viii. 14 ; Gal. v. 18.

Divers (ποικίλαις).   In Pastorals only here and Tit. iii. 3. Lit. *variegated, of different tints.*   See on *manifold wisdom,* Eph. iii. 10.*

7. **Ever learning.**   From any one who will teach them. See on 1 Tim. v. 13.   It is a graphic picture of a large class, by no means extinct, who are caught and led by the instructions of itinerant religious quacks.

Never able (μηδέποτε δυνάμενα).   Because they have not the right motive, and because they apply to false teachers. Ellicott thinks that there is in δυνάμενα a hint of an unsuccessful endeavour, in better moments, to attain to the truth.

8. **As** (ὃν τρόπον).   The formula occurs in the Synoptic Gospels (see Matt. xxiii. 37 ; L. xiii. 34), and in Acts (i. 11 ; vii. 28), but not in Paul.

Jannes and Jambres.   According to tradition, the names of the chiefs of the magicians who opposed Moses.   Ex. vii. 11, 22.

Of corrupt minds (κατεφθαρμένοι τὸν νοῦν).   Better, *corrupted in mind.*   The verb, N. T.⁰.   Comp. διεφθαρμένων τὸν νοῦν *corrupted in mind,* 1 Tim. vi. 5.

Reprobate (ἀδόκιμοι).   In Pastorals only here and Tit. i. 16.   A Pauline word.   See on Rom. i. 28, and *castaway,* 1 Cor. ix. 27.

9. **Shall proceed** (προκόψουσιν).   See on ch. ii. 16.

---

* Holtzmann, on Tit. iii. 3, has an apt comment: "Im Dienste eines *bunten* Getriebes von Begierden."   Weizsäcker: "Von allerlei Begierden umgetrieben."

Folly (ἄνοια). Only here and L. vi. 11 (note). The *senselessness* of their teaching, with an implication of its immoral character.

Manifest (ἔκδηλος). N. T.⁰. LXX, 3 Macc. iii. 19 ; vi. 5.

10. **Hast fully known** (παρηκολούθησας). Better, *thou didst follow.* See on 1 Tim. iv. 6.   ⁰P.

Manner of life (ἀγωγῇ). Or *conduct.* N. T.⁰. LXX, mostly 2d and 3d Maccabees. Often in Class., but mostly in a transitive sense, *leading, conducting.*

Purpose (προθέσει). See on Acts xi. 23 ; Rom. ix. 11. In Paul, only of the divine purpose.

Longsuffering, charity, patience. For *longsuffering*, see on Jas. v. 7. For *charity* rend. *love*, and see on Gal. v. 22. For *patience*, see on 2 Pet. i. 6 ; Jas. v. 7.

11. **Persecutions, afflictions** (διωγμοῖς, παθήμασιν). Διωγμός *persecution*, only here in Pastorals. Occasionally in Paul. Πάθημα *suffering*, only here in Pastorals. Often in Paul, usually in the sense of *sufferings*, but twice of sinful *passions*, Rom. vii. 5 ; Gal. v. 24.

Antioch, Iconium, Lystra. See Acts xiii. 50 ; xiv. 2 ff.; xiv. 19. These cities may have been selected as illustrations because Timothy was at home in that region. See Acts xvi. 1, 2. Antioch is mentioned by Paul, Gal. ii. 11. Iconium and Lystra nowhere in his letters.

Delivered (ἐρύσατο). Often in Paul. Originally, *to draw to one's self ;* to *draw out* from peril. Paul, in Rom. xi. 26, applies the prophecy of Isa. lix. 20 to Christ, who is called ὁ ῥυόμενος *the deliverer*, LXX.

12. **Who will live** (οἱ θέλοντες ζῆν). *Whose will is* to live, or who *are bent on* living.

Godly (εὐσεβῶς). Only here and Tit. ii. 12. Comp. κατ᾽ εὐσέβειαν *according to godliness,* 1 Tim. vi. 3 ; Tit. i. 1 ; and ἐν πάσῃ εὐσεβείᾳ *in all godliness,* 1 Tim. ii. 2. See also 1 Tim. iv. 7 ; vi. 11, and on *godliness,* 1 Tim. ii. 2.

Shall suffer persecution (διωχθήσονται). In this sense only here in Pastorals.

13. **Seducers** (γόητες). N. T.⁰. Better, *impostors* or *deceivers.* From γοᾶν *to howl.* Originally, one who *chants* spells ; *a wizard, sorcerer.* Hence, *a cheat.*

Shall wax worse and worse (προκόψουσιν ἐπὶ τὸ χεῖρον). Lit. *shall proceed to the worse.* The formula, Past⁰. Comp. ver. 9 and ch. ii. 16.

Deceiving (πλανῶντες). Properly, *leading astray.* See on πλάνοις *seducing,* 1 Tim. iv. 1.

14. **Hast been assured of** (ἐπιστώθης). N. T.⁰. Quite often in LXX. So 2 Sam. vii. 16, *shall be established* (of the house of David) : Ps. lxxvii. 37, *steadfast* in his covenant.

15. **From a child** (ἀπὸ βρέφους). Mostly in Luke. ⁰P. Only here in Pastorals. See on 1 Pet. ii. 2. Comp. Mk. ix. 21, ἐκ παιδιόθεν *from a child.*

The holy Scriptures (ἱερὰ γράμματα). Note particularly the absence of the article. Γράμματα is used in N. T. in several senses. Of *characters of the alphabet* (2 Cor. iii. 7; Gal. vi. 11) : of *a document* (L. xvi. 6, take thy *bill*): of *epistles* (Acts xxviii. 21) : of *the writings of an author collectively* (J. v. 47) : of *learning* (Acts xxvi. 24, πολλά γράμματα much *learning*). In LXX, ἐπιστάμενος γράμματα *knowing how to read* (Isa. xxix. 11, 12). The Holy Scriptures are nowhere called ἱερὰ γράμματα in N. T. In LXX, γράμματα is never used of sacred writings of any kind. Both Josephus and Philo use τὰ ἱερὰ γράμματα for the O. T. Scriptures.* The

---

* Joseph. *Ant. Proem.* 3, 4 ; x. 10, 4. Philo, *Vit. Mos.* 3, 39 ; *De Praem. et Poen.* § 14 ; *Leg. ad Gai.* § 29.

words here should be rendered *sacred learning*. The books
in the writer's mind were no doubt the O. T. Scriptures, in
which Timothy, like every Jewish boy, had been instructed ;
but he does not mean to designate those books as ἱερὰ γράμματα. He means *the learning* acquired from Scripture by
the rabbinic methods, according to which the O. T. books
were carefully searched for meanings hidden in each word
and letter, and especially for messianic intimations. Specimens of such learning may be seen here and there in the
writings of Paul, as 1 Cor. ix. 9 f. ; x. 1 f. ; Gal. iii. 16 f. ;
iv. 21 f. In Acts iv. 13, the council, having heard Peter's
speech, in which he interpreted Ps. cxviii. 22 and Isa.
xxviii. 16 of Christ, at once perceived that Peter and John
were ἀγράμματοι, not versed in the methods of the schools.
Before Agrippa, Paul drew the doctrine of the Resurrection
from the O. T., whereupon Festus exclaimed, "*much learning* (πολλὰ γράμματα, thy acquaintance with the exegesis of
the schools) hath made thee mad" (Acts xxvi. 24). To
Agrippa, who was "expert in all customs and questions which
are among the Jews" (Acts xxvi. 3), the address of Paul, a
pupil of Hillel, was not surprising, although he declared that
Paul's reasoning did not appeal to him. In J. vii. 15, when
Jesus taught in the temple, the Jews wondered, and said :
"How knoweth this man *letters ?*" That a Jew should know
the Scriptures was not strange. The wonder lay in the exe-
getical skill of one who had not been trained by the literary
methods of the time.

To make thee wise (σε σοφίσαι). Only here and 2 Pet.
i. 16. See note there on *cunningly devised*. To give thee
understanding of that which lies behind the letter ; to enable
thee to detect in the O. T. books various hidden allusions to
Christ ; to draw from the O. T. the mystery of messianic
salvation, and to interpret the O. T. with Christ as the key.
This gives significance to the following words, *through faith
which is in Christ Jesus.* Jesus Christ was the key of Scripture, and through faith in him Scripture became a power
unto salvation. The false teachers also had their learning,

but used it in expounding Jewish fables, genealogies, etc.
Hence, their expositions, instead of making wise unto salvation, were vain babblings ; profane and old wives' fables
(1 Tim. iv. 7 ; 2 Tim. ii. 16).   Const. *through faith*, etc.,
with *make wise*, not with *salvation*.

16. **All Scripture** (πᾶσα γραφὴ).   Better, *every* Scripture,
that is, every *passage* of Scripture.   Scripture as a whole is
αἱ γραφαί or αἱ γραφαὶ ἅγιαι.   Ἱερά is never used with γραφή.
Γραφή is the single passage, usually defined by *this*, or *that*,
or *the*, or *which saith*.*

Is given by inspiration of God (θεόπνευστος).   N. T.º.
ºLXX.   From θεὸς *God* and πνεῖν *to breathe*.   *God-breathed*.
The word tells us nothing of the peculiar character or limits
of inspiration beyond the fact that it proceeds from God.   In
construction omit *is*, and rend. as attributive of γραφὴ *every*
divinely-inspired Scripture.

And is profitable (καὶ ὠφέλιμος).   According to A. V.,
καὶ *and* is merely the copula between two predicates of γραφὴ.
It is divinely-inspired and is profitable.   According to the
interpretation given above, καὶ has the force of *also*.   Every
divinely-inspired Scripture is, besides being so inspired and
for that reason, *also* profitable, etc.   Ὠφέλιμος *profitable*,
Pastº.   See on 1 Tim. iv. 8.

For doctrine (πρὸς διδασκαλίαν).   Better, *teaching*.   Comp.
to make thee wise, ver. 15.

Reproof (ἐλεγμόν).   Better, *conviction*.   N. T.º.   ºClass.
Comparatively frequent in LXX, mostly in the sense of
rebuke: sometimes *curse, punishment*.   See Ps. of Sol. x. 1,
but the reading is disputed with ἐλέγχῳ.   See on the verb
ἐλέγχειν, J. iii. 20.

---

* The few passages which are cited in favour of the use of γραφὴ for
Scripture as a whole, as J. ii. 22 ; xvii. 12 ; Gal. iii. 22, are not decisive.
They can all be assigned, with much appearance of probability, to definite
O. T. passages.

Correction (ἐπανόρθωσιν). N. T.⁰. Twice in LXX. Restoring to an upright state (ὀρθός erect); *setting right*.

Instruction (παιδείαν). Better, *chastisement* or *discipline*. See on Eph. vi. 4. In LXX mostly *correction* or *discipline*, sometimes *admonition*. Specially of God's chastisement by means of sorrow and evil.

17. **Perfect** (ἄρτιος). N. T.⁰. ⁰LXX. Rev. *complete;* but the idea is rather that of mutual, symmetrical adjustment of all that goes to make the man : harmonious combination of different qualities and powers. Comp. κατάρτισις *perfecting*, 2 Cor. xiii. 9 : καταρτισμός *perfecting* (as accomplished), Eph. iv. 12 : καταρτίσαι *make perfect* or *bring into complete adjustment*, Heb. xiii. 21.

Thoroughly furnished (ἐξηρτισμένος). The same root as ἄρτιος. It fills out the idea of ἄρτιος; *fitted out*. Only here and Acts xi. 5 (note). ⁰Class.

Unto all good works (πρὸς πᾶν ἔργον ἀγαθὸν). More correctly, *every good work*. Any writing which can produce such profitable results vindicates itself as inspired of God. It is to be noted that the test of the divine inspiration of Scripture is here placed in its practical usefulness.

CHAPTER IV.

1. **I charge** (διαμαρτύρομαι). See on 1 Tim. v. 21.

At his appearing (καὶ τὴν ἐπιφάνειαν). Rend. " *and by* his appearing," ἐπιφάνειαν thus depending on διαμαρτύρομαι, and the accusative being the ordinary accusative of conjuration, with which *by* must be supplied. The A.V. follows the reading κατὰ *at*. For ἐπιφάνεια *appearing*, see on 1 Tim. vi. 14; 2 Th. ii. 8. For βασιλεία *kingdom*, see on L. vi. 20.

2. **Be instant** (ἐπίστηθι). Better, *be ready*. Once in Paul, 1 Th. v. 3. Frequent in Luke and Acts. Lit. *stand by, be at hand, be present*. *To come suddenly upon*, L. ii. 38. Hence, *be ready*. *Instant* signifies *urgent, importunate, persevering*. Lat. *instare to press upon*. Thus Latimer, " I preached at the *instant* request of a curate." So N. T., Rom. xii. 12, " Continuing *instant* in prayer."

In season (εὐκαίρως). Only here and Mk. xiv. 11. LXX once, Sir. xviii. 22. Comp. εὐκαιρεῖν *to have leisure* or *opportunity*, Mk. vi. 31 ; 1 Cor. xvi. 12 : εὐκαιρία *opportunity*, Matt. xxvi. 16 : εὔκαιρος *seasonable, convenient*, Mk. vi. 21 ; Heb. iv. 16.

Out of season (ἀκαίρως). N. T.⁰. LXX once, Sir. xxxv. 4. Comp. ἀκαιρεῖσθαι *to lack opportunity*, Philip. iv. 10. Timothy is not advised to disregard opportuneness, but to discharge his duty to those with whom he deals, whether it be welcome or not.

Reprove (ἔλεγξον). Rather, *convict* of their errors. See on 1 Tim. v. 20 and J. iii. 20. In Paul, 1 Cor. xiv. 24 ; Eph. v. 11, 13. Comp. ἐλεγμόν *conviction*, ch. iii. 16.

Rebuke (ἐπιτίμησον). In Pastorals only here. ⁰P. Mostly in the Synoptic Gospels, where it is frequent. It has two meanings : *rebuke*, as Matt. viii. 26 ; L. xvii. 3, and *charge*, as Matt. xii. 16 ; xvi. 20, commonly followed by ἵνα *that* or λέγων *saying* (Matt. xx. 31; Mk. i. 25 ; iii. 12 ; viii. 30 ; L. iv. 35), but see L. ix. 21. The word implies a *sharp, severe* rebuke, with, possibly, a suggestion in some cases of impending penalty (τιμή); charge *on pain of*. This might go to justify the rendering of Holtzmann and von Soden, *threaten*. To charge on pain of penalty for disobedience implies a *menace*, in this case of future judgment.

Exhort (παρακάλεσον). See on *consolation*, L. vi. 24 ; *comfort*, Acts ix. 31. Tischendorf changes the order of the three imperatives, reading ἔλεγξον, παρακάλεσον, ἐπιτίμησον. In that case there is a climax : first *convict* of error, then, *exhort* to forsake error, finally *threaten* with the penalty of persistence in error.

With all longsuffering and doctrine (ἐν πάσῃ μακροθυμίᾳ καὶ διδαχῇ). Πάσῃ, *every possible exhibition of* longsuffering, etc. For *doctrine* rend. *teaching*. The combination is suggestive. Longsuffering is to be maintained against the temp· tations to anger presented by the obstinacy and perverseness of certain hearers ; and such are to be met, not merely with rebuke, but also with sound and reasonable instruction in the truth. So Calvin : " Those who are strong only in fervour and sharpness, but are not fortified with solid doctrine, weary themselves in their vigorous efforts, make a great noise, rave, . . . make no headway because they build without founda· tion." Men will not be won to the truth by scolding. "They should understand what they hear, and learn to perceive why they are rebuked " (Bahnsen). Διδαχή *teaching*, only here and Tit. i. 9 in Pastorals. The usual word is διδασκαλία. Paul uses both.

ι. For (γάρ). Ground for the preceding exhortations in the future opposition to sound teaching.

Endure (ἀνέξονται). Only here in Pastorals. Mostly in Paul. Comp. Acts xviii. 14 ; 2 Cor. xi. 4 ; Heb. xiii. 22.

Sound doctrine (τῆς ὑγιαινούσης διδασκαλίας). Or *healthful teaching*. The A. V. overlooks the article which is important. *The* teaching plays a prominent part in these Epistles, and signifies more than teaching in general. See on 1 Tim. i. 10.

Shall they heap to themselves teachers (ἑαυτοῖς ἐπισωρεύσουσιν διδασκάλους). A vigorous and graphic statement. Ἐπισωρεύειν *to heap up*, N. T.º. Comp. σεσωρευμένα *laden*, ch. iii. 6. The word is ironical ; shall invite teachers *en*

masse.* In periods of unsettled faith, scepticism, and mere
curious speculation in matters of religion, teachers of all
kinds swarm like the flies in Egypt. The demand creates
the supply. The hearers invite and shape their own preachers.
If the people desire a calf to worship, a ministerial calf-maker
is readily found. " The master of superstition is the people,
and in all superstition wise men follow fools " (Bacon, *Ess.*
xvii).

Having itching ears (κνηθόμενοι τὴν ἀκοήν). Or, *being tickled
in their hearing.* Κνήθειν to tickle, N. T.⁰. ⁰LXX. Κνηθόμενοι
itching. Hesychius explains, "hearing for mere gratification."
Clement of Alexandria describes certain teachers as "scratch-
ing and tickling, in no human way, the ears of those who
eagerly desire to be scratched" (*Strom.* v). Seneca says:
"Some come to *hear*, not to *learn*, just as we go to the theatre,
for pleasure, to delight our ears with the speaking or the voice
or the plays " (*Ep.* 108). 'Ακοή, A. V. *ears*, in N. T. *a report*,
as Matt. iv. 24; xiv. 1; xxiv. 6: in the plural, *ears* (never
ear in singular), as Mk. vii. 35; L. vii. 1: *hearing*, either *the
act*, as Acts xxviii. 26; Rom. x. 17, or *the sense*, 1 Cor.
xii. 17, here, and ver. 4.

4. **Shall be turned unto fables** (ἐπὶ τοὺς μύθους ἐκτραπή-
σονται). More correctly, *will turn aside.* The passive has a
middle sense. For *fables* see on 1 Tim. i. 4.

5. **Watch thou** (σὺ νῆφε). See on 1 Th. v. 6, and on
ἀνανήψωσιν *recover*, 2 Tim. ii. 26.

Endure afflictions (κακοπάθησον). Or *suffer hardship.*
See on ch. ii. 9, and comp. ch. iv. 5.

Of an evangelist (εὐαγγελιστοῦ). Here, Acts xxi. 8 and
Eph. iv. 11. In the last passage, a special function, with

---

* Weizsäcker's *sich herzieht* is feeble. Better von Soden, *sich aufsammeln;*
or Bahnsen, *in Masse herbei schaffen;* or Hofmann, *hinzuhäufen.*

apostles, prophets, pastors, and teachers.   A travelling minister, whose work was not confined to a particular church.   So
Philip, Acts viii. 5–13, 26–40.   A helper of the apostles.   An
apostle, as such, was an evangelist (1 Cor. i. 17), but every
evangelist was not an apostle.   In *The Teaching of the Twelve
Apostles* (about 100 A.D.) it is prescribed that an apostle shall
not remain in one place longer than two days, and that when
he departs he shall take nothing with him except enough
bread to last until his next station (ch. xi).

Make full proof of thy ministry (τὴν διακονίαν σου πληρο-
φόρησον).   Better, *fulfil* or *fully perform*.   In Pastorals only
here and ver. 17.   See on L. i. 1.   In LXX once, Eccl.
viii. 11, *is fully persuaded*.   Only in this passage in the active
voice.   Comp. πληρώσαντες τὴν διακονίαν *having fulfilled their
ministration*, Acts xii. 25: ἐπλήρου τὸν δρόμον *was fulfilling
his course*, Acts xiii. 25, and τὸν δρόμον τετέλεκα *I have finished
the course*, ver. 7.   For διακονίαν *ministry*, see on 1 Tim. i. 12.

6. **For I am now ready to be offered** (ἐγὼ γὰρ ἤδη σπέν-
δομαι).   *I*, emphatic contrast with σὺ *thou*, ver. 5.   *Already*.
What he is now suffering is the beginning of the end.   Σπέν-
δεσθαι *to be poured out as a libation*, only here and Philip.
ii. 17 (note).   In the active voice quite often in LXX.

Departure (ἀναλύσεως).   N. T.º.   ºLXX.   Comp. ἀναλῦσαι
to depart, Philip. i. 23.   The figure is explained by some of
loosing a ship from its moorings; by others of breaking
camp.   In Philippians the latter is the more probable explanation, because Paul's situation in the custody of the
Praetorians at Rome would naturally suggest a military
metaphor, and because he is habitually sparing of nautical
metaphors.   Comp. 2 Cor. v. 1, and Clement of Rome, *ad
Corinth.* xliv : "Blessed are the presbyters who have gone
before, seeing that their *departure* (ἀνάλυσιν) was fruitful
and ripe."

7. **I have fought** a good fight (τὸν καλὸν ἀγῶνα ἠγώνισμαι).
For *a* good fight rend. *the* good fight.   For the phrase, see

on 1 Tim. vi. 12.   Comp. Philip. i. 27, 30; 1 Cor. ix. 25;
Col. ii. 1; 1 Th. ii. 2; Eph. vi. 11 ff.

Course (δρόμον).   Metaphor from the race-course.   Only
here and Acts xiii. 25; xx. 24: comp. 1 Cor. ix. 24; Gal. ii. 2;
v. 7; Rom. ix. 16; Philip. ii. 16; iii. 12–14.

I have kept the faith (τὴν πίστιν τετήρηκα).   The phrase
N. T.°.   For τηρεῖν *to keep*, see on 1 Tim. v. 22; vi. 14.

8.   **Henceforth** (λοιπὸν).   Lit. *as to what remains*. Λοιπὸν
or τὸ λοιπὸν either *finally*, as 2 Cor. xiii. 11; or *henceforth*
as here, Mk. xiv. 41; 1 Cor. vii. 29, Heb. x. 13: or *for the
rest, besides*, as 1 Th. iv. 1 (note); 2 Th. iii. 1.

There is laid up (ἀπόκειται).   Or laid *away*.   In Pastorals only here.   In Paul, see Col. i. 5 (note).   L. xix. 20 of
the pound *laid up* in a napkin.

A crown of righteousness (ὁ τῆς δικαιοσύνης στέφανος).
The phrase N. T.°.   See on στεφανοῦται *is crowned*, ch. ii. 5.
Rend. *the* crown.

Judge (κριτής).   Comp. ver. 1.   Mostly in Luke and Acts.
°P.   Only here in Pastorals.   Applied to Christ, Acts x. 42 ·
Jas. v. 9; to God, Heb. xii. 23; Jas. iv. 12.

Shall give (ἀποδώσει).   Most frequent in Synoptic Gos-
pels.   It may mean to give *over* or *away*, as Matt. xxvii. 58;
Acts v. 8; Heb. xii. 16: or *to give back, recompense*, as here,
Matt. vi. 4, 6, 18; Rom. ii. 6.

At that day (ἐν ἐκείνῃ τῇ ἡμέρᾳ).   See on ch. i. 12.

That love his appearing (τοῖς ἠγαπηκόσι τὴν ἐπιφάνειαν
αὐτοῦ).   For *love* rend. *have loved*.   *Appearing*, Christ's second coming: see on 1 Tim. vi. 14; 2 Th. ii. 8.   The phrase
N. T.°.   Some have interpreted *appearing* as Christ's *first*

coming into the world, as ch. i. 10; but the other sense is according to the analogy of 1 Cor. ii. 9; Philip. iii. 20; Heb. ix. 28.

9. Do thy diligence (σπούδασον). Earnestly endeavour. See on ch. ii. 15, and comp. ch. i. 3. *Do diligence* and *give diligence* (2 Pet. i. 10) are old English phrases. So Chaucer:

> 'And night and day dide ever his diligence
> Hir for to please."
>
> *Manciple's T.* 141.

> "And ech of hem doth al his diligence
> To doon un-to the feste reverence."
>
> *Clerke's T.* 195

10. Demas. A contraction of Demetrius or Demarchus. He is mentioned Col. iv. 13 and Philem. 24. It is supposed that he was a Thessalonian. On leaving Paul he went to Thessalonica; and in Philemon his name is mentioned next to that of Aristarchus the Thessalonian. That no epithet is attached to his name in Col. iv. 14 (comp. "Luke the beloved physician") may be a shadow of Demas's behaviour mentioned here, in case Colossians was written later than 2d Timothy.

Hath forsaken (ἐγκατέλειπεν). In Pastorals here and ver. 16. See on 2 Cor. iv. 9. The compounded preposition ἐν indicates a condition or circumstances *in* which one has been left, as the common phrase *left in the lurch*. Comp. Germ. *im Stiche.*

Having loved (ἀγαπήσας). The participle is explanatory, *because* he loved.

This present world (τὸν νῦν αἰῶνα). See on 1 Tim. vi. 17. Contrast *love his appearing*, ver. 8.

Crescens (Κρήσκης). N. T.⁰. Unknown.

Galatia (Γαλατίαν). Most probably Galatia. See Introd. to Galatians. Eusebius (*H. E.* iii. 4) says: "Paul testifies that Crescens was sent to Gaul (Γαλλίαν)." Tischendorf adopts this reading.

Dalmatia (Δαλματίαν). Part of the country known generally as Illyricum, along the eastern coast of the Adriatic. See Rom. xv. 19.

11. **Luke.** See Introd. to Luke. His connection with Paul appears first in Acts xvi. 10. He remained at Philippi after Paul's departure, and was there seven years later, when Paul revisited the city (Acts xx. 5, 6). He accompanied Paul to Jerusalem (Acts xxi. 15), after which we lose sight of him until he appears at Caesarea (Acts xxvii. 2), whence he accompanies Paul to Rome. He is mentioned Col. iv. 14 and Philem. 24.

Take (ἀναλαβὼν). In N. T. mostly in Acts. See on Acts xxiii. 31, and comp. Acts xx. 13, 14.

Mark. Mentioned Col. iv. 10; Philem. 24; 1 Pet. v. 13. Probably John Mark (Acts xii. 12, 25; xv. 37), called the cousin of Barnabas (Col. iv. 10). The first mention of him since the separation from Paul (Acts xv. 39) occurs in Colossians and Philemon. He is commended to the church at Colossae. In 1st Peter he sends salutations to Asia. In both Colossians and Philemon his name appears along with that of Demas. In Colossians he is named shortly before Luke and along with Aristarchus who does not appear here. He (Mark) is about to come to Asia where 2d Timothy finds him. The appearance in Colossians of Aristarchus with Mark and of Demas with Luke is probably the point of connection with the representation in 2d Timothy.

Profitable for the ministry (εὔχρηστος εἰς διακονίαν). Εὔχρηστος profitable, only here, ch. ii. 21, Philem. 11. For for the ministry rend. for ministering or for service, and see on 1 Tim. i. 12.

12. Tychicus. A comparatively uncommon name in N. T., but found in inscriptions of Asia Minor and on Asiatic coins. He is mentioned Acts xx. 4, 5; Eph. vi. 21; Col. iv. 7. In Acts xx. 4 he is described as a native of proconsular Asia.

13. The cloak (φελόνην).* Hesychius, however, explains as a γλωσσόκομον, originally a case for keeping the mouth-pieces of wind-instruments; thence, generally, *a box.* Γλωσσόκομον is the word for the disciples' treasury-chest (*bag*, J. xii. 6). Also a box for transporting or preserving parchments. Specimens have been found at Herculaneum. In LXX, 2 Sam. vi. 11, the *ark* of the Lord (but the reading varies): in 2 Chron. xxiv. 8, the *chest* placed by order of Joash at the gate of the temple, to receive contributions for its repair. Joseph. *Ant.* vi. 1, 2, of the *coffer* into which the jewels of gold were put for a trespass-offering when the ark was sent back (1 Sam. vi. 8). Phrynicus † defines it as "a receptacle for books, clothes, silver, or anything else." Φαιλόνης or φαινόλης *a wrapper of parchments*, was translated figuratively in Latin by *toga* or *paenula* "a cloak," sometimes of leather; also the *wrapping* which a shopkeeper put round fish or olives; also the parchment cover for papyrus rolls. Accordingly it is claimed that Timothy is here bidden to bring, not a cloak, but a roll-case. So the Syriac Version. There seems to be no sufficient reason for abandoning the translation of A. V.

Carpus. Not mentioned elsewhere.

The books (βιβλία). Βίβλος or βιβλίον was the term most widely used by the Greeks for *book* or *volume.* The usual derivation is from βύβλος *the Egyptian papyrus.* Comp. Lat. *liber* "the inner bark of a tree," also "book." ‡   Pliny

---

* The word appears in different forms. T. R. φαιλόνης. Also φαινόλης, φελώνης, φαιλώνης.

† A Greek sophist of Bithynia in the second half of the third century, author of a selection of Attic verbs and nouns excluding all but the best Attic forms, and arranged alphabetically.

‡ On the βύβλος see Hdt. ii. 92, and Rawlinson's notes in his Translation.

(*Nat. Hist.* xiii. 11) says that the pith of the papyrus plant was cut in slices and laid in rows, over which other rows were laid crosswise, and the whole was massed by pressure. The name for the blank papyrus sheets was χάρτης (charta) *paper*. See on 2 J. 12. Timothy is here requested to bring some papyrus documents which are distinguished from the vellum manuscripts.

Parchments (μεμβράνας). N. T.⁰. Manuscripts written on parchment or vellum. Strictly speaking, vellum was made from the skins of young calves, and the common parchment from those of sheep, goats, or antelopes. It was a more durable material than papyrus and more expensive. The Latin name was *membrana*, and also *pergamena* or *pergamina*, from Pergamum in Mysia where it was extensively manufactured, and from which it was introduced into Greece. As to the character and contents of these documents which Timothy is requested to bring, we are of course entirely ignorant.*

14. Alexander the coppersmith. Comp. 1. Tim. i. 20, and Acts xix. 33. The same person is probably meant in all three cases.

Did me much evil (πολλά μοι κακὰ ἐνεδείξατο). Lit. *shewed me much ill-treatment.* Comp. 1 Tim. i. 16.

May the Lord reward (ἀποδώσει). More correctly *shall reward.* A. V. follows the reading ἀποδῴη.

15. Greatly withstood (λίαν ἀντέστη). Comp. ch. iii. 8, and Gal. ii. 11. This may refer to the occurrences at Ephesus (Acts xix. 33), or to Alexander's attitude during Paul's trial. The former is more probable. Λίαν *greatly*, not in Paul, except in the compound ὑπερλίαν, 2 Cor. xi. 5; xii. 11. Only here in Pastorals. Mostly in Synoptic Gospels.

---

* Much curious and useful information on the subject of ancient bookmaking is contained in Theodor Birt's *Das antike Buchwesen in seinem Verhältniss zur Litteratur*, Berlin, 1882.

16. **At my first answer** (ἐν τῇ πρώτῃ μου ἀπολογίᾳ). Ἀπολογία *defence in a judicial trial.* Comp. Acts xxv. 16. Also *against private persons,* as 1 Cor. ix. 3 ; 2 Cor. vii. 11. *Defence of the gospel against its adversaries,* as Philip. i. 7, 16 ; comp. 1 Pet. iii. 15 (note). It is impossible to decide to what this refers. On the assumption of a second imprisonment of Paul (see Introduction) it would probably refer to a preliminary hearing before the main trial. It is not improbable that the writer had before his mind the situation of Paul as described in Philip. i, since this Epistle shows at many points the influence of the Philippian letter. It should be noted, however, that ἀπολογία in Philip. i. 7, 16, has no specific reference to Paul's trial, but refers to the defence of the gospel under any and all circumstances. In any case, the first Roman imprisonment cannot be alluded to here. On that supposition, the omission of all reference to Timothy's presence and personal ministry at that time, and the words about his first defence, which must have taken place before Timothy left Rome (Philip. ii. 19–23) and which is here related as a piece of news, are quite inexplicable.

Stood with me (παρεγένετο). As a patron or an advocate. The verb mostly in Luke and Acts : once in Paul, 1 Cor. xvi. 3 : only here in Pastorals. It means *to place one's self beside ;* hence, *to come to,* and this latter sense is almost universal in N. T. In the sense of coming to or standing by one as a friend, only here.

Be laid to their charge (αὐτοῖς λογισθείη). Mostly in Paul : only here in Pastorals. See on Rom. iv. 3, 5 ; 1 Cor. xiii. 5.

17. **Strengthened** (ἐνεδυνάμωσεν). See on 1 Tim. i. 12.

The preaching (τὸ κήρυγμα). Better, *the* message (*par excellence*), the gospel message. Usually with a defining word, as *of Jonah; of Jesus Christ; my* preaching ; *our* preaching. Absolutely, as here, 1 Cor. i. 21 ; Tit. i. 3.

Might be fully known (πληροφορηθῇ).   See on ver. 5.
Lit. *might be fulfilled;* fully carried out by being proclaimed
before rulers in the capital of the world.   Comp. Rom.
xv. 19; Acts xxiii. 11; xxviii. 31; Philip. i. 12–14.

Out of the mouth of the lion (ἐκ στόματος λέοντος).
Figurative expression for danger of death.   Comp. 1 Cor.
xv. 32.   As usual, all manner of special references have been
imagined : the lions of the amphitheatre; Nero; the chief
accuser; the Jews; the Devil.

18. **Every evil work** (παντὸς ἔργου πονηροῦ).   Every
design and attempt against him and his work.   Πονηρός
evil cannot be limited to evil on its active side.   See on
1 Cor. v. 13.   The word is connected at the root with πένεσθαι
to be needy, and πονεῖν *to toil;* and this connection opens a
glimpse of that sentiment which associated badness with a
poor and toiling condition.   The word means originally *full
of* or *oppressed by labours;* thence, *that which brings annoy-
ance or toil*.   Comp. ἡμέρα πονηρά *evil day*, Eph. v. 16;
vi. 13 : ἕλκος πονηρὸν *a grievous sore*, Apoc. xvi. 2.

Heavenly kingdom (τὴν βασιλείαν τὴν ἐπουράνιον).   The
phrase N. T.°.   Ἐπουράνιος *heavenly* only here in Pastorals.
Mostly in Paul and Hebrews.   *Heavenly kingdom*, here the
future, glorified life, as 1 Cor. vi. 9, 10; xv. 50; Luke
xiii. 29.   In the same sense, *kingdom of Christ and of God*,
Eph. v. 5; *kingdom of their Father*, Matt. xiii. 43; *my
Father's kingdom*, Matt. xxvi. 29; *kingdom prepared for you*,
Matt. xxv. 34; *eternal kingdom of our Lord and Saviour
Jesus Christ*, 2 Pet. i. 11.

19. **Salute** (ἄσπασαι).   Very often in Paul.   The singular only here and Tit. iii. 15.

Prisca and Aquila.   They appear in Corinth, Acts xviii.
2, 3; in Ephesus, Acts xviii. 18, 26; 1 Cor. xvi. 19.

Onesiphorus. *Profit bringer.* Comp. ch. i. 16. One of the punning names so common among slaves. Comp. Chresimus, Chrestus, Onesimus, Symphorus, all of which signify *useful* or *helpful.*

20. **Erastus.** In Acts xix. 22, sent by Paul with Timothy to Macedonia from Ephesus. In Rom. xvi. 23, the city-treasurer who sends salutations. He cannot be certainly identified with the one mentioned here. The writer merely selects names of well-known companions of Paul.

Trophimus. See Acts xx. 4; xxi. 9.

Sick (ἀσθενοῦντα). By Paul mostly in a moral sense, as *weak in the faith,* Rom. iv. 19; the law was *weak,* Rom. viii. 3; the *weak brother,* 1 Cor. viii. 11. Of bodily sickness, Philip. ii. 26, 27.

21. **Eubulus, Pudens, Linus, Claudia.** N. T.°.

22. **The Lord Jesus Christ be with thy spirit.** Omit *Jesus Christ.* The closing benediction only here in this form.

THE EPISTLE TO TITUS.

CHAPTER I.

1. An apostle — according to the faith of God's elect, etc. The norm of the apostolate in each of the three Epistles is unique, and not Pauline. In 1 Tim., *according to the commandment of God:* in 2 Tim., *according to the promise of life in Christ Jesus.* Κατὰ *according to,* not *for* the faith, but corresponding to the norm or standard of faith which is set for God's elect.

And acknowledging of the truth (καὶ ἐπίγνωσιν ἀληθείας). For *acknowledging* rend. *knowledge.* For the phrase, see on 1 Tim. ii. 4. Governed, like πίστιν *faith,* by κατὰ. The writer is an apostle according to the faith of God's elect, and according to the truth which is contained in the faith, as that truth is intelligently apprehended and held.

Which is after godliness (τῆς κατ' εὐσέβειαν). Or *according to* godliness. Comp. 1 Tim. vi. 3. This addition describes the peculiar and essential character of the truth which is held and known by God's elect, namely, that it is concerned with the fear and obedience of God — all that constitutes true piety. See on 1 Tim. i. 10.

2. In hope of eternal life (ἐπ' ἐλπίδι ζωῆς αἰωνίου). Const. with *Apostle,* ver. 1.* Ἐπὶ *resting upon.*

---

* Not with πίστιν, nor ἐπίγνωσιν, nor ἀληθείας, neither of which rest upon hope; nor with τῆς κατ' εὐσέβειαν, which is a defining clause complete in itself.

God that cannot lie (ὁ ἀψευδὴς θεὸς). Ἀψευδὴς, N. T.°.
Once in LXX, Wisd. vii. 17. Comp. Rom. iii. 4 ; Heb. vi. 18.
Paul expresses the idea positively, by ἀληθής *truthful*, Rom.
iii. 4.

Before the world began (πρὸ χρόνων αἰωνίων). Lit.
before eternal times. Before time began to be reckoned by
aeons. See on 2 Tim. i. 9, and additional note on 2 Th. i. 9.

3. **In due times** (καιροῖς ἰδίοις). Better, *in his* (or *its*)
own seasons. See on 1 Tim. ii. 6.

Through preaching (ἐν κηρύγματι). Rather, *in a proclamation*. See on 2 Tim. iv. 17.

Which is committed unto me (ὃ ἐπιστεύθην ἐγὼ). Better,
wherewith I was intrusted. See on 1 Tim. i. 11.

4. **Own** (γνησίῳ). See on 1 Tim. i. 2.

According to the common faith (κατὰ κοινὴν πίστιν).
The phrase N. T.°. Κοινός *common*, usually in contrast with
καθαρός *pure* or ἅγιος *holy*, as Acts x. 14; xi. 8 ; Apoc.
xxi. 27. In the sense of *general* as here, Acts ii. 44 ; iv. 32 ;
Jude 3. Comp. 2 Pet. i. 1. The "catholic" faith. Κατὰ
according to, as ver. 1.

5. **In Crete.** Crete is one of the largest islands in the
Mediterranean. By the mythological writers it was called
Aeria, Doliché, Idaea, Telchinia. According to tradition,
Minos first gave laws to the Cretans, conquered the Aegean
pirates, and established a navy. After the Trojan war the
principal cities of the island formed themselves into several
republics, mostly independent. The chief cities were Cnos-
sus, Cydonia, Gortyna, and Lyctus. Crete was annexed to
the Roman Empire B.C. 67. About Paul's visiting the island
we have no information whatever beyond the hints in this
Epistle. There is no absolute proof that Paul was ever there

before the voyage to Rome.   Although on that voyage some
time appears to have been spent at Crete, there is no notice of
Paul having received any greeting from the members of the
Christian churches there.   According to this Epistle, Paul
and Titus had worked there together.   Paul went away, and
left Titus to organise the churches founded by himself.   He
sent this letter by Zenas and Apollos (iii. 13), and announced
in it the coming of Artemas or of Tychicus.   On their arrival
Titus was to join Paul at Nicopolis, where Paul was propos-
ing to winter.

Shouldst set in order (ἐπιδιορθώσῃ).   N. T.º.   Lit. *to
set straight besides* or *farther;* that is, should arrange what
remained to be set in order after Paul's departure.   Used
by medical writers of setting broken limbs or straightening
crooked ones.   Διόρθωσις *reformation*, Heb. ix. 10 : διόρθωμα
correction, Acts xxiv. 3.

Ordain elders (καταστήσῃς πρεσβυτέρους).   Καθιστάναι
appoint or *constitute*.   In Paul only Rom. v. 19.   For the
sense here comp. Matt. xxiv. 45, 47 ; L. xii. 14 ; Acts vi. 3.
The meaning of the injunction is, that Titus should appoint,
out of the number of elderly men of approved Christian
reputation, certain ones to be overseers (ἐπίσκοποι) of the
churches in the several cities.   The eldership was not a distinct church office.   See on 1 Tim. v. 1.

I had appointed (διεταξάμην).   Better, *I gave thee charge.*
Mostly in Luke and Acts.

6. **Faithful children** (τέκνα πιστά).   Better, *believing children ;* or, as Rev., *children that believe.*   Comp. 1 Tim. iii. 4.

Not accused of riot (μὴ ἐν κατηγορίᾳ ἀσωτίας).   Lit. *not
in accusation of profligacy.*   For κατηγορία see on 1 Tim. v. 19.
Ἀσωτία, lit. *unsavingness ;* hence, *dissoluteness, profligacy.*
Comp. L. xv. 13, of the prodigal son, who lived *unsavingly*
(ἀσώτως).   Only here, Eph. v. 18, and 1 Pet. iv. 4 (note).

7. A bishop (τὸν ἐπίσκοπον). See on 1 Tim. iii. 1; v. 1.
Rend. *the* bishop.   It will be observed that the qualifications
of the elders are fixed by those of the bishop. Appoint elders
who shall be unaccused, etc., *for* the bishop must be unaccused,
etc. The overseers must have the qualifications of approved
presbyters.

Steward of God (θεοῦ οἰκονόμον). Comp. 1 Cor. iv. 1, 2;
1 Pet. iv. 10; and see on Rom. xvi. 23; L. xvi. 1.   The
phrase N. T.⁰.

Selfwilled (αὐθάδη). Only here and 2 Pet. ii. 10 (note).

Soon angry (ὀργίλον). N. T.⁰.   Rarely in LXX and
Class. *Irascible.*

8. A lover of hospitality (φιλόξενον). Better, *hospitable*.
See on 1 Tim. iii. 2.

A lover of good men (φιλάγαθον). N. T.⁰.   Better,
lover of good.

Temperate (ἐγκρατῆ). N. T.⁰.   Originally, *having power
over; possessed of;* hence, *controlling, keeping in hand*.
Ἐγκράτεια *temperance*, Acts xxiv. 25; Gal. v. 23; 2 Pet. i. 6.
Ἐγκρατεύεσθαι *to contain one's self*, 1 Cor. vii. 9; ix. 25.

9. Holding fast (ἀντεχόμενον). Only here in Pastorals.
In Paul, 1 Th. v. 14 (note).

The faithful word (τοῦ πιστοῦ λόγου). The *trustworthy,
reliable* word. Comp. 1 Tim. i. 15 (note).

As he hath been taught (κατὰ τὴν διδαχὴν). Lit. *according to the teaching*. Const. with *word*. Agreeing with the
apostolic teaching. For διδαχή *teaching* see on 2 Tim. iv. 2.

May be able by sound doctrine both to exhort (δυνατὸς
ᾖ καὶ παρακαλεῖν ἐν τῇ διδασκαλίᾳ τῇ ὑγιαινούσῃ).   Rend.

"may be able both to exhort in the sound teaching." For δυνατὸς *able* or *powerful*, see on 2 Tim. i. 12. Used by Paul in the phrase εἰ δυνατόν *if it be possible*, Rom. xii. 18; Gal. iv. 15 : τὸ δυνατόν *that which is possible*, Rom. ix. 22 : of God, Rom. iv. 21 ; xi. 23 : of men, in the ethical sense, Rom. xv. 1 ; 2 Cor. xii. 10 ; xiii. 9.

Convince (ἐλέγχειν). Better, *convict.* See on J. iii. 20, and ἐλεγμὸν, 2 Tim. iii. 16.

The gainsayers (τοὺς ἀντιλέγοντας). In Pastorals only here and ch. ii. 9. Once in Paul, Rom. x. 21, cit. Mostly in Luke and Acts. *Gainsay*, Angl. Sax. *gegn* (Germ. *gegen*) "against," and "say." Wiclif, L. xxi. 15 : "For I schal gyue to you mouth and wysdom, to whiche alle youre aduersaries schulen not mowe agenstonde, and agenseye."

10. Vain talkers (ματαιολόγοι). N. T.⁰. ⁰LXX, ⁰Class. See on *vain jangling*, 1 Tim. i. 6.

Deceivers (φρεναπάται). N. T.⁰. ⁰LXX, ⁰Class. See on φρεναπατᾶν *to deceive*, Gal. vi. 3.

They of the circumcision (οἱ ἐκ τῆς περιτομῆς). The phrase only here in Pastorals. Ὅι ἐκ περιτομῆς, Acts x. 45 ; xi. 2 ; Rom. iv. 12 ; Gal. ii. 12 ; Col. iv. 11. There can be no doubt of the presence of Jews in Crete. Tacitus (*Hist.* v. 2) even makes the absurd statement that the Jews were Cretan exiles ; and that from their residence in the vicinity of the Cretan Mount Ida they were called *Idaei*, whence *Judaei*. There appears to have been some confusion between the Palestinians and the Philistines — the *Cherethim* or *Cherethites*, who, in Ezek. xxv. 16 ; Zeph. ii. 5 are called in LXX Κρῆτες. Jews were in the island in considerable numbers between the death of Alexander and the final destruction of Jerusalem. In 1 Macc. xv. 23 the Cretan city of Gortyna is mentioned among the places to which letters were written by Lucius, the Roman consul, on behalf of the Jews, when Simon Maccabaeus

renewed the treaty which his brother Judas had made with
Rome.   Josephus (*Ant.* xvii. 12, 1 ; *Bell. Jud.* ii. 7, 1) says
that Herod's pseudo-son Alexander imposed on the Cretan
Jews on his way to Italy.   Philo (*Leg. ad Cai.* § 36) makes
the Jewish envoys say to Caligula that all the principal
islands of the Mediterranean, including Crete, were full of
Jews.

11. **Whose mouths must be stopped** (οὓς δεὶ ἐπιστομίζειν).   Lit. *whom it is necessary to silence.*   Ἐπιστομίζειν,
N. T.º.   ºLXX.   Originally, *to put something into the mouth*,
as a bit into a horse's mouth.   Ἐπιστόμιον is the *stop* of a
water-pipe or of a hydraulic organ.   Comp. φιμοῦν *to muzzle*,
1 Tim. v. 18.

Who subvert (οἵτινες ἀνατρέπουσιν).   The double relative
is explanatory of *must ; inasmuch as they*, etc.   For *subvert*
rend. *overthrow.*   See on 2 Tim. ii. 18.

Houses (οἴκους).   Families.

12. **One of themselves** (τις ἐξ αὐτῶν).   Ἀυτῶν refers to
the gainsayers, vv. 9, 10.   Τις refers to Epimenides, contemporary with Solon, and born in Crete B.C. 659.   A legend
relates that, going by his father's order in search of a sheep,
he lay down in a cave, where he fell asleep and slept for fifty
years.   He then appeared with long hair and a flowing beard,
and with an astonishing knowledge of medicine and natural
history.   It was said that he had the power of sending his
soul out of his body and recalling it at pleasure, and that he
had familiar intercourse with the gods and possessed the
power of prophecy.   He was sent for to Athens at the request
of the inhabitants, in order to pave the way for the legislation
of Solon by purifications and propitiatory sacrifices, intended
to allay the feuds and party-discussions which prevailed in
the city.   In return for his services he refused the Athenians'
offers of wealth and public honours, and asked only a branch
of the sacred olive, and a decree of perpetual friendship

between Athens and his native city. He is said to have lived to the age of 157 years, and divine honours were paid him by the Cretans after his death. He composed a Theogony, and poems concerning religious mysteries. He wrote also a poem on the Argonautic Expedition, and other works. Jerome mentions his treatise *On Oracles and Responses*, from which the quotation in this verse is supposed to have been taken. According to Diogenes Laertius (i. 10) Epimenides, in order to remove a pestilence from Athens, turned some sheep loose at the Areopagus, and wherever they lay down sacrificed to the proper god : whence, he says, there are still to be found, in different demes of the Athenians, anonymous altars. Comp. Acts xvii. 22, 23.*

The Cretans, etc. The words Κρῆτες — ἀργαί form a hexameter line.

Always (ἀεί). Habitually.

Liars (ψεῦσται). In Pastorals here and 1 Tim. i. 10. Once in Paul, Rom. iii. 4. Mostly in John. The Cretan habit of lying passed into a verb, κρητίζειν *to speak like a Cretan = to lie :* also into a noun, κρητισμός *Cretan behaviour = lying.* Similarly, the licentiousness of Corinth appeared in the verb κορινθιάζεσθαι *to practise whoredom*, and in the noun κορινθιαστής *a whoremonger.* Comp. Ov. *Artis Amat.* i. 296.

> " non hoc, centum quae sustinet urbes
> Quamvis sit mendax, Creta negare potest."

> " Crete, which a hundred cities doth maintain,
> Cannot deny this, though to lying given."

A familiar saying was τρία κάππα κάκιστα *the three worst K's,* Κρῆτες, Καππάδοκαι, Κίλικες *Cretans, Cappadocians, Cilicians.*

Evil beasts (κακὰ θηρία). Rude, cruel, and brutal.

---

* Readers of Goethe will recall his " Festspiel," *Des Epimenides Erwachen. Werke,* Bd. XVIII.

Slow-bellies (γαστέρες ἀργαί). Better, *idle-bellies*. Rev. gives the correct idea, *idle gluttons*. They are so given to gluttony that they are mere *bellies*. Comp. Philip. iii. 19. Γαστὴρ, elsewhere in N. T. always in connection with child-bearing. So mostly in LXX, but in a few instances as here. See Job xx. 23; Ps. xvi. 14; Sir. xxxvii. 5. In Job xx. 14 as the rendering of קֶרֶב *bowels*. Ἀργός *idle*, °P. However such words may have befitted the pagan seer, it is not pleasant to regard them as taken up and indorsed by the great Christian apostle, who thus is made to stigmatise as liars, beasts, and gluttons a whole people, among whom he had himself so successfully laboured that several churches had been founded in a short time. They are strange words from a venerable Christian minister to a younger minister to whom he had intrusted the care of those very souls; and, in any case, are superfluous, as addressed to one who must have known the characteristics of the Cretans quite as well as the writer himself.

13. **Sharply** (ἀποτόμως). Only here and 2 Cor. xiii. 10 (note). Paul has ἀποτομία *severity*, Rom. xi. 22 (note). LXX, ἀποτόμως *severely*, only Wisd. v. 22; ἀπότομος *severe* (not in N. T.), Wisd. v. 20; xi. 10; xii. 9. From ἀποτέμνειν *to cut off*. It signifies *abrupt, harsh, summary* dealing.

14. **Not giving heed** (μὴ προσέχοντες). Reprove sharply, that they may be sound in the faith, and may show their soundness by not giving heed, etc. See on 1 Tim. i. 4.

To Jewish fables (Ἰουδαϊκοῖς μύθοις). See on 1 Tim. i. 4. Note *Jewish*. The nature of these we do not know.

Commandments of men (ἐντολαῖς ἀνθρώπων). See on 1 Tim. vi. 14. Comp. Col. ii. 22. Prescriptions concerning abstinence from meats, marriage, etc. The *men* are probably *those of the circumcision*, ver. 10. What they teach theoretically, by means of *the myths*, they bring to bear practically, by means of *their precepts*.

That turn from the truth (ἀποστρεφομένων τὴν ἀλήθειαν).
Comp. 2 Tim. iv. 4, where *the truth* and *fables* appear in
contrast.

15. Unto the pure (τοῖς καθαροῖς). The pure in heart
and conscience. See 2 Tim. i. 3.

All things are pure. Comp. 1 Tim. iv. 4, 5; Acts x. 15;
Mk. vii. 15, 18, 19; 1 Cor. x. 26, 30; Rom. xiv. 20. The
aphorism is suggested by *the commandments of men*, ver. 14.

Unto them that are defiled (τοῖς μεμιαμμένοις). Only
here in Pastorals. See also J. xviii. 28 (note); Heb. xii. 15;
Jude 8. Only in J. xviii. 28 in a ceremonial sense. Elsewhere of moral pollution.

Nothing is pure. Their moral pollution taints everything
with its own quality. The purest things become suggestors
and ministers of impurity.

Mind and conscience (ὁ νοῦς καὶ ἡ συνείδησις). For *νοῦς*
see on Rom. vii. 23: for *συνείδησις*, on 1 Pet. iii. 16.

16. They profess (ὁμολογοῦσιν). Better, *confess*. See on
2 Cor. ix. 13, and comp. 1 Tim. vi. 12. Not *loudly and publicly profess* (as Huther), but *confess* as opposed to *deny*
(J. i. 20); comp. Heb. xi. 13; Rom. x. 9, 10.

Abominable (βδελυκτοὶ). N. T.º. ºClass. LXX, Prov.
xvii. 15; Sir. xli. 5; 2 Macc. i. 27. See on βδέλυγμα *abomin-
ation*, Matt. xxiv. 15, and comp. Apoc. xvii. 4, 5; xxi. 27.
The kindred verb βδελύσσεσθαι *abhor*, Rom. ii. 22; Apoc.
xxi. 8.

Reprobate (ἀδόκιμοι). See on Rom. i. 28; 1 Cor. ix. 27,
and comp. 2 Tim. iii. 8. The phrase *reprobate unto every good
work*, N. T.º.

CHAPTER II.

1. Speak thou (λάλει). See on Matt. xxviii. 18; J. viii. 26.

Become (πρέπει). Originally, *to stand out; be conspicuous.*
Thus Homer, *Od.* viii. 172: μετὰ δὲ πρέπει ἀγρομένοισιν *he is
conspicuous among those who are assembled.* Eurip. *Hel.* 215;
Ζεὺς πρέπων δι᾽ αἰθέρος *Zeus shining clearly through the aether.*
Hence, *to become conspicuously fit; to become; beseem.* In
N. T. in the impersonal forms πρέπον ἐστὶν *it is becoming*
(Matt. iii. 15); πρέπει *it becometh* (Eph. v. 3); ἔπρεπεν *it
became* (Heb. ii. 10). With a subject nominative, 1 Tim. ii. 10;
Heb. vii. 26.

2. Aged men (πρεσβύτας). Only here, L. i. 18; Philem. 9.
To be understood of natural age, not of ecclesiastical position.
Note that 1 Tim. iii, in treating of church officers, deals only
with Bishops and Deacons. Nothing is said of Presbyters
until ch. v, where Timothy's relations to individual members of
the church are prescribed. These church members are classified in this and the following verses as *old men, old women,
younger men, servants.* In LXX πρεσβύτης is occasionally
interchanged with πρεσβευτής *ambassador.* See 2 Chron.
xxxii. 31; 1 Macc. xiii. 21; xiv. 21, 22; 2 Macc. xi. 34.

3. Aged women (πρεσβύτιδας). N. T.º. See on πρεσ-
βύτεραι, 1 Tim. v. 2.

Behaviour (καταστήματι). N. T.º. See on καταστολή
apparel, 1 Tim. ii. 9. It means, primarily, *condition* or *state.*
Once in LXX, 3 Macc. v. 45, κατάστημα μανιῶδες *the mad-
dened state* into which the war-elephants were excited.
Hence the *state* in which one habitually bears himself — his
deportment or *demeanour.*

As becometh holiness (ἱεροπρεπεῖς). N. T.º. LXX,
4 Macc. ix. 25; xi. 20. In the *Theages* (wrongly ascribed

to Plato), τῷ υἱεῖ τὸ ὄνομα ἔθου καὶ ἱεροπρεπές *you have given your son* (*Theages*) *an honorable and reverend name* (122 D). It means *beseeming a sacred place, person,* or *matter.* Thus Athenaeus, vii, of one who had given a sacred banquet, says that the table was ornamented ἱεροπρεπέστατα *in a manner most appropriate to the sacred circumstances.* The meaning here is *becoming those who are engaged in sacred service.* This is the more striking if, as there is reason to believe, the πρεσβύτιδες represented a quasi-official position in the church. See on 1 Tim. v. 3, and comp. 1 Tim. ii. 10; Eph. v. 3.*

False accusers (διαβόλους). Better, *slanderers.* See on Matt. iv. 1, and 1 Tim. iii. 6, 11.

Given to much wine (οἴνῳ πολλῷ δεδουλωμένας). More correctly, *enslaved* to much wine. The verb only here in Pastorals. Comp. 1 Tim. iii. 8.

Teachers of good things (καλοδιδασκάλους). N. T.⁰. ⁰LXX, ⁰Class.

4. They may teach (σωφρονίζωσι). Better, *school* or *train.* N. T.⁰. ⁰LXX. The verb means *to make sane or sober-minded; to recall a person to his senses;* hence, *to moderate, chasten, discipline.*

To love their husbands, to love their children (φιλάνδρους εἶναι, φιλοτέκνους). Lit. *to be husband-lovers, children-lovers.* Both adjectives N. T.⁰. ⁰LXX. Φίλανδρος in Class. not in this sense, but *loving men* or *masculine habits; lewd.* In the better sense often in epitaphs. An inscription at Pergamum has the following : Ἰούλιος Βάσσος Ὀτακιλίᾳ Πώλλῃ τῇ γλυκυτάτῃ γυναικί, φιλάνδρῳ καὶ φιλοτέκνῳ συμβιωσάσῃ ἀμέμπτως ἔτη λ' *Julius Bassus to Otacilia Polla my sweetest wife, who loved her husband and children and lived with me blamelessly for thirty years.*

---

* In accordance with this view von Soden renders *priesterlich.* The A.V. is better than the Rev. *reverent,* which is colourless.

5. **Keepers at home** (οἰκουργούς). Wrong. Rend. *workers at home.* N. T.º.   ºLXX, ºClass.*

Good (ἀγαθάς). Not attributive of *workers at home*, but independent. Rend. *kindly.* The mistress of the house is to add to her thrift, energy, and strict discipline, benign, gracious, heartily kind demeanour. Comp. Matt. xx. 15; 1 Pet. ii. 18; Acts ix. 36. See on Acts xi. 24; Rom. v. 7.†

Obedient (ὑποτασσομένας). Better, *subject* or *in subjection.* Frequent in Paul, but not often in the active voice. See on Jas. iv. 7; Rom. viii. 7; Philip. iii. 21; and comp. 1 Cor. xiv. 34; Eph. v. 22; Col. iii. 18.

7. **In all things** (περὶ πάντα). Lit. *concerning* all things. The exact phrase, N. T.º. For analogous use of περὶ comp. L. x. 40, 41; Acts xix. 25; 1 Tim. i. 19; vi. 4, 21; 2 Tim. iii. 8.

Shewing thyself (σεαυτὸν παρεχόμενος). See on 1 Tim. i. 4. The phrase N. T.º. but occurs in Class., as, to show one's self *holy* or *righteous; wise* or *skilful; παρέχειν ἑαυτὸν σπάνιον* to make himself scarce. ‡

Incorruptness (ἀφθορίαν). Const. with *shewing.* N. T.º. ºClass. LXX once, Hag. ii. 18. Omit *sincerity.*

8. **Sound speech** (λόγον ὑγιῆ). Ὑγιής *sound,* only here in Pastorals. The usual form is the participle, as ὑγιαινόντων λόγων, 2 Tim. i. 13; ὑγιαίνουσι λόγοις, 1 Tim. vi. 3.

---

* A.V. follows the T. R. οἰκουρούς. Even with this reading the rendering is not accurate. The meaning is not *stayers* at home, but *keepers* or *guardians* of the household.

† Some interesting remarks on the use of ἀγαθός by Homer may be found in Gladstone's *Homer and the Homeric Age,* ii. 419 ff.

‡ See Aristoph. *Vesp.* 949: Plato, *Euthyphro,* 3 D; *Protag.* 312 A: Xen. *Cyrop.* II. i. 22; VIII. i. 39. Deissmann cites one instance in an inscription at Carpathus, second century B.C., ἀνέγκλητον αὐτὸν παρέσχηται *may show himself blameless;* and another from Mylasa in Caria, first century B.C., χρήσιμον ἑαυτὸν παρέσχηται *may show himself useful.*

That cannot be condemned (ἀκατάγνωστον). N. T.º.
ºClass. See 2 Macc. iv. 47.

He that is of the contrary part (ὁ ἐξ ἐναντίας). The
phrase N. T.º. See Mk. xv. 39. The heathen opposer is
meant. Comp. *blasphemed*, ver. 5, and 1 Tim. vi. 1. 'Εναν-
τίος *contrary*, in Paul only 1 Th. ii. 15.

May be ashamed (ἐντραπῇ). Only here in Pastorals. In
Paul, 1 Cor. iv. 14; 2 Th. iii. 14, see notes on both, and on
Matt. xxi. 37.

Evil thing (φαῦλον). Only here in Pastorals. In Paul,
Rom. ix. 11; 2 Cor. v. 10. See on J. iii. 20.

9. To please them well in all things (ἐν πᾶσιν εὐαρέστ-
ους εἶναι). Wrong. Const. *in all things* with *to be in subjection*. Note the position of ἐν πᾶσιν in 1 Tim. iii. 11;
iv. 15; 2 Tim. ii. 7; iv. 5, and comp. ὑπακούειν κατὰ πάντα
obey in all things, Col. iii. 20, 22; and ὑποτάσσεται — ἐν παντί
is subject in everything, Eph. v. 24. 'Ευάρεστος *well pleasing*,
only here in Pastorals. Almost exclusively in Paul. See
also Heb. xiii. 21. 'Ευαρέστως *acceptably*, Heb. xii. 28.

10. Purloining (νοσφιζομένους). Only here and Acts v. 2, 3.
LXX, Josh. vii. 1; 2 Macc. iv. 32. Often in Class. From
νόσφι *apart*. The fundamental idea of the word is *to put far
away from another; to set apart for one's self;* hence *to purloin*
and appropriate to one's own use. *Purloin* is akin to *prolong:*
prolongyn or *purlongyn* "to put fer awey." Old French, *por-
loignier* or *purloignier*.

Shewing all good fidelity (πᾶσαν πίστιν ἐνδεικνυμένος
ἀγαθήν). The phrase N. T.º. This is the only instance in
N. T. of ἀγαθός with πίστις.

Adorn the doctrine (τὴν διδασκαλίαν κοσμῶσιν). The
phrase N. T.º. For κοσμῶσιν *adorn*, see on 1 Tim. ii. 9.

11. This *teaching* or *doctrine* which is to be adorned by the lives of God's servants — the teaching of the gospel — is now stated in vv. 11–15.

The grace of God (ἡ χάρις τοῦ θεοῦ). A common Pauline phrase. The exact phrase only here in Pastorals. It is the ultimate ground of salvation. Comp. 2 Tim. i. 9; Eph. ii. 5, 8; Gal. i. 15.

That bringeth salvation (σωτήριος). Lit. *saving*. N. T.°. Const. with χάρις *grace*. The saving grace of God.

Hath appeared (ἐπεφάνη). Only in Pastorals, Luke, and Acts. In the active voice, *to bring to light, show*. See on ἐπιφάνεια *appearing*, 1 Tim. vi. 14.

To all men. Const. with *that bringeth salvation*, not with *hath appeared*. The grace of God which is saving for all men. Comp. 1 Tim. ii. 4.

12. **Teaching** (παιδεύουσα). Better, *instructing* or *training*. The saving economy of God is educative. Comp. Heb. xii. 4–11, and see on 1 Tim. i. 20.

Ungodliness (ἀσέβειαν). In Pastorals only here and 2 Tim. ii. 16. The contrary of εὐσέβεια, for which see on 1 Tim. ii. 2.

Worldly lusts (κοσμικὰς ἐπιθυμίας). The phrase N. T.°. Κοσμικὸς *worldly*, only here and Heb. ix. 1. On the ethical sense in κόσμος *the world*, see on Acts xvii. 24, and J. i. 9.

13. **Looking for** (προσδεχόμενοι). In Pastorals only here. Comp. Mk. xv. 43; L. ii. 25; xii. 36. In this sense not in Paul. Primarily, *to receive to one's self, admit, accept*. So L. xv. 2; Rom. xvi. 2; Philip. ii. 29. That which is *accepted* in faith, is *awaited* expectantly.

That blessed hope (τὴν μακαρίαν ἐλπίδα). The phrase N. T.°. Μακάριος *blessed*, very often in the Gospels. See on

Matt. v. 3. In Pastorals, with the exception of this passage, always of God. In Paul, only of men, and so usually in the Gospels. Ἐλπίδα *hope*, the *object* of hope. Why the hope is called *blessed*, appears from 2 Tim. iv. 8; Philip. iii. 20, etc. Comp. Jude 21, and 1 Pet. i. 13.

And the glorious appearing (καὶ ἐπιφάνειαν τῆς δόξης). Καὶ is explanatory, introducing the definition of the character of the thing hoped for. Looking for the object of hope, *even* the appearing, etc. *Glorious appearing* is a specimen of the vicious hendiadys by which the force of so many passages has been impaired or destroyed in translation. Rend. *appearing of the glory*.

Of the great God and our Saviour Jesus Christ (τοῦ μεγάλου θεοῦ καὶ σωτῆρος ἡμῶν Χριστοῦ Ἰησοῦ). For *Jesus Christ* rend. *Christ Jesus*. Μέγας *great* with *God*, N. T.º, but often in LXX. According to A.V. two persons are indicated, God and Christ. Rev. with others rend. *of our great God and Saviour Christ Jesus*, thus indicating one person, and asserting the deity of Christ. I adopt the latter, although the arguments and authorities in favour of the two renderings are very evenly balanced.*

14. **Gave himself for us** (ἔδωκεν ἑαυτὸν ὑπὲρ ἡμῶν). See on 1 Tim. ii. 6, and comp. Gal. i. 4. Ὑπὲρ *on behalf of;* not *instead of*.

---

* For *one* person are urged: 1. That the two appellations θεὸς and σωτήρ are included under a single article. 2. That σωτήρ with ἡμῶν, where there are two appellatives, has the article in every case, except 1 Tim. i. 1; and that therefore its omission here indicates that it is taken with θεοῦ under the regimen of τοῦ. 3. That ὅς in ver. 14 is singular and refers to Christ, indicating that only one person is spoken of in ver. 13. 4. The analogy of 2 Pet. i. 1, 11; iii. 18. 5. The declarations concerning Christ in Col. i. 15; 2 Th. i. 7; 1 Pet. iv. 13; Col. ii. 9. For *two* persons are urged: 1. The fact that θεὸς is never found connected directly with Ἰησοῦς Χριστὸς as an attribute. 2. The frequency with which God and Christ are presented in the N. T. as distinct from each other, as having a common relation to men in the economy of grace, makes it probable that the same kind of union is intended here, and not a presentation of Christ as God. 3. The evident reference of θεοῦ in ver. 11 to God the Father. 4. The analogy of 2 Th. i. 12.

Might redeem (λυτρώσηται). Only here, L. **xxiv.** 21; 1 Pet. i. 18. See on 1 Tim. ii. 6. Neither λύτρον *ransom*, λύτρωσις *redemption*, nor λυτρωτής *redeemer* occur in Paul. He has the figure of *purchase* (ἀγοράζεσθαι, ἐξαγοράζεσθαι), 1 Cor. vi. 20; vii. 23; Gal. iii. 13; iv. 5. Comp. Apoc. v. 9; xiv. 3, 4; 2 Pet. ii. 1.

Iniquity (ἀνομίας). Only here in Pastorals. Lit. *lawlessness*. See on 1 J. iii. 4.

Might purify (καθαρίσῃ). In Pastorals only here. Mostly in Synoptic Gospels and Hebrews. In Paul, 2 Cor. vii. 1; Eph. v. 26. °Class. Often in LXX.

A peculiar people (λαὸν περιούσιον). Λαός *people* only here in Pastorals. In Paul ten times, always in citations. Most frequently in Luke and Acts; often in Hebrews and Apocalypse. Περιούσιος N. T.°. A few times in LXX, always with λαός. See Ex. xix. 5; xxiii. 22; Deut. vii. 6; xiv. 2; xxvi. 18. The phrase was originally applied to the people of Israel, but is transferred here to believers in the Messiah — Jews and Gentiles. Comp. 1 Pet. ii. 10. Περιούσιος is from the participle of περιεῖναι *to be over and above:* hence περιουσία *abundance, plenty*. Περιούσιος also means *possessed over and above*, that is, specially selected for one's own ; exempt from ordinary laws of distribution. Hence correctly represented by *peculiar*, derived from *peculium, a private purse*, a special acquisition of a member of a family distinct from the property administered for the good of the whole family. Accordingly the sense is given in Eph. i. 14, where believers are said to have been *sealed* εἰς ἀπολύτρωσιν τῆς περιποιήσεως *with a view to redemption of possession*, or *redemption which will give possession*, thus = *acquisition*. So 1 Pet. ii. 9, where Christians are styled λαὸς εἰς περιποίησιν *a people for acquisition*, to be acquired by God as his *peculiar* possession. Comp. 1 Th. v. 9; 2 Th. ii. 14, and περιποιεῖσθαι *to acquire*, Acts **xx.** 28. The phrase καθαρίζειν λαὸν *to purify the people*, in LXX, Neh. xii. 30; Judith **xvi. 18.**

Zealous (ζηλωτήν). Lit. *a zealot.* Comp. Acts xxi. 20 ; xxii. 3 ; 1 Pet. iii. 13. Only here in Pastorals. In Paul, 1 Cor. xiv. 12 ; Gal. i. 14. For the word as a title, see on *the Canaanite*, Matt. x. 4, and Mk. iii. 18.

Authority (ἐπιταγῆς). See on 1 Tim. i. 1.

Despise (περιφρονείτω). N. T.°. Occasionally in Class. From περὶ *beyond*, φρονεῖν *to be minded.* To set one's self in thought beyond ; hence *contemn, despise.* Comp. 1 Tim. iv. 12. The exhortation is connected with *authority.* Titus is to claim respect for his office and for himself as bearing it.

CHAPTER III.

1. **Put them in mind** (ὑπομίμνησκε αὐτοὺς). See on 2 Tim. ii. 14, and on ὑπόμνησιν *reminding*, 2 Tim. i. 5.

Principalities and powers (ἀρχαῖς ἐξουσίαις). Omit *and.* Principalities which are authorities. Ἀρχή *beginning* = *that which begins : the leader, principality.* See on Col. i. 16 ; Jude 6 ; Acts x. 11. Only here in Pastorals. Ἐξουσία *right, authority.* See on Mk. ii. 10 ; J. i. 12 ; Col. i. 16. Only here in Pastorals. For the combination *principalities and powers*, see on L. xx. 20.

To obey magistrates (πειθαρχεῖν). Comp. Acts v. 29, 32 ; xxvii. 21. See on Acts v. 29. The idea of *magistrates* is contained in the word itself ; but it is quite proper to render as Rev. *to be obedient.* Rare in LXX.

Ready to every good work (πρὸς πᾶν ἔργον ἀγαθὸν ἑτοίμους εἶναι). The phrase N. T.°. Ἕτοιμος *ready*, only here in Pastorals. Comp. ἑτοιμασία *readiness* or *preparation*, Eph. vi. 15 (note).

2. **No brawlers** (ἀμάχους). Better as Rev., *not to be contentious.* See on 1 Tim. iii. 3. Past°.

3. Divers — pleasures (ἡδοναῖς ποικίλαις). Ἡδονή *pleasure*, only here in Pastorals. ᴼP. See on Jas. iv. 1. For ποικίλαις *divers*, see on 2 Tim. iii. 6.

Malice (κακίᾳ). Only here in Pastorals. See on Jas. i. 21. In N. T. κακία is *a special form of vice*, not viciousness in general, as Cicero, *Tusc.* iv. 15, who explains by "*vitiositas*, a viciousness which includes all vices." Calvin, on Eph. iv. 32, defines as "a viciousness of mind opposed to humanity and fairness, and commonly styled *malignity*." The homily ascribed to Clement of Rome, describes κακία as the *forerunner* (προοδοίπορον) *of our sins* (x). *Malice* is a correct translation.

4. Kindness (χρηστότης). Only here in Pastorals. Elsewhere only in Paul. See on Rom. iii. 12, and on *easy*, Matt. xi. 30.

Love (φιλανθρωπία). *Love* is too vague. It is love toward *men;* comp. ver. 2. Only here and Acts xxviii. 2: φιλανθρώπως *kindly*, Acts xxvii. 3 (note). While it cannot be asserted that the heretical characteristics noted in the Pastoral Epistles point collectively to any specific form of error, it is true, nevertheless, that certain characteristics of the economy of grace are emphasised, which are directly opposed to Gnostic ideas. Thus the exhortation that supplications be made for *all men*, supported by the statement that God wills that all men should be saved and come to the knowledge of the truth (1 Tim. ii. 1, 4), is in the teeth of the Gnostic distinction between men of spirit and men of matter, and of the Gnostic principle that the knowledge (ἐπίγνωσις) of truth was only for a limited, intellectual class. To the same effect is the frequent recurrence of *all*, *for all*, in connection with the saving and enlightening gifts of God (1 Tim. ii. 6; iv. 10; vi. 13; Tit. ii. 11). So here: not only has the saving grace of God appeared *unto all* (ch. ii. 11), but it has revealed itself as kindness and love to man as man.

5. Not by works of righteousness which we have done (οὐκ ἐξ ἔργων τῶν ἐν δικαιοσύνῃ ἃ ἐποιήσαμεν). Lit. *not by* *works, those namely in righteousness, which we did.* The thought is entirely Pauline. 'Εξ ἔργων, strictly, *out of, in consequence of* works. 'Εν δικαιοσύνῃ *in the sphere of righteousness;* as legally righteous men. Comp. Eph. ii. 9. *We did:* emphatic. Comp. Rom. x. 5; Gal. iii. 10, 12; v. 3.

According to his mercy (κατὰ τὸ αὐτοῦ ἔλεος). The phrase only 1 Pet. i. 3. Comp. Rom. xv. 9; Eph. ii. 4; Jude 21.

By the washing of regeneration (διὰ λουτροῦ παλινγενεσίας). Λουτρόν only here and Eph. v. 26. It does not mean the act of bathing, but *the bath, the laver.* Παλινγενεσία only here and Matt. xix. 28, where it is used of the final restoration of all things. The phrase *laver of regeneration* distinctly refers to baptism, in connection with which and through which as a medium regeneration is conceived as taking place. Comp. Rom. vi. 3–5. It is true that nothing is said of *faith;* but baptism implies faith on the part of its recipient. It has no regenerating effect apart from faith; and the renewing of the Holy Spirit is not bestowed if faith be wanting.

Renewing (ἀνακαινώσεως). Only here and Rom. xii. 2. Comp. 2 Cor. v. 17. Paul has ἀνακαινοῦν *to renew,* 2 Cor. iv. 16; Col. iii. 10: ἀνακαίνωσις *renewing,* Rom. xii. 2. 'Ανακαινίζειν *to renew,* only Heb. vi. 6. The connection of the genitive is disputed. Some make it dependent on λουτροῦ *bath,* so that the bath of baptism is conceived as implying regeneration and renewing of the Holy Spirit. Others construe with *renewing* only, ἀνακαινώσεως being dependent on διὰ; through the laver of regeneration and (through) the renewing, etc. The former seems the more probable. The phrase *renewing of the Holy Spirit* only here. In N. T. the Spirit or the Holy Spirit is joined in the genitive with the following words: *comfort, joy, power, love, demonstration, manifestation, earnest, ministration, fellowship, promise, fruit, unity, sword, sanctification.*

6. **Shed** (ἐξέχεεν). Or *poured forth.* Only here in Pastorals. Most frequent in Apocalypse. The pouring out of

the Spirit is an O. T. metaphor. See Joel iii. 1, 2, cit. in
Acts ii. 17, 18; Zech. xii. 10. In Paul the verb occurs but
once, of shedding blood, Rom. iii. 15, cit.

7. Being justified (δικαιωθέντες). In Pastorals only here
and 1 Tim. iii. 16 (note). See Introd. vi. Justification is
conceived as taking place before the outpouring of the Spirit.

By his grace (τῇ ἐκείνου χάριτι). By the grace of Jesus
Christ. See Acts xv. 11; 2 Cor. viii. 9; xiii. 14; Rom. v. 6;
Gal. i. 6.

We should be made heirs (κληρονόμοι γενηθῶμεν). Κληρονόμος heir only here in Pastorals. A favourite idea of Paul.
See Rom. iv. 13; viii. 17; Gal. iii. 29. Heirship of eternal
life is the result of justification. So, clearly, Rom. v. It is
attested and confirmed by the Holy Spirit. 2 Cor. v. 5;
Eph. i. 14.

According to the hope of eternal life (κατ᾽ ἐλπίδα ζωῆς
αἰωνίου). Const. *of eternal life* with *heirs*, and rend. *heirs of
eternal life according to hope.* Comp. Rom. iv. 18; v. 2;
viii. 24; Gal. v. 5; Col. i. 5, 27; Tit. i. 2; 1 Pet. i. 3;
1 J. iii. 2, 3.

8. Affirm constantly (διαβεβαιοῦσθαι). Past⁰. See on
1 Tim. i. 7. *Constantly*, not *continually*, but *uniformly* and
consistently. So *Book of Common Prayer*, " Collect for Saint
John Baptist's Day," " and after his example constantly speak
the truth." Rend. *affirm steadfastly.*

Might be careful (φροντίζωσιν). N. T.⁰. Quite often in
LXX. Frequent in Class. *To think* or *consider;* hence to
take *careful* thought, *ponder, be anxious about.*

To maintain (προΐστασθαι). Mostly in Pastorals, and
usually in the sense of ruling, as Rom. xii. 8; 1 Th. v. 12;
1 Tim. iii. 4, 5. The sense here is *to be forward in.**

---

* The attempts to resolve the meaning into *practise* are mostly suspicious.
Of the four examples cited by Alford, two at least, Thucyd. viii. 75, and Soph.

Profitable (ὠφέλιμα). Past⁰. ᵒLXX. Comp. 1 Tim. iv. 8; 2 Tim. iii. 16.

9. **Foolish questions, etc.** See on 2 Tim. ii. 23. For *genealogies* see on 1 Tim. i. 4.

Strivings about the law (μάχας νομικὰς). The phrase N. T.⁰. Comp. 1 Tim. i. 7. Νομικός mostly in Luke. Everywhere except here a *lawyer*, with the article or τὶς.

Unprofitable (ἀνωφελεῖς). Only here and Heb. vii. 18.

Vain (μάταιοι). Only here in Pastorals. Twice in Paul, 1 Cor. iii. 20, cit. ; xv. 17 (note). Very frequent in LXX. The sense is *aimless* or *resultless*, as μάταιος εὐχή a prayer *which cannot obtain fulfilment*. The questions, genealogies, etc., lead to no attainment or advancement in godliness. Comp. ματαιολογία *jangling*, 1 Tim. i. 6 : ματαιολόγοι *vain talkers*, ver. 10 : ματαιότης *vanity*, Rom. viii. 20 ; Eph. iv. 17: ἐματαιώθησαν *were made vain*, Rom. i. 21 : μάτην *in vain*, Matt. xv. 9.

10. **A man that is an heretic** (αἱρετικὸν ἄνθρωπον). Ἁιρετικός *heretical*, N. T.⁰. For αἵρεσις *heresy* see on 1 Pet. ii. 1.

Admonition (νουθεσίαν). Only here, 1 Cor. x. 11 ; Eph. vi. 4 (note). See on νουθετεῖν *to admonish*, Acts xx. 31.

11. **Is subverted** (ἐξέστραπται). N. T.⁰. More than *turned away* from the right path : rather, *turned inside out*. Comp. LXX, Deut. xxxii. 20.

Sinneth (ἁμαρτάνει). See on 1 J. i. 9 ; Matt. i. 21, and *trespasses*, Matt. vi. 14.

Elect. 980, have clearly the sense of *taking the lead*. When Plutarch says of Aspasia οὐ κοσμίου προεστῶσα ἐργασίας, he means that she *superintended* an unseemly employment ; she was *at the head* of an establishment. Notwithstanding all criticisms to the contrary, the Vulgate was on the right track, *bonis operibus praeesse*.

Condemned of himself (αὐτοκατάκριτος). Better as Rev., *self-condemned*. N. T.⁰. ⁰LXX, ⁰Class.

12. **Nicopolis.** There were several cities of this name, one in Cilicia, one in Thrace, and one in Epirus. It is uncertain which one is meant here.

To winter (παραχειμάσαι). Comp. Acts xxvii. 12; xxviii. 11; 1 Cor. xvi. 6. The noun παραχειμασία *wintering*, Acts xxvii. 12.

12. **Ours** (ἡμέτεροι). Our brethren in Crete.

For necessary uses (εἰς τὰς ἀναγκαίας χρείας). The phrase N. T.⁰. With reference to whatever occasion may demand them.

Unfruitful (ἄκαρποι). Only here in Pastorals. In Paul, 1 Cor. xiv. 14; Eph. v. 11. Not only in supplying the needs, but in cultivating Christian graces in themselves by acts of Christian service.

15. **Them that love us in the faith** (τοὺς φιλοῦντας ἡμᾶς ἐν πίστει). Better, *in faith*. The phrase N. T.⁰. Φιλεῖν *to love*, only here in Pastorals, and in Paul, only 1 Cor. xvi. 22. See on ἀγάπη *love*, Gal. v. 22. Const. *in faith* with *that love us*.

LISTS OF WORDS FOUND ONLY IN THE PASTORAL EPISTLES, AND IN THE PASTORAL EPISTLES AND NOT IN PAUL'S WRITINGS.

PASTORALS ONLY.		PASTORALS AND NOT IN PAUL.	
ἀγαθοεργέω	ἀπόδεκτος	αἰτία	εἰσφέρω
ἀγνεία	ἀποδοχή	ἀμελέω	ἐκτρέπομαι
ἀγωγή	ἀποθησαυρίζω	ἀνατρέπω	ἐκφέρω
ἀδηλότης	ἀποτρέπομαι	ἄνοια	ἐμπίπτω
ἀθλέω	ἀπρόσιτος	ἀντιλαμβάνομαι	ἐμπλέκω
αἰδώς	ἄρτιος	ἀνυπότα.στος	ἐξαρτίζω
αἱρετικός	ἄσπονδος	ἀνωφελής	ἐξήκοντα
αἰσχροκερδής	ἀστοχέω	ἀπόλαυσις	ἐπακολουθέω
ἀκαίρως	αὐθεντέω	ἀπολείπω	ἐπίθεσις
ἀκατάγνωστος	αὐτοκατάκριτος	ἀποπλανάω	ἐπιλαμβάνομαι
ἀκρατής	ἀφθορία	ἀργός	ἐπιμελέομαι
ἄλλως	ἀφιλάγαθος	ἀργύρεος	ἐπισκοπή
ἄμαχος	ἀψευδής	ἀρνέομαι	ἐπίσταμαι
ἀμοιβή		ἄσπιλος	ἐπιτίθημι
ἀναζωπυρέω	βαθμός	αὐθάδης	ἐπιτιμάω
ἀνάλυσις	βδελυκτός	ἀφιλάργυρος	ἐπιφαίνω
ἀνανήφω	βέλτιον	ἀχάριστος	εὐεργεσία
ἀναψύχω	βλαβερός		εὐκαίρως
ἀνδραποδιστής		βέβηλος	εὐσέβεια
ἀνδροφόνος	γάγγραινα	βίος	εὐσεβέω
ἀνεξίκακος	γενεαλογία	βλάσφημος	
ἀνεπαίσχυντος	γόης	βραδύνω	ζήτησις
ἀνεπίλημπτος	γραώδης	βρέφος	ζωγρέω
ἀνήμερος	γυμνασία	βυθίζω	ζωογονέω
ἀνόσιος	γυναικάριον		
ἀντιδιατίθεμαι		γεωργός	ἡδονή
ἀντίθεσις	δειλία	γυμνάζω	ἡσύχιος
ἀντίλυτρον	διαβεβαιόομαι		
ἀπαίδευτος	διάβολος, as adj.	δεσπότης	θηρίον
ἀπέραντος	διάγω	διπλόος	θνήσκω
ἀπόβλητος	διαπαρατριβή	δρόμος	
		δυνάστης	ἱματισμος

PASTORALS ONLY.		PASTORALS AND NOT IN PAUL.	
διατροφή	καταστολή	κακοπαθέω	παραιτέομαι
διδακτικός	καταστρηνιάω	κακοῦργος	παρακολουθέω
δίλογος	καταφθείρω	καταστροφή	πειθαρχέω
διώκτης	καυστηριάζομαι	κατηγορία	περίεργος
	κενοφωνία	κῆρυξ	περιέρχομαι
ἐγκρατής	κνήθω	κοσμέω	περιΐστημι
ἑδραίωμα	κοινωνικός	κοσμικός	περιποιέομαι
ἔκγονος	κόσμιος	κριτής	ποικίλος
ἔκδηλος	κοσμίως (alt. for	κτίσμα	πολυτελής
ἐκζήτησις	κοσμίῳ)		πρεσβυτέριον
ἐκστρέφομαι		λαός (in Paul al-	πρεσβύτερος
ἔλαττον, as adv.	λογομαχέω	ways in citn.)	προάγω
ἐλεγμός	λογομαχία	λείπω	πρόδηλος
ἐνδύνω		λέων	προδότης
ἔντευξις	μάμμη	λίαν	προπετής
ἐντρέφομαι	ματαιολογία	λοιδορία	προσέρχομαι
ἐπαγγέλλομαι in	ματαιολόγος	λυτρόομαι	προσέχω
sense of pro-	μεμβράνα		προσμένω
fessing	μετάλημψις	μαργαρίτης	πυκνός
ἐπανόρθωσις	μηδέποτε	μαρτυρία	
ἐπαρκέω	μητρολῴης	μάχομαι	σοφίζω
ἐπιδιορθόω	μονόομαι	μελετάω	σπαταλάω
ἐπίορκος		μέντοι	στερεός
ἐπιπλήσσω	νεόφυτος	μεταλαμβάνω	στεφανόω
ἐπιστομίζω	νεωτερικός	μήποτε	στρατιώτης
ἐπισωρεύω	νηφάλιος	μιαίνω	σωματικός
ἑτεροδιδασκαλέω	νομίμως	μῦθος	σωφροσύνη
εὐμετάδοτος	νοσέω		
εὐσεβῶς		νεότης	
	ξενοδοχέω	νίπτω	τάχειον
ἤρεμος		νομή	
	οἰκοδεσποτέω	νομικός	ὑβρίζω
θεόπνευστος	οἰκουργός	νομοδιδάσκαλος	ὑγιαίνω
θεοσέβεια	ὁμολογουμένως	νοσφίζομαι	ὑγιής
	ὀργίλος		ὑπομιμνήσκω
ἱεροπρεπής	ὀρθοτομέω	ξύλινος	ὑπόμνησις
Ἰουδαϊκός			ὕστερος
	παραθήκη	ὀρέγομαι	
	ὅσιος		
καλοδιδάσκαλος	πάροινος		φιλανθρωπία
καταλέγομαι	πατρολῴης	παλιγγενεσία	φιλάργυρος
κατάστημα	περιούσιος (citn.)	παραδέχομαι	φιλόξενος

PASTORALS ONLY.		PASTORALS AND NOT IN PAUL.	
περιπείρω	ὑγιαίνω, metaphor-	χαλεπός	χείρων
περιφρονέω	ical use of the	χειμών	χρυσός
πιστόομαι	participle as at-		
πλέγμα	tributive		
πλήκτης	ὑδροποτέω		
πορισμός	ὑπερπλεονάζω		
πραγματία	ὑπόνοια		
πραϋπαθία	ὑποτύπωσις		
πρεσβῦτις	ὑψηλοφρονέω		
πρόγονος			
πρόκριμα	φελόνης		
πρόσκλισις	φιλάγαθος		
	φίλανδρος		
ῥητῶς	φιλαργυρία		
	φίλαυτος		
σεμνότης	φιλήδονος		
σκέπασμα	φιλόθεος		
στόμαχος	φιλότεκνος		
στρατολογέω	φλύαρος		
στυγητός	φρεναπάτης		
συνκακοπαθέω	φροντίζω		
σωτήριος			
σωφρονίζ	χαλκεύς		
σωφρονισμός	χρήσιμος		
σωφρόνως			
σώφρων	ψευδολόγος		
	ψευδώνυμος		
τεκνογονέω			
τεκνογονία	ὠφέλιμος		
τεκνοτροφέω			
τυφόομαι			

These lists have been made directly from Moulton and Geden's Concordance.

A LIST OF PHRASES WHICH OCCUR ONLY IN THE PASTORAL EPISTLES.

Χριστὸς Ἰησοῦς ἡ ἐλπὶς ἡμῶν, 1 Tim. i. 1.

τέκνον ἐν πίστει, 1 Tim. i. 2.

νόμος κεῖται, 1 Tim. i. 9.

ἡ ὑγιαίνουσα διδασκαλία, 1 Tim. i. 10.

τὸ εὐαγγέλιον τῆς δόξης τοῦ μακαρίου θεοῦ, 1 Tim. i. 11.

ὁ μακάριος θεὸς, 1 Tim. i. 11.

πιστὸς ὁ λόγος, 1 Tim. i. 15.

πάσης ἀποδοχῆς ἄξιος, 1 Tim. i. 15.

πίστις καὶ ἀγαθή συνείδησις, 1 Tim. i. 19.

πρῶτον πάντων, 1 Tim. ii. 1.

οἱ ἐν ὑπεροχῇ, 1 Tim. ii. 2.

εἰς ἐπίγνωσιν ἀληθείας ἐλθεῖν, 1 Tim. ii. 4.

καιροῖς ἰδίοις, 1 Tim. ii. 6.

διδάσκαλος ἐθνῶν (of Paul), 1 Tim. ii. 7.

ἐν πίστει καὶ ἀληθείᾳ, 1 Tim. ii. 7.

ἐπαίροντες ὁσίους χεῖρας, 1 Tim. ii. 8.

χωρὶς ὀργῆς καὶ διαλογισμῶν, 1 Tim. ii. 8.

ἔχων ἐν ὑποταγῇ, 1 Tim. iii. 4.

ἐμπιπτεῖν εἰς κρίμα, 1 Tim. iii. 6.

τὸ μυστήριον τῆς πίστεως, 1 Tim. iii. 9.

οἶκος θεοῦ (of the church), 1 Tim. iii. 15.

στύλος καὶ ἑδραίωμα τῆς ἀληθείας, 1 Tim. iii. 15.

ἐδικαιώθη ἐν πνεύματι (of Christ), 1 Tim. iii. 16.

ἐν ὑστέροις καιροῖς, 1 Tim. iv. 1.

ἀφίστασθαι τῆς πίστεως, 1 Tim. iv. 1.

ἐπαγγελίαν ἔχειν, 1 Tim. iv. 8.

νῦν (with an article and adjectively, as ὁ νῦν αἰών; ζωῆς τῆς νῦν), 1 Tim. iv. 8; vi. 7.

ὄντως (with an article and adjectively, as τὰς ὄντως χήρας), 1 Tim. v. 3.

ἀμοιβὰς ἀποδιδόναι, 1 Tim. v. 4.

ἔχειν κρίμα, 1 Tim. v. 12.

ἐκλεκτοὶ ἄγγελοι, 1 Tim. v. 21.

χωρὶς προκρίματος, 1 Tim. v. 21.

προέρχεσθαι ὑγιαίνουσι λόγοις, 1 Tim. vi. 3.

ἡ κατ᾽ εὐσέβειαν διδασκαλία, 1 Tim. vi. 3.

ἄνθρωπος θεοῦ, 1 Tim. vi. 11.

ἀγωνίζεσθαι τὸν καλὸν ἀγῶνα, 1 Tim. vi. 12.

ὁμολογεῖν τὴν καλὴν ὁμολογίαν, 1 Tim. vi. 12.

μαρτυρεῖν τὴν καλὴν ὁμολογίαν, 1 Tim. vi. 13.

δυνάστης (of God), 1 Tim. vi. 15.

οἱ κυριεύοντες for κύριοι, 1 Tim. vi. 15.

ἔχειν ἀθανασίαν, 1 Tim. vi. 16.

ἀπόστολος κατά —, 1 Tim. i. 1; 2 Tim. i. 1; Tit. i. 1.

ἐπαγγελία ζωῆς, 2 Tim. i. 1.

ἀπὸ προγόνων, 2 Tim. i. 3.

ἐν καθαρᾷ συνειδήσει, 1 Tim. iii. 9; 2 Tim. i. 3.

πίστις ἐνῴκησεν, 2 Tim. i. 5.

κλῆσις ἁγία, 2 Tim. i. 9.

πρὸ χρόνων αἰωνίων, 2 Tim. i. 9; Tit. i. 2.

σωτηρία ἡ ἐν Χριστῷ Ἰησοῦ, 2 Tim. ii. 10.

νομὴν ἔχειν, 2 Tim. ii. 17.

θεμέλιος τοῦ θεοῦ, 2 Tim. ii. 19.

ἡ τοῦ διαβόλου παγίς, 2 Tim. ii. 26.

τοῦτο γίνωσκε, 2 Tim. iii. 1.

διώκειν (in sense of persecute), 2 Tim. iii. 12.

προκόπτειν ἐπὶ τὸ χεῖρον, 2 Tim. iii. 13.

ἱερὰ γράμματα, 2 Tim. iii. 15.

ἑαυτοῖς ἐπισωρεύειν διδασκάλους, 2 Tim. iv. 3.

κνηθόμενοι τὴν ἀκοήν, 2 Tim. iv. 3.

ὁ τῆς δικαιοσύνης στέφανος, 2 Tim. iv. 8.

τοῖς ἠγαπηκόσι τὴν ἐπιφάνειαν αὐτοῦ, 2 Tim. iv. 8.

παραγίνομαι (in the sense of standing by as a friend), 2 Tim. iv. 16.

κατὰ κοινὴν πίστιν, Tit. i. 4.

σεαυτὸν παρέχεσθαι, Tit. ii. 7.

ὁ ἐξ ἐναντίας, Tit. ii. 8.

πᾶσαν πίστιν ἐνδείκνυσθαι ἀγαθήν, Tit. ii. 10.

τὴν διδασκαλίαν κοσμεῖν, Tit. ii. 10.

ἡ χάρις τοῦ θεοῦ σωτήριος, Tit. ii. 11.

κοσμικαὶ ἐπιθυμίαι, Tit. ii. 12.

ἡ μακαρία ἐλπίς, Tit. ii. 13.

ὁ μέγας θεός, Tit. ii. 13.

μάχαι νομικαί, Tit. iii. 9.

οἱ φιλοῦντες ἡμᾶς ἐν πίστει, Tit. iii. 15.

THE EPISTLE TO THE HEBREWS.

THE EPISTLE TO THE HEBREWS.

INTRODUCTION.

" Who wrote the Epistle God only knows." Such was the verdict of Origen, and modern criticism has gotten no farther. That it is not the work of Paul is the almost unanimous judgment of modern scholars. Its authenticity as a Pauline writing has been challenged from the earliest times. In the Eastern church, both Clement and Origen regarded the Greek Epistle as Paul's only in a secondary sense; Clement holding that it was written by Paul in Hebrew and translated by Luke. Origen knew only that some held Clement of Rome and some Luke to be the author. Its position and designation in the Peshitto Version shows that it was regarded as not strictly one of Paul's epistles, but as an appendix to the collection. Eusebius's testimony is inconsistent. He holds a Hebrew original, and a translation by Clement, and cites the letter as Pauline (*H. E.* 38). Again, he expressly classifies it with *antilegomena* (vi. 13); but in iii. 25 he evades the question, naming the Pauline Epistles as *homologumena*, but without stating their number.

In the West the epistle was known to Clement of Rome, who frequently quotes it, but without naming the author. The Pauline authorship was expressly denied by Hippolytus: the Muratorian Canon does not mention it, and reckons only seven churches to which Paul wrote: Tertullian in Africa apparently knew nothing of a Pauline Epistle to the Hebrews, but spoke of an Epistle of Barnabas to the Hebrews. It was not recognised by Cyprian. From the fourth century its canonical authority was admitted in the West, partly on

the assumption of its Pauline authorship; but the influence of the earlier suspicion remained, and Jerome declared
that the custom of the Latins did not receive it as St. Paul's.
Augustine agreed substantially with Jerome. It was author-
ised as canonical by two councils of Carthage (397, 419 A.D.);
but the language of the former council was peculiar: "Thirteen Epistles of Paul, and one of the same to the Hebrews."
The decree of the latter council was "fourteen Epistles of
Paul."

From this time the canonical authority and authorship of
the epistle were generally accepted until the age of the
Reformation, when the old doubts were revived by Cajetan
and Erasmus. The council of Trent (1545–1563) decreed
fourteen Pauline Epistles; yet different views have been
current among Roman Catholic theologians, as Bellarmine,
Estius, and others. Luther denied the Pauline authorship,
and placed the epistle along with James, Jude, and the Apocalypse, after "the right-certain, main books of the New
Testament." Melanchthon treated it as anonymous. The
Magdeburg Centuriators (1559–1574) denied that it was
Paul's, as did Calvin. Under Beza's influence it was separated from the Pauline letters in the Gallican Confession
(1571). The Belgic and Helvetic Confessions declared it
Pauline. The hypothesis of the Pauline authorship was conclusively overthrown by Bleek in 1868.

The conclusion of modern scholarship rests upon:

(1) THE STYLE AND DICTION. — While Paul's style is
marked by frequent irregularities, anacolutha, unclosed parentheses, and mixed metaphors, this epistle is written in a
flowing, symmetrical, and artistically elaborated style. The
difference is as marked as that between a chapter of Gibbon
and one of Sartor Resartus. The rhetorical art of Hebrews
appears in the careful arrangement of the words, the rhyth-
mical structure of sentences, and the sonorous compounds.
The paragraphs are sometimes arranged in a regular series of
premises and conclusions, with parentheses which do not lose
their connection with the main topic, while the whole is
developed in regular sequence, without anacolutha.

(2) THE METHODS OF THOUGHT AND THE POINTS OF VIEW. — These differ from those of the Pauline Epistles. The two do not materially disagree. They reach, substantially, the same conclusions, but by different processes and from different positions. The points of emphasis differ. Topics which, in the Pauline letters, are in the foreground, in Hebrews fall into the shade or are wholly passed over. (*a*) *The conception of faith.* In Paul, faith is belief in Jesus Christ as a means of justification, involving a sharp opposition to the works of the law as meriting salvation. In Hebrews, faith is trust in the divine promises as distinguished from seeing their realisation, a phase of faith which appears rarely in Paul. Both agree that faith is the only true medium of righteousness; but Hebrews sets forth two great factors of faith, namely, that God *is*, and that he is a rewarder of them which diligently seek him.

(*b*) *The mode of presenting the contrast between the covenant of works and the covenant of grace through faith.* Both Paul and the author of Hebrews recognise a relation and connection between the two covenants. The one prefigures and prepares the way for the other. The Christian church is "the Israel of God," "the people of God," "the seed of Abraham." Both teach that forgiveness of sin and true fellowship with God cannot be attained through the law, and that Christianity represents the life-giving Spirit, and Judaism the letter which killeth. Both assert the abrogation of the old covenant by Christ. Paul, however, views Judaism almost entirely as a law to be fulfilled by men; while our writer regards it as a system of institutions designed to represent a fellowship between God and his worshippers. Paul, accordingly, shows that the law cannot put man into right relation with God, because man cannot fulfil it; while Hebrews shows that the institutions of the old covenant cannot, by reason of their imperfection, establish a real fellowship with God. To Paul, the reason why the old covenant did not satisfy lay, not in the law, which "is holy and just and good," but in the relation of man to the law, as unable to fulfil its demands. It cannot effect justification, and it works to make man con-

scious of his sin, and to drive him to the true source of righteousness.   To our writer the reason is to be sought in the
fact that the atoning and purifying institutions of the law
cannot remove the sins which prevent fellowship with God.

From Paul's point of view he might have been expected to
show that, in the Old Testament economy, it devolved on the
sacrificial institution, centred in the high-priesthood, to meet
the want which was not met by legal obedience.   To his
assertion that men could not fulfil the demands of the law, it
might have been answered that the sacrifices, not in being
works of the law, but in being ordained by God himself as
atonements for sin, changed men's defective righteousness into
a righteousness which justified them before God.   But Paul
does not meet this.   He nowhere shows the insufficiency of
the Old Testament sacrifices.   He does not treat the doctrine
of the high-priesthood of Christ.   He regards the system of
sacrifices less as a divinely-ordained means of atonement than
as a work performed by men, and therefore in the line of
other works of the law.

This gap is filled by the writer to the Hebrews, in showing
that the ceremonial economy did not and could not effect
true fellowship with God.   He, no doubt, perceived as clearly
as Paul that the observance of the ritual was of the nature
of legal works ; but he speaks of the ritual system as only a
presumed means of grace intended to define and enforce the
idea of fellowship with God, and to give temporary comfort
to the worshipper, but practically impotent to institute and
maintain such fellowship in any true and deep sense.   Therefore he emphasises the topic of the priesthood.   He dwells
on the imperfect and transient nature of the priestly office :
he shows that the Levitical priesthood was only a foreshadow-
ing of a better and permanent priesthood.   Christ as the
great high priest, who appears nowhere in the Pauline Epistles, is the central figure in the Epistle to the Hebrews.   He
treats of the ritual system and its appliances as mere types
of an enduring reality : he characterises the whole body of
Levitical ordinances and ceremonies as fleshly ; and through
all runs the one, sad note, accentuated again and again,

"they can never take away sins : " "they can never make the comers thereunto perfect : " "they are mere ordinances of the flesh, imposed until the time of reformation."

(c) *The view of the condition in which the subject of the law's dominion is placed.*   To Paul it is a condition of bondage, because the law is a body of demands which man must fulfil (Rom. vii.).   To our writer it is a condition of unsatisfied longing for forgiveness and fellowship, because of the insufficiency of the ritual atonement.   Accordingly, Hebrews points to the satisfaction of this longing in Christ, the great high priest, perfecting by one offering those who are being sanctified, purging the conscience from dead works to serve the living God.   Paul points to the fact that Christ has put an end to the tyranny of the law, and has substituted freedom for bondage.   The conception of *freedom* does not appear in Hebrews.   Neither ἐλεύθερος, ἐλευθερία, nor ἐλευθεροῦν occur in the epistle.

(d) *The doctrine of the resurrection of Christ.*   This emerges everywhere in Paul's epistles.   There is but one allusion to it in Hebrews (xiii. 20), although it is implied in the doctrine of Christ's high-priesthood, he being a priest "according to the power of an indissoluble life" (vii. 16).

(e) *The Gentiles.*   There is no mention of the Gentiles in relation to the new covenant, a topic which constantly recurs in Paul.

(f) *Sin.*   Sin is not treated with reference to its origin as by Paul.   The vocabulary of terms for sin is smaller than in the Pauline writings.

(g) *Repentance.*   The denial of the possibility of repentance after a lapse (vi. 4–6, comp. x. 26–29) is not Pauline.

(3) THE USE OF DIVINE TITLES. — Κύριος *lord*, very common in Paul, is comparatively rare in Hebrews.   Similarly, ᾽Ιησοῦς Χριστός *Jesus Christ*, which occurs thirty times in Romans alone.   Χριστός ᾽Ιησοῦς, which is characteristically Pauline, does not appear at all, neither does σωτὴρ *saviour*, which is found in Ephesians and Philippians.

(4) THE GENERAL SCHEME OF TREATMENT. — This is broader than that of Paul, viewing man not only in his

relation to the law, but to God's original ideal, and to the harmony with God's entire economy in nature and revelation. Man, nature, history, alike illustrate the incarnation. The Son of God, through whom the worlds were made, is the heir of all things, and, as creator and heir, interprets all life. He not only creates, but *bears on* all things by the word of his power toward the consummation—complete harmony with the divine archetype. As high priest he makes God and man at one in every sphere of being. He stands for the solidarity of humanity. He is not perfected without the community of sons (xi. 40). He is himself a son, a partaker of human nature.

With Paul, the law is chiefly a law of ordinances to be replaced by the gospel. It is abolished in Christ. It cannot be perfectly observed. It generates the knowledge of sin. It cannot generate righteousness. Christianity is a manifestation of the righteousness of God apart from the law. Faith is counted for righteousness to him that worketh not but believeth. The law works wrath, and is unto death. It is subsidiary, with a special view to the concrete development of sin.

Equally our epistle shows the insufficiency of the law to reconcile men to God, but in a different way. Paul emphasises the substitution of the gospel for the law: Hebrews the germ of a saving economy contained in the law, and the necessity of its development by the gospel. Paul does not overlook the fact that the law was our pedagogue to bring us to Christ, but he does not show *how*, as our writer does. The latter emphasises the unity of the divine plan, shows how the Levitical institutions pointed forward to Christ, and how the heavenly archetype was foreshadowed in the ritual system. With all Paul's strong assertion of the holiness of the law, he never dwells on it with the sad tenderness for the vanishing system which marks the Epistle to the Hebrews. With Paul the break with the law was sharp and complete. The law, as a champion of which he had been a persecutor of Christ, is thrown into sharp relief against Christ and the gospel. With James and Peter the case was different. It would not be strange if some writing should issue from their circle as "the last voice of the apostles of the circumcision," contemplating with affectionate sympathy that through which they had been led to see the meaning of the gospel, and finding in it "a welcome, though imperfect source of consolation, instead of a crushing burden, as in Paul's case" (Westcott).

(5) THE PERSONAL AUTHORITY OF THE WRITER IS WHOLLY IN THE BACKGROUND. — This is in marked contrast with the epistles of Paul. He appears to place himself in the second generation of believers to whom the salvation preached by Christ had been certified by ear-witnesses; while Paul refuses to be regarded as a pupil of the apostles, and claims to have received the gospel directly from the Lord, and to have been certified of it by the Spirit.

If Paul was not the author, who was? One claim is about as good as another, and no claim has any substantial support. That of Apollos is founded solely upon Acts xviii. 24 f. ; 1 Cor. i. 12 ; ii. 4 ff. The most that can be deduced from these is that Apollos *might* have written it. There is no evidence that he wrote anything, and that he was learned and mighty in the Scriptures might easily have been true of others. Some modern critics incline to Barnabas, on the strength of the words of Tertullian alluded to above, but this is as unsatisfactory as the rest.

As regards the *destination* of the epistle, we are equally in the dark. By ecclesiastical writers from the earliest time it is cited under the title *to the Hebrews*, a fact which is entitled to some weight. It is evidently addressed to a definite circle of readers, and that circle could hardly have been a mixed church of Jews and Gentiles, since it would have been impossible in that case for the letter to avoid allusions to the relations between the two, whereas it contains no allusion to Gentile Christians.

An hypothesis which has obtained considerable currency in modern criticism is, that the epistle was not addressed to Jewish Christians at all, but to Gentile Christians, as a warning against relapsing into heathenism, by showing them from the Old Testament the superiority of Christianity to Judaism.*

---

* So Pfleiderer, von Soden, Jülicher, Weizsäcker, McGiffert.

But this hypothesis presents formidable difficulties. This would seem to be a roundabout way of impressing Gentiles with the superior claims of Christianity. It would appear to have been the more natural course to institute a direct comparison between Christianity and paganism. See on ch. xiii. 7–15.

It is true that Gentile Christians were familiar with the Old Testament, and that Paul's epistles to Gentile readers contain frequent allusions to it ; and, further, that Clement of Rome, in his epistle to the Gentile church at Corinth, makes much use of the Epistle to the Hebrews, and cites freely from the Old Testament. But to illustrate one's thoughts and arguments by occasional references to the Old Testament is a very different thing from drawing out an elaborate argument on the basis of a contrast between a new and an older order, designed to show, not only that the new is superior to the old, but that the new is enfolded in the old and developed from it. To this there is no parallel in the New Testament in writings addressed to Gentiles. It would have been superfluous to prove, as this epistle does, that the old order did not satisfy. The Gentiles never supposed that it did.

Moreover, in almost every case of Paul's allusion to the Jewish institutions, the reference is called out by some feature of the Mosaic economy which lay directly in his track and compelled him to deal with it. Thus, in Romans, he is forced to discuss the doctrine of salvation by faith with reference to the Jewish doctrine of salvation by the works of the law. The Galatians had been tempted by Judaising emissaries to return to the law of circumcision. In Corinth, Paul's authority and teaching had been assailed by Jewish aggressors. In Philippians we have no allusion to the law until the writer comes to deal with "the dogs," "the evil workers," "the concision." In Colossians, Jewish ceremonialism is a distinct factor of the heresy which is attacked ; but nowhere in Paul's epistles is there a didactic development of a thesis from the point of view of the Old Testament economy collectively.

The same remarks will apply to the case of Clement of Rome.   In his Epistle to the Corinthians there are about twenty allusions to the Epistle to the Hebrews or quotations from it.   Two of these relate to the majesty of God; one to Christ as high priest; in two or three there is a mere imitation of the phraseology of Hebrews, and the most of the passages are practical exhortations to the cultivation of moral virtues, enforced by allusions to the Old Testament worthies. Any of these passages might have occurred in an address to either Jews or Gentiles.   They prove nothing as to the point in question.   If we did not know from other sources that Clement's epistle was addressed to a Gentile church, we could not infer that fact from these quotations and allusions. Moreover, Clement's fondness for the Old Testament and the Epistle to the Hebrews is easily explained, if, as there is very good reason for believing, Clement himself was of Jewish origin, a Hellenist.[*]

The whole argument of the Epistle to the Hebrews is *technically* Jewish, and not of a character to appeal to Gentile readers.   The argument, for example, for the superiority of Christ to the angels, would have much force addressed to Jews, since the doctrine of the communication of the Mosaic revelation through the ministration of angels was a familiar tradition.   Between the writer and Jewish readers there would be no question as to the angelic mediation of the Sinaitic legislation; but the point would have no interest and no pertinency for the average Gentile.   The Jew would readily apprehend that no theophany is a *direct* manifestation of God to the physical sense.   The Gentile mode of thought would be the other way.   The Jew would understand that angels were the administrators of the old covenant, and would instinctively catch the turn of the whole argument to the effect that with the exaltation of Christ the angelic sway of the old dispensation ceased.

The same thing might be said of the doctrine of the high-priesthood of Christ.   If this was a point to make with Gen-

---

[*] See Lightfoot's *Clement of Rome*, Vol. I., p. 59 ff.

tiles, it is strange that Paul nowhere alludes to it; and what did the Gentile care about Melchisedec or the relation of Christ's priesthood to his?

It is indeed true that, in the practical warnings of the epistle, nothing is directly said about apostasy to Judaism; but the admonitions are enforced by distinctively Jewish references, as, for example, the warning against failure to enter into God's rest, which is pointed by the example of the Israelites in failing to enter Canaan. Would a writer have said to a Gentile convert that, in case of his committing wilful sin, there was no expiation for him? But he might properly say to a Jewish Christian, who was tempted to return to Judaism: "If you abandon Christ, and return to Judaism, you have no more sacrifice for sins. Your whole system of Levitical sacrifices is abolished. It is Christ or nothing."

It is very strongly urged that the warning against departing from the living God (iii. 12) might very properly be given to Gentiles as against a relapse into heathenism, while it would be utterly inappropriate to a Jewish Christian, because the living God is common to both Jews and Christians; and a relapse into Judaism could not, therefore, be a departure from the living God. But the objection overlooks the intent of the whole epistle, which is to show that the living God of the Jewish economy has revealed himself in the Christian economy, thereby superseding the former. It is the God of the Christian dispensation who is commended to the readers; the living God under a new and grander manifestation of life. God who spake by the prophets, now speaks by his Son, the effulgence of his glory and the very image of his substance. To go back to the old economy of types and shadows, the economy of partial access to God, would be literally to depart from the living God. It would be, practically, to deny him as a living God, by denying all development and expansion in his revelation of his own life, and confining that revelation to the narrow limits of the Mosaic system; in other words, to identify the living God with the dead system. To depart from Christ, the Life, and to seek the God of the Old Testament revelation, would be to fall back from a living to a dead God.

Again, it is claimed that the words at the beginning of Chapter VI. could not be properly addressed to Jewish Christians: that only a heathen would need to lay such a foundation on his first acceptance of Christ. On the contrary, all the points here enumerated would have had to be expounded to a Jew on becoming a Christian. See notes on that passage.

A still more difficult question is the *local* destination of the epistle. By those who supposed it to be the work of Paul, attempts were made to place this destination within the circle of Paul's recorded missionary labours; and it was accordingly assigned to almost every place visited or supposed to have been visited by him, — Macedonia, Corinth, Antioch, Spain, etc.

A plausible hypothesis assigned its destination to Jewish Christians in Alexandria. This was based on the fact that the Muratorian Canon (170–210), while omitting Hebrews, notes an Epistle to the Alexandrians (*Ad Alexandrinos*). It was argued that, since the Canon contains a list both of Paul's genuine epistles and of those falsely ascribed to him, and since Hebrews is not mentioned, the Alexandrian epistle can mean only the Epistle to the Hebrews. It was further urged that Alexandria had, next to Jerusalem, the largest resident Jewish population in the world, and that at Leontopolis in Egypt was another temple, with the arrangements of which the notices in Hebrews corresponded more nearly than with those of the Jerusalem temple.* Moreover, the Alexandrian character of the phraseology of the epistle was supposed to point to Alexandrian readers.

But, (*a*) We have no positive history of the church in Egypt in apostolic times. (*b*) Although there are numerous notices of the epistle by early Alexandrian writers, there is no hint of its having been addressed to their own church. (*c*) In the Muratorian Canon the Epistle to the Alexandrians is distinctly stated to be a forgery in the name of Paul.

---

* This temple was founded B.C. 180–145 by Onias, one of the high-priestly family. The building was a deserted temple of Pasht, the cat-goddess. A description is given by Josephus *B. J.* vii. 10, 3; *Cont. Ap.* ii. 2.

(*d*) It cannot be shown that the temple at Leontopolis exercised the same power over the Alexandrian Jews as the temple
at Jerusalem did over the Palestinian Jews.   Even in Egypt
the Jerusalem temple was recognised as the true centre of
worship.   Moreover, the Christian church at Alexandria was
a mixed church.   (*e*) The furniture of the temple at Jerusalem was more like that of the tabernacle described in
Hebrews than that of the Egyptian temple.

A widely-accepted view is that the epistle was addressed
to Jewish Christians in Palestine and Jerusalem.   Unmixed
Jewish-Christian churches were to be found nowhere else; and
only there would there be likely to exist that attachment to the
old worship which is assumed in the epistle, while it treats
only incidentally of those rites to which, in the Dispersion,
the greatest importance was naturally assigned — ablutions,
etc.   The claim that the epistle was addressed to Rome
involves a mixed church.   The Roman church became more
Gentile after Paul's residence in Rome.   On the assumption
that Jewish Christians were addressed, it is difficult to account
for the Roman destination, unless the letter was intended for
a distinct circle of Jewish Christians in Rome, which is not
impossible.   That the epistle was used by Clement proves
nothing.   The phrase ἀσπάζονται ὑμᾶς οἱ ἀπὸ τῆς Ἰταλίας *they
from Italy salute you* might seem to point to Rome as the residence of the parties saluted; but that is by no means certain.
The meaning of the expression must first be settled.   It may
mean " those in Italy send greeting from Italy," or, " those
who are from Italy (whose home is there, but who are now
with me) send greeting to you (whoever may be addressed)."
The latter meaning is the more probable; but on that supposition the words afford no reliable indication of the residence
of those addressed.   They mean merely that certain Italians
in the writer's company greet the writer's correspondents,
who may have been in Palestine, Asia, or Egypt.*

---

* An able defence of the Roman hypothesis may be found in Réville, *Les
Origines de l'Épiscopat.*   While these sheets are going through the press,
I have received the first number of Preuschen's *Zeitschrift für die neutest.
Wissenschaft und die Kunde des Urchristenthums,* containing Harnack's

The Palestinian hypothesis is not free from difficulty. It appears, at first sight, unlikely that the author would have written in Greek to Palestinian Jewish Christians, whose language was Aramaic, and would have used the Septuagint exclusively in citations from the Old Testament. Nevertheless, Greek was understood and spoken in Palestine : many Greek-speaking Jews resided in Jerusalem (Acts vi. 9), and there were in that city synagogues of the Cyrenians and Alexandrians, in which Greek and the Septuagint would certainly be used. The Hellenists were numerous and influential enough to carry their point in the matter of ministration to their widows (Acts vi. 1 ff.). Finally, it is not impossible that the writer of the epistle was not sufficiently acquainted with Aramaic to write effectively in that language.

The decisive settlement of the date of the epistle is practically given up by critics. The most that can be done is to try and fix approximately the limits within which the composition was possible.* Only one point is definitely fixed. It must have been written before Clement's Epistle to the Corinthians (95). If addressed to Jewish Christians, or indeed to Gentiles, it is highly probable that it was written before the destruction of Jerusalem (70), since it is most unlikely that the writer would have omitted all allusion to an event which furnished such a striking confirmation of his teaching. This probability would be strengthened if it could be proved that the Jewish sacrifices were still being offered at the time when the epistle was composed: but this cannot be conclusively

---

ingenious paper, *Probabilia über die Adresse und den Verfasser des Hebräer-briefs.* He holds that the epistle was addressed to a Christian community — a house-church in Rome: that it was written by Aquila and Prisca, principally by the latter, and that, so far from being addressed especially to Hebrew Christians, it entirely ignores the difference between Hebrews and Gentiles.

* The results of even this attempt vary considerably. Bleek, 68–69: Lünemann, 65–67 : Riehm, 64–66 : Ebrard, end of 62 : De Wette, 63–67 : Tholuck and Wieseler, about 64 : Alford, 68–70 : Salmon, before 63 : Westcott, 64–67 : Jülicher, not before 70 : Weiss, near 67 : Harnack, 65–95 : McGiffert, 81–96. One of the fairest and ablest discussions is by Harnack, *Chronologie der altchristlichen Litteratur.* Jülicher's discussion, in his *Einleitung in das Neue Testament,* will also repay study.

shown. The use of the present tense in viii. 4 ff. ; ix. 6, 9 ;
x. 1 ff. ; xiii. 10 ff., is not decisive. Attempts to identify the
persecution alluded to in x. 2 are the merest guess-work. To
refer it to the Neronian persecution (64) is to assume that it
was addressed to Rome, and is, therefore, to beg the question.
The reference of x. 36 and xii. 3 to the persecution of Domitian
(95), is utterly without foundation, to say nothing of the
fact that it is not certain that those two passages refer to
persecution at all. Against a date near 95 is the use of the
epistle by Clement, unless the Roman address can be proved.
Otherwise, some time would be required for it to obtain
such currency and recognition as would account for Clement's
familiarity with it. Against a very late date is also the fact
that Timothy appears as an active evangelist, which could
hardly have been the case if the letter was written as late
as 90. Against a very early date is the admitted fact that a
second generation of Christians is addressed ; and that the
references to persecution apparently point to a comparatively
distant time. If we are to lay stress on the omission of all
reference to the destruction of Jerusalem, as I think we must
do, it seems to me that the epistle was written not far from 67.

There is no reason for disputing the author's acquaintance
with the writings of Paul, as there is none for asserting his
dependence upon them. There are lexical resemblances and
resemblances in thought and phrasing, but nothing to show
that the writer of Hebrews drew upon Paul to any considerable extent. The coincidences with Galatians which are
pointed out are superficial, and may be fairly traced to common Jewish ideas with which both writers were familiar. As
to Romans, Ephesians, and Corinthians, the resemblances are,
in a number of cases, due to quotation from the same source ;
in other cases they occur in warnings from the example of the
Israelites ; in others again there is a coincidence of a current
phrase, such as "if God permit," which any author might use.
In some other instances cited the resemblance is too remote
to be significant.

As to the influence of Philo, we may freely admit the evidences of the writer's Alexandrian training, and the possibility,

perhaps probability, of his acquaintance with Philo's writings.* The epistle does exhibit certain points of resemblance to Philo, such as similar forms of quotation, similar use of Old Testament passages and narratives, and statements like those of Philo, such as those respecting the sinlessness of the Logos-Priest, the heavenly home of the patriarchs, and the λόγος τομεύς *the dividing word* (iv. 12) : but Philo's meaning differs radically from that of the epistle.   Our writer's Christology has no affinity with that of Philo.   On certain leading topics, such as the two ages of the world, the mediation of the law by angels, the Sabbath-rest, the heavenly sanctuary, and the heavenly Jerusalem, he exhibits more affinity with Palestinian than with Alexandrian thought.   The most that can be claimed is that the Epistle to the Hebrews returns echoes of Philo, and exhibits formal and limited resemblances to him.†

---

* Although critics are not unanimous on this point. It is disputed by Tholuck, Riehm, and Wieseler, and Weiss is evidently inclined to agree with them.

† A valuable discussion of the subject is that of Riehm, *Lehrbegriff des Hebraerbriefs,* § 27.

LITERATURE.

There is a want of good commentaries in English. The principal ones are:

H. Alford, in his Greek Testament.

B. F. Westcott, *The Epistle to the Hebrews, Greek Text with Notes and Essays.*

A. B. Bruce, *The Epistle to the Hebrews.*

English Translations of Lünemann and Delitzsch.

F. Rendall, *The Epistle to the Hebrews.*

G. Milligan, *The Epistle to the Hebrews, with Critical Introduction.*

In German are:

Fried. Bleek, *Der Hebräerbrief erklärt.*

Fr. Delitzsch, *Kommentar zum Briefe an die Hebräer.*

A. Tholuck, *Kommentar zum Briefe an die Hebräer.*

H. A. Ebrard, *Kommentar über den Hebräerbrief.*

G. Lünemann, in the Meyer series.

W. M. L. De Wette, in *Kurzgefasstes exegetisches Handbuch zum Neuen Testament.*

B. Weiss, *Kritisch-exegetisch Handbuch über den Brief an die Hebräer.* Issued as an alternate of Lünemann in Meyer.

On the doctrinal aspects of the epistle:

Ed. Reuss, *L'Épitre aux Hébreux. Essai d'une Traduction Nouvelle, accompagné d'un Commentaire Théologique.*

Ed. K. A. Riehm, *Der Lehrbegriff des Hebräerberbriefes.*

Eug. Ménégoz, *La Théologie de l'Épitre aux Hébreux.*

There may also be noted:

K. Wieseler, *Untersuchung über den Hebräerbrief, namentlich seinen Verfasser und seine Leser.*

J. H. R. Biesenthal, *Epistola Pauli ad Hebraeos, cum Rabbinico Commentario.*

Theo. Zahn, *Einleitung in das Neue Testament, § 47.*

THE EPISTLE TO THE HEBREWS.

CHAPTER I.

THEME OF THE EPISTLE. — God has given a revelation of
salvation in two stages. The first was preparatory and transient, and is completed. The second, the revelation through
Jesus Christ, is final. The readers who have accepted this
second revelation are warned against returning to the economy of the first.

1. God. Both stages of the revelation were given by God.

At sundry times (πολυμερῶς). Rend. *in many parts.*
N. T.°. °LXX, but πολυμερής Wisd. vii. 22. In the first
stage of his revelation, God spake, not *at once*, giving a complete revelation of his being and will; but in many separate
revelations, each of which set forth only a portion of the truth.
The truth as a whole never comes to light in the O. T. It
appears fragmentarily, in successive acts, as the periods of
the Patriarchs, Moses, the Kingdom, etc. One prophet has
one, another another element of the truth to proclaim.

In divers manners (πολυτρόπως). Rend. *in many ways.*
N. T.°. LXX, 4 Macc. iii. 21. This refers to the difference
of the various revelations in contents and form. Not the different ways in which God imparted his revelations to the
prophets, but the different ways in which he spoke by the
prophets to the fathers: in one way through Moses, in another
through Elijah, in others through Isaiah, Ezekiel, etc. At
the founding of the Old Testament kingdom of God, the

character of the revelation was elementary : later it was of
a character to appeal to a more matured spiritual sense, a
deeper understanding and a higher conception of the law.
The revelation differed according to the faithfulness or
unfaithfulness of the covenant-people.   Comp. Eph. iii. 10,
the many-tinted wisdom of God, which is associated with this
passage by Clement of Alexandria (*Strom.* i. 4, 27).   " Fitly,
therefore, did the apostle call the wisdom of God *many-
tinted*, as showing its power to benefit us *in many parts* and
in many ways."

Spake (λαλήσας).   See on Matt. xxviii. 18.   Often in the
Epistle of the announcement of the divine will by *men*, as
vii. 14 ; ix. 19 : by *angels*, as ii. 2 : by *God himself* or *Christ*,
as ii. 3 ; v. 5 ; xii. 25.   In Paul, almost always of men : once
of Christ, 2 Cor. xiii. 3 : once of the Law, personified, Rom.
iii. 9.

In time past (πάλαι).   Better, *of old*.   The time of the
Old Testament revelation.   It indicates a revelation, not
only given, but completed in the past.

Unto the fathers (τοῖς πατράσιν).   Thus absolutely,
J. vii. 22 ; Rom. ix. 5 ; xv. 8.   More commonly with *your*
or *our*.

By the prophets (ἐν τοῖς προφήταις).   Rend. "*in* the
prophets," which does not mean *in the collection of prophetic
writings*, as J. vi. 45 ; Acts xiii. 40, but rather *in the prophets
themselves* as the vessels of divine inspiration.   God spake *in*
them and *from* them.   Thus Philo : "The prophet is an inter-
preter, echoing *from within* (ἔνδοθεν) the sayings of God"
(*De Praemiis et Poenis*, § 9)

2. **In these last times** (ἐπ' ἐσχάτου τῶν ἡμερῶν τούτων).
Lit. *at the last of these days*.   The exact phrase only here ;
but comp. 1 Pet. v. 20 and Jude 18.   LXX, ἐπ' ἐσχάτου τῶν
ἡμερῶν *at the last of the days*, Num. xxiv. 14 ; Deut. iv. 30 ;

Jer. xxiii. 20; xxv. 18; Dan. x. 14.   The writer conceives the history of the world in its relation to divine revelation as falling into two great periods.   The first he calls αἱ ἡμέραι αὗται *these days* (i. 2), and ὁ καιρὸς ὁ ἐνεστηκώς *the present season* (ix. 9).   The second he describes as καιρὸς διορθώσεως *the season of reformation* (ix. 10), which is ὁ καιρὸς ὁ μέλλων *the season to come:* comp. ἡ οἰκουμένη ἡ μέλλουσα *the world to come* (ii. 5); μέλλων αἰών *the age to come* (vi. 5); πόλις ἡ μέλλουσα *the city to come* (xii. 14).   The first period is the period of the old covenant; the second that of the new covenant.   The second period does not begin with Christ's first appearing.   His appearing and public ministry are at the end of the first period but still within it.   The dividing-point between the two periods is the συντέλεια τοῦ αἰῶνος *the consummation of the age,* mentioned in ix. 26.   This does not mean the same thing as *at the last of these days* (i. 2), which is the end of the first period denoted by *these days,* but the conclusion of the first and the beginning of the second period, at which Christ appeared to put away sin by the sacrifice of himself.   This is the end of the καιρὸς ἐνεστηκώς *the present season:* this is the limit of the validity of the old sacrificial offerings : this is the inauguration of the *time of reformation.* The phrase ἐπ' ἐσχάτου τῶν ἡμερῶν τούτων therefore signifies, in the last days of the first period, when Christ was speaking on earth, and before his crucifixion, which marked the beginning of the second period, the better age of the new covenant.

Hath spoken unto us (ἐλάλησεν ἡμῖν).   Rend. *spake,* referring to the time of Christ's teaching in the flesh.   *To us* God spake as to the fathers of old.

By his son (ἐν υἱῷ).   Lit. *in a son.*   Note the absence of the article.   Attention is directed, not to Christ's divine personality, but to his filial relation.   While the former revelation was given through a definite class, *the* prophets, the new revelation is given through one who is a son as distinguished from a prophet.   He belongs to another category.   The revelation was a *son-revelation.*   See ch. ii. 10–18.   Christ's high

priesthood is the central fact of the epistle, and his sonship
is bound up with his priesthood. See ch. v. 5. For a similar use of υἱός *son*, without the article, applied to Christ, see
ch. iii. 6; v. 8; vii. 28.

Whom he hath appointed heir of all things (ὃν ἔθηκεν
κληρονόμον πάντων). For ἔθηκεν *appointed*, see on J. xv. 16.
For κληρονόμος *heir*, see on *inheritance*, 1 Pet. i. 4; and comp.
on Christ as heir, Mk. xii. 1–12. God eternally predestined
the Son to be the possessor and sovereign of all things.
Comp. Ps. lxxxix. 28. Heirship goes with sonship. See
Rom. viii. 17; Gal. iv. 7. Christ *attained* the messianic
lordship through incarnation. Something was *acquired* as
the result of his incarnation which he did not possess before
it, and could not have possessed without it. Equality with
God was his birthright; but out of his human life, death,
and resurrection came a type of sovereignty which could pertain to him only through his triumph over human sin in the
flesh (see ver. 3), through his identification with men as their
brother. Messianic lordship could not pertain to his preincarnate state: it is a matter of function, not of inherent power
and majesty. He was *essentially* Son of God; he must *become*
Son of man.

By whom also he made the worlds (δι᾽ οὗ καὶ ἐποίησεν
τοὺς αἰῶνας). Διὰ commonly expresses secondary agency;
but, in some instances, it is used of God's direct agency. See
1 Cor. i. 1; 2 Cor. i. 1; Gal. iv. 7. Christ is here represented as a mediate agency in creation. The phrase is, clearly,
coloured by the Alexandrian conception, but differs from it in
that Christ is not represented as a mere instrument, a passive
tool, but rather as a coöperating agent. "Every being, to
reach existence, must have passed through the thought and
will of the Logos" (Godet); yet "the Son can do nothing
of himself but what he seeth the Father doing" (J. v. 19).
With this passage Col. i. 16 should be studied. There it is
said that all things, collectively (τὰ πάντα), were created *in*
him (ἐν αὐτῷ) and *through* him (δι᾽ αὐτοῦ as here). The

former expression enlarges and completes the latter. Δι’
αὐτοῦ represents Christ as the mediate instrument. Ἐν
αὐτῷ indicates that "all the laws and purposes which guide
the creation and government of the universe reside in him,
the Eternal Word, as their meeting-point."* Comp. J. i. 3 ;
1 Cor. viii. 6. For τοὺς αἰῶνας *the worlds*, see additional note
on 2 Th. i. 9. Rend. for *by whom also he made*, *by whom
he also made*. The emphasis is on *made*, not on *worlds :* on
the fact of creation, not on *what was created*. In the writer's
thought heirship goes with creation. Christ is heir of what
he made, and because he made it. As πάντων, in the preceding clause, regards all things taken singly, αἰῶνας regards
them in cycles. Ἀιῶνας does not mean *times*, as if representing the Son as the creator of all time and times, but creation
unfolded in time through successive aeons. All that, in successive periods of time, has come to pass, has come to pass
through him. Comp. 1 Cor. x. 11 ; Eph. iii. 21 ; Heb. ix. 26 ;
1 Tim. i. 17 ; LXX, Tob. xiii. 6, 10 ; Eccl. iii. 11. See also
Clement of Rome, *Ad Corinth.* xxxv, ὁ δημιουργὸς καὶ πατὴρ
τῶν αἰώνων *the Creator and Father of the ages*. Besides this
expression, the writer speaks of the world as κόσμος (iv. 3 ;
x. 5) ; ἡ οἰκουμένη (i. 6), and τὰ πάντα (i. 3).

3. **Being** (ὤν). Representing *absolute* being. See on J. i. 1.
Christ's absolute being is exhibited in two aspects, which
follow :

The brightness of his glory (ἀπαύγασμα τῆς δόξης αὐτοῦ).
Of *God's* glory. For *brightness* rend. *effulgence*. Ἀπαύγασμα,
N.T.⁰. LXX, only Wisd. vii. 26. ⁰Class. It is an Alexandrian word, and occurs in Philo.† Interpretation is divided
between *effulgence* and *reflection*. ‡ *Effulgence* or *outraying*

---

* Lightfoot, on Col. i. 16.
† See *De Concupisc.* xi : *De Opif. Mund.* § li : *De Plant. No.* § xii.
‡ *Effulgence* is the rendering of the Greek fathers and of the majority of
modern interpreters. The few instances of the word elsewhere give little
help toward a decision, since in most if not all of them the meaning is disputed. The reader will do well to consult Theodoret on this passage ;
Athanasius, *Contra Arianos*, Orat. ii ; Origen on John xxxii. 18, and *Hom.*

accords better with the thought of the passage ; for the writer
is treating of the *preincarnate* Son ; and, as Alford justly
remarks, "the Son of God is, in this his essential majesty, the
expression and the sole expression of the divine light ; not, as
in his incarnation, its *reflection.*" The consensus of the Greek
fathers to this effect is of great weight. The meaning then
is, that the Son is the *outraying* of the divine glory, exhibiting in himself the glory and majesty of the divine Being.
"God lets his glory issue from himself, so that there arises
thereby a *light-being* like himself" (Weiss). Δόξα *glory* is
the expression of the divine attributes collectively. It is the
unfolded fulness of the divine perfections, differing from
μορφὴ θεοῦ *form of God* (Philip. ii. 6), in that μορφὴ is the
immediate, proper, personal investiture of the divine essence.
Δόξα *is attached* to deity : μορφὴ is identified with the inmost
being of deity. Δόξα is used of various visible displays of
divine light and splendour, as Exod. xxiv. 17 ; Deut. v. 24 ;
Exod. xl. 34 ; Num. xiv. 10 ; xv. 19, 42 ; Ezek. x. 4 ; xliii.
4, 5 ; i. 28 ; iii. 23 ; Lev. ix. 23, etc. We come nearer to
the sense of the word in this passage in the story of Moses's
vision of the divine glory, Exod. xxxiii. 18–23 ; xxxiv. 5, 7.

The express image of his person (χαρακτὴρ τῆς ὑποστάσεως αὐτοῦ). Rend. *the very image* (or *impress*) *of his substance.* The primary sense of ὑπόστασις *substance* is *something
which stands underneath ; foundation, ground of hope* or *confidence,* and so, *assurance* itself. In a philosophical sense, *substantial nature ;* the real nature of anything which underlies
and supports its outward form and properties. In N. T.,
2 Cor. ix. 4 ; xi. 17 ; Heb. iii. 14 ; xi. 1, signifying in every
instance *ground of confidence* or *confidence.* In LXX, it represents fifteen different words, and, in some cases, it is hard
to understand its meaning, notably 1 Sam. xiii. 21. In Ruth
i. 12 ; Ps. xxxvii. 8 ; Ezek. xix. 5, it means *ground of hope :*
in Judg. vi. 4 ; Wisd. xvi. 21, *sustenance :* in Ps. xxxviii. 5 ;

---

on *Jer.* ix. 4 ; Chrysostom, *Hom.* ii. 2. See also Riehm, *Lehrbegriff des
Hebräerbriefes,* 278, 300, 408, 412.

cxxxviii. 15, *the substance or material of the human frame:* in
1 Sam. xiii. 23; Ezek. xxvi. 11, *an outpost* or *garrison:* in
Deut. xi. 6; Job xxii. 20, *possessions.* The theological sense,
person, is later than the apostolic age. Here, *substantial
nature, essence.* Χαρακτὴρ from χαράσσειν *to engrave* or
inscribe, originally *a graving-tool;* also the *die* on which a
device is cut. It seems to have lost that meaning, and always
signifies *the impression* made by the die or graver. Hence,
mark, stamp, as the image on a coin (so often) which indicates
its nature and value, or the device impressed by a signet.
N. T.°. LXX, Lev. xiii. 28; 2 Macc. iv. 10; 4 Macc. xv. 4.
The kindred χάραγμα *mark,* Acts xvii. 29; Apoc. xiii. 16, 17.
Here the essential being of God is conceived as setting its
distinctive stamp upon Christ, coming into definite and characteristic expression in his person, so that the Son bears the
exact impress of the divine nature and character.

And upholding all things (φέρων τε τὰ πάντα). Rend.
maintaining. *Upholding* conveys too much the idea of the
passive support of a burden. "The Son is not an Atlas, sustaining the dead weight of the world" (quoted by Westcott).
Neither is the sense that of *ruling* or *guiding,* as Philo (*De
Cherub.* § xi), who describes the divine word as "the steers-
man and pilot of the all." It implies *sustaining,* but also
movement. It deals with a burden, not as a dead weight, but
as in continual movement; as Weiss puts it, "with the all in
all its changes and transformations throughout the aeons."
It is concerned, not only with sustaining the weight of the
universe, but also with maintaining its coherence and carrying on its development. What is said of God, Col. i. 17, is
here said or implied of Christ: τὰ πάντα ἐν αὐτῷ συνέστηκεν
all things (collectively, the universe) *consist* or *maintain their
coherence in him.* So the Logos is called by Philo *the bond*
(δεσμὸς) *of the universe;* but the maintenance of the coherence
implies the guidance and propulsion of all the parts to a
definite end. *All things* (τὰ πάντα) collectively considered;
the universe; all things in their unity. See ch. ii. 10; Rom.
viii. 32; xi. 36; 1 Cor. viii. 6; Eph. i. 10; Col. i. 16.

By the word of his power (τῷ ῥήματι τῆς δυνάμεως αὐτοῦ)..
The phrase N. T.°., but comp. L. i. 37, and see note. *The
word* is that in which the Son's power manifests itself. 'Αυτοῦ
his refers to Christ. Nothing in the context suggests any
other reference. The world was called into being by the
word of God (ch. xi. 3), and is maintained by him who is
"the very image of God's substance."

When he had by himself purged our sins (καθαρισμὸν
τῶν ἁμαρτιῶν ποιησάμενος). Omit *by himself;* * yet a similar
thought is implied in the middle voice, ποιησάμενος, which
indicates that the work of purification was done by Christ
personally, and was not something which he *caused to be done*
by some other agent. *Purged*, lit. *having made purification.*
The phrase N. T.°. LXX, Job vii. 21. Καθαρισμός *purification* occurs in Mark, Luke, John, 2d Peter, °P., and only here
in Hebrews. The verb καθαρίζειν *to purify* is not often used
in N. T. of cleansing from *sin.* See 2 Cor. vii. 1 ; 1 J. i. 7, 9.
Of cleansing *the conscience*, Heb. ix. 14. Of cleansing
meats and *vessels*, Matt. xxiii. 25, 26 ; Mk. vii. 19 ; Acts x. 15 ;
xi. 9. Of cleansing *the heart*, Acts xv. 9. The meaning
here is cleansing *of* sins. In the phrase " to cleanse *from*
sin," always with ἀπὸ *from.* In carrying on all things toward
their destined end of conformity to the divine archetype, the
Son must confront and deal with the fact of sin, which had
thrown the world into disorder, and drawn it out of God's
order. In the thought of making purification of sins is
already foreshadowed the work of Christ as high priest,
which plays so prominent a part in the epistle.

Sat down on the right hand of the majesty on high (ἐκάθισεν ἐν δεξιᾷ τῆς μεγαλωσύνης ἐν ὑψηλοῖς). Comp. Ps. cx. 1 ;
ch. viii. 1 ; x. 12 ; xii. 2 ; Eph. i. 20 ; Apoc. iii. 21. The
verb denotes a *solemn, formal* act ; the assumption of a position of dignity and authority. The reference is to Christ's
ascension. In his exalted state he will still be bearing on all

---

* The A. V. follows the T. R. δι' ἑαυτοῦ, which is a gloss.

things toward their consummation, still dealing with sin as the great high priest in the heavenly sanctuary. This is elaborated later. See ch. viii; ix. 12 ff. Μεγαλωσύνη *majesty*, only here, ch. viii. 1; Jude 25. Quite often in LXX. There is suggested, not a contrast with his humiliation, but his resumption of his original dignity, described in the former part of this verse. 'Εν ὑψηλοῖς, lit. *in the high places.* Const. with *sat down*, not with *majesty.* The phrase N. T.⁰. LXX, Ps. xcii. 4; cxii. 5. 'Εν τοῖς ὑψίστοις *in the highest* (*places*), in the Gospels, and only in doxologies. See Matt. xxi. 9; Mk. xi. 10; L. ii. 14. 'Εν τοῖς ἐπουρανίοις *in the heavenly* (*places*), only in Eph. See i. 3, 20; ii. 6; iii. 10; vi. 12.

4. The detailed development of the argument is now introduced. The point is to show the superiority of the agent of the new dispensation to the agents of the old—the angels and Moses. Christ's superiority to the angels is first discussed.

Being made so much better than the angels (τοσούτῳ κρείττων γενόμενος τῶν ἀγγέλων). The informal and abrupt introduction of this topic goes to show that the writer was addressing Jewish Christians, who were familiar with the prominent part ascribed to angels in the O. T. economy, especially in the giving of the law. See on Gal. iii. 9. For *being made*, rend. *having become;* which is to be taken in close connection with *sat down*, etc., and in contrast with ὢν *being*, ver. 3. It is not denied that the Son was essentially and eternally superior to the angels; but his glorification was conditioned upon his fulfilment of the requirements of his human state, and it is this that is emphasised. After having passed through the experience described in Philip. ii. 6–8, he sat down on the right hand of the divine majesty as *messianic* sovereign, and so *became* or *proved to be* what in reality he was from eternity, superior to the angels. Τοσούτῳ—ὅσῳ *so much—as.* Never used by Paul. Κρείττων *better, superior*, rare in Paul, and always neuter and adverbial. In Hebrews thirteen times. See also 1 Pet. iii. 17; 2 Pet. ii. 21. Often

in LXX. It does not indicate here *moral excellence*, but *dignity* and *power*. He *became* superior to the angels, resuming
his preincarnate dignity, as he had been, for a brief period,
less or lower than the angels (ch. ii. 7). The superiority of
Messiah to the angels was affirmed in rabbinical writings.

He hath by inheritance obtained (κεκληρονόμηκεν). More
neatly, as Rev., *hath inherited*, as a son. See ver. 2, and comp.
Rom. viii. 17. For the verb, see on Acts xiii. 19, and 1 Pet. i. 4.

More excellent (διαφορώτερον). Διάφορος only once outside of Hebrews, Rom. xii. 6. The comparative only in
Hebrews. In the sense of *more excellent*, only in later writers.
Its earlier sense is *different*. The idea of *difference* is that
which radically distinguishes it from κρείττων *better*. Here
it presents the comparative of a comparative conception.
The Son's name differs from that of the angels, and is *more
different* for good.

Than they (παρ' αὐτούς). Lit. *beside* or *in comparison with
them*. Παρά, indicating comparison, occurs a few times in
Luke, as iii. 13; xiii. 2; xviii. 4. In Hebrews always to
mark comparison, except xi. 11, 12.

5. The writer proceeds to establish the superiority of the
Son to the angels by O. T. testimony. It is a mode of argument which does not appeal strongly to us. Dr. Bruce
suggests that there are evidences that the writer himself
developed it perfunctorily and without much interest in it.
The seven following quotations are intended to show the surpassing excellence of Christ's name as set forth in Scripture.
The quotations present difficulty in that they appear, in great
part, to be used in a sense and with an application different
from those which they originally had. All that can be said
is, that the writer takes these passages as messianic, and
applies them accordingly; and that we must distinguish
between the doctrine and the method of argumentation peculiar to the time and people. Certain passages in Paul are
open to the same objection, as Gal. iii. 16; iv. 22–25.

To which (τίνι). Note the author's characteristic use of the question to express denial. Comp. ver. 14; ii. 3; iii. 17; vii. 11; xii. 7.

First quotation from Ps. ii. 7. The Psalm is addressed as a congratulatory ode to a king of Judah, declaring his coming triumph over the surrounding nations, and calling on them to render homage to the God of Israel. The king is called *Son of Jahveh*, and is said to be "begotten" on the day on which he is publicly recognised as king. Words of the same Psalm are quoted Acts iv. 25, and these words Acts xiii. 33.

Thou art my Son. Note the emphatic position of υἱός *son*. See on ver. 4. In the O. T. *son* is applied to angels *collectively*, but never *individually*. See Ps. xxix. 1; lxxxix. 6. Similarly, *son* is applied to the chosen nation, Ex. iv. 22; Hos. xi. 1, but to no individual of the nation.

Have I begotten (γεγέννηκα). Recognised thee publicly as sovereign; established thee in an *official* sonship-relation. This official installation appears to have its N. T. counterpart in the resurrection of Christ. In Acts xiii. 33, this is distinctly asserted; and in Rom. i. 4, Paul says that Christ was "powerfully declared" to be the Son of God by the resurrection from the dead. Comp. Col. i. 18; Apoc. i. 5.*

Second quotation, 2 Sam. vii. 14. The reference is to Solomon. David proposes to build a temple. Nathan tells him that this shall be done by Solomon, whom Jahveh will adopt as his son. In 2 Cor. vi. 18, Paul applies the passage to followers of the Messiah, understanding the original as referring to all the spiritual children of David.

---

* Opinions differ as to the sense in which this expression is applied to the Messiah. Origen, Athanasius, Lünemann, Alford, Bleek, *the eternal generation of the Son :* Chrysostom, Theodoret, Eusebius, Gregory of Nyssa, *the generation of the Son in time :* De Wette, *the manifestation of Jesus to men as the Son of God :* von Soden, *the establishment of the Son as heir in the world to come.* The reference to the resurrection is held by Delitzsch, Westcott, Weiss, Calvin. According to these different explanations, σήμερον *to-day* will signify *eternity*, the time of *the incarnation*, the time of *the first prophetic announcement of Christ as Son*, the time of *the ascension.*

A father — a son (εἰς πατέρα — εἰς υἱόν).   Lit. *for* or *as a father — son.*   This usage of εἰς mostly in O. T. citations or established formulas.   See Matt. xix. 5; L. ii. 34; Acts xix. 27; 1 Cor. iv. 3.

6. Third quotation, marking the relation of angels to the Son.

And again, when he bringeth in, etc. (ὅταν δὲ πάλιν εἰσαγάγῃ).   Const. *again* with *bringeth in.*   "When he *a second time bringeth* the first-begotten into the world."   Referring to the second coming of Christ.   Others explain *again* as introducing a new citation as in ver. 5; but this would require the reading πάλιν δὲ ὅταν *and again, when.*   In Hebrews, πάλιν, when joined to a verb, always means *a second time.*   See v. 12; vi. 1, 2.   It will be observed that in this verse, and in vv. 7, 8, God is conceived as *spoken of* rather than as *speaking;* the subject of λέγει *saith* being indefinite.   This mode of introducing citations differs from that of Paul.   The author's conception of the inspiration of Scripture leads him to regard all utterances of Scripture, without regard to their connection, as distinct utterances of God, or the Holy Spirit, or the Son of God; whereas, by Paul, they are designated either as utterances of Scripture in general, or of individual writers.   Very common in this Epistle are the expressions, "God *saith, said, spake, testifieth,*" or the like.   See ch. ii. 11, 13; iii. 7; iv. 4, 7; vii. 21; x. 5, 8, 15, 30.   Comp. with these Rom. i. 17; ii. 24; iv. 17; vii. 7; ix. 13; x. 5, 16, 20, 21; xi. 2.   Ὅταν εἰσαγάγῃ *whenever he shall have brought.*   The event is conceived as occurring at an indefinite time in the future, but is viewed as complete.   Comp. J. xvi. 4; Acts xxiv. 22.   This use of ὅταν with the aorist subjunctive never describes an event or series of events as completed in the past.

The first-begotten (τὸν πρωτότοκον).   Mostly in Paul and Hebrews.   Comp. Rom. viii. 29; Col. i. 15, 18; Apoc. i. 5.   Μονογενής *only-begotten* (J. i. 14, 18; iii. 16, 18; 1 J. iv. 9, never by Paul) describes the unique relation of the Son to the Father in his divine nature: πρωτότοκος *first-begotten* describes the relation of the risen Christ in his glorified humanity to man. The comparison implied in the word is not limited to angels. He is the first-born in relation to the creation, the dead, the new manhood, etc. See Col. i. 15, 18. The rabbinical writers applied the title *first-born* even to God. Philo (*De Confus. Ling.* § 14) speaks of the Logos as πρωτόγονος or πρεσβύτατος υἱός *the first-born* or *eldest son.*

And let all the angels of God worship him (καὶ προσκυνησάτωσαν αὐτῷ πάντες ἄγγελοι θεοῦ). Προσκυνεῖν *to worship* mostly in the Gospels, Acts, and Apocrypha. In Paul only 1 Cor. xiv. 25. Very often in LXX. Originally, *to kiss the hand to:* thence, *to do homage to.* Not necessarily of an act of *religious* reverence (see Matt. ix. 18; xx. 20), but often in N. T. in that sense. Usually translated *worship,* whether a religious sense is intended or not: see on Acts x. 25. The quotation is not found in the Hebrew of the O. T., but is cited literally from LXX, Deut. xxxii. 43. It appears substantially in Ps. xcvi. 7. For the writer of Hebrews the LXX was Scripture, and is quoted throughout without regard to its correspondence with the Hebrew.

7. Fourth quotation, Ps. ciii. 4, varies slightly from LXX in substituting *a flame of fire* for *flaming fire.*

Who maketh his angels spirits (ὁ ποιῶν τοὺς ἀγγέλους αὐτοῦ πνεύματα). For *spirits* rend. *winds.** This meaning is supported by the context of the Psalm, and by J. iii. 8. Πνεῦμα often in this sense in Class. In LXX, 1 K. xviii. 45; xix. 11; 2 K. iii. 17; Job i. 19. Of *breath* in N. T., 2 Th. ii. 8; Apoc. xi. 11. In Hebrew, *spirit* and *wind* are synonymous. The thought is according to the rabbinical idea of

---

* Bleek, Ebrard, Lünemann, Toy, rend. "who maketh winds his messengers and flames of fire his servants." This is defended on the ground of the previous "who maketh clouds his chariots." But in the Hebrew the order of our passage is transposed; and according to this rendering there would be no allusion to angels.

the variableness of the angelic nature. Angels were supposed to live only as they ministered. Thus it was said:
"God does with his angels whatever he will. When he
wishes he makes them sitting : sometimes he makes them
standing : sometimes he makes them winds, sometimes fire."
"The subjection of the angels is such that they must submit
even to be changed into elements."   "The angel said to
Manoah, 'I know not to the image of what I am made; for
God changes us each hour: wherefore then dost thou ask
my name? Sometimes he makes us fire, sometimes wind.'"
The emphasis, therefore, is not on the fact that the angels
are merely servants, but that their being is such that they
are only what God makes them according to the needs of
their service, and are, therefore, changeable, in contrast with
the Son, who is ruler and unchangeable. There would be
no pertinency in the statement that God makes his angels
spirits, which goes without saying. The Rabbis conceived
the angels as perishable. One of them is cited as saying,
"Day by day the angels of service are created out of the fire-
stream, and sing a song, and disappear, as is said in Lam. iii.
23, 'they are new every morning.'" For λειτουργοὺς *ministers*,
see on *ministration*, L. i. 23, and *ministered*, Acts xiii. 2.

8. Fifth quotation, Ps. xlv. 7, 8. A nuptial ode addressed
to an Israelitish king. The general sense is that the Messiah's
kingdom is eternal and righteously administered.

Thy throne, O God (ὁ θρόνος σου ὁ θεὸς). I retain the
vocative, although the translation of the Hebrew is doubtful.
The following renderings have been proposed : "thy throne
(which is a throne) of God": "thy throne is (a throne) of
God": "God is thy throne." Some suspect that the Hebrew
text is defective.

Forever and ever (εἰς τὸν αἰῶνα τοῦ αἰῶνος). Lit. *unto the
aeon of the aeon.** See additional note on 2 Th. i. 9.

* This is the reading of the LXX, and is followed by Tischendorf and
Weiss. Westcott and Hort bracket τοῦ αἰῶνος.

A sceptre of righteousness (ἡ ῥάβδος τῆς εὐθύτητος)
Rend. *the* sceptre. The phrase N. T.⁰. ⁰LXX. Ἐυθύτης,
lit. *straightness*, N. T.⁰. It occurs in LXX.

9. Iniquity (ἀνομίαν). Lit. *lawlessness*.

Hath anointed (ἔχρισεν). See on *Christ*, Matt. **i. 1.** The
ideas of the royal and the festive unction are combined.
The thought includes the royal anointing and the fulness
of blessing and festivity which attend the enthronement.

Oil of gladness (ἔλαιον ἀγαλλιάσεως). The phrase N.T.⁰.
⁰LXX. Ἀγαλλίασις *exultant* joy. Comp. L. i. 44 ; Acts
ii. 46, and the verb ἀγαλλιᾶσθαι, Matt. v. 12 ; L. x. 21, etc.
The noun only here in Hebrews, and the verb does not occur.

Fellows (μετόχους). With exception of L. v. 7, only in
Hebrews. Lit. *partakers*. In the Psalm it is applied to
other kings : here to angels.

10. Sixth quotation (10–12), exhibiting the superior dignity of the Son as creator in contrast with the creature.
Ps. ci. 26–28. The Psalm declares the eternity of Jahveh.

And — in the beginning (καὶ — κατ' ἀρχάς). *And* connects
what follows with *unto the Son he saith*, etc., ver. 8. Κατ'
ἀρχὰς *in the beginning*, N. T.⁰. Often in Class., LXX only
Ps. cxviii. 152. The more usual formula is ἐν ἀρχῇ or ἀπ'
ἀρχῆς.

Hast laid the foundation (ἐθεμελίωσας). Only here in
Hebrews. In Paul, Eph. iii. 18 ; Col. i. 23.

11. They (αὐτοί). The heavens : not heaven and earth.

Remainest (διαμένεις). Note the present tense : *not shalt
remain*. Permanency is the characteristic of God in the
absolute and eternal present.

12. Vesture (περιβόλαιον). Only here and 1 Cor. xi. 5. From περιβάλλειν to throw around : a wrapper, mantle.

Shalt thou fold them up (ἐλίξεις αὐτούς). Rather, roll them up. A scribal error for ἀλλάξεις shalt change. After these words the LXX repeats ὡς ἱμάτιον as a garment from ver. 11.

Shall not fail (οὐκ ἐκλείψουσιν). Shall not be ended. With this exception the verb only in Luke's Gospel. See L. xvi. 9; xxii. 32; xxiii. 45. Very frequent in LXX.

13. Seventh quotation, Ps. cix. No one of the angels was ever enthroned at God's right hand.

Sit (κάθου). Or be sitting, as distinguished from ἐκάθισεν, ver. 3, which marked the act of assuming the place.

On my right hand (ἐκ δεξιῶν μοῦ). Lit. "from my right hand." The usual formula is ἐν δεξίᾳ. The genitive indicates moving from the right hand and taking the seat. The meaning is, "be associated with me in my royal dignity." Comp. Dan. vii. 13, 14, and the combination of the Psalm and Daniel in Christ's words, Mk. xiv. 62. Comp. also Matt. xxiv. 30; Acts ii. 34; 1 Cor. xv 25; 1 Pet. iii. 22.

14. Ministering spirits (λειτουργικὰ πνεύματα). Summing up the function of the angels as compared with Christ. Christ's is the highest dignity. He is co-ruler with God. The angels are servants, appointed for service to God for the sake of (διὰ) the heirs of redemption. Λειτουργικὰ ministering, N. T.°. See on ministers, ver. 7.

CHAPTER II.

The opening words of this chapter illustrate the writer's habit of introducing his practical exhortations into the body of his argument, unlike Paul, who defers them until the end. Comp. ch. iii. 7–19; v. 11.

1. Therefore (διὰ τοῦτο). Because you have received a revelation superior to that of the old dispensation, and given to you through one who is superior to the angels.

To give the more earnest heed (περισσοτέρως προσέχειν). Lit. *to give heed more abundantly.* Προσέχειν *to give heed,* lit. *to hold (the mind) to.* ᵒP. The full phrase in Job vii. 17. Mostly in Luke, Acts, and the Pastorals. See on 1 Tim. i. 4. Περισσοτέρως *more abundantly,* in Hebrews only here and xiii. 19 : elsewhere only in Paul.

To the things which we have heard (τοῖς ἀκουσθεῖσιν). Lit. *to the things which were heard,* that is, from the messengers of the gospel. Comp. the phrase ὁ λόγος τῆς ἀκοῆς *the word of hearing,* ch. iv. 2 ; 1 Th. ii. 13. 'Ευαγγέλιον *gospel* does not occur in the Epistle, and εὐαγγελίζεσθαι *to proclaim good tidings,* only twice.

We should let them slip (παραρυῶμεν). Rend. *should drift past them.* N. T.ᵒ. From παρὰ *by* and ῥεῖν *to flow.* Of the snow slipping off from the soldiers' bodies, Xen. *Anab.* iv. 4, 11 : of a ring slipping from the finger, Plut. *Amat.* 754 : see also LXX, Prov. iii. 21, and Symmachus's rendering of Prov. iv. 21, "let not my words *flow past* (παραρρυησάτωσαν) before thine eyes." The idea is in sharp contrast with *giving earnest heed.* Lapse from truth and goodness is more often the result of inattention than of design. Drifting is a mark of death : giving heed, of life. The log drifts with the tide : the ship breasts the adverse waves, because some one is giving earnest heed.

2. The word spoken by angels (ὁ δι' ἀγγέλων λαληθεὶς λόγος). The Mosaic legislation which was conveyed through the mediation of angels. Comp. Deut. xxxiii. 2 ; Acts vii. 38, 53 ; Gal. iii. 19, on which see note. The agency of angels indicates the limitations of the legal dispensation; its character as a dispensation of the flesh. Hence its importance in this discussion. The abolition of the old limitations is the

emancipation of man from subordination to the angels. The
O. T. is made to furnish proof that such subordination is
inconsistent with man's ultimate destiny to sovereignty over
all creation.

Was steadfast (ἐγένετο βέβαιος). Rend. *proved sure:*
realised itself in the event as securely founded in the divine
holiness, and eternal in its principles and obligations. Comp.
Matt. v. 18.

Transgression and disobedience (παράβασις καὶ παρακοή).
Παράβασις is *a stepping over the line;* the violation of a positive divine enactment. See on Rom. ii. 23. Παρακοή, only
in Paul and Hebrews, is a disobedience which results from
neglecting to *hear;* from letting things *drift by.* It is noticeable how often in O.T. obedience is described as hearing, and
disobedience as refusing to hear. See Ex. xv. 26; xix. 5, 8;
xxiii. 22; Josh. i. 18; Isa. xxviii. 12; xxx. 9; Jer. xi. 10;
xxxii. 23; xxxv. 16. Comp. Acts vii. 57.

A just recompense of reward (ἔνδικον μισθαποδοσίαν).
Ἔνδικος *just,* only here and Rom. iii. 8. ᴼLXX, quite
frequent in Class., but mainly in poetry. The meaning is
substantially the same as δίκαιος as it appears in the familiar
phrase δίκαιός εἰμι with the infinitive : thus, δίκαιός εἰμι κολάζειν *I am right to punish,* that is, *I have a right,* etc., right or
justice being regarded as working within a definite circle.
Μισθαποδοσία *recompense* only in Hebrews. Comp. x. 35;
xi. 26. ᴼLXX, ᴼClass., where the word is μισθοδοσία. From
μισθός *wages* and ἀποδιδόναι *to pay off* or *discharge.* The
reference is, primarily, to the punishments suffered by the
Israelites in the wilderness. Comp. ch. iii. 16; x. 28
1 Cor. x. 5, 6.

3. **How shall we escape** (πῶς ἡμεῖς ἐκφευξόμεθα). The
rhetorical question expressing denial. *We* is emphatic. *We,*
to whom God has spoken by his Son, and who, therefore, have
so much the more reason for giving heed. Ἐκφευξόμεθα, lit.

flee out from. The English *escape* conveys the same idea, but contains a picture which is not in the Greek word, namely, *to slip out of one's cape, ex cappâ,* and so get away. Comp. French *échapper.* In Italian we have *scappare* "to escape," and also *incappare* "to fall into a snare," and *incappuciare* "to wrap up in a hood or cape; to mask."

If we neglect (ἀμελήσαντες). Lit. *having neglected.* Rare in N. T., ᴼP. Comp. Matt. xxii. 5; 1 Tim. iv. 14. The thought falls in with *drift past,* ver. 1.

Salvation (σωτηρίαν). Characterising the new dispensation, as *the word* (ver. 2) characterises the old. Not the *teaching* or *word* of salvation, but the *salvation itself* which is the gift of the gospel, to be obtained by purification from sin through the agency of the Son (ch. i. 3).

Which (ἥτις). Explanatory. A salvation which may be described as one which was first spoken by the Lord, etc.

At the first began to be spoken (ἀρχὴν λαβοῦσα λαλεῖσθαι). Lit. *having taken beginning to be spoken.* Rend. *which, having at the first been spoken.* The phrase N. T.ᴼ.

By the Lord (διὰ τοῦ κυρίου). Const. with ἀρχὴν λαβοῦσα, not with λαλεῖσθαι. It is *the beginning,* not *the speaking* which is emphasised.

Was confirmed (ἐβεβαιώθη). It was *sure* (βέβαιος) even as was the word spoken by angels (ver. 2), and it was *confirmed,* proved to be real, by the testimony of ear-witnesses.

By them that heard (ὑπὸ τῶν ἀκουσάντων). We heard it (ver. 1) from those who heard, the immediate followers of the Lord. The writer thus puts himself in the second generation of Christians. They are not said to have heard the gospel directly from the Lord. Paul, on the other hand, claims that he received the gospel directly from Christ (Gal. i. 11).

4. God also bearing them witness (συνεπιμαρτυροῦντος τοῦ θεοῦ). The verb N. T.⁰: σύν *along with other witnesses:* ἐπὶ *giving additional* testimony : μαρτυρεῖν *to bear witness.*

With signs and wonders (σημείοις τε καὶ τέρασιν). A very common combination in N. T. See Matt. xxiv. 24; Mk. xiii. 22; J. iv. 48; Acts ii. 43; 2 Cor. xii. 11, etc. See on Matt. xxiv. 24.

Divers miracles (ποικίλαις δυνάμεσιν). Rend. *powers.* No doubt these include miracles, see Acts ii. 22; 2 Cor. xii. 12; but *powers* signifies, not the miraculous *manifestations*, as *signs* and *wonders*, but the miraculous *energies* of God as displayed in his various forms of witness.

Gifts (μερισμοῖς). Rend. *distributions* or *impartations.*

Of the Holy Ghost. The genitive is objective : distributions of the one gift of the Holy Spirit in different measure and in different ways. Comp. 1 Cor. xii. 4–11.

According to his will (κατὰ τὴν αὐτοῦ θέλησιν). Θέλησις *willing :* his *act* of will. N. T.⁰. Const. with *distributions.* The Spirit was imparted and distributed as God willed. The hortatory digression ends here. The subject of the Son's superiority to the angels is resumed.

5. The writer's object is to show that the *salvation*, the new order of things inaugurated by Christ, is in pursuance of the original purpose of creation, to wit, that universal dominion was to pertain to man, and not to angels. The great salvation means lordship of the world to be. This purpose is carried out in Christ, who, in becoming man, became temporarily subject to the earthly dispensation of which angels were the administrators. This was in order that he might acquire universal lordship *as man.* Being now exalted above angels, he does away with the angelic administration, and, in the world to come, will carry humanity with him to

the position of universal lordship. This thought is developed by means of Ps. viii. Having set Christ above the angels, the writer must reconcile that claim with the historical fact of Christ's humiliation in his incarnate state. The Psalm presents a paradox in the antithesis of *lower than the angels* and *all things under his feet.* From the Psalm is drawn the statement of a *temporary* subordination of Christ to angels, followed by his *permanent* exaltation over them.

Hath — put in subjection (ὑπέταξεν). The word suggests an economy; not merely subjecting the angels, but *arranging* or *marshalling* them under a new order. See 1 Cor. xv. 27, 28; Eph. i. 22; Philip. iii. 21.

The world to come (τὴν οἰκουμένην τὴν μέλλουσαν). See on ch. i. 2. For ἡ οἰκουμένη the *inhabited* (*land* or *country*) see on L. ii. 1. *The world to come* means the new order of things inaugurated by the sacrifice of Christ.

6. **In a certain place** (πού). Only here and ch. iv. 4, signifying indefinite quotation. It does not mean that the writer is ignorant of the author or of the place, but assumes that the readers know it, and that it is a matter of no moment who said it or where it is written.

Testified (διεμαρτύρατο). Mostly in Luke and Acts. Only here in Hebrews. In Paul only in 1st Thessalonians. See on 1 Th. ii. 12. It implies a *solemn, earnest* testimony.

What is man. The Hebrew interrogation, מָה *what, what kind of,* implies "*how small* or *insignificant*" compared with the array of the heavenly bodies; not "*how great* is man."

The son of man. Hebrew *son of Adam,* with a reference to his earthly nature as formed out of the dust. Very often in Ezekiel as a form of address to the prophet, LXX, υἱὲ ἀνθρώπου *son of man.* The direct reference of these words cannot be to the Messiah, yet one is reminded that *the Son of man* was Christ's own title for himself.

Visitest (ἐπισκέπτῃ). The primary sense of the verb is *to look upon;* hence, *to look after* or *inspect; to visit* in order to inspect or help. Similarly the Latin *visere* means both *to look at* and *to visit.* An ἐπίσκοπος is *an overlooker,* and ἐπισκοπὴ is *visitation.* The verb only here in Hebrews, ᵒP., very often in LXX. See on Matt. xxv. 36. Here in the sense of *graciously and helpfully regarding; caring for.*

Thou madest him a little lower than the angels (ἠλάττωσας αὐτὸν βραχύ τι παρ᾽ ἀγγέλους). Rend. *thou didst for some little time make him lower than the angels.* Ἐλαττοῦν *to make less* or *inferior,* only here, ver. 9, and J. iii. 30. Often in LXX (principally Sirach). Βραχύ τι, the Hebrew as A.V. *a little;* of *degree.* The LXX translators interpreted it, apparently, of *time,* "for some little time." Although there is precedent for both meanings in both Class. and N. T., the idea of time better suits the whole line of thought, and would probably, as Robertson Smith observes, have appeared to a Greek reader the more natural interpretation. For this sense see Isa. lvii. 17; Acts v. 34. He who has been described as superior to the angels, was, for a short time, on the same plane with man, and identified with an economy which was under the administration of angels. This temporary subordination to angels was followed by permanent elevation over them. Παρ᾽ ἀγγέλους. The Hebrew is מֵאֱלֹהִים *than God.* *Elohim* is used in a wide sense in O. T.: see, for instance, Ps. lxxxii. 6, where God addresses the judges by that title, and declares that he himself called them to their office and gave them their name and dignity. Comp. J. x. 34 and Ps. xxix. 1, LXX υἱοὶ θεοῦ *sons of God,* A.V. *mighty.* The LXX translators understand it, not as representing the personal God, but that which is divine, in which sense it would be appropriate to angels as having divine qualities.

8. **For** (γάρ). Explanatory. Thou hast put all things in subjection under his feet, *that is to say,* nothing is excepted.

That is not put under him (αὐτῷ ἀνυπότακτον). Lit. "*unsubjected* to him." The adjective only here and 1 Tim. i. 9 ᶜ

Tit. i. 6. But this ideal is not yet a reality. We see not yet all things subjected to him, but we do see the germinal fulfilment of the prophecy in Jesus' life, suffering, and death.

9. Jesus—made a little lower, etc. Repeated from ver. 7. To be subordinated to the angels is the same as being "made under the law," Gal. iv. 4. In that chapter Paul shows that the law under which the church in its state of pupilage was kept (Gal. iii. 23; iv. 3) was instituted through the mediation of angels (Gal. iii. 19). Then, as interchangeable with *under the law*, Paul has "enslaved *under the elements* (ὑπὸ τὰ στοιχεῖα) of the world" (Gal. iv. 3, 9). These elements are *elemental forces* or *spirits*, as appears from a correct interpretation of Col. ii. 8, 20.* The subjection to elemental spirits is only another form of subjection to the angels of the law, and our author uses this doctrine to show the mutable nature of angels in contrast with the immutable perfection of the Son (see ch. i. 7, 8). This accords with the Epistle to the Colossians which deals with the heresy of angel-worship, and in which the worship of angels is represented as connected with the service of elemental or cosmic forces. Very striking is Col. ii. 15. When the bond of the law was rendered void in Christ's crucifixion, that ministry of angels which waited on the giving of the law was set aside by God (ἀπεκδυσάμενος *having stripped off*), revealing Christ as the head of every principality and power. God made a *show* or *display* of them (ἐδειγμάτισεν) as subordinate and subject to Christ. He thus *boldly* (ἐν παρρησίᾳ), by a bold stroke, put his own chosen ministers in subjection before the eyes of the world. See on Col. ii. 15. The use of the human name, Jesus, at this point, is significant. In this epistle that name usually furnishes the key to the argument of the passage in which it occurs. See ch. iii. 1; vi. 20; xii. 2.

---

* On this subject see T. K. Abbott, *International Commentary* on Col. ii. 8, and compare Lightfoot, *Commentary on Colossians*, ad loc. Also von Soden ad loc. in *Hand-Commentar on Colossians;* Professor Hincks in *Journal of Biblical Literature*, Vol. XV., 1896 ; Otto Everling, *Die paulinische Angelologie und Daemonologie*, p. 65 ff.

For the suffering of death crowned with glory and honour (διὰ τὸ πάθημα τοῦ θανάτου δόξῃ καὶ τιμῇ ἐστεφανωμένον). The usual interpretation connects *for the suffering of death* with *made lower than the angels*, meaning that Jesus was subordinated to the angels for the suffering of death. But *for the suffering of death* should be connected with *crowned*, etc. Διὰ should be rendered *because of*. Jesus was crowned with glory and honour because of the suffering of death. Christ's exaltation and preëminence over the angels was won through humiliation and death. For *crowned*, see on 2 Tim. ii. 5. Exaltation was the logical result of Christ's humiliation (comp. Philip. ii. 9), not simply its recompense (comp. Matt. xxiii. 12; L. xiv. 11; xviii. 14). He was glorified *in* humiliation. "The humiliation is only the glory not yet begun." *

By the grace of God (χάριτι θεοῦ). God manifested his grace in giving Christ the opportunity of tasting death for every man, and so abolishing death as a curse. The same thought of glory in humiliation is expressed in J. i. 14. To be called to the office of "apostle and high-priest of our confession" (ch. iii. 1), an office which involved personal humiliation and death, was to be "crowned with glory and honour," and was a signal token of God's favour. Note J. xii. 23, 28; xiii. 31, 32, in which Jesus speaks of his approaching passion as itself his glorification. Comp. Heb. iii. 3. It was desirable to show to Jews who were tempted to stumble at the doctrine of a crucified Messiah (Gal. iii. 13), that there was a glory in humiliation.†

Should taste death (γεύσηται θανάτου). The phrase is found several times in the Gospels, as Matt. xvi. 28; Mk. ix. 1; L. ix. 27; J. viii. 52. See on L. ix. 27; J. viii. 52.

---

* Schmidt, Art. "Stand doppelter Christi," Herzog, *Real Encyc.*

† Findlay, *Expositor*, 3d ser. ix. 229, calls attention to the fact that ἠλαττωμένον and ἐστεφανωμένον are in the same tense and grammatical form, indicating contemporary rather than successive states. For χάριτι θεοῦ *by the grace of God*, some texts read χωρὶς θεοῦ *apart from God*. So Weiss. On this reading interpretations differ, as, *apart from divinity: forsaken by God; for all, God only excepted* (!).

The following statement justifies the bold assertion of ver. 9. With a view to the recoil of Jewish readers from the thought of a suffering Messiah (1 Cor. i. 23), the writer will show that Jesus' suffering and death were according to the divine fitness of things.

10. **It became** (ἔπρεπεν). Not *logical necessity* (δεῖ, ver. 1), nor *obligation growing out of circumstances* (ὤφειλεν, ver. 17), but an *inner fitness* in God's dealing. Dr. Robertson Smith observes : " The whole course of nature and grace must find its explanation in God; and not merely in an abstract divine *arbitrium*, but in that which befits the divine nature."

For whom — by whom (δι' ὅν — δι' οὗ). *For whom*, that is, *for whose sake* all things exist. God is the *final* cause of all things. This is not = εἰς αὐτὸν τὰ πάντα *unto whom are all things*, Rom. xi. 36; which signifies that all things have their *realisation* in God; while this means that all things have their *reason* in God. *By whom, through whose agency*, all things came into being. On διὰ applied to God, see on ch. i. 2. These two emphasise the idea of fitness. It was becoming even to a God who is the beginning and the end of all things.

In bringing many sons unto glory (πολλοὺς υἱοὺς εἰς δόξαν ἀγαγόντα). Const. *bringing* with *him;** not with *captain*, which would mean " to perfect the captain, etc., as one who led many sons, etc." Ἀγαγόντα is not to be explained *who had brought*, or *after he had brought*, with a reference to the O. T. saints, " after he had brought many O. T. sons of God unto glory "; but rather, *bringing as he did*, or *in bringing*, as A. V.† *Many sons*, since their leader himself was a son. *Unto glory*, in accordance with the glory with which he himself had been crowned (ver. 9). The *glory* is not dis-

---

* For the construction see Moulton's Winer, p. 402 ; and for similar instances, L. i. 74 ; Acts xi. 12 ; xv. 22 ; xxv. 27.

† The Vulgate has " qui multos filios in gloriam *adduxerat.*" For the construction see Burton, *New Testament Moods and Tenses*, § 149.

tinguished from the *salvation* immediately following. For
the combination *salvation* and *glory* see 2 Tim. ii. 10;
Apoc. xix. 1.

To make perfect (τελειῶσαι). Lit. *to carry to the goal* or
consummation. The "perfecting" of Jesus corresponds to his
being "crowned with glory and honour," although it is not a
mere synonym for that phrase; for the writer conceives the
perfecting not as an *act* but as a *process*. "To make perfect"
does not imply moral imperfection in Jesus, but only the
consummation of that human experience of sorrow and pain
through which he must pass in order to become the leader of
his people's salvation.

The captain of their salvation (τὸν ἀρχηγὸν τῆς σωτηρίας
αὐτῶν). Comp. Acts v. 31. Ἀρχηγὸς *captain*, quite frequent
in LXX and Class. Rev. renders *author*, which misses the
fact that the Son *precedes* the saved on the path to glory.
The idea is rather *leader*, and is fairly expressed by *captain*.

11. In order to bring many sons unto glory, Christ assumes
to them the relation of *brother*.

He that sanctifieth (ὁ ἁγιάζων). Sanctification is the path
to glorification. Comp. Heb. x. 14.

Of one (ἐξ ἑνὸς). Probably God, although the phrase may
signify *of one piece*, or *of one whole*. Jesus and his people
alike have God for their father. Therefore they are brethren, and Christ, notwithstanding his superior dignity, is not
ashamed to call them by that name.

12. This acknowledgment as brethren the writer represents as prophetically announced by Messiah in Ps. xxii. 22.
The Psalm is the utterance of a sufferer crying to God for
help in the midst of enemies. The Psalmist declares that
God has answered his prayer, and that he will give public
thanks therefor.

Unto my brethren (τοῖς ἀδελφοῖς μου).   His brethren in the worshipping assembly.   This is applied by our writer to the human brotherhood at large, and Christ is represented as identifying himself with them in thanksgiving.

Will I sing praise unto thee (ὑμνήσω σε).   Rare in N. T. Matt. xxvi. 30; Mk. xiv. 26; Acts xvi. 25.   Lit. *hymn thee.* Often in the Greek liturgies.

13. **I will put my trust, etc.** Isa. viii. 17, 18.   The passage occurs in an invective against the people's folly in trusting to any help but God's during the Syro-Israelitish war under Ahaz.   The prophet is commanded to denounce those who trusted to soothsayers and not to God, and to bind and seal God's testimony to the righteous party who maintained their confidence in him — a party comprising the disciples of Isaiah, and in whom lies the prophet's hope for the future of Israel.   Isaiah declares his own faith in God, and announces that he and his children have been appointed as living symbols of the divine will, so that there is no need of applying to necromancers.   The names of the children are Shear-jashub *a remnant shall return,* and Maher-shalal-hash-baz *haste-spoil-hurry-prey.*   These names will teach Israel that Assyria will spoil Damascus and Samaria; and that, in the midst of foreign invasion, God will still be with Judah, and will make a nation of the remnant which the war shall leave.   The prophet and his children are thus omens of the nation's fortunes.   The children were babes at this time, and "the only unity which existed among them was that which exists between every father and his children, and that which resulted from their belonging to the same prophetic household and all bearing symbolic names (without knowledge of the fact on the part of the children)." *   Our writer ignores the historical sense of the words, takes a part of a sentence and puts a messianic meaning into it, inferring from it the oneness of Jesus and his people, and the necessity of his assuming their nature in order to be one with them.   He treats the two parts of the

---

* Professor Toy, *Quotations in the New Testament.*

passage separately, emphasising in the first part Messiah's trust in God in common with his human brethren, and inserting ἐγὼ *I* into the LXX text in order to call special attention to the speaker as Messiah. In the second part, he expresses the readiness of himself and his children to carry out God's will.

14. The children (τὰ παιδία). Children of men, the subjects of Christ's redemption.

Are partakers of flesh and blood (κεκοινώνηκεν αἵματος καὶ σαρκός). For κεκοινώνηκεν see on Rom. xii. 13. For *flesh and blood* the correct text reads *blood and flesh*. In rabbinical writers a standing phrase for human nature in contrast with God.

Likewise (παραπλησίως). Rend. *in like manner.* N. T.º. Expressing general similarity. He took his place *alongside* (παρὰ) and *near* (πλησίος) : *near by.*

Took part (μετέσχεν). The verb only in Hebrews and Paul. The distinction between it and κεκοινώνηκεν *were partakers* is correctly stated by Westcott; the latter marking the characteristic sharing of the common fleshly nature as it pertains to the human race at large, and the former signifying the unique fact of the incarnation as a voluntary acceptance of humanity.

He might destroy (καταργήσῃ). Rend. *bring to nought.* See on *cumbereth*, L. xiii. 7, and *make of none effect*, Rom. iii. 3. The word occurs 27 times in N. T., and is rendered in 17 different ways in A. V.

Him that had the power of death (τὸν τὸ κράτος ἔχοντα τοῦ θανάτου). Not power *over* death, but *sovereignty* or *dominion of death*, a sovereignty of which death is the realm. Comp. Rom. v. 21, "Sin reigned *in* death."

That is the devil. An explanation has been sought in the Jewish doctrine which identified Satan with Sammaël, the angel of death, who, according to the later Jews, tempted Eve.   This is fanciful, and has no value, to say nothing of the fact that Michael and not Sammaël was the angel of death to the Israelites.   The O. T. nowhere identifies Satan with the serpent in Eden.   That identification is found in Wisd. ii. 24, and is adopted Apoc. xii. 9.   The devil has not power to inflict death, nor is death, as such, done away by the bringing of the devil to nought.   The sense of the passage is that Satan's dominion in the region of death is seen in the existence and power of the fear of death as the penalty of sin (comp. *through fear of death*, ver. 15).   The fear of death as implying rejection by God is distinctly to be seen in O. T. It appears in the utterances of many of the Psalmists.   There is a consciousness of the lack of a pledge that God will not, in any special case, rise up against one.   Along with this goes the conception of Satan as the accuser, see Zech. iii. This idea may possibly give colouring to this passage.   Even before death the accuser exercises sway, and keeps God's people in bondage so long as they are oppressed with the fear of death as indicating the lack of full acceptance with God.   How strongly this argument would appeal to Hebrew readers of the Epistle is clear from rabbinical theology, which often speaks of the fear of death, and the accuser as a constant companion of man's life.   Jesus assumes the mortal flesh and blood which are subject to this bondage.   He proves himself to be both exempt from the fear of death and victorious over the accuser.   He never lost his sense of oneness with God, so that death was not to him a sign of separation from God's grace.   It was a step in his appointed career; a means ($\delta\iota\grave{\alpha}$ $\tau o\hat{v}$ $\theta\alpha\nu\acute{\alpha}\tau o\nu$) whereby he accomplished his vocation as Saviour.   His human brethren share his exemption from the bondage of the fear of death, and of the accusing power of Satan.   " He that believeth on the Son *hath* eternal life."   " Whether we live or die we are the Lord's." *

---

* I desire to acknowledge my obligation in the notes on this passage to the very suggestive series of articles by Dr. W. Robertson Smith on " Christ and the Angels," *Expositor*, 2d ser. Vols., II., III.

15. Deliver (ἀπαλλάξῃ). Only here in Hebrews, and besides, only L. xii. 58; Acts xix. 12. Tolerably often in LXX. Very common in Class. Used here absolutely, not with δουλείας bondage, reading deliver from bondage.

Subject to bondage (ἔνοχοι δουλείας). Ἔνοχοι from ἐν in and ἔχειν to hold. Lit. holden of bondage. See on Jas. ii. 10. Comp. the verb ἐνέχειν, Mk. vi. 19 (note), and Gal. v. 1. Δουλεία bondage only in Hebrews and Paul.

16. Verily (δήπου). N. T.⁰. Doubtless, as is well known.

Took not on him (οὐ ἐπιλαμβάνεται). Rend. he doth not take hold. Comp. Matt. xiv. 31; Mk. viii. 23; Acts xviii. 17. Absolutely, in the sense of help, Sir. iv. 11. The Greek and Latin fathers explained the verb in the sense of appropriating. He did not appropriate the nature of angels. Angels did not need to be delivered from the fear of death.

The nature of angels (ἀγγέλων). The nature is not in the Greek, and does not need to be supplied if ἐπιλαμβάνεται is properly translated. Rend. not of angels doth he take hold. It is not angels who receive his help.

The seed of Abraham. The one family of God, consisting of believers of both dispensations, but called by its O. T. name. See Ps. cv. 6; Isa. xli. 8, and comp. Gal. iii. 29. The O. T. name is selected because the writer is addressing Jews. The entire statement in vv. 16, 17 is not a mere repetition of vv. 14, 15. It carries out the line of thought and adds to it, while at the same time it presents a parallel argument to that in vv. 14, 15. Thus: vv. 14, 15, Christ took part of flesh and blood that he might deliver the children of God from the fear of death and the accusations of Satan: vv. 16, 17, Christ takes hold of the seed of Abraham, the church of God, and is made like unto his brethren, tempted as they are, in order that he may be a faithful high priest, making reconciliation for sin, thus doing away with the fear of death, and enabling his people to draw near to God with boldness. Comp. ch. iv. 15, 16. Christ gives that peculiar help the necessity of which was exhibited in the O. T. econ· omy under which the original seed of Abraham lived. The fear of death, arising from the consciousness of sin, could be relieved only by the intervention of the priest who stood between God and the sinner, and made reconciliation for sin. Jesus steps into the place of the high priest, and perfectly fulfils the priestly office. By his actual participation in the sorrows and temptations of humanity he is fitted to be a true sympathiser with human infirmity and temptation (ch. v. 2), a merciful and faithful high priest, making reconciliation for sin, and thus abolishing the fear of death.

17. **Wherefore** (ὅθεν). ᵒP. Often in Hebrews.

In all things to be made like unto his brethren (κατὰ πάντα τοῖς ἀδελφοῖς ὁμοιωθῆναι). Comp. Philip. ii. 7, ἐν ὁμοιώματι ἀνθρώπων γενόμενος *having become in the likeness of men*. Likeness is asserted without qualification. There was a complete and real likeness to humanity, a likeness which was closest just where the traces of the curse of sin were most apparent — in poverty, temptation, and violent and unmerited death.

It behooved (ὤφειλεν). Indicating an obligation growing out of the position which Christ assumed: something which he *owed* to his position as the helper of his people.

That he might be a merciful and faithful high priest (ἵνα ἐλεήμων γένηται καὶ πιστὸς ἀρχιερεὺς). Rend. *that he might be compassionate, and so* (in consequence of being compassionate), *a faithful high priest*. The keynote of the Epistle, the high-priesthood of Christ, which is intimated in ch. i. 3, is here for the first time distinctly struck. Having shown that Christ delivers from the fear of death by nullifying the accusing power of sin, he now shows that he does this in his capacity of high priest, for which office it was

necessary that he should be made like unto his human brethren.   In the O. T. economy, the fear of death was especially
connected with the approach to God of an impure worshipper
(see Num. xviii. 3, 5).   This fear was mitigated or removed
by the intervention of the Levitical priest, since it was the
special charge of the priest so to discharge the service of the
tabernacle that there might be no outbreak of divine wrath
on the children of Israel (Num. xviii. 5).   Γένηται *might
show himself to be*, or *prove to be*.   The idea of compassion
as an attribute of priests is not found in the O. T.   On the
contrary, the fault of the priests was their frequent lack of
sympathy with the people (see Hos. iv. 4–9).   In the later
Jewish history, and in N. T. times, the priestly aristocracy
of the Sadducees was notoriously unfeeling and cruel.   The
idea of a compassionate and faithful high priest would appeal
powerfully to Jewish readers, who knew the deficiency of the
Aaronic priesthood in that particular.   Πιστὸς *faithful*, as an
attribute of a priest, appears in 1 Sam. ii. 35.   The idea there
is *fidelity*.   He will do all that is in God's mind.   Comp.
Heb. iii. 2.   This implies *trustworthiness*.   The idea here is,
faithful in filling out the true ideal of the priesthood (ch.
v. 1, 2), by being not a mere ceremonialist but a compassionate man.

In things pertaining to God (τὰ πρὸς τὸν θεόν).   Comp.
Rom. xv. 17.   A technical phrase in Jewish liturgical language to denote the functions of worship.   Const. with *a
faithful high priest*, not with *compassionate*.

To make reconciliation (εἰς τὸ ἱλάσκεθαι).   See on *propitiation*, Rom. iii. 25.   The verb only here and L. xviii. 13.

18. **In that he himself hath suffered being tempted** (ἐν
ᾧ γὰρ πέπονθεν αὐτὸς πειρασθείς).   Rend. *for having himself
been tempted in that which he suffered*.   The emphasis is on
having been tempted.   Christ is the succourer of the tempted
because he has himself been tempted.   Ἐν ᾧ is not *inasmuch*

as, but means *in that which*. 'Εν ᾧ πέπονθεν qualifies πειρασθείς, explaining in what the temptation consisted, namely, *in
suffering.**

CHAPTER III.

1. The leading ideas of the preceding section are echoed
in this verse: *brethren*, of whom Christ made himself the
brother: *holy*, in virtue of the work of the sanctifier.

Wherefore (ὅθεν). Drawing a conclusion from ch. ii. 9–18.

Holy brethren (ἀδελφοὶ ἅγιοι). The phrase N. T.°. 'Αδελ-
φοὶ *brethren*, in address, is not found in the Gospels. In Acts
mostly ἄνδρες ἀδελφοὶ *brother men*. In Paul, ἀδ. ἀγαπητοί
brethren beloved, or ἀδ. ἀγαπ. καὶ ἐπιπόθητοι *brethren beloved
and longed for* (once, Philip. iv. 1), ἀδ. ἠγαπημένοι ὑπὸ τοῦ
θεοῦ and τοῦ κυρίου *brethren beloved of God* or *of the Lord*, and
ἀδ. μου *my brethren*. In James mostly ἀδ. μου. In Hebrews,
except here, ἀδελφοὶ simply. *Holy* brethren (see ch. ii. 11)
are worshippers of God, taking the place of God's O. T.
people, as called and consecrated to ethical and spiritual
service according to the Christian ideal.

Partakers of a heavenly calling (κλήσεως ἐπουρανίου μέτοχοι). Μέτοχοι *partakers* only in Hebrews except L. v. 7.
See on μετέσχεν *took part*, ch. ii. 14. The phrase *heavenly
calling* N. T.°. Comp. τῆς ἄνω κλήσεως *the upward calling*,
Philip. iii. 14. The expression points to the lordship of the
world to be (ch. ii. 5); and the world to be is the abiding
world, the place of realities as contrasted with types and

---

* Dr. W. Robertson Smith objects that Jesus was *in all points* tempted
like as we are (ch. iv. 15), and that not every temptation arises out of the
painful experiences of life. But the great point is that Christ is able to
succour the tempted because he has himself experienced temptation. The
peculiar nature of his temptation, and the points of its correspondence with
ours, are not in question. One point is selected out of the whole range of
possible causes of temptation, and that the most prominent and obvious
point — *suffering*.

shadows. The calling comes from that world and is to that world. See ch. xiii. 14.

Consider (κατανοήσατε).* Attentively, thoughtfully (κατά). See on Jas. i. 23. The writer's habit is to use the communicative *we* or *us* identifying himself with his readers.

The apostle and high priest (τὸν ἀπόστολον καὶ ἀρχιερέα). In calling Jesus *apostle*, the writer is thinking of Moses as one *sent* by God to lead Israel to Canaan. Comp. LXX, where ἀποστέλλειν *to send* is often used of Moses. See Ex. iii.–vii. Often of Jesus, as L. x. 16; J. iii. 17; v. 36; vi. 29.

Of our profession (τῆς ὁμολογίας ἡμῶν). Rend. *confession* for *profession*. The apostle and high priest whom we confess. Comp. 1 Tim. vi. 12.

2. **Who was faithful** (πιστὸν ὄντα). Rend. "*is* faithful." A general designation of inherent character. He *is* faithful as he ever *was*.

To him that appointed him (τῷ ποιήσαντι αὐτόν). *Constituted* him apostle and high priest. Some render *created*, referring to Christ's humanity or to his eternal generation. So the Old Latin, *creatori suo;* but this does not suit the context. Ποιεῖν often in Class. in the sense of *institute*, as sacrifices, funerals, assemblies, etc., and in the middle voice of *adoption* as a son. See 1 Sam. xii. 6; Mk. iii. 14; Acts ii. 36.

As also Moses (ὡς καὶ Μωυσῆς). The highest example of human fidelity known to the readers.

In all his house (ἐν ὅλῳ τῷ οἴκῳ αὐτοῦ). Const. with *was faithful*. Jesus was faithful even as Moses was faithful.

---

* Some interesting data and remarks on the use of "I," "we" and "you" in the Epistle may be found in Harnack's article, "Probabilia über die Adresse und den Verfasser des Hebräerbriefs," in Preuschen's *Zeitschrift für die neutestamentliche Wissenschaft und die Kunde des Urchristenthums,* Heft i. s. 24.

The subject of the high-priesthood of Christ, introduced
in this verse, is not carried out in detail by showing the
superiority of Jesus to earthly high priests. This is reserved
for chs. v.–vii. Instead, the writer proceeds to show that
Christ is superior to Moses, as he has already shown his
superiority to angels. He will thus have shown Christ's
superiority to both the agencies by which the old covenant
was mediated. The subject is a delicate one to treat for
Jewish readers to whom Moses was the object of the deepest
veneration; but the treatment displays tact by placing Moses
in the foreground beside Christ as an example of fidelity to
his commission. Justice is thus done to the familiar historical record, and to God's own testimony, Num. xii. 7. The
general sense of the comparison is that Moses was as faithful
as any *servant* in a house can be, while Christ was not a servant in the house, but a son, and displayed his fidelity in that
capacity.

3. **Was counted worthy** ($\dot{\eta}\xi\acute{\iota}\omega\tau\alpha\iota$). Used both of *reward*
which is due (1 Tim. v. 17) and of punishment (Heb. x. 29).

Of more glory ($\pi\lambda\epsilon\acute{\iota}o\nu o\varsigma$ $\delta\acute{o}\xi\eta\varsigma$). Comp. ch. ii. 8, 9.

Inasmuch as ($\kappa\alpha\theta'$ $\acute{o}\sigma o\nu$). Rend. *by so much as*. The
argument is based on the general principle that the founder
of a house is entitled to more honour than the house and its
individual servants. There is an apparent confusion in the
working out, since both God and Christ appear as *builders*,
and Moses figures both as the house and as a servant in the
house. The point of the whole, however, is that Moses was
a *part* of the O. T. system — a servant in the house; while
Christ, as one with God who established all things, was the
founder and establisher of both the Old and the New Testament economies.

4. **He that built all things is God** ($\acute{o}$ $\pi\acute{a}\nu\tau\alpha$ $\kappa\alpha\tau\alpha\sigma\kappa\epsilon\upsilon\acute{a}\sigma\alpha\varsigma$
$\theta\epsilon\acute{o}\varsigma$). The verb includes not only *erection*, but *furnishing*
with the entire equipment. See ch. ix. 2; 1 Pet. ii. 10. The

verb °P. The application of *built* or *established* to Christ
(ver. 3) is guarded against possible misapprehension. Christ
is the establisher, but not by any independent will or agency.
As the Son he is *he that built*, but it is as one with God *who
built all things*. The *special* foundership of Christ does not
contradict or exclude the *general* foundership of God.*

5. **And** Moses. Καὶ *and* introduces the further development of the thought of vv. 2, 3 — *fidelity*, and the corresponding honour. It is not a second proof of the superiority
of Christ to Moses. See Num. xii. 7.

A servant (θεράπων). N. T.°. Comp. Apoc. xv. 3. Often
in LXX, mostly as translation of עֶבֶד *servant, slave, bondman*.
Also, when coupled with the name of a deity, a *worshipper,
devotee*. Sometimes applied to angels or prophets. Of Moses,
θεράπων κυρίου *servant of the Lord*, Wisd. x. 16. In Class.
and N. T. the word emphasises the performance of a present service, without reference to the condition of the doer,
whether bond or free. An ethical character attaches to it,
as to the kindred verb θεραπεύειν: service of an affectionate,
hearty character, performed with care and fidelity. Hence
the relation of the θεράπων is of a nobler and freer character
than that of the δοῦλος or bondservant. The verb is used of
a physician's tendance of the sick. Xenophon (*Mem.* iv. 3, 9)
uses it of the gods *taking care* of men, and, on the other
hand, of men's worshipping the gods (ii, 1. 28). See Eurip.
Iph. Taur. 1105; and on *heal*, Matt. viii. 7; L. v. 15, and
on *is worshipped*, Acts xvii. 25.

For a testimony of those things which were to be spoken
(εἰς μαρτύριον τῶν λαληθησομένων). Ἐις *for*, with the whole

---

* The older expositors regarded ὁ θεὸς as predicate, and ὁ πάντα κατασκευ-
άσας as designating Christ; and explained, "now he that founded all things
(Christ) must be God," thus using the passage as a proof of Christ's deity.
But this would be entirely irrelevant. The writer is not trying to show that
Christ was greater than Moses because he was God, but because of his fidelity as a son instead of as a servant. This is the point which he goes on to
elaborate.

preceding clause. Moses' faithful service in God's house was *for a testimony*, etc.   The *things which were to be spoken* are *the revelations afterward to be given in Christ*.   Others, however, explain of the things which Moses himself was afterward to speak to the people by God's command, referring to Num. xii. 8.   According to this explanation, the fidelity hitherto exhibited by Moses ought to command respect for all that he might say in future.   But (1) in the present connection that thought is insignificant.   (2) It would be an exaggeration to speak of Moses's fidelity to God throughout his whole official career as a witness of the things which he was to speak to the people by God's command.   (3) The future participle requires a reference to a time subsequent to Moses's ministry.   The meaning is that Moses, in his entire ministry, was but a testimony to what was to be spoken in the future by another and a greater than he.   Comp. Deut. xviii. 15, explained of Christ in Acts iii. 22, 23.

6. **But Christ.** Replacing the human name *Jesus*, and being the *official* name which marks his position over the house.

As a son (ὡς υἱὸς).   The fidelity of Moses and the fidelity of Christ are exhibited in different spheres : of Moses in that of servant ; of Christ in that of son.

Over his own house (ἐπὶ τὸν οἶκον αὐτοῦ).   Comp. ch. x. 21, and notice ἐπὶ *over* his house, and ἐν *in* all his house, of Moses.   For "*his own* house" rend. "*his* house," referring to God.   Reference to Christ would destroy the parallel.   It is said by some that the matter of respective positions is irrelevant : that the main point is *fidelity*, and that therefore it does not matter whether Moses was a son or a servant, provided he was faithful.   But the writer evidently feels that Christ's position as a son *enhanced* his fidelity.   Comp. ch. v. 8.   The implication is that Christ's position involved peculiar difficulties and temptations.

Whose house (οὗ).   God's house.   The church is nowhere called the house of Christ.

We (ἡμεῖς). Even as was the house in which Moses served. The Christian community is thus emphatically designated as *the house of God*, implying the transitoriness of the Mosaic system. Comp. 1 Cor. iii. 16, 17; 2 Cor. vi. 16; Eph. ii. 22; 1 Pet. iv. 17.

Hold fast (κατάσχωμεν). The verb is used in N. T. as here, 1 Th. v. 21; Philem. 13; of *restraining* or *preventing*, L. iv. 42; of *holding back* or *holding down* with an evil purpose, Rom. i. 18; 2 Th. ii. 7; of *holding one's course toward*, *bearing down for*, Acts xxvii. 40.

The confidence and the rejoicing of the hope (τὴν παρρησίαν καὶ τὸ καύχημα τῆς ἐλπίδος). The combination *confidence and rejoicing* N. T.°. *Rejoicing or boasting of hope* N. T.°, but comp. 1 Th. ii. 19. For παρρησία *confidence* see on 1 Tim. iii. 13. The entire group of words, καύχημα *ground of glorying*, καύχησις *act of glorying*, and καυχᾶσθαι *to glory*, is peculiarly Pauline. Outside of the Pauline letters καυχᾶσθαι occurs only Jas. i. 9; iv. 16; καύχησις only Jas. iv. 16; and καύχημα only here. The thought here is that the condition of being and continuing the house of God is the holding fast of the hope in Christ (ἐλπίδος of the *object* of hope) and in the consummation of God's kingdom in him; making these the ground of boasting; exultantly confessing and proclaiming this hope. There must be, not only confidence, but *joyful* confidence. Comp. Rom. v. 3; Eph. iii. 12, 13; Philip. iii. 3.

Firm unto the end (μέχρι τέλους βεβαίαν). Textually, there is some doubt about these words. Westcott and Hort bracket them. Tischendorf retains, and Weiss rejects them. The latter part of this verse marks the transition to the lesson of the wilderness-life of the exodus; the writer fearing that the fate of the exodus-generation may be repeated in the experience of his readers. We are God's house if we steadfastly hold fast our Christian hope, and do not lose our faith as Israel did in the wilderness. The exhortation to faith is thrown into the form of warning against unbelief.

Faith is the condition of realising the divine promise. The section is introduced by a citation from Ps. xcv. 7, 8.

7. **Wherefore as the Holy Ghost saith** (διὸ καθὼς λέγει τὸ πνεῦμα τὸ ἅγιον). See on ch. i. 6. The formula *the Spirit the holy (Spirit)* is common in the N. T. with the exception of the Catholic Epistles, where it does not occur. The construction of the passage is as follows : Διὸ *wherefore* is connected with βλέπετε *take heed*, ver. 12. The point is *the writer's* warning, not the warning of *the citation*. The whole citation including the introductory formula, down to *rest*, ver. 11, is parenthetical.

To-day if ye will hear his voice (σήμερον ἐὰν τῆς φωνῆς αὐτοῦ ἀκούσητε). The Hebrew reads, *O that you would hear his voice to-day.* *To-day* is prophetically interpreted by the writer as referring to the Christian present, the time of salvation inaugurated by the appearance of Christ.

8. **Harden not** (μὴ σκληρύνητε). In N. T. mostly in this epistle. Comp. Acts xix. 9; Rom. ix. 18, see note. The group of kindred words consists of σκληρός *hard* (see on Matt. xxv. 24; Jude 14); σκληρότης *hardness* (Rom. ii. 5); σκληρύνειν *to harden* (Acts xix. 9; Rom. ix. 18); and the compounds σκληροκαρδία *hardness of heart* (Matt. xix. 8; Mk. x. 5), and σκληροτράχηλος *stiff-necked* (Acts vii. 5). All occur in LXX, with the addition of σκληρῶς *hardly, painfully* (not in N. T.).

In the provocation (ἐν τῷ παραπικρασμῷ). Only here and ver. 15. In LXX only Ps. xciv. 8. The verb παραπικραίνειν *to provoke*, only in ver. 16. Often in LXX. The simple verb πικραίνειν *to make bitter*, Col. iii. 19; Apoc. viii. 11; x. 9, 10. From πικρός *bitter, pungent*: hence *to stir up to bitterness, to irritate*. Comp. LXX Ezek. ii. 4.

In the day (κατὰ τὴν ἡμέραν). Κατὰ in a temporal sense, as Acts xii. 1; xix. 23; xxvii. 27. Comp. κατ' ἀρχάς *in the beginning*, ch. i. 10.

Of temptation (τοῦ πειρασμοῦ). Rend. "of *the* temptation," referring to a definite event, the murmuring against Moses at Rephidim on account of the lack of water, Ex. xvii. 1–7. In that passage the LXX gives for the two proper names *Massah* and *Meribah*, πειρασμὸς *temptation*, which is correct, and λοιδόρησις *railing* or *reviling*, which is loose, since Meribah signifies *strife*.* In Ps. xciv, LXX renders *Meribah* παραπικρασμός *provocation*, which is inexact, and *Massah* πειρασμὸς *temptation*, which is correct.

9. **When** (οὗ). Rend. *where*. See οὗ after ἔρημος *wilderness*, Deut. viii. 15.

Tempted me, proved me (ἐπείρασαν ἐν δοκιμασίᾳ). Lit. *tried (me) in proving*. The text differs from LXX, which reads ἐπείρασαν, ἐδοκίμασαν *tempted, proved*, as A. V. The phrase here means *tempted by putting to the test*. Comp. ἐκπειράζειν to tempt or *try with a view to seeing how far one can go*. See on 1 Cor. x. 9.

And saw my works (καὶ εἶδον τὰ ἔργα μου). Some construe *my works* with both verbs: *tried and saw my works :* but it is better to supply *me* after ἐπείρασαν *tempted*, to take *works* with *saw* only, and to give καὶ the force of *and yet* (see on L. xviii. 7). "They tempted and yet saw my works;" *although* they saw my works. The Hebrew is "tried me, proved me, yea saw my works."

Forty years. In LXX this is connected with *saw my works*. In the Hebrew *forty years* begins the next clause.

10. **Wherefore I was grieved** (διὸ προσώχθισα). The Hebrew omits *wherefore*. It was inserted because of the transfer of *forty years* to the preceding clause. The verb

* Comp. τοῦ ὕδατος λοιδορίας, Num. xx. 24, and ὕδωρ Ἀντιλογίας, Num. xx. 13 ; xxvii. 14 ; Deut. xxxii. 51 ; xxxiii. 8 ; Ps. lxxx. 7 ; cv. 32. The LXX has preserved the proper names only in Ezek. xlvii. 19, Μαριμὼθ, and xlviii. 28, Βαριμὼθ.

προσώχθισα *I was grieved*, only here and ver. 17.   In LXX for קוֹא *to spue out;* גּעַל *to exclude, reject, abhor;* מאַס *to repudiate*.

11. So I sware (ὡς). Rend. "*according as* I sware": the ὡς correlating the oath and the disobedience.

They shall not enter into my rest (εἰ ἐλεύσονται εἰς τὴν κατάπαυσίν μου). Lit. *if they shall enter*, etc. A common Hebraistic formula in oaths. Where God is speaking, as here, the ellipsis is "may I not be Jehovah *if* they shall enter." Where man is speaking, "so may God punish me *if*"; or "God do so to me and more *if*." Comp. Mk. viii. 12: LXX, Gen. xiv. 23; Deut. i. 35; 1 K. i. 51; ii. 8. Sometimes the ellipsis is filled out, as 1 Sam. iii. 17; 2 Sam. iii. 35. Κατάπαυσιν *rest*, only in Hebrews, and Acts vii. 49. The verb καταπαύειν *to lay to rest* also only in Acts and Hebrews. In Class. the verb sometimes means *to kill* or *to depose from* power. In the original citation the reference is to Canaan. Paul uses κληρονομία *inheritance* in a similar sense.

12. Note how the following exhortation is colored by the O. T. citation : *evil heart; the to-day; be hardened; take heed* (βλέπετε). See to it. Often in warnings or admonitions : sometimes with ἀπὸ *from*, with genitive of that against which the warning is given, as Mk. viii. 15; xii. 38; but so only in the Gospels. In construction connect with διὸ, ver. 7; *therefore beware*.

Lest there be (μή ποτε ἔσται). The indicative with μὴ *lest* shows that with the *fear* that the event *may* occur, there is blended a *suspicion* that it *will* occur.

In any of you (ἔν τινι ὑμῶν). They are appealed to individually.

An evil heart of unbelief (καρδία πονηρὰ ἀπιστίας). The whole phrase N. T.º. Neither do the combinations *evil heart*

or *heart of unbelief* occur elsewhere.   In LXX, among nearly
a thousand instances of καρδία *heart*, καρδία πονηρὰ *evil heart*
appears only five times, and in three of the five in apocryphal
books.   See Sir. ix. 1; Bar. i. 22; ii. 8.   In LXX proper,
Jer. xvi. 12; xviii. 12.   'Απιστίας *of unbelief*, specifies that
in which the more general πονηρὰ *evil* consists.   An evil heart
is an unbelieving heart.

In departing from the living God (ἐν τῷ ἀποστῆναι ἀπὸ
θεοῦ ζῶντος).   The characteristic of unbelief.   Faith is personal union with God.   Unbelief separates from God.   The
phrase *living God* is common to both Testaments.   For the
bearing of the words upon the question of the Gentile destination of the Epistle, see Introduction.

13.   **While it is called to-day** (ἄχρις οὗ τὸ σήμερον καλεῖται).
Lit. *so long as the to-day is being named*.   The article points
to the former expression — *the* "to-day" of ver. 7.   It is the
day of grace, while salvation through Christ is still attainable.

Through the deceitfulness of sin (ἀπάτῃ τῆς ἁμαρτίας).
'Απάτη is rather *a trick, stratagem, deceit*, than the quality of
deceitfulness.   The warning is against being hardened by a
trick which their sin may play them.   Note the article, *the*
or *his* sin — the sin of departing from the living God.   The
particular deceit in this case would be the illusion of faithfulness to the past.

14.   **We are made partakers of Christ** (μέτοχοι γὰρ τοῦ
Χριστοῦ γεγόναμεν).   Rend. *we are become fellows with Christ.*
For *fellows* see L. v. 7; Heb. i. 9.   It marks even a closer
relation than "brethren."   See L. xxii. 30; Rom. viii. 17;
Apoc. iii. 21.

Beginning of our confidence (τὴν ἀρχὴν τῆς ὑποστάσεως).
The believing confidence with which we began our Christian
life.   For ὑπόστασις *confidence* see on ch. i. 3.   The Greek
fathers render *substance;* that in virtue of which we are
believers.

Unto the end (μέχρι τέλους). Better, *the consummation.*
It is more than mere *termination.* It is the point into
which the whole life of faith finally gathers itself up. See
Rom. vi. 21; 2 Cor. xi. 15; Philip. iii. 19; Heb. vi. 8;
1 Pet. i. 9.

15. **While it is said** (ἐν τῷ λέγεσθαι). The formula by
which the writer reverts to the previous citation. Connect
with *if we hold fast.* The exhortation of ver. 12 answered to
Ps. xcv; so the condition of fulfilment in ver. 14 is declared
to rest on the same Scripture. Only *on the ground of what is
said* in that Psalm does the holding fast come to pass. Rend.
therefore, " We are fellows of Christ if we hold the beginning of our confidence steadfast unto the end, seeing it is
said," etc.

16. **For some, when they had heard, did provoke** (τίνες
γὰρ ἀκούσαντες παρεπίκραναν). Rend. *who, when they heard,
did provoke?* The interrogative τίνες calls special attention
to those who provoked God. The writer would say, " My
warning against apostasy is not superfluous or irrelevant:
for, consider: *who* were they that provoked God? They were
those who had fairly begun their journey to Canaan, as you
have begun your Christian course. *They* provoked God, so
may *you.*

Howbeit not all (ἀλλ' οὐ πάντες). Wrong. The interrogation should be continued. Who were they? But (ἀλλ')
why do I ask? *Were they not all who came out of Egypt by
Moses?* They were so numerous that they practically constituted the whole generation of the exodus. So far from its
being true that a good ending necessarily follows a good
beginning, a whole generation of God's chosen people failed
to reach the Land of Promise because they provoked God.

17. The interrogation still continued. " With whom was
he displeased forty years? Was it not with them?" etc.

Carcasses (τὰ κῶλα). N. T.⁰. LXX for פֶּגֶר *a corpse.*
Κῶλον properly *a limb.* The idea of *dismemberment* underlies
the use of the word. Comp. Num. xiv. 29 (LXX), and
1 Cor. x. 5, of the rebellious Israelites, who κατεστρώθησαν
ἐν τῇ ἐρήμῳ *were strewn down along in the wilderness.*

18. **To them that believed not** (τοῖς ἀπειθήσασιν). Rend.
to them that disobeyed.

CHAPTER IV.

Christian salvation, having been presented as lordship over
the world to come, and as deliverance from the fear of death,
is now to be presented as participation in the rest of God. The
purpose of vv. 1–11 is to confirm the hope of that rest, and
to warn against forfeiting it. There is a possibility of your
forfeiting it. The rest of God was proclaimed to your forefathers, but they did not enter into it because of their unbelief. It has been proclaimed to you. You may fail as did
they, and for the same reason.

1. **Being left** (καταλειπομένης). Still remaining: not *being
neglected.* It is not a reason for fearing that is given, but a
circumstance connected with the thing to be avoided. As
there is now left a promise, let us fear. *Being left* announces
the thought which is afterward emphasised, and on which
the whole treatment of the subject turns—that *God's original
promise of rest remains unchanged, and still holds good.* Such
being the case, he who doubts the promise itself, or thinks
that it is too late for him to enjoy its fulfilment, runs a risk.

Should seem to come short (δοκῇ ὑστερηκέναι). According to this rendering, the meaning is that one must avoid *the
appearance* of having failed to enter into the rest; the perfect tense (ὑστερηκέναι) placing the reader at the parousia,
when judgment will be pronounced. This is forced, tame,
and irrelevant to the previous discussion. Rend. *lest any*

one of you think he has come too late for it. This accords with the previous admonitions against unbelief. For one to think that he has come too late to inherit the promise is to disbelieve an immutable promise of God. Hence the writer may well say, "Since this promise *remains*, let us *fear* to distrust it." ʽΥστερεῖν is *to be behind; to come late; to come short;* hence, *to suffer need*, as Philip. iv. 12; of material deficiency, L. xv. 14; J. ii. 3; of moral and spiritual shortcoming, Rom. iii. 23; 1 Cor. viii. 8; Heb. xii. 15.

2. **For unto us was the gospel preached** (καὶ γὰρ ἐσμεν εὐηγγελισμένοι). Lit. *we have had good tidings proclaimed to us.* The translation of the A. V. is unfortunate, since it conveys the technical and conventional idea of *preaching the gospel*, which is entirely out of place here. The reference is to the special announcement of the rest of God; the glad tidings that God has provided a rest for his people. This announcement was made to the fathers, and signified to them the promise of the rest in Canaan. It has been proclaimed to us, and to us is the announcement of the heavenly rest. The emphasis is on the entire statement, "we have had the good tidings proclaimed to us," rather than on *we* as contrasted with *they*.

The word preached (ὁ λόγος τῆς ἀκοῆς). Lit. *the word of the message.* See on 1 Th. ii. 13.

Not being mixed with faith in them that heard it (μὴ συνκεκερασμένους τῇ πίστει τοῖς ἀκούσασιν). Rend. *because not incorporated by faith in them that heard.** A body of obedient hearers with whom the erring Israelites were not in-

---

* There is a difference of reading: συνκεκερασμένους and συνκεκερασμένος. According to the former, the participle agrees with ἐκείνους *them:* "the word did not profit them, (they) not having been united, etc.," or, "since they were not united." According to the latter, the participle agrees with ὁ λόγος *the word:* "the word not having been united, etc." I prefer the second reading, although the external authority for the other is stronger. . So Tischendorf and Weiss. Westcott and Hort read συνκεκερασμένους, but suspect a primitive corruption. Westcott, however, adopts the other in his commentary.

corporated would be an idea foreign to the discussion. Moreover, in ch. iii. 16, the writer has declared that there were practically no believing hearers. He says that although the good tidings were announced to them, they did not profit them. The word did not profit them because it (the word) was not assimilated by faith in those that heard. They did not make the promise of rest their own. Their history was marked by continual renewals and rejections of the promise.

3. **For we which have believed do enter into rest** (εἰσερχόμεθα γὰρ εἰς τὴν κατάπαυσιν οἱ πιστεύσαντες). I say by faith, *for*, we believers, who embraced the Christian faith when it was offered to us (note the aorist participle), *do* enter into the rest. Ἐισερχόμεθα, categorical; not *are entering* or *are on the way to*, but entering into the rest is a fact which characterises us as believers.

As he said (καθὼς εἴρηκεν). We enter *in accordance with the saying* which follows.

As I have sworn—if they shall enter. The statement is somewhat obscure. The meaning is, *we* (who believed) enter into rest in accordance with God's declaration that *they* (who did not believe) should *not* enter. The point is *faith* as the condition of entering into the rest.

Although the works were finished (καίτοι τῶν ἔργων γενηθέντων). This is an awkward and indirect way of saying, "these unbelievers did not enter into God's rest, although he had provided that rest into which they might have entered." The providing of the rest is implied in the completion of God's works. The writer assumes the readers' acquaintance with the narrative of the creation in Genesis.

4. What was implied in the preceding verse is now stated.

Did rest from all his works (κατέπαυσεν — ἀπὸ πάντων τῶν ἔργων αὐτοῦ). The verb only in Hebrews and Acts xiv. 18. *Works*, plural, following LXX. The Hebrew has *work*.

5. **In this place** (ἐν τούτῳ). The passage already cited, ver. 3. It is cited again to show that the rest was not entered into.

6. The rest was not appropriated by those under Moses, nor, in the full sense, by those under Joshua, nor in David's time.

It remaineth that some must enter therein (ἀπολείπεται τινὰς εἰσελθεῖν εἰς αὐτήν). Ἀπολείπεται, "remains *over from* past times." The promise has not been appropriated. It must be appropriated in accordance with God's provision. The rest was not provided for nothing. God's provision of a rest implies and involves that some enter into it. But the appropriation is yet in the future. It *remains* that some enter in.

They to whom it was first preached (οἱ πρότερον εὐαγγελισθέντες). Lit. *they who were first the subjects of the announcement of the glad tidings*. It is desirable to avoid the word *preached*. See on ver. 2. The Israelites under Moses and Joshua are meant.

Because of unbelief (δι' ἀπείθειαν). Rend. for *unbelief*, *disobedience*. Comp. ch. iii. 18. Ἀπείθεια *disobedience* is the active manifestation of ἀπιστία *unbelief*.

7. **Again he limiteth a certain day** (πάλιν τινὰ ὁρίζει ἡμέραν). For *limiteth* rend. *defineth*. For the verb see on *declared*, Rom. i. 4. The meaning is, he gives another opportunity of securing the rest, and calls the period in which the opportunity is offered *to-day*.

In David. The date of the composition of Ps. xcv is uncertain. In LXX (xciv) it is called a Psalm of David. In the words *in David* the writer may adopt the LXX title, or may mean simply *in the Psalms*. In the Hebrew the Psalm has no inscription.

After so long a time (μετὰ τοσοῦτον χρόνον). The time between Joshua and David. After this long interval he renews the promise in the Psalm.

As it is said (καθὼς προείρηται). Rend. *as it hath been before said;* referring to the citations, ch. iii. 7, 8, 15.

8. But it might be said that under Joshua the people did enter into the promised rest. He therefore shows that Israel's rest in Canaan did not fulfil the divine ideal of the rest.

Jesus ('Ιησοῦς). Rend. *Joshua*, and see on Matt. i. 21.

After this (μετὰ ταῦτα). After the entrance into Canaan under Joshua.

9. **There remaineth therefore a rest** (ἄρα ἀπολείπεται σαββατισμὸς). *Remaineth*, since in the days of neither Moses, Joshua, or David was the rest appropriated. He passes over the fact that the rest had not been entered into at any later period of Israel's history. Man's portion in the divine rest inaugurated at creation has never been really appropriated: but *it still remaineth*. This statement is justified by the new word for "rest" which enters at this point, σαββατισμὸς instead of κατάπαυσις. Σαββατισμὸς, N. T.°, °LXX, °Class., signifies a *keeping Sabbath*. The *Sabbath* rest points back to God's original rest, and marks the *ideal* rest — the rest of perfect adjustment of all things to God, such as ensued upon the completion of his creative work, when he pronounced all things good. This falls in with the ground-thought of the Epistle, the restoration of all things to God's archetype. The sin and unbelief of Israel were incompatible with that rest. It must remain unappropriated until harmony with God is restored. The Sabbath-rest is the consummation of the new creation in Christ, through whose priestly mediation reconciliation with God will come to pass.

For the people of God (τῷ λαῷ τοῦ θεοῦ). For the phrase see Rom. ix. 25; xi. 1; 1 Pet. ii. 10, and comp. *Israel of*

God, Gal. vi. 16.   The *true* Israel, who inherit the promise by faith in Christ.

10.   Only in such a Sabbath-rest is found the counterpart of God's rest on the seventh day.

For he that is entered into his rest (ὁ γὰρ εἰσελθὼν εἰς τὴν κατάπαυσιν αὐτοῦ).   Whoever has once entered.*   *His*, God's.   The aorist marks the completeness of the appropriation — once and for all.

He also hath ceased from his own works (καὶ αὐτὸς κατέπαυσεν ἀπὸ τῶν ἔργων αὐτοῦ).   Omit *own*.   The statement is a general proposition: any one who has entered into God's rest has ceased from his works.

As God did from his (ὥσπερ ἀπὸ τῶν ἰδίων ὁ θεός).   Rend. *as God (did) from his own*.   Ἰδίων *own* signifies more than mere possession.   Rather, works *peculiarly* his own, thus hinting at the perfect nature of the original works of creation as corresponding with God's nature and bearing his impress.   The blessing of the Sabbath-rest is thus put as a cessation from labours.   The basis of the conception is Jewish, the rest of the Sabbath being conceived as mere abstinence from labour, and not according to Christ's conception of the Sabbath, as a season of refreshment and beneficent activity, Mk. ii. 27; J. v. 17.   Our writer's conception is not the rabbinical conception of cessation of work, but rather of the cessation of the weariness and pain which accompany human labor.   Comp. Apoc. xiv. 13; xxi. 4; L. xi. 7; xviii. 5; Gal. vi. 17.

11.   This promise of rest carries with it a special responsibility for the people of God.

Let us labour therefore (σπουδάσωμεν οὖν).   For the verb, see on Eph. iv. 3.   *Give diligence*, not *hasten*, which is the primary meaning.

---

* Not as Ebrard and Alford, *he that entered*, referring to Christ, and contrasted with Joshua.   Jesus is not mentioned in the entire passage, iii. 7–iv. 9.

That rest (ἐκείνην τὴν κατάπαυσιν). The Sabbath-rest of God, instituted at creation, promised to the fathers, forfeited by their unbelief, remaining to us on the condition of faith.

Lest any man fall after the same example of unbelief (ἵνα μὴ ἐν τῷ αὐτῷ τις ὑποδείγματι πέσῃ τῆς ἀπειθείας). Πέσῃ *fall* is to be taken absolutely ; not, *fall into the same example.* Ὑπόδειγμα *example,* mostly in Hebrews. Rejected as unclassical by the Attic rhetoricians. Originally *a sign* which suggests something : *a partial suggestion* as distinct from *a complete expression.* See ch. viii. 5 ; ix. 23. Thus Christ's washing of the disciples' feet (J. xiii. 15) was a *typical suggestion* of the whole field and duty of ministry. See on 1 Pet. ii. 6. It is not easy to give the exact force of ἐν *in.* Strictly speaking, the " example of disobedience " is conceived as that in which the falling takes place. The fall is viewed in the sphere of example. Comp. 2 Macc. iv. 30 ; 1 Cor. ii. 7. Rend. *that no man fall in the same example of disobedience :* the same as that in which they fell.

12. The exhortation is enforced by reference to the character of the revelation which sets forth the rest of God. The message of God which promises the rest and urges to seek it, is no dead, formal precept, but is instinct with living energy.

The word of God (ὁ λόγος τοῦ θεοῦ). That which God speaks through *any* medium. The primary reference is to God's declarations concerning his rest. The fathers explained it of the *personal* Word as in the Fourth Gospel. But in the Epistle there is no approach to any definite use of λόγος with reference to Christ, not even in the description of his relation to God in ch. i, where, if anywhere, it might have been expected. In ch. vi. 5 and xi. 3 we find ῥῆμα. Everywhere in the Epistle Christ appears as *the Son,* not as *the Word.* In this passage, the following predicates, ἐνεργὴς, τομώτερος, κριτικὸς, would hardly be applied to the Logos, and in ver. 14 he is styled *Jesus the Son of God.*

Quick and powerful (ζῶν καὶ ἐνεργὴς). Note the emphatic position of ζῶν *living*. *Living* is the word of God, since it is the word of "the living God" (ch. iii. 12). Living in its essence. For ἐνεργὴς *active, energising*, and kindred words, see on J. i. 12; Philip. iii. 21; Col. i. 29; Philem. 6. Manifesting itself actively in the world and in men's hearts. Comp. 1 Pet. i. 23.

Sharper than any two-edged sword (τομώτερος ὑπὲρ πᾶσαν μάχαιραν δίστομον). Τομώτερος *sharper* from τέμνειν *to cut*, N. T.⁰. ⁰LXX. The word of God has an incisive and penetrating quality. It lays bare self-delusions and moral sophisms. For the comparison of the word of God or of men to a sword, see Ps. lvii. 4; lix. 7; lxiv. 3; Eph. vi. 17. Philo calls his Logos ὁ τομεύς *the cutter*, as cutting chaos into distinct things, and so creating a kosmos. Ὑπὲρ *than*, is literally, *above*. Πᾶσαν *any*, is *every*. Δίστομον only here and Apoc. i. 16; ii. 12, lit. *two-mouthed*. In LXX always of a sword. See Judg. iii. 16; Ps. cxlix. 6; Prov. v. 4; Sir. xxi. 3. In Class. of a cave with *a twofold mouth* (Soph. *Philoct.* 16); of *double-branching* roads (Soph. *Oed. Col.* 900); of rivers with *two mouths* (Polyb. xxxiv. 10, 5). Στόμα *mouth*, of the *edge* of a sword, L. xxi. 24; Heb. xi. 34. Often in LXX, as Gen. xxxiv. 26; Josh. x. 28, 33, 35, 37, 39; Judg. i. 8. So occasionally in Class., as Homer, *Il.* xv. 389. Κατεσθίειν or κατέσθειν *to devour* is used of the sword, Deut. xxxii. 42; 2 Sam. ii. 26; Isa. xxxi. 8; Jer. ii. 30, etc. Μάχαιρα *sword*, in Class. *a dirk* or *dagger:* rarely, a *carving knife;* later, a *bent* sword or *sabre* as contrasted with a *straight, thrusting* sword, ξίφος (not in N. T. but occasionally in LXX). Ῥομφαία, L. ii. 35 (see note), elsewhere only in Apocalypse, very often in LXX, is a large broadsword. In LXX of Goliath's sword, 1 Sam. xvii. 51

Piercing (διικνούμενος). Lit. *coming through*. N. T.⁰.

Even to the dividing asunder of soul and spirit and of the joints and marrow (ἄχρι μερισμοῦ ψυχῆς καὶ πνεύματος ἁρμῶν τε καὶ μυελῶν). Μερισμὸς dividing, only here and ch. ii. 4, is not to be understood of dividing soul *from* spirit or joints *from* marrow. Soul and spirit cannot be said to be separated in any such sense as this, and joints and marrow are not in contact with each other. Μερισμὸς is the *act* of division; not the *point* or *line* of division. Joints and marrow are not to be taken in a literal and material sense.* In rendering, construe *soul, spirit, joints, marrow*, as all dependent on *dividing*. Joints and marrow (ἁρμῶν, μυελῶν, N. T.°) are to be taken figuratively as joints and marrow of soul and spirit. This figurative sense is exemplified in classical usage, as Eurip. *Hippol.* 255, " to form moderate friendships, and not πρὸς ἄκρον μυελὸν ψυχῆς to the deep *marrow* of the soul." The conception of *depth* applied to the soul is on the same figurative line. See Aesch. *Agam.* 778; Eurip. *Bacch.* 203. Attempts to explain on any psychological basis are futile. The form of expression is poetical, and signifies that the word penetrates to the inmost recesses of our spiritual being as a sword cuts through the joints and marrow of the body. The separation is not of one part from another, but operates in each department of the spiritual nature. The expression is expanded and defined by the next clause.

A discerner (κριτικὸς). N. T.°. °LXX. The word carries on the thought of *dividing*. From κρίνειν to *divide* or *separate*, which runs into the sense of *judge*, the usual meaning in N. T., judgment involving the *sifting out* and *analysis* of evidence. In κριτικὸς the ideas of *discrimination* and *judgment* are blended. Vulg. *discretor*.

Of the thoughts and intents of the heart (ἐνθυμήσεων καὶ ἐννοιῶν καρδίας). The A. V. is loose and inaccurate. Ἐνθύμησις rare in N. T. See Matt. ix. 4; Acts xvii. 29. Comp. ἐνθυμεῖσθαι, Matt. i. 20; ix. 4. In every instance, both of the noun and of the verb, the sense is *pondering* or *thinking*

---

* As Delitzsch, whose note on this passage **is one of the curiosities of exegesis**, and a specimen of literalism run mad.

out. Rend. *the reflections.* Έννοια, only here and 1 Pet. iv. 1.
It is *the definite conception* which follows ἐνθύμησις   Rend.
conceptions.

13. From the word of God the writer proceeds to God
himself as cognisant of all things; thus giving a second
ground for the exhortation of ver. 11.

Creature (κτίσις). See on Rom. viii. 19; 2 Cor. v. 17;
Col. i. 15. Here in the sense of *thing created.*

Opened (τετραχηλισμένα). N. T.°. °LXX. Only later
Greek. Evidently connected with τράχηλος *neck, throat.*
The exact metaphor, however, it is impossible to determine.
The following are the principal explanations proposed : *taken
by the throat,* as an athlete grasps an adversary ; *exposed,* as
a malefactor's neck is bent back, and his face exposed to the
spectators ; or, as the necks of victims at the altar are drawn
back and exposed to the knife. The idea at the root seems
to be the bending back of the neck, and the last explanation,
better than any other, suits the previous figure of the sword.
The custom of drawing back the victim's neck for sacrifice
is familiar to all classical students. See Hom. *Il.* i. 459;
ii. 422; Pindar, *Ol.* xiii. 114. The victim's throat bared to
the sacrificial knife is a powerful figure of the complete ex-
posure of all created intelligence to the eye of him whose
word is as a two-edged sword.

With whom we have to do (πρὸς ὃν ἡμῖν ὁ λόγος). Rend.
with whom is our reckoning; that is *to whom we have to give
account.**

14. Chapter ii. 17, 18 is now resumed. This and the following verse more naturally form the conclusion of the preceding section than the introduction to the following one.

---

* Not as Lünemann, Alford, Bleek, Calvin, De Wette, *toward whom a
relation exists for us,* on which Weiss correctly remarks that this sense of
λόγος is unbiblical.

Great high priest (μέγαν). Emphasising Christ's priestly character to Jewish readers, as superior to that of the Levitical priests. He is holding up the *ideal* priesthood.

Passed into the heavens (διεληλυθότα τοὺς οὐρανούς). Rend. " passed *through* the heavens." Through, and up to the throne of God of which he wields the power, and is thus able to fulfil for his followers the divine promise of rest.

Jesus the Son of God. The name *Jesus* applied to the high priest is forcible as recalling the historical, human person, who was tempted like his brethren. We are thus prepared for what is said in ver. 15 concerning his sympathising character.

15. We have not an high priest who cannot, etc. Whatever may be thought to the contrary ; whatever contrary conclusion may be drawn from the character of the Levitical priests, or from Christ's exalted dignity and purity.

Touched with the feeling (συνπαθῆσαι). Only here and ch. x. 34. This is more than *knowledge* of human infirmity. It is *feeling* it by reason of a common experience *with* (σύν) men.

Infirmities (ἀσθενείαις). Not *sufferings*, but *weaknesses*, moral and physical, which predispose to sin and facilitate it.

Like as we are (καθ᾽ ὁμοιότητα). Lit. *according to likeness.* Ἡμῶν *of us* or *our* is to be understood, or, as some, ἡμῖν, according to his likeness *to us.*

Without sin (χωρὶς ἁμαρτίας). This, of course, implies that he was not led into sin by temptation, and also that no temptation aroused in him sin already present and dormant. It is not meant that temptation arising from sin external to himself was not applied to him.

16. **Come**—**unto** ($\pi\rho\sigma\epsilon\rho\chi\acute{\omega}\mu\epsilon\theta\alpha$). °P., often in Hebrews, and commonly in the same sense as here—approach to God through the O. T. sacrifices or the sacrifice of Christ. Paul's word $\pi\rho\sigma\alpha\gamma\omega\gamma\acute{\eta}$ *access* expresses the same idea.* See Eph. ii. 18 ; iii. 12. The phrase *come boldly* expresses a thought which the Epistle emphasises—that Christianity is the religion of *free access* to God. Comp. 2 Cor. iii. 12, 13.

Unto the throne of grace ($\tau\hat{\omega}\ \theta\rho\acute{\delta}\nu\omega\ \tau\hat{\eta}s\ \chi\acute{\alpha}\rho\iota\tau\sigma s$). The phrase N. T.°.   Throne *of glory*, Matt. xix. 28 ; xxv. 31 : *of majesty*, Heb. viii. 1.   In Apoc. *throne* occurs over forty times, either *the* throne, or *his* throne, or throne *of God*. Once throne *of the beast*, xvi. 10.   *Throne of grace* expresses grace as the gift of divine power.

Mercy—**grace** ($\check{\epsilon}\lambda\epsilon\sigma s$—$\chi\acute{\alpha}\rho\iota\nu$). *Mercy* for past sins ; *grace* for future work, trial, and resistance to temptation.

To help in time of need ($\epsilon\grave{\iota}s\ \epsilon\check{\upsilon}\kappa\alpha\iota\rho\sigma\nu\ \beta\sigma\acute{\eta}\theta\epsilon\iota\alpha\nu$).   Lit. *for seasonable help*, or *help in good time;* before it is too late ; while there is still time to seek God's rest.   Others, however, explain, *when it is needed;* or, *before temptation leads to sin.*

CHAPTER V.

The doctrine of the high-priesthood of Christ.

The Hebrew Christians were not familiar with Christ under the aspect of a high priest. They did not understand the application of the title and office to him. They could not infer it from his early life, since he was not of the lineage of Aaron, nor from his ministry, since he claimed no special privilege of access to the temple, performed no priestly functions, and contradicted the whole Jewish conception of the priesthood.

---

* Though some, as Meyer and Ellicott, insist on the transitive sense—
introduction.

1. **Every high priest** (πᾶς ἀρχιερεὺς).   Every Levitical high priest.   Αρχιερεὺς °P.

Taken (λαμβανόμενος).   Rend. *being taken,* or *since he is taken:* not *who is taken.*   The point is that the high priest's efficiency for men depends on his being taken from among men.

Is ordained (καθίσταται).   Constituted priest.   See on Tit. i. 5.

For men (ὑπὲρ ἀνθρώπων).   *On behalf of* men.

In things pertaining to God (τὰ πρὸς τὸν θεόν).   As respects his relation to God.   See on ch. ii. 17.

That he may offer (ἵνα προσφέρῃ).   Προσφέρειν, lit. *to bring to* (*the altar*).   Comp. Matt. v. 23.   °P., who, however, has the kindred noun προσφορὰ *offering.*   Very often in LXX ; nineteen times in Hebrews, and always, with one exception (ch. xii. 7), in the technical sense, as here.

Gifts—sacrifices (δῶρα—θυσίας).   Δῶρα *offerings generally:* θυσίας *bloody* sacrifices.   The distinction, however, is not constantly observed.   Thus, θυσίαι, of unbloody offerings, Gen. iv. 3, 5 ; Lev. ii. 1 ; Num. v. 15 : δῶρα, of bloody offerings, Gen. iv. 4 ; Lev. i. 2, 3, 10.

For sins (ὑπὲρ ἁμαρτιῶν).   In this the priest's efficiency is especially called out, and he who has not genuine compassion for the sinful cannot do this efficiently.   Hence the words which follow.

2. **Have compassion** (μετριοπαθεῖν).   N. T.°.   °LXX. °Class.   Originally of the rational regulation of the natural passions, as opposed to the Stoic ἀπάθεια, which involved the crushing out of the passions.   Often, in later Greek, of moderating anger.   It is not identical with συμπαθῆσαι (ch. iv. 5),

but signifies *to be moderate* or *tender* in judgment toward
another's errors.   Here it denotes a state of feeling toward
the ignorant and erring which is neither too severe nor too
tolerant.   The high priest must not be betrayed into irritation at sin and ignorance, neither must he be weakly indul-
gent.

The ignorant (τοῖς ἀγνοοῦσι).   Comp. ἀγνοημάτων *ignorances*, ch. ix. 7, and Num. xv. 22–31, where the distinction
is drawn between sins of ignorance and sins of presumption.
Atonement for sins of ignorance was required by the Levitical law as a means of educating the moral perception, and
of showing that sin and defilement might exist unsuspected:
that God saw evil where men did not, and that his test of
purity was stricter than theirs.

For that he himself also is compassed with infirmity
(ἐπεὶ καὶ αὐτὸς περίκειται ἀσθένειαν).   Sympathy belongs to
the high-priestly office, and grows out of the sense of personal infirmity.   The verb is graphic :   *has infirmity lying
round him.*   Comp. ch. xii. 1, of the *encompassing* (περικείμενον) cloud of witnesses.   Ἀσθένειαν, the *moral* weakness
which makes men capable of sin.   This is denied in the case
of Christ.   See ch. vii. 28.

3. **He ought** (ὀφείλει).   It is his duty, growing out of
the fact of his own infirmity.

4. The high priest must be divinely called.   One thus
compassed with infirmity would shrink from such an office
unless called to it by God.

He that is called (καλούμενος).   The A. V. follows T. R.,
ὁ καλούμενος.   The article should be omitted.   Rend. *but being
called by God (he taketh it), as did Aaron.*

5. **Did not glorify himself to be made high priest.**
Ἐδόξασεν *glorified* is general, and is more specifically defined
by γενηθῆναι ἀρχιερέα *to be made high priest.*

But he that said unto him, Thou art my Son, etc. Supply *glorified him.* He did not glorify himself, but God who styled him "son" glorified him. *Thou art my Son* is introduced thus in close connection with the call to the priesthood, in recognition of the fact that the priesthood of Christ had its basis in his sonship. "Christ's priestly vocation ceases to be an accident in his history, and becomes an essential characteristic of his position as Son: sonship, christhood, priestliness, inseparably interwoven" (Bruce).

6. **Thou art a priest forever, etc.** According to this verse Christ is prophetically pointed out in Ps. cx as an eternal priest, independent of fleshly descent, a king, and superior in dignity to the Levitical priests.

According to the order (κατὰ τὴν τάξιν). According to the rank which Melchisedec held. Almost = *like*. For Melchisedec see ch. vii.

7. He is now to show that Christ was under training for the priesthood, and describes the process of training.

Who (ὅς). Nominative to ἔμαθεν *learned*, ver. 8, to which all the participles are preparatory.

In the days of his flesh (ἐν ταῖς ἡμέραις τῆς σαρκὸς αὐτοῦ). During his mortal life.

When he had offered up prayers and supplications (δεήσεις τε καὶ ἱκετηρίας προσενέγκας). Δεήσεις special, definite requests: ἱκετηρίας, N. T.⁰, is properly an adjective, *pertaining to* or *fit for suppliants*, with ῥάβδους staves or ἐλαίας olive-branches understood. The olive-branch bound round with wool was held forth by a suppliant in token of his character as such. The phrase προσφέρειν δεήσεις N. T.⁰.*

---

* In his volume on Hebrews (1899) Professor Bruce abandons the view held by him in his *Humiliation of Christ*, p. 30, that, in the use of the sacrificial expression προσενέγκας, the writer conceived Christ's prayer in Gethsemane as a sacrificial offering, and found in it a parallel with the offering which the Levitical high priest presented for himself; a view which must be regarded as fanciful. See Weiss ad loc.

Unto him that was able to save him from death (πρὸς τὸν δυνάμενον σώζειν αὐτὸν ἐκ θανάτου). Const. with *prayers and supplications*, not with *offered*.   *To save him from death* may mean to deliver him from *the fear of death*, from *the anguish of death*, or from *remaining a prey to death*.   In either case, the statement connects itself with the thought of Christ's real humanity.   He was under the pressure of a sore human need which required divine help, thus showing that he was like unto his brethren.   He appealed to one who could answer his prayer.   The purport of the prayer is not stated.   It is at least suggested by Matt. xxvi. 39.

And was heard in that he feared (καὶ εἰσακουσθεὶς ἀπὸ τῆς εὐλαβείας). Rend. *was heard on account of his godly fear*. Ἐυλάβεια only here and ch. xii. 28.   The verb εὐλαβεῖσθαι *to act cautiously, beware, fear*, only ch. xi. 7.   The image in the word is that of *a cautious taking hold* (λαμβάνειν) and *careful and respectful handling:* hence piety of a *devout* and *circumspect* character, as that of Christ, who in his prayer took account of all things, not only his own desire, but his Father's will.   Ἐυλάβεια is ascribed to Christ as a human trait, see ch. xii. 28.   He was *heard*, for his prayer was answered, whatever it may have been.   God was able to save him from death altogether.   He did not do this.   He was able to sustain him under the anguish of death, and to give him strength to suffer the Father's will: he was also able to deliver him from death by resurrection: both these he did.   It is not impossible that both these may be combined in the statement *he was heard*.*

8. **Though he were a Son** (καίπερ ὢν υἱός).   For *were* rend. *was*.   His training for the priesthood involved suffering, even though he was a son.   Connect with ἔμαθεν *learned*, not with the preceding clause, which would mean that his position as a son did not exempt him from the obligation to

---

* The rendering *he was heard (and so delivered) from his fear (that which he feared)* is untenable because εὐλάβεια cannot mean the *object* of fear.   The rendering *he was heard by him who was his fear* is absurd.

godly fear, which is true as a fact (see ver. 7), but is not the
point of emphasis here.

Learned he obedience (ἔμαθεν τὴν ὑπακοήν). Omit *he*,
since the subject of ἔμαθεν *learned* is ὃς *who*, ver. 7. Jesus
did not have to learn to obey, see J. viii. 29; but he required
the special discipline of a severe human experience as a training for his office as a high priest who could be touched with
the feeling of human infirmities. He did not need to be disciplined out of any inclination to disobedience; but, as Alford
puts it, "the special course of submission by which he became
perfected as our high priest was gone through in time, and
was a matter of acquirement and practice." This is no more
strange than his growth in wisdom, L. ii. 52. *Growth* in
experience was an essential part of his humanity.

By the things which he suffered (ἀφ᾽ ὧν ἔπαθεν). Or
from the things, etc. Note the word-play, ἔμαθεν ἔπαθεν.
So Croesus, addressing Cyrus, says, τὰ δέ μοι παθήματα, ἐόντα
ἀχάριστα, μαθήματα γέγονεν, "my *sufferings*, though painful,
have proved to be *lessons*" (Hdt. i. 207): so Soph. *Trach.*
142, μήτ᾽ ἐκμάθοις παθοῦσα, "mayst thou not *learn* by *suffering*."

9. **And being made perfect** (καὶ τελειωθεὶς). Comp. ch.
ii. 10. The fundamental idea in τελειοῦν is the bringing of
a person or thing to the goal fixed by God. Comp. ch. vii.
11, 19; ix. 9; x. 1, 14; xi. 40; xii. 23. Here of Christ's
having reached the end which was contemplated in his
divinely-appointed discipline for the priesthood. The consummation was attained in his death, Philip. ii. 8: his *obedience* extended even unto death.

The author of eternal salvation (αἴτιος σωτηρίας αἰωνίου).
Ἀίτιος, N. T.°, an adjective, *causing*. Comp. *captain of salvation*, Heb. ii. 10. The phrase σωτηρία αἰώνιος *eternal salvation* N. T.°, but see LXX, Isa. xv. 17. Not *everlasting*
salvation, but a salvation of which all the conditions, attainments, privileges, and rewards transcend the conditions and
limitations of time.

Unto all them that obey him (πᾶσιν τοῖς ὑπακούουσιν
αὐτῷ). *Obey* points to *obedience*, ver. 8, and *salvation* to *save*,
ver. 7. If the *captain* of salvation must learn obedience, so
must his followers. Comp. 2 Th. i. 8.

10. **Called of God** (προσαγορευθεὶς ὑπὸ τοῦ θεοῦ). Rend.
since he was addressed or *saluted by God*. God recognised and
saluted him as that which he had *become* by passing through
and completing his earthly discipline. Προσαγορεύειν *to address* N. T.⁰. A few times in LXX.

11. From this point the comparison of Christ with Melchisedec would naturally be developed; but the author digresses
into a complaint of the imperfect spiritual attainment of his
readers, and a remonstrance and admonition extending to the
end of ch. vi.

Of whom (περὶ οὗ). Rend. *concerning which.* Not Melchisedec, but the *topic* that Christ is a priest after the order
of Melchisedec, a topic to which great importance is attached.
Can it be imagined that the discussion of such a topic would
appeal to a Gentile audience as a reason for not relapsing into
paganism?

We have many things to say (πολὺς ἡμῖν ὁ λόγος). Lit.
the discourse is abundant unto us. We refers to the writer
himself.

Hard to be uttered (δυσερμήνευτος λέγειν). Lit. *hard of
interpretation to speak.* The A.V. entirely misses the idea of
interpretation. Rev. better, *hard of interpretation.* Δυσερμήνευτος N. T.⁰.   ⁰LXX.   ⁰Class.

Ye are dull of hearing (νωθροὶ γεγόνατε ταῖς ἀκοαῖς). Rend.
ye have grown dull in your hearing. For ἀκοὴ *hearing* see on
2 Tim. iv. 3. The verb implies a deterioration on the hearers'
part. Νωθροὶ only here and ch. vi. 12. From νη *not* and

ὠθεῖν *to push.* Hence *slow, sluggish.** Mostly in later Greek,
although Plato uses it much in the same sense as here. "When
they have to face study they are *stupid* (νωθροί) and cannot
remember." *Theaet.* 144 B. In LXX, Prov. xxii. 29;
Sir. iv. 29; xi. 12. Sometimes = *low, mean, obscure.* So
in Proverbs, but in Sirach *slack, slow.*

12. **When for the time ye ought to be teachers** (ὀφείλον-
τες εἶναι διδάσκαλοι διὰ τὸν χρόνον). Rend. *for when ye ought
to be teachers by reason of the time.* A. V. entirely obscures
the true meaning, which is that, because of the time during
which the readers have been under instruction, they ought to
be able to instruct others.

Again (πάλιν). Not with *teach you,* as A.V., but with *ye
have need.* The position of the word is emphatic. *Again* ye
have need of being taught the very rudiments of divine truth
which ye were taught long ago.

Which be (τινὰ). A.V. takes the pronoun as interrogative
(τίνα). Better *indefinite* as subject of διδάσκειν *teach.* Rend.
"ye have need that *some one* teach you."

The first principles of the oracles (τὰ στοιχεῖα τῆς ἀρχῆς
τῶν λογίων). Lit. *the rudiments of the beginning of the oracles.*
The phrase στοιχεῖα τῆς ἀρχῆς N. T.° It is = *primary elements.* For στοιχεῖα see on Gal. iv. 3. Λόγιον is a diminutive,
meaning strictly a *brief* utterance, and used both in classical
and biblical Greek of *divine* utterances. In Class. of *prose
oracles.* Philo uses it of the O. T. prophecies, and his treatise
on the Ten Commandments is entitled περὶ τῶν δέκα λογίων.
In LXX often generally — "the *word* or *words* of the Lord,"
see Num. xxiv. 16; Deut. xxxiii. 9; Ps. xi. 6; xvii. 30, etc.
It was used of the *sayings* of Jesus, see Polycarp, *Ad Phil.* vii.
From the time of Philo, of any sacred writing, whether dis-

---

* Schmidt, *Synon.,* says it is best represented by the German nöhlen *to
dawdle.*

course or narrative. Papias and Irenaeus have τὰ κυριακὰ
λόγια *dominical oracles.** The meaning here is *the O. T.*
sayings, especially those pointing to Christ.

And are become (καὶ γεγόνατε). As in ver. 11, implying
degeneracy. The time was when you needed the strong meat
of the word.

Milk (γάλακτος). Comp. 1 Cor. iii. 2. Answering to
rudiments.

Strong meat (στερεᾶς τροφῆς). Lit. *solid* meat. See on
steadfast, 1 Pet. v. 9. More advanced doctrinal teaching.
The explanation of the Melchisedec priesthood to which the
writer was about to pass involved the exhibition for the first
time of the opposition of the N. T. economy of salvation to
that of the old, and of the imperfection and abrogation of the
O. T. priesthood. To apprehend this consequence of N. T.
revelation required alert and matured minds. This is why
he pauses to dwell on the sluggish mental and spiritual condition of his readers.

13. **Useth** (μετέχων). Rend. *partakes of.* See on ch. i. 9;
ii. 14; iii. 1, 14.

Unskilful (ἄπειρος). N. T.º. Rend. *unskilled* or *in-*
experienced.

In the word of righteousness (λόγου δικαιοσύνης). The
phrase N. T.º. The genitive δικαιοσύνης *of righteousness* is
combined in N. T. with *way, God, gift, instruments, servants,*
law, ministration, fruit and *fruits, ministers, hope, breastplate,*
crown, king, preacher. It is a mistake to attempt to give the
phrase here a concrete meaning. It signifies simply a word
of normally right character. It is not = *the Christian revelation,*
which would require the article. Probably, however, in the

---

* An interesting discussion of the word may be found in Lightfoot's
Essays on Supernatural Religion, p. 172 ff.

foreground of the writer's thought was the word spoken by
the Son (ch. i. 2); the salvation which at first was spoken
by the Lord (ch. ii. 3).*

A babe (νήπιος). See on Rom. ii. 20; 1 Cor. iii. 1;
Eph. iv. 14.

14. Strong meat belongeth to them that are of full age
(τελείων δέ ἐστιν ἡ στερεὰ τροφή). This rendering is clumsy.
Rend. *solid food is for full-grown men.* For τελείων *full-grown,*
see on 1 Cor. ii. 6. Often by Paul, as here, in contrast with
νήπιοι *immature Christians.* See 1 Cor. ii. 6; iii. 1; xiii. 11;
Eph. iv. 4. Paul has the verb νηπιάζειν *to be a child* in
1 Cor. xiv. 20.

By reason of use (διὰ τὴν ἕξιν). For *use* rend. *habitude.*
N. T.º. It is the condition produced by past exercise. Not
the *process,* as A. V., but the *result.*

Their senses (τὰ αἰσθητήρια). N. T.º. Organs of perception; perceptive faculties of the mind. In LXX see
Jer. iv. 19; 4 Macc. ii. 22.

Exercised (γεγυμνασμένα). See on 2 Pet. ii. 14, and
1 Tim. iv. 7.

Good and evil. Not moral good and evil, but wholesome
and corrupt doctrine. The implication is that the readers'
condition is such as to prevent them from making this
distinction.

CHAPTER VI.

Some difficulty attaches to the first three verses, because
the writer combines two thoughts: his own intention to proceed from elementary to more advanced teachings, and his

---

* Surely not, as Lünemann, *the gospel message as centring in the doctrine
of justification by faith,* which would be dragged in by the ears.

readers' advance to that higher grade of spiritual receptiveness on which the effectiveness of his teaching must depend. The mistake in interpretation has been in insisting that the three verses treat only the one or the other thought. Observe that διὸ *wherefore* is connected with the rebuke in ch. v. 11, 12; and that that rebuke is directly connected with the announcement of the doctrine of the Melchisedec priesthood of Christ. The course of thought is as follows : Christ is a priest after the order of Melchisedec (ch. v. 10). There is much to be said on this subject, and it is hard to explain, because you have become dull, and need elementary teaching, whereas, by reason of your long Christian standing, you ought to be teachers yourselves (ch. v. 11, 12). For you all recognise the principle that baby-food is for babes, and solid food only for men, whose powers have been trained by habitual exercise (ch. v. 13, 14). *Wherefore*, in order that you may be aroused from your sluggishness and have your perceptions brought up to the matured condition which befits men in Christ, and in order that I may, at the same time, complete the development of my theme, I propose that we together move forward to completion : I to the full exposition of the subject of Christ's high-priesthood, and you to that maturity of discernment which becomes you. This will require us both to leave the rudimentary stage of teaching concerning Christ.

1. Leaving the principles of the doctrines of Christ

(ἀφέντες τὸν τῆς ἀρχῆς τοῦ Χριστοῦ λόγον). Lit. *leaving the word of the beginning concerning Christ*. Ἀφέντες *leaving* or *dismissing* does not imply ceasing to believe in elementary truths or to regard them as important, but leaving them "as a builder leaves his foundation in erecting his building" (Bruce). *The word of the beginning of Christ* is practically = *the rudiments of the beginning*, ch. v. 12; that rudimentary view of Christ's person and office which unfolds into the doctrine of his priesthood. Up to this point the writer has shown only that the permanent elements of the old covenant remain and are exalted in Christ. The more difficult point,

which it will require matured perception to grasp, is that
Christ's priesthood involves the entire abolition of the old
covenant.

Let us go on unto perfection (ἐπὶ τὴν τελειότητα φερώ-
μεθα). Lit. *let us be borne on to completeness*. The participial clause, *leaving*, etc., is related to the verbal clause as
expressing a necessary accompaniment or consequence of the
latter. *Let us be borne on to completeness, and, because of this,
leave*, etc. This sense is not given by the Rev. Τελειότης
only here and Col. iii. 14. Rend. *completeness*. The completeness is viewed as pertaining to both the writer and the
readers. He proposes to fully develop his theme : they are
exhorted to strive for that full Christian manhood which will
fit them to receive the fully-developed discussion.

Not laying again the foundation (μὴ πάλιν θεμέλιον κατα-
βαλλόμενοι). Not explanatory of *leaving*, etc. The following
words, describing the elements of the foundation, — repentance, baptisms, etc., — simply illustrate in a general way
the proposal to proceed to the exposition of the doctrine of
Christ's priesthood. The illustrative proposition is that a
building is not completed by lingering at the foundation ;
and so Christian maturity is not to be attained by going back
to subjects which belong to the earliest stage of Christian
instruction. He purposely selects for his illustration things
which belong to the very initiation of Christian life.

Dead works (νεκρῶν ἔργων). The phrase only in Hebrews.
Comp. ch. ix. 14. Not sinful works in the ordinary sense of
the term, but works without the element of life which comes
through faith in the living God. There is a sharp opposition,
therefore, between dead works and faith. They are contraries.
This truth must be one of the very first things expounded to
a Jew embracing Christianity.

2. **Doctrine of baptisms** (βαπτισμῶν διδαχὴν).* Not lay-

---

* There is a difference of reading : διδαχὴν, Westcott and Hort, Weiss :
διδαχῆς, Tischendorf, Rev. T. If the latter, the arrangement may be (a) two

ing again as a foundation the teaching (διδαχὴν) of baptisms.
Βαπτισμός only here, ch. ix. 10, and Mk. vii. 4.   The common
form is βάπτισμα.   Neither word in LXX or Class.   The
meaning here is *lustral rites in general*, and may include the
baptism of John and Christian baptism.   The teaching would
cover all such rites, their relations and comparative significance, and it would be necessary in the case of a Jewish
convert to Christianity who might not perceive, for example,
any difference between Jewish lustrations and Christian
baptism.

Laying on of hands.   See on 1 Tim. iv. 14.   A Jewish
and a Christian practice.

Resurrection — eternal judgment.   Both resurrection and
future judgment were Jewish tenets requiring exposition to
Jewish converts as regarded their relations to the same doctrines as taught by Christianity.   The resurrection of Christ
as involving the resurrection of believers would, of itself,
change the whole aspect of the doctrine of resurrection as
held by a Jew.   'Αιωνίου *eternal* certainly cannot here signify
everlasting.   It expresses rather a judgment which shall transcend all temporal judgments; which shall be conducted on
principles different from those of earthly tribunals, and the
decisions of which shall be according to the standards of the
economy of a world beyond time.   See additional note on
2 Th. i. 9.   The phrase *eternal judgment* N. T.º.   Comp.
κρίμα τὸ μέλλον *the judgment to come*, Acts xxiv. 25.

3. **If God permit** (ἐάνπερ ἐπιτρέπῃ ὁ θεός).   The exact
formula N. T.º.   Comp. 1 Cor. xvi. 7; Acts xviii. 21.   Pagan
parallels are τῶν θεῶν θελόντων *if the gods will;* θεῶν ἐπιτρεπ-

---

distinct genitives, *of teaching, of baptisms*: (*b*) διδαχῆς dependent on βαπτισμῶν, *baptisms accompanied with teaching*: (*c*) διδαχῆς governing βαπτισμῶν, *teaching of baptisms*.   (*a*) is not in accord with the structure of what
precedes and follows, since all the particulars of the foundation are designated by double expressions: (*b*) is unusual and difficult to explain with the
plural βαπτισμῶν, since baptism with teaching would mean Christian baptism,
and βαπτισμῶν is not limited to Christian baptism: (*c*) is preferable if διδαχῆς
is to be read.

ὄντων *the gods permitting*, and θεῶν βουλομένων *if the gods desire*. An ominous hint is conveyed that the spiritual dulness of the readers may prevent the writer from developing his theme and them from receiving his higher instruction. The issue is dependent on the power which God may impart to his teaching, but his efforts may be thwarted by the impossibility of repentance on their part. No such impossibility is imposed by God, but it may reside in a moral condition which precludes the efficient action of the agencies which work for repentance, so that God cannot permit the desired consequence to follow the word of teaching.

4. **Impossible** (ἀδύνατον). It is impossible to dilute this word into *difficult*.

Those who were once enlightened (τοὺς ἅπαξ φωτισθέντας). Rend. "*once for all* enlightened." Ἅπαξ is frequent in the Epistle. Comp. ch. ix. 7, 26, 27, 28; x. 2; xii. 26, 27. Indicating that the enlightenment ought to have sufficed to prevent them from falling away; not that it does not admit of repetition. *Enlightened*, through the revelation of God in Christ, the true light, and through the power of the Spirit. Φωτίζειν in LXX usually *to teach* or *instruct;* see Ps. cxviii. 130; 2 K. xii. 2; xvii. 27. Comp. in N. T. J. i. 9; Eph. i. 18; iii. 9; Heb. x. 32. Erasmus gives the correct explanation: "Who once for all have left the darkness of their former life, having been enlightened by the gospel teaching." There is no ground for explaining the word here of baptism, although the fathers from the time of Justin Martyr used φωτίζειν and φωτισμός in that sense, and this usage continued down to the Reformation. See Just. Mart. *Apol.* i. 62. Chrysostom entitled his 59th Homily, addressed to candidates for baptism, πρὸς τοὺς μέλλοντας φωτίζεσθαι *to those who are about to be enlightened;* and justified this name for baptism by this passage and x. 32. The Peshitto translates this passage, "who have once (for all) descended to baptism." The N. T. gives no example of this usage.*

---

* See a good note by Alford, *Commentary* ad loc.

Tasted of the heavenly gift (γευσαμένους τῆς δωρεᾶς τῆς ἐπουρανίου). For γευσαμένους *tasted*, comp. ch. ii. 9. The meaning is, *have consciously partaken of.* Comp. 1 Pet. ii. 3, and τρώγων *eateth*, J. vi. 56. The heavenly gift is the Holy Spirit. It is true that this is distinctly specified in the next clause, but the two clauses belong together.*

Partakers of the Holy Ghost (μετόχους πνεύματος ἁγίου). "*Heavenly* gift" emphasises the *heavenly quality* of the gift. *The Holy Ghost* is the gift itself which possesses the heavenly quality.

5. **The good word of God** (καλὸν θεοῦ ῥῆμα). The gospel of Christ as preached. Comp. ch. ii. 3. To *the word* are attached *life* (Acts v. 20); *spirit and life* (J. vi. 63); *salvation* (Acts xi. 14); *cleansing* (Eph. v. 26); especially *the impartation of the Spirit* (J. iii. 34; Acts v. 32; x. 44; Eph. vi. 17; Heb. ii. 4).

Powers of the world to come (δυνάμεις μέλλοντος αἰῶνος). Not foretastes of heavenly bliss. *The world to come* is the world of men under the new order which is to enter with the fulfilment of Christ's work. See on *these last days*, ch. i. 2. These powers are characteristic of that period, and in so far as that dispensation is inaugurated here and now, they assert and manifest themselves.

6. **If they shall fall away** (καὶ παραπεσόντας). Lit. *and having fallen away.* Comp. πέσῃ *fall*, ch. iv. 11. Παραπίπτειν, N. T.°. It means *to deviate, turn aside.* Comp. LXX, Ezek. xiv. 13; xv. 8.

To renew them again (πάλιν ἀνακαινίζειν). The verb N. T.°. 'Ανακαινοῦν *to renew*, 2 Cor. iv. 16; Col. iii. 10.

---

* The number and variety of explanations of *the heavenly gift* are bewildering: the Lord's Supper; regeneration in general, as distinguished from the special communication of the Spirit in baptism; persuasion of eternal life; righteousness; forgiveness of sins; peace which results from forgiveness; faith; the gospel; the heavenly light which produces the enlightenment; the abundant grace of Christianity.

Seeing they crucify to themselves — afresh (ἀνασταυρ-οῦντας ἑαυτοῖς). In the Roman classical use of the word, ἀνά has only the meaning *up:* to nail *up* on the cross. Here in the sense of *anew*, an idea for which classical writers had no occasion in connection with crucifying.* Ἑαυτοῖς for *themselves*. So that Christ is no more available for them. They declare that Christ's crucifixion has not the meaning or the virtue which they formerly attached to it.

The Son of God. Marking the enormity of the offence.

Put him to an open shame (παραδειγματίζοντας). N. T.°. Rarely in LXX. Comp. Num. xxv. 4, *hang them up.* From παρά *beside*, δεικνύναι *to show* or *point out.* To put something alongside of a thing by way of commending it to imitation or avoidance. *To make an example of;* thence *to expose to public disgrace.* Δεῖγμα *example*, only Jude 7. Δειγματίζειν *to make a public show* or *example*, Matt. i. 19; Col. ii. 15. See additional note at the end of this chapter.

7. The inevitableness of the punishment illustrated by a familiar fact of nature.

The earth (γῆ). Or *the land.* Personified. Comp. αὐτο-μάτη ἡ γῆ *the land of itself*, Mk. iv. 28, see note.

Which drinketh in (ἡ πιοῦσα). Appropriates the heavenly gift of rain, the richness of which is indicated by *that cometh oft upon it.*

Herbs (βοτάνην). Grass, fodder. N. T.°.

---

* Principal Edwards, *Expositor's Bible*, explains, "they cannot be re-newed after falling away *if they persist in crucifying.*" Surely nothing could be farther from the writer's meaning. Some of the older commentators, referring *renew them* to baptism, take *crucify* and *put to an open shame* as explanatory of ἀνακαινίζειν, thus : *to renew them to repentance which would be a recrucifying.* They refer to Paul's declaration, Rom. vi. 3, that in baptism is signified the crucifixion of the old man with Christ. If baptism were repeated, Christ would be recrucified. But *Christ* is not crucified in baptism ; only *the old man.*

Meet for them by whom it is dressed (εὔθετον ἐκείνοις δι' οὓς καὶ γεωργεῖται). For εὔθετον, lit. *well placed*, thence *fit* or *appropriate*, see L. ix. 62; xiv. 35. Γεωργεῖν *to till the ground*, N. T.[o]. Rend. *tilled*. *Dress* is properly to *trim*. The natural result of the ground's receiving and absorbing the rains is fruitfulness, which redounds to the benefit of those who cultivate it.

Receiveth blessing from God (μεταλαμβάνει εὐλογίας ἀπὸ τοῦ θεοῦ). Rend. *partaketh of blessing*. The blessing is increased fruitfulness. Comp. Matt. xiii. 12; J. xv. 2.

8. But that which beareth thorns and briers (ἐκφέρουσα δὲ ἀκάνθας καὶ τριβόλους). Wrong. As given in A. V. the illustration throws no light on the subject. It puts the contrast as between two kinds of soil, the one well-watered and fertile, the other unwatered and sterile. This would illustrate the contrast between those who have and those who have not enjoyed gospel privileges. On the contrary the contrast is between two classes of *Christians* under equally favorable conditions, out of which they develop opposite results. Rend. *but if it (the ground that receives the rain) bear thorns and thistles*, etc. Ἄκανθαι *thorns*, from ἀκή *a point*. Τρίβολος, from τρεῖς *three* and βέλος *a dart;* having three darts or points. A ball with sharp iron spikes, on three of which it rested, while the fourth projected upward, was called *tribulus* or *tribolus*, or *caltrop*. These were scattered over the ground by Roman soldiers in order to impede the enemy's cavalry. A kind of thorn or thistle, a land-caltrop, was called *tribulus* So Virgil,

> " Subit aspera silva,
> Lappaeque tribulique."
>
> *Georg.* i. 153.

Is rejected (ἀδόκιμος). Lit. *unapproved*. See on *reprobate*, Rom. i. 28.

Nigh unto cursing (κατάρας ἐγγύς). See on Gal. iii. 10. Enhancing the idea of *rejected*. It is exposed to the peril of abandonment to perpetual barrenness.

Whose end is to be burned (ἧς τὸ τέλος εἰς καῦσιν). Ἧς *whose, of which,* may be referred to *cursing* — the end of which cursing : but better to the main subject, γῆ *the land.* Τέλος is *consummation* rather than *termination.* Εἰς καῦσιν, lit. *unto burning.* Comp. LXX, Isa. xl. 16. The consummation of the cursed land is burning. Comp. J. xv. 6. The field of thorns and thistles is burned over and abandoned to barrenness.*

9. But the writer refuses to believe that his readers will incur such a fate.

Beloved (ἀγαπητοί). Only here in the epistle. It often suggests an argument. See 1 Cor. x. 14; xv. 58; 2 Cor. vii. 1.

We are persuaded (πεπείσμεθα). We are firmly convinced. The verb indicates a past hesitation overcome.

Better things (τὰ κρείσσονα). The article gives a collective force, the better *state of things,* the going on unto perfection (ver. 1). For κρείσσονα *better,* see on ch. i. 4.

That accompany salvation (ἐχόμενα σωτηρίας). Ἔχεσθαι with a genitive is a common Greek idiom meaning *to hold one's self to* a person or thing ; hence to be closely joined to it. So in a local sense, Mk. i. 38; in a temporal sense, L. xiii. 33, *next.* He is persuaded that they will give heed to all things which attend the work of salvation and will enjoy all that attaches to a saved condition.

10. He is encouraged in this confidence by the fact that they are still as formerly engaged in Christian ministries.

Your work and labour of love (τοῦ ἔργου ὑμῶν καὶ τῆς ἀγάπης). Omit *labour.* The A.V. follows T. R. τοῦ κόπου. Rend. *your work and the love which ye shewed,* etc.

---

* The reference to Sodom and Gomorrah (Lünemann, Bleek) is forced, and perhaps equally so that of Westcott to volcanic fires. There is no thought of *purification* by fire, which would be foreign to the subject.

Which ye have shewed toward his name (ἧς ἐνεδείξασθε εἰς τὸ ὄνομα αὐτοῦ).   The verb means, strictly, to show something *in* one's self; or to show one's self in something.   Similar praise is bestowed in ch. x. 32.   They have shown both love and work toward God's name.   That does not look like crucifying Christ.   God is not *unjust*, as he would show himself to be if he were forgetful of this.

11. **We desire** (ἐπιθυμοῦμεν).   Strongly, earnestly.   Comp. Matt. xiii. 17 ; L. xxii. 15.   The manifestations just mentioned make the writer desire that they may exhibit more of the spirit which animates their beneficent works.

Each (ἕκαστον).   He is concerned, not only for the body of believers, but for each member.

To the full assurance of hope unto the end (πρὸς τὴν πληροφορίαν τῆς ἐλπίδος ἄχρι τέλους).   That is, we desire that each of you exhibit the same diligence to develop your hope, which is in danger of failing, into full assurance, unto the end of the present season of trial with its happy consummation.   Comp. Rom. viii. 24.   For πληροφορία see on 1 Th. i. 5, and comp. Rom. iv. 21 ; xiv. 5.   It is practically the same whether we translate *full development* or *full assurance*.   The two meanings coalesce.   Hope develops into full assurance.

12. **Slothful** (νωθροί).   See on ch. v. 11.   Or *sluggish*, as you will become if you lose hope.

Followers (μιμηταί).   Rend. *imitators*.

Faith and patience (πίστεως καὶ μακροθυμίας).   For *patience* rend. *longsuffering*, and see on Jas. v. 7.   Faith and longsuffering go together.   Faith does not win its inheritance without persevering endurance ; hence longsuffering is not only presented as an independent quality, but is predicated of faith.

Inherit (κληρονομούντων). Notice the present participle, *are inheriting.* Their present faith and perseverance are now making for their final inheritance. Comp. Eph. i. 14.

13. Illustration of the longsuffering of faith by the example of Abraham. The necessity for emphasising this element of faith lay in the growing discouragement of the Jewish Christians at the long delay of Christ's second coming. Comp. ch. xi. Abraham became a sojourner in the land of the promise, looking for the heavenly city (ch. xi. 9, 10). All the instances cited in that chapter illustrate the *long outlook* of faith, involving patient waiting and endurance. The example of Abraham shows, first, that the promise of God is sure.

Because he could swear by no greater (ἐπεὶ κατ' οὐδενὸς εἶχεν μείζονος ὀμόσαι). Lit. *since he had (the power) to swear by no one greater.*

By himself (καθ' ἑαυτοῦ). Comp. Gen. xxii. 16. N. T.°, but see LXX, Am. vi. 8.

14. **Surely blessing I will bless thee** (εἰ μήν εὐλογῶν εὐλο-γήσω σε). Ἐι μήν as a formula of swearing N. T.°. In LXX, see Num. xiv. 23, 28, 35; Isa. xlv. 23; Ezek. xxxiii. 27; xxxiv. 8. *Blessing I will bless* is a Hebraism, emphasising the idea contained in the verb. Comp. LXX, Gen. xxii. 17; Num. xxv. 10; Deut. xv. 4.*

15. **After he had patiently endured** (μακροθυμήσας). Pointing back to μακροθυμία *longsuffering*, ver. 12.

---

* Bleek holds that the form εἰ μήν arose from a confusion of the Hebraistic εἰ μή (comp. Heb. אִם) and the Greek ἦ μήν. Thayer (*Lex.*) says this must be the explanation unless εἰ came by itacism from ἦ. So Winer-Schmiedel, *N. T. Gramm.* § 5, 15. Deissmann, however (*Neue Bibelstudien*, Pt. II., p. 33 ff.), gives instances of εἰ (εἶ?) μήν from papyri before Christ, a hundred years older than this epistle, and from the same country in which the LXX was prepared. See also Blass, *N. T. Gramm.* Ss. 9, 60, 254.

He obtained (ἐπέτυχεν). The compounded preposition ἐπὶ has the force of *upon: to light* or *hit upon.* The verb indicates that Abraham did not personally receive the *entire* fulfilment of the promise, but only the germ of its fulfilment. It was partially fulfilled in the birth of Isaac. See Rom. iv. 18.

The security of the divine promise illustrated by the analogy of human practice.

16. **And an oath for confirmation is to them an end of all strife** (καὶ πάσης αὐτοῖς ἀντιλογίας πέρας εἰς βεβαίωσιν ὁ ὅρκος). For " *an* oath," rend. " *the* oath ": generic. Const. *for confirmation* with *end.* "The oath is final for confirmation." Πέρας is *the outermost point;* the point beyond which one cannot go. With this exception always in N. T. in the plural, of *the ends of the earth.* See Matt. xii. 42; Rom. x. 18. So often in LXX. Ἀντιλογία, strictly *contradiction,* only. in Hebrews and Jude 11, on which see note.

17. **Wherein** (ἐν ᾧ). Referring to the whole previous clause. In accordance with this universal human custom.

Willing (βουλόμενος). Rend. *being minded.* See on Matt. i. 19.

The immutability (τὸ ἀμετάθετον). The adjective used substantively. Only here and ver. 18.

Confirmed (ἐμεσίτευσεν). Rend. *interposed* or *mediated.* Comp. μεσίτης *mediator.* From μέσος *midst.* Placed himself *between* himself and the heritors of the promise.

18. **Two immutable things** (δύο πραγμάτων ἀμεταθέτων). His word and his oath.

Strong consolation (ἰσχυρὰν παράκλησιν). Ἰσχυρὸς *strong* implies indwelling strength embodied or put forth either

aggressively or as an obstacle to resistance ; as an army or a fortress.   For *consolation* rend. *encouragement*, and see on L. vi. 24 ; 1 Cor. xiv. 3.

Who have fled for refuge (οἱ καταφυγόντες).   Only here and Acts xiv. 6.   The compound verb is well rendered by A. V., since, as distinguished from the simple φεύγειν *to flee*, it expresses flight to a definite place or person for safety. Hence often used in connection with an altar or a sanctuary. The distinction between the simple and the compound verb is illustrated in Hdt. iv. 23, where, speaking of the barbarous tribe of the Iyrcae, he says, " Whoever *flees* (φεύγων) *and betakes himself for refuge* (καταφύγῃ) to them, receives wrong from no one."   So Xen., *Hellen.* 1, 6, 16 : " Conon, fled (ἔφευγε) in swift vessels, and *betakes himself for refuge* (καταφεύγει) to Mitylene."

To lay hold upon the hope set before us (κρατῆσαι τῆς προκειμένης ἐλπίδος).   For κρατῆσαι *to lay fast hold*, see on Mk. vii. 3 ; Acts iii. 11 ; Col. ii. 19.   Προκειμένης *lying before* or *set before; destined* or *appointed*.   Mostly in Hebrews. Comp. 2 Cor. viii. 12 ; Jude 7.*

19. An anchor of the soul (ἄγκυραν τῆς ψυχῆς).   The same figure is implied 1 Tim. i. 19.

Sure and steadfast (ἀσφαλῆ τε καὶ βεβαίαν).   The distinction between the two adjectives expresses the relation of the same object to different tests applied from without. Ἀσφαλῆ, *ἀ* not, σφάλλειν *to make totter*, and so *to baffle* or *foil*.   Hence, secure against all attempts to break the hold. Βεβαίαν *sustaining one's steps in going* (βαίνειν *to go*): not breaking down under what steps upon it.

Which entereth into that within the veil (εἰσερχομένην εἰς τὸ ἐσώτερον τοῦ καταπετάσματος).   Const. the participle

---

* Lünemann takes καταφυγόντες absolutely, and makes κρατῆσαι τῆς προκ. ἐλπ. depend on παράκ. ἐχ. *that we who have fled for refuge might have strong consolation to lay hold*, etc.

εἰσερχομένην entering with *anchor.*   Ἐσώτερον only here and
Acts xvi. 24.   Comparative, of something *farther* within.
So ἐσωτέραν φυλακήν "the *inner* prison," Acts xvi. 24.   Καταπέτασμα *veil,* ᵒClass.   Commonly in N. T. of the veil of the
temple or tabernacle.   See Matt. xxvii. 51; Heb. ix. 3.
That within the veil is the unseen, eternal reality of the heavenly world.*   Two figures are combined: (*a*) the world a
sea; the soul a ship; the hidden bottom of the deep the
hidden reality of the heavenly world.   (*b*) The present life
the forecourt of the temple ; the future blessedness the shrine
within the veil.   The soul, as a tempest-tossed ship, is held
by the anchor: the soul in the outer court of the temple is
fastened by faith to the blessed reality within the shrine.

20. **Whither the forerunner is for us entered** (ὅπου πρόδρομος ὑπὲρ ἡμῶν εἰσῆλθεν).   Ὅπου, strictly *where,* instead of
ὅποι *whither* (not in N. T.), but more significant as indicating
an *abiding* there.   Πρόδρομος *forerunner,* N. T.ᵒ.   It expresses
an entirely new idea, lying completely outside of the Levitical system.   The Levitical high priest did not enter the
sanctuary as a forerunner, but only as the people's representative.   He entered a place into which none might follow him ;
in the people's stead, and not as their pioneer.   The peculiarity of the new economy is that Christ as high priest goes
nowhere where his people cannot follow him.   He introduces
man into full fellowship with God.   The A. V. entirely
misses this point by rendering "*the* forerunner," as if the
idea of a high priest being a forerunner were perfectly familiar.   Rend. *whither as a forerunner Jesus entered.*   Comp.
ch. x. 19.

Made a high priest (ἀρχιερεὺς γενόμενος).   Rend. *having
become a high priest,* etc.   *Become,* because his office must be
inaugurated by his suffering human life and his death.

---

* Two other arrangements are proposed: (*a*) ἀσφαλῆ, βεβαίαν, εἰσερχομένην with ἐλπίδα understood: *hope, sure, steadfast, entering,* etc. (*b*) ἀσφαλῆ
and βεβαίαν with ἄγκυραν, and εἰσερχ. with ἐλπ. *a hope which enters,* etc. (*and
which is) an anchor sure and steadfast.*

Additional Note on Verses 4–6.

The passage has created much discussion and much distress, as appearing to teach the impossibility of restoration after a moral and spiritual lapse. It is to be observed: (1) That the case stated is that of persons who once knew, loved, and believed Christian truth, and who experienced the saving, animating, and enlightening energy of the Holy Spirit, and who lapsed into indifference and unbelief. (2) The questions whether it is possible for those who have once experienced the power of the gospel to fall away and be lost, and whether, supposing a lapse possible, those who fall away can ever be restored by repentance — do not belong here. The possibility of a fall is clearly assumed. (3) The sin in the case supposed is the relinquishment of the spiritual gifts and powers accompanying faith in Christ, and rejecting Christ himself. (4) The significance of this sin lies in the mental and spiritual condition which it betrays. It is the recoil of conviction from Christ and the adoption of the contrary conviction. (5) The writer does not touch the question of the possibility of *God's* renewing such to repentance. He merely puts his own hypothetical case, and says that, in the nature of such a case, the ordinary considerations and means which are applied to induce men to embrace the gospel no longer appeal to the subjects supposed. He contemplates nothing beyond such agencies, and asserts that these are powerless because the man has brought himself into a condition where they can no longer exert any power. Whether God will ever reclaim by ways of his own is a point which is not even touched. Destruction of the faculty of spiritual discernment is the natural outcome of deliberate and persistent sin, and the instrument of its punishment. Note, "renew unto *repentance.*" God promises pardon on penitence, but not penitence on sin. See a powerful passage in Coleridge's *Moral and Religious Aphorisms*, Amer. ed., Vol. I., p. 191.

CHAPTER VII.

The Melchisedec-priesthood of Christ. — Christ can be a priest without Aaronic descent, and his priesthood is of a higher and older type than the Levitical.

1. For this Melchisedec, etc. See Gen. xiv. 18–20; Ps. cx.

2. First being by interpretation King of righteousness (πρῶτον μὲν ἑρμηνευόμενος βασιλεὺς δικαιοσύνης). The *first* designation is the literal interpretation of the Hebrew name. *Being interpreted* belongs only to this designation. So Joseph. *Ant.* 1, 10, 2 : σημαίνει δε τοῦτο βασιλεὺς δίκαιος "and this (the name Melchisedec) signifies *righteous king.*"

And after that also (ἔπειτα δὲ καὶ). Then follows a designation derived from his character, *king of peace*. Supply *being;* not *being interpreted*.

Salem. Commonly regarded as the site of Jerusalem. It has also been supposed to represent Σαλείμ *Salim*, mentioned in J. iii. 23. Jerome says that the place retained that name in his day, and that the ruins of Melchisedec's palace were shown there.* The ancient name of Jerusalem was Jebus. Others, again, suppose that Salem is not the name of a place, but is merely the appellation of Melchisedec. The passage in Genesis, however, points to a place, and the writer might naturally have desired to indicate the typical meaning of the city over which Melchisedec reigned.

3. Without father, without mother, without descent (ἀπάτωρ, ἀμήτωρ, ἀγενεαλόγητος). The three adjectives N. T.°, °LXX. The meaning is that there is no record concerning his parentage. This is significant as indicating a different type of priesthood from the Levitical, in which genealogy was of prime importance. No man might exercise priestly functions who was not of the lineage of Aaron.

Having neither beginning of days nor end of life. That is to say, history is silent concerning his birth and death.

But made like unto the Son of God (ἀφωμοιωμένος δὲ τῷ υἱῷ τοῦ θεοῦ). The verb N. T.°. *Made like* or *likened*, not *like*. "The resemblance lies in the Biblical representation, and not primarily in Melchisedec himself" (Westcott).

---

* *Ep. ad Evangelium*, § 7.   Stanley thinks that the meeting of Abraham and Melchisedec was at Gerizim.   Ewald at a point north of Jerusalem.

Son of *God*, not Son of *man*, for the likeness to Jesus as Son of man would not hold; Jesus, as man, having had both birth and death.   The words *likened unto the Son of God* stand independently.   Not to be connected with the following sentence, so as to read *abideth a priest continually like the Son of God;* for, as a priest, Melchisedec, chronologically, was prior to Christ; and, therefore, it is not likeness with respect to priesthood that is asserted.   The likeness is in respect to the things just predicated of Melchisedec.   Christ as Son of God was without father, mother, beginning or end of days; and, in these points, Melchisedec is likened in Scripture to him.

Abideth a priest continually (μένει ἱερεὺς εἰς τὸ διηνεκές). Διηνεκής from διαφέρειν *to bear through;* borne on through ages, continuous.   Only in Hebrews.   There is no historical account of the termination of Melchisedec's priesthood.   The tenure of his office is uninterrupted.   The emphasis is on the eternal duration of the ideal priesthood, and the writer explains the Psalm as asserting eternal duration as the mark of the Melchisedec order.   Accordingly, he presents the following characteristics of the ideal priesthood: *royal, righteous, peace-promoting, personal* and *not inherited, eternal.* Comp. Isa. ix. 6, 7; xi. 4, 10; xxxii. 17; lii. 7.   It is, of course, evident to the most superficial reader that such exposition of O. T. scripture is entirely artificial, and that it amounts to nothing as proof of the writer's position.   Melchisedec is not shown to be an eternal high priest because his death-record is lost; nor to be properly likened unto the Son of God because there is no notice of his birth and parentage.

4. The superiority of the Melchisedec priesthood to the Levitical.

Consider (θεωρεῖτε).   Only here in Hebrews and [O]P. Except this passage, confined to the Synoptic Gospels, Acts, and Johannine writings.   See on L. x. 18; J. i. 18.

How great (πηλίκος).   Only here and Gal. vi. 11.

The patriarch (ὁ πατριάρχης). Only here and in Acts.

The tenth (δεκάτην). Properly an adjective, but used as a noun for *tithe*. Only in Hebrews, as is the kindred verb δεκατοῦν to *impose* or *take tithes*. ᾿Αποδεκατοῖν to *exact tithes*, Heb. vii. 5. Comp. Matt. xxiii. 23; L. xi. 42.

Of the spoils (ἐκ τῶν ἀκροθινίων). The noun N. T.°, from ἄκρον *topmost point*, and θίς *a heap*. The top of the pile: the "pick" of the spoil.

5. If Melchisedec was greater than Abraham, he was greater than Abraham's descendants, including the tribe of Levi.

They that are of the sons of Levi who receive, etc. (οἱ ἐκ τῶν υἱῶν Λευεὶ λαμβάνοντες). Those *out of* the sons of Levi who become priests. Not those who receive the priesthood *from* the sons of Levi. Not all Levites were priests, but only those of the house of Aaron.

The office of the priesthood (τὴν ἱερατίαν). Only here and L. i. 9.

A commandment (ἐντολὴν). A special injunction. See on Jas. ii. 8; Eph. ii. 15.

To take tithes (ἀποδεκατοῖν). See on ver. 4.

That is of their brethren, though they come out of the loins of Abraham. The people, the brethren of the Levites, are descended from their common ancestor, Abraham, yet the Levites exact tithes from them.

6. **But he whose descent is not counted from them** (ὁ δὲ μὴ γενεαλογούμενος ἐξ αὐτῶν). Lit. *he who is not genealogically derived from them:* Melchisedec. The verb N. T.°.

Received tithes of Abraham.   Melchisedec, who has no part in the Levitical genealogy, and therefore no legal right to exact tithes, took tithes from the patriarch himself.   Hence he was greater than Abraham.   The right of the Levitical priest to receive tithes was only a *legal* right, conferred by special statute, and therefore implied no *intrinsic* superiority to his brethren; but Melchisedec, though having no legal right, received tithes from Abraham as a voluntary gift, which implied Abraham's recognition of his *personal* greatness.

And hath blessed him that had the promises.   Melchisedec accepted the position accorded to him by Abraham's gift of tithes by bestowing on Abraham his blessing, and Abraham recognised his superiority by accepting his blessing. He who had received the divine promises might have been supposed to be above being blessed by any man.   The significance of this acceptance is brought out in the next verse.

7. **Without all contradiction** (χωρὶς πάσης ἀντιλογίας). Asserting a principle which no one thinks of questioning: **it** is *the less* who is blessed, and *the greater* who blesses.

8. **Here** (ὧδε).   In the Levitical economy.

Men that die receive tithes.   The emphasis is on ἀποθνήσκοντες *dying*.   The Levites are dying men, who pass away in due course, and are succeeded by others.

But there (ἐκεῖ δὲ).   In the case of Melchisedec.

(He receiveth them of whom) it is witnessed that he liveth (μαρτυρούμενος ὅτι ζῇ).   The Greek is very condensed : *being attested that he liveth.*   The A. V. fills it out correctly. Melchisedec does not appear in Scripture as one who dies, and whose office passes to another.   See on *abideth continually*, ver. 3.

9. **Levi himself, in the person of Abraham, was tithed by Melchisedec.**

As I may say (ὡς ἔπος εἰπεῖν). = *so to speak.* N. T.⁰.
⁰LXX. Introducing an unusual statement, or one which
may appear paradoxical or startling to the reader, as this
statement certainly is, to a modern reader at least.

In Abraham (δι' Ἀβραάμ). Lit. *through* Abraham.

10. **In the loins of his father** (ἐν τῇ ὀσφύϊ τοῦ πατρὸς).
His own father; not of Abraham.

When Melchisedec met him. In the person of Abraham.
The whole Jewish law, its ordinances and priesthood, are
regarded as potentially in Abraham. When Abraham paid
tithes, Levi paid tithes. When Abraham was blessed, Israel
was blessed. It is a kind of reasoning which would appeal
to Hebrews, who so strongly emphasised the solidarity of
their race. Comp. Rom. ix. 4, 5.

11. In Christ, as the Melchisedec-priest, the ideal of the
priesthood is realised.

Perfection (τελείωσις). Only here and L. i. 45. The
act or *process* of consummating. By this word is signified
the establishment of a perfect fellowship between God and
the worshipper. See ch. ix. 9; x. 1.

Priesthood (ἱερωσύνης). Only in Hebrews. See vv. 12,
14. It expresses the *abstract notion* of the priest's office;
while ἱερατία, ver. 5, expresses the priestly *service*.

For under it the people received the law (γὰρ ἐπ' αὐτῆς
νενομοθέτηται). *Under,* rather *on the basis of.* The verb lit.
the law has been laid down. Only here and ch. viii. 6.

What further need (τίς ἔτι χρεία). Ἔτι *after that,* assuming
that there was perfection through the Levitical priesthood.

Another priest (ἕτερον ἱερέα). Not merely *another,* but **a**
different kind of priest. See on Matt. vi. 24.

Should rise (ἀνίστασθαι). In Hebrews only here and ver. 15, both times in connection with *priest*.

12. **Being changed** (μετατιθεμένης). Or *transferred* to another order. See on Gal. i. 6.

A change (μετάθεσις). A *transfer* to a new basis. Only in Hebrews. See ch. xi. 5; xii. 27. The inferiority of the Levitical priesthood is inferred from the fact that another priesthood was promised. If perfection was possible at all under the Mosaic economy, it must come through the Levitical priesthood, since that priesthood was, in a sense, the basis of the law. The whole legal system centred in it. The fundamental idea of the law was that of a people united with God. Sin, the obstacle to this ideal union, was dealt with through the priesthood. If the law failed to effect complete fellowship with God, the priesthood was shown to be a failure, and must be abolished; and the change of the priesthood involved the abolition of the entire legal system.

13. As the law prescribed that the priesthood should be of the order of Aaron, a new priesthood, not of that order, must set aside the law.

Pertaineth to another tribe (φυλῆς ἑτέρας μετέσχηκεν). Lit. *hath partaken of another tribe.* Not only *another*, but a *different* tribe; one not specially set apart to sacerdotal service.

Of which no man gave attendance at the altar (ἀφ' ἧς οὐδεὶς προσέσχηκεν τῷ θυσιαστηρίῳ). Προσέχειν originally *to bring to; bring the mind to; attend to.* See on ch. ii. 1. Θυσιαστήριον *altar*, ᵒClass. Strictly an altar for the sacrifice of victims; but used of the altar of incense, L. i. 11; Apoc. viii. 3; comp. Ex. xxx. 1. See on Acts xvii. 23. It was also used of the enclosure in which the altar stood. See Ignat. *Eph.* v; *Trall.* vii. See Lightfoot's interesting note, *Ignatius and Polycarp*, Vol. II., p. 43.

14. **Evident** (πρόδηλον). Obvious. See on 1 Tim. v. 24.

Sprang (ἀνατέταλκεν). Rend. *hath sprung.* In N. T. always of the rising of a heavenly body, sun or star, except L. xii. 54, of a cloud, and here. See LXX, Gen. xxxii. 31; Ex. xxii. 3; Num. xxiv. 17; Judg. ix. 33; Isa. xiv. 12; lx. 1; Mal. iv. 2. Also of the springing up of plants, Gen. ii. 5; iii. 18; Deut. xxix. 23; of the growing of the beard, 2 Sam. x. 5.

15. **Evident** (κατάδηλον). N. T.º. *Thoroughly* evident. Not referring to that which is declared to be πρόδηλον *evident* in ver. 14, viz., that Christ sprang out of Judah, but to the general proposition — the unsatisfactory character of the Levitical priesthood.

Similitude (ὁμοιότητα). Better, *likeness:* answering to *made like,* ver. 3, and emphasising the personal resemblance to Melchisedec.

16. **The law of a carnal commandment** (νόμον ἐντολῆς σαρκίνης). The phrase N. T.º. Νόμον *the norm* or *standard,* as Rom. vii. 21, 23. Ἐντολῆς, the *specific precept* of the Mosaic law regarding Levitical priests. Comp. Eph. ii. 15. Σαρκίνης *fleshly,* indicates that the conditions of the Levitical priesthood had reference to the body. Fitness for office was determined largely by physical considerations. The priest must be of proper descent, without bodily blemish, ceremonially pure. See ch. ix. 1–5, 10, and comp. Rom. viii. 3. Such a priesthood cannot be eternal.

After the power of an endless life (κατὰ δύναμιν ζωῆς ἀκαταλύτου). Δύναμιν *inherent virtue.* Rend. for *endless,* *indissoluble.* Comp. καταλυθῇ *loosened down,* of a tent, 2 Cor. v. 1; of the stones of the temple, Matt. xxiv. 2. Jesus was high priest in virtue of the energy of indissoluble life which dwelt in him, unlike the priests who die, **ver. 8.** This truth the writer finds in the Psalm.

18, 19. The structure of the passage is as follows : The two verses contain a proposition in two parts. The verb γίνεται *is* or *comes to pass* is common to both parts. 'Ουδὲν— ὁ νόμος is parenthetical. Rend. " for there is a disannulling of a foregoing commandment, because of its weakness and unprofitableness (for the law made nothing perfect), and the bringing in thereupon of a better hope through which we draw nigh unto God."

18. **There is verily a disannulling of the commandment going before** (ἀθέτησις μὲν γὰρ γίνεται προαγούσης ἐντολῆς). *Verily* is superfluous. 'Αθέτησις only here and ch. ix. 26 ; a very few times in LXX: The fundamental idea is the doing away of something established (θετόν). The verb ἀθετεῖν *to make void, do away with,* is common in N. T. and in LXX, where it represents fifteen different Hebrew words, meaning *to deal falsely, to make merchandise of, to abhor, to transgress, to rebel, to break an oath,* etc. The noun, in a technical, legal sense, is found in a number of papyri from 98 to 271 A.D., meaning the making void of a document. It appears in the formula εἰς ἀθέτησιν καὶ ἀκύρωσιν *for annulling and cancelling.* Προαγούσης ἐντολῆς, rend. *of a foregoing commandment.* The expression is indefinite, applying to any commandment which might be superseded, although the commandment in ver. 16 is probably in the writer's mind. *Foregoing,* not emphasising mere precedence in time, but rather the preliminary character of the commandment as destined to be done away by a later ordinance. With *foregoing* comp. 1 Tim. i. 18 ; v. 24.

For the weakness and unprofitableness thereof (διὰ τὸ αὐτῆς ἀσθενὲς καὶ ἀνωφελές). Rend. " because of its weakness and unprofitableness." It could not bring men into close fellowship with God. See Rom. v. 20 ; viii. 3 ; Gal. iii. 21. 'Ανωφελής *unprofitable,* only here and Tit. iii. 9.

19. **For the law made nothing perfect** (οὐδὲν γὰρ ἐτελείωσεν ὁ νόμος). Parenthetical. The A.V. overlooks the parenthesis, ignores the connection of *bringing in* with *disannulling,*

translates δὲ *but* instead of *and*, and supplies *did ;* thus making
an opposition between *the law which made nothing perfect* and
the bringing in of a better hope, which did make something
perfect.   What the writer means to say is that, according to
the Psalm, there takes place, on the one hand, a disannulling
of the preliminary commandment because it was weak and
unprofitable, unable to perfect anything, and on the other
hand, the introduction of a better hope.

The bringing in of a better hope (ἐπεισαγωγὴ κρείττονος
ἐλπίδος).   Ἐπεισαγωγὴ N. T.º, ºLXX, is "a bringing in
upon" (ἐπὶ), upon the ground formerly occupied by the commandment.   So Rev., correctly, "a bringing in *thereupon*."
For κρείττων *better*, see on ch. i. 4.   The comparison is not
between *the hope* conveyed by the commandment, and the
better hope introduced by the gospel, but between *the commandment* which was characteristic of the law (Eph. ii. 15)
and *the hope* which characterised the gospel (Rom. v. 2-5 ;
viii. 24).

By the which we draw nigh to God (δι' ἧς ἐγγίζομεν τῷ
θεῷ).   Giving the reason why the hope is better.   Christianity
is the religion of good hope because by it men first enter
into intimate fellowship with God.   The old priesthood could
not effect this.

20-24.   A third argument to show the inferiority of the
old priesthood.   It is twofold : (*a*) the new priesthood was
established with the oath of God ; (*b*) it is held perpetually
by one person, in contrast with the old priesthood which was
administered by a succession of priests.

20.   **Not without an oath** (οὐ χωρὶς ὀρκωμοσίας).   The
A.V. is, on the whole, better than Rev. by inserting *he was
made priest.*   Ὁρκωμοσία only in Hebrews.   In LXX see
Ezek. xvii. 18 ; 1 Esdr. ix. 93.   For *an oath* rend. *the taking
of an oath.*

21. For those priests were made (οἱ μὲν γὰρ—εἰσὶν ἱερεῖς γεγονότες). Rend. *for they have been made priests.* Lit. *are priests, having become such.*

Without an oath. Without the taking of an oath by God. Scripture says nothing of an oath of God when he appointed Aaron and his posterity to the priesthood.

But this with an oath (ὁ δὲ μετὰ ὁρκωμοσίας). Rend. *but he with the taking of an oath.* The taking of the oath *accompanied* (μετὰ) the inauguration into the priesthood.

That said (λέγοντος). Better, *saith.* Still says, since the promise is realised in Christ's priesthood.

22. Was Jesus made a surety of a better testament (κρείττονος διαθήκης γέγονεν ἔγγυος Ἰησοῦς). Ἔγγυος *surety*, N. T.°. Comp. Sir. xxix. 15, 16 ; 2 Macc. x. 28. Occasionally in Class., where also occur ἐγγυᾶν *to give as a pledge*, ἐγγύη *surety*, ἐγγύησις *giving in surety*, ἐγγυητής *one who gives security*, and ἐγγυητός *plighted*, always of a wife. The idea underlying all these words is that of putting something *into one's hand* (ἐν *in*, γύαλον *hollow of the hand*) as a pledge. For *testament* rend. *covenant* and see on ch. ix. 16. The thought of a covenant is introduced for the first time, and foreshadows ch. viii. 6–13. It adds to the thought of the inferiority of the Levitical priesthood that of the inferiority of the *dispensation* which it represented.

23. Were many priests (πλείονές εἰσιν γεγονότες ἱερεῖς). Comp. ver. 21 for the construction. Rend. *have been made priests many in number.*

Because they were not suffered to continue (διὰ τὸ κωλύεσθαι παραμένειν). Rend. *because they are hindered from continuing.* Παραμένειν " to abide *by* their ministration."

24. Hath an unchangeable priesthood (ἀπαράβατον ἔχει τὴν ἱερωσύνην). Rend. *hath his priesthood unchangeable.* The A.V.

misses the possessive force of the article, *his* priesthood, and the emphasis on *unchangeable*, ἀπαράβατος, N.T.⁰.   ⁰LXX.   This may be explained either as *inviolable*, or *which does not pass over to another*.   Comp. Ex. xxxii. 8 ; Sir. xxiii. 18.   Usage is in favour of the former meaning, but the other falls in better with the course of thought.

25.   **To the uttermost** (εἰς τὸ παντελές).   Παντελής *all-complete*, only here and L. xiii. 11.   Not *perpetually*, but *perfectly*.

Come unto God (προσερχομένους τῷ θεῷ).   The verb ⁰P., and in this sense only in Hebrews and 1 Pet. ii. 4.   See a peculiar usage in 1 Tim. vi. 3.   Comp. ἐγγίζειν *to draw near*, Jas. iv. 8 ; Heb. vii. 19.

To make intercession for them (εἰς τὸ ἐντυγχάνειν ὑπὲρ αὐτῶν).   The verb only here in Hebrews.   Comp. ὑπερεντυγ-χάνειν, Rom. viii. 26, see note.   See also on ἐντεύξεις *supplications*, 1 Tim. ii. 1.   The idea is not *intercession*, but *intervention*.   It includes every form of Christ's identifying himself with human interests.*   The attempt has been made to trace this idea to Philo, who alludes to the λόγος ἱκέτης *the supplant Logos*, and the λόγος παράκλητος *the advocate-Logos*. But the Logos is not treated by Philo as a divine-human personality intervening for men, but as a poetical personification allegorically considered.   In one instance the suppliant Logos is the cry of the oppressed Israelites ; in another, Moses, as the allegorical representative of the universal reason of mankind.   It represents certain functions of human reason and speech.   Again, the suppliant is the visible Cosmos striving to realise its ideal.

26–28.   Sketch of the ideal priest.

26.   **Became us** (ἡμῖν ἔπρεπεν).   See on ch. ii. 10.   For the verb see on Tit. ii. 1.   There was an essential fitness in the gift of our great high priest.   Comp. ch. ii. 17.

---

* See Westcott's note.

Holy (ὅσιος). See on L. i. 75. Always with a relation to God; never of moral excellence as related to men. Of Christ, Acts ii. 27; xiii. 35: of a bishop, Tit. i. 8.

Harmless (ἄκακος). Rend. *guileless.* Free from malice and craft. Only here and Rom. xvi. 18. *Undefiled* (ἀμίαντος), see on 1 Pet. i. 4.

Separate (κεχωρισμένος). Rend. *separated:* denoting a condition realised in Christ's exaltation. Comp. Rom. vi. 10.

Higher than the heavens (ὑψηλότερος τῶν οὐρανῶν). Comp. Eph. iv. 10; Heb. iv. 14.

27. Who needeth not **daily** (καθ᾽ ἡμέραν). Apparently inconsistent with ch. ix. 7: but the sense is, " who hath no need day by day as the high priest had (year by year) to offer sacrifices," etc. The great point is *repetition*, whether daily or yearly.*

Once (ἐφάπαξ). Rend. *once for all.* Contrasted with *daily.*

When he offered up himself (ἑαυτὸν ἀνενέγκας). A new thought. For the first time Christ appears as *victim.* Comp. ch. ix. 12, 14; Eph. v. 2.

28. Summarising the contents of vv. 26, 27. — The law constitutes *weak* men high priests. God's sworn declaration constitutes a son, perfected forevermore. ᾽Ανθρώπους *men,* many in number as contrasted with one Son. ῎Εχοντας ἀσ-

---

* All explanations must be rejected which seek to modify the sense of καθ᾽ ἡμέραν, as " on each *day of atonement* "; or " very often "; or " as the high priest daily feels the need." It is urged by some (as Ménégoz) that the high priest took part in the daily sacrifices; but if such participation took place it was only occasional. Bleek thinks that the ceremonies of the great Day of Atonement were throughout before the writer's mind as the archetypal features of the high priest's ministry, and that these were in some sort reproduced in the daily sacrifices.

θένειαν *having infirmity*, stronger than ἀσθενεῖς *weak*, which might imply only special exhibitions of weakness, while *having infirmity* indicates a general characteristic.   See on J. xvi. 22.

A son.   Again the high-priesthood is bound up with son ship, as in ch. v. 5, 6.

CHAPTER VIII.

Christ's fulfilment of his high-priestly office as related to the Aaronic priesthood. — Christ's ministry is superior to that of the Levitical priests as he himself is superior to them.

1. **Of the things which we have spoken** (ἐπὶ τοῖς λεγομ-ένοις).   The A. V. is wrong.   Ἐπὶ is *in the case of*, or *in the consideration of:* not *of*, nor *in addition to*.   Τοῖς λεγομένοις "the things which *are being* spoken": the matters now under discussion.

The sum (κεφάλαιον).   Rend. *the chief point*.   It is not the sum of what precedes, but the main point of the present discussion.   This point is that Christ is the minister of a better sanctuary, connected with a better covenant.

Such an high priest (τοιοῦτον).   Taken up from ch. vii. 26.

Is set (ἐκάθισεν).   Repeating ch. i. 3.   Rend. *sat down.*

The throne of the majesty (τοῦ θρόνου τῆς μεγαλωσύνης).   See on ch. i. 3.   The phrase N. T.º.

In the heavens (ἐν τοῖς οὐρανοῖς).   Const. with *sat down*, not with *majesty*, which is complete in itself and needs no qualifying epithet.

2. **A minister** (λειτουργὸς).   Sat down as a minister.   From an old adjective λεῖτος or λέϊτος (found only in this com-

pound), *belonging to the people*, and ἔργον *work*. Hence, originally, the service of the state in a public office. In LXX
and N. T. λειτουργὸς *minister*, λειτουργεῖν *to minister*, and λειτουργία *ministry* are used both of priestly service to God and
of service to men. Λειτουργία in LXX rarely of the service
of the priests, often of the Levites. See 1 K. i. 4; xix. 21;
2 K. iv. 43; vi. 15. Λειτουργοὺς, Heb. i. 7, in the general
sense of *servants of God*.

Of the sanctuary (τῶν ἁγίων). The heavenly sanctuary.
Τὰ ἅγια *the most holy place*, Heb. ix. 8, 12, 25; x. 19; xiii. 11.
Comp. ἅγια ἁγίων *holy of holies*, Heb. ix. 3. Ἅγια *holy places
generally*, but with special reference to the innermost sanctuary, Heb. ix. 24.

The true tabernacle (τῆς σκηνῆς τῆς ἀληθινῆς). Explanatory of τῶν ἁγίων. The form of expression is emphatic: *the
tabernacle, the genuine one*, as compared with the tabernacle
in the wilderness. For ἀληθινός *real, genuine*, see on J. i. 9.
Σκηνή *a tent*. For different shades of meaning, comp.
Matt. xvii. 4; L. xvi. 9; Acts vii. 43. In this epistle always
of the tabernacle in the wilderness.

3. A priest is appointed to offer gifts and sacrifices.
Therefore Christ, a high priest, must have gifts and sacrifices to offer, and a sanctuary in which to offer them.

Wherefore it is of necessity (ὅθεν ἀναγκαῖον). Rend.
wherefore it is necessary.

Somewhat to offer (ὃ προσενέγκῃ). Lit. *what he may offer.*
The construction is unusual. Comp. Acts xxi. 16. The
statement is a truism, unless it be assumed that the Hebrew
Christians were ignorant of the doctrine of Christ's priesthood.

4. Rend. "Now if he were on earth he would not be a
priest at all, seeing that there are those who offer the gifts

according to the law." Christ could not be a priest on earth,
because there is an order of priests already established by law;
and as Christ was not of the tribe of Levi (ch. vii. 13, 14)
he could have nothing in common with them.

5. **Who serve unto the example and shadow of heavenly
things** (οἵτινες ὑποδείγματι καὶ σκιᾷ λατρεύουσιν τῶν ἐπουρανίων). The connection is, "there are those who offer the gifts
according to the law, such as (οἵτινες) serve," etc.   For λατρεύουσιν *serve*, see on 2 Tim. i. 3.   Omit *unto*.   Rend. *serve
the copy and shadow*, etc., or, as Rev., *that which is a copy and
shadow*.   For ὑπόδειγμα *copy*, see on 1 Pet. v. 3; 2 Pet. ii. 6.
Comp. Heb. ix. 23.   Τῶν ἐπουρανίων "of heavenly *things*."
Τὰ ἐπουράνια in N. T. usually "heavenly *places*."   See
Eph. i. 3; ii. 6; iii. 10; vi. 12: "heavenly *things*," J. iii. 12;
Philip. ii. 10; Heb. ix. 23.*

As Moses was admonished (καθὼς κεχρημάτισται Μωυσῆς).
By God.   This, and the remainder of the verse, explain the
words *copy and shadow*.   For χρηματίζειν see on Matt. ii. 12;
L. ii. 26; Acts xi. 26.   Comp. χρηματισμός *answer* (of God),
Rom. xi. 4.   In Ex. xl. 1, where Moses is commanded to
make the tabernacle, God is expressly named.

To make (ἐπιτελεῖν).   The margin of Rev. *complete* may
easily convey a wrong idea.   The sense is *to carry out* or *exe-
cute* the plan given to him.

For, See (ὅρα γάρ).   Γάρ *for* is not a part of the quotation,
but is argumentative.   Moses was admonished, *for* God said
"See," etc.

That thou make (ποιήσεις).   A direct command.   "See,
thou shalt make."

Pattern (τύπον).   See on 1 Pet. v. 3.   The meaning is
that, in all essential features, the Levitical system of worship

---

* Westcott suggests "heavenly order." Lünemann supplies ἁγίων *sanctuary*.

was a copy of a heavenly reality. This was pressed into an
absurd literalism by the Rabbins, who held that there were
in heaven original models of the tabernacle and of all its
appurtenances, and that these were shown to Moses in the
Mount. The writer draws out of this vulgar conception the
thought that the material tabernacle was an emblem of a
spiritual, heavenly sanctuary. The Levitical priests, therefore, serve only a copy and shadow.

6. **But now** ($\nu\hat{v}\nu$ $\delta\grave{\epsilon}$). N$\hat{v}\nu$ is logical: as the case now
stands. The statement of ver. 4 is taken up. "If he were
on earth he could not be a priest," etc., but *now*, since Christ
is a priest, and must have a sanctuary and an offering, he has
a more excellent ministry.

He hath obtained a more excellent ministry ($\delta\iota\alpha\phi\rho\omega$-
$\tau\acute{\epsilon}\rho\alpha\varsigma$ $\tau\acute{\epsilon}\tau\upsilon\chi\epsilon\nu$ $\lambda\epsilon\iota\tau\upsilon\rho\gamma\acute{\iota}\alpha\varsigma$). The ministry of the heavenly
sanctuary.

He is the mediator of a better covenant ($\kappa\rho\epsilon\acute{\iota}\tau\tau\upsilon\acute{o}\varsigma$ $\grave{\epsilon}\sigma\tau\iota\nu$
$\delta\iota\alpha\theta\acute{\eta}\kappa\eta\varsigma$ $\mu\epsilon\sigma\acute{\iota}\tau\eta\varsigma$). For $\mu\epsilon\sigma\acute{\iota}\tau\eta\varsigma$ *mediator*, see on Gal. iii. 19.
Both here and in the following chapter, the ideas of the
sanctuary and the covenant are closely united. God's covenant was embodied in the sanctuary. The ark was "the ark
of the covenant"; the tables of the law were "the tables of
the covenant." The essence of a covenant is the establishment of a relationship. The sanctuary was the meeting-place
of God and man. The ritual of sacrifice adjusted the sinner's
relation to a holy God. All the furniture and all the ordinances of the tabernacle assumed the covenant between God
and his people. Thus the two ideas belong together. The
minister of the Levitical sanctuary was the mediator of the
old covenant. A new covenant implies a new ministry, a
better covenant implies a better ministry. Christ's priesthood implies a sanctuary. The new sanctuary implies a new
covenant. This covenant is a better covenant because it

Was established upon better promises ($\grave{\epsilon}\pi\grave{\iota}$ $\kappa\rho\epsilon\acute{\iota}\tau\tau\upsilon\sigma\iota\nu$
$\grave{\epsilon}\pi\alpha\gamma\gamma\epsilon\lambda\acute{\iota}\alpha\iota\varsigma$ $\nu\epsilon\nu\upsilon\mu\upsilon\theta\acute{\epsilon}\tau\eta\tau\alpha\iota$). For *established* rend. *enacted.*

Νομοθετεῖν to enact a law, only here and ch. vii. 11. A few times in LXX: Νομοθεσία enacting, only Rom. ix. 4: νομοθέτης lawgiver, only Jas. iv. 12. The better covenant was *enacted* as truly as was the law. See ver. 10. The new covenant was a new law—the perfect law, the law of liberty, Jas. i. 25.

7. The statement that a better covenant was enacted upon better promises is justified by the very existence of that second covenant. "If that first covenant had been faultless, there would no place have been sought for a second." The argument is like that in ch. vii. 11 (see note). Notice the imperfect tense ἐζητεῖτο, lit. *would have been being sought.* A search would not have been going on. This implies a sense of dissatisfaction while the old covenant was still in force, and a looking about for something better. This hint is now expanded. It is to be shown that the Levitical system answered to a covenant which was recognised as imperfect and transitory by an O. T. prophet, since he spoke of a divine purpose to establish a new covenant.

8. **For finding fault with them** (μεμφόμενος αὐτοὺς).*
Them signifies the possessors of the first covenant. The prophet says what follows by way of blame. The passage cited is Jer. xxxviii, LXX (A.V. xxxi), 31–34. The writer assumes that Jeremiah's new covenant means the Christian covenant.

I will make (συντελέσω). Rend. *I will conclude* or *consummate*. See on L. iv. 13. Only here in Hebrews, and once in Paul, Rom. ix. 28, a citation.

With the house (ἐπὶ). The preposition marking direction toward.

---

* Westcott and Hort and Tischendorf read αὐτούς. Weiss and Rev. T. retain the T. R. αὐτοῖς. If the latter, the more probable construction is with *he saith :* "he saith to them," taking μεμφόμενος absolutely. If αὐτούς, the pronoun will be governed by μεμφόμενος, " blaming them."

A new covenant (διαθήκην καινήν). Always καινὴ in the phrase *new covenant*, except Heb. xii. 24, where we have νέα. For the distinction see note there, and on Matt. xxvi. 29.

9. **In the day when I took** (ἐν ἡμέρᾳ ἐπιλαβομένου μου). An unusual construction. Lit. *in the day of me having taken hold.* Comp. J. iv. 39.

10. **The covenant which I will make** (ἡ διαθήκη ἣν διαθήσομαι). The noun and the verb are cognate — *the arrangement which I will arrange.* A *covenant* (διαθήκη) is something *arranged* (διατίθεσθαι) between two parties. See the same combination, Acts iii. 25.

I will put my laws (διδοὺς νόμους μου). Lit. *giving my laws:* const. with *I will make:* "the covenant which I will make *by giving* my laws."

Mind (διάνοιαν). The moral understanding. See on Mk. xii. 30; L. i. 51. *Hearts*, καρδίας, see on Rom. i. 21; x. 10.

A God — a people (εἰς θεόν — εἰς λαόν). Lit. *unto* a God, etc. A Hebraistic form of expression, εἰς signifying the destination of the substantive verb. The sense is, I will be to them *to serve as* a God; or my being as related to them will *amount to* my being a God to them. Comp. Matt. xix. 5; 2 Cor. vi. 18; Heb. i. 5.

11. **His neighbour** (τὸν πολίτην). Lit. *his citizen:* his *fellow-citizen.**

Know the Lord (γνῶθι τὸν κύριον). As if commending God to the knowledge of one who is ignorant of him.

All shall know (πάντες εἰδήσουσιν). Observe the two words for *know:* γνῶθι of the recognition of a stranger; εἰδήσουσιν

---

* Codex A, LXX, has τὸν ἀδελφόν *his brother,* and for τὸν ἀδελφόν in the following clause, τὸν πλησίον *his neighbour.*

of an absolute acquaintance as of one born under God's covenant.

From the least to the greatest (ἀπὸ μικροῦ ἕως μεγάλου αὐτῶν). Lit. *from the little unto the great of them.* This knowledge of God will be without distinction of age or station.

12. **Merciful** (ἵλεως). Only here and Matt. xvi. 22, see note.

Unrighteousness (ἀδικίαις). *Unrighteousnesses.* The only occurrence of the word in the plural. For ἀδικία see on 2 Pet. ii. 13.

Their sins and their iniquities (τῶν ἁμαρτιῶν αὐτῶν). Omit *and their iniquities.** For ἁμαρτία *sin*, see on Matt. i. 21; and for both ἀδικία and ἁμαρτία, on 1 J. i. 9. Comp. 1 J. v. 17.

Will I remember no more (οὐ μὴ μνησθῶ ἔτι). Lit. *I will by no means remember any more.*

13. **In that he saith a new covenant** (ἐν τῷ λέγειν καινήν). Lit. "in his saying *new.*"

He hath made the first old (πεπαλαίωκεν τὴν πρώτην). Παλαιοῦν *to make old*, only in Hebrews and L. xii. 33. Comp. Heb. i. 11.

Now that which decayeth and waxeth old (τὸ δὲ παλαιούμενον καὶ γηράσκον). Rend. *but that which is becoming old and waxing aged.* Γηράσκειν (only here and J. xxi. 18) adds the idea of *infirmity* to that of *age.*

Is ready to vanish away (ἐγγὺς ἀφανισμοῦ). Lit. *is nigh unto vanishing.* Ἀφανισμός *vanishing*, N. T.⁰. Often in LXX. Class. rare and late. The whole statement indicates that the writer regarded the Sinaitic covenant, even in Jeremiah's

---

* καὶ τῶν ἀνομιῶν αὐτῶν, T. R.

time, as obsolete, and that Jeremiah himself so regarded it.
When God announced a new covenant he proclaimed the
insufficiency of the old, and the promise of a new covenant
carried with it the promise of the abrogation of the old.
The new covenant is so shaped as to avoid the defects of
the old one, and some one has remarked that, in one aspect,
it is a criticism of the Sinaitic covenant.   The following
are its provisions : (1) The law will no more be merely
external, but a law written in the heart. Comp. 2 Cor. iii. 3.
(2) The people will be on intimate and affectionate terms
with God, so that the knowledge of God will be general.
(3) Sin will be dealt with more radically and effectively.

CHAPTER IX.

The new scene and conditions of Christ's high-priestly work
—the higher sanctuary and the better covenant (ch. viii. 1–6)
—are presented with more detail.

1. **Ordinances of divine service** (δικαιώματα λατρείας).
For δικαίωμα *ordinance*, see on Rom. v. 16.   For λατρεία
service, see on L. i. 74 ; Apoc. xxii. 3 ; Philip. iii. 3 ;
2 Tim. i. 3.   The meaning is ordinances directed to or
adapted for divine service.

A worldly sanctuary (τὸ ἅγιον κοσμικόν).   The A. V. misses
the force of the article.   Rend. *and its sanctuary a sanctuary
of this world*.   Τὸ ἅγιον in the sense of *sanctuary* only here.
Elsewhere the plural τὰ ἅγια.   Κοσμικόν *of this world* in contrast with the heavenly sanctuary to be mentioned later.*

2. **Was made** (κατεσκευάσθη).   See on ch. iii. 3.

---

* The rendering *well-ordered, seemly*, is contrary to usage. Κοσμικός has
three meanings : *relating to the universe ; of the world ; worldly*, with an
ethical sense — having the character of the sinful world. The word for
seemly is κόσμιος, 1 Tim. ii. 9 ; iii. 2.

The first. The first *tabernacle*, that is, the first *division* of the tabernacle. He speaks of the two divisions as two tabernacles.

Candlestick (λυχνία). Rend. *lampstand.* See on Matt. v. 15; Apoc. i. 12. Description in Ex. xxv. 31–37. Comp. Zech. iv.

The table and the shewbread (ἡ τράπεζα καὶ ἡ πρόθεσις τῶν ἀρτῶν). See Ex. xxv. 23–30; xxxv. 13; 2 Chron. ii. 4; xiii. 11. The table and the loaves are treated as one item. Lit. *the table and the setting forth of the loaves*, that is, *the table with its loaves set forth.* See on Mk. ii. 26; Acts xi. 23.

Which is called the sanctuary (ἥτις — ἅγια). Since it was thus furnished. See on ch. viii. 2.

3. **After the second veil** (μετὰ τὸ δεύτερον καταπέτασμα). According to Ex. xxvi. 31–37 there were two veils, the one before the door of the tent and the other before the sanctuary. After passing the first veil and entering the tent, the worshipper would see before him the second veil behind which was the holy of holies. The writer calls this also *a tabernacle*, ver. 2.

4. **The golden censer** (χρυσοῦν θυμιατήριον). The noun N. T.⁰. It may mean either *censer* or *altar of incense.* In LXX the altar of incense is called θυσιαστήριον θυμιάματος, Ex. xxx. 1, 27; Lev. iv. 7: comp. L. i. 11. Θυμιατήριον is used of *a censer*, 2 Chron. xxvi. 19; Ezek. viii. 11; 4 Macc. vii. 11. These are the only instances of the word in LXX: accordingly, never in LXX of the altar of incense. Josephus uses it for both. The golden censer is not mentioned in O. T. as a part of the furniture of the holy of holies. The facts of the case then are as follows: (*a*) according to Ex. xxxi the incense-altar was in the holy place, not in the holy of holies; (*b*) Philo and Josephus use θυμιατήριον

for the altar of incense; * (c) there is no mention in O. T. of a censer set apart for the day of atonement; (d) the high priest was to *enter* with incense, so that the ark might be veiled by the smoke (Lev. xvi. 12). Hence the censer could not have been kept in the holy of holies; (e) the writer clearly speaks of an abiding-place of the θυμιατήριον in a particular division of the tabernacle. There is evidently a discrepancy, probably owing to the fact that the writer drew his information from the O. T. by which he might have been led into error. Thus Ex. xxvi. 35, there are mentioned in the holy place *without the veil* only the candlestick and the table, and not the incense-altar. Again, when the standing-place of the incense altar was mentioned, the expressions were open to misconstruction: see Ex. xxx. 6; xl. 5. On the day of atonement, the incense-altar, like the most holy place, was sprinkled with blood. This might have given rise to the impression that it was in the holy of holies.

With gold (χρυσίῳ). Properly, *wrought* gold.

Wherein (ἐν ᾗ). But according to Ex. xvi. 34; Num. xvii. 10, neither the pot of manna nor Aaron's rod was in the ark, but "before the testimony"; while in Ex. xxv. 16, Moses was commanded to put only the tables of the law into the ark; and in 1 K. viii. 9 it is said of the ark in the temple, "there was nothing in the ark save the two tables of stone." The writer follows the rabbinical tradition that the pot of manna and the rod were inside of the ark.

Golden pot (στάμνος χρυσῆ). Στάμνος, N. T.⁰, a few times in LXX, rare in Class. *Golden* is an addition of the LXX. Comp. Ex. xvi. 33.

5. **Cherubim of glory** (χερουβεὶν δόξης). Setting forth or exhibiting the divine glory. The word signifies *living crea-*

---

tures, and they are described as ζῶα. Hence usually with the neuter article τά. See Isa. vi. 2, 3 ; Ezek. i. 5–10 ; x. 5–20, and comp. Apoc. iv. 6–8. Nothing could be more infelicitous than the A.V. rendering of ζῶα *beasts.*

Shadowing the mercy-seat (*κατασκιάζοντα τὸ ἱλαστήριον*). Κατασκιάζειν, N. T.⁰, ⁰LXX, occasionally in Class. Throwing their shadow *down* upon the mercy-seat. For ἱλαστήριον, see on Rom. iii. 25. Used in LXX to translate כַּפֹּרֶת *the place of covering sin,* the throne of mercy above the ark.

Particularly (*κατὰ μέρος*). In detail ; his main point being the twofold division of the tabernacle. The phrase N. T.⁰. Note the completeness of the list of articles of furniture in the tabernacle, even to the inclusion of things which had no connection with worship ; also the emphasis on the costliness of the articles — gold. The writer will say all that can be said for this transitory, shadowy tabernacle ; but all that he can say about the costliness of the apparatus only emphasises the inferior and unspiritual character of the worship. The vessels are superior to the service.*

6. The inferiority of the ancient system was proved by the old tabernacle itself : by its division into two parts, both of which were inaccessible to the people.

Always (*διὰ παντός*). Rend. *continually.* The phrase is usually found in connection with matters involving relations to God — worship, sacrifice, etc. See Matt. xviii. 10 ; L. xxiv. 53 ; Acts ii. 25 ; x. 2 ; 2 Th. iii. 16 ; Heb. xiii. 5.

Accomplishing (*ἐπιτελοῦντες*). See on ch. viii. 5, and Gal. iii. 3. The verb is used of performing religious services by Herodotus. See i. 167 ; ii. 63, 122 ; iv. 186.

7. **Errors** (*ἀγνοημάτων*). Lit. *ignorances.* See on ch. v. 2.

---

* Professor Bruce's remarks on this point are worth reading : *The Epistle to the Hebrews,* p. 310 ff.

8. The Holy Ghost. Speaking through the appliances and forms of worship. The intimation is that God intended to emphasise, in the old economy itself, the fact of his inaccessibility, in order to create the desire for full access and to prepare the way for this.

The way into the holiest of all (τὴν τῶν ἁγίων ὁδὸν). Lit. *the way of the holies*. For the construction comp. ὁδὸν ἐθνῶν *way of the Gentiles*, Mk. x. 5. The phrase N. T.°. Τῶν ἁγίων as in vv. 12, 24, 25; x. 19.

While as the first tabernacle was yet standing (ἔτι τῆς πρώτης σκηνῆς ἐχούσης στάσιν). By the first tabernacle is meant the first *division*. The point is that the division of the tabernacle showed the limitations of the Levitical system, and kept the people from coming directly to God. Of this limitation the holy place, just outside the second veil, was specially significant; for the holy place barred priests and people alike from the holy of holies. The priests could not pass out of it into the holy of holies; the people could not pass through it to that sanctuary, since they were not allowed in the holy place. The priests in the holy place stood between the people and God as revealed in the shrine. Ἐχούσης στάσιν, lit. *had standing*. The phrase N. T.°. Στάσις, everywhere in N. T. except here, is used in its secondary sense of *faction, sedition, insurrection*. Here in its original sense. Note that the sense is not *physical* and *local* as the A.V. implies, but *remained a recognised institution*.

9. Which (ἥτις). The first division of the tabernacle. The double relative directs attention to the emphasis which belongs to the first tabernacle. The way into the holiest was not yet manifest while the first tabernacle continued to be a recognised institution, *seeing that* the first tabernacle was a parable, etc.

A figure (παραβολὴ). Outside of the Synoptic Gospels, only here and ch. xi. 19. Here of a visible symbol or type. See on Matt. xiii. 3.

For the time then present (εἰς τὸν καιρὸν τὸν ἐνεστηκότα). Rend. *now* present, as contrasted with the "time of reformation," ver. 10.   See on *these last days*, ch. i. 2.   'Εἰς *for; with reference to; applying to.*   Καιρὸς *season* is used instead of *αἰὼν age*, because "the time" is conceived by the writer as a critical point, — a turning-point, at which the old system is to take its departure.   For ἐνεστηκότα *present*, see on Gal. i. 4, and comp. Rom. viii. 38; 1 Cor. iii. 22.

In which (καθ᾽ ἥν).   The A.V. wrongly assumes a reference to *the tabernacle;* whereas the reference is to *the parable.* Rend. *according to which.*

Were offered — could not (προσφέρονται μὴ δυνάμεναι). Rend. "*are* offered" or "*are being offered*"; and for "could not," "cannot."

Make him that did the service perfect (τελειῶσαι τὸν λατρεύοντα).   Rend. as Rev. "make the worshipper perfect." See ch. vii. 11.

As pertaining to the conscience (κατὰ συνείδησιν).   Having shown that the division of the tabernacle proved the imperfection of the worship, the writer will now show that the Levitical ritual did not accomplish the true end of religion. The radical defect of the Levitical system was its inability to deal with *the conscience*, and thus bring about the "perfection" which is the ideal of true religion.   That ideal contemplated the cleansing and renewal of the inner man; not merely the removal of ceremonial uncleanness, or the formal expiation of sins.   Comp. Matt. xxiii. 25, 26.   For συνείδησις *conscience*, see on 1 Pet. iii. 16.

10.   The impotence of the gifts and sacrifices lay in the fact that they were only symbolic ordinances.

Which stood in (ἐπὶ).   The passage should be read thus: "according to which are offered gifts and sacrifices which cannot perfect the worshipper as touching the conscience, being mere ordinances of the flesh *on the ground of* (ἐπὶ *resting upon*) meats," etc.

Meats and drinks and divers washings (βρώμασιν καὶ πόμασιν καὶ διαφόροις βαπτισμοῖς). Βρώμασιν, clean and unclean *meats.* Πόμασιν *drinks,* concerning which the Levitical law laid down no prescriptions except as to abstinence in the case of a Nazarite vow, and of the priests when they were about to officiate. See Num. vi. 3; Lev. x. 9. For βαπτισμοῖς *washings* see on ch. vi. 2.

And carnal ordinances (δικαιώματα σαρκὸς). Omit *and.* The phrase is a general description of *meats,* etc. Lit. *ordinances of the flesh.*

Imposed (ἐπικείμενα). Some interpreters find in this the suggestion of *a burden,* which these ceremonial observances assuredly were. Comp. Acts xv. 10. This, however, is not probable.

Until the time of reformation (μέχρι καιροῦ διορθώσεως). Διόρθωσις N. T.[o], [o]LXX, occasionally in Class. Διόρθωμα *correction, amendment,* Acts xxiv. 2. Διόρθωσις lit. *making straight:* used by medical writers of straightening a distorted limb. The verb διορθοῦν (not in N. T.) in LXX of *mending one's ways,* Jer. vii. 3, 5; Wisd. ix. 18. Of *setting up* or *establishing,* Isa. xvi. 5; lxii. 7. " The time of reformation " is the Christian age, when God made with his people a better covenant. It was inaugurated by the death of Christ. See on ch. i. 2. The gifts and offerings were only provisional, to tide the people over to the better time.

11. The time of reformation introduces a higher sanctuary, a better offering, a more radical salvation.

Having come (παραγενόμενος). Having appeared in the world. Only here in Hebrews, and only once in Paul, 1 Cor. xvi. 3. Most frequent in Luke and Acts.

Of good things to come (τῶν γενομένων ἀγαθῶν). According-ing to this reading the A. V. is wrong. It should be "of the good things *realised*," or *that have come to pass*. The A. V. follows the reading μελλόντων *about to be*. So Tischendorf and Rev. T. Weiss with Westcott and Hort read γενομένων. Blessings not merely prophetic or objects of hope, but actually attained ; free approach to God, the better covenant, personal communion with God, the purging of the conscience.

Through a greater and more perfect tabernacle (διά). The preposition is instrumental. Comp. ver. 12. Const. with ἀρχιερεὺς *high priest*, and as qualifying it. "A high priest *with* a greater and more perfect tabernacle." It has been shown that the new high priest must have a sanctuary and an offering (ch. viii. 2–6). Accordingly, as the Levitical priests were attached to (were priests *with*) an inferior taber-nacle, so Christ appears *with* a greater and more perfect tabernacle. For this use of διά see Rom. ii. 27; xiv. 20 ; 2 Cor. ii. 4; iii. 11. Note the article with *tabernacle*, *his* greater, etc.*

---

* By some interpreters διά is explained as local, *passing through*, and τῆς μείζονος — σκηνῆς is construed with εἰσῆλθεν, ver. 12. Thus: "Christ having appeared as a high priest of the good things accomplished, entered into the holiest, *passing through* the greater and more perfect tabernacle." That is, as the Levitical high priest had to pass through the holy place in order to reach the holy of holies, so Christ passed through a holy place greater and more perfect than that of the ancient tabernacle, in order to reach the heavenly sanctuary. All kinds of explanations are given of this intermediate holy place ; as, *the lower spaces of the heavens: Christ's human nature : his holy life : the church on earth : the world*, etc. It is to be said that this local sense of διά emphasises a subordinate point, of which nothing is made in the epistle ; which is not even stated. In other words, nothing in the epistle is made to turn on the fact of the high priest's passing through one place in order to reach another. The emphatic point is Christ's entering the heavenly sanctuary. His passing through the heavens (ch. iv. 14) or through anything else, is a mere incident having no typical significance. The construction advocated by Rendall, *Epistle to the Hebrews*, should be noticed : "High priest of good things which came through the greater and more perfect taber-nacle." But not the greater tabernacle, but Christ is everywhere represented as the agent of the good things of the new dispensation. The new sanctuary which Christ must have as high priest is an *accompaniment* of his position and ministry.

That is to say not of this building (τοῦτ᾽ ἔστιν οὐ ταύτης τῆς κτίσεως). For *building* rend. *creation*. See on Rom.viii. 19; 2 Cor. v. 17; Col. i. 15. The meaning is, not belonging to this natural creation either in its materials or its maker.

12. **By the blood of goats and calves** (δι᾽ αἵματος τράγων καὶ μόσχων). Διὰ *with*, as ver. 11. Μόσχος originally *a tender shoot* or *sprout :* then *offspring* generally. Everywhere in the Bible *calf* or *bullock*, and always masculine.

His own blood. The distinction is not between the different *bloods*, but between the *victims*. The difference of blood is unimportant. Regarded merely as blood, Christ's offering is not superior to the Levitical sacrifice. If Christianity gives us *only* the shedding of blood, even Christ's blood, it does not give us a real or an efficient atonement. Whatever significance may attach to the blood is derived from something else. See on ver. 14.

Once (ἐφάπαξ). Rend. *once for all.*

Having obtained eternal redemption (αἰωνίαν λύτρωσιν εὑράμενος). Having *found* and *won* by his act of entrance into the heavenly sanctuary. This is better than to explain " entered the sanctuary after having obtained redemption by his life, death, and resurrection "; for the work of redemption is crowned and completed by Christ's ascension to glory and his ministry in heaven (see Rom. vi). Even in the old sanctuary the rite of the Day of Atonement was not complete until the blood had been offered in the sanctuary. *Eternal*, see on. ch. vi. 2. Not mere *duration* is contemplated, but *quality ;* a redemption answering in its quality to that age when all the conditions of time shall be no more : a redemption not ritual, but profoundly ethical and spiritual. Λύτρωσιν *redemption*, only here, L. i. 68 ; ii. 38. See on *might redeem*, Tit. ii. 4.

13–14. Justifying the preceding words, and answering the question, *What has Christ to offer ?*

13. **Ashes of a heifer** (σποδὸς δαμάλεως). Σποδός *ashes*, only here, Matt. xi. 21; L. x. 13, in both instances in the phrase *sackcloth and ashes*. Often in LXX. Δάμαλις *heifer*, N. T.º. The two examples selected cover the entire legal provision for removing uncleanness, whether contracted by sin or by contact with death. "The blood of bulls and goats" refers to the sin-offerings, perhaps especially to the annual atonement (Lev. xvi); "the ashes of a heifer" to the occasional sacrifice of the red heifer (Num. xix) for purification from uncleanness contracted by contact with the dead. The Levitical law required *two* remedies: the Christian economy furnishes *one* for all phases of defilement.

Sprinkling the unclean (ῥαντίζουσα τοὺς κεκοινωμένους). For *sprinkling* see on 1 Pet. i. 2. The verb only in Hebrews, except Mk. vii. 4. For *the unclean* rend. *them that have been defiled*. The literal rendering of the participle brings out better the *incidental* or *occasional* character of the defilement.

14. **Through the eternal spirit** (διὰ πνεύματος αἰωνίου). For *the* rend. *an*. Διὰ *through* = *by virtue of*. Not the Holy Spirit, who is never so designated, but Christ's own human spirit: the higher element of Christ's being in his human life, which was charged with the eternal principle of the divine life. Comp. Rom. i. 4; 1 Cor. xv. 45; 1 Pet. iii. 18; Heb. vii. 16. This is the key to the doctrine of Christ's sacrifice. The significance and value of his atonement lie in the personal quality and motive of Christ himself which are back of the sacrificial act. The offering was the offering of Christ's deepest self — his inmost personality. Therein consists the attraction of the cross; not to the shedding of blood, but to Christ himself. This is Christ's own declaration, J. xii. 32. "I will draw all men unto *me*." Therein consists its potency for men: not in Christ's satisfaction of justice by suffering a legal penalty, but in that the cross is the supreme expression of a divine spirit of love, truth, mercy, brotherhood, faith, ministry, unselfishness, holiness, — a spirit which goes out to men with divine intensity of pur-

pose and yearning to draw them into its own sphere, and to
make them partakers of its own eternal quality. This was a
fact before the foundation of the world, is a fact to-day, and
will be a fact so long as any life remains unreconciled to God.
Atonement is eternal in virtue of the eternal spirit of Christ
through which he offered himself to God.

Offered himself without spot (ἑαυτὸν προσήνεγκεν ἄμω-
μον). The two other elements which give superior validity
to Christ's sacrifice. It was *voluntary*, a *self-offering*, unlike
that of brute beasts who had no volition and no sense of the
reason why they were offered. It was *spotless*. He was a
perfectly righteous, sinless being, perfectly and voluntarily
obedient to the Father's will, even unto the suffering of death.
The legal victims were only physically unblemished according
to ceremonial standards. Ἄμωμος in LXX, technically, of
victims, Ex. xxix. 1; Lev. i. 3, 10, etc.

Purge your conscience (καθαριεῖ τὴν συνείδησιν ἡμῶν).
For *your* rend. *our*. The superior *nature* of Christ's sacrifice
appears in its deeper *effect*. While the Levitical sacrifice accomplished only formal, ritual expiation, leaving the inner
man unaffected, while it wrought externally and dealt with
specific sins, the effect of Christ's sacrifice goes to the centre
of the moral and spiritual life, and cleanses the very fountain-
head of being, thus doing its work where only an eternal
spirit can do it. Καθαρίζειν to *purge* is not a classical word.
In Class. καθαιρεῖν (also in LXX): but καθαρίζειν appears in
inscriptions in a ritual sense, and with ἀπὸ *from*, as here,*
thus showing that the word was not confined to biblical and
ecclesiastical Greek.

From dead works (ἀπὸ νεκρῶν ἔργων). The effect of
Christ's sacrifice upon the conscience transmits itself to the
works, and fills them with the living energy of the eternal

---

* See Deissmann *Neue Bibelstudien*, Pt. II., p. 43.   He gives one specimen,
93 or 91 B.C.

spirit.   It changes the character of works by purging them
of the element of death.   This element belongs not only to
works which are acknowledged as sinful and are committed
by sinful men, but to works which go under the name of
religious, yet are performed in a merely legal spirit.   None
the less, because it is preëminently the religion of faith, does
Christianity apply the severest and most radical of tests to
works.   Professor Bruce truthfully says that "the severest
test of Christ's power to redeem is his ability to loose the
bonds springing out of a legal religion, by which many are
bound who have escaped the dominion of gross, sinful habits."

15.   The efficacy of Christ's sacrifice is bound up with a
covenant.   His priesthood involves a new and a better covenant.   See ch. viii. 6–13.   That covenant involves his death.

For this cause ($\delta\iota\grave{a}$ $\tau o\hat{v}\tau o$).   Indicating the close relation
between the cleansing power of Christ's blood and the new
covenant.

Mediator of the new testament ($\delta\iota a\theta\acute{\eta}\kappa\eta s$ $\kappa a\iota\nu\hat{\eta}s$ $\mu\epsilon\sigma\acute{\iota}\tau\eta s$).
For *the new testament* rend. *a new covenant*.   See on next verse.
For $\mu\epsilon\sigma\acute{\iota}\tau\eta s$ *mediator*, see on Gal. iii. 19, 20.

By means of death ($\theta a\nu\acute{a}\tau o\nu$ $\gamma\epsilon\nu\upsilon\mu\acute{\epsilon}\nu o\nu$).   Rend. *a death
having taken place.*

For the redemption of the transgressions ($\epsilon i s$ $\mathring{a}\pi o\lambda\acute{\nu}$-
$\tau\rho\omega\sigma\iota\nu$ $\tau\hat{\omega}\nu$ $\pi a\rho a\beta\acute{a}\sigma\epsilon\omega\nu$).   The phrase *redemption of transgressions* (that is, *from* transgressions) only here.   'A$\pi o\lambda\acute{\nu}\tau\rho\omega\sigma\iota s$
ın N. T. mostly absolutely :   *the* redemption, or *your* redemp-
tion, or simply *redemption*.   Twice with genitive of that
which is redeemed, Rom. viii. 23 ; Eph. i. 14.   Only once
in LXX, Dan. iv. 32.   For $\pi a\rho\acute{a}\beta a\sigma\iota s$ *transgression*, see on
Rom. ii. 23.

Under the first testament ($\mathring{\epsilon}\pi\acute{\iota}$).   On the basis of :   estim-
ated according to the standard of the provisions of the first

covenant, and to be atoned for in the way which it prescribed. By this expression he emphasises the insufficiency of every other atoning provision, selecting the system which represented the most elaborate and complete atonement for sin prior to Christ. The intimation is in the same direction with that of the phrase *through an eternal spirit*—that the ideal redemption must be eternal.

They which are called (οἱ κεκλημένοι). Without regard to nationality. The scope of the new covenant was wider than that of the old. Comp. Acts ii. 39. In ch. iii. 1, the readers are addressed as "partakers of a *heavenly* calling," which corresponds with "eternal inheritance" here. Those who obtain this inheritance are designated as "called." See Eph. i. 18; 1 Th. ii. 12; v. 24; 1 Pet. iii. 9.

Of eternal inheritance (τῆς αἰωνίου κληρονομίας). Rend. "*the* eternal inheritance": something recognised as a fact. For κληρονομία *inheritance*, see on 1 Pet. i. 4, and comp. Eph. i. 14. The whole statement implies that the provisions of the Levitical system were inadequate to procure and insure full salvation.

16. **For where a testament is** (ὅπου γὰρ διαθήκη). "The English Version has involved this passage in hopeless obscurity by introducing the idea of a testament and a testator." This statement of Rendall (*Epistle to the Hebrews*, p. 159) is none too strong. That interpretation, however, is maintained by a very strong array of modern expositors.* It is based upon κληρονομία *inheritance;* it being claimed that this word changes the whole current of thought. Hence it is said that the new covenant established by Christ is here represented

---

* As Bleek, Alford, Lünemann, Dwight, De Wette, Weiss, Briggs, Bruce, Rev. Vers., Lightfoot (on Gal. iii. 15), Thayer (Lex.), Edwards. Weizsäcker and von Soden both render *Stiftung* "foundation"; *a basis*, formally established, on which certain benefits are insured to those who accept it. Such a basis might be of the nature either of a covenant or a testament. Bruce includes both under the word. Vaughan renders "arrangement," whether of *relations* (covenant) or of *possessions* (testament).

as a testamentary disposition on his part, which could become operative in putting the heirs in possession of the inheritance only through the death of Christ.   See Additional Note at the end of this chapter.

There must also of necessity be the death of the testator (θάνατον ἀνάγκη φέρεσθαι τοῦ διαθεμένου). Rend. *it is necessary that the death of the institutor (of the covenant) should be borne.* With the rendering *testament*, φέρεσθαι is well-nigh inexplicable. If *covenant* the meaning is not difficult. If he had meant to say *it is necessary that the institutor die*, he might better have used γένεσθαι : "it is necessary that the death of the institutor *take place*"; but he meant to say that it was necessary that the institutor die *representatively;* that death should be *borne* for him by an animal victim. If we render *testament*, it follows that the death of the testator himself is referred to, for which θάνατον φέρεσθαι is a very unusual and awkward expression.

17. **For a testament is of force after men are dead** (διαθήκη γὰρ ἐπὶ νεκροῖς βεβαία). Rend. "for a covenant is of force (or sure) over (or upon) dead (victims)." Comp. Soph. *Elect.* 237 ; Eurip. *Ion.* 228; Aesch. *Eumen.* 316 ; Hdt. iv. 162. See also Lev. xxi. 5.

Otherwise it is of no strength at all while the testator liveth (ἐπεὶ μὴ τότε ἰσχύει ὅτε ζῇ ὁ διαθέμενος). Rend. "since it hath not then force when the institutor is alive": until he has been representatively slain.

18. **Whereupon** (ὅθεν). Rend. *wherefore*, or *for which reason:* on the general principle that a covenant must be ratified by death.

Neither the first testament was dedicated without blood (οὐδὲ ἡ πρώτη χωρὶς αἵματος ἐνκεκαίνισται). Rend. "neither hath the first (covenant) been inaugurated without blood." There is surely no excuse for inserting *testament* here, as

A. V., since the allusion is clearly to the ratification of a covenant with blood.   But further, as this and the verses immediately following are intended to furnish a historical illustration of the statements in vv. 16, 17, we seem forced either to render *covenant* in those verses, or to assume that the transaction here related was the ratification of a will and testament, or to find our writer guilty of using an illustration which turns on a point entirely different from the matter which he is illustrating.   Thus : a testament is of force after men are dead.   It has no force so long as the testator is alive. *Wherefore*, the first *covenant* was ratified by slaying victims and sprinkling their blood.   For the incident see Ex. xxiv. 8.   Ἐνκαινίζειν only here and ch. x. 20.   LXX, *to renew*, 1 Sam. xi. 14; 2 Chron. xv. 8 ; Ps. l. 10 : *to dedicate*, 1 K. viii. 63; 1 Macc. iv. 36.   Comp. τὰ ἐνκαίνια *the feast of dedication*, J. x. 22.   Rend. οὐδὲ *neither*, as A. V., and not *not even*, in which case the meaning would be, "not even the first covenant, although its ministries did not perfect the worshipper as touching the conscience," a thought which would be foreign to the point, which is merely the analogy in the matter of death.

19.   The statement of verse 18 historically confirmed by the story of the establishment of the law-covenant, Ex. xxiv.

Of calves and goats (τῶν μόσχων καὶ τῶν τράγων).   Not mentioned in the O. T. account.   The goat was always for a sin-offering, and the sacrifices on this occasion were oxen, and are described as burnt offerings and sacrifices of peace, Ex. xxiv. 5.   In the original covenant with Abraham a she-goat and a heifer are specially mentioned, Gen. xv. 9.

Water, scarlet wool, hyssop — sprinkled the book (ὕδατος, ἐρίου κοκκίνου, ὑσσώπου αὐτό τε τὸ βιβλίον ἐράντισεν).   None of these are mentioned in the O. T. account, which the writer appears to have filled up from the details of subsequent usage. Comp. the additions in vv. 5, 10.   It will also be observed that the sacrifices on the occasion of establishing the law-

covenant were not made according to the Mosaic ritual.
They were offered, not by the priests, but by the young
men, Ex. xxiv. 5.   For κόκκινος *scarlet*, see on Matt.
xxvii. 6. Ύσσωπος *hyssop* appears in Ex. xii. 22; Lev.
xiv. 4, 6, 49; Num. xix. 6, 18; Ps. li. 9; J. xix. 29. Mostly
in connection with lustral ceremonies. The vexed question
of the precise botanical character of the plant has never been
decisively settled.*

22. The historical facts are summed up, emphasising one
point—cleansing by blood.

Almost all things (σχεδὸν—πάντα). The A. V. is wrong.
Σχεδὸν *almost* or *nearly* is prefixed to the entire clause, and
applies to both its members. Rend. "and I may almost say,
it is in blood," etc. *Almost* provides for such exceptions as
Ex. xix. 10; xxxii. 30–32; v. 11–13; Lev. xv. 5; xvi. 26–28;
xxii. 6; Num. xvi. 46–48; xxxi. 23, 24; Ps. li. 1–17;
xxxii. 1, 2.

And without shedding of blood is no remission (καὶ
χωρὶς αἱματεκχυσίας οὐ γίνεται ἄφεσις). This sentence also
is covered by "I may almost say." It does not state that
without shedding of blood there is no remission of sins, which
"would be in conflict with the history and literature of the
Old Testament." †   See exceptions above. Ἁιματεκχυσία
shedding of blood, N. T.°, °LXX, °Class. Οὐ γίνεται ἄφεσις,
lit. *remission does not take place* or *ensue*. For ἄφεσις see on
Jas. v. 15; most frequent in Luke and Acts. In Hebrews
only here and ch. x. 18. Commonly with a genitive, in the
phrase *remission of sins:* but sometimes absolutely as here,
Mk. iii. 29; L. iv. 18.

---

* Those who are curious about the matter will find it discussed in Riehm's
Handwörterbuch des biblischen Alterthums, and in the article in Hastings's
Dictionary of the Bible, by Dr. George E. Post of Beyrout, than whom there
is no more competent authority.

† Dr. Briggs, *Messiah of the Apostles*, p. 266.

23. The heavenly sanctuary required a better purification than the Levitical.

The patterns of things in the heavens. The earthly tabernacle and its furniture. See on ch. viii. 5.

With these (τούτοις). Things specified in ver. 19.

With better sacrifices (κρείττοσι θυσίαις). How can it be said that the heavenly things needed cleansing? It is not easy to answer. Various explanations have been proposed, which the student will find collected in Alford's note on this passage. The expression is rhetorical and figurative, and appears to be founded on that feature of the Levitical ritual according to which the high priest was required, on the Great Day of Atonement, to make an atonement for the sanctuary, "because of the uncleanness of the children of Israel." He was to do this also for the tabernacle of the congregation, and for the great altar. See Lev. xvi. 16 ff. The rite implied that even the holy of holies had contracted defilement from the people's sin. Similarly, the atoning blood of Christ is conceived as purifying the things of the heavenly sanctuary which had been defiled by the sins of men. "If the heavenly city of God, with its Holy Place, is, conformably with the promise, destined for the covenant-people, that they may there attain to perfect fellowship with God, then their guilt has defiled these holy things as well as the earthly, and they must be purified in the same way as the typical law appointed for the latter, only not by the blood of an imperfect, but of a perfect sacrifice" (Delitzsch).*

24. Under the old covenant, the bloodshedding was symbolical : the death of the institutor was by proxy. In the ratification of the new covenant, Christ himself was the covenant-victim, and a real cleansing power attaches to his blood as the offering of his eternal spirit.

---

* See also Riehm, *Lehrbegriff des Hebräerbriefes*, p. 542.

The holy places made with hands (χειροποίητα ἅγια). For *holy places* rend. *a holy place*, the plural being used of the sanctuary. Christ is not entered into a *hand-made* sanctuary.

Figures (ἀντίτυπα). Or *figure*. Only here and 1 Pet. iii. 21, see note. Answering to the patterns in the heavens, ch. viii. 5. Rev. *like in pattern*.

Now to appear (νῦν ἐμφανισθῆναι). *Now*, not only in contrast with the time of the old, typical economy, but also implying a continually-present manifestation, *for us*, *now*, as at his first entrance into the heavenly sanctuary. Ἐμφανισθῆναι, rend. *to be manifested*. Better than *to appear*, because it exhibits the manifestation of Christ as something *brought about* as the result of a new and better economy, and distinctly contemplated in the institution of that economy. Christ is made openly manifest before the face of God. The Levitical priest was compelled to shroud the ark and the shekinah with incense-smoke, that he might not look upon God face to face.

25. **Nor yet that** (οὐ δ᾽ ἵνα). Supply *did he enter*. "Nor yet did he enter that he might offer," etc.

He should offer himself often (πολλάκις προσφέρῃ ἑαυτόν). His offering did not need repetition like the Levitical sacrifices. *Offer himself* refers rather to Christ's entrance into the heavenly sanctuary and presentation of himself before God, than to his offering on the cross. See on ver. 14. The sacrifice on the cross is described by παθεῖν *suffer*, ver. 26, and is introduced as a distinct thought. The point is that, being once in the heavenly sanctuary, Christ was not compelled to renew often his presentation of himself there, since, in that case, it would be necessary for him to *suffer* often. Each separate offering would necessitate a corresponding suffering.

26. **Since the foundation of the world** (ἀπὸ καταβολῆς κόσμου). For, from the foundation of the world, sin required atonement by sacrifice ; and, therefore, if Christ had been a victim like others, which must be offered repeatedly, he would have had to suffer repeatedly from the foundation of the world. If his sacrifice, like the animal atonements, had availed for a time only, he would have been obliged to repeat his offering whenever that time expired; and, since his atonement was designed to be universal, it would have been necessary for him to appear repeatedly upon earth, and to die repeatedly from the foundation of the world. Comp. 1 Pet. i. 20 ; Apoc. xiii. 8.*

In the end of the world (ἐπὶ συντελείᾳ τῶν αἰώνων). In N. T. συντέλεια *consummation,* always with αἰὼν *age.* With the plural αἰώνων only here. Everywhere else συντέλεια αἰῶνος. The A. V. gives a wrong impression as of the end of this visible world. The true sense is *the consummation of the ages:* that is to say, Christ appeared when the former ages had reached their moral consummation under the old Levitical economy. Comp. ch. i. 2.

To put away sin (εἰς ἀθέτησιν τῆς ἁμαρτίας). Lit. *for the putting away of sin.* For ἀθέτησις see on ch. vii. 18. Note the singular number, *sin.* The sacrifice of Christ dealt with sin as a principle : the Levitical sacrifices with individual transgressions.

27. That there is no place for a repeated offering of Christ is further shown by reference to the lot of men in general. The very idea is absurd ; for men die once, and judgment

---

* If the question of the retrospective value of Christ's sacrifice is raised here, some light is thrown upon it by the expression "through his eternal spirit," ver. 14. An eternal spirit is independent of time, and acts performed under its inspiration are valid for all time. Christ offered himself in spirit before the foundation of the world. Was not the act of his eternal spirit the core of the whole preparatory system of sacrifice ? What I take to be the correct interpretation of Rom. iii. 25, as given in the notes on that passage, agrees with this.

follows.   Christ was man, and Christ died.   He will not
come to earth to live and die again.   Christ died, but judgment did not follow in his case.   On the contrary, he became
judge of all.

It is appointed (ἀπόκειται).   Lit. *is laid by in store.*
Comp. L. xix. 20; Col. i. 5 (see note); 2 Tim. iv. 8.

28. **Christ.**   Emphasising him, as the figure to which the
old economy pointed.

Was once offered (ἅπαξ προσενεχθεὶς).   Lit. *having been
offered once for all.*   Note the passive in contrast with *offer
himself*, ver. 25.   He was *appointed* to die as truly as we.
Comp. L. xxiv. 26; Matt. xxvi. 53, 54; Ps. xl. 7, 8.

To bear (ἀνενεγκεῖν).   Not in the sense of *bearing a sin-
offering up to the cross;* for ἁμαρτία never means a sin-offering ; nor in the sense of *putting away;* but signifying *to take
upon himself and bear as a burden.*

Unto them that look for him (τοῖς αὐτὸν ἀπεκδεχομένοις).
Rend. *await him.*   For the verb, see on Philip. iii. 20.   This
second coming with salvation is only for those who await
him in faith.

Shall he appear (ὀφθήσεται).   The usual verb for the
appearance of Christ after his resurrection.

The second time (ἐκ δευτέρου).   A phrase quite common
in N. T., but not in Paul.   The idea is, beginning *from* the
second : the second in a series taken as the point of departure.   As among men judgment follows as the second thing
after death, so, when Christ shall appear for the second time,
he will appear as the sinless Saviour.

Unto salvation (εἰς σωτηρίαν).   Not as a sinner to be
judged, but as the Saviour of mankind.   It is not said that

he will appear as judge, but only that he will not share the judgment which befalls all men after death. Still the phrase may imply that he will award salvation, as judge, to such as have believed on him.

ADDITIONAL NOTE ON VERSE 16.

Against the rendering *testament* for διαθήκη, and in favour of retaining *covenant*, are the following considerations : (*a*) *The abruptness of the change, and its interruption of the line of reasoning.* It is introduced into the middle of a continuous argument, in which the new covenant is compared and contrasted with the Mosaic covenant (ch. viii. 6–x. 18). (*b*) The turning-point, both of the analogy and of the contrast, is that both covenants were inaugurated and ratified by *death :* not *ordinary, natural* death, but sacrificial, violent death, accompanied with bloodshedding as an essential feature. Such a death is plainly indicated in ver. 15. If διαθήκη signifies *testament,* θάνατον *death* in ver. 16 must mean natural death without bloodshed. (*c*) The figure of a testament would not appeal to Hebrews in connection with an inheritance. On the contrary, the idea of the κληρονομία was always associated in the Hebrew mind with the inheritance of Canaan, and that inheritance with the idea of a covenant. See Deut. iv. 20–23; 1 Chron. xvi. 15–18; Ps. cv. 8–11. (*d*) In LXX, from which our writer habitually quotes, διαθήκη has universally the meaning of *covenant.* It occurs about 350 times, mostly representing בְּרִית *covenant.* In the Apocryphal books it has the same sense, except in Sir. xxxviii. 33, where it signifies *disposition* or *arrangement.* Διατίθεσθαι *to dispose* or *arrange* represents כָּרַת *to cut off, hew, divide.* The phrase כָּרַת בְּרִת *to cut* (i.e., *make*) *a covenant,* is very common. The verb marks a *disposing* by the divine will, to which man becomes a party by assent; while συντίθεσθαι indicates an arrangement between two equal parties. There is not a trace of the meaning *testament* in the Greek O. T. In the classics διαθήκη is usually *testament.* Philo uses the word in the sense of *covenant,* but also shows how it acquired that of *testament* (*De Mutatione Nominum,* § 6 ff.). The Vulgate has *testamentum,* even where the sense of *covenant* is indisputable. See Ex. xxx. 26; Num. xiv. 44; 2 K. vi. 15; Jer. iii. 16; Mal. iii. 1; L. i. 72; Acts iii. 25; vii. 8. Also in N.T. quotations from the O.T., where, in its translation of the O. T., it uses *foedus.* See Jer. xxxi. 31, cit. Heb. viii. 8. For διατίθεσθαι of making a covenant, see Heb. viii. 10; Acts iii. 25; Heb. x. 16. (*e*) The ratification of a covenant by the sacrifice of a victim is attested by Gen. xv. 10; Ps. l. 5; Jer. xxxiv. 18. This is suggested also by the phrase כָּרַת בְּרִת *to cut a covenant,* which finds abundant analogy in both Greek and Latin. Thus we have ὅρκια τάμνειν *to cut oaths,* that is, to sacrifice a victim in attestation (Hom. *Il.* ii. 124; *Od.* xxiv. 483; Hdt. vii. 132). Similarly, σπονδὰς τέμωμεν *let us cut* (*make*) *a league*

(Eurip. *Hel.* 1235): φίλια τέμνεσθαι *to cement friendship* by sacrificing a victim; lit. *to cut* friendship (Eurip. *Suppl.* 375). In Latin, *foedus ferire to strike* a league: *foedus ictum a ratified* league, ratified by a *blow* (*ictus*). (*f*) If *testament* is the correct translation in vv. 16, 17, the writer is fairly chargeable with a rhetorical blunder; for ver. 18 ff. is plainly intended as a historical illustration of the propositions in vv. 16, 17, and the illustration turns on a point entirely different from the matter illustrated. The writer is made to say, " A *will* is of no force until after the testator's death; *therefore* the first *covenant* was ratified with the blood of victims.

CHAPTER X.

1-18. A summary restatement of the matters discussed from ch. viii. 1.

1. The arrangement of the verse is much disputed. Rend. " The law, with the same sacrifices which they continually renew year by year, can never make the comers thereunto perfect." *

A shadow (σκιὰν). The emphasis is on this thought. The legal system was a shadow. Σκιὰ is *a rude outline, an adumbration*, contrasted with εἰκὼν, *the archetypal* or *ideal pattern*. Σκιὰ does not accurately exhibit the figure itself. Comp. ch. viii. 5.

Of good things to come (τῶν μελλόντων ἀγαθῶν). From the point of view of the law.

The very image of the things (αὐτὴν τὴν εἰκόνα τῶν πραγμάτων). For εἰκὼν *image*, see on Apoc. xiii. 14 ; Philip. ii. 7. Πραγμάτων *things* expresses a little more distinctly than μελλόντων ἀγαθῶν the idea of *facts* and *realities*.

---

* Others take κατ' ἐνιαυτὸν with the whole clause, ταῖς αὐταῖς — προσφέρουσιν, and εἰς τὸ διηνεκὲς with τελειῶσαι : thus : "with the same sacrifices which they offer year by year make perfect forever" (Westcott and von Soden). Others, κατ' ἐνιαυτὸν with all that follows to τελειῶσαι (Alford, Ebrard, Delitzsch). Others, κατ' ἐνιαυτὸν with ταῖς αὐταῖς, and εἰς τὸ διηνεκὲς with προσφέρουσιν : "with the same sacrifices every year which they offer continually " (Lünemann).

Can (δύνανται). Δύναται might be expected with ὁ νόμος *the law* as the subject. If δύνανται, the plural, is retained, the clause *the law — image of the things* must be taken absolutely, the construction of the sentence breaking off suddenly, and the subject being changed from *the law* to *the priests:* "The priests can never," etc. It is better to read δύναται in the singular, with Tischendorf, Westcott and Hort, and Weiss.

Continually (εἰς τὸ διηνεκὲς). See on ch. vii. 3, and comp. vv. 12, 14. Const. with *offer.*

2. **To be offered** (προσφερόμεναι). The present participle brings out more forcibly the continuous repetition: "Ceased *being offered.*"

3. **A remembrance of sins** (ἀνάμνησις ἁμαρτιῶν). Each successive sacrifice was a fresh reminder of sins to be atoned for; so far were the sacrifices from satisfying the conscience of the worshipper. Ἀνάμνησις, lit. *a calling to mind.* Comp. ver. 17, and see LXX, Num. v. 15.

5. Confirming the assertion of ver. 4 by a citation, Ps. xl. 7–9, the theme of which is that deliverance from sin is not obtained by animal sacrifices, but by fulfilling God's will. The quotation does not agree with either the Hebrew or the LXX, and the Hebrew and LXX do not agree. The writer supposes the words to be spoken by Messiah when he enters the world as Saviour. The obedience to the divine will, which the Psalmist contrasts with sacrifices, our writer makes to consist in Christ's offering once for all. According to him, the course of thought in the Psalm is as follows : "Thou, O God, desirest not the sacrifice of beasts, but thou hast prepared my body as a single sacrifice, and so I come to do thy will, as was predicted of me, by the sacrifice of myself." Christ did not yield to God's will as authoritative constraint. The constraint lay in his own eternal spirit. His sacrifice was no less his own will than God's will.

Sacrifice and offering (θυσίαν καὶ προσφορὰν). The animal-offering and the meal-offering.

6. Burnt offerings and sacrifices for sin (ὁλοκαυτώματα καὶ περὶ ἁμαρτίας). The burnt-offering and the sin-offering.

7. In the volume of the book (ἐν κεφαλίδι βιβλίου). Κεφαλίς, N. T.⁰, is a diminutive, meaning *little head*. Lat. *capitellum* or *capitulum*. The *extremity* or *end*, as the capital of a column. See Ex. xxvi. 32, 37. Sometimes the column itself, as Ex. xl. 18; Num. iii. 36. Said to be used of the *tips* or *knobs* of the rollers around which parchments were rolled, but no instances are cited. *A roll of parchment*, *a book-roll*, Ezek. ii. 9. Meaning here the Scriptures of the O. T. for Hebrew מְגִלָּה. Κεφαλίς is found in LXX with βιβλίου *book*, only Ezek. ii. 9; Ps. xxxix. 7. For βιβλίον *book*, see on 2 Tim. iv. 13.

8. Above when he said (ἀνώτερον λέγων). Lit. *saying above*. Introducing a partial repetition of the quotation.

9. He taketh away the first that he may establish the second. Removes that which God does not will, the animal-sacrifice, that he may establish that which God does will, the offering of an obedient will.

10. By the which will (ἐν ᾧ θελήματι). The will of God as fulfilled in Christ.

We are sanctified (ἡγιασμένοι ἐσμὲν). Lit. *we are having been sanctified;* that is, in a sanctified state, as having become partakers of the spirit of Christ. This is the work of the eternal spirit, whose will is the very will of God. It draws men into its own sphere, and makes them partakers of its holiness (Heb. xii. 10).

Once for all (ἐφάπαξ). Const. with *are sanctified*. The sanctification of the Levitical offerings was only temporary,

and had to be repeated. Christ's one offering "perfected
forever them that are sanctified" (ver. 14).* This thought
is elaborated in vv. 11–14.

11. **Every** priest (πᾶς). Suggesting *many* priests. Comp.
ch. vii. 23.

Standeth (ἕστηκεν). Servile attitude, contrasted with that
of the exalted Saviour, ch. i. 3.

Daily — often — the same. The wearisome round of daily
offerings, always the same, contrasted with the one offering,
once for all.

Take away (περιελεῖν). Only here in connection with sin.
See on 2 Cor. iii. 16. The verb literally means *to strip off
all round.* See Gen. xli. 42 (of a ring): Gen. xxxviii. 14;
Deut. xxi. 13 (of clothes). Comp. εὐπερίστατος, Heb. xii. 1,
see note, and περίκειται ἀσθένειαν *is compassed about with weakness*, Heb. v. 2. See also *clothed with shame*, and with *cursing*,
Ps. xxxv. 26; cix. 18.

12. **Forever** (εἰς τὸ διηνεκὲς). Const. with *offered.* The
reason appears in ver. 14. It is according to the usage of the
epistle to place this phrase *after* that which it qualifies. Thus
one sacrifice forever is contrasted with *the same sacrifices often.*
This agrees also with what follows. He offered one sacrifice
forever, and then sat down, awaiting its eternal result.†

14. **He hath perfected forever** (τετελείωκεν εἰς τὸ διηνεκὲς).
Note the continued emphasis upon the τελείωσις *perfection.*
Comp. ch. vii. 11, 19; ix. 9; x. 1; xii. 2. No more sacrifices
are needed. The reign of the Great High Priest is not to be
interrupted by the duty of sacrifice.

---

* Westcott takes ἐφάπαξ with the entire sentence: Alford with *offering.*
It is true that the writer insists on the *offering* of Christ being "once for all"
(ch. vii. 27; ix. 12, 26, 28; x. 12, 14), but here this connection would seem
to require the article τῆς ἐφάπαξ.

† Others construe with *sat down.* So Lünemann, Bleek, De Wette.

15–17. Repetition of the passage already cited from Jeremiah in ch. viii. 10–12. The nerve of the citation is ver. 17.

18. **There is no more offering for sin.** Forgiveness of sin is the characteristic of the new covenant. In Jeremiah complete pardon of sins is promised. If the pardon is complete, there is left no place for the Levitical sacrifices under the new covenant. At this point the doctrinal portion of the epistle ends.

19. **To enter into the holiest** (εἰς τὴν εἴσοδον τῶν ἁγίων). Lit. *for the entering of the holiest.* The phrase παρρησία εἰς *boldness unto,* N. T.º. Παρρησία with περὶ *concerning,* J. xvi. 25; with πρὸς *with reference to,* 2 Cor. vii. 4; 1 J. iii. 21; v. 14. Εἴσοδος in N. T. habitually of the *act* of entering.

By the blood (ἐν τῷ αἵματι). Lit. "*in* the blood": in the power or virtue of.

20. **By a new and living way which he hath consecrated for us** (ἣν ἐνεκαίνισεν ἡμῖν ὁδὸν πρόσφατον καὶ ζῶσαν). The A. V. is wrong. Ἣν *which* is to be construed with εἴσοδον *entrance.* Thus: "having boldness for the entrance which he has inaugurated (or opened) for us—a way new and living." For ἐνεκαίνισεν see on ch. ix. 18. The way must be *opened,* for every other way is closed. Ἐνκαινίζειν in LXX of the inauguration of a house, kingdom, temple, altar. See Deut. xx. 5; 1 Sam. xi. 14; 1 K. viii. 63; 2 Chron. xv. 8. Πρόσφατον *new,* N. T.º. In LXX, see Num. vi. 3; Deut. xxxii. 17; Ps. lxxx. 9; Eccles. i. 9. The derivation appears to be πρὸς *near to,* and φατός *slain* (from πέφαμαι, the perfect of φένειν *to kill*). According to this the original sense would be *newly-slain;* and the word was used of one so recently dead as to retain the appearance of life: also, generally, of things which have not lost their character or appearance by the lapse of time; of fishes, fruits, oil, etc., which are *fresh;* of anger which has not had time to cool. Later the meaning

was weakened into *new*.*   Note that the contrast is not
between a new and an old way, but between a new way and
no way.   So long as the old division of the tabernacle existed,
the way into the holiest was not opened, ch. ix. 8.   *Ζῶσαν*
living.   A *living way* seems a strange expression, but comp.
Peter's *living stones*, 1 Pet. ii. 5.   Christ styles himself both
way and *life*.   The bold figure answers to the fact.   The new
way is *through* a life *to* life.

Through the veil (διὰ τοῦ καταπετάσματος).   The veil of
the holy of holies is rent.   Christ's work does not stop short
of the believer's *complete* access to God himself.

That is to say his flesh (τοῦτ᾽ ἔστιν τῆς σαρκὸς αὐτοῦ).
Const. with *veil:* the veil which consisted in his flesh.   His
flesh was the state through which he had to pass before he
entered heaven for us.   See ch. ii. 9–18; v. 7–9; x. 5.
When he put off that state, the veil of the temple was rent.
He passed through humanity to glory as the forerunner of
his people, ch. vi. 20.

21. **A high priest** (ἱερέα μέγαν).   Lit. *a great priest.*
Comp. Lev. xxi. 10, LXX.   Not merely = ἀρχιερεὺς *high*
priest, but emphasising Christ's superior *greatness* as high
priest.

House of God (οἶκον τοῦ θεοῦ).   In the Gospels always of
the temple.   Not found in Paul.   Once in the Pastorals,
of the church, 1 Tim. iii. 15, and so 1 Pet. iv. 17.   Here
the whole Christian family.   Comp. 1 Cor. iii. 16, 17;
2 Cor. vi. 16; Eph. ii. 22.

22. **Let us draw near** (προσερχώμεθα).   See on ch. iv. 16.

With a true heart (μετὰ ἀληθινῆς καρδίας).   A right and
genuine inward attitude toward God.   For the phrase comp.

---

* The derivation from πρὸ *before* and σφάζειν *to slay* is more than suspicious.

LXX, Isa. xxxviii. 3. N. T.°. For ἀληθινῆς see on J. i. 9,
and comp. Heb. viii. 2 ; ix. 24. A true heart is required to
enter the true sanctuary. The phrase means more than *in
sincerity*. Sincerity is included, but with it all that enters
into a right attitude toward God as revealed in our Great
High Priest, — gladness, freedom, enthusiasm, bold appropriation of all the privileges of sonship.

In full assurance of faith (ἐν πληροφορίᾳ πίστεως). Full
conviction engendered by faith. See on ch. vi. 11. Faith is
the basis of all right relation to God.

Sprinkled from an evil conscience (ῥεραντισμένοι — ἀπὸ
συνειδήσεως πονηρᾶς). This qualification for a right approach
to God is stated typologically. As the priests were sprinkled
with the sacrificial blood and washed with water before ministering, so do you who have now the privilege and standing of
priests in approaching God, draw near, priestlike, as sharers
in an economy which purges the conscience (ch. ix. 14),
having your consciences purged. Your own hearts must
experience the effects of the great sacrifice of Christ, —
pardon, moral renewal, deliverance from a legal spirit. On
the priesthood of believers see 1 Pet. ii. 5, 9 ; Ex. xix. 6 ;
Isa. lxi. 6. This idea is dominated in our epistle by that of
Christ's priesthood ; but it is not excluded, and is implied
throughout. See ch. xiii. 15. For *sprinkled*, see on 1 Pet. i. 2.

Bodies washed (λελουσμένοι τὸ σῶμα). Also typological.
Most expositors refer to baptism. The most significant passage in that direction is 1 Pet. iii. 21 ; comp. Eph. v. 26 ;
Tit. iii. 5. It may be, though I doubt if the idea is emphasised. I incline, with Dr. Bruce, to think that it indicates
generally the thoroughness of the cleansing process undergone
by one who surrenders himself, soul, body, and spirit, to God.

23. **Profession of our faith** (τὴν ὁμολογίαν τῆς ἐλπίδος).
Rend. "confession of our hope." *Faith* does not appear
among Ms. readings. It is an innovation of the translators.

Hope is the rendering of Tyndale, Coverdale, the Great Bible, the Geneva, the Bishops', and Rheims.   On *confession* see on 2 Cor. ix. 13, and comp. notes on 1 Tim. vi. 12, 13.   The phrase *confession of hope* N. T.⁰.   They are steadfastly to confess their hope in God's promise and salvation.   Comp. ch. iii. 6; vi. 11, 18; vii. 19.   *Hope* is here = *the object of hope*.

Without wavering (ἀκλινῆ).   N. T.⁰.

24.   **Let us consider one another** (κατανοῶμεν ἀλλήλους). Take careful note of each other's spiritual welfare.   For the verb see on Jas. i. 23.   It denotes *attentive, continuous* care. Comp. Heb. iii. 1.

To provoke (εἰς παροξυσμὸν).   Lit. *with a view to incitement.* Only here and Acts xv. 39.   From παροξύνειν *to sharpen.* Hence to *stimulate.*   In Acts xv. 39, the *result* of provocation; *irritation* or *contention.*   Here the *act* of incitement.   Twice in LXX, Deut. xxix. 28 (27); Jer. xxxix. (xxxii.) 3, 7; for the Hebrew קֶצֶף *anger, wrath, altercation.*   The Hebrew derivation is from קָצַף *a splinter.*   The new economy demands mutual care on the part of the members of the Christian community.   Comp. 1 Cor. xii. 25.   They must stir up each other's religious affections and ministries.

25.   **The assembling of ourselves together** (ἐπισυναγωγὴν ἑαυτῶν).   Ἐπισυναγωγή only here and 2 Th. ii. 1, see note. The *act* of assembling, although some explain *assembly.*   The antithesis is, "not forsaking assembling, but exhorting in assembly."   Lünemann aptly says that the idea of apostasy which would be conveyed by the rendering *assembly* or *congregation* is excluded by ἔθος *habit* or *custom*, which implies an often recurring act on the part of the same persons.

As the manner of some is (καθὼς ἔθος τισίν).   For *manner* rend. *custom.*   Lit. *as is custom unto some.*   Ἔθος mostly in Luke and Acts.   Comp. L. i. 9; J. xix. 40.

Ye see the day approaching (βλέπετε ἐγγίζουσαν τὴν ἡμέραν). The day of Christ's second coming, bringing with it the judgment of Israel. He could say "ye see," because they were familiar with Christ's prophecy concerning the destruction of the temple; and they would see this crisis approaching in the disturbances which heralded the Jewish war.

26. **We sin wilfully** (ἑκουσίως ἁμαρτανόντων ἡμῶν). Ἑκουσίως *wilfully*, only here and 1 Pet. v. 2. Comp. Philem. 14, κατ᾽ ἐκούσιον *of free will*. See LXX, Num. xv. 3. The wilful sin is the abandonment of Christianity for Judaism.

The knowledge (ἐπίγνωσιν). Only here in Hebrews. Very common in Paul. For the word, and the phrase *knowledge of the truth*, see on 1 Tim. ii. 4. *The truth* is the revelation through Christ.

There remaineth no more sacrifice for sins (οὐκέτι περὶ ἁμαρτιῶν ἀπολείπεται θυσία). Of course not. For the Levitical sacrifices are abolished. It is Christ's sacrifice or none.

27. **But a certain fearful looking for** (φοβερὰ δέ τις ἐκδοχή). Rend. "a kind of fearful expectation." Ἐκδοχὴ N. T.°, °LXX.

Fiery indignation (πυρὸς ζῆλος). For ζῆλος see on Jas. iii. 14. The radical idea of the word is *ferment of spirit* (ζεῖν *to boil;* see Acts xviii. 25; Rom. xii. 11). This idea takes on different aspects in ζῆλος, as *indignation*, Acts v. 17; *zeal*, J. ii. 17; Rom. x. 2; 2 Cor. vii. 7; xi. 2; Philip. iii. 6; *envy*, Rom. xiii. 13; 1 Cor. iii. 3; Gal. v. 20. In the last sense often with ἔρις *strife*. The phrase *fiery indignation*, lit. *indignation of fire* (N. T.°) is an adaptation from Isa. xxvi. 11.

The adversaries (τοὺς ὑπεναντίους). **Only here and Col.** ii. 14. Often in LXX.

28. **He that despised** (ἀθετήσας τις). Lit. *one* that despised; *any* transgressor. The verb only here in Hebrews.
The kindred noun ἀθέτησις only in Hebrews. See ch. vii. 18;
ix. 26.

Died (ἀποθνήσκει). Lit. *dieth*. According to the ordinance as it *now* stands in the law.

Without mercy (χωρὶς οἰκτιρμῶν). The phrase N. T.⁰.
For the noun see on 2 Cor. i. 3.

Under two or three witnesses (ἐπὶ δυσὶν ἢ τρισὶν μάρτυσιν).
As in LXX, Deut. xvii. 6. ’Επὶ with dative signifying *on
condition of* two or three witnesses testifying. Comp. 1 Tim.
v. 17, where the same phrase occurs with the genitive, *before,
in the presence of*. Comp. also Deut. xix. 15.

29. **Of how much** (πόσῳ). Not qualifying χείρονος *sorer*,
but the whole clause: "by how much think ye shall he be
thought worthy of sorer punishment."

Punishment (τιμωρίας). N. T.⁰. Occasionally in LXX,
frequent in Class. Originally *assistance;* assistance to one
who has been wronged; punishment. With no sense of
chastisement. It is purely retributive.*

Trodden under foot (καταπατήσας) Only here in Hebrews.
⁰P. Frequent in LXX for *spoiling, defeating, treating contemptuously*. The strong term is purposely selected in order
to convey the sense of the fearful outrage involved in forsaking Christ and returning to Judaism.

---

* The distinction sometimes asserted between τιμωρία *retribution*, and
κόλασις *chastisement* for the amendment of the subject, does not hold in N. T.
Neither κόλασις nor κολάζειν convey any sense of chastisement. See Acts iv. 21;
2 Pet. ii. 9; Matt. xxv. 46; 1 J. iv. 18; nor is there a trace of this meaning
of either noun or verb in LXX. See Trench, *New Testament Synonyms*, § VII,
and Schmidt, *Synonymik*, § 167, 1, 3. The prevailing sense of κόλασις in Class.
is *a check* applied to prevent excess.

Hath counted an unholy thing (κοινὸν ἡγησάμενος). Ἡγεῖσ-θαι *to count* or *deem* means a conscious judgment resting on a deliberate weighing of the facts. See Rom. xii. 10 ; Philip. ii. 3. Here it implies a deliberate, contemptuous rejection of the gifts of the new covenant. The fundamental idea of κοινὸς is *shared by all, public.* Thus Acts ii. 44 ; iv. 32 ; Tit. i. 4 ; Jude 3. Out of this grows the idea of *not sacred ;* not set apart for particular uses by purification, and so (ceremonially) *unclean* or *defiled*, as Mk. vii. 2, 5 ; Acts x. 14, 28 ; xi. 8. In these cases it is not implied that the thing is defiled or filthy in itself, but only unclean through the absence of that which would set it apart. Comp. Rom. xiv. 14. Here the word admits of two explanations : (1) that Christ's blood was counted *common*, having no more sacred character or specific worth than the blood of any ordinary person ; (2) that in refusing to regard Christ's blood as that of an atoner and redeemer, it was implied that his blood was *unclean* as being that of a transgressor. The former seems preferable. There was no specific virtue in Christ's blood *as blood ;* but a peculiar and unique virtue attached to it as the offering of his eternal spirit (ch. ix. 14), as the blood shed in ratification of a sacred covenant established by God, and as having sanctifying virtue. This view is further justified by the combination of *blood* and *spirit*, as sources of sanctification allied in the writer's mind.

Hath done despite unto the spirit of grace (καὶ τὸ πνεῦμα τῆς χάριτος ἐνυβρίσας). Ἐνυβρίζειν *to insult*, N. T.⁰. The simple verb ὑβρίζειν in Matthew, Luke, Acts, and Pastorals. It will be observed that the work of the Holy Spirit does not receive in this epistle the emphasis which marks it in some other portions of the N. T.

30. **We know him that hath said** (οἴδαμεν γὰρ τὸν εἰπόντα). The retribution (τιμωρία) is certain, because assured by the word of God in Scripture.

Vengeance (ἐκδίκησις). An unfortunate translation, since it conveys the idea of *vindictiveness* which does not reside in

the Greek word. It is the full meting out of justice to all
parties. The quotation is an adaptation of the LXX of
Deut. xxxii. 35. The second citation is literally from LXX
of Deut. xxxii. 36.

31. To fall, etc. Comp. LXX, 2 Sam. xxiv. 14; Sir. ii. 18.

Of the living God. The living God, revealed in the living
Christ, will not suffer his sacrificial gift and his covenant to
be slighted and insulted with impunity. See on ch. iii. 12.

32. After ye were illuminated ($\phi\omega\tau\iota\sigma\theta\acute{\epsilon}\nu\tau\epsilon\varsigma$). See on
ch. vi. 4.

A great fight ($\pi o\lambda\lambda\grave{\eta}\nu$ $\check{a}\theta\lambda\eta\sigma\iota\nu$). Ἄθλησις N. T.°, °LXX.
See on $\grave{a}\theta\lambda\mathring{\eta}$ *strive*, 2 Tim. ii. 5. See Introduction, on the
allusions in the epistle to persecution.

33. Whilst ye were made a gazing-stock ($\theta\epsilon a\tau\rho\iota\zeta\acute{o}\mu\epsilon\nu o\iota$).
N. T.°. °LXX, °Class. Lit. *exhibited in the theatre*. Comp.
1 Cor. iv. 9.

Whilst ye became companions ($\kappa o\iota\nu\omega\nu o\grave{\iota}$ $\gamma\epsilon\nu\eta\theta\acute{\epsilon}\nu\tau\epsilon\varsigma$).
Rend. *by becoming partakers*. More than companionship is
implied. For $\kappa o\iota\nu\omega\nu o\grave{\iota}$ see on L. v. 10. The noun and its
kindred verb in N. T. almost exclusively of ethical and spir-
itual relations, as 1 Tim. v. 22; 1 Pet. iv. 13; 2 J. 11;
1 Cor. x. 18; 2 Cor. i. 7; Philem. 17. Even when applied
to pecuniary contributions they imply Christian fellowship as
the basis of the liberality. See on Rom. xii. 13; xv. 27;
Philip. iv. 15.

Of them that were so used ($\tau\hat{\omega}\nu$ $o\check{v}\tau\omega\varsigma$ $\grave{a}\nu a\sigma\tau\rho\epsilon\phi o\mu\acute{\epsilon}\nu\omega\nu$).
Rend. "of them that fared thus." Others render "who con-
ducted themselves thus"; endured their persecutions so
bravely. But the $o\check{v}\tau\omega\varsigma$ can refer only to *made a gazing-
stock*.

34. **For ye had compassion of me in my bonds** (καὶ γὰρ τοῖς δεσμίοις συνεπαθήσατε). Entirely wrong, following T. R. τοῖς δεσμοῖς μου. Rend. "ye had compassion on the prisoners." So Vulg. *vinctis compassi estis.* The corrupt reading has furnished one of the stock arguments for the Pauline authorship of the Epistle.

Took joyfully (μετὰ χαρᾶς προσεδέξασθε). The verb primarily *to receive to one's self, accept,* as here. Comp. L. xv. 2; Philip. ii. 29. Mostly, in N. T. however, *to wait for, expect,* as Mk. xv. 43; L. ii. 25, 38; Acts xxiii. 21.

Spoiling (ἁρπαγὴν). Only here, Matt. xxiii. 25; L. xi. 39. Allied with ἁρπάζειν *to snatch away.*

Of your goods (τῶν ὑπαρχόντων ὑμῶν). The verb ὑπάρχειν means originally *to begin,* or *begin to be;* hence of anything that has begun to be, *to come forth, be there;* then simply *to be.* Accordingly the phrase ὑπάρχει μοί τι means *there is something to me, I have something.* See Acts iii. 6; iv. 37; xxviii. 7. Hence τὰ ὑπάρχοντα *things which are to one; possessions, goods.* See Matt. xix. 21; xxiv. 27; L. viii. 3; Acts iv. 32.*

Knowing in yourselves that ye have, etc. (γινώσκοντες ἔχειν ἑαυτοὺς). Rend. "knowing that ye yourselves have a better," etc. The A.V. follows T. R. ἐν ἑαυτοῖς.† Ye yourselves in contrast with your spoilers.

Substance (ὕπαρξιν). Only here and Acts ii. 45. Occasionally in LXX. Rend. *possession.*

---

* It is sometimes claimed that ὑπάρχειν as distinguished from εἶναι implies a reference to an antecedent condition. That is true in some instances, but the reference is not inherent in the verb ; since sometimes there is implied a reference to a future condition, and sometimes the verb is used simply in the sense of εἶναι *to be* absolutely.

† Others, as Alford and Lünemann, adopt the reading ἑαυτοῖς *for yourselves.* Westcott, and Rev. marg., reading ἑαυτοὺς, render it as the object of ἔχειν, "knowing that ye had yourselves for a better possession," and referring to L. xxi. 19. According to this the sense is, "your true selves remained untouched. You saved them out of the wreck of your possessions." This is foreign to the tone of the epistle, and must be regarded as artificial.

35. **Confidence** (τὴν παρρησίαν). Rend. *boldness*. The boldness and courage which you manifested under persecution.

36. **Ye might receive the promise** (κομίσησθε τὴν ἐπαγγελίαν). Comp. ch. xi. 13, 39, and see on 1 Pet. i. 8. The verb implies, not mere *obtaining*, but receiving and carrying away for use and enjoyment.

37. **A little while** (μικρὸν ὅσον ὅσον). Strictly, *a very little while*. The phrase N. T.º. It is not part of the quotation, but is taken from Isa. xxvi. 20, the only instance. See Aristoph. *Wasps*, 213.

He that shall come will come (ὁ ἐρχόμενος ἥξει). Rend. "he that cometh will come." In the Hebrew (Hab. ii. 3) the subject of the sentence is the vision of the extermination of the Chaldees. "The vision — will surely come." As rendered in the LXX, either Jehovah or Messiah must be the subject. The passage was referred to Messiah by the later Jewish theologians, and is so taken by our writer, as is shown by the article before ἐρχόμενος. Comp. Matt. xi. 3; xxi. 9; J. xi. 27. Similarly he refers ἥξει *shall come* to the final coming of Messiah to judge the world.

38. **Now the just shall live by faith** (ὁ δὲ δίκαιός (μου) ἐκ πίστεως ζήσεται). Cited by Paul, Rom. i. 17; Gal. iii. 11.* In the original prophecy the just man is contrasted with the haughty Chaldaean invaders, who are puffed up and not upright. Through his steadfast obedience to God he shall be kept alive in the time of confusion and destruction.

But if any man draw back (καὶ ἐὰν ὑποστείληται). Omit *if any man*. Rend. "and if he draw back," that is, the just

---

* The Hebrew reads, "the just shall live by his constancy." LXX, "the just shall live by my faith," or (Cod. A) "my just one shall live by faith." Μου does not appear in Romans or Galatians.

man. The possibility of the lapse of even the just is assumed. See on ch. vi. 4–6. The verb only here, Acts xx. 20, 27; Gal. ii. 12. See on Acts xx. 20. Rare in LXX.

Shall have no pleasure (οὐκ εὐδοκεῖ). Rend. "hath no pleasure." "If he draw back — in him," not in the Hebrew, which reads, "behold, puffed up within him is his soul, it is not upright." The clauses of the LXX are transposed here.

39. **But we are not of them who draw back** (ἡμεῖς δὲ οὐκ ἐσμὲν ὑποστολῆς). Lit. *we are not of shrinking back*. Ὑποστολὴ N.T.°, °LXX, °Class. Εἶναι with genitive marks the quality or peculiarity of a person or thing. Comp. ch. xii. 11 χαρᾶς εἶναι *to be of joy, joyful*. We do not partake of drawing back, which is characteristic of recreants.

Unto perdition (εἰς ἀπώλειαν). Or *destruction*. Drawing back *makes for* and *terminates in* (εἰς) *destruction*.

Of them that believe (πίστεως). Rend. *of faith*. The phrase εἶναι πίστεως *to be of faith*, N. T.°.

Saving (περιποίησιν). See on 1 Th. v. 9.

CHAPTER XI.

The concluding statement of ch. x suggests the following discussion of the nature of faith and of its fruits as called out by God's revelation from the earliest time.

1. **Faith** (πίστις). Without the article, indicating that it is treated in its abstract conception, and not merely as Christian faith. It is important that the preliminary definition should be clearly understood, since the following examples illustrate it. The key is furnished by ver. 27, *as seeing him who is invisible*. Faith apprehends as a real fact what is not revealed to the senses. It rests on that fact, acts upon it,

and is upheld by it in the face of all that seems to contradict it. Faith is a real seeing. See Introduction, p. 363.

Substance (ὑπόστασις). See on ch. i. 3 and iii. 14. On the whole, the Rev. *assurance* gives the true meaning. The definition has a scholastic and philosophic quality, as might be expected from a pupil of the Alexandrian schools. The meaning *substance, real being,* given by A. V., Vulg., and many earlier interpreters, *suggests* the true sense, but is philosophically inaccurate. *Substance,* as used by these translators, is *substantial nature;* the real nature of a thing which underlies and supports its outward form or properties. In this sense it is very appropriate in ch. i. 3, in describing the nature of the Son as the image or impress of God's essential being: but in this sense it is improperly applied to faith, which is *an act* of the moral intelligence directed at an object; or *a condition* which sustains a certain relation to the object. It cannot be said that faith is substantial being. It *apprehends* reality: it is that to which the unseen objects of hope become real and substantial. *Assurance* gives the true idea. It is the firm grasp of faith on unseen fact.

Evidence (ἔλεγχος). N. T.⁰. Quite often in LXX for יָכַח to *reprove, rebuke, punish, blame.* See Prov. i. 23; Wisd. ii. 14; Sir. xvi. 12. See especially on the kindred verb ἐλέγχειν, J. iii. 20. Rend. *conviction.* Observe that ὑπόστασις and ἔλεγχος are not two distinct and independent conceptions, in which case καί would have been added; but they stand in apposition. Ἔλεγχος is really included in ὑπόστασις, but adds to the simple idea of assurance a suggestion of influences operating to produce conviction which carry the force of demonstration. The word often signifies a process of proof or demonstration. So von Soden: "a being convinced. Therefore not a rash, feebly-grounded hypothesis, a dream of hope, the child of a wish."

Of things (πραγμάτων). Πρᾶγμα is, strictly, a thing *done;* an accomplished fact. It introduces a wider conception than ἐλπιζομένων *things hoped for;* embracing not only future realities, but all that does not fall under the cognisance of the senses, whether past, present, or future.

2. **For by it** (ἐν ταύτῃ γὰρ). Lit. *for in this*. Rend. *therein:* in the sphere and exercise of faith: as believers. Comp. 1 Tim. v. 10. *For* introduces a proof of the preceding statement concerning the nature of faith. Faith has power to see and realise the unseen, *for* the experience of the fathers proves it.

The elders obtained a good report (ἐμαρτυρηθήσαν οἱ πρεσβύτεροι). *The elders* for the more common *the fathers:* the saints of the O. T. dispensation, many of whose names are recorded in this chapter. Ἐμαρτυρηθήσαν, lit. *were borne witness to.* God bore witness to them in the victory of their faith over all obstacles, and their characters and deeds as men of faith were recorded in Scripture. For this use of μαρτυρεῖν in the passive, see Acts vi. 3; x. 22; xvi. 12; Rom. iii. 21; Heb. vii. 8, 17. Notice that the statement in this verse does not begin the list of examples, which commences with ver. 4, but is closely attached to the definition in ver. 1 as a comprehensive justification of it.

3. Neither does this verse belong to the list of historical instances from Genesis, in which men exercised faith. It is merely the first instance presented in O. T. history of an opportunity for the exercise of faith as the assurance and conviction of things not seen. Like ver. 2, it is closely connected with the definition. It contains the exposition of the nature of faith, by showing that in its earliest and most general expression — belief in the creation of the visible universe by God — it is a conviction of something not apprehensible by sense.*

---

* The assumption that this verse furnishes the first item in the catalogue of O. T. examples of faith, gives rise to such explanations as that of Michaelis, which is indorsed by Bleek; that the writer thought of the earliest men as attaining only by faith the knowledge that God made the world, and that he expressed himself so generally because that fact is not expressly related of them, and because their conduct did not indicate a living faith.

We understand (νοοῦμεν). Νοεῖν signifies *to perceive with the νοῦς* or reflective intelligence. In Class. of seeing with the eyes, sometimes with ὀφθαλμοῖς expressed; but as early as Homer it is distinguished from the mere physical act of vision, as perception of the mind consequent upon seeing. Thus, τὸν δὲ ἰδὼν ἐνόησε and *seeing him he perceived* (*Il.* xi. 599): οὐκ ἴδον οὐδ᾽ ἐνόησα I *neither saw nor perceived* (*Od.* xiii. 318). In N. T. never of the mere physical act. Here is meant the inward perception and apprehension of the visible creation as the work of God, which follows the sight of the phenomena of nature.

The worlds (τοὺς αἰῶνας). Lit. *the ages*. The world or worlds as the product of successive aeons. See on ch. i. 2.

Were framed (κατηρτίσθαι). Put together; adjusted; the parts fitted to each other. See on Gal. vi. 1; Matt. xxi. 16; L. vi. 40. Of the *preparing* and *fixing* in heaven of the sun and moon, LXX, Ps. lxxiii. 16; lxxxviii. 37 : of *building* a wall, 2 Esdr. iv. 12, 13, 16. See also Ps. xxxix. 6. Rend. *have been framed*. The A. V. gives the impression of one giving his assent to *an account* of creation; but the perfect tense exhibits the faith of one who is actually contemplating creation itself.

By the word of God (ῥήματι θεοῦ). Comp. Gen. i; Ps. xxxiii. 6; cxviii. 5.

So that things which are seen were not made of things which do appear (εἰς τὸ μὴ ἐκ φαινομένων τὸ βλεπόμενον γεγονέναι). For *things which are seen*, rend. *that which is seen*. For *were not made* rend. *hath not been made*. ᾽Εις τὸ followed by the infinitive signifies *result*, not *purpose*. We perceive that the worlds have been framed by the word of God, so that (this being the case) that which is visible has not arisen out of that which is seen.* Μὴ *not* negatives the remainder

---

* Some, however, insist that εἰς τὸ, etc., indicates *purpose* or *design*. So Westcott, who says, "the worlds were made, etc., *to the end that* that which

of the clause taken as a whole. In other words, the proposition denied is, *that which is seen arose out of visible things.* By many early interpreters μὴ was transposed, and construed with φαινομένων alone, signifying "that which is seen has arisen from things which do *not* appear." These things were explained as chaos, the invisible creative powers of God, etc.

4. **Abel offered unto God** (Ἄβελ προσήνεγκεν τῷ θεῷ). For the phrase see ch. ix. 14.

A more excellent sacrifice (πλείονα θυσίαν). Greater in value in God's eyes. For πλείων in this sense, see ch. iii. 3 ; Matt. vi. 25; L. xi. 31; xii. 23. In Paul never in this sense. Others explain *a more abundant* sacrifice, referring to the material character of the offerings. See Gen. iv. 4. But the difference between the offerings of Abel and Cain, considered in themselves, is largely a matter of speculation, and, as Lünemann justly remarks, such an interpretation accentuates unduly a purely external feature.*

By which he obtained witness (δι' ἧς ἐμαρτυρήθη). Lit. *was witnessed to,* as ver. 2. The pronoun *which* may refer either to the sacrifice or to faith. Better the latter, as is apparent from ver. 2, and probably from ver. 7, although the relation there is somewhat different.

is seen (be known) to have arisen not from things which appear." According to this, faith certifies not only *the fact* of creation by the word of God, but also God's *design* that creation should be believed to have taken place *only* by his word, calling the world out of nothing; and should not be believed to have arisen out of visible things. It must be allowed that εἰς τὸ followed by the infinitive, in every one of the eight other instances in this epistle, expresses purpose ; and further, that such is its more frequent meaning everywhere. But (*a*) such is not its *universal* meaning. See Rom. i. 20; xii. 3; 2 Cor. viii. 6; Gal. iii. 17 ; 1 Th. ii. 16.   (*b*) On this explanation something is imported into the passage which neither the sense nor the construction requires, and which is laboured and unnatural.   (*c*) Γεγονέναι thus becomes excessively awkward. Alford justly says that, on this hypothesis, γεγονέναι ought to have been some subjective word ; not, as it is now, a mere record of a past fact.   The sense of *result* is held by Bleek, Alford, Weizsäcker, Burton.

* That some external difference was recognised is most likely. See the peculiar reading of LXX, Gen. iv. 7.

Righteous (δίκαιος). Abel is called *righteous* by Christ himself, Matt. xxiii. 35. Comp. 1 J. iii. 12. See on Rom. i. 17.

God testifying of his gifts (μαρτυροῦντος ἐπὶ τοῖς δώροις αὐτοῦ τοῦ θεοῦ). Defining more specifically the general *was witnessed to*. God bore witness by his acceptance of the gifts. Ἐπί marks the fact *on* which the witness was based.

Yet speaketh (ἔτι λαλεῖ). Comp. Gen. iv. 10. *Still*, although ages have passed since his death. Comp. ch. xii. 24. Not that his voice still cries to God (so Bleek and others), but that by his faith he still speaks to us in the O. T. Scriptures, though dead. Const. ἔτι *yet* with λαλεῖ *speaketh*; not with *being dead*, in the logical sense, "*even* being dead," as Rom. iii. 7.*

5. Enoch. Gen. v. 21–24. Comp. Sir. xliv. 16; xlix. 14; Wisd. iv. 10.

Was translated (μετετέθη). The verb used of Enoch's translation, LXX, Gen. v. 24. In Acts vii. 16 of the transporting of the remains of Jacob and his sons to Sychem. In Gal. i. 6, of the sudden change in the religious attitude of the Galatians. In Heb. vii. 12, of the change in the priesthood.

That he should not see death (τοῦ μὴ ἰδεῖν θάνατον). This may signify *the purpose* of his translation, but probably refers to *the result*. He was translated *so that he did not* see death. Comp. Matt. xxi. 32; Acts vii. 19; Rom. vii. 3.†

Was not found because God had translated him (οὐχ ηὑρίσκετο διότι μετέθηκεν αὐτὸν ὁ θεός). Cited from LXX, Gen. v. 24. For *had translated* rend. *translated*.

He had this testimony (μεμαρτύρηται). Rev. properly preserves the force of the perfect tense, "he *hath had* witness *borne* to him." The testimony still stands on record.

---

* T. R. reads λαλεῖται *is spoken about.*
† See Burton's *New Testament Moods and Tenses*, § 398.

That he pleased God. Rend. *hath pleased.* Comp. LXX, Gen. v. 22, 24. Faith was exhibited by Enoch in walking with God (comp. A. V. Gen. v. 22, "*walked* with God," and LXX, εὐαρέστησε *pleased* God). Faith creates close personal relation.

6. **To please** (εὐαρεστῆσαι). The aorist gives the sense of *at all*, stating the verbal idea without time, as a universal proposition. Comp. Rom. viii. 8.

Cometh (προσερχόμενον). See on ch. iv. 16. *Must* (δεῖ). An essential obligation. In the nature of the case. *That he is* (ὅτι ἔστιν). Faith in God involves belief in his existence although he is unseen.

Is a rewarder (μισθαποδότης γίνεται). Note the difference of the verb : not simply *exists*, but *comes to pass as; proves to be*, habitually, so that he who approaches God has, through faith, the assurance that his seeking God will result in good to himself. Μισθαποδότης *rewarder*, N. T.⁰. Comp. μισθ-αποδοσία *recompense of reward*, ch. ii. 2 (note) ; x. 35 ; xi. 26.

Of them that diligently seek him (τοῖς ἐκζητοῦσιν αὐτὸν). Lit. *unto them that seek him out.* Comp. Acts xv. 17 ; Heb. xii. 17 ; 1 Pet. i. 10. The verb is used of seeking God, Rom. iii. 11. God's beneficent will and attitude toward the seeker are not always apparent at the first approach. In such cases there is occasion for faith, in the face of delay, that diligent seeking will find its reward. One is reminded of Jesus' lessons on importunity in seeking God, L. xi. 5–10 ; xviii. 1–8.

> " He hides himself so wondrously
>   As though there were no God;
> He is least seen when all the powers
>   Of ill are most abroad.
> Or he deserts us at the hour
>   The fight is almost lost,
> And seems to leave us to ourselves
>   Just when we need him most.

It is not so, but so it looks ;
And we lose courage then ;
And doubts will come if God hath kept
His promises to men."

Faber.

7. Noah. Gen. vi.

Being warned of God (χρηματισθείς). *Of God* is not in
the text. See on Matt. ii. 12; L. ii. 26; Acts xi. 26; and
comp. Heb. viii. 5.

Of things not seen as yet (περὶ τῶν μηδέπω βλεπομένων).
Const. with εὐλαβηθείς, and rend. "by faith Noah, being
warned, having reverent care concerning things not seen as
yet, prepared an ark," etc. Thus χρηματισθείς *warned* is
taken absolutely.* *The things not seen* were the well-known
contents of the revelation to Noah, Gen. vi. 13 ff., as apprehended by Noah's faith.

Moved with fear (εὐλαβηθείς). N. T.°. Often in Class.
and LXX. See on εὐλάβεια *godly fear*, ch. v. 7. The A. V.
gives the impression that Noah acted under the influence of
fright. Rev. improves on this a little by rendering *godly
fear*. The true idea is *pious care*, a reverent circumspection
with regard to things enjoined by God, and as yet unseen,
yet confidently expected on the strength of God's word.

Prepared (κατεσκεύασεν). Built and equipped. See on
ch. iii. 3.

An ark (κιβωτὸν). Originally, *a wooden chest*. Also of
the ark of the covenant in the temple and tabernacle, as
ch. ix. 4; Apoc. xi. 19. Of Noah's ark, Matt. xxiv. 38;
L. xvii. 27; 1 Pet. iii. 20. Λάρναξ *a chest* is found in Class.

---

* The more usual interpretation is that of the A. V. But, as was long ago
discerned by Grotius, and is clearly shown by Weiss and von Soden, the subjective negative μηδέπω agrees much better with the subjective quality (*reverent care*) than with the announcement of an objective fact (*being warned of
things*, etc.).

in the same sense.   Every classical scholar will recall the
charming fragment of Simonides on Danae and her infant
son Perseus exposed in an ark:

'Ότε λάρνακι ἐν δαιδαλέᾳ ἄνεμος
Βρέμε πνέων κ. τ. λ.

Also of the ark of Deucalion, the mythic Noah.

By the which (δι' ἧς).   By faith: although some refer it
to the ark.

He condemned the world (κατέκρινεν τὸν κόσμον).   His
faith was exhibited in building the ark on the mere strength
of God's declaration, while as yet there were no signs of the
flood.   By his faith thus manifested he announced the condemnation of the world to destruction.   *World* is to be taken
as in 2 Pet. ii. 5.   It is not used in Hebrews in the ethical
sense so common in John and Paul—the world as alien from
God.   The meaning of the statement is not that Noah condemned the conduct of his contemporaries by the contrast
presented by his own faith, after the analogy of Matt. xii. 41;
Rom. ii. 27.

And became heir (καὶ — ἐγένετο κληρονόμος).   This is not
an independent clause, but is dependent on δι' ἧς *by which*.
It is connected by καὶ with the preceding clause, and the two
clauses are parallel, describing the lot of Noah and his family.
Became heir is practically = *became partaker of*.   The literal
sense of *heir* must not be pressed.   Certainly not "inherited
the righteousness of Abel and Enoch."   But righteousness
came to Noah in virtue of his intimate fellowship with God.
Of him as of Enoch, it is said that "he walked with God,"
Gen. vi. 9.   Because of this fellowship he was a son of God
and an heir of righteousness.

Of the righteousness which is by faith (τῆς κατὰ πίστιν
δικαιοσύνης).   In the O. T. Noah is the first to receive the
title of δίκαιος *righteous*, Gen. vi. 9; comp. Ezek. xiv. 14, 20;
Sir. xliv. 17.   Κατὰ πίστιν, lit. *according to faith*, comp.

Matt. ix. 29; Tit. i. 1, 4. Paul has δικαιοσύνη and δίκαιος *from* or *out of faith* (ἐκ πίστεως), *by faith* (διὰ πίστεως), *founded on faith* (ἐπὶ τῇ πίστει), and *of faith* (πίστεως), none of which are found either in Hebrews or in the Pastorals. Κατὰ πίστιν signifies *according to faith* as a standard; but the conception at bottom is not essentially different from Paul's, unless there be imported into his conception the scholastic fiction of imputed righteousness. Paul, in Rom. iv, is at pains to show that the Christian conception of righteousness by faith has its parallel in Abraham, and that the doctrine of justification by faith is no new thing. Faith is the ground and the germ of righteousness. Our writer here lays down the absolute and universal standard of righteousness for the men of both dispensations — *according to faith*. Hence, like Paul, he cites the words of Hab. ii. 4. See ch. x. 38.

8. Paul exhibits faith as the element of personal righteousness in Abraham. In these verses (8–22) faith, according to the opening definition in this chapter, is that assurance and conviction of unseen things which caused Abraham and the patriarchs to rely confidently upon the future fulfilment of the divine promises.

When he was called to go out—obeyed (καλούμενος ἐξελθεῖν ὑπήκουσεν). A. V. is wrong. Ἐξελθεῖν *to go out* should be construed with ὑπήκουσεν *obeyed*, and καλούμενος *being called* is to be taken absolutely. Καλούμενος, the present participle, indicates Abraham's immediate obedience to the call: *while he was yet being called*. Rend. "when he was called obeyed to go out." The infinitive explains the more general *obeyed*, by specifying that in which his obedience was shown. For the construction, see Acts xv. 10; 1 Th. i. 9; Heb. v. 5. For the narrative, see Gen. xii. 1–6, and comp. Acts vii. 2–5.

Whither he went (ποῦ ἔρχεται). Note the picturesque continued present tense, "whither he is going," as of Abraham on his journey.

9. **He sojourned in** (παρῴκησεν εἰς). The verb lit. *to dwell beside* or *among*. Πάροικος, a foreigner dwelling in a state without rights of citizenship. In Class. only in the sense of *neighbour*. See on L. xxiv. 18. The verb of rest with the preposition of motion (only here) signifies that he went *into* the land and *dwelt there*. Usually with *ἐν in*, but sometimes with the simple accusative, as L. xxiv. 18; Gen. xvii. 8; Ex. vi. 4.

Land of promise (γῆν τῆς ἐπαγγελίας). Note the article, omitted in A. V., *the* promise : the land which was designated in *the* promise of God. See Gen. xii. 7; xiii. 15. The phrase N. T.°. There is no corresponding phrase in O. T.

Strange (ἀλλοτρίαν). *Another* (ἄλλη) land than his own. So LXX, Gen. xv. 13. Comp. Acts vii. 6.

In tabernacles (ἐν σκηναῖς). Or *tents*, as a migratory people, without a permanent home.

The heirs with him (τῶν συνκληρονόμων). Joint-heirs or fellow-heirs. °LXX, °Class. See Rom. viii. 17; Eph. iii. 6; 1 Pet. iii. 7. The three, Abraham, Isaac, and Jacob, are mentioned because they cover the entire period of the sojourn in Canaan. Faith inspired these to endure patiently their unsettled life, since it assured them of a permanent home in the future.

10. **For he looked for a city which hath foundations** (ἐξεδέχετο γὰρ τὴν τοὺς θεμελίους ἔχουσαν πόλιν). The sense is impaired in A. V. by the omission of the articles, *the* city, *the* foundations. Passing over the immediate subject of God's promise to Abraham — his inheritance of the land in which he sojourns — the writer fastens the patriarch's faith upon the heavenly fulfilment of the promise — the perfected community of God, which, he assumes, was contained in the original promise. By *the city* he means the heavenly Jerusalem, and his statement is that Abraham's faith looked for-

ward to that. The idea of the new or heavenly Jerusalem
was familiar to the Jews. See ch. xii. 22; xiii. 14; Gal.
iv. 26; Apoc. iii. 12; xxi. 2. The Rabbins regarded it as
an actual city. For *the foundations* comp. Apoc. xxi. 14.
In ascribing to the patriarchs an assured faith in heaven as
the end and reward of their wanderings, the writer oversteps
the limits of history; but evidently imports into the patriarchal faith the contents of a later and more developed faith
— that of himself and his readers.

Builder and maker (τεχνίτης καὶ δημιουργὸς). Τεχνίτης
artificer, architect. Comp. Acts xix. 24 (note), 38; Apoc.
xviii. 22, and LXX, 1 Chron. xxix. 5; Cant. vii. 1; Wisd.
viii. 6; xiv. 2; Sir. ix. 17. Δημιουργὸς N. T.°, originally
a workman for the public (δῆμος); generally, *framer, builder.*
It is used by Xenophon and Plato of the maker of the world
(Xen. *Mem.* i. 4, 9; Plato, *Tim.* 40 C; *Repub.* 530 A). It
was appropriated by the Neo-Platonists as the designation of
God. To the Gnostics, the Demiurge was a limited, secondary God, who created the world; since there was no possibility of direct contact between the supreme, incommunicable
God and the visible world.

11. **Sarah.** Faith prevailing against natural impossibili-
ties. See Rom. iv. 19–22. Both Abraham and Sarah doubted
at first (Gen. xvii. 17; xviii. 12); but both became persuaded of the truthfulness of the promise.

Herself (αὐτὴ). She who at first doubted.

To conceive seed (εἰς καταβολὴν σπέρματος). In every
other instance in N. T. καταβολή means *foundation,* and
appears in the phrase καταβολὴ κόσμου *foundation of the
world.* Originally it means *throwing down;* hence, the *depos-
iting* of the male seed in the womb. The sentence may be
explained either, "received strength as regarded the deposi-
tion of seed," to fructify it; or, "received strength for the
foundation of a posterity," σπέρμα being rendered in accord-

ance with ch. ii. 16 ; xi. 18, and καταβολή in the sense of *foundation*, as everywhere else in N. T.

And was delivered of a child when she was past age (καὶ παρὰ καιρὸν ἡλικίας). *Was delivered of a child* not in the text. Καὶ *and that*. Rend. "received strength," etc., "and that when she was past age." Παρὰ καιρὸν ἡλικίας, lit. *past the season of age*. For ἡλικία see on *stature*, L. xii. 25.

12. **As good as dead** (νενεκρωμένου). Comp. Rom. iv. 19. *As good as* is an addition of A. V. The Greek reads *and that a dead man*. Comp. νέκρωσιν *deadness* applied to Sarah, Rom. iv. 19.

Stars—sand. See Gen. xxii. 17; xxxii. 12.

By the seashore (παρὰ τὸ χεῖλος τῆς θαλάσσης). Lit. *by the lip of the sea*. The phrase N. T.⁰. Very often in LXX, as Gen. xxii. 17; Ex. xiv. 30: *lip of a river*, Gen. xli. 17; Ex. vii. 15: *of a brook*, Deut. ii. 36; iii. 12: *of Jordan*, 2 K. ii. 13. So in Class. The vigour thus supernaturally imparted to Abraham does not appear to have exhausted itself in the generation of Isaac; since, according to Gen. xxv. 2, Abraham became by Keturah the father of six sons after the death of Sarah.

13. **In faith** (κατὰ πίστιν). See on ver. 7.

Not having received (μὴ κομισάμενοι). See on ch. x. 36. They died according to faith, inasmuch as they did not receive. They died under the regimen of faith, and not of sight. For the phrase κομίζειν τὰς ἐπαγγελίας *to receive the promises*, comp. ch. x. 36; xi. 39.

Having seen them afar off (πόρρωθεν αὐτὰς ἰδόντες). By faith ; *from* afar.

Were persuaded of them and embraced them (ἀσπασάμενοι). The A. V. completely destroys the beauty of this

verse. It reads *were persuaded*, following T. R. πεισθέντες,
and translates ἀσπασάμενοι *embraced*, which is a sort of infer-
ential rendering of the original sense *to salute* or *greet*. Rend.
"having seen them from afar and greeted them" : as seamen
wave their greeting to a country seen far off on the horizon,
on which they cannot land. Lünemann appropriately quotes
Virgil, *Aen.* iii. 522 :

> " Cum procul obscuros collis humilemque videmus
> Italiam. Italiam primus conclamat Achates,
> Italiam laeto socii clamore salutant."

Confessed that they were strangers and pilgrims (ὁμο-
λογήσαντες ὅτι ξένοι καὶ παρεπίδημοι). They admitted and
accepted the fact with the resignation of faith, and with the
assurance of future rest. Comp. Gen. xxiii. 4; xxiv. 37;
xxviii. 4; xlvii. 9; Ps. xxxix. 12; cxix. 19, 54. For παρεπίδημοι *sojourners*, see on 1 Pet. i. 1. In the anonymous
Epistle to Diognetus, an apologetic letter, probably of the
second century, and one of the gems of early Christian literature, occur the following words concerning Christians : "They
inhabit their own country, but as sojourners: they take part
in all things as citizens, and endure all things as aliens : every
foreign country is theirs, and every country is foreign."

14. **Declare plainly** (ἐμφανίζουσιν). ᵒP. See on **J. xiv. 21.**
Occasionally in LXX. Rend. "make it manifest."

They seek a country (πατρίδα ἐπιζητοῦσιν). The verb
is found in LXX, chiefly in the sense of seeking after God or
another deity. See 2 K. i. 3, 6; iii. 11; viii. 8; xxii. 18;
2 Chron. xviii. 6. Comp. ἐπιζητουμένη πόλις *a city sought
after* (Zion), Isa. lxii. 12. Πατρίς is a *native* country; a
fatherland. Only here and in Gospels and Acts. Quite
often in LXX.

15. **If they had been mindful** (εἰ ἐμνημόνευον). In N. T.
habitually *remember*. So invariably in LXX. The meaning
here is, that if, in their declaration (ver. 14) that they were

seeking a country, they had called to mind the country from which they came out, they could have returned thither, so that it is evident that they did not mean that country.*

To have returned (ἀνακάμψαι). Rend. "to return." Lit. *bend their way back again* (ἀνα).

16. **Now they desire** (νῦν ὀρέγονται). Νῦν *now* is logical: as the case now stands. For ὀρέγονται *desire*, see on 1 Tim. iii. 1.

Is not ashamed (οὐκ ἐπαισχύνεται). Because they have commended themselves to God by their faith, so that he acknowledges them as his own. Comp. ch. ii. 11; Mk. viii. 28, 38; Rom. i. 16; 2 Tim. i. 8, 16.

To be called their God (θεὸς ἐπικαλεῖσθαι αὐτῶν). Lit. *to be surnamed*. Comp. Acts iv. 36; x. 5, 18, 32. God was called the God of Abraham, of Isaac, and of Jacob. See Ex. iii. 6.

For he hath prepared for them a city (ἡτοίμασεν γὰρ αὐτοῖς πόλιν). Comp. Matt. xxv. 34; J. xiv. 2; Apoc. xxi. 2. *City* is significant, as showing that the fulfilment of God's promise lies in introducing them into the perfection of *social* life. Comp. Apoc. iii. 12; xxi. 2, 10; xxii. 19.

---

* Some interpreters render ἐμνημόνευον *mentioned*, citing 1 Th. i. 3, and Heb. xi. 22, where the verb is followed by περί with the genitive. In both these cases, however, the meaning *remember* is quite possible. Grammatical testimony is confusing. There are instances in Class. where the verb signifies *mention*, as Plato, *Legg.* 646 B, with accusative: also with περί and genitive. Winer says positively that verbs of making mention do not take a genitive in the N. T. (xxx, 10, c). On the other hand, the verb in the sense of *remember*, though mostly with the genitive, is sometimes found with the accusative, as Matt. xvi. 9; 1 Th. ii. 9; 2 Tim. ii. 8. So in Class. Neither Class. nor N. T. furnishes any sufficient reason why the verb in Heb. xi. 22 should not be rendered *remembered*. Περί is constantly used in connection with mental operations, as φροντίζειν. The kindred verb μιμνήσκεσθαι is used with περί and the genitive meaning *remember;* see Tob. iv. 1, and comp. Homer, *Od.* vii, 192; Hdt. i, 36: ix, 45; Plato, *Phileb.* 31 A. Μνημόσυνος *memorial* is found with περί and genitive, Ex. xxviii. 12.

17. **When he was tried offered up** (προσενήνοχεν πειραζόμενος). The full sense of the statement is missed in A.V. The meaning is that *while the trial is yet in progress*, Abraham *hath already offered up* his son, before the trial has come to an issue, by the act of his obedient will, through faith in God. Comp. Jas. ii. 21.

He that had received (ὁ ἀναδεξάμενος). The verb only here and Acts xxviii. 7. It means *to accept; to welcome* and *entertain*. So Rev. *gladly received*.

Accounting (λογισάμενος). See on 1 Pet. v. 12; Rom. iv. 5; viii. 18.

From whence (ὅθεν). Rend. *wherefore:* because of his faith in God's power and truthfulness. Ὅθεν, though occasionally in a local sense in N. T., as Matt. xii. 44; L. xi. 24; Acts xiv. 26, is much more common in the logical or causal sense, *wherefore, on which account.* So in every other instance in Hebrews. In the local sense it would mean *from the dead.*

Also he received him in a figure (αὐτὸν καὶ ἐν παραβολῇ ἐκομίσατο). Καὶ marks the receiving as answering to the faith. As Abraham believed in God's power to restore Isaac, so, because of his faith, he *also* received him. For ἐκομίσατο *received* see on ch. x. 36. Ἐν παραβολῇ *in a parable.* Since the sacrifice did not take place as a literal slaughter, there could not be a literal restoration from death. There was a real offering in Abraham's will, but not a real death of Isaac. Isaac's death took place symbolically, in the sacrifice of the ram: correspondingly, the restoration was only a symbolic restoration from the dead. Some expositors, among whom is Westcott, explain thus: Abraham accounted that God was able to raise Isaac from the dead, from which he received him *at birth*, in that Isaac sprung from one *dead* (νενεκρωμένου, ver. 12). This is extremely laboured and artificial.*

---

* The varieties of interpretation are endless. A list of the principal ones may be found in Westcott. One should be noticed, according to which *is*

20. Blessed (εὐλόγησεν). See on J. xii. 13.

Concerning things to come (καὶ περὶ μελλόντων). A.V.
omits καὶ which gives an emphasis to the following words.
Isaac pronounced a blessing, *and that* concerning things to
come; things beyond the lifetime of Jacob and Esau. See
Gen. xxvii. 29, 39. The blessing was an act of faith. Isaac's
confidence in the power of his blessing to convey the good
which it promised was "the assurance of things hoped for,
the conviction of things not seen," founded on the promise
of Gen. xvii. 5.

21. When he died (ἀποθνήσκων). Rend. "when dying."
It is quite superfluous to explain this as emphasising the
strength in contrast with the weakness of approaching death;
or that, in the birth of Joseph's two sons before Jacob's death,
Jacob discerned a monition to adopt them into the direct line
of his own sons. The meaning is simply that these events
took place in Jacob's last hours.

Blessed each (ἕκαστον εὐλόγησεν). See Gen. xlviii. 17–20.
Each son received a separate and distinct blessing, although
Joseph had expected only one common blessing for both.
Jacob's discernment of faith appeared in this, as in the pre-
cedence assigned to the younger son.

And worshipped leaning on the top of his staff (καὶ
προσεκύνησεν ἐπὶ τὸ ἄκρον τῆς ῥάβδου αὐτοῦ). From the LXX
of Gen. xlvii. 31. It seems to have been loosely included by
our writer among the incidents of Jacob's last hours (ἀποθνήσκων), although it belongs to a different part of the nar-

---

παραβολῇ is explained *in venture* or *risk*, from παραβάλλειν *to throw beside,
to expose*. The *verb* sometimes has this meaning in Class., and once in LXX,
2 Macc. iv. 38; but there is no instance of the *noun* παραβολή in that sense,
either in N. T., LXX, or Class. Thayer cites one or two doubtful cases in
later Greek. According to this interpretation the clause would read, "from
whence he received him in risking him." Lünemann explains: "on which
account he received him on the ground of *the giving up*," taking παραβολή in
the sense of *surrender*.

rative. The promise given by Joseph to remove his father's
remains to the family sepulchre may have been regarded
as preparatory to the blessing, or introduced in order to
emphasise the devotional character of the entire proceeding.
The words *upon the head of his staff* are from the LXX;
the Hebrew being "Jacob bowed himself upon *the head
of the bed*." Comp. 1 K. i. 47. According to its vowel-points
the same Hebrew word signifies either *staff* or *bed*. The
LXX has chosen the former, and renders by ῥάβδος *staff*.
According to the Hebrew, the meaning is that Jacob, having
been sitting during the conversation, lay down when it was
finished, probably overcome by weakness, and breathing a
prayer as he fell back on his pillow.*

22. **When he died** (τελευτῶν). Comp. Gen. l. 26, LXX.
The verb means *to finish* or *close*, with *life* understood.
Always in this sense in N. T. See Matt. ii. 19; ix. 18;
L. vii. 2, etc. Never used by Paul. Rend. " when near his
end."

Made mention of (περὶ — ἐμνημόνευσεν). See on ver. 15.
A.V. has *remembered* in marg. *Remembered* is appropriate
here. Joseph on his death-bed remembered the promise of
God to give the land of Canaan to the seed of Abraham
(Gen. xii. 7; xiii. 15; xv. 7), and also the prediction to
Abraham that his descendants should pass four hundred
years in bondage in a strange land, and should afterward be
brought out thence, Gen. xv. 13, 14.

The departing of the children of Israel (τῆς ἐξόδου τῶν
υἱῶν Ἰσραήλ). Ἔξοδος only here, L. ix. 31 (note) and

---

* A formidable mass of hermeneutic rubbish has accumulated about this
passage : for instance, that the act of Jacob implied the worship of the staff ;
or that the staff was Joseph's, and that the patriarch paid formal reverence
to the staff as a tribute to Joseph's position, a view common among the
Fathers ; or that worship was paid to some image or symbol of power on
the head of the staff, from which has been drawn the justification of image-
worship.

2 Pet. i. 15 (note). 'Οι υἱοὶ 'Ισραὴλ is one of several phrases
in N. T. denoting the chosen people. There are also *house*
(οἶκος) and *people* (λαὸς) *of Israel*, and *Israel of God*, and
Israel according to the flesh.

And gave commandment (καὶ ἐνετείλατο). **Καὶ** *and so ;*
in consequence of his remembering the prophecy of the
exodus. The verb indicates a *specific* injunction (ἐντολή).
See on 1 Tim. vi. 14.

23. **Of his parents** (ὑπὸ τῶν πατέρων αὐτοῦ). Lit. *by his
fathers*. Comp. Ex. ii. 2. Πατέρες *fathers*, according to a
late Greek usage, is employed like γονεῖς *parents*. Similarly
the Lat. *patres* and *soceri*, including *both* parents, or father
and mother in law.

Proper (ἀστεῖον). Only here and Acts vii. 20, on which
see note. Rend. " comely."

Commandment (διάταγμα). N. T.⁰. Rend. "mandate."

24. **When he was come to years** (μέγας γενόμενος). Lit.
having become great. Comp. LXX, Ex. ii. 11. Often in the
phrase μικροὶ καὶ μεγάλοι *small and great ; young and old*.
See Acts xxvi. 22; Heb. viii. 11; Apoc. xi. 8; xiii. 16, etc.

25. **To suffer affliction with** (συνκακουχεῖσθαι). N. T.⁰,
⁰LXX, ⁰Class. The verb κακουχεῖν *to treat ill*, ver. 37 ;
ch. xiii. 3; LXX, 1 K. ii. 26; xi. 39. Rend. " to be evil
entreated."

Than to enjoy the pleasures of sin for a season (ἢ πρόσ-
καιρον ἔχειν ἁμαρτίας ἀπόλαυσιν). Lit. *than to have temporary
enjoyment of sin*. The emphasis is first on *temporary* and
then on *sin*. For ἀπόλαυσις *enjoyment*, see on 1 Tim. vi. 17.
Πρόσκαιρος *for a season, temporary*, rare in N. T. ⁰LXX.
Once in Paul, see 2 Cor. iv. 18.

26. **Esteeming the reproach of Christ** (ἡγησάμενος τὸν ὀνειδισμὸν τοῦ Χριστοῦ). The participle gives the reason for his choice of affliction instead of sin: *since he esteemed*. "The reproach of Christ" is the reproach peculiar to Christ; such as he endured. The writer uses it as a current form of expression, colouring the story of Moses with a Christian tinge. Comp. Rom. xv. 3; Heb. xiii. 13; 2 Cor. i. 5; Col. i. 24; Philip. iii. 14; 1 Pet. iv. 14. The phrase is applied to Moses as enduring at the hands of the Egyptians and of the rebellious Israelites the reproach which any faithful servant of God will endure, and which was endured in a notable way by Christ.

He had respect unto (ἀπέβλεπεν εἰς). N. T.º. Lit. *he looked away* (from the treasures of Egypt, etc.) *unto* the recompense.

27. **He forsook Egypt** (κατέλιπεν Ἀιγυπτον). After he had killed the Egyptian, Ex. ii. 15. Not in the general exodus. The historical order of events is preserved: the flight to Midian, the Passover, the Exodus, the passage of the Red Sea.

The wrath (τὸν θυμὸν). Only here in Hebrews. See on J. iii. 36.

He endured (ἐκαρτέρησεν). N. T.º. Occasionally in LXX. Often in Class. He was *stanch* and *steadfast*.

As seeing him who is invisible (τὸν ἀόρατον ὡς ὁρῶν). Since he saw, etc. The emphasis is on *invisible*, pointing back to the introductory definition of faith. The word is used of God, Col. i. 15; 1 Tim. i. 17.

28. **Kept the passover** (πεποίηκεν τὸ πάσχα). Rend. "hath instituted the passover." The perfect tense indicates the continued significance of the service down to the time of writing. The phrase ποιεῖν τὸ πάσχα in N. T. only here and Matt. xxvi. 18. The usual N. T. phrase is φαγεῖν τὸ πάσχα

to eat the Passover. See Matt. xxvi. 17; Mk. xiv. 12;
L. xxii. 11. Ποιεῖν τὸ πάσχα unquestionably means *to keep*
or *celebrate* the Passover, as Matt. xxvi. 18; Ex. xii. 48;
Num. ix. 2, 4, 6, 10, 13; Deut. xvi. 1: but the verb is elastic.
The corresponding Hebrew verb עָשָׂה, among other meanings, signifies *to create* (Gen. i. 7; ii. 2); *to establish* (Eccl.
ii. 5, 6, 8); *to constitute* (1 K. xii. 31, 32); *to make ready* or
prepare (Judg. xiii. 15; *to prepare as a sacrifice* (Ps. lxvi. 15).
In all these instances it is rendered in LXX by ποιεῖν. In
N. T. we find ποιεῖν ἄριστον or δεῖπνον *to prepare a breakfast*
or *dinner*. Accordingly ποιεῖν may properly be used here of
the *instituting* of the Passover. Moreover the two following
clauses clearly indicate that the writer is referring to the
original institution.

The sprinkling of blood (τὴν πρόσχυσιν τοῦ αἵματος).
Πρόσχυσις *affusion*, N. T.⁰, ⁰LXX, ⁰Class. From προσχεῖν
to pour on. In the post-Exodus legislation the blood which,
in the original institution, was sprinkled on the door-posts
and lintels (Ex. xii. 22), was thrown upon the altar (Deut.
xvi. 6), and προσχεῖν in LXX is used of this act almost
without exception. See Ex. xxiv. 6; xxix. 16; Lev. i. 5, 11;
iii. 2, 8, 13, etc.

Lest he that destroyed the first-born should touch them
(ἵνα μὴ ὁ ὀλοθρεύων τὰ πρωτότοκα θίγῃ αὐτῶν). Rend. " that
the destroyer of the first-born should not touch them," a
rendering which brings out more sharply the preventive
purpose of the sprinkling of blood. Ὀλοθρεύειν *to destroy*,
N. T.⁰, ⁰Class. Ὁ ὀλοθρεύων is used in the narrative of
Ex. xi. 23 for *the destroying angel*. The kindred noun ὀλο-
θρευτής *destroyer* (⁰LXX, ⁰Class.) occurs in 1 Cor. x. 10 of
the plague in Num. xvi. 46–50. For θίγῃ *should touch*, see
on Col. ii. 21.

29. Passed through (διέβησαν). Only three times in
N. T. See L. xvi. 26; Acts xvi. 9. The simple βαίνειν does
not occur in N. T.

The Red Sea (τὴν Ἐρυθρὰν Θάλασσαν). Called by the Israelites *the sea*, Ex. xiv. 2, 9, 16, 21, 28, etc., and, specially, the sea of Sûph (*sedge, seeds*). In LXX always as here except Judg. xi. 16, where it is θάλασσα Σίφ, i.e. *Sûph*. By the Greeks the name was at first applied to the whole ocean from the coast of Ethiopia to the island of Taprobana or Ceylon. Afterward, when they learned of the existence of an Indian Ocean, they applied the name merely to the sea below Arabia, and to the Arabian and Persian gulfs.

Which the Egyptians assaying to do (ἧς πεῖραν λαβόντες οἱ Ἀιγύπτιοι). The A.V. has *assaying*, according to the older English usage. *Assay* is now chiefly used of the testing of precious metals; but in the sense of *try* it is found in Piers Ploughman, Gower, Chaucer, Shakespeare. Lit. *of which* (*sea*) *the Egyptians having taken trial*. The phrase πεῖραν λαμβάνειν *to take trial* occurs also in LXX, Deut. xxviii. 56. In N. T. only here and ver. 36.

Were drowned (κατεπόθησαν). Lit. *were drunk down*. See on Matt. xxiii. 24. Comp. LXX, Ex. xv. 4, and in N. T. 1 Cor. xv. 54; 2 Cor. ii. 7; v. 4.

30. **Compassed about** (κυκλωθέντα). Comp. L. xxi. 20; J. x. 24. °P.

31. **The harlot Rahab** (Ῥαὰβ ἡ πόρνη). See Josh. ii; vi. 17, and comp. Jas. ii. 25. Rahab's occupation is stated without mincing, and the lodging of the spies at her house was probably not a matter of accident. Very amusing are the efforts of some earlier expositors to evade the fact of a harlot's *faith*, by rendering πόρνη *landlady*.

Perished not with (οὐ συναπώλετο). N. T.°. In LXX see Num. xvi. 26; Ps. xxv. 9; xxvii. 3.

Them that believed not (τοῖς ἀπειθήσασιν). Rend. "them that were disobedient." Simple disbelief is expressed by ἀπιστεῖν, ἀπιστία: disbelief as it manifests itself in disobedience, by ἀπειθεῖν. ᾿Απειθεῖν is ἀπιστεῖν on its active side. See on J. iii. 36, and comp. Heb. iii. 18; iv. 6, 11; Rom. xi. 30, 32, contrasting with Rom. xi. 20, 23. ᾿Απειθεῖν here describes the failure to be persuaded that God had given the land to the Israelites, and the consequent refusal to surrender Jericho. Rahab's faith is shown Josh. ii. 9–11.

When she had received the spies (δεξαμένη τοὺς κατασκόπους). Rend. "having received." For this sense of friendly reception as a guest see L. x. 8, 10. Κατάσκοπος *a spy*, N. T.º. LXX, Gen. xlii. 9, 11, 14; 1 Sam. xxvi. 4.

With peace (μετ᾽ εἰρήνης). The phrase only here and Acts xv. 33. Quite often in LXX, as Gen. xv. 15; xxvi. 29; Ex. xviii. 23; Deut. xx. 20; Judg. viii. 9. In N. T. ἐν εἰρήνῃ *in peace* (Acts xvi. 36; Jas. ii. 16): εἰς εἰρήνην *into peace* (Mk. v. 34; L. vii. 50; viii. 48); both these very often in LXX. Rahab received the spies without enmity, and did not allow them to suffer harm from others. An interesting parallel is furnished by Dante, *Purg.* ii. 99, in the case of the pilot-angel who conveys souls to the shore of Purgatory.

> " He, sooth to say, for three months past has taken
> Whoever wished to enter, *with all peace* " (without interposing any
> obstacle.) *

32. To tell (διηγούμενον). Lit. *the time will fail me telling:* if I tell. See on Mk. ix. 9, and comp. Mk. v. 16; L. viii. 39; ix. 10; Acts ix. 27, and διήγησις *narrative* (A. V. *declaration*), L. i. 1.

Gideon, etc. These names of the four judges are not enumerated in chronological order. Samuel is closely connected with David as in the history, but with τε καὶ as introducing the new order of the prophets.

---

* " Veramente da tre mesi egli ha tolto
   Chi ha voluto entrar *con tutta pace.*"

33. **Through faith** (διὰ πίστεως). This formula is now substituted for the instrumental dative πίστει *by faith*. The reason for the change cannot perhaps be accurately formulated, but will be appreciated by one who *feels* the Greek idiom, as better suiting the more general illustrations which follow.

Subdued kingdoms (κατηγωνίσαντο βασιλείας). The verb N. T.°, °LXX, signifies *fought down;* overcame by struggle, as Barak, Judg. iv; Gideon, Judg. vii; Jephthah, Judg. xi; David, 2 Sam. v.

Wrought righteousness (ἠργάσαντο δικαιοσύνην). For the phrase comp. Acts x. 35. Referring not merely to their personal virtues, but to the public exercise of these as leaders, as 2 Sam. viii. 15; 1 Chron. xviii. 14; 1 Sam. xii. 4. Faith showed itself in the association of righteousness with power. Comp. Isa. ix. 7; liv. 14; 1 K. x. 9.

Obtained promises (ἐπέτυχον ἐπαγγελιῶν). See on ch. vi. 15.

Stopped (ἔφραξαν). The verb means *to fence in; block up.* Rare in N. T. See Rom. iii. 19; 2 Cor. xi. 10, and comp. φραγμός *a fence*, Matt. xxi. 33; Eph. ii. 14. Occasionally in LXX, as Job xxxviii. 8; Prov. xxi. 13; Zech. xiv. 5. The reference is no doubt to Daniel, Dan. vi. 22; comp. 1 Macc. ii. 60.

34. **Quenched the violence of fire** (ἔσβεσαν δύναμιν πυρός). Rend. "the power of fire." Reference to the three Hebrews, Dan. iii; comp. 1 Macc. ii. 59.

Edge of the sword (στόματα μαχαίρης). Lit. *mouths of the sword.* See on ch. iv. 12. The plural *edges* indicates frequent assaults.

Out of weakness (ἀπὸ ἀσθενείας). Rend. "*from* weakness." For the sense of ἀπὸ *from*, see L. v. 15. The meaning is not confined to sickness, as in the case of Hezekiah (2 K. xx; Isa. xxxviii). The main reference is probably to Samson, Judg. xvi. 28 ff.

The armies of the aliens (παρεμβολὰς ἀλλοτρίων). Omit both *the's* in translation. For παρεμβολὰς see on Acts xxi. 34. Very often in LXX. *Aliens*, foreign foes or invaders.

35. **Women.** The recorded raisings from the dead are mostly for women. See 1 K. xvii. 17 ff.; 2 K. iv. 17 ff. Comp. L. vii. 11 ff.; J. xi; Acts ix. The reference here is to the first two.

Raised to life again (ἐξ ἀναστάσεως). Rend. "by a resurrection"; and for the force of ἐξ comp. Rom. i. 4.*

Were tortured (ἐτυμπανίσθησαν). N. T.⁰. LXX once, 1 Sam. xxi. 13. Originally *to beat a drum* (τύμπανον). Hence *to beat, to cudgel*. The A. V. of 1 Sam. xxi. 13, describing the feigned madness of David, renders ἐτυμπάνιζεν "*he scrabbled* on the doors of the gate," meaning that he beat the doors like a madman. Τύμπανον means *a drum* or *a drumstick;* hence *a cudgel;* so Aristoph. *Plut.* 476, where it is associated with κύφων *a pillory.* Comp. 2 Macc. vi. 19, 28. The meaning here is, *were beaten to death with clubs*, the word being used to represent cruel torture in general.

Not accepting deliverance (οὐ προσδεξάμενοι τὴν ἀπολύτρωσιν). For the verb, see on ch. x. 34. *The* (τὴν) deliverance offered at the price of denying their faith. See 2 Macc. vi. 21–27.

A better resurrection (κρείττονος ἀναστάσεως). Better than a resurrection like those granted to the women above mentioned, which gave merely a continuation of life on earth. Comp. 2. Macc. vii. 9, 14.

---

* Not as Westcott: "Resurrection, which is the transition from death to life, is that *out of which* the departed were received."

36. **Of cruel mockings** (ἐμπαιγμῶν). N. T.⁰, ⁰Class.
Rare in LXX. *Cruel* is an insertion of A. V. Rend. " of
mockings." Ἐμπαιγμονὴ *mockery* (⁰LXX, ⁰Class.) is found
2 Pet. iii. 3 (note); and ἐμπαίκτης *mocker* or *scoffer*, 2 Pet.
iii. 3; Jude 18. Ἐμπαίζειν *to mock* is quite frequent in the
Synoptic Gospels, and occurs also in LXX.

37. **They were stoned** (ἐλιθάσθησαν). A characteristic
Jewish punishment. See 2 Chron. xxiv. 20; Matt. xxiii. 37;
J. x. 31; Acts v. 26; vii. 59; xiv. 19. The verb λιθοβολεῖν
is also used in Matthew, Luke, and Acts, and once in this
epistle, xii. 20.

Were sawn asunder (ἐπρίσθησαν). N. T.⁰ As Isaiah,
according to tradition.

Were tempted (ἐπειράσθησαν). If the reading is correct,
which seems probable, the reference is probably to induce-
ments offered them to abandon their loyalty to God. It has
seemed to many out of place, because occurring in the midst
of a list of different forms of violent death.*

38. **Of whom the world was not worthy** (ὧν οὐκ ἦν ἄξιος
ὁ κόσμος). This clause falls into the series of participles
which precedes it; the form of the relative sentence being
adopted because of the lack of a proper participial phrase to
express the statement. At the same time it prepares the way
for the following clause in which the participial construction
is resumed. Rend. " they went about in sheepskins and goat-
skins, being destitute, afflicted, evil-entreated, men of whom
the world was not worthy, wandering in deserts," etc. By *the
world* (κόσμος) is not meant the *corrupt* world, as in John and
Paul (see on ver. 7), but the world considered as an economy
which was unworthy of these, because ruled by sense and not
by faith. Their plane of life was higher.

---

* Accordingly a variety of readings has been proposed: ἐπυρώθησαν, ἐπρήσ-
θαν, ἐπυρίσθησαν *they were burned*: ἐπάρθησαν *they were pierced*: ἐπειράθησαν
they were impaled: ἐπηρώθησαν *they were mutilated*: ἐσπειράσθησαν *they were
broken on the wheel*: ἐπράθησαν *they were sold*.

They wandered (πλανώμενοι). Lit. *wandering* or *straying*, apart from the homes and the intercourse of men.

Caves of the earth (ὀπαῖς τῆς γῆς). 'Οπή only here and Jas. iii. 11. It means *a hole;* primarily a place through which one can *see* (ὄπωπα). In LXX *the cleft* of the rock in which God placed Moses, Ex. xxxiii. 22: *a window, a latticed opening*, Eccl. xii. 3: *the eye-socket*, Zech. xiv. 12: *a hole in the wall*, Ezek. viii. 7: *a hole in a tree*, 4 Macc. xiv. 16.

39. **Having obtained a good report** (μαρτυρηθέντες). Rend. " having had witness borne to them." See on ver. 2.

40. **Having provided** (προβλεψαμένου). N. T.º.

For us (περὶ ἡμῶν). The better thing is for *us*. It was not for them: they lived in the assurance of a future time better than their own, and in this assurance of faith, did their work and bore their burden in their own time. It is one of the achievements of faith to be cheerfully willing to be only a stage to some better thing which we cannot share.

That they without us should not be made perfect (ἵνα μὴ χωρὶς ἡμῶν τελειωθῶσιν). Each successive stage of history gathers up into itself the fruit of preceding stages. This passage teaches the solidarity of humanity in its work as well as in itself. The man of the present requires the work and suffering and achievement of the men of the past to complete him and his work. The future men will, in like manner, require the work and suffering and achievement of the men of to-day to complete them. The whole creation, in all its successive aeons, moves *together* toward

" The one far-off, divine event."

CHAPTER XII.

1. **Therefore** (τοιγαροῦν). An emphatic particle, strongly affirming the facts on which the following exhortation is based.

We also are compassed (καὶ ἡμεῖς). According to this the sense would be, those described in ch. xi were compassed with a cloud of witnesses, and *we also* are so compassed.   Wrong. The *we also* should be construed with *let us run*.   "Therefore *let us also* (as they did) run our appointed race with patience."

Seeing we are compassed about with so great a cloud of witnesses (τοσοῦτον ἔχοντες περικείμενον ἡμῖν νέφος μαρτύρων).   Lit. *having so great a cloud of witnesses lying around us.*   Νέφος *cloud*, N.T.⁰, means a great mass of cloud covering the entire visible space of the heavens, and therefore without definite form, or a single large mass in which definite outlines are not emphasised or distinguished.   It thus differs from νεφέλη, which is a detached and sharply outlined cloud. Νέφος is therefore more appropriate to the author's image, which is that of a vast encompassing and overhanging mass. The use of cloud for a mass of living beings is familiar in poetry.   Thus Homer, *a cloud of footmen* (*Il.* xxiii. 133): *of Trojans* (*Il.* xvi. 66).   Themistocles, addressing the Athenians, says of the host of Xerxes, "we have had the fortune to save both ourselves and Greece by repelling *so great a cloud of men*" (Hdt. viii. 109).   Spenser, *F. Q.* i. 1, 23 :

> "A cloud of cumbrous gnattes doe him molest."

Milton, *Par. L.* i. 340 :

> "A pitchy cloud of locusts."

Witnesses (μαρτύρων) does not mean *spectators*, but those who have borne witness to the truth, as those enumerated in ch. xi. Yet the idea of spectators is implied, and is really the principal idea.   The writer's picture is that of an arena in which the Christians whom he addresses are contending in a race, while the vast host of the heroes of faith who, after having borne witness to the truth, have entered into their heavenly rest, watches the contest from the encircling tiers of the arena, compassing and overhanging it like a cloud, filled with lively interest and sympathy, and lending heavenly aid.   How striking the contrast of this conception with that of Kaulbach's familiar "Battle of the Huns," in which the slain warriors are depicted rising from the field and renewing the fight in the upper air with aggravated fury.

Weight (ὄγκον). N. T.⁰, ⁰LXX. Lit. *bulk, mass*. Often in Class. Sometimes metaphorically of a person, *dignity, importance, pretension:* of a writer's style, *loftiness, majesty, impressiveness*. Rend. "encumbrance," according to the figure of the racer who puts away everything which may hinder his running. So the readers are exhorted to lay aside every worldly hindrance or embarrassment to their Christian career.

And the sin which doth so easily beset (καὶ τὴν εὐπερίστατον ἁμαρτίαν). Καὶ adds to the general *encumbrance* a specific encumbrance or hindrance. Ἐυπερίστατος N. T.⁰, ⁰LXX, ⁰Class. From εὐ *readily, deftly, cleverly*, and περίστασθαι *to place itself round*. Hence, of a sin which readily or easily encircles and entangles the Christian runner, like a long, loose robe clinging to his limbs. *Beset* is a good rendering, meaning *to surround*. In earlier English especially of surrounding crowns, etc., with jewels. So Gower, *Conf. Am.* i. 127:

> " With golde and riche stones beset."

Shakespeare, *Two Gent. Ver.* v. 3 :

> " The thicket is beset ; he cannot 'scape."

The sin may be any evil propensity. The sin of unbelief naturally suggests itself here.

With patience (δἰ ὑπομονῆς). Ὑπομονὴ includes both passive endurance and active persistence. See on 2 Pet. i. 6, and Jas. v. 7. For this use of δἰ *with*, see on ch. ix. 11.

The race (τὸν ἀγῶνα). Instead of a specific word for *race* (δρόμος), the general term *contest* is used. For προκείμενον *set before*, see on ch. vi. 18.

2. **Looking** (ἀφορῶντες). Only here and Philip. ii. 23. In LXX see 4 Macc. xvii. 10. Looking *away* from every-

thing which may distract.   Comp. Philip. iii. 13, 14, and
ἀπέβλεπεν he had respect, lit. looked away, Heb. xi. 26.   Wetstein cites Arrian, Epictet. ii. 19, 29 : εἰς τὸν θεὸν ἀφορῶντες
ἐν παντὶ μικρῷ καὶ μεγάλῳ looking away unto God in everything small and great.

Jesus.   Having presented a long catalogue of witnesses
under the old covenant, he now presents Jesus, the mediator
of the new covenant, and the supreme witness.   See Apoc.
i. 5; iii. 14; 1 Tim. vi. 13.

The author and finisher of our faith (τὸν τῆς πίστεως
ἀρχηγὸν καὶ τελειωτὴν).   The A. V. is misleading, and nar-
rows the scope of the passage.   For author, rend. leader or
captain, and see on ch. ii. 10.   For finisher, rend. perfecter.
For our faith, rend. faith or the faith.   Not our Christian
faith, but faith absolutely, as exhibited in the whole range
of believers from Abel to Christ.   Christ cannot be called
the author or originator of faith, since the faith here treated
existed and worked before Christ.   Christ is the leader or
captain of faith, in that he is the perfecter of faith.   In himself he furnished the perfect development, the supreme example of faith, and in virtue of this he is the leader of the whole
believing host in all time.   Notice the recurrence of the
favorite idea of perfecting.   Comp. ch. ii. 10; v. 9; vi. 1;
vii. 11, 19, 28; ix. 9; x. 1, 14; xi. 40.   Τελειωτής perfecter,
N. T.°, °LXX, °Class.

For the joy that was set before him (ἀντὶ τῆς προκειμένης αὐτῷ χαρᾶς).   Ἀντὶ in its usual sense, in exchange for.
Προκειμένης lying before, present.   The joy was the full,
divine beatitude of his preincarnate life in the bosom of the
Father ; the glory which he had with God before the world
was.   In exchange for this he accepted the cross and the
shame.   The contrast is designed between the struggle which,
for the present, is alone set before the readers (ver. 1), and
the joy which was already present to Christ.   The heroic
character of his faith appears in his renouncing a joy already

in possession in exchange for shame and death. The passage thus falls in with Philip. ii. 6–8.*

The cross (σταυρὸν). Comp. Philip. ii. 8. °LXX. Originally *an upright stake* or *pale*. Σταυροῦν *to drive down a stake; to crucify*. Comp. the use of ξύλον *wood* or *tree* for the cross, Acts v. 30; x. 39; 1 Pet. ii. 24. See on L. xxiii. 31.

The shame (αἰσχύνης). Attendant upon a malefactor's death.

Is set down, etc. See ch. i. 3, 13; viii. 1; x. 12. Notice the tenses: *endured*, aorist, completed: *hath sat down*, perfect, he remains seated and reigning.

3. **For consider** (ἀναλογίσασθε γὰρ). Γὰρ *for* introduces the reason for the exhortation to look unto Jesus. Look unto him, *for* a comparison with him will show you how much more he had to endure than you have. Ἀναλογίζεσθαι N. T.°. Comp. 3 Macc. vii. 7. It means *to reckon up; to consider in the way of comparison.*

Contradiction of sinners (ὑπὸ τῶν ἁμαρτωλῶν ἀντιλογίαν). *Contradiction* or *gainsaying*. See on ch. vi. 16, and comp. ch. vii. 7. See on *gainsaying*, Jude 11. *Of sinners*, ὑπὸ *by*, *at the hands of.*

Against himself (εἰς ἑαυτούς). According to this text we should render "against themselves." Comp. Num. xvi. 38.

---

* The interpretation of the passage has been dominated by the assumption that *the joy set before him* must refer to a future prize which Christ was to receive in return for his sufferings, "without which," says Weiss, "he would not have been able to endure them." Accordingly, ἀντὶ is explained *for the sake of* or *to obtain* the joy, and *the joy* is defined as *the heavenly reward*, or the joy *of being the redeemer of his brethren*. This sense of ἀντὶ is legitimate, although it enfolds the meaning of *exchange* (see, for instance, Matt. xvii. 27; xx. 28, and the formula ἀνθ' ὧν *because*). At any rate, its use here in that sense creates a feeling of awkwardness. We should rather expect ἕνεκα, or ὑπὲρ or διὰ with the accusative. Moreover, Christ did not endure cross and shame for the sake of heavenly reward, and the redemption of his brethren can hardly be called something to which he looked forward with *faith*.

The explanation will then be that Christ endured the gain-saying of sinners, who, in opposing him, were enemies of their own souls.   The reading ἑαυτοὺς, however, is doubtful, and both Tischendorf and Weiss read ἑαυτὸν *himself*, which I prefer.

Lest ye be wearied and faint in your minds (*ἵνα μὴ κάμητε ταῖς ψυχαῖς ὑμῶν ἐκλυόμενοι*).   Rend. "that ye be not weary, fainting in your minds."   Ἐκλύειν is *to loosen;* hence, *to relax, exhaust.*   So often in LXX.   See Deut. xx. 3 ; Judg. viii. 15 ; 1 Sam. xiv. 28.   Comp. Matt. xv. 32 ; Mk. viii. 3 ; Gal. vi. 9.

4. **Unto blood** (*μέχρις αἵματος*).   Your strife against sin has not entailed the shedding of your blood, as did that of many of the O. T. worthies, and of Jesus himself.   See ch. xi. 35, 37.   Of Jesus it is said, Philip. ii. 8, "he became obedient *to the extent of death* (*μέχρι θανάτου*).   Comp. 2 Macc. xiii. 14.

Striving against sin (*πρὸς τὴν ἁμαρτίαν ἀνταγωνιζόμενοι*). The verb N. T.º.   LXX, 4 Macc. xvii. 14.   Sin is personified.

5. **Ye have forgotten** (*ἐκλέλησθε*).   N. T.º.   Common in Class., ºLXX.   The simple verb λανθάνειν means *to escape notice; to be unseen* or *unknown.*   Middle and passive, *to let a thing escape; forget.*   Some render interrogatively, "have ye forgotten?"

Speaketh unto you (*ὑμῖν διαλέγεται*).   The verb always in the sense of *mutual converse* or *discussion.*   See Mk. ix. 34; Acts xvii. 2 ; xviii. 19.   Rend. "reasoneth with you."

My son, etc.   From Prov. iii. 11, 12.   Comp. Job v. 17.

Despise not (*μὴ ὀλιγώρει*).   N. T.º.   LXX only in this passage.   Quite often in Class.   It means *to make little of* (*ὀλίγος*).

Chastening (παιδείας)。 Mostly in Hebrews。 **See on** Eph. vi。 4, and 2 Tim. iii。 16.

6。 **He chasteneth** (παιδεύει). See on L。 xxiii. 16。

Scourgeth (μαστιγοῖ). Not very common, but found in all the four Gospels。 Hebrews only here. Quite often in LXX.

Receiveth (παραδέχεται). Admits to filial privileges: acknowledges as his own. Of receiving the word of God, Mk. iv. 20: of receiving delegates from a body, Acts xv. 4: of adopting or approving customs, Acts xvi. 21.

7。 **If ye endure chastening** (εἰς παιδείαν ὑπομένετε). Rend. "it is for chastening that ye endure." A. V. follows the reading of T. R. εἰ *if.* Do not faint at affliction. Its purpose is disciplinary. Παιδεία is here *the end* or *result* of discipline. In ver. 5 it is *the process.*

God dealeth with you as with sons (ὡς υἱοῖς ὑμῖν προσφέρεται ὁ θεὸς). The verb means *to bring to:* often *to bring an offering* to the altar, as Matt. v. 23, 24; viii. 4. In the passive voice with the dative, *to be borne toward one;* hence, *to attack, assail, deal with, behave toward.* See Thucyd. i. 140; Eurip. *Cycl.* 176; Hdt. vii. 6. The afflictive dealing of God with you is an *evidence* that you are sons。

What son is he whom the father, etc. (τίς υἱὸς). Some interpreters render, "who is a son whom the father?" etc. That is, no one is a son who is without paternal chastening. The A. V. is better. The idea expressed by the other rendering appears in the next verse.

8。 **Of which all are partakers** (ἧς μέτοχοι γεγόνασι πάντες). Rend. "of which all have been made partakers." For μέτοχοι *partakers* see on ch. iii. 14。 *All,* that is, all sons of God.

Bastards (νόθοι). N. T.⁰. See Wisd. iv. 3. They might think that they would not suffer if they were really God's sons; whereas the reverse is the case. If they did not suffer, they would not be God's sons.

9. **Furthermore** (εἶτα). Everywhere else in N. T. this particle marks a succession of time or incident. See Mk. iv. 17; viii. 25; L. viii. 12; 1 Cor. xv. 5, 7. Here it introduces a new phase of the subject under discussion.

Fathers of our flesh (τοὺς μὲν τῆς σαρκὸς ἡμῶν πατέρας). Up to this point the suffering of Christians has been explained by God's fatherly relation to them. Now the emphatic point is that their fathers, with whom God is compared, were only *earthly, human* parents. The phrase πατέρες τῆς σαρκὸς N. T.⁰, but kindred expressions are found Rom. iv. 1; ix. 3; Gal. iv. 29; Heb. ii. 14.

Which corrected (παιδευτάς). Lit. "we have had fathers of our flesh *as chasteners.*" Only here and Rom. ii. 20. In LXX, Sir. xxxvii. 19; Hos. v. 2; 4 Macc. v. 34; ix. 6.

Shall we not much rather be in subjection (οὐ πολὺ μᾶλλον ὑποταγησόμεθα). The comparison is between the respect paid to a fallible, human parent, which may grow out of the natural relation, or may be due to fear, and the complete subjection to the divine Father.

To the Father of spirits (τῷ πατρὶ τῶν πνευμάτων). Contrasted with *fathers of the flesh.* Their relation to us is limited; his is universal. They are related to us on the fleshly side; he is the creator of our essential life. Our relation to him is on the side of our eternal being. Comp. J. iv. 23, 24; Zech. xii. 1; Isa. lvii. 16. The phrase N. T.⁰. Comp. LXX, Num. xvi. 22; xxvii. 16; Apoc. xxii. 6. Clement of Rome styles God *the benefactor* (εὐεργέτης) *of spirits, the creator and overseer* (κτίστης, ἐπίσκοπος) of every spirit, and *the lord* (δεσπότης) *of spirits. Ad Corinth.* lix, lxiv.

And live (καὶ ζήσομεν). Have true life; not limited to the future life. Comp. J. v. 26; vi. 57; 1 J. v. 11; Apoc. xi. 11; Acts xvi. 28; Rom. vi. 11; xiv. 8; 1 J. iv. 9, and see on *living God*, Heb. iii. 12.

10. Much difficulty and confusion have attached to the interpretation of this verse, growing out of : (*a*) the relations of the several clauses ; (*b*) the meaning of *for a few days*, and how much is covered by it. The difficulties have been aggravated by the determination of commentators to treat the verse by itself, confining the relation of its clauses within its own limits, attempting to throw them into pairs, in which attempt none of them have succeeded, and entirely overlooking relations to the preceding verse.

For a few days (πρὸς ὀλίγας ἡμέρας). This clause is directly related to *be in subjection to the Father of spirits and live*, and points a contrast. On the one hand, subjection to the Father of spirits, the source of all life, has an *eternal* significance. Subjection to his fatherly discipline means, not only the everlasting life of the future, but present life, eternal in quality, developed even while the discipline is in progress. Subjection to the Father of spirits and life go together. On the other hand, the discipline of the human father is brief in duration, and its significance is confined to the present life. In other words, the offset to *for a few days* is in ver. 9. To read *for a few days* into the two latter clauses of the verse which describes the heavenly discipline, and to say that both the chastening of the earthly and of the heavenly father are of brief duration, is to introduce abruptly into a sharp contrast between the two disciplines a point of resemblance. The dominant idea in πρὸς is not mere *duration*, but duration as related to *significance:* that is to say, "*for* a few days" means, during just that space of time in which the chastisement had force and meaning. See, for instances, L. viii. 13; J. v. 35; 1 Th. ii. 17; 2 Cor. vii. 8. The *few days* can scarcely refer to the whole lifetime, since, even from the ancient point of view of the continuance of parental author-

ıty, parental discipline is not applied throughout the lifetime.
It signifies rather the brief period of childhood and youth.

After their own pleasure (κατὰ τὸ δοκοῦν αὐτοῖς). Better,
as seemed good to them. The αὐτοῖς has a slightly emphatic
force, as contrasted with a higher intelligence. The thought
links itself with παιδευτὰς, in ver. 9, and is explained by *as
seemed good to them*, and is placed in contrast with subjection
to the Father of spirits. The human parents were short-
sighted, fallible, sometimes moved by passion rather than by
sound judgment, and, therefore, often mistaken in their disciplinary methods. What seemed good *to them* was not always
best *for us.* No such possibility of error attaches to the
Father of spirits.

But he for our profit (ὁ δὲ ἐπὶ τὸ συμφέρον). The contrast is with what is implied in *as seemed good to them.* The
human parent may *not* have dealt with us to our profit.
Συμφέρειν means *to bring together: to collect* or *contribute in
order to help:* hence, *to help* or *be profitable.* Often imper-
sonally, συμφέρει *it is expedient,* as Matt. v. 29; xviii. 6;
J. xi. 50. The neuter participle, as here, *advantage, profit,*
1 Cor. xii. 7; 2 Cor. xii. 1. There is a backward reference
to *live,* ver. 9, the result of subjection to the Father of spirits; and this is expanded and defined in the final clause,
namely:

That we might be partakers of his holiness (εἰς τὸ
μεταλαβεῖν τῆς ἁγιότητος αὐτοῦ). Lit. *unto the partaking of
his holiness.* Εἰς marks the *final purpose* of chastening.
Holiness is life. Shall we not be subject to the Father of
spirits and live? For, in contrast with the temporary, fault-
ful chastening of the human parent, which, at best, prepares
for work and success in time and in worldly things, his chastening results in holiness and eternal life.

11. **No chastening for the present seemeth** (πᾶσα μὲν
παιδεία πρὸς μὲν τὸ παρὸν οὐ δοκεῖ). Lit. *all chastening —*

doth not seem. Πᾶσα *of all sorts,* divine and human. The
A. V., by joining οὐ *not* to πᾶσα *all,* and rendering *no chastisement,* weakens the emphasis on the idea *every kind of* chastisement. Πρὸς μὲν τὸ παρὸν *for the present.* For the force
of πρὸς see on ver. 10. Not merely *during* the present, but
for the present regarded as the time in which its application
is necessary and salutary. Μὲν indicates that the suffering
present is to be offset by a fruitful future — *but* (δὲ) *afterward.*

To be joyous but grievous (χαρᾶς εἶναι ἀλλὰ λύπης).
Lit. *to be of joy but of grief.*

It yieldeth the peaceable fruit of righteousness (καρπὸν εἰρηνικὸν ἀποδίδωσιν δικαιοσύνης). Perhaps with a suggestion of *recompense* for the longsuffering and waiting, since
ἀποδιδόναι often signifies "to give back." The phrase ἀποδιδόναι καρπὸν only here and Apoc. xxii. 2. Καρπὸν *fruit*
with διδόναι *to give,* Matt. xiii. 8; Mk. iv. 8: with ποιεῖν *to
make* or *produce,* often in Synoptic Gospels, as Matt. iii. 8, 10;
vii. 17; L. iii. 8; vi. 43, etc.: with φέρειν *to bear,* always
and only in John, J. xii. 24; xv. 2, 4, 5, 8, 16: with βλασ-
τάνειν *to bring forth,* Jas. v. 18. Εἰρηνικός *peaceable,* in N. T.
only here and Jas. iii. 17, as an epithet of wisdom. Quite
often in LXX of *men, the heart,* especially of *words* and *sacrifices.* The phrase καρπός εἰρηνικός *peaceable fruit* (omit *the*),
N. T.⁰, ⁰LXX. The phrase *fruit of righteousness,* Philip.
i. 11; Jas. iii. 18, and LXX, Prov. iii. 9; xi. 30; xiii. 2;
Am. vi. 13: comp. Ps. i. 3; lvii. 11. The genitive *of
righteousness* is explicative or appositional; fruit which *consists in* righteousness or *is* righteousness.

Unto them which are exercised thereby (τοῖς δι' αὐτῆς
γεγυμνασμένοις). Who have been subjected to the severe
discipline of suffering, and have patiently undergone it. For
the verb see on 1 Tim. iv. 7. Rend. "it yieldeth peaceable
fruit unto them that have been exercised thereby, even the
fruit of righteousness." This preserves the Greek order, and
puts *righteousness* in its proper, emphatic position.

12. **Wherefore** (διό). Because chastening is thus necessary, and serves for wholesome discipline, and issues in
holiness.

Lift up (ἀνορθώσατε). Found in L. xiii. 13; Acts xv. 16
(cit ͫ.). Occasionally in LXX. It signifies to *set up*, *make*,
erect. In O. T. *to establish*, as a throne (2 Sam. vii. 13, 16);
a house (2 Sam. vii. 26; 1 Chron. xvii. 24); *to raise up one
who is down* (Ps. cxlv. 9; Sir. xi. 12). In Acts xv. 16, *to
build anew*. By medical writers, *to straighten; to set* dislocated parts of the body. See L. xiii. 13.* The translation
here should be more general: not *lift up*, which is inappropriate to *paralyzed knees*, but *set right; brace*. As falling in
with the thought of this passage, comp. the LXX of Ps.
xvii. 35, which, for the A. V. "thy gentleness hath made me
great," gives "thy discipline hath established me or set me
up." See also Ps. xix. 8.

The hands which hang down (τὰς παρειμένας χεῖρας).
Rend. *the slackened* or *weakened hands*. Comp. Isa. xxxv. 3;
Sir. xxv. 23; 2 Sam. iv. 1. The verb παριέναι (only here
and L. xi. 42) originally means *to let pass, disregard, neglect;*
thence *to relax, loosen*. See Clem. Rom. *Ad Corinth.* xxxiv,
who associates it with νωθρὸς *slothful* (comp. Heb. v. 11).

And the feeble knees (καὶ τὰ παραλελυμένα γόνατα). For
feeble rend. *palsied*. See on L. v. 18.

13. **Make straight paths for your feet** (τροχιὰς ὀρθὰς
ποιεῖτε τοῖς ποσὶν ὑμῶν). After the LXX of Prov. iv. 26.
The corresponding Hebrew means *to tear, to cut into:* hence
to cut through as a path; *to make firm* or *plain*. Ὀρθός N. T.
only here and Acts xiv. 10; commonly *straight* or *upright*,
but also *right, safe, happy*. Comp. Prov. viii. 6; xv. 14;

---

* A copious list of references to Hippocrates and Galen may be found in
W. K. Hobart's *Medical Language of St. Luke*, p. 22.

xxi. 8. Here, not in the sense of *straight* as distinguished
from *crooked*, but more generally, *right, plain*, by implication
even or *smooth*.* Τροχιά N. T.º is literally *a wheel-track*
(τροχός *a wheel*). Very rare in profane Greek. Τοῖς ποσὶν
ὑμῶν "*for* your feet," not *with*. That is, exert yourselves
to make the course clear for yourselves and your fellow-
Christians, so that there be no stumbling and laming.

That which is lame (τὸ χωλὸν). Χωλός *lame, halting*, only
in Synoptic Gospels and Acts. Mostly in the literal sense.
Proverbial in Isa. xxxiii. 23. Metaphorically here, and partly
Matt. xviii. 8; Mk. ix. 45. The verb χωλαίνειν *to be lame* or
to make lame (not in N. T.) is used metaphorically in LXX,
Ps. xviii. 45; 1 K. xviii. 21, where the A.V. "how long halt
ye between two opinions" is ἕως πότε ὑμεῖς χωλανεῖτε ἐπ'
ἀμφοτέραις ταῖς ἰγνύαις *how long do ye go lame on both your
hams?* Τὸ χωλὸν here signifies the lame *part* or *limb*.

Be turned out of the way (ἐκτραπῇ). Rend. "be put out
of joint." The A.V. is according to the more usual meaning
of the verb, which, in N. T., is confined, with this exception,
to the Pastoral Epistles. See 1 Tim. i. 6; v. 15; 2 Tim. iv. 4.
LXX only Am. v. 8. But it is also used by medical writers
in the passive, with the meaning *to be wrenched* or *dislocated*.†
There is nothing strange in the use of this word in a medical
sense by our writer, whose work bears the stamp of Alexandria. The Greeks received their knowledge of surgery
from the Egyptians, and mural paintings and documents,
and even hieroglyphic symbols, prove that that people had
attained remarkable proficiency in the science. Herodotus

---

* So von Soden, "not the *direction* but the *surface:* ὀρθαὶ = *smooth, without stones or holes.*"

† Stephens, *Thes.*, gives *detorquere*, and cites a number of instances from
medical writers in which ἐκτροπή and ἐκτρόπιον are used of an everted eyelid,
in which the lid is turned outward. Celsus says that when the eyelids refuse
to come together, the lower lid hanging and dragging, and unable to unite
with the upper, the Greeks call it ἐκτρόπιον.

(ch. iii. 131) mentions a medical school at Cyrene in Africa, and says that the pupils of that school were regarded as the second best physicians in all Greece. At the time of Galen (163 A.D.) the medical school of Alexandria was the most famous in the world, and Galen himself studied there. Celsus (first half of the first century A.D.), in the 7th book of his treatise *De Artibus*, treats of surgical operations according to the views of the Alexandrian schools. The commonly-accepted rendering of the A. V., besides giving a conception which is very tame, presents two incongruities: the association of *going astray* with *lameness*, and of *healing* with *straying*. The other rendering gives a lively and consistent image. Make the paths smooth and even, so that the lame limb be not dislocated by stones or pitfalls. Do everything to avoid aggravating the weakness of a fellow-Christian. Rather try to heal it. Τὸ χωλὸν may refer either to an individual or to a section of the church which is weak and vacillating.

14. **Follow peace** (εἰρήνην διώκετε). Comp. LXX, Ps. xxiii. 14, and Rom. xiv. 19; 1 Pet. iii. 11. The verb is used of the pursuit of moral and spiritual ends, Rom. ix. 30, 31; xii. 13; 1 Cor. xiv. 1; Philip. iii. 12, 14; 1 Th. v. 15; 1 Tim. vi. 11; 2 Tim. ii. 22.

Holiness (ἁγιασμόν). See on Rom. vi. 19.

15. **Looking diligently** (ἐπισκοποῦντες). A.V. gives *diligently* as the force of ἐπὶ; but ἐπὶ signifies *direction* rather than *intensity*. The idea is *exercising oversight*. Only here and 1 Pet. v. 2.

Fail of (ὑστερῶν ἀπὸ). Rend. "fall back from," implying a previous attainment. The present participle marks something in progress: "lest any one *be falling* back."

Root of bitterness (ῥίζα πικρίας). From LXX, Deut. xxix. 18. A bad man in the church. Ῥίζα *of a person*, 1 Macc. i. 10.

Springing up (ἄνω φύουσα). The participle pictures the springing up in progress; the root gradually revealing its pernicious character.

Trouble (ἐνοχλῇ). Only here and L. vi. 18, see note.

Many be defiled (μιανθῶσιν οἱ πολλοί). Rend. "*the* many": the majority of the church. For the verb see on J. xviii. 28.

16. **Fornicator** (πόρνος). In the literal sense, as always in N. T.

Profane person (βέβηλος). See on 1 Tim. i. 9.

As Esau. Only the epithet *profane* is applied to Esau, not *fornicator*.

For one morsel of meat (ἀντὶ βρώσεως μιᾶς). Βρῶσις, lit. *the act* of eating, as 1 Cor. viii. 4; Rom. xiv. 17: "one *eating* of meat." Sometimes *corrosion*, as Matt. vi. 19. Sometimes of *that which is eaten*, J. vi. 27, 55.

Sold (ἀπέδετο). The word occurs in the narrative of Gen. xxv. 31, 33, LXX. In N. T. often of *discharging an obligation; paying back*. *To sell*, Acts v. 8; vii. 9.

His birthright (τὰ πρωτοτοκία). N. T.°, °Class. In this form only in the later Greek translations of the O.T. Πρωτοτοκεῖον, a very few times, almost all in this narrative.

17. **He found no place of repentance** (μετανοίας γὰρ τόπον οὐχ εὗρεν). The phrase *place of repentance* N. T.°. This does not mean that Esau was rendered incapable of repentance, which is clearly contradicted by what follows; nor that he was not able to persuade Isaac to change his mind and to recall the blessing already bestowed on Jacob and give it to him. This is unnatural, forced, and highly improbable. The words *place of repentance* mean *an opportunity to repair by*

repenting. He found no way to reverse by repentance what he had done. The *penalty* could not be reversed in the nature of the case. This is clear from Isaac's words, Gen. xxvii. 33.

Sought it carefully (ἐκζητήσας). See on 1 Pet. i. 10. Comp. Heb. xi. 6. See also on *questionings*, 1 Tim. i. 4.

18. Following this allusion to Esau, and perhaps suggested by it, is a passage setting forth the privileges of the Christian birthright and of Christian citizenship in contrast with those under the old covenant.

The mount that might be touched and that burned with fire (ψηλαφωμένῳ καὶ κεκαυμένῳ πυρὶ). Ὄρει *mount* is omitted by the best texts, but should be understood.* Ψηλαφᾶν is rare in N. T. and LXX; fairly frequent in Class. Radically, it is akin to ψᾶν *to rub, wipe;* hence feeling on the surface, as Gen. xxvii. 12, 21, 22, LXX: a touch which communicates only a superficial effect. It need not imply contact with an object at all, but simply the movement of the hands feeling *after* something. Hence often of the groping of the blind, as Deut. xxviii. 29; Isa. lix. 10; Job v. 14. Appropriate here as indicating mere superficial contact. The present participle *that is being touched*, means simply that the mountain was something material and tangible. The A. V. *which might be touched*, although not literally correct, conveys the true sense.

That burned with fire (κεκαυμένῳ πυρὶ). See Ex. xix. 18; Deut. iv. 11; v. 4; ix. 15. The participle is passive, *set on fire; kindled with fire:* not attributive of πυρὶ, *enkindled fire.*

---

* This is preferable to the Vulg. adopted by Westcott, *ad tractabilem et accensibilem ignem* "to a palpable and kindled fire," thus making ψηλαφωμένῳ qualify πυρί. It destroys the antithesis clearly intended between the material Mount Sinai and the spiritual, heavenly Mount Zion, and leads us to expect as the antithesis of *material* fire, some other kind of fire. The other rendering is required by Σιὼν ὄρει, ver. 22. Moreover, ψηλαφωμένῳ as an epithet of πυρί is unnatural.

Blackness, darkness, tempest (γνόφῳ, ζόφῳ, θυέλλῃ).
Γνόφος (N. T.°) and ζόφος (elsewhere only 2 Peter and Jude)
belong to the same family. As distinguished from σκότος
darkness that conceals, as opposed to light, these words
signify *half-darkness, gloom, nebulousness;* as the darkness of
evening or the gathering gloom of death. It is a darkness
which does not entirely conceal colour. Thus δνόφος, the
earlier and poetic form of γνόφος, is used by Homer of water
which appears dark against the underlying rock, or is tinged
by mire. Γνόφος and σκότος appear together, Ex. x. 22;
xiv. 20; Deut. iv. 11; v. 22. Γνόφος alone, Ex. xx. 21.
Ζόφος only in the later version of Symmachus. See on J. i. 5.
Θύελλα N. T.°, from θύειν *to boil* or *foam*. It is a brief,
violent, sudden, destructive blast, sometimes working upward
and carrying objects into the upper air; hence found with
ἀείρειν *to lift* and ἀναρπάζειν *to snatch up* (see Hom. *Od.* xx. 63).
It may also come from above and dash down to the ground
(Hom. *Il.* xii. 253). Sometimes it indicates the mere force of
the wind, as ἀνέμοιο θύελλα (Hom. *Od.* xii. 409; *Il.* vi. 346).

19. **Sound of a trumpet** (σάλπιγγος ἤχῳ). See Ex. xix. 16,
19; xx. 18. ἮΗχος *a noise*, almost entirely in Luke and Acts.
See L. iv. 37; Acts ii. 2; comp. LXX, 1 Sam. xiv. 19. Of
the roar of the waves, L. xxi. 25; comp. LXX, Ps. lxiv. 7;
lxxvi. 17. *A rumour* or *report*, see on L. iv. 37, and comp.
LXX, 1 Sam. iv. 16; Ps. ix. 6. It does not occur in the
O. T. narrative of the giving of the law, where we have φωνή
voice; see LXX, Ex. xix. 13, 16, 19; xx. 18. For φωνή σάλπιγγος *voice of a trumpet* in N. T., see Apoc. i. 10; iv. 1;
viii. 13. Σάλπιγξ is a *war-trumpet.*

Voice of words (φωνῇ ῥημάτων). See Ex. xix. 19; Deut.
iv. 12; v. 22, 24, 26.

Entreated (παρῃτήσαντο). See on 1 Tim. iv. 7.

Be spoken to them any more (προστεθῆναι αὐτοῖς). Lit.
be added. See on L. iii. 19; xx. 11; Acts xii. 3. *To*

them refers to the hearers, not to the things heard. Rend. "that no word more should be spoken unto them." Comp. Ex. xx. 19 ; Deut. v. 25 ; xviii. 16.

20. That which was commanded (τὸ διαστελλόμενον). See on Mk. vii. 36 ; Acts xv. 24.

Touch (θίγῃ). Elsewhere in N. T. only ch. xi. 28 and Col. ii. 21. LXX only Ex. xix. 12. It implies a touching or grasping which affects the object (comp. ver. 18 on ψηλα-φᾶν). In Class. often of touching or handling some sacred object which may be desecrated by the one who lays hands on it. See Soph. *Philoct.* 667 ; *Oed. Tyr.* 891, 899. So here, the touch of the mountain was *profanation*.

Shall be stoned (λιθοβοληθήσεται). Found in Matthew, Luke, and Acts. In LXX see Ex. xix. 13. Comp. ἐλιθάσθη-σαν, ch. xi. 37. The correct text omits *or thrust through with a dart*.

21. The sight (τὸ φανταζόμενον). N. T.°. LXX, Wisd. vi. 16 ; Sir. xxxi. 5. Rend. "the appearance ": that which was made to appear.

I exceedingly fear and quake (ἔκφοβός εἰμι καὶ ἔντρομος). Lit. *I am frightened away* (or *out*) *and trembling.* Ἔκφοβός only here and Mk. ix. 6. Comp. LXX, Deut. ix. 19. Ἔν-τρομος, only Acts vii. 32 ; xvi. 29. Rare in LXX.

22. The heavenly Jerusalem. See on Gal. iv. 26. The spiritual mountain and city where God dwells and reigns. Comp. Dante *Inf.* i. 128 :

"Quivi è la sua cittade, e l'alto seggio." *

Comp. Ps. ii. 6 ; xlviii. 2, 3 ; l. 2 ; lxxviii. 68 ; cx. 2 ; Isa. xviii. 7 ; Joel ii. 32 ; Mic. iv. 1, 2 ; Am. i. 2.

---

* "Here is his city and his lofty seat."

To an innumerable company of angels (μυριάσιν ἀγγέ-λων). On this whole passage (22–24) it is to be observed that it is arranged in a series of clauses connected by καὶ. Accordingly μυριάσιν to *myriads* or *tens of thousands* stands by itself, and πανηγύρει *festal assembly* goes with ἀγγέλων *angels*. Μυριάς (see L. xii. 1 ; Acts xix. 19 ; Apoc. v. 11 ; quite often in LXX) is strictly the number *ten thousand*. In the plural, *an innumerable multitude*. So A. V. here. Rend. "to an innumerable multitude," placing a comma after μυριά-σιν, and connecting *of angels* with the next clause. This use of μυριάσιν without a qualifying genitive is justified by numerous examples. See Gen. xxiv. 60 ; Deut. xxxii. 30 ; xxxiii. 2 ; 1 Sam. xviii. 7, 8 ; Ps. xc. 7 ; Cant. v. 10 ; Dan. vii. 10 ; xi. 12 ; Sir. xlvii. 6 ; 2 Macc. viii. 20 ; Jude 14. Χιλιάδες *thousands* is used in the same way. See Isa. lxx. 22 ; Dan. vii. 10.

23. **To the general assembly** (πανηγύρει). Const. with ἀγγέλων *of angels*, with comma after *angels*. Rend. "to a festal assembly of angels." This and the next clause show what the myriads consist of, —a host of angels and redeemed men. Πανήγυρις, N. T.⁰, is *a gathering to celebrate a solemnity*, as public games, etc. : a public, festal assembly. Frequently joined with ἑορτή *feast*. See Ezek. xlvii. 11 ; Hos. ii. 11 ; ix. 5. The verb πανηγυρίζειν *to celebrate* or *attend a public festival*, *to keep holiday*, occurs occasionally in Class. : not in N. T. : LXX once, Isa. lxvi. 10. The *festal* assembly of angels maintains the contrast between the old and the new dispensation. The host of angels through whose ministration the law was given (see on ch. ii. 2, and Gal. iii. 19) officiated at a scene of terror. Christian believers are now introduced to a *festal* host, surrounding the exalted Son of man, who has purged away sins, and is enthroned at God's right hand (ch. i. 3).

And church of the first-born which are written in heaven (καὶ ἐκκλησίᾳ πρωτοτόκων ἀπογεγραμμένων ἐν οὐρανοῖς).

This forms a distinct clause; "and to the church," etc.   For
ἐκκλησία *assembly* or *church*, see on Matt. xvi. 18; 1 Th. i. 1.
The "myriads" embrace not only angels, but redeemed men,
enrolled as citizens of the heavenly commonwealth, and entitled to the rights and privileges of first-born sons.   Πρωτότοκος *first-born* is applied mostly to Christ in N. T.   See Rom.
viii. 29; Col. i. 15, 18; Heb. i. 6; Apoc. i. 5.   Comp.
Heb. xi. 28, and L. ii. 7.   Properly applied to Christians by
virtue of their union with Christ, "the first-born of all creation," "the first-born from the dead," as sharing his sonship
and heirship.   See Rom. viii. 14–17, 29.   The word also
points to Christians as the true *Israel* of God.   The analogy
is suggested with the first-born of Israel, to whom peculiar
sanctity attached, and whose consecration to himself God
enjoined (Ex. xiii. 1, 11–16); and with the further application of the term *first-born* to Israel as a people, Ex. iv. 22.
The way was thus prepared for its application to the Messiah.   There seems, moreover, to be a clear reference to the
case of Esau (ver. 16).   Esau was the first-born of the twin
sons of Isaac (Gen. xxv. 25).   He sold his birthright (πρωτοτοκία), and thus forfeited the privilege of the first-born.   The
assembly to which Christian believers are introduced is composed of those who have not thus parted with their birthright,
but have retained the privileges of the first-born.   The phrase
"church of the first-born" includes all who have possessed
and retained their heavenly birthright, living or dead, of both
dispensations: the whole Israel of God, although it is quite
likely that the Christian church may have been most prominent in the writer's thought.

Which are written in heaven (ἀπογεγραμμένων ἐν οὐρανοῖς).   ᾽Απογράφειν, only here and L. ii. 1, 3, 5, means *to write
off* or *copy;*   to enter in a register the names, property, and
income of men.   Hence, ἀπογραφή *an enrolment*.   See on
L. ii. 1, 2.   Here, inscribed as members of the heavenly commonwealth; citizens of heaven; Philip. iv. 3; Apoc. iii. 5;
xiii. 8, etc.   See for the image, Ex. xxxii. 32; Ps. lxix. 28;
Isa. iv. 3; Dan. xii. 1; L. x. 20.

To God the judge of all (κριτῇ θεῷ πάντων). Rend. "a judge who is God of all." Comp. Dan. vii. 9 ff. God of all his first-born, of those whom he chastens, of all who are in filial relations with him under both covenants, and who, therefore, need not fear to draw near to him as judge.

Spirits of just men made perfect (πνεύμασι δικαίων τετελειωμένων). The departed spirits of the righteous of both dispensations, who have completed their course after having undergone their earthly discipline. Notice again the idea of τελείωσις, not attained under the old covenant, but only through the work of Christ, the benefits of which the disembodied saints of the O. T. share with departed Christian believers. Comp. ch. xi. 40.

24. **The mediator of the new covenant** (διαθήκης νέας μεσίτῃ). See ch. vii. 22; viii. 6, 8, 9, 10; ix. 15. For *covenant*, see on ch. ix. 6 ff. For *the* new covenant, rend. *a* new covenant. Nέα *new*, only here applied to the covenant in N. T. The word elsewhere is καινή. For the distinction, see on Matt. xxvi. 29. It is better not to press the distinction, since νέος, in certain cases, clearly has the sense of *quality* rather than of *time*, as 1 Cor. v. 7; Col. iii. 10, and probably here, where to confine the sense to *recent* would seem to limit it unduly. In the light of all that the writer has said respecting the better quality of the Christian covenant, superseding the old, outworn, insufficient covenant, he may naturally be supposed to have had in mind something besides its mere recentness. Moreover, all through the contrast from ver. 18, the thought of earlier and later is not once touched, but only that of inferior and better; repellency and invitation; terrors and delights; fear and confidence. Note that the privilege of approaching the Mediator *in person* is emphasised.

Blood of sprinkling (αἵματι ῥαντισμοῦ). Ῥαντισμός *sprinkling* only here and 1 Pet. i. 2, see note. The phrase *blood of sprinkling* N. T.º. ºLXX, where we find ὕδωρ ῥαντισμοῦ *water of sprinkling*, Num. xix. 9, 13, 20, 21. For the verb ῥαντίζειν *to sprinkle*, see on ch. ix. 13. The mention of blood naturally follows that of a covenant, since no covenant is ratified without blood (ch. ix. 16). The phrase is sufficiently explained by ch. ix. 16–22.

Speaketh better things (κρεῖττον λαλοῦντι). For "better things" rend. "better." The blood is personified, and its voice is contrasted with that of Abel, whose blood cried from the ground for vengeance upon his murderer (Gen. iv. 10). The voice of Christ's blood calls for mercy and forgiveness.

Than that of Abel (παρὰ τὸν Ἄβελ). Rend. "than Abel." Comp. ch. xi. 4, where Abel himself speaks.

25. **See—refuse** (βλέπετε—παραιτήσησθε). For βλέπετε *see*, see on ch. iii. 12. For παραιτήσησθε *refuse*, see on 1 Tim. iv. 7

Him that speaketh (τὸν λαλοῦντα). Through his blood. Rend. "that is speaking," the participle denoting something that is going on.

They (ἐκεῖνοι). The people of the Exodus. See ch. iv. 2. The words from *for if they* to the end of the verse are parenthetical.

That spake on earth (ἐπὶ γῆς τὸν χρηματίζοντα). For *spake* rend. *warned*, and see on ch. viii. 5. Ἐπὶ γῆς *upon earth* should not be construed with *refused* nor *warned*, but with the whole clause. "If on earth they escaped not, refusing him that warned."

If we turn away (ἀποστρεφομενοι). Lit. *turning away*. The present participle, possibly with reference to the relapse into Judaism as already in progress.

From him that speaketh from heaven (τὸν ἀπ᾽ οὐρανῶν). Lit. *from him from the heavens*. Supply as A. V. *that speaketh.*

'Ο ἀπ' οὐρανοῦ or οὐρανῶν does not occur in N. T. elsewhere.
Wherever ἀπ' οὐρ. appears, some act or thing is always
named which proceeds from heaven.   See Matt. xxiv. 29;
Mk. viii. 11; L. ix. 54; xvii. 29; xxi. 11; xxii. 43; J. vi. 38;
1 Th. i. 7.   The speaker from heaven is still God, but speaking through his Son.   The thought connects itself with that
of Christ carrying his blood into the heavenly sanctuary, from
which he exerts his power on behalf of men.   See ch. ix. 12, 24.
This will be the clearer if we throw out the idea of Christ
presenting his blood to an angry God as a propitiation, and
interceding with him to pardon sin.   See note on ch. vii. 25.

26. Whose voice (οὗ ἡ φωνὴ).   Connect, after the parenthesis, with *speaketh better*, etc., ver. 24.

Shook (ἐσάλευσεν).   See on L. xxi. 26, and comp. σάλος
tossing or *swell* of the sea, L. xxi. 25.   See Judg. v. 4;
Ps. cxiii. 7.

He hath promised (ἐπήγγελται).   See Hag. ii. 6.   The
quotation is adapted from LXX, which reads : " Yet once
will I shake the heaven and the earth and the sea and the
dry land."   The Hebrew for "yet once" reads "yet a little
while."   In Haggai's prophecy, he comforts the people for
their sorrow that the second temple is so inferior to the first,
predicting that Jehovah will move heaven and earth and sea
and land, and will fill the house with his glory; and the glory
of the latter house shall exceed that of the former.   The discipline begun on Sinai will then have its consummation.
This shaking of heaven and earth was typified by the material shaking at Sinai.   The shaking predicted by the prophet
is applied by our writer to the downfall of worldly powers
before the kingdom of Christ, ver. 28; comp. ch. i. 8, and
see Zech. xiv.

27. This word " yet once more " (τὸ δέ Ἔτι ἄπαξ).   Attention is called to this phrase as specially significant, because
it indicates that the shaking prophesied by Haggai is to be

final. It is to precede the new heaven and the new earth.
Isa. lxv. 17; lxvi. 22; 2 Pet. iii. 13; Apoc. xxi. 1.

Signifieth (δηλοῖ). From δῆλος *manifest, evident.* To
make manifest *to the mind.* Used of indications which lead
the mind to conclusions about the origin or character of
things. See Thucyd. i. 3; Aesch. *Pers.* 518. Comp. 1 Cor.
iii. 13; Heb. ix. 8; 1 Pet. i. 11. Appropriate to prophetic
revelations.

The removing (τὴν μετάθεσιν). See on ch. vii. 12. For
the thought comp. 1 J. ii. 17; 1 Cor. vii. 31.

As of things that are made (ὡς πεποιημένων). Made
indeed by God, who also makes the new heaven and the new
earth (Isa. lxv. 17; lxvi. 22), but made to pass away.

That the things which cannot be shaken may remain
(ἵνα μείνῃ τὰ μὴ σαλευόμενα). Whether we consider the
things which are shaken, the old heavens and earth which
pass away, or the new heaven and earth which cannot be
shaken, both are πεποιημένα *made* by God. The writer
perceives this, and therefore adds to *as of things that are
made* a clause stating that they were made (by God himself)
to pass away. Accordingly, ἵνα *in order that* is to be connected with πεποιημένων, after which the comma should be
removed. Rend. "the removal of things made in order that
they might await the things which are not shaken." Μένειν
is used in this sense, *await*, Acts xx. 5, 23, and often in Class.*

28. **Receiving a kingdom** (βασιλείαν παραλαμβάνοντες).
The participle gives no note of time, but simply indicates the
fact that Christians as such receive. The compounded prep-

---

* Another mode of rendering is "things which are made to the end that
the things which cannot be shaken may abide." To this it is justly objected
that μείνῃ is thus compelled to assume an elliptical sense: "Come into the
place of the things removed and so abide"; for as Alford remarks, "things
which cannot be shaken *remaining* merely, would be a matter of course."

osition παρὰ adds to the idea of *receiving* that of *transmission* or *communication*. They receive *from* God. See Dan. vii. 18. Βασιλεία in the sense of the kingdom of Christ, in this epistle only here and ch. i. 8 (citⁿ). See on Matt. iii. 2; L. vi. 20.

Let us have grace (ἔχωμεν χάριν). For *grace* rend. *thankfulness*. See L. xvii. 9; 1 Tim. i. 12 · 2 Tim. i. 3. Comp. Ps. l. 23.

Acceptably (εὐαρέστως). N. T.⁰, ⁰LXX. Ἐυαρεστεῖν *to be well pleasing*, ch. xi. 5, 6; xiii. 16. For the adjective εὐάρεστος *well pleasing*, see on Tit. ii. 9.

With reverence (μετὰ εὐλαβείας). Rend. "with pious care." *Reverence* is translated from T. R. αἰδοῦς (see on 1 Tim. ii. 9). See on ch. v. 7; xi. 7.

Fear (δέους). N. T.⁰. See 2 Macc. iii. 17, 30; xii. 22; xiii. 16; xv. 23. Its fundamental idea is *timid apprehension of danger;* while φόβος is the terror which seizes one when the danger appears. Schmidt (*Synon.* 139, 10) illustrates happily. In a primitive forest an undefined sense of possible danger possesses one, and makes his heart beat quickly at every rustle of a leaf. This is δέος. When the voice and tread of a wild beast are distinctly heard close at hand, the δέος becomes φόβος. The phrase "with pious care and fear" is not explanatory of *acceptably*. These are to *accompany* (μετὰ) acceptable service. They do not imply a cringing or slavish feeling, but grow out of the warning in ver. 25, which runs through the two following verses, and implies that the catastrophe of ver. 27 will be final, leaving no more opportunity to retrieve the refusal of God's invitation to the privileges of the new covenant, or the relapse into the superseded economy of Judaism.

29. **For our God is a consuming fire** (καὶ γὰρ ὁ θεὸς ἡμῶν πῦρ καταναλίσκον). See Ex. xxiv. 17; Deut. iv. 24;

ix. 3 ; Mal. iii. 2; iv. 1.   The verb N. T.⁰, a few times in
LXX.   Often in Class., especially Xenophon.   Originally
to use up, *spend*, *lavish*, as property : thence *to consume* as
with fire.   The simple verb ἀναλίσκειν *to expend* occurs
L. ix. 54; Gal. v. 15; 2 Th. ii. 8.   Ὁ θεὸς ἡμῶν is not *our*
God as compared with the God of the Jews.   He is the God
of both covenants (see ch. i. 1, 2, and notes); but though
now revealed in Jesus Christ, and offering all the privileges
of the new covenant (vv. 22–24), his anger burns against
those who reject these privileges.

CHAPTER XIII.

1. **Let brotherly love continue** (φιλαδελφία μενέτω).   Φιλαδελφία in Paul, Rom. xii. 10; 1 Th. iv. 9.   As a proper
name, Apoc. i. 11; iii. 7.   It is not necessary to suppose
that the admonition implies signs of estrangement among
those addressed.   Comp. ch. iii. 13; vi. 10; x. 24; xii. 12–15.

2. **Be not forgetful to entertain strangers** (τῆς φιλο·
ξενίας μὴ ἐπιλανθάνεσθε).   Lit. *be not forgetful of hospitality*.
Φιλοξενία only here and Rom. xii. 13.   ⁰LXX.   Φιλόξενος
hospitable, 1 Tim. iii. 2; Tit. i. 8; 1 Pet. iv. 9.   The rendering of Rev. *to show love unto strangers*, is affected.   On the
injunction comp. Rom. xii. 13; 1 Tim. iii. 2; Tit. i. 8;
1 Pet. iv. 9, and see Clem. Rom. *Ad Corinth.* x, xi, xii.   The
virtue of hospitality is not distinctively Christian.   It appears
with the very beginnings of history, largely as the result of
nomadic conditions.   It was peculiarly an Oriental virtue.
In the Egyptian Book of the Dead, commendatory judgment
is awarded to him who has fed the hungry and clothed the
naked.   The O. T. abounds in illustrations, and the practice
of hospitality among the Arabs and Bedoueen is familiar
through the writings of travellers in the East.*   Great stress

---

* See Dr. W. M. Thomson, *The Land and the Book;* Burckhardt, *Notes
on the Bedouins and Wahâbys;* Lane, *Modern Egyptians;* Palgrave, *Central
and Eastern Arabia;* Trumbull, *Oriental Social Life;* etc.

was laid on the duty by the Greeks, as appears constantly in Homer and elsewhere. Hospitality was regarded as a religious duty. The stranger was held to be under the special protection of Zeus, who was called ξένιος, *the god of the stranger*. The Romans regarded any violation of the rites of hospitality as impiety. Cicero says: "It seems to me eminently becoming that the homes of distinguished men should be open to distinguished guests, and that it is an honour to the Republic that foreigners should not lack this kind of liberality in our city" (*De Off.* ii. 18).

Have entertained angels unawares (ἔλαθόν τινες ξενίσαντες ἀγγέλους). The Greek idiom is, "were not apparent as entertaining angels." The verb ἔλαθον *were concealed* represents the adverb *unawares*. For similar instances see Mk. xiv. 8; Acts xii. 16; Aristoph. *Wasps*, 517; Hdt. i. 44; Hom. *Il.* xiii. 273. Ξενίζειν *to receive as a guest*, mostly in Acts. In LXX only in the apocryphal books. In later Greek, *to surprise with a novelty;* passive, *to be surprised* or *shocked.* So 1 Pet. iv. 4, 12; comp. 2 Ep. of Clem. of Rome (so called), xvii. *To be a stranger* or *to be strange*, once in N. T., Acts xvii. 20. Ξενισμός *amazement, perplexity*, not in N. T. LXX, Prov. xv. 17. Comp. Ignatius, *Eph.* xix. The allusion to the unconscious entertainment of angels is probably to Gen. xviii, xix, but the idea was familiar in Greek literature. The Greeks thought that any stranger might be a god in disguise. See Hom. *Od.* i. 96 ff.; iii. 329–370; xvii. 485. Comp. also the beautiful story of Baucis and Philemon as related by Ovid (*Metam.* viii. 626–724). The thought appears in our Lord's words, Matt. xxv. 34–46.

3. **Them that are in bonds** (τῶν δεσμίων). See on ch. x. 34.

As bound with them (ὡς συνδεδεμένοι). N. T.º. As if you were fellow-prisoners. Comp. 1 Cor. xii. 14–26; 2 Cor. xi. 29. Public intercession for prisoners has formed a part of the service of the church from the earliest times. See the prayer at the close of Clem. Rom *Ad Corinth.* lix. It also occurs in the daily morning service of the synagogue.

Which suffer adversity (κακουχουμένων). Rend. *are evil entreated*. See on ch. xi. 37.

As being yourselves also in the body (ὡς καὶ αὐτοὶ ὄντες ἐν σώματι). As subject like them to bodily sufferings. Not *in the body — the church*, which would require the article. The expression ἐν σώματι in the sense of being still alive, only in 2 Cor. xii. 2.

4. **Marriage is honourable in all** (τίμιος ὁ γάμος ἐν πᾶσιν). Γάμος everywhere else in N. T. *a wedding* or *wedding feast*, often in the plural, as Matt. xxii. 2, 3, 4; L. xii. 36. Τίμιος *honourable* or *held in honour*. Often in N. T. *precious*, of gold, stones, etc., as 1 Cor. iii. 12; Apoc. xvii. 4; xviii. 12: of life, Acts xx. 24: the fruits of the earth, Jas. v. 7; the blood of Christ, 1 Pet. i. 19; the divine promises, 2 Pet. i. 4. Rend. "let marriage be had in honour." The statement is hortatory, as suiting the character of the entire context, and especially the γὰρ *for;* "for whoremongers," etc. Ἐν πᾶσιν "in all respects," as 1 Tim. iii. 11; 2 Tim. iv. 5; Tit. ii. 9; Col. i. 18; Philip. iv. 12. If as A. V., the more natural expression would be παρὰ πᾶσιν, as Matt. xix. 26; Acts xxvi. 8; Rom. ii. 13; 2 Th. i. 6; Jas. i. 27. Ἐν πᾶσιν *in all things* appears in this chapter, ver. 18.* There are many points in which marriage is to be honoured besides the avoidance of illicit connections. See on 1 Thess. iv. 6.

God will judge (κρινεῖ ὁ θεός). Note the emphatic position of ὁ θεός. *He* will judge and condemn infractions of the marriage-bond, however social sentiment may condone them.

5. **Let your conversation be without covetousness** (ἀφιλάργυρος ὁ τρόπος). Τρόπος originally *turn* or *direction*. Hence *way, manner, fashion; way* or *manner of life*. In this sense N. T.⁰. Elsewhere often in the phrase ὅν τρόπον or

---

* Calvin, taking πᾶσιν as masculine, explains that marriage is not to be denied to any class of men, as to priests. Others explain that marriage is not to be avoided on ascetic grounds by any one.

καθ' ὃν τρόπον *in* or *according to the way in which.* See
Matt. xxiii. 37; L. xiii. 34; Acts i. 11; xv. 11; xxvii. 25.
The meaning here is *character* or *moral disposition.* Ἀφιλάρ-
γυρος *without covetousness,* only here and 1 Tim. iii. 3, see note.

Be content with such things as ye have (ἀρκούμενοι τοῖς
παροῦσιν). Lit. *being contented with the things which are at
hand.* For ἀρκεῖν *to suffice,* see L. iii. 14; J. vi. 7; 1 Tim. vi. 8.
On the compounds αὐτάρκης *self-sufficient* and αὐτάρκεια *self-
sufficiency,* see on 2 Cor. ix. 8; Philip. iv. 11.

For he hath said (αὐτὸς γὰρ εἴρηκεν). Rend. for "he
himself." God himself. For εἴρηκεν *hath said,* see ch. i. 13;
iv. 3, 4; x. 9.

I will never leave nor forsake thee (οὐ μή σε ἀνῶ οὐδ' οὐ
μή σε ἐγκαταλίπω). Comp. Gen. xxviii. 15; Josh. i. 5;
Deut. xxxi. 6. None of these, however, give the saying in
the form in which it appears here. This appears to be a
combination or general adaptation of those passages. For
"never," rend. "by no means" or "in no wise." Ἀνῶ from
ἀνίημι. In Acts xvi. 26; xxvii. 40, *to loosen:* Eph. vi. 9,
to give up or *forbear.* Somewhat in this last sense here: "I
will in no wise *give thee up,* or *let thee go.*" I will not relax
my hold on thee. For ἐγκαταλίπω *forsake,* see on 2 Tim. iv. 10.

So that we may boldly say (ὥστε θαρροῦντας ἡμᾶς λέγειν).
Lit. *so that, being of good courage, we say.* Θαρρεῖν *to be con-
fident* or *bold,* only here in Hebrews. Elsewhere only in Paul.
The kindred form θαρσεῖν is used in N. T. only in the im-
perative θάρσει or θαρσεῖτε *take courage.* See Matt. ix. 2;
Mk. vi. 50; J. xvi. 33; Acts xxiii. 11.

The Lord is my helper, etc. From LXX, Ps. cxvii. 6,
with slight alteration. Here, *what shall man do unto me* is
an independent clause. LXX inserts *and:* "my helper *and*
I will not fear," and connects the last clause with "fear":
"I will not fear what man will do."

7–15. The following passage presents many difficulties of detail, but its general sense is clear. It sums up in a striking way the main topics of the epistle, bringing them all to bear upon the conclusion that Judaism and Christianity are mutually exclusive, and thus enforcing the warning against a relapse into Judaism. It goes to show, in connection with other features of the epistle, the absurdity of the hypothesis that the epistle was intended as a warning to Gentile Christians against a relapse into Paganism.*

7. Remember them which have the rule over you (μνημονεύετε τῶν ἡγουμένων ὑμῶν). Remember, with a view to observing their admonitions. For τῶν ἡγουμένων *those who lead* or *rule*, see on 1 Th. v. 13. Used of both civil and ecclesiastical rulers. Clement of Rome, among a great variety of names for church functionaries, has both ἡγούμενοι and προηγούμενοι (see *Ad Corinth.* i, xxi). Comp. Acts xv. 22. In LXX frequently, of various forms of authority, and in later Greek of bishops and abbots. For "which have the rule," rend. "which *had*," etc.

Who have spoken (οἵτινες ἐλάλησαν). Rend. "spake," and comp. ch. ii. 3, 4.

Follow (μιμεῖσθε). Rend. "imitate." See on ch. vi. 12.

Considering (ἀναθεωροῦντες). Only here and Acts xvii. 23, see note. The compound verb means to observe *attentively*. The simple verb θεωρεῖν implies a spiritual or mental interest in the object. See on J. i. 18.

---

* The hypothesis that the letter was called out by "an amateur attachment to Levitical institutions" on the part of Gentile Christians, leading to the adoption of an eclectic system in which Jewish elements figured, is too shadowy to call for serious refutation. That Judaism became a "fad" for a time in certain circles, is a well-known fact, which has its analogy in the affectation of Buddhism by certain individuals in modern times. But there is no historical evidence that in the Gentile church this affectation of Judaism ever assumed the proportions of a movement, or afforded a menace to Gentile Christianity sufficiently serious to call out such a production as the Epistle to the Hebrews.

The end of their conversation (τὴν ἔκβασιν τῆς ἀναστρο-
φῆς). Ἔκβασις only here and 1 Cor. x. 13 (note). It means
outcome or *issue*. See Wisd. viii. 8. In 1 Cor. x. 13, *way
out.* Comp. Wisd. ii. 17. Ἀναστροφή is *life in intercourse
with men.* See on 1 Pet. i. 15. *Conversation,* in the older
sense of that word, is a good rendering, as it is also a nearly
literal rendering of the Greek word. The reference is to the
end of their life ; what kind of an end they made ; possibly,
but not necessarily, with an allusion to cases of martyrdom.
What, now, was the subject of these teachers' faith which is
commended to imitation ? It is stated in the next verse.

8. **Jesus Christ the same** (Ἰησοῦς Χριστὸς ὁ αὐτός). The
A.V. is slipshod, leaving the sentence without connection,
or in apparent apposition with *the end of their conversation.*
In translation this is commonly corrected by inserting *is :*
"Jesus Christ *is* the same," etc. But even thus the real
point of the statement is missed. No doubt the old teachers
believed in the unchangeableness of Jesus Christ; but that
fact is not represented as the subject of their faith, which
would be irrelevant and somewhat flat. The emphatic point
of the statement is *Christ.* They lived and died in the faith
that Jesus is THE CHRIST — the Messiah. The readers were
tempted to surrender this faith and to return to Judaism
which denied Jesus's messiahship (comp. ch. x. 29). Hence
the writer says, "hold fast and imitate their faith in Jesus
as *the Christ.* He is ever the same. He must be to you,
to-day, what he was to them, yesterday, and will be forever
to the heavenly hosts — CHRIST. Rend. therefore "Jesus is
Christ." Observe that our writer rarely uses the formula
Jesus Christ. In ch. x. 10 it occurs in a passage in which
the messianic mission of Jesus is emphasised (see vv. 5, 9),
and in xiii. 21, in a liturgical formula. The temptation to
forsake Jesus as Messiah is treated in the next verse.

9. **Be not carried about** (μὴ παραφέρεσθε). A.V. follows
T. R. περιφέρεσθε. Rend. "carried *away.*" The present tense
indicates a present and active danger.

With divers and strange doctrines (διδαχαῖς ποικίλαις καὶ
ξέναις). For "doctrines" rend. "teachings." These teachings
represent various phases of one radical error — the denial of
Jesus's messiahship and of his messianic economy as superseding Judaism and all other means of salvation.   Among
them the writer's mind would naturally turn to the prescriptions concerning clean and unclean meats and sacrificial
festivals.   See next clause.   These teachings were *various*
as contrasted with the *one* teaching of the gospel; they
were *strange* as they differed from that teaching.   Comp.
Gal. i. 6–9.   For ποικίλαις see on 2 Tim. iii. 16.

That the heart be established (βεβαιοῦσθαι τὴν καρδίαν).
There is an emphasis on *heart* as well as on *grace*.   These
strange teachings all emphasised *externalism*, in contrast with
Christianity, which insisted upon the purification of the heart
and conscience.   The contrast is strongly stated in ch. ix. 9,
14, and the Epistle constantly directs the readers to *the heart*
as the true point of contact with God, and the source of all
departures from him.   See ch. iii. 8, 10, 12, 15; iv. 7, 12;
viii. 10; especially x. 22.   Hence, the writer says, "it is good
that the solid basis of your assurance before God be in the
heart, purged from an evil conscience, so that you can draw
near to God with a firmly-established confidence, with a true
heart, in full assurance of faith": ch. x. 22; comp. 1 Th.
iii. 13; 2 Tim. ii. 22.

With grace, not with meats (χάριτι οὐ βρώμασιν).   The
heart is the proper seat of the work of grace.   Free grace
is the motive-power of Christ's sacrifice (2 Cor. viii. 9;
Gal. i. 15); it is behind the blood of the new covenant,
and is the energetic principle of its saving operation.   See
Rom. v. 2, 15; 1 Cor. xv. 10; Eph. ii. 5, 7, 8; 2 Th. ii. 16;
Heb. ii. 9; iv. 16; x. 29.   *With meats* stands for the whole
system of ceremonial observances, in contrast with grace,
working on the heart.   See ch. ix. 10.   This ceremonial system
yielded no permanent benefit to those who lived under it.
See ch. vii. 25; ix. 9, 13, 14; x. 1, 2, 4.

Which have not profited them that have been occupied therein (ἐν οἷς οὐκ ὠφελήθησαν οἱ περιπατοῦντες). Lit. *in the which they who walked were not profited.* Περιπατεῖν *to walk about* is often used to express habitual practice or general conduct of life. See Rom. vi. 4; 2 Cor. x. 3; Eph. ii. 10; Col. iii. 7; iv. 5.

10. Those who persist in adhering to the Jewish economy can have no part in the blessing of the new covenant. The two are mutually exclusive. The statement is cast in the mould of the Jewish sacrificial ritual, and in the figure of eating a sacrificial meal.

We have an altar (ἔχομεν θυσιαστήριον). It is a mistake to try to find in the Christian economy some specific object answering to *altar* — either the cross, or the eucharistic table, or Christ himself. Rather the ideas of approach to God, — sacrifice, atonement, pardon and acceptance, salvation, — are gathered up and generally represented in the figure of an altar, even as the Jewish altar was the point at which all these ideas converged. The application in this broader and more general sense is illustrated by Ignatius : " If one be not within the altar (ἐντὸς τοῦ θυσιαστηρίου, the sacred precinct), he lacketh the bread of God. . . . Whosoever, therefore, cometh not to the congregation (ἐπὶ τὸ αὐτὸ), he doth thereby show his pride, and hath separated himself," *Eph.* v. Ignatius here uses the word, not of a literal altar, but of the church. Comp. *Trall.* vii. Again : " Hasten to come together as to one temple, even God; to one altar, even to one Jesus Christ," *Magn.* vii.

Of which — to eat (ἐξ οὗ — φαγεῖν). The foundation of the figure is the sacrifice of the peace- or thank-offering, in which the worshippers partook of the sacrifice. See Lev. vii. 29–35 ; Deut. xii. 6 ; xxvii. 7. The peace-offerings were either public or private. The two lambs offered every year at Pentecost (Lev. xxiii. 19) were a public offering, and their flesh was eaten only by the officiating priests, and within the

holy place.   The other public peace-offerings, after the priests
had received their share, were eaten by the offerers themselves.   Jehovah thus condescended to be the guest of his
worshippers.   The large scale on which such festivals were
sometimes celebrated is illustrated in 1 K. viii. 63.   In private peace-offerings, the breast of the victim belonged to the
Lord, who gave it to the priests (Lev. vii. 30), and the right
shoulder was given directly to the priests by Israel (Lev.
vii. 32).   After the ritual of waving, the entrails were consumed, and the rest was eaten by the priest or the worshippers and their invited guests, among whom were specially
included the poor and the Levites.

Right (*ἐξουσίαν*).   See on J. i. 12.

Which serve the tabernacle (*οἱ τῇ σκηνῇ λατρεύοντες*).
This does not mean the priests only, but the worshippers
also.   *Σκηνή tabernacle* is used figuratively for the whole ceremonial economy.   A reference to the priests alone is entirely
foreign to the context, and to the whole drift of the discussion which contrasts the privileges of Christians at large (*we*)
with those of Israel at large.   The writer is speaking in the
present tense, of institutions in operation in his own time, to
which *tabernacle*, in any other than a figurative sense, would
be inappropriate.   Moreover, *λατρεύειν to serve* is used
throughout the N. T., with the single exception of Heb.
viii. 5, of the service of the worshipper and not of the priest.

11. The statement that the adherents of the old economy
are excluded from the privileges of the new is justified by
an illustrative argument drawn from the ceremonies of the
Great Day of Atonement.   See Lev. xvi, and comp. Heb.
ix. 7.   Of the victims offered on that occasion neither people
nor priest were allowed to eat.   The blood of the bullock
and of one of the goats was carried into the sanctuary and
sprinkled upon the mercy-seat, and afterward on the horns
of the great altar outside ; and the bodies of the slain animals
were burned in a clean place outside of the camp or city.

Beasts (ζώων). Lit. *living creatures.* The victims for the Day of Atonement were a bullock and two young goats for sin-offerings, and two rams for burnt-offerings. Only one goat, chosen by lot, was slain ; the other served as the scape-goat. Ζῷον *animal* is not used elsewhere of a sacrificial victim, either in N. T. or LXX. The word in N. T. mostly in Apocalypse. See on Apoc. i. 16 ; iv. 6.

Without the camp (ἔξω τῆς παρεμβολῆς). Burning without the camp was also required in the case of victims offered at the consecration of the priests, Ex. xxix. 14 ; at the sin-offering for the priest, Lev. iv. 11, 12 ; and at the sin-offering for the congregation, Lev. iv. 21. For παρεμβολή *camp*, see on Acts xxi. 34.

12. **That he might sanctify the people** (ἵνα ἁγιάσῃ τὸν λαόν). Ἁγιάζειν *to sanctify* had a peculiar significance to Jews. It meant *to set them apart as holy.* Hence, the Israelites were called ἅγιοι, as separated from other nations and consecrated to God. Our writer extends the application of the word to Christians. For Christ's work he claims the same efficacy which the Jew claimed for the special call of God to Israel, and for the operation of the Jewish sacrificial system. The office of his atoning work is *to sanctify ;* to make for himself a holy nation (ἔθνος ἅγιον), a people " prepared for the Lord " (L. i. 17) ; a true Israel of God. Ὁ λαός *the people*, or λαός μου *my people*, occurs constantly in O. T. as a designation of Israel, and also in N. T. See, in this epistle, ch. v. 3 ; vii. 5, 11, 27 ; ix. 7, 19. The N. T. extends the title to all who, under the new dispensation, occupy the position of Israel. See 1 Pet. ii. 10 ; Matt. i. 21 ; L. ii. 10 ; Heb. iv. 9 ; viii. 10 ; x. 30 ; xi. 25.

With his own blood (διὰ τοῦ ἰδίου αἵματος). In contrast with the blood of animal-sacrifices. Comp. ch. ix. 12, 28.

Suffered (ἔπαθεν). Used of Christ in Hebrews, 1st Peter, and Acts, but not in Paul, who, however, has παθήματα τοῦ Χριστοῦ *sufferings of Christ*, 2 Cor. i. 5 ; Philip. iii. 10 (αὐτοῦ).

Without the gate (ἔξω τῆς πύλης).   *Gate* is substituted for *camp* (ver. 11), as more appropriate to a city.

13. **Bearing his reproach** (τὸν ὀνειδισμὸν αὐτοῦ φέροντες). The reproach of exclusion from the Jewish commonwealth.

14. **For here have we no continuing city** (οὐ γὰρ ἔχο-μεν ὧδε μένουσαν πόλιν).   *Here*, on earth.   *Continuing* city. Let us go forth without the gate to Jesus ; for the system which has its centre in Jerusalem, the Holy City, is no more ours.   We are excluded from its religious fellowship by embracing the faith of him who suffered without the gate. The city itself is not abiding.   As a *holy* city, it is the centre and representative of a system of shadows and figures (ch. viii. 5 ; ix. 9, 23, 24 ; x. 1), which is to be shaken and removed, even as is the city itself (xii. 27) ; viii. 13 ; ix. 10 ; x. 9, 18.   If the epistle had been written after the destruction of Jerusalem a reference to that event could hardly have been avoided here.

One to come (τὴν μέλλουσαν).   Rend. "that which is to come."   The heavenly Jerusalem.   Comp. ch. xi. 10, 13-16.

The course of thought in vv. 9-14 is as follows : Be not carried away with divers and strange teachings, for example, those concerning meats and drinks and sacrificial feasts.   It is good that *the heart* be established, rather than that *the body* should be ceremonially pure ; and that the heart be estab-lished by the grace of God in Christ, which alone can give inward peace, a pure conscience, an established rest and secur-ity — rather than by the consciousness of having partaken of meats ceremonially clean : for those whose religious life was under the regimen of this ceremonial system derived no per-manent profit from it.   Not only so, the two systems exclude each other.   You cannot hold by the Levitical system and enjoy the blessings of Christian salvation.   It is the sacrifice of Christ through which you become partakers of grace.   It is impossible to obtain grace through meats ; for meats rep-

resent the economy which denies Christ ; and, by seeking
establishment through meats, you exclude yourselves from
the economy which is the only vehicle of grace.

Accordingly, we have an altar and a sacrifice from which
the votary of Leviticalism is excluded.   By the Levitical
law it was forbidden to eat the flesh of the victim offered on
the Great Day of Atonement ; so that, if the Levitical law
still holds for you, you cannot partake of the Christian's
atoning victim.   The law under which you are prohibits you.
According to that law, there is nothing to eat of in an atoning
sacrifice, since the body of the victim is burned.   Neither
priest nor people have anything more to do with it, and,
therefore, it is carried outside of the camp or city, outside of
the region of O. T. covenant-fellowship.   Similarly, so long
as you hold by Judaism, participation in Christ's atoning
sacrifice is impossible for you.   It is outside your religious
sphere, like the body of the victim outside the gate.   You
cannot eat of our altar.

The blood of the Levitical victim was carried into the
holy of holies and remained there.   If you seek the benefit
of *that* blood, it must be *within* the camp, at the Levitical
tabernacle or temple.   And you cannot have the benefit of
Christ's blood, for that compels you to go outside the gate,
where he suffered.   According to the O. T. law, you could
partake of the benefit of the blood, but you could not eat of
the body.   Christ's sacrifice gives you both body and blood
as spiritual food ; but these you must seek outside of Judaism.   Thus, by means of the O. T. ritual itself, it is shown
that the Jewish and the Christian systems exclude each
other.   Christ must be sought outside of the Jewish pale.

15. **By him therefore** (δι' αὐτοῦ).   Rend. "through him."
Omit *therefore*.   A. V. follows T. R. οὖν.   Through Jesus,
and not through the Jewish ritual.

Let us offer (ἀναφέρωμεν).   Lit. *bring up* the offering to
the altar.   See Jas. ii. 21, where the full phrase occurs.   For
the phrase *offer up through Jesus Christ*, comp. 1 Pet. ii. 5.

The sacrifice of praise (θυσίαν αἰνέσεως). The Levitical term for a thank-offering. See LXX, Lev. vii. 2, 3, 5 ; 2 Chron. xxix. 31 ; xxxiii. 16 ; Ps. xlix. 14, 23 ; cvi. 22 ; cxv. 8. Αἰνεσις *praise*, N. T.⁰. Often in LXX, ⁰Class. For "*the* sacrifice" rend. "*a* sacrifice." The sacrifice of thanks-giving is to take the place of the animal sacrifice. For the emphasis on thanksgiving in N. T. see Eph. v. 20 ; Col. i. 12 ; 1 Th. v. 18. The Rabbins had a saying, "in the future time all sacrifices shall cease ; but praises shall not cease." Philo says : "They offer the best sacrifice who glorify with hymns the saviour and benefactor, God."

That is the fruit of our lips (τουτέστιν καρπὸν χειλέων). Omit *our*. From LXX of Hos. xiv. 3, where the Hebrew reads, "we will account our lips as calves " (offered in sacrifice). Comp. Isa. lvii. 19.

Giving thanks to his name (ὁμολογούντων τῷ ὀνόματι αὐτοῦ). The phrase N. T.⁰, ⁰LXX. Rend. "of lips which make confession to his name."

16. **But to do good and to communicate forget not** (τῆς δὲ εὐποιΐας καὶ κοινωνίας μὴ ἐπιλανθάνεσθε). Lit. *but be not forgetful of doing good and communicating*. Ἐυποιΐα *benefi-cence*, N. T.⁰, ⁰LXX, ⁰Class. For κοινωνία *communication*, of alms, etc., see on L. v. 10 ; Acts ii. 42. See also Rom. xv. 26 ; 2 Cor. viii. 4 ; ix. 13. Comp. the verb κοινωνεῖν *to impart*, Rom. xii. 13 ; xv. 27 ; Philip. iv. 15.

17. **They watch** (ἀγρυπνοῦσιν). See on Mk. xiii. 33, and comp. L. xxi. 36 ; Eph. vi. 18.

With grief (στενάζοντες). Lit. *groaning*. See Rom. viii. 23 ; 2 Cor. v. 2, 4 ; Jas. v. 9.

Unprofitable (ἀλυσιτελὲς). N. T.⁰, ⁰LXX. From *ἀ not*, and λυσιτελής *paying for expenses*. Hence, *what does not pay; unprofitable*.

I may be restored to you (ἀποκατασταθῶ ὑμῖν).   Not implying imprisonment, but enforced absence through sickness or other cause.

20. The God of peace.   Not an O. T. phrase, and found only in Paul and Hebrews.   See Rom. xv. 33; xvi. 20; 1 Cor. xiv. 33; Philip. iv. 9; 1 Th. v. 23; 2 Th. iii. 16. The phrase signifies *God who is the author and giver of peace.*

Who brought again from the dead (ὁ ἀναγαγὼν ἐκ νεκρῶν). The only direct reference in the epistle to the resurrection of Christ.   Ch. vi. 2 refers to the resurrection of the dead generally.   'Ανάγειν of raising the dead, only Rom. x. 7. Rend. "brought up," and comp. Wisd. xvi. 13.   'Ανά in this compound, never in N. T. in the sense of *again.*   See on L. viii. 22; Acts xii. 4; xvi. 34; xxvii. 3.   The verb often as a nautical term, to bring a vessel *up* from the land to the deep water; to put to sea.

That great shepherd of the sheep (τὸν ποιμένα τῶν προβάτων τὸν μέγαν).   The Greek order is, "the shepherd of the sheep the great (shepherd)."   Comp. J. x. 2, 11, 14; 1 Pet. ii. 25, and see Isa. lxiii. 11.   Of God, Ezek. xxxiv.

Through the blood of the everlasting covenant (ἐν αἵματι διαθήκης αἰωνίου).   Rend. "in the blood of an eternal covenant."   See Zech. ix. 11.   The phrase *eternal covenant* N. T.⁰.   Common in LXX; see Gen. ix. 16; xvii. 19; Lev. xxiv. 8; 2 Sam. xxiii. 5; Jer. xxxix. 40; Ezek. xvi. 60. Const. with *the great shepherd of the sheep.*   It may be granted that the raising of Christ from the dead, viewed as the consummation of the plan of salvation, was in the sphere of the blood of the covenant; nevertheless, the covenant is nowhere in the N. T. associated with the resurrection, but frequently with death, especially in this epistle.   See Matt. xxvi. 28; L. xxii. 20; Heb. ix. 15, 16, 17, 20.   The connection of the blood of the covenant with Christ's pastoral office gives a thoroughly scriptural sense, and one which exactly fits into

the context.   Christ becomes the great shepherd solely
through the blood of the covenant.   Comp. Acts xx. 28.
Through this is brought about the new relation of the
church with God described in ch. viii. 10 ff.   This tallies
perfectly with the conception of "the God of peace"; and
the great Shepherd will assert the power of the eternal
covenant of reconciliation and peace by perfecting his flock
in every good work to do his will, working in them that
which is well pleasing in his sight.   With this agree Jer. l.
5, 19; Ezek. xxxiv. 25, and the entire chapter, see especially
vv. 12–15, 23, 31.   In these verses the Shepherd of the
Covenant appears as guiding, tending his flock, and leading
them into fair and safe pastures.   Comp. Isa. lxiii. 11–14,
and Apoc. vii. 17, see note on ποιμανεῖ *shall shepherd.*   Ἐν
αἵματι "*in* the blood," is *in virtue of*, or *in the power of* the
blood.

21. **Make you perfect** (καταρτίσαι ὑμᾶς).   The verb is
aptly chosen, since the readers are addressed as a body — the
flock of Christ.   The prayer is for the complete mutual
adjustment of all the members of the flock into a perfected
whole, fitted to do the perfect will of God.   See on 1 Pet. v. 10,
and comp. notes on 2 Tim. iii. 17; 1 Cor. i. 10; 2 Cor. xiii. 11.
Ignatius uses the word of the church's being joined (κατηρ-
τισμένοι) in common subjection to the Bishops and the Presbytery (*Eph.* ii), and of himself as one *composed* or *settled*
into union (εἰς ἔνωσιν), that is, avoiding division in the
church (*Philad.* viii); and again to the *Smyrnaeans* (i) "I
have perceived that ye are *settled* or *compacted* in faith im-
movable, being, as it were, nailed on the cross of the Lord
Jesus Christ in flesh and in spirit."

In every good work (ἐν παντὶ ἀγαθῷ).   A.V. follows T. R.
ἔργῳ *work.*   Rend. "in every good thing."

To do his will (εἰς τὸ ποιῆσαι τὸ θέλημα αὐτοῦ).   **To the**
end that you do, etc.

Working in you (ποιῶν ἐν ἡμῖν). Rend. "in *us*." A.V.
follows T. R. ὑμῖν *you*. For "working" rend. "doing."
The word plays on ποιῆσαι *to do*. "Make you perfect *to do*
his will, he *doing* in us what is well-pleasing in his sight."

That which is well-pleasing in his sight (τὸ εὐάρεστον
ἐνώπιον αὐτοῦ). Comp. Eph. v. 10. The phrase N. T.⁰.
Ἐυάρεστον usually with the simple dative, as Rom. xii. 1;
xiv. 8; Eph. v. 10; Philip. iv. 18. Comp. 1 J. iii. 22.

22. Suffer the word of exhortation (ἀνέχεσθε τοῦ λόγου
τῆς παρακλήσεως). For "suffer," rend. "bear with." See
Acts xviii. 14; 2 Cor. xi. 1; 2 Tim. iv. 3. Do not become
impatient at my counsels in this letter. *The word of exhortation* refers to the entire epistle which he regards as hortatory rather than didactic or consolatory. The phrase only
in Acts xiii. 15.

I have written a letter unto you (ἐπέστειλα ὑμῖν). A.V.
supplies *a letter*. Rend. "I have written unto you." The
verb only here, Acts xv. 20; xxi. 25. Lit. *to send*, not letters only. Sometimes with ἐπιστολαὶ or ἐπιστολὰς *letters*
added, as Neh. vi. 19; 1 Macc. xii. 7. In N. T. always of
sending a letter.

In a few words (διὰ βραχέων). There is a suggestion of
apology. Do not grow impatient. The letter is short. The
phrase N. T.⁰, but comp. δι' ὀλίγων, 1 Pet. v. 12, and ἐν
ὀλίγῳ *briefly*, Eph. iii. 3.

23. Our brother Timothy (τὸν ἀδελφὸν ἡμῶν Τιμόθεον).
Paul's habit, when using ὁ ἀδελφός *brother* with a proper
name, is to put the proper name first. See Rom. xvi. 23;
1 Cor. i. 1; xvi. 12; 2 Cor. i. 1; ii. 13; Philip. ii. 25.

Set at liberty (ἀπολελυμένον). Nothing is known of the
fact referred to. Ἀπολύειν of releasing from confinement,
Matt. xxvii. 15; J. xix. 10; Acts iii. 13; iv. 21, 23; v. 40.

24. **They of Italy** (οἱ ἀπὸ τῆς Ἰταλίας). This may mean, "those who are in Italy send greeting from Italy"; or, "those of Italy (Italian Christians with the writer at the time) send greeting' from the place at which the letter is being written. See Introduction. The phrase affords no reliable indication as to the residence of the persons addressed.

WORDS WHICH OCCUR ONLY IN HEBREWS.

ἀγενεαλόγητος	γενεαλογέομαι	εὐθύτης	μετέπειτα
ἀγνόημα	γεωργέομαι	εὐλάβεια	μετριοπαθέω
ἀθέτησις	γνόφος	εὐλαβέομαι	μηδέπω
ἄθλησις		εὐπερίστατος	μηλωτή
αἴγειος	δάμαλις	εὐποιΐα	μήν
αἱματεκχυσία	δεκάτη		μισθαποδοσία
αἴνεσις	δεκατόω	θεατρίζομαι	μισθαποδότης
αἰσθητήριον	δέος	θέλησις	μυελός
αἴτιος	δέρμα	θεράπων	
ἀκατάλυτος	δημιουργός	θύελλα	νέφος
ἀκλινής	δήπου	θυματήριον	νόθος
ἀκροθίνιον	διάταγμα		νομοθετέω
ἀλυσιτελής	διαφορώτερος	ἱερωσύνη	νωθρός
ἀμετάθετος	διηνεκής	ἱκετήριος	
ἀμήτωρ	δικνέομαι		ὄγκος
ἀνακαινίζω	διόρθωσις	καθαρότης	ὀλιγωρέω
ἀναλογίζομαι	δοκιμασία	κακουχέομαι	ὀλοθρεύω
ἀναρίθμητος	δυσερμήνευτος	καρτερέω	ὁμοιότης
ἀνασταυρόω		καταγωνίζομαι	ὀρκωμοσία
ἀνταγωνίζομαι	ἐάνπερ	κατάδηλος	
ἀντικαθίστημι	ἔγγυος	καταναλίσκω	πανήγυρις
ἀπαράβατος	ἐκβαίνω	κατασκιάζω	παραδειγματίζω
ἀπάτωρ	ἐκδοχή	κατάσκοπος	παραπικραίνω
ἀπαύγασμα	ἐκλανθάνομαι	καῦσις	παραπικρασμός
ἄπειρος	ἔκτρομος	κεφαλίς	παραπίπτω
ἀποβλέπω	ἔλεγχος	κοπή	παραπλησίως
ἀπόστολος (of	ἐμπαιγμός	κριτικός	παραρέω
Christ)	ἐνκαινίζω	κῶλον	πεῖρα
ἁρμός	ἐνυβρίζω		πήγνυμι
ἀφανής	ἕξις	λειτουργικός	πολυμερῶς
ἀφανισμός	ἐπεισαγωγή	λευειτικός	πολυτρόπως
ἀφομοιόομαι	ἐπιλείπω		πρίζω
	ἔπος	μερισμός	προβλέπομαι
βοηθός	εὐαρεστέω	μεσιτεύω	πρόδρομος
βοτάνη	εὐαρέστως	μετάθεσις	προσαγορεύω

προσοχθίζω   συνδέομαι   τράγος   φαντάζομαι
πρόσφατος   συνεπιμαρτυρέω   τραχηλίζομαι   φοβερός
πρόσχυσις   συνκακουχέομαι   τρίμηνος
πρωτοτόκια   συνπαθέω   τροχία   χαρακτήρ
                                  τυμπανίζω   χερουβείν

σαββατισμός   τελειωτής
στάμνος   τιμωρία   ὑπείκω
συναπόλλυμαι   τομός   ὑποστολή

WORDS FOUND IN HEBREWS AND ELSEWHERE, BUT NOT IN PAUL.

ἀγγαλλίασις
ἄγκυρα
αἰτία *
ἄκανθαι
ἄκρον
ἀμελέω *
ἀμίαντος
ἀναδέχομαι
ἀναθεωρέω
ἀνακάμπτω
ἀνατέλλω
ἀναφέρω
ἀνορθόω
ἀντιλογία
ἀντίτυπος
ἀνυπότακτος *
ἀνώτερον
ἀνωφελής *
ἀπαλλάσσω
ἀποβάλλω
ἀπογράφομαι
ἀποδεκατόω
ἀποδοκιμάζω
ἀποκαθίστημι
ἀπόλαυσις *
ἀπολείπω
ἀπολύω
ἀρνέομαι *
ἁρπαγή
ἀρχηγός
ἀρχιερεύς

ἀσάλευτος
ἀστεῖος
ἄστρον
ἀφιλάργυρος *

βαπτισμός
βέβηλος *
βλαστάνω
βοήθεια
βραχύς

γάμος
γηράσκω
γυμνάζω *

διαβαίνω
διαλέγομαι
διαστέλλομαι
διατίθεμαι
διηγέομαι
δίστομος

ἔθος
εἰρηνικός
εἰσάγω
εἴσειμι
εἰσφέρω *
ἐκλείπω
ἑκουσίως
ἐκτρέπομαι *
ἐκφέρω *

ἔκφοβος
ἔλαιον
ἐλαττόω
ἐλεήμων
ἐμπίπτω *
ἐμφανίζω
ἐνθύμησις
ἔννοια
ἐνοχλέω
ἐντέλλομαι
ἔντρομος
ἐξάγω
ἔξοδος
ἐπιγράφω
ἐπιδείκνυμι
ἐπίθεσις *
ἐπιλαμβάνομαι *
ἐπισκέπτομαι
ἐπισκοπέω
ἐπίσταμαι *
ἐπιστέλλω
ἔριον
ἑρμηνεύω
ἐρυθρός
ἐσώτερος
εὔθετος
εὔκαιρος
ἐχθές

ζόφος
ζῶον

ἦχος

θεωρέω
θηρίον *

ἰάομαι
ἱερατεία
ἱερεύς
ἱλάσκομαι
ἵλεως
ἱμάτιον

καθαρισμός
καίτοι
κάμνω
καταπατέω
κατάπαυσις
καταπαύω
καταπέτασμα
κατασκευάζω
καταφεύγω
κεφάλαιον
κίβωτος
κλίνω
κοινόω
κόκκινος
κοσμικός *
κριτής *
κυκλόω

λανθάνω
λέων *

λιθοβολέω
λούω
λύτρωσις
λυχνία

μάννα
μαστιγόω
μάστιξ
μεγαλωσύνη
μεταλαμβάνω *
μέτοχος
μήποτε *
μιαίνω *
μονογενής
μόσχος
μυριάς

ξενίζω
ξηρός

ὅθεν
ὁλοκαύτωμα
ὀμνύω
ὀπή
ὀρέγομαι *
ὀρθός

ὅρκος
ὅσιος *
ὀστέον

παλαιόω
παντελής
πάντοθεν
παραβολή
παραδέχομαι *
παραιτέομαι *
παραλύομαι
παραφέρω
παρεμβολή
παρεπίδημος
παρίημι
παροικέω
παροξυσμός
πατριάρχης
πατρίς
περιέρχομαι *
περικαλύπτω
περίκειμαι
πλῆθος
ποικίλος *
πολίτης

πόρρωθεν
πρεσβύτερος *
προάγω *
πρόδηλος *
προσέρχομαι *
προσέχω *
προσφέρω
πύλη

ῥαντίζω
ῥαντισμός

σείω
σκηνή
σπήλαιον
σποδός
στάσις
στερεός *
στεφανόω *
συναντάω
συντέλεια
σχεδόν

ταῦρος
τάχειον * (variant)

τελείωσις
τελευτάω
τεχνίτης
τρίβολος
τροφή

ὑετός
ὑμνέω
ὕπαρξις
ὑπόδειγμα
ὑποκάτω
ὑποπόδιον
ὕσσωπος
ὕστερον
ὕψιστος

φύω

χείρων *
χρονίζω
χρύσεος *
χωλός

ψηλαφάω

INDICES.

INDEX OF ENGLISH WORDS.

INDEX OF GREEK WORDS.

καταγι;ωσκω, 101
καταγωνίζομαι, 532
κατάδηλος, 461
καταδουλόω, 97
κατακρίνω, 517
καταλαμβάνω, 45
καταλέγομαι, 261
καταλείπω, 32, 420, 528
καταλύω, 106
κατὰ μέρος, 477
καταναλίσκω, 559
κατανοέω, 410, 502
καταπατέω, 504
κατάπαυσις, 417, 426
καταπαύω, 422
καταπέτασμα, 453, 475, 500
καταπίνω, 530
κατάρα, 86, 117, 447
καταργέω, 65, 156, 161, 292, 404
καταρτίζω, 33, 171, 512, 574
κατασκευάζω, 411, 516
κατασκιάζω, 477
κατασκοπέω, 96
κατάσκοπος, 531
κατάστημα, 222, 340
καταστολή, 221
καταστρηνιάω, 262
καταστροφή, 301
καταφεύγω, 452
καταφθείρω, 313
κατεσθίω, 163
κατευθύνω, 34
κατέχω, 51, 64, 65, 414
κατηγορία, 268, 333
κατηχέω, 174
κατ᾽ ἰδίαν, 94
καῦσις, 448
καυστηριάζομαι, 244
καυχάομαι, 179, 414
καύχημα, 173, 414
καύχησις, 414
κεῖμαι, 33, 207

κέλευσμα, 42
κενοδοξία, 170
κενόδοξος, 170
κενός, 20, 33, 301
κενοφωνία, 283, 302
κεφάλαιον, 467
κεφαλίς, 497
κήρυγμα, 328, 332
κῆρυξ, 220
κηρύσσω, 160, 220, 241
κιβωτός, 516
κλέπτης, 44, 45
κληρονομέω, 154, 386, 450
κληρονομία, 486, 494
κληρονόμος, 132, 138, 350, 380, 517
κλῆσις, 57, 291, 409
κλίμα, 92
κνήθω, 321
κοιλία, 89
κοιμάομαι, 39, 40
κοινός, 332, 505
κοινόω, 483
κοινωνέω, 174, 269, 404
κοινωνία, 100, 572
κοινωνικός, 282
κοινωνός, 506
κόκκινος, 488
κολακία, 23
κόλασις, 504
κομίζω, 508, 521, 524
κοπιάω, 249, 266, 297
κόπος, 15, 25, 180
κοσμέω, 221, 343
κοσμικός, 344, 474
κόσμιος, 222, 229
κόσμος, 179, 212, 381, 517, 534
κράζω, 137
κρατέω, 452
κράτος, 404
κρείττων or κρείσσων, 385, 448, 470,
   490, 533, 556
κρίμα, 232, 263